# THE ROMAN REVOLUTION
## OF CONSTANTINE

The reign of the emperor Constantine (306–337) was as revolutionary for the transformation of Rome's Mediterranean empire as that of Augustus, the first emperor three centuries earlier. The abandonment of Rome signaled the increasing importance of frontier zones in northern and central Europe and the Middle East. The foundation of Constantinople as a new imperial residence and the rise of Greek as the language of administration previewed the establishment of a separate eastern Roman empire. Constantine's patronage of Christianity required both a new theology of the Christian Trinity and a new political image of a Christian emperor. Raymond Van Dam explores and interprets each of these events. His book complements accounts of the role of Christianity by highlighting ideological and cultural aspects of the transition to a post-Roman world.

Raymond Van Dam is Professor of History and Director of the Interdepartmental Program in Greek and Roman History at the University of Michigan. He is the author of numerous books, most recently *Families and Friends in Late Roman Cappadocia* and *Becoming Christian: The Conversion of Roman Cappadocia.*

D1559052

# THE ROMAN REVOLUTION OF CONSTANTINE

RAYMOND VAN DAM

UNIVERSITY OF MICHIGAN

CAMBRIDGE
UNIVERSITY PRESS

CAMBRIDGE UNIVERSITY PRESS
Cambridge, New York, Melbourne, Madrid, Cape Town, Singapore,
São Paulo, Delhi, Dubai, Tokyo, Mexico City

Cambridge University Press
32 Avenue of the Americas, New York, NY 10013-2473, USA

www.cambridge.org
Information on this title: www.cambridge.org/9780521133012

First published 2007
Reprinted 2008
First paperback edition 2009

A catalog record for this publication is available from the British Library.

Library of Congress Cataloging in Publication Data
Van Dam, Raymond.
The Roman revolution of Constantine / Raymond Van Dam.
    p.  cm.
Appendices include material in Latin with English translation.
Includes bibliographical references and index.
ISBN 978-0-521-88209-5 (hardback)
1. Constantine I, Emperor of Rome, d. 337. 2. Church history – Primitive and
early church, ca. 30-600. I. Title.
BR180.V36 2007
937'.08092–dc22                    2007008119

ISBN 978-0-521-88209-5 Hardback
ISBN 978-0-521-13301-2 Paperback

*For Jody*
*"The look, the light in your eyes"*
*— George Strait, "Carried Away"*

# CONTENTS

�֎ ✾ ✾

# PREFACE

AN EARLY INTEREST IN CLASSICAL STUDIES LED ME INSTEAD TO LATE antiquity. As an undergraduate I was fortunate to study with a classics professor who enjoyed reading patristics texts; as a graduate student I wrote my doctoral dissertation under the supervision of a distinguished historian of the later Roman empire. Their direction expanded my sense of antiquity to include early Christianity and early medieval and early Byzantine history. Now their influence lives on in my own teaching and research. As a teacher I assign my students to read books and articles by Dick Whittaker, my dissertation supervisor. As a researcher I consult volumes of church fathers from the library of Bob Otten, my undergraduate classics professor. At Caesarea in Palestine scholars such as Jerome studied in the great library founded by Origen and augmented by bishop Eusebius. Among the books they read were the writings of Origen and Eusebius. All of us who work as professors deeply appreciate this fulfilling sense of intellectual continuity from our teachers to our students.

Courses on the Roman empire, late antiquity, early Christianity, medieval history, and Byzantine history without fail include Constantine. Since one delight of teaching such courses is the anticipation of the inevitable arguments, over the decades the best critics of my ideas about Constantine and his age have been students, both undergraduates and graduates. During the past several years it has been my privilege to enjoy the company of a remarkable group of graduate students here at the University of Michigan. These students have completed their degrees in my home department of history, my two adjunct departments of classical studies and Near Eastern studies, the Interdepartmental Program in Classical Art and Archaeology, and now our new Interdepartmental Program in Greek and Roman History. Many of them have taught with me as graduate student instructors; they have also shaped my thinking about late antiquity through their own research on ancient and postclassical history. The highest reward of teaching is the intellectual stimulation of learning from students.

Research is simultaneously a solitary undertaking and a collegial enterprise. We think and write alone, but we also read the books and articles of hundreds of scholars from around the world. The output of publications on Constantine and related issues is both overwhelmingly large and impressively brilliant. A quick count reveals that I have met in person only a small percentage of the contemporary authors cited in my bibliography. It is hence all the more gratifying to acknowledge my pleasure in having met the rest of you in your scholarship.

One essential requirement for research is the kindness of friends. My department generously awarded me a one-semester leave from teaching. The comments from the audience at a seminar organized by the Miller Center for Historical Studies at the University of Maryland were most stimulating, and Ken Holum, Marsha Rozenblit, Art Eckstein, and Jeannie Rutenburg were gracious hosts. Noel Lenski sent me an advance copy of his excellent *Cambridge Companion to the Age of Constantine*. Kent Rigsby and Geoffrey Schmalz kindly read and commented on early drafts. As a senior editor at Cambridge University Press, Beatrice Rehl has been an encouraging friend and a wonderful patron saint for all of us in ancient studies.

# ABBREVIATIONS

❊ ❊ ❊

| | |
|---|---|
| ACW | Ancient Christian Writers (Westminster) |
| Budé | Collection des Universités de France publiée sous le patronage de l'Association Guillaume Budé (Paris) |
| CChr. | Corpus Christianorum (Turnhout) |
| *CIL* | *Corpus inscriptionum latinarum* (Berlin) |
| CSEL | Corpus scriptorum ecclesiasticorum latinorum (Vienna) |
| FC | Fathers of the Church (Washington, D.C.) |
| GCS | Die griechischen christlichen Schriftsteller der ersten Jahrhunderte (Berlin) |
| *ICUR* | *Inscriptiones Christianae urbis Romae septimo saeculo antiquiores*, ed. J. B. de Rossi (Rome, 1857–1888), 2 vols. |
| *ICUR* nova series | *Inscriptiones Christianae urbis Romae septimo saeculo antiquiores*, nova series, ed. A. Silvagni, A. Ferrua et al. (Rome and Vatican City, 1922-) |
| *IGR* | *Inscriptiones graecae ad res romanas pertinentes*, ed. R. Cagnat et al. (Paris, 1906–1927), Vols. 1, 3–4 |
| *ILCV* | *Inscriptiones latinae Christianae veteres*, ed. E. Diehl (Berlin, 1925–1931), 3 vols. |
| *ILS* | *Inscriptiones latinae selectae*, ed. H. Dessau (reprint: Berlin, 1962), 3 vols. in 5 |
| LCL | Loeb Classical Library (Cambridge, MA) |
| *MAMA* | *Monumenta Asiae Minoris antiqua.* Vol. 1 = Calder (1928). Vol. 4 = Buckler, Calder and Guthrie (1933). Vol. 5 = Cox and Cameron (1937). Vol. 6 = Buckler and Calder (1939). Vol. 7 = Calder (1956) |
| MGH | Monumenta Germaniae historica (Berlin, Hannover, and Leipzig) |

| | |
|---|---|
| NPNF | A Select Library of Nicene and Post-Nicene Fathers of the Christian Church (reprint: Grand Rapids) |
| *OGIS* | *Orientis graeci inscriptiones selectae: supplementum sylloges inscriptionum graecarum*, ed. W. Dittenberger (Leipzig, 1903–1905), 2 vols. |
| *PG* | *Patrologia graeca* (Paris) |
| *PL* | *Patrologia latina* (Paris) |
| *PLRE* | *The Prosopography of the Later Roman Empire* (Cambridge). Vol. 1, A.D. 260–395, ed. A. H. M. Jones, J. R. Martindale, and J. Morris (1971). Vol. 2, A.D. 395–527, ed. J. R. Martindale (1980) |
| SChr. | Sources chrétiennes (Paris) |
| *SIG³* | *Sylloge inscriptionum graecarum*, ed. W. Dittenberger (Third edition: Leipzig, 1915–1924), 4 vols. |
| *TAM* | *Tituli Asiae Minoris*. Vol. 2 = Kalinka (1930–1944). Vol. 3 = Heberdey (1941). |
| Teubner | Bibliotheca scriptorum graecorum et romanorum Teubneriana (Leipzig and Stuttgart) |
| TTH | Translated Texts for Historians (Liverpool) |

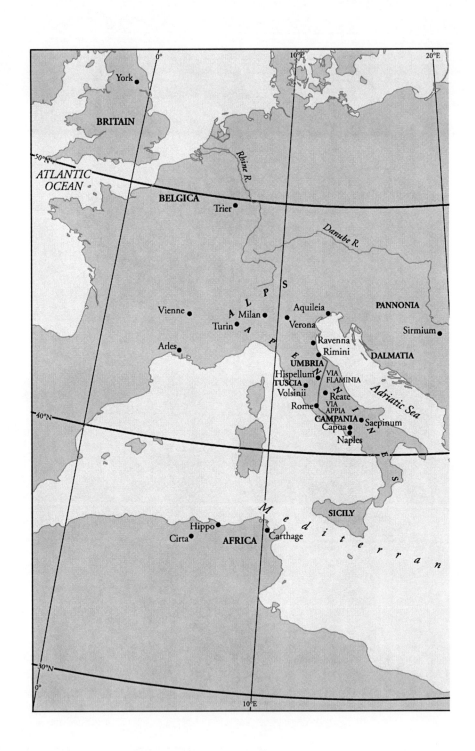

York •

**BRITAIN**

*ATLANTIC*
*OCEAN*

50°N

*Rhine R.*

**BELGICA**

Trier •

*Danube R.*

**PANNONIA**

Vienne •

A
*L*
*P*
*S*

Milan •

Aquileia •

Turin •

*A*

Verona •

Sirmium •

*P*

Ravenna •

**DALMATIA**

Arles •

*E*

Rimini •

**UMBRIA**

*N*

VIA
FLAMINIA

Hispellum •

*Adriatic Sea*

**TUSCIA**

Volsinii •

*N*

Reate •

Rome •

VIA
APPIA

**CAMPANIA**

Saepinum •

Capua •

*I*

40°N

Naples •

*N*

*E*

*S*

**SICILY**

*M e d i t e r r a n*

Hippo •

Cirta •

**AFRICA**

Carthage •

30°N

0°

0°

10°E

20°E

10°E

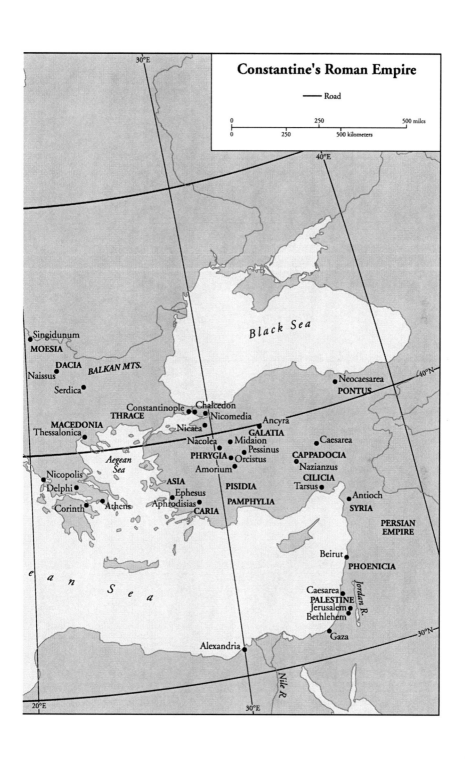

## Constantine's Roman Empire

——— Road

| 0 | | 250 | | 500 miles |
| 0 | 250 | | 500 kilometers | |

*Black Sea*

Singidunum
**MOESIA**
**DACIA** *BALKAN MTS.*
Naissus
Serdica

Neocaesarea
**PONTUS**

Constantinople  Chalcedon
**THRACE**  Nicomedia
Nicaea
**MACEDONIA**  **GALATIA**  Ancyra
Thessalonica  Nacolea  Midaion  **CAPPADOCIA**  Caesarea
**PHRYGIA**  Pessinus
Amorium  Orcistus  Nazianzus
*Aegean Sea*  **CILICIA**
Nicopolis  **ASIA**  Tarsus
Delphi  Ephesus  **PISIDIA**  Antioch
Corinth  Athens  Aphrodisias  **PAMPHYLIA**  **SYRIA**
**CARIA**

**PERSIAN EMPIRE**

Beirut
**PHOENICIA**

*e a n*  *S e a*

Caesarea
**PALESTINE**
Jerusalem
Bethlehem  *Jordan R.*
Gaza

Alexandria

*Nile R.*

# AUGUSTUS AND CONSTANTINE

## INTRODUCTION

J ULIAN WAS ONE OF THE FEW ROMAN EMPERORS WHO HAD CARE-
fully studied Roman history. During the summer of 362 he arrived
at Antioch to prepare for an invasion of the Persian empire. In
December the city's residents enjoyed the Saturnalia, a lively festival celebrated with games, gambling, and an inversion of social standing as masters and slaves temporarily exchanged roles. Such a raucous
festival might have reminded Julian that his own career had been a
bit "Saturnalian" in its unforeseen trajectory. As a young man he had
avidly studied classical culture, presumably with the hope of becoming
a sophist or a philosopher. Instead, and quite unexpectedly, the book-
worm had become an emperor. But now, rather than contemplating his
own wry twist of fate, Julian decided to evaluate and rank his predecessors on the imperial throne. In the midst of a festival that celebrated
role reversal the emperor returned to his original scholarly vocation by
writing history.[1]

---

[1] For the significance of Antioch in the later Roman empire, see Van Dam (forthcoming).

One of those predecessors was Constantine. Julian's recollections of his uncle were scarred by a painfully personal resentment. After Constantine's death in May 337 troops had murdered several of his relatives, including a half-brother who was Julian's father. One tradition claimed that Constantine himself had already ordered these executions after discovering a plot; Julian would eventually blame Constantius, one of the three sons of Constantine who had succeeded as emperors. Still only a little boy, Julian had been spared and allowed to grow up under the implacable supervision of his cousin Constantius. When he finally did learn about this massacre of his relatives, he claimed that only the intervention of Hermes, a patron deity of eloquence, had rescued him from his despair.[2]

In his treatise about his predecessors Julian imagined a tribunal of gods to evaluate the emperors. In light of Julian's own love of Platonic philosophy it is no surprise that they agreed that the best had been Marcus Aurelius, a paradigmatic example of a philosopher-king. Constantine had had no chance in this competition. When the judges had invited him to argue his case, Constantine proudly noted his military victories over rival emperors and barbarians. But before this heavenly court the satyr Silenus snidely dismissed these accomplishments as "flowerbeds of Adonis," mere passing fancies that blossomed briefly and then wilted. In his estimation Constantine had been so devoted to the pursuit of pleasure that he might have been a chef or a hairdresser.[3]

Writing historical satire about his predecessors could reinforce Julian's smugness about his own future prospects. In the previous year the death of Constantius had averted a civil war and left Julian as the sole emperor. Constantine had reigned as emperor for over thirty years, and then Constantius for another twenty-four. Still only in his early thirties, Julian might have anticipated an even longer reign for himself. If he were successful in his Persian expedition, if he were able to revive cities

---

[2] Plot: Philostorgius, *HE* 2.16, with Chapter 3, for the relationship between Constantine and his half-brothers. Despair and Hermes: Julian, *Orat.* 7.230A-231B.

[3] Julian, *Caesares* 328D-329D, Constantine and Silenus, 335A-B, chef, hairdresser, with Bidez (1930) 300, and Bowersock (1978) 101, both dating this treatise to December 362, and Gleason (1986), on the celebration of the Saturnalia. For Julian's interest in imitating Marcus Aurelius, see Eutropius, *Breviarium* 10.16.3.

and their pagan cults, then he could prove Silenus to be correct, as his accomplishments reduced the lengthy reigns of his uncle and his cousin to insignificance. He could still be the most consequential emperor of the Constantinian dynasty.

Instead, as the festivities of the Saturnalia might have portended, both Julian's version of Roman history and his vision of the future were to be turned upside-down. Six months later he was dead, killed in battle. He had also been wrong in his satirical evaluation of Constantine. As the last, fleeting pagan emperor Julian now seems to have been the oddity. Constantine meanwhile has become one of the towering figures of both Roman and early Christian history.

The most important book about Roman history from the twentieth century is Ronald Syme's *The Roman Revolution*. In this book Syme analyzed the transition from the Republic to the rule of emperors by focusing on the career of Augustus, the first emperor. His narrative of Augustus' rise to prominence and the details of his reign was seductively compelling, in part because he proposed a distinctive political interpretation of the basis of the first emperor's power. Augustus' contemporaries had already been arguing over whether the emperor had truly restored the old Republic, as he himself claimed, or whether he had instituted a monarchy in disguise. Syme cut through this conundrum over the legal and institutional framework by dismissing the Roman constitution as "a screen and a sham." He also downplayed the importance of Augustus' own ambitions in favor of highlighting "the identity of the agents and ministers of power." "Emphasis is laid . . . not upon the personality and acts of Augustus, but upon his adherents and partisans." If relationships and alliances were more important than institutions or personalities, then Syme's task was to plot the replacement of one group of ruling elites by another. His Augustus hence presided both as a great patron at the center of many networks of personal obligations and as the representative of the interests of new factions. "There is always an oligarchy somewhere, open or concealed."[4]

---

[4] Argument over Augustus' motives: Tacitus, *Annales* 1.9–10. Syme (1939) vii, personality, 15, screen and sham, 325, identity, 346, oligarchy. In a supplementary study

Syme's vision has had a powerful afterlife. Not only did it influence subsequent accounts of Augustus and the origins of the Roman principate; it also defined a distinctive style of interpreting Roman history. Syme's emphasis on networks legitimated the importance of prosopography, the study of the career patterns of notables and their personal connections, as a useful tool of historical analysis. His emphasis on oligarchy reasserted the significance of the history of elites that had long been at the heart of so many studies of the ancient world: "Roman history, Republican or Imperial, is the history of the governing class." His emphasis on political scheming provided a license to hunt for the unspoken intrigues and hidden motives in all writings of the era and essentially transformed contemporary literary masterpieces into patriotic manifestoes orchestrated from the center by Augustus and his cronies through "the systematic exploitation of literature on the grand scale." Syme approached Augustus' reign from both ends through his reverence for the interpretive perspectives of Sallust, a pre-Augustan historian who had lamented a decline in values already during the late Republic, and Tacitus, a post-Augustan historian who would mock the pretenses of the first emperors. By inheriting their moralizing nostalgia for a lost Republic, Syme adopted a deprecatory perspective on Augustus himself as "a chill and mature terrorist." His account of Augustus was hence political history at its grandest and most critical, simultaneously a scathing critique and a begrudging panegyric that tempered its distaste for the emperor's ruthlessness at suppressing personal liberty with admiration for his success at imposing stable government.[5]

In subsequent centuries Augustus remained an intriguing figure. Already in the later second century bishop Melito of Sardis argued that the coincidence of Augustus' rule and the birth of Jesus was a conclusive

of the Augustan regime Syme reiterated his theory about oligarchy and his dislike of biography: see Syme (1986) 13, "Oligarchy is imposed as the guiding theme, the link from age to age whatever be the form and name of government," 14, "biographies of emperors are a menace and an impediment to the understanding of history in its structure and processes."

[5] Syme (1939) 7, governing class, 19, terrorist, 460, exploitation. For an excellent assessment of Syme's use of prosopography, see Galsterer (1990).

demonstration of the providential intersection of Roman empire and Christian church: "our teaching flourished along with an empire that had a splendid foundation." Emperors too were aware of Augustus' lingering reputation. Constantine issued an edict that repealed the penalties on celibacy in Augustus' "ancient law." In his evaluation of his predecessors Julian allowed Augustus to speak before the tribunal of gods about his achievements, which included his success at ending the civil wars, his respect for philosophy, and his firm administration of the state. When the gods subsequently questioned Augustus, their only criticism was to dismiss him as a "model maker," because he had fabricated some new gods, among them Julius Caesar, his father by adoption. They also complained that he was a "chameleon" and a "monster of many shapes." Even Julian's gods could not quite define Augustus' many facets.[6]

Since Augustus was still a significant presence during the fourth century, it is perhaps predictable that modern scholarship on late Roman emperors and aristocrats, with regard to interests, approach, and tone, has often followed the lead of Augustus' most powerful modern interpreter. Syme's influence is directly apparent in analyses of Constantine, in three linked perspectives. One is an emphasis on a close reading of the ancient evidence, especially the literary texts, as sources whose contents and intentions require repeated scrutiny. Since some ancient documents were so flattering of Constantine and others so disparaging, source criticism (including prosopography) will always be a mainstay of scholarship on Constantine. A second important influence is a focus on the emperor's politics. This approach tries to resolve Constantine's sometimes bewildering inconsistencies about his attitudes toward Christianity and paganism in terms of his political needs and strategies. It also highlights the influence of his supporters, who soon of course included bishops. In some cases these bishops would become so powerful that they were seemingly able to compel Constantine to accept their own preferred policy of intolerance toward heterodox churchmen.

---

[6] Teaching: Eusebius, *HE* 4.26.7–8, citing a lost treatise by Melito. Celibacy: *CTh* 8.16.1, issued in 320. Julian, *Caesares* 309A-C, chameleon, monster, 325C-327A, Augustus' speech, 332C-333A, critique.

Even though one bishop, Eusebius of Caesarea, carefully defined the emperor as "a loyal son of the church," the supposed underlying reality is that more aggressive bishops like Athanasius of Alexandria and Eusebius of Nicomedia had simply overwhelmed this "artful negotiator, patient consensus builder, and ardent judicial reformer." A final important influence concerns the sincerity of Constantine's commitment to Christianity. Not only was Constantine sometimes fickle in his attitudes toward Christianity; he also seemingly used Christian policies in order to advance a political agenda. The question of the sincerity of Constantine's religious commitment is hence an analogue of the question about the sincerity of Augustus' political claim to have restored the Republic. Because each pronouncement can readily seem disingenuous, Constantine is as vulnerable as Augustus to Syme's sort of dark, skeptical style of historical interpretation.[7]

---

[7] Source criticism can even include an attempt to explain a vision of Constantine as the witnessing of a solar halo: see Weiss (2003). Quotations about Constantine's politics from Drake (2000) 357. For the modern emphasis on Constantine's motives, see Brandt (1998) 32, "die übergeordnete Frage, ob Konstantins Begünstigung des Christentums auf politisches Kalkül oder auf religiöse Überzeugung zurückzuführen ist." But for criticism of the emphasis on Constantine's personal beliefs, see Dagron (2003) 128: "we have to stop . . . speculating about the sincerity or the depth of his faith."

Scholarship on the prosopography of late antiquity has flourished with a proliferation of specialist studies and large handbooks such as *The Prosopography of the Later Roman Empire, Consuls of the Later Roman Empire*, and *Prosopographie chrétienne du Bas-Empire;* for appreciative overviews of the impact of prosopography, see Eck (2003), Martindale (2003), and Mathisen (2003). For the reign of Constantine prosopographical studies have typically focused on the religious preferences of the top magistrates, such as consuls, praetorian prefects, and prefects of Rome. The first Christian consul served in 317, and about a dozen more during the 320s and 330s; praetorian prefects and prefects of Rome who were certainly or probably Christians also served during the 320s and 330s: see von Haehling (1978) 513–21, and Barnes (1994a), revising Barnes (1989a). But this emphasis on the top Christian magistrates can be misleading about the nature of the Constantinian revolution, and in particular about the continuity (or discontinuity) from the Tetrarchs to Constantine. Almost all top magistrates (excepting perhaps emperors' relatives) would have held lesser offices, such as provincial governorships,

Another approach to Augustus has focused on his public representation. From the beginning of his rise to sole rule, he and his advisors
were experimenting with various public identities, as communicated in
various media. As a result, how the emperor presented himself or how
others represented him far overshadowed his actions and convictions.
The other great modern book about Augustus' reign is Paul Zanker's
*The Power of Images in the Age of Augustus*. His approach was both a
complement to Syme's perspective and an antidote. Because Syme had
approached Augustus' reign with the assumption that the emperor and
his cronies used literature and art to conceal their power, he was always
looking for the true underlying reality of imperial rule. In contrast,
Zanker assumed that Augustus and his supporters used art and iconography in order to reveal the emperor and to project favorable images.
Syme presented Augustus as a manipulative dissimulator, and Zanker as
an equally manipulative self-promoter. While Syme's Augustus seemed
to live in the shadows, Zanker's Augustus was always on public display.

Zanker emphasized the invention of "a whole new method of visual
communication" that included a "completely new pictorial vocabulary."
At first Augustus and his rivals used images based on the portraits of

perhaps two decades or so before their consulships or prefectures. For instance,
Amnius Anicius Julianus, consul in 322 and prefect of Rome from 326 to 329,
had been proconsul of Africa in the early fourth century: see *PLRE* 1:473–74,
"Amnius Anicius Iulianus 23." Sextus Anicius Paulinus, consul in 325 and prefect of Rome from 331 to 333, had likewise been proconsul of Africa: see *PLRE*
1:679–80, "Sextus Anicius Paulinus 15." Because these men might well have held
these lesser imperial offices under Diocletian and the Tetrarchs, the question facing modern scholars is whether this continuity of magistrates was matched by
continuity of religious preferences. One possibility is that these men had held
lesser offices under pagan emperors despite their Christianity; note Eusebius,
*HE* 8.1.2, for a claim that Christians were serving as provincial magistrates under
the Tetrarchs. Another possibility is that these men had previously been pagans
but converted to Christianity before serving as high magistrates under Constantine. Eusebius noted that of Constantine's magistrates, although "some preferred
paganism," most had acknowledged "the saving faith." But he also complained
that some men only pretended to accept Christianity, perhaps to improve their
job prospects: see Eusebius, *Vita Constantini* 2.44, magistrates, 4.54.2–3, pretense.

Hellenistic rulers; then he adopted a new harmonious style of portraiture "inspired by the Classical canon." He also gradually shifted away from overt self-glorification to advertisement of his religious piety and political traditionalism. In this new era he restored temples, dedicated offerings, and enhanced priesthoods; he also promoted the standing of senators and restored the functioning of old Republican offices and institutions. The basis of Augustus' prestige and authority was now a repeated public display of modesty and deference.[8]

Zanker furthermore stressed Augustus' self-conscious use of Roman legends and the early history of the Republic in his public imagery. The centerpiece of Augustus' new forum at Rome was a temple dedicated to Mars the Avenger that celebrated his ultimate victory in the civil wars. The decoration of the temple also emphasized how Augustus' rule was a natural outcome of Roman history. Inside the temple were statues of Mars, the father of Romulus according to legend, and Venus, an ancestor of Aeneas according to myth. Romulus and Aeneas were central figures in legends about the foundation of Rome. Alongside those statues of Mars and Venus was another of Julius Caesar, Augustus' father by adoption. By implication Augustus was the new founder of Rome, the proper successor to both Aeneas and Romulus. In one of the colonnades that flanked the courtyard in front of the temple Augustus erected a row of statues of the worthiest ancestors in his Julian family. In the opposite colonnade he set up a corresponding row of statues of eminent leaders and generals from the Republic. The juxtaposition of these statues clearly highlighted the importance of Augustus' dynasty in Roman history. "These portrait galleries thus offered a revised version of history suited to the purposes of Augustan Rome." By the end of Augustus' reign the iconography of this "new official mythology" had become "a single integrated system of images": "the message was comprehensible to all." People hence used this visual language throughout the empire, in Italy to decorate their houses with depictions of Augustan ideals, in the provinces to embellish temples in honor of the emperor. In Zanker's perspective, for Romans "an image was more powerful than

[8] Zanker (1988) 3, visual communication, 98, canon, 101, pictorial vocabulary.

the reality." Augustus had invented himself as a Republican emperor, and many Romans had accepted his self-representation. In his appropriation of traditional imagery Augustus had become a true champion of the Republic.[9]

One imposing requirement for interpreting the past is to forget the future. In hindsight the actual course of events may seem to have been a natural, almost inevitable, outcome: Roman Republic becomes empire, and Roman empire becomes Christian empire. But this sort of retrospective teleology thoroughly obscures the underlying contingency of past events and the fundamental uncertainty of our modern interpretations. Even as Augustus absorbed past traditions, his success seemed to challenge the expectations of those same traditions. A Republican emperor was a contradiction in terms, because centuries earlier the Republic had been founded as the opposite of monarchy. Panels of magistrates had replaced monarchy, the annual tenures of these magistrates had replaced the lifetime rule of a king, and the election of magistrates had replaced dynastic succession. Now, although Augustus and subsequent emperors carefully avoided calling themselves "kings," their mere presence as sole rulers with lifetime tenure and a preference for dynastic succession was a denial of the essence of the Republic.

A Christian emperor was no less of a contradiction in terms. Before Constantine churchmen had not anticipated the possibility, and their

---

[9] Zanker (1988) 114, comprehensible, 193, mythology, 211, portrait galleries, 237, integrated system, 238, image. The visual language of Constantine's reign deserves a similar study. For his portraits, see L'Orange (1984), and Fittschen and Zanker (1985). For imperial buildings, see Mayer (2002), interpreting the monuments "aus dem ideologischen Diskurs zwischen dem Kaiser und der jeweiligen gesellschaftlichen Elite" (p. 5). For churches, see Klein (1999c): "So wie der Neubau und die Ausstattung der Heiligtümer im Erneuerungsprogramm des Augustus die wichtigsten und vornehmsten Aufgaben waren, so waren für Constantin die neuen Basiliken Zeugnisse offizieller Staatsarchitektur und dienten somit der Propaganda kaiserlicher Politik" (p. 212). Elsner (2000a) 177–78, stresses the importance of investigating Constantinian building projects and images "as aspects of a concerted and developing visual strategy over three decades."

hope of a Christian ruler had instead highlighted the return of Jesus
Christ "at the end of time." As they were once thought to have explained
to an emperor, Christ's "heavenly and angelic empire" would succeed
the Roman empire, not replace it. A generation after Constantine, his
nephew Julian was still trying to analyze the rise of Christianity. In his
perspective, the success of Christians would have surprised both Jesus
and the apostle Paul, "both of whom never had even the hope that you
[Christians] would someday attain such power." Even Jesus had not
foreseen a Christian emperor. As a result, the reign of Constantine had
been so unexpected that, like the reign of Augustus as a Republican
emperor, it introduced "a whole new way of thinking" about emperors. The greatest challenge that the reign of Constantine posed, for
both Christians and non-Christians, was simply imagining a Christian
emperor.[10]

Modern scholarship has typically insisted that Constantine's involvement with Christianity was the defining characteristic of his long reign.
Already in their titles many books advertise this association between
emperor and Christianity: *Constantine the Great and the Christian
Church; The Conversion of Constantine and Pagan Rome; Constantine
and the Conversion of Europe; Constantine and Eusebius; The Christianity of Constantine the Great; Constantine and the Bishops; Constantine and
the Christian Empire.* In these books the usual issues about Christianity
take priority: the timing and exact nature of Constantine's conversion
to Christianity, the inconsistency between his patronage for Christianity and his continuing support for some aspects of pagan cults, his
involvement in the controversies over Donatist Christianity and Arian
Christianity, his role at the council of Nicaea, his supportive relationship
with anti-Nicene churchmen like Eusebius of Caesarea, and the tension
between his opposition to the use of coercive force and the intrigues of
bishops. Even studies that examine ostensibly non-religious aspects of
Constantine's reign, such as his legislation about marriage and families,

---

[10] Explanation to Domitian: Eusebius, *HE* 3.20.4, alluding to Jesus' saying in
John 18:36: "My kingdom is not of this world." Jesus and Paul: Julian, *Contra
Galilaeos* 1.206A. Quotation about thinking from Zanker (1988) 263.

cannot avoid evaluating (even if downplaying) the extent of Christian influence on these laws.[11]

In contrast, this book about Constantine highlights different, and often alternative, perspectives on the significance of his reign. In many situations Christianity was not Constantine's primary concern. Because the practical obstacles to establishing imperial rule were overwhelming, becoming emperor, surviving as emperor, and imposing his authority were more pressing worries. Constantine spent almost twenty years eliminating his rivals, even as he remained committed to protecting the frontiers and conducting military campaigns against neighbors. He had to prioritize his attention between the northern frontiers and the eastern frontier. He had to cope with the underlying strains that had long characterized the Roman empire, such as the social resentment resulting from the promotion of the amenities of Rome at the expense of the provinces, the cultural contrast between Latin West and Greek East, and the extraordinary diversity of local religious cults. Once established as emperor, he had to consider his future legacy, and in particular the problem of imperial succession. Before Constantine was a Christian emperor, he was a typical emperor.[12]

---

[11] Titles: Baynes (1931), Alföldi (1948), Jones (1962), Barnes (1981), Elliott (1996), Drake (2000), Odahl (2004). For a typical claim about the role of Christianity, see Elliott (1996) 1, "Constantine's importance is due to his christianizing mission." For the motives behind Constantine's legislation, see Evans Grubbs (1995) 317: "Thorough examination . . . does not support the often expressed view that his marriage laws clearly reflect Christian teachings and a peculiarly 'Christian' perspective," and Humfress (2006) 207, on recent scholarship "undermining the idea of a general Christian influence on the extant corpus of Constantinian legislation."

[12] Already in late antiquity historians could evaluate Constantine against non-Christian criteria, as the first emperor to found a city named after himself, the first emperor to have condoned the greed of his courtiers, the first emperor to have appointed barbarians as consuls, or the emperor responsible for the collapse of the frontiers: see Orosius, *Historiae adversum paganos* 28.27, city; Ammianus Marcellinus, *Res gestae* 16.8.12, courtiers, 21.10.8, barbarians; Zosimus, *Historia nova* 2.34, frontiers; with Warmington (1999) 166, on fourth-century historians: "They . . . are applying to him [Constantine] the same traditional standard of

The first section of chapters examines two consequential issues, the fate of Rome in the later empire and ideas about imperial succession. The nominal starting point is Constantine's response to a petition from some cities in central Italy. In his reply Constantine agreed to their request to construct a new temple that would be dedicated to his imperial dynasty. In the early empire cities in Italy had shared in the special esteem of Rome, and they too had enjoyed enhanced privileges. But increasingly emperors had spent more time near the frontiers, and they had promoted more provincials as imperial magistrates. By agreeing to this petition Constantine hence seemed to be restoring an older prestige and luster to cities in central Italy, and also to Rome itself. At the same time he was publicizing new ideas about imperial succession. Under the Tetrarchy, the rule of four concurrent emperors that had preceded his reign, emperors' sons had been repeatedly overlooked in the selection of successors. In contrast, Constantine ensured the succession of his own sons by reviving the expectation of dynastic succession. In the process he also burnished his own reputation, because many subsequent emperors would represent themselves as his ideological and spiritual heirs. In his response to these Italian cities Constantine was now promoting both the importance of central Italy and Rome in the empire and the succession of his sons.

The second section of chapters considers two other important issues, the firmness of emperors' decisions about religious affairs and the impact of Latin in the Greek East. Despite his visits to Rome, Constantine nevertheless founded Constantinople as New Rome in the East. The presence of this new capital raised concerns among Greek provincials about both Constantine's religious preferences and his cultural preferences. The nominal starting point this time is the emperor's responses to a series of petitions from the citizens of a small town in Phrygia. The

judgement as they had to all the earlier emperors." One historian, by matching odd characterizations with puzzling chronological periods, seemed to imply that Constantine's life had proceeded backward from adulthood to boyhood: see *Epitome de Caesaribus* 41.16, "For [the first] ten years [of his reign] he was truly extraordinary. For the next twelve years he was a bandit. For the last ten years he was a little boy, because of his unrestrained generosity."

citizens hoped for a promotion in the rank of their town, and to support their request they stressed their religious piety. But even though Constantine had already demonstrated his own Christianity, these citizens never mentioned Christianity. Perhaps the vagaries of previous imperial policies about religion had made them cautious about an appeal to religious solidarity. These citizens also submitted their petition in Latin. Since the Tetrarchic emperors had promoted the use of Latin even in the Greek East, these citizens presumably thought that Constantine still shared his predecessors' convictions about the hegemony of Latin. These Greek provincials hence decided to represent themselves to the emperor not as Christians, but as Romans who were capable of using Latin.

The final section of chapters evaluates the problem of imagining a Christian emperor. This analysis defines Christianity in terms of identity rather than beliefs. Being a Christian emperor certainly raised practical problems for Constantine, for instance about his readiness to use coercive force or his attitudes toward bishops. Even more important, it raised ideological issues about self-presentation. Constantine had to decide how to identify himself in public; and in turn others, both Christians and non-Christians, had to decide how to think about him. Already during his lifetime there were many possibilities for imagining a Christian emperor. Constantine himself often followed the lead of the Tetrarchic emperors, who had defined themselves and their rule in terms of divine legitimation. Even though he eventually promoted a different God, he retained their emphasis on a theology of emperorship. The Tetrarchic emperors had identified themselves with pagan gods; once Constantine supported Christianity, he likewise emphasized his intimacy with, even identification with, Jesus Christ. But at the same time churchmen were arguing over the proper doctrinal articulation of the relationship between Jesus Christ the Son and God the Father. As a result, the controversies over these schemes of representation often overlapped, with the same issues and the same terminology. The theological search for the identity of Jesus Christ and the political search for the identity of a Christian emperor were complementary aspects of the same discourse about power and representation. In these disputes

Constantine was not simply a participant. He also became a symbolic medium, as churchmen (and Constantine himself) articulated their ideas about both theology and politics by using a lexicon of images of a divine Son and a Christian emperor.

At the center of these searches was Eusebius of Caesarea. Eusebius survived the persecutions under the Tetrarchic emperors and became bishop of Caesarea in Palestine. He attended the council at Nicaea in 325, which considered the doctrinal controversies about the Trinity. At this council he met Constantine. Subsequently he received supportive letters from Constantine, delivered panegyrics in honor of the emperor, and finally composed a laudatory biography of the emperor. Modern scholars have hence often not treated Eusebius kindly as a historian, and his *Life of Constantine* has been especially criticized as an inadequate historical source. Even sympathetic scholars fault *Life* for its deficiencies as "a sober historical account" or for presenting "so tendentious a picture in favor of Constantine," as if Eusebius had knowingly falsified the emperor through his excessive praise.[13]

In fact, Eusebius did not *mis*represent the emperor. Instead, he had deliberately represented the emperor in a particular way that happened to correspond to and support his own doctrines. Throughout his career Eusebius was a theologian and apologist first, and a historian second. Just as in his *Ecclesiastical History* he had articulated a unique perspective that supported his own understanding of the importance of Christianity in the Roman world, so in *Life* he constructed an image of Constantine that was compatible with his own theological stance. Although it is proper for us to disagree with Eusebius' interpretations, it is quite unfair to

[13] Quotations from Cameron and Hall (1999) 7 (sober), and Lenski (2006a) 5 (tendentious); note that historians of late antiquity were likewise already criticizing Eusebius for his excessive flattery of Constantine: see Chapter 12, with Droge (1992), for an excellent summation of Eusebius' historical vision, and Warmington (1993), for Eusebius' manipulative citations of Constantine's edicts. Athanasius' writings too are frequently, but misleadingly, characterized as "tendentious" or "political caricature": see Barnes (1993) 126. For an important corrective interpretation of Athanasius' *Historia Arianorum*, see Kannengiesser (2001).

criticize him for doing exactly what we modern historians are supposed to do: argue a point of view. Like Eusebius, we too fashion images of Constantine that fit into our own interpretive stances, and in our scholarly disputes we too conjure up new identities for the first Christian emperor. As we repeatedly construct Constantine, we are Eusebius' true heirs.

Constantine is one of the best documented of the Roman emperors, and a political narrative of his life and reign is straightforward enough. The empire seemed to be collapsing when he was born at Naissus in the early 270s. His father, Constantius, became a junior emperor in the Tetrarchy, the college of four emperors, in 293, and he succeeded Diocletian and Maximian as one of the senior emperors in 305. When Constantius died at York in the next year, his troops proclaimed his son emperor. In 312 Constantine defeated Maxentius, a rival emperor, at Rome, and in 324 he eliminated Licinius, his last rival. He celebrated the dedication of Constantinople in 330, and upon his death in 337 he was buried in his new capital. His successors were his three sons, Constantine II, Constantius II, and Constans.

Modern studies often adopt significant dates from Constantine's life as the basic framework for this entire period of Roman history. Just as Eusebius of Caesarea turned the biography of Constantine into theology, modern historians likewise transform that same biography into an "age of Constantine." Such an emphasis on his (or any emperor's) biography can distort our understanding of the later Roman empire, since it gives too much credit to his capacity for influencing historical changes and too little credit to the larger social and cultural transitions. Constantine certainly could choose how to represent himself, not least because so many images were available, as an emperor of the North or an emperor of the Mediterranean, as an emperor of Rome or an emperor of Constantinople, as an heir of the Tetrarchic imperial system or the founder of a new imperial dynasty, as a Latin emperor or a Greek emperor, as an Arian Christian emperor or a Nicene Christian emperor, as a friend of God or a friend of Christ. But in each case he was responding to larger trends over which he had little influence, such as the increasing importance of the frontier zones at the expense of the Mediterranean core of the empire, the decreasing significance of Rome, the possibility that the Greek East might become a separate empire, the uncertainty over the relationship between emperors and gods, and the conflicts over Christian Trinitarian doctrines. During the fourth century the discourse about "emperor" was hence an aspect of a more comprehensive discourse about "empire," in particular concerning the future of Romanness, Greekness, and Christianity. In each case the outcome was quite unexpected: a Roman empire that no longer had to include Rome, a Greek empire in the eastern provinces that still used Latin, a Christian empire that was consistently at odds about defining orthodox Christianity.

Any analysis of such an obviously important historical figure as Constantine can easily become a bit overdetermined. Some events that seem in retrospect to have been vitally significant innovations may in fact have been quite petty at the time. One innovation of Constantine's reign was the regular wearing of the imperial diadem. Some of the emperors during the later third century had already experimented with wearing a diadem, perhaps because it conjured up memories of Alexander the Great, the greatest conqueror in the East. Portraits of Constantine wearing a diadem first appeared on his coins during his war with Licinius in 324 and soon after he had taken control of the eastern provinces. At first he was depicted wearing a plain band diadem, but over the years the diadem seems to have become more elaborate, decorated with rosettes, leaves, and jewels. Subsequent historians credited him as the first to have worn a diadem studded with pearls and gems: "none of the previous emperors had ever worn something like that." This new emblem conjured up various explanations. One historian suggested that Constantine started wearing a diadem in order to fulfill the implication of a Psalm in which the king thanked God for his crown of precious stones. Another claimed that he wore a "beautiful crown" as "a symbol of his sole rule and his victory over his enemies." These historians interpreted Constantine's diadem either as a sign of his new religion or as a reminder of his military success at reunifying the empire.[14]

A diadem quickly became a common badge of imperial rule, along with a purple robe and golden slippers. Already during the fourth century receiving a diadem was a standard component in the ceremonial assumption of emperorship. The various types of diadems were used to differentiate the relative ranks of co-emperors. Soon one legend claimed that Helena had sent to her son Constantine a diadem formed from one of the nails used to crucify Jesus Christ. Through its refashioning as an imperial diadem, this implement of torture and persecution had become the "nail of the Roman empire." Jesus' crown of thorns had been swapped for an imperial diadem of nails, and by wearing this diadem "Constantine also transmitted the faith to subsequent emperors." For both the historians of antiquity and modern scholars Constantine's diadem represented the reunification of the empire, the emergence of Christian emperors, and the triumph of Christianity.[15]

But already in antiquity other commentators offered a more mundane explanation that ignored these great religious and political transformations. In their estimation, Constantine was just vain. One historian suggested that Constantine had started wearing a diadem because "his hair was receding from his forehead." Another solution for his embarrassment over his baldness was apparently the concoction of a scented

[14] According to *Epitome de Caesaribus* 35.5, the emperor Aurelian "was the first among the Romans to wear a diadem on his head." Portraits: Bruun (1966) 44–45, 147, 660, and Bastien (1992–1994) 1:143–66. Constantine's diadem: *Epitome de Caesaribus* 41.14, *Chronicon Paschale* s.a. 330; previous emperors: John Malalas, *Chronographia* 13.8, citing Psalm 21:3 (= LXX 20:4); symbol: *Vita Constantini* 24, ed. Opitz (1934) 557.

[15] Symbols of imperial rule: Pacatus, *Panegyrici latini* 2(12).45.1–2, warning any potential usurper against covering his shoulders with "royal purple," his feet with "gold and gems," and his head with a diadem; with the excellent survey of the changing significance of the diadem in Kolb (2001) 76–79, 105–8, 113–14, 201–4. Ambrose, *De obitu Theodosii* 47, faith, 48, nail.

lotion that subsequently took its name from the emperor: *Sapo Constantini*, "Constantine's Hair Gel." Perhaps we modern historians should take seriously the possibility that Julian's assessment of his uncle as a "hairdresser" had been based on credible family gossip. Augustus was thought to have inserted lifts in his shoes to make himself appear taller; perhaps Constantine the Great had started wearing a diadem to avoid being known as Constantine the Bald.[16]

[16]  Receding hair, scented soap: Polemius Silvius, *Laterculus* V, "Breviarium temporum." Various medical writers included recipes for "Constantine's Lotion," apparently a shampoo or medicinal application: see Mazzini (1992), and Callu (1995), suggesting that this emphasis on personal narcissism was an attempt to minimize the autocratic implications of wearing a diadem. Note also Themistius, *Orat.* 6.81c, a recommendation that the emperor Valens remember his own oration to the senate and gaze into it as if into a mirror, so that "you might arrange more attractively not your hair but your rule over the Romans." Although Heather and Moncur (2001) 195n.195, suggest that this was a reference to Nero, Constantine was a more immediate predecessor and a more appropriate reference for a joking allusion at Constantinople. Augustus' shoes: Suetonius, *Augustus* 73.

For use of Constantine's physical appearance as a nickname, note that "according to a popular saying" he was known as Trachala, "thick-necked": see *Epitome de Caesaribus* 41.16, with Bruun (1995), evaluating whether this nickname was a compliment ("strong-necked") or a critique ("proud-necked").

# A ROMAN EMPIRE WITHOUT ROME

## SECTION ONE

H OPE AND TREPIDATION. APPROACHING AN EMPEROR CON-
jured up conflicting feelings in petitioners. Because emperors were a highly anticipated source of justice, generosity,
and assistance, they were expected to demonstrate their
accessibility and civility. When Theodosius visited Rome, he had
enjoyed bantering with the crowds. To reinforce this image of himself as an ordinary citizen, he had also "banished terror." But despite
their best intentions, emperors often projected an aura of menace and
intimidation. Emperors were frightening figures, usually surrounded
by high-ranking advisers and armed bodyguards and with no constitu-
tional restrictions on their exercise of power. Even as one orator praised
Theodosius for his affability at Rome, he also admitted that he was still
terrified to speak in his presence. Another orator had calmed his nerves
in front of Constantine by openly acknowledging his uneasiness. "It
is no small task to ask the emperor of the entire world for a personal
favor, . . . to compose the words, to speak without fear, to stop at the
right time, to await a response."[1]

[1] Theodosius at Rome: Claudian, *De sexto consulatu Honorii* 59–61. Pacatus, *Panegyrici latini* 2(12).1.1, terror, 47.3, accessibility. No small task: *Panegyrici latini*

Petitioners and communities approached emperors and their courts either directly in person or through letters. In a direct meeting an envoy might address the emperor with a panegyric. However nervewracking for the panegyrist, the formal occasion at least imposed a framework of traditional protocol, since the orator generally followed the demands of the rhetorical genre and the emperor was expected to listen respectfully. Petitions presented to the court as letters were often just as formulaic, essentially miniature panegyrics that followed similar guidelines. These petitions combined praise for the emperor and his accomplishments with lists of grievances and requests for benefactions or honors. Petitions hence involved a certain amount of guesswork, as petitioners tried to imagine what an emperor might like to hear and to suggest remedies that they hoped he would adopt. Petitions were simultaneously deferential, trying to reflect the emperor's image of himself, and didactic, trying to bend his response in a favorable manner.

The emperor Constantine acquired a reputation for reading, listening to, thinking about, and responding directly to embassies and petitions from provincials. His reign was especially rich in petitions, in particular with regard to Christianity. Many of these petitions arose from theological controversies involving the Donatists in North Africa and the supporters and opponents of the priest Arius in the East. At the council of Nicaea, in fact, in the interest of unanimity Constantine publicly burned the many petitions submitted by rival churchmen. Other petitions concerned nominally non-Christian topics, such as municipal affairs. Toward the end of his reign Constantine received a petition from central Italy. This petition had been sent by the cities of Umbria, a region north of Rome, or perhaps more specifically by Hispellum (now Spello), a leading city in the region which certainly stood to benefit the most from a favorable response. This petition requested autonomy for both Hispellum and Umbria from a neighboring region and its dominant city. Even as it presented specific requests, however, this petition

5(8).9.3, with Rees (2002) 9, for an evocation of "the imposing atmosphere surrounding such occasions."

also seemed to hint at some uncertainty about how to approach Constantine.[2]

One hesitation involved religion. Because Constantine was a Christian emperor who consistently publicized his patronage of ecclesiastical affairs, it is natural to assume that his preference for Christianity would somehow influence his responses to petitions. In their petition Hispellum and the other cities did define their autonomy in terms of religion. But significantly, their petition did not mention Christianity at all. These cities instead requested the institution of their own festival and the construction of their own temple in honor of Constantine's dynasty. Equally significantly, in his reply Constantine did not mention Christianity either. He clearly considered other issues to be more important. The obsession of modern scholars with the Christianity of the first Christian emperor has obscured other important, perhaps even more consequential, transformations that he initiated or influenced. Dynastic succession was one such alteration. In a break from the model of his Tetrarchic predecessors, Constantine was planning to reinstate hereditary succession to imperial rule. In his letter to these cities in Umbria his concern over the succession of his own sons seems to have taken priority over considerations about specific religious beliefs.

A second hesitation in this petition involved Constantine's absence from Italy and Rome. Although Constantine visited Rome three times between 312 and 326, thereafter during the final eleven years of his reign he usually resided in cities on or near the northern frontiers, including Constantinople. This new capital relentlessly acquired more benefits and advantages, among them the *ius Italicum*, the highly prized "Italian right" that deemed the city to be a part of Italy and a shareholder in its privileges. The foundation of a new permanent capital in the East and the expansion of its prestige in turn led to a demotion in the standing of

---

[2] Constantine's reputation: *Epitome de Caesaribus* 41.14, "legere ipse scribere meditari audire legationes et querimonias provinciarum." For a survey of petitions during the Donatist and Arian controversies, see Millar (1977) 584–607, and Chapter 10. Burning of petitions: Socrates, *HE* 1.8.18–19.

Rome in particular, and of central and southern Italy in general. "Italy" seems to have changed location: even as Constantinople was becoming more "Italian," cities in Italy were becoming more "provincial." Rome and its inhabitants had to adapt; so did many small towns in peninsular Italy. In its petition Hispellum had become an Italian city that seemed to sense it was losing contact with an increasingly distant emperor, and in its appeal for the patronage of a remote emperor Hispellum seemed to be behaving instead like a faraway provincial city. Its petition was symptomatic of a grand reversal in the relationship between capital and frontier regions, and hence in the definitions of center and periphery. By the end of Constantine's reign it was apparent that Rome and other cities in peninsular Italy were no longer central in the Roman world. These cities were now on the edge, in a marginal hinterland, seemingly forgotten and ignored.[3]

In their petition Hispellum and the other cities in Umbria clearly felt more comfortable talking about modifications of old customs than about simply building a new temple and creating a new festival. They hoped that Constantine would be more of a traditionalist than an innovator, more interested in reviving their former prestige than in promoting unexpected innovations (Chapter 1). Constantine seems to have appreciated the opportunity to present himself as a conservative restorer, especially since he was in fact cutting back on his interest in Rome and central Italy in favor of his new capital at Constantinople (Chapter 2), and since he was trying to promote his own sons and other relatives as a new imperial dynasty (Chapter 3). His new capital and his new dynasty both needed the legitimacy of a proper history (Chapter 4). In his rescript to Hispellum the emperor hoped to invent a new future by claiming to revive the past. Even as he looked forward by publicizing himself and his new dynasty, he insisted that his decision preserved old traditions.

---

[3]   See *CTh* 14.13.1, for the restoration of the *ius Italicum* to Constantinople in the early 370s, with Dagron (1974) 62–63, discussing when the capital had first received this right. In the early fifth century the possession of *ius Italicum* entitled Constantinople to acquire the prerogatives of "old Rome": see *CJ* 11.21.

# CONSTANTINE'S RESCRIPT TO HISPELLUM

## CHAPTER ONE

CONSTANTINE REPLIED TO THE PETITION FROM HISPELLUM and the other Umbrian cities sometime after late December 333, and most likely before mid-September 335. During this period he was either in or near Constantinople, or he was campaigning in the Balkans. Unless there had been a long delay in his response, the cities had presumably sent their petition shortly before.[1]

### ITALY FOREVER

Hispellum and these other cities in Umbria were reacting in part to fairly recent changes in the administration of Italy. Already during Augustus' reign the peninsula had been divided into eleven geographical *regiones*. The region that included Rome was, of course, the first region, and through his patronage and favoritism Augustus made clear that no other city in the empire, in particular one of the great cities in the East such as Alexandria or Antioch, would become a rival: "hereafter Rome would never be anywhere but in Rome." In central Italy north

---

[1] For discussion of the date, an edition of the Latin text, and a translation of the rescript, see Appendix 1.

of Rome the upper Tiber River divided Etruria (sometimes known as Tuscia) as the seventh region from Umbria to its east as the sixth region. Since central and southern Italy shared in the elevated prestige of Rome, from the beginning the cities of peninsular Italy had long had a favored standing within the empire. "Italy tended to be treated by the emperors as something of an extension of the city of Rome." Augustus and his successors funded municipal buildings, temples, walls, and aqueducts, provided aid after natural disasters, and built or repaired roads everywhere. Hispellum was located on the Via Flaminia, the great highway that linked Rome with northeastern Italy. It now acquired the rank of a Julian colony, and to compensate for its awkward site on the end of a mountain spur it received additional land from the territories of neighboring cities. Augustus had furthermore donated land along the upper Clitumnus River that the city administered as a public resort for bathing. Even the first emperors with backgrounds in the provinces, Trajan, Hadrian, and Antoninus Pius, continued to favor Italy, and their reigns during the first half of the second century in fact marked a high point in imperial generosity and patronage. Italy forever: one dedication at Rome pointedly praised Trajan for having provided for "the eternal [welfare] of *his* Italy."[2]

[2]  Regions of Umbria and Etruria: Pliny the Elder, *Historia naturalis* 3.50–53, 112–14, with the review of the evidence in Thomsen (1947) 120–25, 230–36, and the list of *correctores* in Chastagnol (1963) 358–60. Quotation about Rome from Nicolet (1991) 193, in an excellent discussion of Augustus' organization of administrative space in Italy; quotation about Italy from Patterson (2003) 97, in an excellent overview of imperial generosity in Italy during the early empire; Eck (1994), argues that the interaction between emperors and Italian cities was more extensive than the surviving documents suggest. Hispellum as Colonia Julia: *CIL* 11.2.1:771, no. 5278, and *Liber coloniarum*, ed. Campbell (2000) 174, with note *ad loc.* Additional land: "Hyginus," *Constitutio limitum*, ed. Campbell (2000) 142. Public bath: Pliny, *Ep.* 8.8.6, with Duncan-Jones (1982) 31, for Pliny's own dedication at Hispellum. For the patronage of Italy by provincial emperors, see Woolf (1990) 226–27, on the alimentary schemes: "the *alimenta* were set up as a means of symbolically binding the emperor and Italy closer together at a time when there was anxiety that they were drifting apart." His Italy: *ILS* 2.1:532, no. 6106, "aeternitati Italiae suae prospexit."

Along with specific gifts and honors Italian cities enjoyed one common advantage that clearly distinguished them from provincial cities. The most important concession for mainland Italy was immunity from the levying of taxes. The payment of taxes was of course necessary for the maintenance of imperial responsibilities, and in particular for financing the army. But it was also a sign of subordination and inferiority. Provincials paid for the privileges of Rome and other Italian cities. As a result, the prestige of Italy elevated the prestige of its administrators, and in the later third century one emperor could still joke that it was more desirable to govern a region of Italy than to reign as a breakaway usurper in Gaul.[3]

This witticism was a last hurrah, however, because with the increasing importance of provincials as soldiers, imperial administrators, senators, and emperors, Italy had been slowly losing its privileged status. Its economic standing had also declined considerably. In Etruria and Umbria, many cities contracted in size and population as municipal buildings fell into disrepair and as columns and marble panels from older monuments were recycled into new dedications. In the countryside villas and rural settlements were abandoned and disappeared. At the end of the third century the emperor Diocletian completed the process of realigning Italy into districts that were effectively the equivalents of provinces, each administered by a governor with the title of *corrector* (later *consularis*). One of these new districts was "Tuscia and Umbria," which combined much of the old regions of Etruria and Umbria.[4]

---

[3] Aurelian's joke: *Epitome de Caesaribus* 35.7, with Nicolet (1994), and Purcell (2000), for surveys of the privileges of early imperial Italy.

[4] For a survey of economic decline in north central Italy during the third and fourth centuries, see Papi (2004). The Verona List mentioned "Tuscia Umbria" as one of the "provinces" in Italy: see *Laterculus Veronensis* 10.5, with Barnes (1982) 203–5, dating the western part of this list between 303 and 314, (1996) 548–50, to late 314. For the province of *Tuscia et Umbria*, later governed by a *consularis*, see *Notitia Dignitatum in partibus Occidentis* 1.57, 2.15, 19.4. Barnes (1982) 218, dates the division of Italy into provinces to the early 290s, Chastagnol (1963) 349–52, precisely to the winter of 290–291. Excellent surveys of the administrative reorganization that marked the "provincialization" of Italy include Ausbüttel (1988) 87–95, stressing

This administrative reorganization overlapped with the loss of fiscal immunity for Italy. Diocletian extended the "oppressive evil of taxes" to northern Italy, and his successor Galerius to peninsular Italy and even the city of Rome. Like cities in the provinces, the cities of Italy now had to accept the responsibility, and the liability, for the collection of taxes within their urban territories. Perhaps not everyone complained equally loudly, because this new burden for the cities offered a new opportunity for local notables. In previous centuries wealthy Italian aristocrats had focused their attention on their rural villas and their involvement in affairs at Rome, and they had been less engaged in their own cities as local patrons. Now, because municipal councilors and magistrates might profit from the supervision of the collection of taxes, local notables had a new incentive to hold offices in their cities. As elsewhere in the Roman empire, in Italy local aristocrats were able to manipulate the assessment and collection of taxes to their advantage by strictly enforcing payment by ordinary peasants while allowing their own arrears to accumulate. The imposition of taxation became, paradoxically, a better stimulus than the earlier direct largess of emperors for encouraging the participation of local notables in municipal affairs.[5]

This involvement gave these local notables in Italy a new motive for promoting the prestige and rank of their own hometowns, and hence of the municipal offices and priesthoods that they might hold. One tactic at hand was the advertisement of an impressive pedigree, and some cities now recalled their earlier founders and revived old foundation myths. Another tactic was an appeal for the continuing intervention of emperors. During the later third and early fourth centuries various emperors,

the important role of the earlier emperors Caracalla and Aurelian, and Lo Cascio (2005) 165–69.

[5] Oppressive evil: Aurelius Victor, *De Caesaribus* 39.31; also Lactantius, *De mortibus persecutorum* 23.1–6, 26.2, with Barnes (1981) 9, 29, for the sequence. For the earlier interest of wealthy Italian élites in their villas and in Rome, see Whittaker (1994b) 142–43: "the basic problem was one of local patronage . . . , the absence of which began to make itself felt in the later first century. . . . The large landowners, who produced the basis of the wealth of the majority of Italian cities, . . . could simply transfer their revenues beyond the reach of the city."

including Tetrarchs, had funded the construction of new municipal buildings in Tuscia and Umbria and the repair of roads, including the Via Flaminia. These lingering displays of imperial patronage might have encouraged cities to ask for more. In particular, cities that had lost ground in the administrative shuffle might resort to petitions to emperors. In their petition to Constantine the cities of Umbria, and in particular Hispellum, were now hoping for an improvement in their standing by being recognized as the equal of the cities in Tuscia.[6]

## "CONTAGIOUS SUPERSTITION"

When the two old regions of Etruria/Tuscia and Umbria were combined into a single new administrative district, Tuscia, and in particular the city of Volsinii (now Bolsena), became dominant. The two regions now celebrated a joint religious festival. But although each region selected a priest, the games were always staged in Tuscia at Volsinii, "according to the tradition of ancient custom." The people of Volsinii had quickly tried to consolidate the momentum of their newly enhanced prominence. The city erected a dedication, and perhaps a statue, in honor of Constantius. After Constantius' son seized control of central Italy in 312, the city erected a statue, and most likely a dedication, in honor of the new emperor. Since Volsinii erected this monument to Constantine apparently soon after his victory, it was perhaps anticipating the emperor's return to celebrate the tenth anniversary of his reign in 315. It furthermore carefully linked the new emperor to earlier Roman history, since Constantine's head on the statue was recut from a head of Augustus. This statue was presumably a reminder to Constantine

---

[6] For the revival of old myths, note Campbell (2000) xliv, on the context for interpreting the *Liber coloniarum*: "the interest in named Italian towns . . . hints at community rivalry in the fourth century." For imperial patronage for cities and roads, see Papi (2004) 65–70: "all roads leading to Rome were improved" (p. 69); but for the abrupt decline of imperial interest for cities in southern Etruria after the Tetrarchs, see Papi (2000) 226–34: "Dal secondo decennio del IV secolo le testimonianze scritte sulle donazioni in Etruria meridionale cessano dappertutto" (p. 234).

that as a new Augustus he should continue imperial patronage for Volsinii.[7]

In their petition the cities of Umbria responded by requesting both relief from a grievance and some favors. By complaining about the difficulties for their priest of traveling over the mountains and through the forests to Volsinii, they seemed to imply that if Constantine truly wanted to imitate Augustus, he should restore the earlier separation between Umbria and Tuscia. In addition, these cities hoped to trump the "ancient custom" of Volsinii by requesting a festival that may have looked back to a still earlier period. They apparently intended to revitalize and update a much older festival at Hispellum, to be celebrated in an ancient sanctuary complex where in fact the inscription of Constantine's reply was found. This complex included a theater, constructed in the later first century B.C., and an amphitheater, constructed during the first century A.D.; archaeologists have also uncovered remains and votive figurines that date as far back as the fifth century B.C. In a neatly evocative symmetry, as central Italy was losing its favored standing in the Roman empire, the region of Umbria planned to reinstate a festival at an archaic religious sanctuary with local roots.[8]

This petition furthermore solicited favors that involved the reputation of the new imperial dynasty. The cities of Umbria requested a new

---

[7] Dedication to Constantius: *CIL* 11.1:426, no. 2697, inscribed on a marble pedestal. Head of Constantine: Giuliano (1991), dating the recutting of the head between 312 and 315, the period of the construction of the Arch of Constantine at Rome. For the likely combination of dedication and statue, see *ILS* 2.1:387, no. 5557a = Grünewald (1990) 224, no. 284, a dedication mentioning statues of Constantine and two of his sons at Canusium in Apulia.

[8] For the religious sanctuary at Hispellum, see Bradley (2000) 244–45, and Amann (2002) 18–25: "Zweifellos war das Heiligtum von Hispellum spätestens im 3./2. Jh. v. Chr. aktiv und verfügte seit augusteischer und auch noch in konstantinischer Zeit über eine beachtliche Breitenwirkung" (p. 21). Coarelli (2001), suggests that the petioners hoped to revive an ancient "centro federale umbro" near Hispellum, and he identifies this imperial temple with the modern church of S. Fedele located near the theater: "La datazione che si deve attribuire a questo edificio, il IV secolo d. C., e la presenza dell'abside – tipica degli edifici del culto imperiale – permette de identificarvi senza possibilità di dubbio il tempio della *gens Flavia*, menzionato nel rescritto" (p. 46).

name for Hispellum that was derived from the emperor's name, and they asked for permission to construct a new temple (*templum*) that would be dedicated to Constantine's "Flavian dynasty." This temple then marked the intersection of grievance and favors, since the cities also suggested that their priest should instead preside over a festival at this new temple. While the priest selected in Tuscia would continue to officiate at the current festival in Volsinii, Umbria hoped to mark its new association with Constantine with a new imperial name for Hispellum, a new imperial temple, and a new imperial festival hosted by its own priest. These imperial benefactions would then become warranties of a new autonomy. Even if they did remain in the same administrative district, a city and a region that received such honors could hardly be expected to be subordinate to a neighboring city and region.

One striking feature of Constantine's rescript, and presumably of the petition too, was the absence of any overt reference to Christianity. Instead, these cities requested a temple, hoped for a new festival that was to include theatrical shows and gladiator games, and conceded that the festival at Volsinii should continue. In their petition the cities of Umbria seemed not to have realized that they were now part of a Christian empire. Nor did Constantine respond in overtly Christian terms. He bestowed upon Hispellum the new name of Flavia Constans and allowed the construction of a new shrine (*aedis*) dedicated to the Flavian dynasty. He permitted a new festival to be celebrated at Hispellum, but also insisted that Volsinii continue to celebrate the old games. The only restriction he imposed concerned the ceremonies at Hispellum: "a shrine dedicated to our name is not to be polluted with the deceits of any contagious superstition."[9]

The meaning and the implications of this restriction on "contagious superstition" are not obvious. On the basis of this restriction,

[9] For a suggestion that Constantine was trying to preserve the traditional games by neutralizing their pagan associations and classifying them as "secular," see Markus (1990) 108–9, and Salzman (2003) 691: "further evidence for how Christian emperors ... sought to re-orient imperial cult to present a more neutral, less offensive aspect to Christian eyes." Note Dvornik (1966) 2:647, for the unlikely suggestion that Constantine included a "gentle correction of a pagan opinion" by substituting *nomen* ("name") in his reply for *numen* ("divinity") in the petition.

most modern discussions of the inscription quickly detour into consideration of Constantine's policies toward pagan cults, and specifically toward pagan sacrifices. These policies were distinctly vague and certainly open to interpretation already during the emperor's reign, not to mention afterward in retrospective partisan evaluations. After his victory over Maxentius at Rome, Constantine joined with his fellow emperor Licinius in early 313 to extend "to both Christians and all people the free power of following the religion that each wishes." This grant of toleration did not mention sacrifices.[10]

In 315 Constantine returned to Rome to commemorate the beginning of the tenth anniversary of his accession as emperor. The celebration included the dedication of a triumphal arch that memorialized the victory over Maxentius. The facades and attic of this arch, however, also advertised the emperor's more generic activities and attributes in a series of iconographic scenes. These scenes were depicted on large sculptured panels and roundels that had been appropriated from earlier monuments honoring the second-century emperors Hadrian and Marcus Aurelius. Some of these imperial activities were neutral in terms of religious practices: the emperor hunting a bear, a boar, and a lion, the emperor addressing the troops, receiving barbarian captives, and distributing gifts to the Roman people. Others were directly religious. Four of the roundels depicted the emperor offering sacrifices to various deities, Silvanus, Diana, Apollo, and Hercules, and one of the panels depicted the emperor preparing to officiate at the traditional sacrifice of a bull, pig, and sheep. In all of these scenes the heads of the original emperors had been recut to resemble Constantine himself or, in two cases, his father, Constantius. Since the senate and people of Rome had constructed and dedicated this arch, presumably they wanted to represent Constantine and his father upholding and respecting the traditional sacrifices. At Rome fitting a new emperor into established religious practices, including participation in sacrifices, was apparently as straightforward as recutting old sculptures.[11]

[10] Letter of 313: Latin version in Lactantius, *De mortibus persecutorum* 48.2, Greek version in Eusebius, *HE* 10.5.4, with additional discussion in Chapter 6.

[11] Photographs and discussion of panels and roundels: L'Orange and von Gerkan (1939) 165–87 + Tafeln 39–42, 46–47, Giuliano (1955) plates 9–24, and Koeppel

Christian commentators, and perhaps Constantine himself, inter-preted these associations differently. Bishop Eusebius of Caesarea claimed that during this visit to Rome in 315 Constantine had offered "prayers of thanksgiving to God, the Emperor of all," as the equivalent of "sacrifices that did not include fire or smoke." In this perspective the emperor seemed to be proposing a Christian alternative to pagan sacrifices, but without banning them. When Constantine wrote to the Persian king Shapur, he included a description of his religious con-victions that indicated his revulsion for "all disgusting blood," but he did not mention any outright ban on sacrifices. At the end of the fourth century Libanius, an unrepentant pagan who might be assumed to be looking to criticize Constantine, nevertheless conceded that the emperor had not changed anything in the traditional forms of pagan worship. Whatever their agenda, both Christians and pagans seemed to recognize that Constantine was quite tolerant in religious matters.[12]

But according to Eusebius, Constantine's stance on sacrifices did in fact eventually become more restrictive. Soon after he defeated Licinius in 324 he had forbidden pagans who held imperial magistracies from offering sacrifices. Eusebius furthermore claimed that the emperor had also issued a more general law against "the abominations of idolatry" that forbade "anyone at all from offering sacrifices." In 341 the emperor Constans (most likely joined by his brother Constantius) seemed to be repeating these restrictions: "superstition is to stop, and the madness of sacrifices is to be abolished." As a warranty for such harshness this edict referred to a "law of the divine emperor, our father." This earlier law

---

(1986) 26–34, 56–75. The identity of the emperor in the two roundels that depicted sacrifices to Apollo and Hercules is disputed. L'Orange and von Gerkan (1939) 168–72 + Tafel 45, and Rohman (1998), identify him as Licinius, Calza (1959–1960), as Constantius. Note that these scenes of sacrifices on the Arch of Constantine rarely figure in modern discussions of Constantine's attitudes toward sacrifices. But as "texts" about Constantine, they are nevertheless similar to the panegyrics, histories, and edicts that modern historians prefer to analyze.

[12] Eusebius, *Vita Constantini* 1.48, smokeless sacrifices, 4.10.1, disgusting blood. No changes: Libanius, *Orat.* 30.6, with Wiemer (1994) 522: "Libanius reflects a per-sistent pagan tradition which insisted that Constantine... did not persecute the pagans."

of Constantine is not extant; but by the mid-360s Libanius noted that attacks on paganism had indeed led to the destruction of temples, the expulsion of priests, and "the abolishment of sacrifices." Even though Constantine's sons were clearly less pragmatic in their attitudes toward pagan cults, they apparently thought that they were simply continuing their father's policies. According to their cousin Julian, "the sons destroyed the ancestral temples that their father had previously dishonored." Constantius in particular had a reputation for being "very pious in the veneration of his father." Since the sons' edict of 341 pointedly linked superstition and sacrifices and specifically appealed to Constantine's precedent, it seems only natural to assume that in his rescript to the cities of Umbria Constantine too, by restricting superstition, had been forbidding the offering of pagan sacrifices at the new temple at Hispellum.[13]

If this was his purpose, he was surprisingly obtuse in saying so. Constantine could be remarkably direct in his reactions to pagan activities.

---

[13] Eusebius, *Vita Constantini* 2.44, restriction on pagan magistrates, 45.1, general restriction, with Corcoran (1996) 315–16, summarizing discussion of the existence of this law about sacrifices, and Heather and Moncur (2001) 49–51, summarizing discussion of Constantine's legislation against paganism. Edict of 341: *CTh* 16.10.2. Since Madalianus, the recipient of this edict, was the vicar of Italy, the edict was issued more likely by Constans than by Constantius: see Seeck (1919) 191. Abolishment of sacrifices: Libanius, *Orat.* 18.23, with Bradbury (1995), on the decline of public sacrifices before Julian's reign. Note that by the later fourth century there were no more altars at Sardis: see Eunapius, *Vitae sophistarum* 503. Ancestral temples: Julian, *Orat.* 7.228B. Constantius' reputation: Aurelius Victor, *De Caesaribus* 42.23, with Curran (2000) 181–93, for a survey of the legislation of Constantius and Constans.

For conventional interpretations of the restriction on "contagious superstition" at Hispellum, see Barnes (1981) 212, "official disapproval of the sacrifices"; Bowersock (1982) 177, "the obvious reference is to sacrifice"; Price (1984) 227, "he entirely abolished sacrifices"; Bradbury (1994) 130, "he would not allow blood sacrifices"; Curran (2000) 181, "he cut animal sacrifice out of the ceremony of the imperial cult"; Odahl (2004) 250, "no sacrifices"; and Lee (2006) 175, "almost certainly a reference to sacrifice." Perhaps Constantine meant to be obscure about the meaning of *superstitio*; note Beard, North, and Price (1998) 1:372: "Constantine may in fact have deliberately played upon the ambiguities of the term, which might usefully evade any precise definition."

In a law of 325 he had already banned gladiators and their "bloody spectacles." He prohibited the celebration of Olympic games in the theater at Chalcedon, and he allowed the despoliation of pagan temples elsewhere. When he had decided to cleanse the pagan images and "impure sacrifices" from the holy site of Mamre in Palestine, he explicitly linked those restrictions with the construction of a new church and the celebration of proper rituals. At Constantinople he eliminated pagan statues, altars, and sacrifices in favor of churches and martyrs' shrines. At Cirta in North Africa, even though a priesthood in honor of the Flavian dynasty had already been founded, Constantine combined the renaming of the city as Constantina with the construction of a church.[14]

The petition of Hispellum and the other Umbrian cities now offered an opportunity to impose similar restrictions in Italy. By the time he replied to their petition Constantine had been an emperor for over twenty-five years, he had already publicized his support for Christianity, and he had no more rivals whose challenges might compel him to temper his policies. He had furthermore already subsidized the construction of

---

[14] Edict on gladiators: *CTh* 15.12.1, issued in October 325; but in 328 Libanius' uncle included gladiatorial combats in the Olympic games at Antioch: see Libanius, *Orat.* 1.5. Olympic games at Chalcedon: Callinicus, *Vita Hypatii* 33.1. Eusebius, *Vita Constantini* 3.48, Constantinople, 51–53, Mamre, 54, despoliation of temples. Priesthood in North Africa and new name for Cirta: Aurelius Victor, *De Caesaribus* 40.28; church: Optatus, Appendix 10.36b.

One of Constantine's important supporters was Lucius Aradius Valerius Proculus, a distinguished senator who served as proconsul of Africa in the early 330s, prefect of Rome in 337–338 and 351–352, and consul of 340. In recognition of his service Constantine honored Proculus in a letter to the magistrates and senate of Rome: see *L'année épigraphique 1934* (1935) 42, no. 158, with the corrections to the preamble in Barnes (1982) 23. But despite this appreciation from a Christian emperor, Proculus was a pagan who held priesthoods at Rome and erected a dedication to Cybele and Attis at Carthage: for the dedication, see *CIL* 8, Supplementum 2.4:2461, no. 24521. Among his offices and honors Proculus listed his tenure as a *pontifex Flavialis*: see *CIL* 6.1:366–67, nos. 1690 ( = *ILS* 1:273, no. 1240), 1691, 1694. It is not clear whether he served as a Flavian priest at Rome; Chastagnol (1962) 100, implies that he may have held this priesthood in North Africa.

churches in cities elsewhere throughout Italy, at Albano, Capua, and Naples. As a result, in this case too Constantine might be expected to have been more overtly enthusiastic in his opposition to pagan shrines and ceremonies and his support of Christianity. Not only might he have explicitly banned pagan sacrifices; he might also have suggested that the people of Hispellum instead construct a church.[15]

In fact, religion, whether pagan cults or Christianity, was most likely not Constantine's primary concern in this rescript. The rationale he himself provided for his decision instead highlighted non-religious concerns. In the preamble of his rescript he emphasized his concern for the welfare of cities. In this case, while Hispellum would have its status enhanced "through the generosity of our beneficence," Volsinii would nevertheless retain its original prestige. In the conclusion the emperor stressed his hope for the preservation of "old institutions." Constantine seems to have been concerned more about restoring an ancestral past than about imposing a new Christian future. Like other emperors, he too wanted to cloak his policies, and in particular his innovations, in the shroud of tradition and antiquarianism. But his most disturbing innovations did not necessarily include the imposition of a new religion at the expense of ancient pagan sacrifices. In this rescript of the mid-330s the innovations he was especially concerned about were the establishment of a new imperial dynasty and the foundation of Constantinople. Only now was Constantine finally making the arrangements for the hereditary succession that would follow his death; and by now the prominence of his new capital in the East was beginning to jeopardize the standing of Rome and other cities in Italy, including Hispellum.[16]

---

[15]  Churches in Italy: *Liber pontificalis* 34.30, Albano, 31, Capua, 32, Naples. Since a temple dedicated to Constantine's family would most likely have included a statue of the emperor, note also the apparent contradiction with the claim in Eusebius, *Vita Constantini* 4.16: "by a law he prevented statues of himself from being erected in the temples of idols."

[16]  Note Arnheim (1972) 51, for Constantine as "a man of antiquarian tastes."

# HIS FAVORITE ROOSTER: OLD ROME AND NEW ROME

## CHAPTER TWO

THIS FEUDING AMONG REGIONS AND CITIES IN CENTRAL ITALY was now incidental to imperial concerns, because increasingly central Italy itself had become peripheral. So had the city of Rome. At the end of the third century a Gallic orator described a map of the Roman world that was being painted on the wall of a new school at Autun. This map highlighted the regions where the four emperors who made up the Tetrarchy had enjoyed recent military successes. Those regions included Egypt, where Diocletian had suppressed a rebellion; Africa, where Maximian had defeated the Moors; Batavia and Britain, where Constantius had overthrown a usurper; and the eastern frontier, where Galerius had triumphed over the Persians. The orator did not mention Rome. If the map had provided a caption for Italy and Rome, then the absence of an emperor and his court would have been all the more glaring. The emperors now resided and campaigned in the frontier zones that enclosed the Roman world and rarely visited the provinces around the Mediterranean center.[1]

---

[1] Map at Autun: *Panegyrici latini* 9(4).20.2–21.3, with Nixon and Rodgers (1994) 146–48, for the dating of this panegyric to the late 290s.

## THE OUTER RIM

This map still noted the activities of emperors in Africa and Egypt. Soon emperors no longer visited those regions either. Constantine's reign confirmed the shift in political significance from the western and southern regions of the empire to the eastern and, especially, the northern regions. Centuries earlier, Roman armies had first expanded outside Italy in campaigns against the rival empire of Carthage in North Africa. During these wars the Roman state had survived a devastating backdoor invasion of Italy across the Alps led by the great Carthaginian general Hannibal. "Italy trembled at the sight of the Carthaginian on the peaks of the Alps." The defeat of the Carthaginian empire heralded the rise of the Roman empire. Its first overseas provinces had been in a ring around the shores of the western Mediterranean, including Sicily, Africa, Spain, and southern Gaul. During the second and first centuries B.C. the Roman empire expanded outward from this core in the western Mediterranean and acquired provinces in the Greek peninsula and western Asia Minor, the regions surrounding the Aegean Sea that had long been the heartland of the classical Greek world. Only later did the empire come to include provinces on its outer rim at the eastern end of the Mediterranean, in central and eastern Asia Minor, and in central and northern Europe. The primary focus of the Roman empire had slowly expanded from Rome and central Italy to include first the regions around the western Mediterranean that had been part of the former Carthaginian empire and then the regions around the Aegean Sea that made up the old Greek world. The provinces on the northern frontier along the Rhine and Danube rivers and on the eastern frontier facing Armenia and Mesopotamia had marked the outer fringes.[2]

In contrast, because Constantine approached Italy, the western Mediterranean, and finally the Aegean from the north, his imperial career reversed both this historical sequence and the consequent political priorities. He had started as a usurper in Britain, proclaimed by his father's troops at York. No provincial capital was as far from the

---

[2]  Italy trembled: *Panegyrici latini* 11(3).10.2

Mediterranean as York. Constantine himself conceded that he had initiated his imperial reign at the far edge of the known world, "at the ocean next to the British people and those regions where it is ordained that the sun sets." Britain could be dismissed as "an island beyond the known world," so remote that in the mid-fourth century even a professional geographer wavered on its whereabouts. Although Constantine soon relocated to the Rhine frontier, his initial power base remained in northern Europe. If confirmation of his standing as a distant outsider to the civilized world of the south were needed, one of his early prominent supporters was Crocus, a king of the Alamans along the upper Danube frontier; another supporter was Bonitus, a Frankish chieftain in northern Gaul. Not surprisingly, Constantine eventually acquired a reputation as the first emperor to have promoted barbarians to high offices, including consulships. When he invaded Italy in a campaign against the emperor Maxentius in 312, he appeared as the commander of "an army of Gauls." While Maxentius was defending Italy with a Mediterranean army of "Romans," "Italians," "Sicilians," and "Carthaginians," Constantine's army of the North consisted of "barbarians, including Germans, other Celtic peoples, and recruits from Britain." In this perspective Constantine might have been just another renegade Gallic emperor, a successor to the rulers of the breakaway empire that had flourished in northern Gaul during the later third century.[3]

---

[3] The ocean: Eusebius, *Vita Constantini* 2.28.2, quoting Constantine's letter to the people of Palestine. Island: Libanius, *Orat.* 59.137, referring to Constans' visit to Britain in early 343. Geographer: *Expositio totius mundi et gentium* 67, with Rougé (1966) 341, on the author's ignorance. Support of Crocus: *Epitome de Caesaribus* 41.3, with *PLRE* 1:233; of Bonitus: Ammianus Marcellinus, *Res gestae* 15.5.33, with *PLRE* 1:163, "Bonitus 1." Reputation: Ammianus Marcellinus, *Res gestae* 21.10.8, 12.25. Army of Gauls: Libanius, *Orat.* 30.6, with Urban (1999) 98–100, for the responses of Constantine's panegyrists to these concerns about his soldiers. Armies of Maxentius and Constantine: Zosimus, *Historia nova* 2.15; also Porphyrius, *Carm.* 18.9–10, addressed to Constantine: "your remote Rhine generates armies for you." According to Julian, *Orat.* 1.34C, addressed to Constantius II, the army of Magnentius, a usurper in the early 350s, included "Celts and Gauls" serving in units "enrolled by your ancestors and father [Constantine]." For the depiction of barbarians in Constantine's army in the panel reliefs on the Arch of Constantine at Rome, see L'Orange and von Gerkan (1939) 41–51.

Even after he had defeated his final rival and emerged as sole emperor in 324, Constantine was rarely far from the long northern frontier that stretched between Trier and Constantinople, from the lower Rhine through northern Italy and the Balkans along the Danube to Thrace. During his exceptionally long reign he never visited the provinces in Spain, Africa, southern Italy and Sicily, Greece, western Asia Minor, Palestine, or Egypt, and he made only one round trip through central Asia Minor to Antioch in Syria. About a year after Constantine became emperor a panegyrist hailed him as *oriens imperator*, an "emperor on the rise." Within a decade of his accession a long panel on the arch commemorating his victory at Rome depicted the arrival of the triumphant emperor at the capital, seated in a four-horse carriage. Over this panel was a large roundel that depicted the god Sol, rising from the ocean on his four-horse chariot. Appropriately enough, this roundel was on the east end of the arch, and its proximity to the panel clearly associated the arrival of the victorious emperor with the rising of the Sun-god. But Constantine had not come to Rome from the east. His uprising had been instead in the north, in Britain. He resembled another victorious emperor who had appeared at Rome "dazzling with the dust from a battle in the north." From the beginning of his reign to the end, Constantine remained fundamentally a northern emperor.[4]

Rome marked the southernmost extent of his absence from the frontiers, and Rome was an odd place to be visited by an emperor who emphasized his association with the northern provinces, who was a career soldier, and who presented himself as a Christian. The capital was a "city of the toga," whose residents were primarily civilians. Some of its notable senators still claimed to be the direct descendants

---

[4]  *Panegyrici latini* 7(6).1.1, rising emperor, 4.3, *illic oriundo*, "by rising there," i.e. in Britain. For descriptions and photographs, see L'Orange and von Gerkan (1939) 72–78, the panel, 162–64, the roundel + Tafeln 1, 3, 12–13, and Giuliano (1955) plates 39, 54. Dust: Martial, *Epigrammata* 8.65.3, in a description of Domitian standing at the triumphal arch that commemorated a campaign on the Danube. In one of the panels on his arch the depiction of Constantine's arrival at Rome in fact ended at this Arch of Domitian: see below. Constantine's Flavian dynasty was furthermore a reminder of Domitian's Flavian dynasty: see Chapter 3.

of the great senators from the late Republic who had commanded the armies that had conquered the Mediterranean. Now they were reduced to pompous claims that stately trips to their country estates qualified as the equivalent of the arduous military campaigns of Alexander the Great and Julius Caesar. Some of these senators were true intellectuals who corrected Latin and Greek texts or edited manuscripts of Livy's historical narrative. Others were, at best, dilettantes, even in Latin literature. One learned visitor, a Greek who was nevertheless familiar with Latin literature, would ridicule their devotion to the tabloid biographies of Marius Maximus and the caustic satires of Juvenal. Many, perhaps most, of these senators were still pagans. In the early fourth century Rome was a civilian, Latin, and pagan capital. In contrast, not only did the foundation of Constantinople conspicuously reaffirm the increasing importance of the northern and eastern frontiers. It furthermore highlighted the importance of the army, Greek culture, and Christianity. Constantinople would become a military, Greek, and Christian capital. The significance of these new factors tended to marginalize Rome. They also marginalized other cities in central Italy.[5]

## BALKAN EMPERORS AT ROME

Constantine had first visited Rome already before he became an emperor. For late Roman emperors, control over Rome still represented imperial legitimacy. After the murder of Severus Alexander in 235 few subsequent emperors could make a proper hereditary claim on the throne, and most became emperors through military coups on the

---

[5] City of the toga: Prudentius, *Peristephanon* 12.56. Ammianus Marcellinus, *Res gestae* 28.4.14, literary tastes at Rome, 18, senators' trips, with Barnes (1998) 65–78, on the Greek substrate of Ammianus' Latin, and Cameron (2004) 350–54, on the revival of interest in Juvenal during the late third and fourth centuries. For Symmachus' editing of Livy, see Symmachus, *Ep.* 9.13, with Bloch (1963) 213–17, and Hedrick (2000) 171–213, on the correction of Latin manuscripts by Roman aristocrats. The pace of the spread of Christianity among the aristocracy at Rome remains contested; Salzman (2002) 73–81, suggests that it was gradual: "aristocrats from Rome and Italy were predominantly pagan well into the last decades of the fourth century" (p. 77).

frontiers. Many of the new emperors nevertheless soon visited Rome, where they might hobnob with the senate and people, promote new construction projects, and participate in traditional festivals. One of these military emperors, Philip the Arab, even presided over the extravagant celebration of the millennium of Rome's foundation in 248. Decius highlighted a connection with central Italy by naming his first son Etruscus. Gallienus celebrated the tenth anniversary of his emperorship at Rome with a magnificent procession and entertainments. Aurelian initiated construction of the huge wall surrounding the city. Emperors clearly wanted to flaunt their successes and acquire legitimacy at Rome. In fact, in an odd reversal that future events would soon turn into irony, Gallienus visited Rome in part to celebrate his devastation of Byzantium, the small city destined to become the New Rome of Constantinople.[6]

Diocletian too used a visit to Rome to reinforce his authority. Within a year after his proclamation as emperor at Nicomedia, he had traveled to Italy in summer 285. This trip may have included a visit to Rome. In late 303 Diocletian certainly visited Rome in order to celebrate the beginning of the year marking the twentieth anniversary of his accession. He also expected to assume a consulship at Rome. His fellow senior emperor Maximian joined him for the festivities, and together they celebrated "at Rome a distinguished triumph over numerous peoples." Over a decade earlier a panegyrist had imagined just such a moment of unanimity: "when these [emperors] return to you [Rome] in triumph, they wish to ride in one chariot, to approach the Capitoline Hill together, and to reside on the Palatine Hill together." Also in attendance was Constantine, a junior military officer who was accompanying Diocletian's court.[7]

---

[6]  Etruscus: Aurelius Victor, *De Caesaribus* 29.1, with Papi (2000) 202–5, on Decius' wife, Herennia Etruscilla. Gallienus: SHA, *Gallieni duo* 6.8–9, 7.2–4, Byzantium, 7.4–9.8, decennalia at Rome. For surveys of construction at Rome during the third century, see Scheithauer (2000) 204–11, and Curran (2000) 5–26.

[7]  For Diocletian in Italy in 285 and the probability of a visit to Rome, see Barnes (1982) 50, (1996) 537. Vicennalia at Rome in 303: Lactantius, *De mortibus persecutorum* 17.1–3. Dual triumph: Eutropius, *Breviarium* 9.27.2; also Jerome, *Chronicon*

A visit from Diocletian and Maximian was both reassuring and potentially unsettling for the senate and people of Rome. Panegyrists might
blithely insist that the emperors had already fulfilled the expectations of
Roman traditions. In a retrospective evaluation one orator celebrated
Diocletian's victory in 285 over Carinus, a rival emperor who had established himself in Italy and briefly resided at Rome, as a return to an
ancestral constitution: "through your might the Republic was liberated
from a most savage domination." The notion of the restoration of the
old Republic was still powerful in particular at Rome, since it seemed
to verify both the eminence of the old capital and the importance of
its senators. But despite the determined traditionalism, emperors who
identified themselves with deities did not fit into this conventional ideology. During the winter of 290–291 the senate had sent a delegation
of its "luminaries" to attend a meeting of Diocletian and Maximian at
Milan. Since Diocletian was by now associating himself with Jupiter and
Maximian with Hercules, these senators would have had to join with
the crowd in "invoking a visible Jupiter who was present and nearby"
and "adoring Hercules as an emperor."[8]

In 303 the emperors arrived at Rome to celebrate their triumph. At
the same time they could show that their identification with deities
was not meant to distance them from the senators and people at the
capital. Instead, they highlighted the correspondence between their religious preferences and the traditional cults. The most renowned shrine
at Rome was the Temple of Jupiter Optimus Maximus on the Capitoline Hill. This eminent temple was as old as the Republic itself, and its
current version was considered to be a manifestation of Rome's eternity.
Diocletian and Maximian now met in this temple. They also celebrated
the twentieth anniversary of their rule by erecting a monument at the

s.a. 304. For the earlier description of Diocletian and Maximian, see *Panegyrici
latini* 10(2).13.2. For the likelihood of Constantine's visit to Rome in 303, see
Barnes (1981) 25.

[8] Carinus at Rome: *ILS* I:138, no. 608, repair of bridge near Ostia; *CJ* 8.53.5, issued
at Rome in January 284. *Panegyrici latini* 11(3).5.3, liberation of Rome, 10.5, Jupiter
and Hercules, 12.2, luminaries of the senate. According to SHA, *Carus et Carinus
et Numerianus* 18.4, the Tetrarchic emperors "greatly revered the Roman senate."

foot of the Capitoline Hill behind the Rostra, the speakers' platform located at the west end of the old Forum. This monument consisted of five tall columns, the middle one topped with a statue of Jupiter, the other four each with a statue of the guardian spirit ("Genius") of an emperor, together representing the two senior emperors and two junior emperors in the Tetrarchy. The reliefs on the one surviving pedestal depicted scenes of sacrifice, with both an emperor and senators participating. The statues and the reliefs of this Monument of Five Columns hence conjured up a longstanding tradition of a communal religious festival in honor of Jupiter and other deities. They were also, however, sharp reminders that the actual moment had been fleeting. Neither Diocletian nor Maximian had stayed. Even though there was now a Tetrarchy of four emperors, none resided in the old capital. Rome would have to be content only with statues.[9]

---

[9] Temple of Jupiter and Rome's eternity: Ammianus Marcellinus, *Res gestae* 22.16.12. Meeting: *Panegyrici latini* 6(7).15.6; Diocletian and Maximian "swore an oath" in the temple, perhaps concerning their plans for a joint abdication: see Nixon (1981).

Only fragments remain of the Monument of Five Columns. L'Orange (1938), classified the fragments as a Tetrarchic monument and identified it with the five columns and their statues depicted in a panel of the Arch of Constantine. For this panel, see Chapter 3; for the inscriptions, Chapter 9. L'Orange included photographs and clear line drawings of the four faces of the surviving pedestal; for additional photographs, with an excellent discussion of the transformation of the Forum, see Kähler (1964). Wrede (1981), argues that the imperial statues were each of the Genius of an emperor rather than of an individual emperor; in that case the monument legitimated the Tetrarchic system rather than specific emperors. At Halicarnassus a provincial governor likewise erected a dedication to Jupiter and the Genius of each of the four Tetrarchic emperors: see *ILS* 1:143, no. 635. Engemann (1984), compares the scenes of sacrifice on the surviving pedestal with Christian sacrifice; Brandt (1998) 64–68, provides a concise summary of the monument; see also Mayer (2002) 176–80, and Elsner (2005) 85, for the theme of public sacrifice as "an iconography focused principally on the emperor's priestly rôle."

The Arcus Novus, a triumphal arch over the Via Lata north of the Capitoline Hill, may also have commemorated this twentieth anniversary: see Curran (2000) 45, although Kolb (1987) 180–83, argues that it celebrated the fifth anniversary of the Caesars in 297. Another monument at Rome included stylized statues

In addition to enhancing their authority and legitimacy, their occasional presence at Rome allowed these emperors to back into an aura of civilization and respectability. Almost all of these emperors were natives of outlying provinces, in particular from the frontier zones along the Danube. Diocletian, his fellow original Tetrarchs, Maximian, Constantius, and Galerius, and their immediate successors, Severus, Maximinus, and Licinius, were military men from Dalmatia, Pannonia, Moesia, Dacia, and Thrace. Later historians tended to fuse the Tetrarchs, their predecessors from the mid-third century, and some of their fourth-century successors as emperors from "Illyricum," which referred in general to the wide zone in the Balkans between the Adriatic Sea and the Danube River that would eventually become the core of the prefecture of Illyricum. Even after its incorporation into the Roman empire this mountainous region had long been seen as untamed, noted primarily as a haven for bandits and a source of fresh recruits for the army. Its inhabitants were so uncivilized that they drank beer rather than wine![10]

As professional soldiers these Balkan emperors had such limited familiarity with classical culture that they seemed to be deficient in "humanity." When they visited Rome, they could readily be characterized as undercivilized despots from the provinces, if not wild animals, then "half-barbarians." Maximian was denigrated as "a ferocious, lustful, obtuse peasant, a Pannonian by birth." Diocletian himself was supposed to have dismissed Severus as a "drunken dancer." In his youth Galerius was known as "cowboy"; as emperor he seemed to be not even a Roman. The refined teacher Lactantius struggled to control his loathing as he

of Tetrarchic emperors; for these two pairs of emperors, found in the Campus Martius and now in the Vatican Museum, see Kolb (2001) 151–53, suggesting that they represented the emperors in the revised Tetrarchy after Diocletian's retirement and before Maxentius' usurpation at Rome.

[10] Emperors from Illyricum: Aurelius Victor, *De Caesaribus* 39.26, "humanitatis parum," 40.1, Maximinus and Severus, with Syme (1971) 179–236, for the prejudices about these emperors, (1983) 66, "the least harm will ensue if those rulers are called Danubian – or even Balkan." Beer: Dio, *Historiae Romanae* 49.36.3; also Ammianus Marcellinus, *Res gestae* 26.8.2, for derision of Valens as a "beer drinker," with Van Dam (2002) 104–5.

described Galerius: "the barbarity in this beast was innate, and his sav-agery was foreign to Roman blood." Julian, the last of the Constantinian dynasty, would be equally appalled when he recalled the background of his own family, "totally rustic, rough, uncouth, repulsive." For centuries the people of Rome had been free from the anxiety of waiting for the barbarians. Then the barbarians had arrived, in the guise of their own emperors.[11]

At Rome and in Italy people might well be suspicious of these out-siders and their policies. Even as these emperors continued to defend Italy and the interior provinces, their pedigrees hinted at new priorities. Italy certainly still retained its prestige because of its longstanding emi-nence, but that seniority also made it appear to be elderly, and hence outdated and decrepit. The strength, and therefore the future, of the empire seemed to be with the soldiers and their commanders from the Balkan regions. In these provinces "military service is the whole of life." When a panegyrist praised one of these Balkan emperors, his com-pliment was all the more dismissive of Italy for its politeness. "Who doubts that for many centuries now, while Italy may indeed have been the ruler of peoples because of the antiquity of her glory, Pannonia [has been ruler] because of her vigor?"[12]

For all the benefits they might derive from visiting Rome, it was nev-ertheless easy for such emperors to be wary and perhaps even dismissive of the needs of Rome and Italy. Galerius was outright hostile. When he invaded Italy in 307 in a strike against rival emperors, his army caused so much destruction that he was accused of having forfeited his title of

---

[11]  Maximian: *Epitome de Caesaribus* 40.10. Lactantius, *De mortibus persecutorum* 9.1, beast, 18.12, Severus, 18.13, Maximinus as *semibarbarus*; also 13.2, for the Tetrarchic emperors as "Goths and Sarmatians." Galerius as Armentarius: Aurelius Victor, *De Caesaribus* 39.24, 40.1, 6; also *Epitome de Caesaribus* 40.15, "pastor armentorum"; with Zecchini (1992), on the stereotypes of Balkan emperors and Gothic kings, and Grant (1992), on denigrating critiques of Tetrarchic emperors. Julian's family: Julian, *Misopogon* 348D.

[12]  Military service: *Panegyrici latini* 11(3).3.9, commenting on Maximian's homeland. Italy and Pannonia: *Panegyrici latini* 10(2).2.2, in a celebration of the emperor Maximian.

"Roman emperor." In particular, because he allowed his soldiers to loot communities in Umbria along the Via Flaminia, he might as well have been a new Hannibal, a "destroyer of Italy." Galerius apparently returned the slight. Until he finally saw the city, he had casually dismissed Rome as no more grand than any other town. He was thought to have ordered the imposition of taxes on Rome and central Italy in retaliation for the subjugation of his homeland of Dacia by the emperor Trajan … a distant two centuries earlier! He was also thought to have suggested that the Roman empire should be renamed the "Dacian empire." Rome and Italy were now not just gradually losing their privileged standing within the empire. An emperor like Galerius wanted to turn the relationship between capital and frontiers completely inside out. Galerius seemed to present himself as a Dacian emperor, rather than a Roman emperor. In his perspective, with his accession Dacia had finally conquered Rome, and the Balkans were now the center of the empire.[13]

The prestige of Rome revived in the early fourth century, first under Maxentius, who spent his entire reign there, then under Constantine. In 312 Constantine returned to Rome, this time as an emperor in his own right. After his victory over Maxentius in October he entered the city hailed as a liberator. Crowds of people greeted his arrival with enthusiasm, and even during the celebration of games they could not stop staring at him. According to a later panegyric, his victory had rescued the city. "Your divine power … awakened Rome when the city was oppressed and completely spent." Constantine furthermore honored the senate by reviving its earlier prestige. During the third century emperors had increasingly preferred to appoint non-senators to imperial magistracies; under Constantine members of the senatorial aristocracy at Rome were encouraged to hold high offices again. He delivered an

---

[13] Galerius' invasion of Italy: Lactantius, *De mortibus persecutorum* 23.5, grudge, 27.2, dismissal of Rome, 27.7–8, "Romanus quondam imperator, nunc populator Italiae," with Lactantius, *Institutiones divinae* 2.16.16, "Romanum nomen apud Cannas paene deletum est." For Lactantius' views about Rome, see Nicholson (1999). Looting of Via Flaminia: *Origo Constantini imperatoris* 3.7. Before retreating, Galerius' army had camped at Interamna, on the Via Flaminia about thirty miles south of Hispellum: *Origo Constantini imperatoris* 3.6.

oration in the senate, and he restored some privileges to senators. In return, the senate bestowed honors on Constantine. It dedicated to him a statue of a deity, and it decreed that he was now the senior emperor within the imperial college. As in the old Roman Republic, "the senate and people of Rome" had adopted and honored their liberator.[14]

In subsequent years Constantine returned to Rome to celebrate important anniversaries. Following campaigns along the Rhine frontier he visited Rome from July to September 315 to celebrate the beginning of the tenth anniversary of his proclamation as emperor. During this visit the senate and people of Rome dedicated the magnificent triumphal arch that commemorated his earlier victory over Maxentius. Through the six long panels in the new frieze that depicted the emperor's campaign in Italy and his activities at Rome, through the many panels, roundels, and statues appropriated from earlier imperial monuments, and through the dedicatory inscriptions, this arch was an especially eloquent text about Constantine, a "panegyric of sculptures." Like panegyrists delivering orations before the emperor, like petitioners presenting requests to the emperor, through the medium of this arch the senate and people of Rome were both applauding the emperor and hoping to shape his behavior. In particular, they hoped to reinstate the priority of Rome itself.[15]

[14] For Maxentius at Rome, see Chapter 3. Constantine at Rome: *Panegyrici latini* 12(9).19, arrival and games, 20.1–2, "verba tua in senatu habita"; 4(10).3.3, divine power. Membership of the senate: *CTh* 15.14.4, with Seeck (1919) 64–65, dating the edict to January 313. Senators holding offices again: Arnheim (1972) 39–73, on the "political impotence" of senators under the Tetrarchs and their revival under Constantine, and Barnes (1981) 46, with Marcone (1992) and Salzman (2002) 31–35, for Constantine's policies toward senators at Rome, and Barnes (1975c), for prefects of Rome under Maxentius serving again as prefects under Constantine. Statue of deity: *Panegyrici latini* 12(9).25.4, with the discussion of Nixon and Rodgers (1994) 331n.157. Senior emperor: Lactantius, *De mortibus persecutorum* 44.11. Senate and people: *Panegyrici latini* 12(9).19.5.

[15] Ruysschaert (1962–1963a) 92, "ce panégyrique de sculptures," in a wonderfully evocative interpretation of the iconography of the arch. For the arch as a traditional senatorial monument, see Elsner (2000a) 171n.28: "The Arch's propaganda...represents *not* Constantine justifying himself...but rather the Senate

The senate and people were first of all grateful for the restoration of peace. Short dedications inscribed in the central passageway of the arch hailed Constantine as "liberator of the city" and "founder of peace." The upper story of the arch included giant statues of Dacians in postures of captivity and mourning, with downcast eyes. Although these statues had been appropriated most likely from an earlier Trajanic monument, in their new location on the arch they represented the renewed submission of Dacia, and by implication of all the Balkan regions, to the majesty of Rome. Constantine's arrival had ensured that Rome would not after all become part of a "Dacian empire." In addition, the panels in the frieze demonstrated how the new emperor himself could be transformed from a provincial warlord into a respectable civilian at Rome. On the panel depicting the siege of Verona Constantine was shown standing among his troops, wearing armor and Gallic trousers; on the panel depicting the battle at the Milvian Bridge he was shown in the company of deities, wearing armor and a sword on his left hip. On the panels depicting the procession of his troops into Rome and his speech to the people in the Forum he was shown still wearing a long military cloak. But on the final panel depicting the distribution of coins to senators and the people, the emperor was shown wearing a toga. From battle-dress to civilian clothing: the man of war from the provinces should become the man of peace at Rome.[16]

> presenting their new emperor with a visual programme that constructs him in the way they hoped he would turn out"; Wilson Jones (2000) 72, emphasizes Constantine "as the driving force." For the contribution of the arch to highlighting Constantine's association with the Sun-god, see Marlowe (2006); also Chapter 3, for additional discussion of the frieze, panels, and roundels.
>
> [16] For discussion of Constantine's clothing as depicted on the frieze, see L'Orange and von Gerkan (1939) 61–62 (Verona), 67 (Milvian Bridge), 74 (procession), 86 (Forum), 96 (distribution); for photos, see L'Orange and von Gerkan (1939) Tafeln 6–17, and Giuliano (1955) plates 30–45. Smith (2002) 143, properly highlights the peculiarity of depicting Constantine wearing the cloak (*chlamys*) that had become the standard uniform for military commanders outside combat: "Here for the first time an emperor wearing the long military cloak addresses the populace of Rome inside the city – and at its civilian epicentre, the Forum Romanum." Such a uniform was a bit too provocative for a capital. By the end of the century

Constantine apparently understood that he should now represent himself as an old-style emperor, a civilian rather than a soldier. His portraits were modeled on earlier images of Augustus, handsome, eternally youthful, clean-shaven. Even though his statue in the Basilica Nova was imposingly huge, the accompanying inscription mentioned his liberation of the city from the yoke of a tyrant and his restoration of the senate and people to their "ancient splendor." At Rome even an oversized emperor acknowledged that he had to accommodate himself to the expectations of the senate and the people.[17]

Through the primary dedication on this arch the senate and people also located Constantine in an appropriate Roman past. This laudatory inscription thanked the emperor for having saved the Republic from "a tyrant and his faction." The model for such distinctly "Republican" behavior was of course the first emperor, Augustus, who centuries earlier in his *Res gestae*, his own account of his "accomplishments," had stressed his role in ending wars, restoring peace, and returning power to the senate and people of Rome. The inscription on the arch was

the emperor Theodosius ordered the prefect of Constantinople to ensure that senators did not wear a "military costume" within the city. Because a military *chlamys* caused "terror," senators were instead to wear "peaceful clothing": see *CTh* 14.10.1, issued in 382. For a possible hint of a statue of Constantine at Rome wearing "civilian clothing," see the fragmentary dedication in *CIL* 6.4.2:3789, no. 36953 = Grünewald (1990) 220, no. 259: "Constantino ma[ximo . . . ] | statuam civili [habitu . . . ] | ex aerario in su[ . . . ]"

[17] Imitation of Augustus: see Wright (1987), discussing Constantine's use of Augustus' image during the first months of his reign and then again in 312, and Smith (1997) 186–87. Inscription on statue: Eusebius, *HE* 9.9.11, *Vita Constantini* 1.40.2. Eusebius published his Greek version of this inscription in *HE* 9 by 314; for the editions of his *HE*, see Chapter 6. His source for this inscription is not obvious. Rather than simply translating Eusebius' version, Rufinus, *HE* 9.9.11, included a slightly different Latin version of the inscription. Rufinus had been a student at Rome most likely during the 360s, and he visited Rome again in the late fourth century: see Murphy (1945) 15–19, 82, 91–92. Because he would have seen this statue during his visits, he may have copied his version of the inscription from the original in Latin, as suggested by Christensen (1989) 300, and Grünewald (1990) 71.

now a miniature *Res gestae* for Constantine, more prescriptive than descriptive, but still eerily reminiscent of Augustus' claim to have saved the Republic from the domination of a faction. But when it came to religion, this inscription was notably noncommittal and attributed the emperor's motivation to "the impulse of a divinity and the greatness of his mind." In another dedication the senate and Roman people hailed Constantine and Licinius (now emperor in the East) as liberators and restorers of the public security and thanked them for deliverance from "the most hideous tyrants." During the next few years the city's magistrates praised Constantine as restorer of the human race and public liberty, enlarger of the Roman empire, and founder of everlasting security and peace. The bland conservatism of these dedications suggests that at Rome people did not quite yet know how to accommodate a Christian emperor and instead preferred to imagine him in a distinctly Republican context. A shared political tradition from a revered antiquity could mask any uncertainties about different religious affiliations. In addition, by stressing the emperor's role in reviving the old Republic, the senators and the people of Rome could remind Constantine of his obligation to patronize the old capital. Only his proper behavior at Rome could ensure his standing as a truly Roman emperor.[18]

Constantine seems to have taken the hint. In July 326 he returned to Rome. This visit again flattered the capital and its traditional social orders. While there Constantine paid his respects to the senate by minting a large medallion that mentioned him on one side and the senate on

---

[18] Dedications on arch: *ILS* 1:156, no. 694, with Alföldi (1948) 63, "a Republican hero of liberty," and L. J. Hall (1998), arguing that both pagans and Christians would have recognized *instinctu divinitatis* as a reference to ideas in Cicero's *De divinatione*. Dedication from senate and people published in Grünewald (1990) 98–100, 217, no. 240, dated between April 30, 313 and the outbreak of civil war between Constantine and Licinius in 316; with Wallace-Hadrill (1990), on the importance of the honors voted for Augustus by the senate and people: "an attempt to bridge the gap between the ideology of the Republic and his own dominance" (p. 168). Dedications from magistrates at Rome before ca. 315: *ILS* 1:156, no. 692, *CIL* 6.1:237, nos. 1143, 1145, *CIL* 6.4.3:3789, no. 36952 = Grünewald (1990) 217–20, nos. 241, 245, 247, 258.

the other. The primary purpose for this visit was to celebrate the end of the twentieth anniversary of his reign. In late spring and early summer of 325 he had been preoccupied with orchestrating a council of bishops at Nicaea, and he had celebrated the beginning of this anniversary in Nicomedia. Since emperors usually celebrated only the beginnings of the years of their decennial anniversaries, the reenactment of this festival in 326 at Rome was exceptional.[19]

## "My Rome"

These visits suggest that Constantine continued to think of Rome as the place to celebrate the major anniversaries of his accession. Yet during these same years it is apparent that he was promoting alternatives. Between 313 and 315 Constantine was again leading campaigns on the Rhine frontier. He spent most of these years in residence at Trier, which had already been his base of operations before he had invaded Italy. During the remainder of the fourth century Trier considerably enhanced its importance as "the distinguished residence of emperors." Three of Constantine's sons, Crispus, Constantine II, and Constans, lived there off and on in succession; in subsequent decades Julian visited, and Trier became a residence again for Valentinian and his sons, Gratian and Valentinian II.[20]

One consequence of the extended residence of emperors in northern Gaul was a redefinition of one of the fundamental images of the Roman empire. For centuries the Mediterranean had been the core of the empire, and Rome had been at the center of the Mediterranean. But this "Great Sea," "Our Sea," as the Romans regarded it, was in fact first called "Mediterranean" only in the early seventh century: "This

---

[19] Medallion: Bruun (1966) 326, no. 272, with Grünewald (1990) 141, for the focus on Rome: "die gesamte Peripherie des Reiches, nahm keinen Anteil an den Vicennalienprägungen." Vicennalia at Nicomedia and Rome: Jerome, *Chronicon* s.a. 326, with Chastagnol (1987), for the celebration of imperial anniversaries at Rome: "seules les vicennales de Constantin ont été répétées..., mais ce fut à titre très exceptionnel" (p. 491).

[20] Residence: Ammianus Marcellinus, *Res gestae* 15.11.9. For more discussion of emperors and Trier, see below.

Great Sea is also Mediterranean, 'Mid-land,' because it flows through the middle of the land all the way to the East, dividing Europe, Africa, and Asia." The Mediterranean became a "midland" sea not during the many centuries when it had been the undivided center of the Roman empire, but only after it had become a frontier zone. In contrast, because it had long been in the middle of an important frontier zone in northern Europe, Trier was already classified as a "mediterranean" capital during the fourth century. Strictly speaking, Trier seemed more deserving of this description, since it truly was "interior," "inland," "landlocked." During the fourth century the "mediterranean" regions of the Roman empire were in northern Gaul. So, apparently, might be the center of the empire and the residence of an emperor. A proper "mediterranean" Roman empire could have its capital in northern Europe. From this perspective it is not surprising that Trier was now called "Belgian Rome."[21]

After an inconclusive war against Licinius in 316–317 Constantine acquired control over the Balkans. Thereafter he often resided near the middle Danube frontier, in particular at Sirmium or Serdica. During his residence in the Balkans he was certainly kept informed about events in Rome. In late 320, for instance, he replied from Serdica to a report from the prefect of Rome about a lightning strike on the Colosseum by allowing the traditional consultation of a diviner. But he also skipped at least one important celebration in Rome. In early March 321 the panegyrist Nazarius celebrated the fifth anniversary of the accession of two of Constantine's sons as Caesars. This orator addressed Constantine as if he were in attendance at Rome. In fact, the emperor was in Serdica or Sirmium. Constantine now spent increasingly more time in the Balkan regions, and he even began to refer to Serdica as "my Rome."[22]

[21] Great Sea as "Mediterranean": Isidore of Seville, *Etymologiae* 12.16.1. Trier as mediterranean city: *Expositio totius mundi et gentium* 58, "civitatem autem maximam dicunt habere quae vocatur Triveris, ubi et habitare dominus dicitur, et est mediterranea." For Trier as Rome, see Vollmer and Rubenbauer (1926), discussing an epitaph from Trier, most likely of the fourth century: "Belgica Roma mei, non mea, digna fuit."

[22] Lightning strike on amphitheater at Rome: *CTh* 16.10.1, dated to December 320. Nazarius' oration: *Panegyrici latini* 4(10).3.1, address to Constantine, with Nixon

Although Constantine returned to Rome to celebrate the tenth and twentieth anniversaries of his accession, during most of the 310s and early 320s he was residing at other cities on the frontiers. In 328 he seems to have accompanied his mother's sarcophagus on its westward journey to Italy, although he probably did not escort it all the way to Rome for burial. His primary concerns were elsewhere. If he did go to Rome in 328 to bury his mother, he inserted that visit between stays in spring at Serdica, "my Rome," and in autumn at Trier, "Belgian Rome." These extended absences from Rome suggest that Constantine was now developing a different perspective on the Roman empire that plainly emphasized its northern frontiers. Constantine's reign was becoming, implicitly and subtly, the fulfillment of earlier challenges to the pre-eminence of Rome. Through his residence at cities like Trier near the Rhine frontier Constantine had seemingly revived the breakaway Gallic empire of the later third century, and through his residence at Sirmium and Serdica in the Balkans he had essentially realized Galerius' dream of a Dacian empire. The mere presence of an emperor now created an imperial capital. When Diocletian and Maximian had met at Milan during the winter of 290–291, a panegyrist claimed that "the seat of empire then seemed to be the place to which each emperor had come." A secret of the later empire was revealed: "Rome" could be made elsewhere than at Rome.[23]

and Rodgers (1994) 338, for the date of this panegyric. In 321 Constantine was at Serdica in February (*CTh* 2.19.2, 9.42.1) and at Sirmium in April (*CTh* 11.19.1). Serdica as Rome: Anonymus post Dionem (=Dio Continuatus), *Frag.* 15.1, ed Müller (1851) 199, Ἡ ἐμὴ Ῥώμη Σαρδικὴ ἐστιν. Note also *Expositio totius mundi et gentium* 57, on Pannonia and specifically Sirmium: "et semper habitatio imper-atorum est." During the usurpation of Magnentius in Italy in the early 350s the senate at Rome apparently supported Constantius, who had moved to the Balkans. Julian, *Orat.* 1.48B, complimented Constantius for saving Rome: "while the tyrant still ruled in Italy, you relocated Rome to Pannonia through its senate"; also *Orat.* 2.97B-C, on senators who "embraced Pannonia in place of Rome."

[23] Helena's death and funeral cortege: Eusebius, *Vita Constantini* 3.46–47.1, with Barnes (1981) 221, (1982) 9n.40, 77n.130, dating her death before January 7, 328, Drijvers (1992) 73, to 328 or early 329, and Bruun (1966) 72, to late 329. In 328 Constantine was at Serdica in May (*CTh* 11.7.4) and at Trier in September (*CTh* 1.4.2).

Since Constantine had visited Rome to celebrate the tenth and twentieth anniversaries of his accession, he was probably expected to return for his thirtieth, either in July 335 for the beginning or in July 336 for the end. "There is only one event that could make Rome happier," a panegyrist had once announced in anticipation of another anniversary, "that it see its defender Constantine and the most blessed Caesars [his sons]." Senators at Rome began to prepare for his arrival. In 334 Anicius Paulinus, a consul and the prefect of Rome, set up dedications to Constantine that thanked him again for having expanded the Republic and the city of Rome. One of these dedications was most likely engraved on a new equestrian statue of Constantine that stood in the old Forum in front of the senate house. Since Anicius Paulinus continued to serve as prefect through 335, he was presumably beginning to preen in anticipation of presiding over the emperor's visit. He was expecting that soon Constantine himself would ride into the Forum.[24]

Hispellum and the other cities of Umbria most likely sent their petition to Constantine now, perhaps likewise in expectation of his visit. Since he would probably be coming from the east through the Balkans, these cities could expect him to travel south down the Italian peninsula and to cross the Apennines on the Via Flaminia. The construction of roads under the Republic had been one important tactic for creating the idea of a unified Italy that was focused on Rome. Almost immediately after his confirmation as sole ruler Augustus had insisted that the generals who had assisted him during the civil wars improve the roads in Italy with the booty from their campaigns. The one road whose repairs he reserved for his own supervision was the Via Flaminia, which passed through north central Italy to link Rome with cities in Umbria. His improvements had included the construction of monuments to himself at each end of the road: a statue on the Milvian Bridge over the

---

Seat of empire: *Panegyrici latini* 11(3).12.2, with Millar (1977) 45–48, on the earlier residences of emperors in cities near the Rhine and Danube frontiers.

[24] One event: *Panegyrici latini* 4(10).38.6. Dedications by Anicius Paulinus: *ILS* 1:157, no. 698, *CIL* 6.1:237, no. 1142 = Grünewald (1990) 218, nos. 242, 243. For the equestrian statue, see Verduchi (1995).

Tiber, and a statue and a commemorative arch at Rimini on the Adriatic coast. Subsequent emperors, including Trajan and Hadrian, had also funded maintenance of the Via Flaminia. This great highway was hence a memorial to the generosity and military success of Augustus and his imperial successors, a reminder of the unification of Italy, and a symbol of the longstanding intimacy between Rome and the cities of Umbria.[25]

In 312 Constantine had apparently marched down the Via Flaminia during his invasion of central Italy. After crossing the Alps into northern Italy he had first marched from west to east and subdued the cities of Susa, Turin, Milan, and Brescia. Maxentius had stationed many of his troops at Verona, presumably in anticipation of an invasion by Licinius from the Balkans. Once Constantine defeated that army, he had headed for the Via Flaminia in order to approach Rome from the north. To celebrate the thirtieth anniversary of his accession the cities of Umbria were probably expecting Constantine to want to re-enact his earlier victorious march by once more riding down the Via Flaminia to the Milvian Bridge, and then through the crowds that would greet him between the Flaminian Gate and the Palatine Hill in Rome. If he were to travel through central Italy down the Via Flaminia, he would pass again through Umbria and near Hispellum. The cities of Umbria, and Hispellum in particular, hoped to benefit from the emperor's presence. Their petition pointedly reminded the emperor that Hispellum was "adjacent and next to the Via Flaminia."[26]

---

[25] Repairs of roads by generals: Suetonius, *Augustus* 30.1. Augustus' repair of Via Flaminia and statues: Augustus, *Res gestae* 20.5, Dio, *Historiae Romanae* 53.22.1–2; with Ashby and Fell (1921), for a discussion of the historical importance of the Via Flaminia and a comprehensive survey of its surviving monuments. Augustus' arch at Rimini: *ILS* 1:24, no. 84. Patterson (2003) 94–96, surveys repairs by other emperors; Laurence (1999) 21–23, discusses the significance of the Via Flaminia for the unification of north central Italy.

[26] Maxentius' troops at Verona: *Panegyrici latini* 4(10).25.3, 12(9).8.1; for the invasion route in 312, see Nixon and Rodgers (1994) 317n.94, and Odahl (2004) 101–5. For a description of travel on the Via Flaminia from Aquileia to Rome as "effortless," see Jerome, *Apologia contra Rufinum* 2.2, "per mollissimum Flaminiae iter." On the Arch of Constantine the panel displaying his arrival at Rome depicted his

The cities of Umbria decided to take advantage of the emperor's expected return to advance their standing and liberate themselves from their obligations to participate in a festival at Volsinii in Tuscia. These cities requested permission to construct a temple in honor of the emperor's Flavian dynasty. If Constantine had indeed replied to this petition in 334, soon after his youngest son had joined him and his other sons in the imperial college at the end of 333, then his favorable response would allow time for the construction of the temple. This temple would then be waiting for Constantine at Hispellum when he returned for his

procession from the Flaminian Gate to the Arch of Domitian (i.e. the Triumphal Gate): see L'Orange and von Gerkan (1939) 74, 79–80 + Tafeln 3, 12–13, 18d, and Giuliano (1955) plates 33, 39. In autumn of 403 the emperor Honorius traveled from Ravenna to Rome on the Via Flaminia; for the crowd that lined the route from the Milvian Bridge to the Palatine Hill, see Claudian, *De sexto consulatu Honorii* 494–522, 543–44.

Constantine may have visited or passed by Hispellum during previous trips along the Via Flaminia. In 315 he may have been at Sirmio in northern Italy in early June: see *CTh* 2.30.1, with the emendation in Barnes (1982) 72. He then traveled south, and in July a few days before entering Rome he was at Aqua Viva, a town north of Rome on the Via Flaminia: see *CTh* 8.18.1, with the emendation in Seeck (1919) 163. Upon leaving Rome in September he went to Milan. In 326 he was at Milan before traveling to Rome. When he left Rome to return to Milan, he passed through Spoletium, another city on the Via Flaminia about fifteen miles south of Hispellum: see *CTh* 16.5.2, with Barnes (1982) 77. In 357 his son Constantius traveled on the Via Flaminia and stopped at Ocriculum on his way to Rome: see Ammianus Marcellinus, *Res gestae* 16.10.4. It was perhaps during this trip that Constantius made a contribution to repair the baths at Spoletium: see *ILS* 1:166, no. 739 = Conti (2004) 144–45, no. 124.

Hispellum was most likely not alone among towns on the Via Flaminia in dedicating a memorial in honor of Constantine. Note in particular the large triumphal arch at Malborghetto, about eight miles north of the Milvian Bridge. Toebelmann (1915) 30–31, and Kuhoff (1991) 156–57, suggest that this arch commemorated the location of Constantine's final encampment before his battle against Maxentius. In that case it would have been similar to the trophy monument that Augustus erected to celebrate the site of his camp before his victory at Actium: see Zachos (2003). Messineo and Calci (1989) 81–83, date this arch to the early fourth century and associate its construction with the tenth or twentieth anniversary of Constantine's reign.

thirtieth anniversary. In 326 Constantius had accompanied his father to
Rome for the twentieth anniversary. Perhaps Constantine would bring
him and his other sons along for the thirtieth anniversary. Then two
generations of the Flavian dynasty, the present and the future, could
celebrate at this temple.[27]

Modern scholars have often interpreted the expansion of the imperial
cult throughout the early Roman empire as an indication of the loyalty
that provincials felt for Roman rule. In return, the celebration of the
attendant festivals and the veneration of the imperial images provided
provincials with a sense of inclusion and membership in the Roman
world. The imperial cult made Roman rule both acceptable and accessible, and through it provincial cities found a way "of making sense of

> At the other end of the Via Flaminia an imperial arch at Fanum Fortunae
> (modern Fano) was rededicated to Constantine. Originally an inscription on this
> arch commemorated Augustus' patronage for the construction of the city's wall:
> see *CIL* 11.2:925, no. 6218 = *ILS* 1:27, no. 104. A new line in honor of Constantine
> was added before this original dedication: see *CIL* 11.2:925, no. 6219 = *ILS* 1:159,
> no. 706 = Grünewald (1990) 216, no. 234. Because this new dedication hailed
> Constantine as "father of lords," the commentary in *ILS* suggests that this line may
> have been engraved on the arch already during the interregnum in 337 between
> Constantine's death in May and the proclamation of his three sons in September.
> During his tenure as governor of the district of Flaminia and Picenum, Lucius
> Turcius Secundus Asterius added another new line after the original dedication to
> Augustus. In this second new line Secundus described his father, Lucius Turcius
> Apronianus, as prefect of Rome; his father started his prefecture in July 339: see
> *PLRE* 1:88, "L. Turcius Apronianus 9," 817, "L. Turcius Secundus signo Asterius
> 6." If Secundus was also responsible for the first new line, then he added the new
> dedication to Constantine after the summer of 339 but before January 350, when
> Constans' death left Constantius as the only surviving son of Constantine: see
> Amici (2000) 189. Note that the name of Fanum Fortunae changed along with the
> rededication of the arch. Under Augustus the city had been a "Julian colony"; by
> the later fourth century its name commemorated Constantine's Flavian dynasty:
> see *Consultatio veteris cuiusdam iurisconsulti* 9.4, "Flavia Fanestri," in an edict
> issued in 365.

[27] For Constantius' visit to Rome in 326, see Barnes (1982) 85. Tabata (1995) 386–
401, properly emphasizes Constantine's concern for "implementing his policy of
reinvigorating municipal life in the empire" (p. 386).

an otherwise incomprehensible intrusion of authority into their world."
Hispellum and the other cities in Umbria now faced the opposite problem. They were trying to cope with the equally incomprehensible withdrawal of imperial favor from central Italy and its cities. Rather than
being conquered, they were being abandoned; and rather than having to accommodate a new overlord, they were trying to revive an old
intimacy. Their solution, again, was the medium of the imperial cult.
A new name for Hispellum, a new temple dedicated to the imperial
dynasty, a new festival, a new series of annual priests, all endorsed by
Constantine: these blessings would be evidence that these cities still
had a significant relationship with a distant emperor. In an unexpected
reversal, these Italian cities were now acting like provincial cities, trying
to come to terms with a remote ruling power. In addition to being a
request for imperial patronage, this petition from the cities of Umbria
was a reminder that the emperor should visit, a hope that he would
visit, an anticipation that he might visit.[28]

## "SECOND ROME"

Constantine, of course, never showed up again, either in Umbria or at
Rome. Letters arrived sometimes, such as the one sent in the names of
Constantine and the Caesars to "their senate" and the magistrates of
Rome. But during the later 320s and the 330s Constantine and his sons
spent most of their time on or near the frontiers. Constantine himself
resided on the northern frontiers or in the region around the Hellespont,
overseeing the transformation of the ancient city of Byzantium into a
new capital. One occasional residence was Nicomedia, where Diocletian
had already sponsored massive construction projects that he had hoped
would make the city "the equal of Rome." In 330 Constantine presided
over the formal dedication of Constantinople. During the next few years
he spent his time in the new capital or campaigning against the Goths
in the Balkans. The farthest west he went was a trip to Singidunum on

---

[28] Quotation from Price (1984) 247. Note also Bowersock (1982) 172, "an unparalled
guarantee of loyalty," 182, "succeeded in making multitudes of citizens in far-flung
regions feel close to the power that controlled them."

the Danube during the summer of 334, which included a nostalgic visit to his hometown of Naissus.[29]

Constantine subsequently celebrated his thirtieth anniversary, both the beginning in July 335 and the end in July 336, in his new capital. His son Constantius furthermore celebrated his own marriage during the festivities in 336. By now Constantinople clearly had become the favored setting for major imperial ceremonies. Diocletian had once contemplated the possibility of establishing a new eastern capital, and his extensive patronage had left such a lasting impression that Nicomedia was thought to have become another district of Rome, the "Eternal City." In contrast, Constantinople now became much more than merely a suburb of Rome. Constantine's patronage for his own new capital was so impressive that it seemed to deserve the "eternal name" itself. Constantine seems to have originally planned that the name for his new capital in the East would be "New Rome" or "Second Rome." The celebration of his thirtieth anniversary in Constantinople was a clear indication that he and his dynasty now preferred Second Rome to First Rome.[30]

First Rome might still have hoped that even if Constantine had not been present for his thirtieth anniversary, he might yet show up for his own funeral. The remains of Helena, his mother, had been brought for burial at Rome in a mausoleum attached to the Church of St. Marcellinus and St. Peter, in a suburb outside the city's walls.

[29]  Letter: *L'année épigraphique 1934* (1935) 42, no. 158 = Grünewald (1990) 220, no. 260. Diocletian and Nicomedia: Lactantius, *De mortibus persecutorum* 7.10; with Millar (1977) 51–52, Foss (1995), and Mayer (2002) 29–31, on the importance of Nicomedia. Constantine's trip in 334: *CTh* 10.15.2, Singidunum in July, 11.39.3, Naissus in August.

[30]  During the celebration of July 336 Constantius married an anonymous cousin who was a daughter of Julius Constantius, Constantine's half-brother: see Eusebius, *Vita Constantini* 4.49. Nicomedia as district of Rome: Ammianus Marcellinus, *Res gestae* 22.9.3, "regio quaedam urbis...aeternae." "Eternal name" for Constantinople: *CTh* 13.5.7, a constitution issued by Constantine in 334. New Rome: according to John the Lydian, *De magistratibus* 2.30, Constantine did not call Constantinople "New Rome" before its consecration. Second Rome: Porphyrius, *Carm.* 4.6, "Ponti nobilitas, altera Roma"; Socrates, *HE* 1.16.1.

Constantine had already bestowed extravagant gifts and endowments upon this church, and Helena was now buried in a large porphyry sarcophagus that had perhaps been designed originally for the emperor himself. Helena's internment seems to have suggested that in the later 320s Constantine was planning to use this huge circular mausoleum for himself and his entire dynasty. A decade later the people of Rome still shared that anticipation. Upon hearing about the emperor's death in 337 the senate and people dedicated a portrait of Constantine that depicted him "enjoying an ethereal repose above the arches of heaven." Presumably they were already looking forward to performing the usual ritual of consecration for a dead emperor. As a result, when the people of Rome heard that he had instead been buried in Constantinople, they were frustrated and angry.[31]

Subsequently Constantine's two daughters were buried in a mausoleum next to the Church of St. Agnes on the outskirts of Rome. One was Constantina, who had been married successively to her cousins Hannibalianus and the emperor Gallus; the other was Helena, who

---

[31] Church of St. Marcellinus and St. Peter: *Liber pontificalis* 34.27, with Krautheimer (1937–1980) 2.2:193–206, Deichmann and Tschira (1957) 74, suggesting that the mausoleum had originally been intended for Constantine, Guyon (1987) 256–58, Krautheimer (1992) 526–30, 545, on Constantine's plans, and Holloway (2004) 86–93. Mausoleum of Helena: Deichmann and Tschira (1957), Pietri (1976) 31–33, Guyon (1987) 217–19, and Curran (2000) 102. This church was built on an imperial estate apparently owned by Helena: see *Liber pontificalis* 34.27; Drijvers (1992) 30–34, hence suggests that Helena had resided in Rome after 312. Johnson (1992), arguing that Helena's body remained in Rome, is to be preferred to Ebersolt (1929–1930), suggesting that her body was eventually moved to Constantinople; for the subsequent transfer of her relics, see Drijvers (1992) 74–76, and Odahl (2004) 225. Portrait: Eusebius, *Vita Constantini* 4.69.2, with Cameron and Hall (1999) 345–50, on the ceremony of consecration. Reaction of Roman people: Aurelius Victor, *De Caesaribus* 41.17, with Price (1987), on the traditional role of the senate in passing posthumous judgment on emperors. Since posthumous dedications and coins honored Constantine with the title of *divus*, the senate at Rome may nevertheless have passed a decree acknowledging the emperor's apotheosis as a god: see Bruun (1954), discussing the philosophical and biblical ideas behind the imagery and legends on the coins, and Amici (2000), for the inscriptions.

had been married to another cousin, the emperor Julian. The historian Ammianus thought that Julian too should have been buried next to the Tiber River in the "eternal city." This was a distinctly odd opinion, since Julian had never visited Rome and he had been the most "Greek" of all the Constantinian emperors. He had never quite fit in the Latin West, and while he was commanding campaigns in Gaul his soldiers had teased him as a "little Greekling." Ammianus likewise, who pointedly described himself too as a former soldier and a Greek, had seemingly little personal regard for the old capital. The very oddness of his comment about Julian is hence a telling indication of the lingering reputation of Rome as the only proper burial place for a Roman emperor, even one so strongly identified with Greek culture.[32]

Constantine instead constructed a mausoleum for his family at Constantinople, which eventually became part of the precinct around the Church of the Holy Apostles. Subsequently his son Constantius was also buried in this mausoleum. The bodies of Constantine II and Constans, the other two sons who succeeded Constantine, were lost after military defeats. After his death in battle against the Persians Julian was buried first in the outskirts of Tarsus, in a tomb across the road from the tomb of Maximinus. In an eerie twist of fate, the tomb of the last pagan emperor faced that of the last of the persecuting emperors. Even though this symmetry probably left many Christians feeling a bit smug over the effectiveness of divine retribution, Julian's remains were nevertheless later moved to Constantinople. His membership in the Constantinian dynasty took priority over his rejection of Christianity and the symbolic

[32] Church of St. Agnes: *Liber pontificalis* 34.23, with Krautheimer (1937–1980) 1.1:34–35, suggesting that Constantine II, not his father Constantine, was the founder of the church. Ammianus Marcellinus, *Res gestae* 15.12.1, little Greekling, 21.1.5, Constantina and Helena, 25.10.5, Julian and eternal city, 31.16.9, soldier and Greek, with Kelly (2003) 590–94, for Julian's imaginary tomb at Rome; Pietri (1976) 47–51, Curran (2000) 128, and Holloway (2004) 93–104, for the mausoleum of the daughters (now Santa Costanza); and Chapter 7, for Julian's Greekness. Eventually emperors' wives were buried with their husbands in the imperial mausoleum next to the Church of the Holy Apostles at Constantinople: see Procopius, *De aedificiis* 1.4.19, with Chapter 12.

proximity of his burial next to one of the most oppressive of the pagan Tetrarchs.[33]

Not only had this mausoleum at the eastern capital become the preferred burial place for members of the Constantinian dynasty. It now also became the preferred burial place for subsequent emperors. Jovian died in Galatia, but his body was sent to Constantinople; Valentinian died in Pannonia, but his body too was sent to the eastern capital; Valens' body was never found after the battle of Hadrianople; Theodosius died at Milan, but his body was sent back to Constantinople for burial in Constantine's mausoleum. In 312 the body of Maxentius, Constantine's rival, had been recovered from the Tiber, mutilated, and discarded for burial, perhaps in his family's mausoleum on the Via Appia. Maxentius has the dubious honor of being the last significant emperor to be interred at Rome during the fourth century. Thereafter the closest imperial tombs during the fourth century were those of Gratian and Valentinian II, buried probably together at Milan.[34]

[33] The body of Constantine II was thrown into a river near Aquileia: *Epitome de Caesaribus* 41.21. Constans was killed at Helena (modern Elne), south of Narbonne: see *Epitome de Caesaribus* 41.23; but he was most likely not buried at the villa of Centcelles near Tarraco: see Kulikowski (2004) 147. Julian's burial at Tarsus: Ammianus Marcellinus, *Res gestae* 25.9.12, 10.4–5, Zosimus, *Historia nova* 3.34.4. Maximinus' tomb: Philostorgius, *HE* 8.1; with Gregory of Nazianzus, *Orat.* 5.18, 21.33, for the spiteful reactions of Christians, and Van Dam (2003b) 31, suggesting that the heresiarch Eunomius' plan to return Julian's body to Constantinople was an attempt to curry favor with Theodosius by providing the emperor with an opportunity to preside over an imperial funeral.

[34] Jovian's burial: Ammianus Marcellinus, *Res gestae* 26.1.3. Return of Theodosius' body to Constantinople: Ambrose, *De obitu Theodosii* 55. Valentinian II was buried at Milan in a "very beautiful porphyry tub that was most appropriate for this purpose": see Ambrose, *Ep.* 25(53).4. His makeshift casket apparently shared a tomb with Gratian: see Ambrose, *De obitu Valentiniani* 79, "non vos [=Gratian and Valentinian] discrevit tumulus." Although Johnson (1991), suggests that Gratian and Valentinian II were buried probably in the chapel of Sant'Aquilino attached to the church of San Lorenzo, McLynn (1994) 164n.25, 176–79, is unsure whether Gratian was buried in Milan.

The emperor Severus, after being defeated and captured at Ravenna by Maximian and Maxentius in 307, was soon killed outside Rome. He was buried in the

## "LITTLE GALLIC ROME"

During the fourth century cities that had become imperial residences benefited enormously. Emperors sponsored extensive construction projects. Trier, for instance, became the most important imperial
residence along the Rhine frontier. Under the Tetrarchy Constantius
resided at Trier or in its vicinity for over a decade, and Constantine
moved there soon after his proclamation as emperor. Even after he
began to expand his authority beyond Gaul, he frequently returned,
and eventually he established at Trier the court of a son, first Crispus and then Constantine II. As a result, this new imperial residence
acquired a new bath complex. Its amphitheater was repaired, and its
"circus maximus" was enlarged enough to be considered a rival to the
legendary Circus at Rome: "in the afternoon the emperor was captivated
by the spectacles in the circus." The emperors furthermore constructed
a new basilica that could serve as an immense reception chamber. A
panegyrist would eventually credit Constantine for his support in the
construction of these "imperial buildings." "All these buildings are of
course the gifts of your presence. . . . Cities and temples blossom in your
footprints, Constantine."[35]

Northern Gaul had become a focal point of the western empire,
and Trier in particular was seen as the great fortress that protected the
interior provinces. In an illustrated calendar from the mid-fourth century Trier was depicted as a brawny Amazon warrior, towering over
a barbarian captive. Even as they grumbled about having to endure

tomb of the emperor Gallienus, located on the Via Appia several miles south of
Rome: see *Epitome de Caesaribus* 40.3, *Origo Constantini imperatoris* 4.10. Maximian had been buried on the outskirts of Milan: see Ambrose, *Ep.* 25(53).4. Maxentius may have been buried with his son Romulus: see Chapter 3. The usurper
Nepotianus, Constantine's nephew who was beheaded at Rome after reigning less
than a month, was probably also buried at Rome: see Eutropius, *Breviarium* 10.11,
and Chapter 3. For details on eastern emperors, see Grierson (1962); in the early
fifth century Honorius was buried at Rome in a mausoleum next to the Church
of St. Peter: see below.

[35] Buildings at Trier: *Panegyrici latini* 6(7).22.5–6, with Wightman (1970) 98–123,
on construction at Trier. Emperor's attendance: Augustine, *Confessiones* 8.6.15.

the chilly overcast weather, senators from Rome duly traveled north to pay homage to their imperial protectors on the frontier. Their presence seemed to imply that the venerable senate itself had been moved from Rome to Trier. Gauls likewise were aware of their region's new importance, and some even concluded that it should take priority over Italy. At Rome one Gallic orator would gently chide the emperor Theodosius for having procrastinated before liberating Gaul from the usurper Magnus Maximus. In his perspective, although the emperor's successes against the Goths in the Balkans and the Persians on the eastern frontier were impressive, Gaul should still have come first in his concerns. "We Gauls are upset at your triumphs."[36]

Then the emperors would leave northern Gaul for other cities. Valentinian was "the last of the great military rulers of the Roman empire." During most of his reign he resided at Trier and campaigned along the Rhine frontier. In fact, after his proclamation as emperor he had moved to Gaul so quickly that a delegation of bishops never caught up with him in northern Italy. By the time they arrived, "they did not meet the emperor, because he was busy in Gaul." After Valentinian's death in 375 his son Gratian continued to reside primarily at Trier, and during his reign Gallic aristocrats held many important imperial offices in the western empire. Because of these military successes and the active participation of Gallic aristocrats, the reigns of Valentinian and Gratian marked a crest in the importance of northern and central Gaul.[37]

Once Gratian departed, however, the citizens of Trier could only dream about the return of a strong emperor. Instead they had to settle for the usurper Magnus Maximus, the last effective emperor to consider Trier as his primary residence. Two hundred years later the historian Gregory of Tours would in fact remember only the usurper Maximus as "the emperor at Trier." Although Maximus' generals did conduct

<hr/>

[36] Illustration in the Calendar of 354: see Salzman (1990), figure 5. Cold weather: Symmachus, *Orat.* 1.16, delivered in honor of the emperor Valentinian at Trier in February 369. Senate at Trier: Ausonius, *Mosella* 402. Theodosius: Pacatus, *Panegyrici latini* 2(12).23.1, we Gauls, 24.3–6, procrastination.

[37] For Valentinian and Gratian at Trier, see Matthews (1975) 32–87; quotation about Valentinian at p. 33. Busy in Gaul: Socrates, *HE* 4.12.4; also Sozomen, *HE* 6.10.5.

successful military operations on the Rhine frontier, the other emperors were reluctant to grant him official recognition. For a few years the Alps were garrisoned on both sides as a barrier, almost a new frontier, between Gaul and Italy, and Maximus was ignored as just another Gallic usurper from the northern regions. In 387 he invaded Italy, like Constantine decades earlier. This time the outcome was different. Although his advance made the emperor Valentinian II and his court scatter, in the next year Maximus was killed by Theodosius' troops. The reputation of Trier as an important imperial residence was now likewise tarnished, and in retrospect its standing as a proper Roman capital seemed as dubious as the illegitimate authority of its last infamous emperor.[38]

Already during the fourth century emperors had occasionally overseen affairs in Gaul from the south. In late 353 Constantius II had celebrated his thirtieth year as an emperor with extravagant entertainments in the theater and circus at Arles. He may well have memorialized the occasion with the erection of an obelisk in the circus. After defeating Maximus, Theodosius sent Valentinian II back to Gaul, where he resided at Trier for at least a year. During this stay Valentinian II published the last known imperial edict issued from Trier, in June 390. But by the time he died in 392, he had already moved south to Vienne, and he was planning to return to Milan. His successor, the usurper Eugenius, for a moment seemed to reverse policy by leading an expedition into northern Gaul. He was the last Roman emperor to campaign along the Rhine frontier, and his general Arbogast led the last Roman army across the Rhine. In 396 the powerful general Stilicho campaigned again along the Rhine frontier. Despite their success, these campaigns in fact previewed a disconcerting future, because both generals were themselves barbarians, Arbogast a Frank and Stilicho a Vandal, and their "Roman" armies consisted largely of contingents of barbarians. On the Rhine frontier barbarian generals were commanding barbarian troops in the name of Rome against fellow barbarians. For northern Gaul Stilicho's

---

[38] Maximus' reputation: Gregory of Tours, *Historiae* 1.45, *De passione et virtutibus sancti Iuliani martyris* 4, *Vita patrum* 2.1. Maximus' generals: Gregory of Tours, *Historiae* 2.9. Garrisoning of Alps: Ambrose, *Ep.* 24.7.

victories were disastrously counter-productive, because upon his departure he seems to have removed many troops. At about the same time the seat of the praetorian prefect of the Gauls was transferred from Trier south to Arles. Now northern Gaul had been abandoned.[39]

Italian aristocrats were probably not sad, since they no longer had to worry about having to make the long journey to the northern Rhine frontier. As Symmachus, one of the more distinguished of the senators at Rome, politely explained to Protadius, a Gallic aristocrat probably from Trier, "none of our [senatorial] class visits the Rhineland, which both the most distinguished emperor and the most powerful magistrate are now abandoning." Protadius was astute enough to take the hint, since he himself also moved south to Italy, first to become prefect of Rome in 401 or 402, then to retire to an estate near Pisa. Gallic aristocrats who stayed home likewise conceded that the reign of Valentinian II had marked a turning point for northern and central Gaul. Afterward emperors no longer resided on the Rhine frontier or even visited. In a retrospective composed over sixty years later, Sidonius noted sadly that even the divine personification of Roma had to admit that ever since the reign of Valentinian II "my Gaul is to this day unfamiliar with the

[39] Constantius at Arles: Ammianus Marcellinus, *Res gestae* 14.5.1, with the discussion of the month, October or November, in Barnes (1993) 314n.32. On the obelisk at Arles, see Henck (2001) 300; for the suggestion that the obelisk had been erected already during Constantine's reign, see Heijmans (1999) 157, and Charron and Heijmans (2001). Last edict from Trier: *CTh* 8.5.50 = *CJ* 12.50.13, dated June 17, 390. For the plans of Valentinian II to return to northern Italy, see Ambrose, *De obitu Valentiniani* 23–24, with McLynn (1994) 335–41, on Theodosius' opposition to his return. Eugenius and Arbogast: Gregory of Tours, *Historiae* 2.9, with Chapter 12. Arbogast the Frank: Paulinus of Milan, *Vita Ambrosii* 30, "count Arbogast made war on his own people, the Franks," with *PLRE* 1:95–97. Stilicho the Vandal: Orosius, *Historiae adversum paganos* 7.38.1; his mother was in fact a Roman: *PLRE* 1:853–58. Stilicho's campaigns: Claudian, *De consulatu Stilichonis* 1.188–245, campaigns against Franks and other barbarians, 2.186, "limite...inermi," *De bello Gothico* 419–23, withdrawal of troops, with Jones (1964) 198. The emperor Honorius did not accompany Stilicho: see Claudian, *De quarto consulatu Honorii* 448, "Honorius absens." Transfer of seat of prefect dated to 395 by Palanque (1973), to 407 by Chastagnol (1973) and Matthews (1975) 333.

omnipotent lords." Already by the early fifth century only southern Gaul still seemed to be in touch with Roman emperors, and hence part of the Roman empire. After the usurper Constantine III invaded Gaul from Britain in 407, he too established his court at Arles.[40]

In 418 the emperor Honorius reinstated a provincial assembly to meet at Arles. The "idleness of usurpers" had interrupted an earlier attempt to found such an assembly; now, having established his court at Ravenna, Honorius would try to use this annual council in order to reassert his authority in Gaul. The emperor insisted that the delegates were to include provincial governors or their representatives, former imperial magistrates with senatorial rank, local landowners, and municipal magistrates. "With this provision we think that there is a great deal of goodwill and advantage for our provincials."[41]

In fact, this new attempt at integrating the interests of the Gallic nobility with the court in northern Italy reflected a much more constricted perspective on the participation of Gaul in the Roman empire. Most of the representatives were to come from the provinces in the southeastern corner of Gaul that was next to northern Italy and closest to the Mediterranean. This southern region had been the first part of Gaul to have been formally incorporated into the Roman empire as a large province known as, simply, *Provincia*, "Province." This region had been very receptive to the influences of a Romanized life style, and already in the early empire Province had been characterized as "more truly Italy than a province." In contrast, western, central, and northern Gaul had been later additions to the empire, conquered by Julius Caesar, then organized into provinces by Augustus, subsequently strongly influenced by Roman civilization, but always somewhat distinct from the Mediterranean heartland of the Roman world. Now, as he defined the participation in this new assembly, Honorius seemed to be reverting to

---

[40] Protadius: Symmachus, *Ep.* 4.28.1, with Matthews (1975) 262, 326–27. My Gaul: Sidonius, *Carm.* 5.356–57, in a panegyric for the emperor Majorian, delivered in 458. Constantine III at Arles: Zosimus, *Historia nova* 5.31.4.

[41] Honorius' edict: *Epistolae Arelatenses* 8, ed. Gundlach (1892) 13–15.

this older, pre-imperial perspective that seemingly again excluded much of western, central, and northern Gaul from the Roman world. Northern Europe was apparently not a part of his empire. Several years earlier the emperor had responded to a request for assistance from the people of Britain with the discouraging suggestion that they should defend themselves. In his edict announcing the formation of this new provincial assembly Honorius likewise dismissed the participation of most of Gaul, this time through a sardonic comment and an equally disparaging silence. Even though the provinces along the Atlantic coast in southwestern Gaul could also send envoys to the assembly, the emperor conceded that these provinces were "more remote." In a more telling omission, the emperor never mentioned the provinces in central and northern Gaul. Their inhabitants evidently were no longer included among "our provincials." Instead, Honorius extolled the virtues of Arles, whose river port received goods from all over the world, as far away as Arabia. In his perspective, the focal point of Gaul was a Mediterranean city near the south coast.[42]

Honorius' comments about this revived provincial assembly seemed to mark a tacit concession of the autonomy of Gaul. Not only did he not take northern and central Gaul into account. He also seemed to concede that Arles had become the equivalent of a new capital in southern Gaul. In the early fifth century the senate at Rome continued to meet, although it was predictably dominated by the interests of Italian notables; the senate at Constantinople, "Second Rome," provided a forum for eastern notables; now this assembly in southern Gaul apparently functioned as a "senate" for the notables of southern Gaul. It is no surprise that Arles was known, precisely at this time, as "little Gallic Rome." Nor is it surprising that in 455 the "pious gathering of the senate" at a town

<hr/>

[42] "Italia verius quam provincia": Pliny the Elder, *Historia naturalis* 3.4.31, with Drinkwater (1983) 5–8, 20, on the renaming of the province of Provincia as Narbonensis, Van Dam (1985a) 37–40, 47–48, on the limits of Honorius' perspective, and Van Dam (1992), (1993) 11–12, 117–18, on the distinctiveness of southern Gaul.

outside Arles declared the Gallic aristocrat Avitus as emperor. Southern Gaul too would now have its own senate, its own Roman emperor, and its own Rome.[43]

Northern, central, and western Gaul meanwhile had to cope with the influx and settlement of barbarian groups. In previous centuries Roman garrisons and military campaigns had tried to maintain a solidly demarcated frontier that matched the firm ideological distinction between "Romans" and "barbarians." Now the ideology was as porous as these frontier zones had always been. As the institutions of the Roman state collapsed, powerful Gallic aristocrats came to resemble barbarian chieftains as local warlords, and the indiscriminate use of military force had effectively become a means of assimilation between Romans and barbarians in northern and central Gaul. At about the same time between the mid-460s and the mid-480s a Frankish king assumed control over an old Roman province in northern Gaul and was buried with the ornaments of a Roman magistrate, while the scion of a distinguished Gallic family inherited his father's military enclave at Soissons and was known as a "king of the Romans." As Romanized barbarians and barbarianized

---

[43] Letter to people of Britain: Zosimus, *Historia nova* 6.10.2. Arles as "Gallula Roma": Ausonius, *Ordo urbium nobilium* 10.2, with Klingshirn (1994) 33–71, on the increasing prominence of late Roman Arles, and the excellent overview of the transformation of late antique Arles in Loseby (1996): "The political and economic pre-eminence of Arles was...an imperial creation" (p. 64). Avitus: Sidonius, *Carm.* 7.571, "pia turba senatus"; also Hydatius, *Chronica* 156: "Avitus, a citizen of Gaul, was proclaimed Augustus by the army of Gaul and by the former imperial magistrates, first at Toulouse and then at Arles." For hints that this new assembly was the equivalent of a Gallic senate, see Heather (1998) 203: "it became a regional forum through which the Gallic aristocracy could express itself as a regional power bloc"; and Kulikowski (2001) 32: "The council provided Gauls with a means of asserting their individual interests short of outright rebellion"; with Vanderspoel (1995) 53–70, for the importance of an independent senate in transforming Constantinople into a proper imperial capital. Note that after the early fifth century native Gallic aristocrats monopolized the prefecture in Gaul: see Sundwall (1915) 8–20, with the list of prefects in *PLRE* 2:1246–47. For the construction, most likely in the early fifth century, of a monumental hall at Arles that was perhaps attached to an official residence, see Heijmans (1998).

Romans blended together, the common denominator was the use of violence. In contrast to southern Gaul, where the notion of a Gallic Roman empire survived until the later fifth century, northern and central Gaul was dominated by outlaw regimes of warlords, both Roman and barbarian.[44]

In these outlying regions the withdrawal of the imperial court led to a contraction in the size of cities. At Trier people found a new use for those old imperial buildings, since a later tradition claimed that they had fortified the amphitheater in order to defeat the barbarians. In the past barbarian prisoners had been condemned to entertain the locals by fighting wild animals in this amphitheater, as a symbolic, and very public, depiction of the successes of Roman troops at defeating the enemies on the Rhine frontier. All of the mayhem was supposed to stay safely outside the frontier or inside the amphitheater. Now, in a neatly eloquent reversal of fortunes, barbarians had crossed the frontier and the citizens of Trier themselves cowered inside the amphitheater, desperate to keep the barbarians out.[45]

Despite their dire straits, they nevertheless continued to insist they were still Romans. In the early fifth century local aristocrats at Trier even "demanded circus games from the emperors, as if that was the best cure for a destroyed city." Salvian, the priest who mentioned this petition, could barely control his indignation at this apparent folly. Holding games now seemed both immoral and unrealistic. Yet this petition may not have been so outrageous. In the face of calamities the celebration of games would be a way of reaffirming the proper order of things, with the Romans victorious and the barbarians defeated. These local notables were furthermore most likely hoping that an emperor would

---

[44] For the Frankish king Childeric and the Roman aristocrat Syagrius, see Van Dam (2005) 196. The best overview of the rise of warlordism in northern Europe is Whittaker (1994a) 248–53, 257–78; also Innes (2000) 165–74. Van Dam (1985a) 169–72, discusses the parallel rise of cults of local Gallic saints that replaced cults of St. Peter and St. Paul.

[45] For the cities in Gaul, see Liebeschuetz (2001) 82–89; also Halsall (1996), for a fine survey of the transformation of Metz. Barbarian prisoners at Trier: *Panegyrici latini* 6(7).12.3, 12(9).23.3. Fortification of arena: Fredegar, *Chronica* 2.60.

preside over the new games in person, just as Constantius had long ago presided at Arles. Trier had been an imperial residence before; perhaps it should be so again. This petition was an implicit invitation for an emperor to come and visit.[46]

## CROSSING THE RUBICON

During the fourth century cities in central Italy had sensed that they too were being abandoned in favor of parvenu frontier capitals like Trier and Constantinople. The poet Porphyrius claimed that the establishment of Constantinople was good for central Italy: "the ornament of Pontus, a sister Rome, enhances the ancient people of Tuscia." He was wrong. Just like Trier a century later, Hispellum and the cities of Umbria were now reduced to requesting a new festival with the hope that the emperor himself would visit and revive their prestige. And despite Constantine's favorable response to this particular petition, most cities in central and southern Italy continued to be overlooked. Since emperors rarely visited, cities now relied instead upon the generosity of senatorial notables or appealed for the assistance of imperial magistrates. The cities of Etruria may have had a reputation for respecting "ancient customs," but in the later fourth century Pisa would have to be content with erecting a statue in honor of a former governor of the district. In central Italy the preservation of ancient tradition no longer had to include the emperor.[47]

Once, long ago, other cities in central and southern Italy had competed with Rome to become dominant in Italy. During the Republic Capua had even been known as "second Rome." In the later empire

[46] Games at Trier: Salvian, *De gubernatione Dei* 6.85, with Van Dam (1985a) 42–45, 149, on Salvian's indignation. In 461 the emperor Majorian did again preside over games in Gaul, but, no surprise, at Arles: see Sidonius, *Ep.* 1.11.10.

[47] Ornament of Pontus: Porphyrius, *Carm.* 18.33–34; this poem is dated to shortly after 324 by Polara (1973) 2:103, 109, to late 324 by Barnes (1975b) 182, 184. Rutilius Namatianus, *De reditu suo* 1.575–76, statue of Claudius Lachanius, 597, ancient customs. Lachanius had served as *consularis* of Tuscia and Umbria in 389: see Matthews (1975) 327. Ausbüttel (1988) 122–25, discusses Italian notables who served as governors in their home regions, and Smith (2003), surveys patrons in Italy during the fourth century.

Capua was still the leading city of Campania, the region south of Rome where many senators owned estates and vacationed on the Bay of Naples. As an acknowledgement of their support Constantine had helped fund the reconstruction of an aqueduct that supplied the entire region around the bay. As recently as 387 the emperor Valentinian II had reached out to the senatorial aristocracy by sanctioning the establishment of a series of pagan holidays at Capua. But only a few years later when Ausonius, a senator from Gaul, was ranking the cities in the empire, he noted that Capua was slipping backward: "it is hardly holding on to eighth place."[48]

Instead, northern Italy, frontier Italy, was becoming increasingly important for emperors, and some of its cities acquired distinguished reputations. On Ausonius' list the city in Italy with the highest rank after Rome was Milan, in seventh place. In ninth place was Aquileia. Situated at the head of the Adriatic Sea, Aquileia was located in a borderland between the eastern and western halves of the empire. Its location made it so strategically important that an emperor who controlled the city could acquire the support of "the inhabitants of Italy." But by describing Aquileia as "an Italian colony opposite the mountains of Illyricum," Ausonius provided a telling commentary on current events. His description seemed to hint that this northern Italian city had lost its moorings and was becoming more Balkan than Mediterranean in its orientation.[49]

The political and cultural associations of northern Italy in general were also open to realignment. As the imperial presence retreated from the Rhine frontier, northern Italy, the old Cisalpine Gaul, became a

[48] Capua as second Rome: Ausonius, *Ordo urbium nobilium* 8.16. Aqueduct: *L'année épigraphique 1939* (1940) 49, no. 151 = Grünewald (1990) 222, no. 277, dated to late 324; also *Liber pontificalis* 34.32. See Bell (1997) 14, for the challenge to Rome during the late Republic from Capua, the "anti-Rome," and Trout (2001), for an excellent interpretation of the calendar of festivals at Capua.

[49] Aquileia as Italian colony: Ausonius, *Ordo urbium nobilium* 9.3. Aquileia and the inhabitants of Italy: Ammianus Marcellinus, *Res gestae* 21.11.3. For Aquileia as the gateway between northern Italy and the Balkan regions, note that Theodosius, marching west from Constantinople, defeated two usurpers near the city, Maximus in 388 and Eugenius in 394: see Chapter 12.

primary focus of the shortened northern frontier of the empire. As the new midpoint of the Gallic and Balkan frontiers it soon became the seat of an imperial court, in cities like Milan and Ravenna. During the long transition from ancient society to medieval civilization northern Italy was already gradually shifting its political allegiances and cultural influences from the Mediterranean back to northern and central Europe. In a reversal of Roman imperialism, barbarians from northern and central Europe were again invading Italy, and northern Italy would become the heartland of the kingdoms of the Goths and then the Lombards in Italy. As a preview of the later expansion of Charlemagne's Frankish empire, already during the sixth century a Frankish kingdom centered on the Rhineland in northern Gaul would claim control over "Lesser Italy," that is, northern Italy. Already in late antiquity this continental region of Italy retained its prominence by becoming more northern, more "Gallic," in its orientation. Through its increasing affiliations with continental Europe northern Italy was, again, more Gaul than Italy.[50]

In contrast, central and southern Italy was marginalized. The heartland of the old Roman Republic and the early empire was now, remarkably, more truly a province than the center. When Sidonius, later bishop of Clermont, traveled to Rome in 467, he seems to have lingered in the cities of northern Italy. Once he came to the Rubicon River, however, he knew that he was leaving "Gaul," Cisalpine Gaul, and entering "old Italy." As he started south, there was nothing more to see: "as soon as I entered the other towns on the Via Flaminia, I left." He certainly did not stop to visit any imperial temple at Hispellum. Traveling in "old Italy" between Ravenna and Rome left Sidonius feeling ill.[51]

[50] For the distinction between *Italia minor* and *Italia maior*, see Gregory of Tours, *Historiae* 3.32, on the Frankish general Buccelen's campaigns in Italy during the 550s, with the discussion of Frankish ambitions in Pohl (2002) 138–39. For the expansion of the Carolingians, see McCormick (1995) 361: "They forcibly removed northern Italy from the Byzantine sphere and so strengthened its transalpine political, cultural and economic links that it looked much like the southernmost extension of northern Europe."

[51] Sidonius' journey: Sidonius, *Ep*. 1.5.7, old Italy, 8, Via Flaminia. For the prominence of northern Italy during the fourth century, see Humphries (1999)

Rome too had to come to terms with the loss of its prestige. During the fourth century it was certainly no longer a regular imperial residence, and it seemed barely to retain its standing as an imperial capital. Although the city had celebrated its millennium in 248 with vast games and shows, it hardly celebrated its next centennial: "to such an extent has concern for the city of Rome dwindled day by day," sighed one historian. The emperor Constans was in northern Italy in late spring of 348, but he apparently had not visited Rome for the centennial in April. In the summer of 352 Constantius regained control of Italy from the usurper Magnentius. At Rome the prefect of the city soon erected an equestrian statue of the emperor in the old Forum, and in the dedication he praised Constantius as the "restorer of the city of Rome." Not only was this prefect expressing the city's gratitude; he may also have been broadcasting his own loyalty to the emperor in anticipation of a visit by Constantius to celebrate the thirtieth anniversary of his emperorship in late 353. Instead, the emperor celebrated the occasion in Arles, and then spent the next few winters at Milan. Unlike their father, Constantine's sons did not have even an initial phase in their reigns during which they paid their respects to Rome, before taking up residence elsewhere. After Constantine few emperors crossed the Rubicon to march on Rome.[52]

---

42: "northern Italy . . . had far outstripped Rome and southern Italy in every way." Note that when Filastrius, bishop of Brescia during the 380s and 390s, mentioned a mythical visit by Hermes Trismegistus to "the province of the Celts," he might have been referring to his home region of northern Italy: see Filastrius, *Diversarum hereseon liber* 10.2. For the inclusion of northern Italy in modern political discussions of "Celtic Europe," see J. H. C. Williams (2001) 6–14.

[52] Dwindling concern: Aurelius Victor, *De Caesaribus* 28.2; also 4.14, 15.4, 28.1, for celebration of previous centennials. Constans in Italy: *CTh* 10.14.2, issued from Milan on June 17, 348, with Kent (1981) 238, on Constans' medallions: "Surprisingly, they offer no specific comment on Rome's eleventh centenary."

Constans had little if any direct contact with Rome. Although he may have visited the capital in 340 (see Chapter 3), in 342 he celebrated the tenth anniversary of his accession as an emperor in Gaul: see the verse inscription on a plate found at Colonia Augusta Raurica (modern Augst), published in Kaufmann-Heinimann (1999) 339 and reprinted in *L'année épigraphique 1999* (2002) 371, no. 1123, with the discussion of its translation in Gordon (2003) 234. Petitioners had to find him

Constantius had in fact visited Rome once before, when he was a little boy. More than thirty years later in 357 he finally returned. At first he had behaved almost like a tourist from a foreign country, and during the formal procession celebrating his arrival his demeanor had been completely implacable, "just as he was accustomed to appear in his provinces." Then he had warmed to the city, and for a month he seems to have thoroughly enjoyed his role as "emperor of the Romans" at Rome. He delivered a speech in the senate house, presided at games, and bantered with the crowds. He was respectful toward the pagan shrines, carefully reading the names of the gods inscribed on the facades of the temples and asking about the builders. He was suitably speechless when he first glimpsed the old Forum, and even more impressed when he surveyed the vast Forum of Trajan. As his contribution to the decoration of the Forum of Trajan he restored the statue of a distinguished senator. Senators were understandably elated and only too ready to guide his tours: "he followed the happy senate through all the streets of the eternal city." But despite these pleasant experiences, Constantius remained an outsider, thoroughly astonished by a monumental grandeur that he seems not to have realized had even existed in his empire. A Persian prince in his entourage seemed to know more about Rome and its traditions. This time when the prefect of the city commemorated

instead in cities close to the frontier. In the summer of 339 bishop Athanasius of Alexandria exiled himself to Rome; but to visit Constans during the early 340s, he went to Milan, Aquileia, and Trier: see Athanasius, *Apologia ad Constantium* 4; also *Apologia ad Constantium* 15, for Constans' attendance at a church in Aquileia; with Barnes (1993) 47–70, 224–26. Proaeresius, a famous sophist at Athens, also visited Constans in Gaul; the emperor then sent him to Rome: see Eunapius, *Vitae sophistarum* 492.

Dedication to Constantius from Neratius Cerealis: *ILS* 1:164, no. 731, "restitutori urbis Romae adque orb[is," with Barnes (1993) 221–22, on Constantius' whereabouts, and Chioffi (1995), on the statue. In mid-354 Eusebia, Constantius' wife, did visit Rome, where "the people and the senate welcomed her with joy." She came alone, however, while "the emperor was on campaign and crossing the Rhine on bridges and boats": see Julian, *Orat.* 3.129B–C, with Ammianus Marcellinus, *Res gestae* 14.10.6, for Constantius' battle against the Alamans on the upper Rhine near Augst.

Constantius' visit, he praised the emperor not for his role at Rome, but as the "enlarger of the Roman empire." Constantius was a true provincial emperor, both a descendant of a provincial family and more comfortable ruling in the provinces. He imagined himself as the "lord of the entire world," and not simply emperor of Rome. When the news came about attacks on the Danube frontier, he immediately left the capital.[53]

During his visit in the summer of 389 Theodosius presented his young son Honorius to the senate. After his father's death in 395 Honorius established his court permanently in northern Italy. Senators from Rome corresponded with court officials and visited often, despite the risks from barbarian marauders in the Balkans. On one trip to Milan Symmachus was forced to make a detour to avoid Visigothic raiders. He and other senators always hoped that the emperor would visit Rome again. In 397 an embassy from the senate invited the emperor to celebrate his upcoming consulship at Rome: "it is necessary to ask again for the arrival of our lord, the emperor." Instead, through the intervention of the prefect of Italy, who resided at the court, Honorius remained in Milan. Symmachus was rather annoyed that senators like himself could be foiled so easily: "the wishes of provincials were preferred to petitions from the senate." From the perspective of a senator at Rome, northern Italy was still a province.[54]

---

[53] Constantius' visit and prince Hormisdas: Ammianus Marcellinus, *Res gestae* 16.10. Emperor of the Romans: Themistius, *Orat.* 3.43d; for the context of this oration at Rome during Constantius' visit, see Heather and Moncur (2001) 114–25. Pagan shrines, happy senate: Symmachus, *Relationes* 3.7. Restoration of statue of Flavius Eugenius: *ILS* 1:274, no. 1244 = Conti (2004) 137–38, no. 114. Dedications to Constantius, "propagatori imperii | Romani," by Memmius Vitrasius Orfitus: *CIL* 6.1:240, nos. 1161, 1162, 6.4.2:3095, no. 31395, with Humphries (2003) 38–41. "Orbis totius dominus": Ammianus Marcellinus, *Res gestae* 15.1.3. For a survey of visits by emperors to Rome during the fourth century, see Barnes (1975a), with the modifications in Barnes (1999) 168, now rejecting a visit by Gratian in 376.

[54] Symmachus, *Ep.* 6.52, arrival, wishes, 7.13, detour in 402, with Humphries (2003), on attempts by senators from Rome to maintain contact with emperors, and Salzman (2004) 85–87, 92, on Symmachus' reluctance to visit imperial capitals like Trier and Milan.

In fact, however, it was Rome that was increasingly seen as a "provincial metropolis." According to one pun, Rome was now so insignificant that it could be dismissed as just an "alleyway." Honorius did return to Rome in autumn of 403 to celebrate a triumph and subsequently assume a consulship for the next year. This visit was perhaps not as reassuring as intended, however. According to the panegyrist Claudian, at the moment of his accession as emperor Honorius had deliberately chosen not to reign in the eastern provinces, in order to reside instead at "my Rome." But these words that Claudian put into the emperor's mouth were a cruel parody of a compliment, since "my Rome" turned out not to be Rome. Honorius in fact spent most of his reign first at Milan and then at Ravenna. With its incessant need for supplies of grain and other provisions, Rome had become an onerous liability for emperors. Rome was an old city, on the decline, "slipping into senility." Emperors might even prefer that its demands would go away.[55]

In late 408 king Alaric and his Visigoths invaded Italy. During the early years of his reign Honorius had been praised at Rome for his assistance in restoring buildings and an aqueduct and in rebuilding the city's walls, gates, and towers. In 405 the senate had even celebrated a victory over one Gothic king in northern Italy by erecting a triumphal arch that was decorated with images of the current emperors. Since

[55] For Rome under Honorius as a "Provinzmetropole," see Mayer (2002) 203–6. Pun: "Oracle of Baalbak," ed. Alexander (1967) 15, γίνεται Ῥώμη ῥύμη. Claudian, *De sexto consulatu Honorii* 73–76, Theodosius and Honorius, 87, my Rome. Honorius resided in Rome from autumn of 403 until at least summer of 404. Soon after his arrival he paid his respects at the tomb of St. Peter: see Augustine, *Serm. Mayence* 61 = *Serm. Dolbeau* 25.26, ed. Dolbeau (1996) 266, "he removed his diadem and beat his breast [at the tomb] where the body of the fisherman is buried," and *Serm. Mayence* 55 = *Serm. Dolbeau* 22.4, ed. Dolbeau (1996) 557, "in order to pray for salvation from the Lord that pious and Christian emperor hurried not to the grandiose temple of an emperor but to the tomb of the fisherman," with the discussion of the dating in Dolbeau (1996) 6, 626–27, 640. Senility: Ammianus Marcellinus, *Res gestae* 14.6.4, with Markus (1970) 26, on the sense of Rome's antiquity already before the sack of 410: "at no time do men seem to have been as ready to speak . . . of Rome in her old age, as in the last decades of the fourth century and the early years of the fifth."

Honorius was still trying to participate in the defense of Rome and central Italy, earlier in 408 he had been in the capital during a debate in the senate over the payment of a large subsidy to Alaric. At the time of the invasion, however, he was back in Ravenna, surrounded by marshy lagoons. He was no longer able, or willing, to offer any assistance. In these dire circumstances a request to celebrate the imperial cult at a new imperial temple would be pointless, since the emperor would certainly be unable to attend. During their journey south the Visigoths most likely passed through Umbria. Narnia, a town on the Via Flaminia about thirty-five miles south of Hispellum, now tried a different defensive tactic. Its inhabitants resorted to "prayer to the divine and worship in ancestral fashion." This appeal to traditional pagan rituals was successful, since thunder and lightning drove off the Visigoths. At Rome refugees from Tuscia recommended that the prefect of the city likewise sanction the use of ancestral pagan rituals.[56]

Instead, the city's notables negotiated with the Visigoths and continued to appeal for Honorius' help. In the next year Alaric compelled the senate to accept Priscus Attalus, the prefect of Rome, as his puppet emperor. Attalus immediately announced his plan to restore the standing of Rome by making "Egypt and the entire eastern empire subject to Italians." His boast seemed to be a challenge not only to the eminence of Constantinople in the eastern empire, but also to Honorius' beleaguered court at Ravenna. This new emperor at Rome seemed to have delusions that Italy, central Italy, could again conquer and preside over a Mediterranean empire.[57]

Soon, however, Alaric deposed Attalus, marched on Rome in 410, and this time pillaged the city. Through their repeated incursions the Visigoths had brought the military campaigns that were characteristic of the outer rim all the way to central Italy. For a few years central Italy would itself become a frontier zone, similar to northern Gaul or the

---

[56] *ILS* 1:175–77, nos. 793, 795, 797, Honorius' assistance at Rome, no. 798, the arch. Zosimus, *Historia nova* 5.29.5–9, Honorius at Rome, 37.3–4, Visigoths' route, 41.1–3, pagan rituals.

[57] Attalus' speech: Sozomen, *HE* 9.8.2; also Zosimus, *Historia nova* 6.7.3.

Balkans. During the previous century the rivals to Rome had included frontier capitals like "Belgian Rome" at Trier and "my Rome" at Serdica. Then "Rome" had been exported to the frontiers; now the frontier had been moved to central Italy. In the early fifth century Rome itself seemed to have become a frontier capital, and it could now be imagined as an "Italian Trier," under constant threat from nearby barbarians. In contrast to New Rome at Constantinople, Rome had now become Old Rome.[58]

In Ravenna the emperor Honorius was perhaps more relieved than dismayed. At first he was distraught when he heard the news of the devastation of Rome. "But it just nibbled from my hands!" Then he was comforted to learn that his favorite rooster, named Roma, was safe. At a moment of panic Honorius was thought to have blurted out his true priorities. If a Rome was to be lost, better the old capital than his pet rooster.[59]

---

[58] For the use of ἡ πρεσβυτέρα Ῥώμη, "older Rome," see Sozomen, *HE* 2.3.3, 34.2; also Council of Chalcedon, *Actio* 17.8, ed. Schwartz (1933–1935) 3:89, explicitly contrasting ἡ πρεσβυτέρα Ῥώμη and ἡ νέα Ῥώμη.

[59] Honorius and Roma: Procopius, *Bella* 3.2.25–26; note that Innocent, bishop of Rome, had also taken refuge in Ravenna: see Orosius, *Historiae adversum paganos* 7.39.2. To be fair to Honorius, he did visit Rome again, perhaps in January 411 to celebrate the twentieth anniversary of his reign (Marcellinus Comes, *Chronicon* s.a. 411), in late summer of 414 (*CTh* 16.5.55), and in spring of 416 to celebrate a triumph (Olympiodorus, *Frag.* 26.2 = Philostorgius, *HE* 12.5). After his death in 423 he was buried in a rotunda attached to the south end of the transept of the Church of St. Peter: see Paul the Deacon, *Historia Romana* 13.7, "corpusque eius iuxta beati Petri apostoli martyrium in mausoleo sepultum est," with Koethe (1931), discussing the medieval transformation of the mausoleum, and Alchermes (1995) 7–8, suggesting that Honorius was establishing a mausoleum for western emperors as a counterpart to the imperial mausoleum at Constantinople. Honorius' wives, the sisters Maria and Thermantia, were also buried in this mausoleum: see Krautheimer (1937–1980) 5:179. For the revival of Rome as an imperial residence from 440 to 475, see Gillett (2001).

# "HOPE IN HIS NAME": THE FLAVIAN DYNASTY

## CHAPTER THREE

D URING THE THIRD AND EARLY FOURTH CENTURIES EMPER-
ors may not have resided long or often in Rome, but they
did not entirely neglect it either. The city and its empire
were thought to have been synonymous from the begin-
ning, and in the later fourth century one historian would credit Romulus, the mythical first king, as the founder of both Rome and the Roman
empire. In this perspective the empire was as old as the city, and to rule
one implied accepting responsibility for the other.[1]

Despite their frequent military campaigns on the frontiers, during
the later third century most emperors still acknowledged the prestige
of Rome and patronized its inhabitants. When Maximian arrived in
the late 290s, the "Roman people" mobbed him already outside the
city's walls. When Diocletian visited in 303, he brought along spoils
from the East, including thirteen elephants that had most likely been
captured from the Persians. The culmination of this beneficial relationship was the announcement of the completion of the gigantic Baths

---

[1] Romulus as founder of empire and city: Eutropius, *Breviarium* 10.1–2, with the
excellent discussion of Eutropius' intentions in Lenski (2002) 185–96.

of Diocletian in the north of the city, which Diocletian, Maximian, and the successor Tetrarchs dedicated to "their Romans." These most recent emperors were now competing with the achievements of their predecessors in the one city with a long enough history of aristocratic munificence and imperial patronage to keep a scorecard. According to one retrospective survey, "each emperor, past and present, wanted to build something in Rome, and each of them constructed some sort of monument in his own name." At Rome people could measure and compare the generosity of each emperor very precisely. The huge Baths of Caracalla had provided seating for 1600 people; these new Baths of Diocletian could accommodate almost twice as many. Even as the significance of the capital faded, the Tetrarchic emperors nevertheless enhanced its amenities.[2]

These gifts and construction projects seemingly validated the special standing of the citizens of Rome and improved their daily lives. For most emperors, however, the public benefits were probably supplementary, because their primary concern was always the promotion of themselves and their families. In this perspective these buildings, no matter how grandiose or how useful, were simply elaborate scaffolding, designed to display the dedications and statues that reminded the citizens of emperors' generosity and authority. Even as emperors competed with the memories of their predecessors, they were each looking forward to the establishment of a family dynasty of successors.

Constantine followed the example of the Tetrarchs by advertising himself at Rome and elsewhere in Italy. But he broke with Tetrarchic practice by also promoting a new Flavian dynasty of his own sons. Eventually the Flavian name became common throughout the empire. After Constantine expanded his control over the eastern provinces, he

---

[2] Maximian at Rome: *Panegyrici latini* 7(6).8.7; this visit is dated to possibly 299 by Barnes (1982) 59. Elephants: Chronographer of 354, *Chronica urbis Romae*, s.v. Diocletianus et Maximianus, ed. Mommsen (1892) 148. Dedication of Baths of Diocletian: *ILS* 1:148, no. 646, "Romanis suis." Each emperor: *Expositio totius mundi et gentium* 55. Number of seats: Olympiodorus, *Frag.* 41, with Purcell (1999), on the increasing mismatch between supply and demand at Rome, and Papi (2004) 53, on a population increase at Rome in the early fourth century.

furthermore founded a new capital that became a rival to Rome. Both new capital and subsequent emperors took their names from Constantine. New Rome became Constantinople, and emperors assumed the name of Flavius.

## MAXENTIUS AND ROME

The emperor Maxentius in particular had cultivated a special relationship with Rome. In 285 Diocletian had appointed Maximian as a fellow emperor. While Diocletian had identified himself with the authority of Jupiter, the supreme god, by adding the title of Jovius to his official name, Maximian had claimed the special patronage of Hercules by adding the title of Herculius. Since in Roman mythology Hercules was associated with the foundation of the city of Rome, his spiritual descendant, "Hercules adored as an emperor," could now also assert a singular connection with the capital. In a panegyric delivered on April 21, the birthday of the foundation of Rome, Maximian Herculius was praised for preserving the tradition of "your family and your name." "You celebrate the foundation of that city as if you had yourself founded it." Apparently in attendance during the performance of this panegyric was Maximian's young son Maxentius. Once this "divine and immortal offspring" became an emperor in 306, he too proclaimed his membership in his father's Herculian dynasty. On coins minted at Rome Maxentius could now present himself, if not as a new founder, then certainly as the "preserver of his own city."[3]

One sign of a new founding was new construction. Maxentius' most extensive construction projects at Rome were just beyond the east end

---

[3] *Panegyrici latini* 10(2).1.3–4, family, foundation, 14.1, offspring, with Rees (2002) 39–50, on this orator's use of the myth of Hercules at Rome. "Imperator Hercules": *Panegyrici latini* 11(3).10.5. The timing and meaning of Maximian's use of the title of Herculius are predictably much contested; for an overview, see Nixon and Rodgers (1994) 44–51, and Chapter 9. On the special relationship between Maximian and Italy, note also *Panegyrici latini* 7(6).10.3: when Maximian had retired in 305, "the whole of Italy and Rome itself . . . trembled and almost stumbled." For Maxentius as Herculius, see Barnes (1982) 24n.11. For the coins with the legend "conservator urbis suae," see Sutherland (1967) 338–47, and Cullhed (1994) 46–49.

of the old Forum, on the north side of the Sacred Way. He completely rebuilt the burned-out Temple of Venus and Roma, the largest temple in the city, which commemorated the eternity of Rome and its venerated status in the divine order. Next to it he constructed an enormous basilica, the Basilica Nova. At one corner of the basilica he constructed a rotunda on the Sacred Way that probably was a temple dedicated in part with a cult in honor of his young son Romulus. In addition, he may have had the colossal bronze statue (originally of Nero) that still stood next to the Colosseum rededicated in honor of his son. A son with a name reminiscent of Rome's original founder presented too good of an opportunity to overlook in the capital, especially when that son was also a grandson of Maximian and Galerius and a great-grandson of Diocletian. These building projects were a conspicuous proclamation of Maxentius' standing at Rome. As a member of the Herculian imperial dynasty and the father of Romulus, he was now the guardian of the capital, and by implication of the entire empire. Unfortunately his son died young. A few miles south of Rome along the Via Appia, Maxentius built a new suburban villa that included a separate rotunda. Since a dedication at the site commemorated the deified Romulus, Maxentius most likely intended this rotunda to become the mausoleum for his imperial dynasty.[4]

Maxentius had become emperor as a usurper, proclaimed by the praetorian guards in defiance of the reorganized Tetrarchy that had excluded

---

[4] On Maxentius' buildings at Rome, see the thorough survey in Coarelli (1986), Cullhed (1994) 49–60, and the excellent summation in Curran (2000) 50–63. For recent archaeology of the Temple of Venus and Roma, see Monaco (2000); for opinions about the rotunda on the Sacred Way, see Richardson (1992) 333–34. Ensoli (2000), in a suggestive survey of changes to the colossal statue, highlights the meaning of the rededicated statue for Maxentius: "il colosso diverrebbe il fulcro architettonico della nuova piazza massenziana" (p. 87); but the inscription with the rededication has not yet been published: see Marlowe (2006) 228. Dedication to deified Romulus: *ILS* 1:153, no. 673, with Pisani Sartorio (2000), discussing Maxentius' combination of palace, mausoleum, and circus; for Romulus' lineage, see Barnes (1982) 31, 38. Maxentius continued to identify his dynasty with the foundation myths of Rome, because after 308 his mints at the capital issued coins that depicted the wolf and twins: see Sutherland (1967) 344.

this son of an original Tetrarch. As he then looked for recognition from the other emperors, he seemed to have found a powerful warranty for his legitimacy in his association with Rome. He had become the resident emperor of the capital, devoted to preserving its privileges and prestige and intent upon constructing a legacy of monuments that linked his own authority with the city's reputation. He even had a dedication in honor of Romulus and his brother Remus, "the founders of the eternal city," erected precisely on April 21, the birthday of the city's foundation. Maxentius' presence at Rome furthermore seemed to give him priority over the other emperors, and he himself would claim that the other emperors "were fighting battles on the frontiers on his behalf." Even an orator who celebrated Maxentius' death would concede the advantage that came from residing in Rome. "Maxentius benefited from the majesty of his city." Maxentius hence promoted an ideology in which he and Rome were inseparable, and both were foremost. Coins minted at Rome depicted him receiving the globe that symbolized universal rule directly from the goddess Roma. According to the legend on one gold coin minted at Rome, Maxentius was now *Princeps imperii Romani*, the leading ruler in the Roman empire. Maxentius ruled at Rome; and because Rome was still the capital of the empire, he deserved to be acknowledged as the senior emperor.[5]

Constantine meanwhile was one of those other emperors on the frontiers. He had spent the first years of his reign likewise looking for legitimacy, but in the remote northern provinces of Britain and the Rhine frontier. He too had started out as a usurper, supported by his father's army in Britain but not accredited by the other emperors who formed the new Tetrarchy. In order to become more than a rebellious military commander with imperial pretensions, he needed recognition

---

[5] Dedication: *ILS* 2.2:XXIII, no. 8935, with Wrede (1981) 140–42, suggesting that Maxentius' emphasis on Mars and his sons Romulus and Remus was a deliberate promotion of the idea of family succession against Tetrarchic notions of succession. *Panegyrici latini* 12(9).3.7, majesty, 14.6, frontiers, with Cullhed (1994) 63–67, on Maxentius' attitude toward Rome. Coins depicting Roma: Sutherland (1967) 372–78, nos. 166, 173, 212. *Princeps*: Sutherland (1967) 373, no. 172, with p. 343, "the first man in any of the territories which looked to Rome as their natural centre."

from other emperors. Galerius begrudgingly acknowledged him as a junior emperor with the title of Caesar. In Italy Maxentius had been joined by his father Maximian, who now came out of retirement. They too needed allies. In the original Tetrarchy Constantius had married a daughter of Maximian; in 307 Constantine followed his father's lead and married Fausta, another daughter of Maximian. This marriage not only linked him with a father-in-law and a brother-in-law who were fellow emperors. It also associated him with their mythical dynasty of Hercules. After Constantine's marriage a panegyrist would celebrate his new membership in the Herculian imperial dynasty: "Herculian emperors forever!"[6]

This association with Maximian and Maxentius soon became a liability for Constantine. In late 308 a conference of senior emperors, including Galerius and Diocletian, again acknowledged Constantine as a Caesar. But this conference did not recognize Maxentius, even though he was ruling as emperor at Rome, and it compelled Maximian to abdicate again. Constantine too soon began cutting his ties to the Herculian dynasty. In 310 he eliminated his father-in-law after an unsuccessful plot, and his designation as Maximian's descendant was literally erased off one dedication. In Gaul a panegyrist soon offered alternative justifications for his rule. This orator now claimed that Constantine was a descendant of the emperor Claudius Gothicus, a "restorer of mankind" who had subsequently become a "companion of the gods." Although Claudius Gothicus had in fact been a rather nondescript emperor during the later 260s, this startling revelation provided Constantine with a hereditary claim on the throne that was older than the Tetrarchy. The orator furthermore stressed the accomplishments of Constantius, another of the original Tetrarchs. During his reign Constantius had been identified with Hercules because of his association with Maximian. But after his death he had become "a god in heaven" through the invitation of Jupiter himself, who had welcomed the former emperor to heaven "by extending his right hand." Constantius may have been a Herculian emperor in life, but after his apotheosis he had become a Jovian deity. As

---

[6] Herculian emperors: *Panegyrici latini* 7(6).2.5; also *ILS* 1:154, no. 681, "Herculian Caesar, be victorious!"

a descendant of Claudius Gothicus and a son of the deified Constantius, Constantine hence had a double claim on imperial rule: "you deserved the empire by birth." Constantine was already the third emperor in his family, and not merely the second. The orator also mentioned Constantine's recent visit to a temple of Apollo in Gaul. During this visit the emperor had essentially identified himself with Apollo in a vision. With this epiphany of Apollo, Constantine had affiliated himself with yet another god to displace his (and his father's) earlier association with Hercules. In his guise as the Sun-god, Apollo was now "the companion of Constantine."[7]

In 312 Constantine severed another tie with the Herculian dynasty by defeating Maxentius, his brother-in-law, outside Rome. Maxentius had become emperor with the support of the praetorian guards, and at this final battle his troops had in addition included the *equites singulares*, an elite cavalry unit. Constantine soon eliminated the praetorian guards for good and demolished their garrison at Rome. As a patron of Christianity he also quickly initiated the construction of churches and shrines. One of the first was the Church of St. John Lateran, which would become the official seat of the city's bishop. This church was immense, almost as large as Maxentius' huge Basilica Nova. Constantine clearly used the site of the church to send a message about the total defeat of Maxentius and his supporters, because the substructures of barracks that had once housed the *equites singulares* now became the foundations for this new church. Since initially this Church of St. John Lateran was known as *Basilica Constantiniana*, a "Constantinian Basilica" now emerged from the rubble of a camp of Maxentius' supporters.[8]

[7] Conference at Carnuntum: Lactantius, *De mortibus persecutorum* 29.1–3. Erasure: *ILS* 1:154, no. 684. *Panegyrici latini* 6(7).2.2, Claudius, 2.4, third emperor, 3.1, by birth, 4.2, god in heaven, 7.3, Jupiter's hand, 21.4–5, vision of Apollo, with Nixon and Rodgers (1994) 219–21, 248–51, reviewing modern interpretations, and Kolb (2001) 64, "die Inkarnation Apollons." For a gold coin minted at Ticinum in 316 with the legend "Soli comiti Constantini Aug," see Bruun (1966) 368, no. 56; also no. 53, for a gold coin depicting Sol and Constantine, discussed in Kolb (2001) 196–200. On Constantine's search for legitimation, see Leadbetter (1998).

[8] Dissolution of praetorian guards: Aurelius Victor, *De Caesaribus* 40.25; garrisons: Zosimus, *Historia nova* 2.17.2. For the participation and punishment of the *equites*

This church was on the southeastern edge of Rome, just inside the city's walls. Many of Maxentius' own building projects had been in the heart of the city, near the old Forum. Constantine now likewise impressed his own patronage and reputation on the city's symbolic center. He renovated the Circus Maximus, completed yet another new bath complex north of the imperial forums, and erected gold and silver statues of himself. In addition, he appropriated credit for his rival's construction projects. One example was a possible rededication of the temple that Maxentius had dedicated in honor of his son. The most conspicuous example of this confiscation of credit was the great Basilica Nova on the edge of the Forum. Constantine remodeled the building, and in the apse at the end of the basilica he erected a colossal statue of himself that quite likely replaced a large statue of Maxentius. "Constantine's military victory cost Maxentius his monumental legacy as well as his life." As a result, the regionary catalogues of Rome referred to this building too as *Basilica Constantiniana*, another "Constantinian Basilica."[9]

singulares, see Speidel (1986). Basilica Constantiniana: *Liber pontificalis* 34.9, with Krautheimer (1983) 12–15, suggesting that the Church of St. John Lateran was founded already within two weeks of Constantine's victory, Curran (2000) 93–96, for the meanings attached to the church, and Liverani (2004), for an archaeological survey of sites in the neighborhood. Maxentius' family had apparently owned property in the vicinity of these barracks, since Fausta, his sister and Constantine's wife, owned "a house on the Lateran" where a council of bishops met in autumn of 313: see Optatus, *Contra Donatistas* 1.23.2, "in domum Faustae in Laterano." Barceló (1992), suggests that some of the reliefs used on the Arch of Constantine had been taken from these former barracks of the *equites singulares*. Constantine also obliterated a cemetery of *equites singulares* located east of the city on the Via Labicana by constructing a new Church of St. Marcellinus and St. Peter: see Deichmann and Tschira (1957) 68–70, Guyon (1987) 30–33, 230–39, Curran (2000) 99–102, and Chapter 2, for the burial of his mother, Helena, in this church.

[9]  Circus, bath, statues: *Panegyrici latini* 4(10).35.5, Aurelius Victor, *De Caesaribus* 40.27–28. Quotation from Curran (2000) 90, who also, pp. 76–90, provides an excellent survey of Constantine's buildings in Rome; Curran accepts the identification of the colossal marble statue in the basilica with the statue described by Eusebius, *HE* 9.9.10–11, *Vita Constantini* 1.40. For a reconstruction of Constantine's modifications to the basilica, see Minoprio (1932); also Kähler (1952),

After establishing himself at Rome, Constantine quickly advertised his dominance by rewriting memories of his opponent. Contrary to Maxentius' own propaganda, this revised interpretation insisted that all along the defeated emperor had been the "murderer of the city." The images and legends on coins were one important form of self-promotion, and some of Constantine's coins seemed to engage in a direct dialogue with Maxentius' slogans. Maxentius had associated himself with memories of Romulus, the founder of Rome and its first king, and the legends on his coins had praised him as the guardian of the city. His propaganda had conjured up reminders of the original monarchy at Rome and presented him as a successor to the original kings. In contrast, Constantine seems to have wanted to locate himself in the context of the Republic that had succeeded that mythical monarchy. The legends on his coins now honored the new ruler at Rome not only as the city's "liberator," but also as its "restorer." Through these slogans Constantine seemed to hint at his willingness to promote a new future for the capital, rather than merely to defend its past reputation.[10]

Another, even more overt tactic for eclipsing Maxentius' prominence at Rome was through buildings. By sponsoring new construction and by replacing dedications, Constantine made clear that his preferences were now dominant. One Constantinian Basilica, the Church of St. John Lateran, represented a conspicuous advertisement of his patronage for Christianity and his annihilation of Maxentius' military support. The other Constantinian Basilica, the Basilica Nova, signified the equally

---

discussing the relationship between the basilica and the statue of Constantine. Basilica Nova as Basilica Constantiniana: *Curiosum* and *Notitia*, ed. Nordh (1949) 78, 100, with the survey of Coarelli (1993) 170–73.

[10] Murderer: *Panegyrici latini* 12(9).18.1, also mentioning the death of a "false Romulus," referring to either Maxentius or his son. Constantine's coins: Sutherland (1967) 387, nos. 303–4, "liberatori urbis suae," 388, no. 312, "restitutor urbis suae." Note that a hostile source would compare Maximian, Maxentius' father, to Tarquin the Proud, the last king of Rome whose overthrow marked the establishment of the Republic: see Lactantius, *De mortibus persecutorum* 28.4. De Decker (1968), argues that Constantine may also have appropriated Maxentius' religious policy of toleration and pluralism at Rome.

conspicuous theft of Maxentius' reputation from the symbolic heart of the city.

## FLAVIAN EMPERORS

Maxentius had been a direct descendant of the imperial Herculian dynasty, and by obliterating his presence at Rome, Constantine was also eradicating any reminders of his family. One historian noted that Constantine tended to belittle the achievements of his imperial predecessors, for instance by calling Augustus a "plaything of fortune," Hadrian a mere "paintbrush," and Marcus Aurelius a "buffoon." Constantine also disparaged Trajan as "wall ivy" for having claimed credit for so many buildings by posting his name everywhere.[11]

This candid evaluation of Trajan was an involuntary peek into Constantine's own boundless capacity for appropriation of his predecessors' monuments. The triumphal arch dedicated to celebrate his victory over Maxentius scavenged sculptures and relief panels from earlier monuments of Trajan, Hadrian, and Marcus Aurelius, in part to display an attractive pastiche of styles and in part to ensure its rapid construction. Most importantly, this confiscation of earlier sculptures served to identify Constantine with ancient imperial traditions by superimposing his image on his predecessors' reworked faces. In a similar fashion the colossal marble statue of himself in the Basilica Nova may have originally been a statue of Trajan, moved from the Forum of Trajan, or of Hadrian, moved from the Temple of Venus and Roma, or even of Maxentius himself, already in the Basilica and now skillfully recut. Perhaps just the head had originally been a head of Hadrian, with its beard carefully shaved off and its hair neatly trimmed. The original right hand of the recycled statue was apparently discarded in favor of a new hand that could grip the shaft of a cross. Constantine's heist of

---

[11] Evaluations of emperors: Anonymus post Dionem (= Dio Continuatus), *Frag.* 15.2, ed Müller (1851) 199; this fragment stops before completing Constantine's assessment of Septimius Severus. Ammianus Marcellinus, *Res gestae* 27.3.7, repeated the joke about Trajan; another historian applied this saying about Trajan directly to Constantine as proof of his vanity: see *Epitome de Caesaribus* 41.13.

Maxentius' monuments was hence another blatant example of his life-long iconographical larceny. In the case of Maxentius' Basilica Nova, he was furthermore able to enlist the support of the senate in sanctioning this transfer of credit. "The Fathers [senators] dedicated all the monuments that Maxentius had magnificently constructed, [including] the shrine of the city and the basilica, to the merits of Flavius."[12]

[12] For the reliefs and roundels reused in the arch, see Chapter 2. Interpretive discussions of the use of *spolia* in the arch include Brenk (1987) 103–7, Peirce (1989) 415, "consciously recalling the ideals of the principate," Alchermes (1994), and Elsner (2000a) 174, "the act of recutting... represents not a rejection of these previous emperors... but rather a bolstering and elevating of Constantine through literally putting him in their shoes." Colossal marble statue: Stuart Jones (1926) 5–6, reviews earlier suggestions that the head originally belonged to a colossal statue of Apollo, Domitian, or Commodus; Harrison (1967) 94, suggests that Constantine first appropriated a statue of Trajan or Hadrian and later added a new head and right hand, Fittschen and Zanker (1985) 149, that it had been a statue of a god, Evers (1991) 794–99, that its head had originally been a bearded Hadrian, Coarelli (1993) 171–72, that it had originally been a statue of Maxentius, Varner (2004) 217–18, 287, that it had been a statue of Hadrian first recut as Maxentius in the guise of Jupiter and then as Constantine, Curran (2000) 82, that it was an original, and Kolb (2001) 208, that it resembled a statue of Jupiter. Other right hand: Stuart Jones (1926) 12, no. 16, L'Orange (1984) 71–74, and Fittschen and Zanker (1985) 148; with Chapter 4, for the modern meanings of the head and hand. Merits of Flavius: Aurelius Victor, *De Caesaribus* 40.26; the basilica was the Basilica Nova, and the *Urbis Fanum* probably the Temple of Venus and Roma that Maxentius had restored. For the possibility that Constantine also appropriated the colossal bronze statue next to the Colosseum, see Ensoli (2000) 86–90.

Scholars continue to debate whether the Arch of Constantine was a new construction of the early fourth century or (less likely) a remodeled version of an earlier Flavian or Hadrianic arch. The proximity of the arch to other Flavian projects might suggest that it was built by or dedicated to a Flavian emperor such as Domitian; its use of Trajanic reliefs and Hadrianic roundels might suggest Hadrian's initiative; and its characteristically late antique syncretism might even suggest initial construction by Maxentius: see Melucco Vaccaro and Ferroni (1993–1994), discussing Domitian and Hadrian, Holloway (2004) 50–53, arguing for Maxentius, and the reassertion of construction under Constantine by Pensabene (1999) and Panella (1999), summarized in Kleiner (2001). Wilson Jones (2000), stresses the "proportional elegance" of the arch (p. 58); hence, "the existing

Constantine's father's official imperial name had been Marcus (or Gaius) Flavius Valerius Constantius. This was certainly not his original name. In the Tetrarchic system new emperors commonly changed their names upon accession, and Constantius' complete official name appeared for the first time only on dedications after he had been promoted to be a Caesar, a junior emperor. He had certainly assumed the name Valerius after being adopted into the original Tetrarchy of emperors established by Diocletian, whose official name was Marcus Aurelius Gaius Valerius Diocletianus at first, later often Gaius Aurelius Valerius Diocletianus. Valerius functioned as Diocletian's family name (the *nomen gentilicium*). It also seems to have become the most significant of his names, since in dedications his name (almost) always included at least Valerius Diocletianus, and the historian Aurelius Victor sometimes referred to him simply as Valerius. Diocletian named his only daughter Valeria, and one of the new provinces resulting from the division of Pannonia Inferior was called Valeria. In addition, like Constantius, the other members of the original Tetrarchy also adopted the name Valerius in their official nomenclature, Maximian as Marcus Aurelius Valerius Maximianus and Galerius as Gaius Galerius (Aurelius) Valerius Maximianus. Subsequent members of the revamped Tetrarchy, Severus, Maximinus, and Licinius, also used Valerius as part of their official names; so did Maxentius and his son Romulus. The adoption of the name Valerius indicated subordination to Diocletian, as well as membership in the Tetrarchic imperial college or at least acceptance of its ideals.[13]

configuration is most economically explained as a Constantinian assemblage" (p. 68). Marlowe (2006), provides an excellent analysis of the visual and ideological relationship between the Arch of Constantine and the colossal statue of the Sun-god behind it. But if Maxentius had initiated construction of the arch, many of her observations would apply even better to his ideological pretensions, since he had in fact rededicated the colossal statue to his son: see above.

[13]   For Constantius' full name, see the references in *PLRE* 1:227–28, "Constantius 12." One dedication added the praenomen Marcus, another the praenomen Gaius: see *ILS* 1:143, 148, nos. 637, 649. A dedication that mentioned Constantius during his governorship of Dalmatia but already included his full imperial name is a forgery: see *CIL* 3, Supplementum 1:1623, no. 9860, with Barnes (1982) 36n.35. For the commonness of name changes, note the account in Lactantius, *De mortibus*

But the origin of the name Flavius remains a mystery. Constantius had been born no later than about 250, and his early career had been in the army. If anything, he might be expected to have included "Aurelius" or "Marcus Aurelius" in his name as an indication of the Roman citizenship that all provincials had received from the edict issued in the early third century by the emperor Caracalla, officially known as Marcus Aurelius Antoninus. In that case Constantius would have been a descendant of one of those recently enfranchised "New Romans" whose name commemorated their imperial benefactor. Instead, Constantius' name before his appointment as Caesar may have been Julius Constantius. Then he became Flavius Valerius Constantius. Upon his promotion to membership in the Tetrarchy he adopted one new name, Valerius, that represented his loyalty to the college of emperors. But he also adopted another new name, Flavius, that seems to have represented his ambitions for himself and his own family. Although in their group portraits the Tetrarchs tended to look alike, images of Constantius consistently highlighted his long curved nose as a unique identifying characteristic. The name of Flavius was the dynastic equivalent of this distinctive physiognomical feature. As a result, while Constantius' standing as a Valerius indicated his solidarity in Diocletian's Tetrarchy, his standing as a Flavius seems to have represented his own new dynastic pretensions.[14]

---

*persecutorum* 19.4. In 305 Diocletian announced Severus and Maximinus as the new Caesars. Since everyone had been expecting Constantine to be selected, "people were uncertain whether Constantine's name had been changed." Diocletian as simply Valerius: Aurelius Victor, *De Caesaribus* 39.1, 8, 13, 18, 29, 30, 36, 46, with Kolb (1987) 16–17, for Diocletian's use of Aurelius to associate himself with the Antonine emperors of the second century, and Cambi (2004) 38: "a political meaning for their names was intended." Province of Valeria: Aurelius Victor, *De Caesaribus* 40.10, Ammianus Marcellinus, *Res gestae* 19.11.4, with Barnes (1982) 223. Note also Coarelli (1993) 171, for the intriguing suggestion that the construction of the Basilica Nova on the Velia was Maxentius' attempt to recall the ancestral tomb of the family of P. Valerius Publicola, one of the legendary founding fathers of the Republic.

[14] Date of Constantius' birth: Barnes (1982) 35. For the widespread adoption of the name Aurelius after the publication of the *Constitutio Antoniniana*, see Salway (1994) 133–36. Julius Constantius: Aurelius Victor, *De Caesaribus* 39.24. Note the overly tidy resolution of Piganiol (1932) 32, who speculates that Constantius'

His son Constantine's official name was Flavius Valerius Constantinus. Since Constantine had been born about fifteen or twenty years before his father became a Caesar and changed his name, this official name had most likely not been his original name. Constantius' three other sons, Constantine's younger half-brothers, had rather bland names, as far as is known. One was Dalmatius, presumably named after the province of Dalmatia that Constantius had once governed; another was Julius Constantius, perhaps a reminder of Constantius' original name before he became emperor; another was Hannibalianus. Constantine's official name of course did not appear on dedications until he became an emperor. But perhaps he had already acquired this name that resembled an official imperial name some years earlier, after his father became an emperor. If so, then it was a name that already carried a double significance, as a potential Valerian member of the Tetrarchy and as a likely Flavian successor to his father.[15]

original name had been Flavius Julius Constantius and even invents names for his anonymous parents, Flavius Delmatius [sic] and Julia Constantia. Constantius' nose: Smith (1997) 180–1, 184–85, "a Constantinian dynastic badge," and L'Orange (1984) 29–31, emphasizing the differences between Constantius' images and those of the other Tetrarchs. For an argument that emperors selected the images of themselves, see Price (1984) 174.

The source of Constantius' name Flavius is open to speculation. One possibility is that an ancestor had changed his name upon entering the Roman army. In the early empire the brother of a German king adopted the name of Flavus, "Mr. Blond," when he served in the Roman army: see Tacitus, *Annales* 2.9. Such a nickname that reflected a recruit's appearance may eventually have been changed to the more distinguished name of Flavius with the adoption of Roman nomenclature. Another possibility is that long ago an ancestor had received Roman citizenship after military service under the Flavian emperors and hence adopted the name Flavius. Yet another possibility highlights a consequence of the *Constitutio Antoniniana*. Salway (1994) 134, notes that praetorians recruited from the Danubian provinces who used the name M. Aurelius were sometimes enrolled in the voting tribe of Flavia. Flavia was a fictitious voting tribe; but perhaps membership in it had somehow influenced Constantius' name.

[15] Some dedications to Constantine added various praenomina, Lucius, Marcus, or Gaius: see *ILS* 1:155, no. 690. For Constantius' governorship of Dalmatia, see *Origo Constantini imperatoris* 1.2. Hannibalianus' name may have been a recollection of

But when Constantine was passed over in the realignment of the Tetrarchy in 305, his name made him a rival rather than a successor. Constantius became a senior emperor with the title of Augustus, while his new subordinate Caesar was Severus. As a nod to Constantius' authority Severus became both a Flavian and a Valerian by adopting the official name of Flavius Valerius Severus. But Constantius may have had reason to suspect the loyalty of Severus, who had been selected as a Caesar because he was a friend of Galerius, the other senior emperor in this reconfigured Tetrarchy. Severus had perhaps not been Constantius' endorsed choice to become a new junior emperor. His preference was most likely his own son, who perhaps by now had already assumed the appropriate name to be an emperor himself. The son, Flavius Valerius Constantinus, was essentially a clone of his father, Flavius Valerius Constantius. Constantine would be a new Constantius, "as if brought back to life." Panegyrists repeatedly commented on the similarity between the two: "nature stamped Constantius' celestial features on Constantine's face." He even had his father's hooked nose! With his distinctive nose and his imperial-sounding name, Flavius Valerius Constantinus would have been an obvious successor to his father.[16]

After his victory over Maxentius in 312 Constantine seems to have sensed the advantages of presenting himself openly, and increasingly exclusively, as a Flavian. One was an improvement in his standing at Rome. He certainly had no incentive to identify himself at Rome with Diocletian's Valerian dynasty of Tetrarchs. In fact, almost a decade

his maternal grandfather: see *PLRE* 1:407–8, "Afranius Hannibalianus 3," and Barnes (1982) 33–34.

[16] For Severus as Galerius' friend, see Lactantius, *De mortibus persecutorum* 18.12, and *Origo Constantini imperatoris* 4.9. Brought back: Eusebius, *Vita Constantini* 1.22.1. Similarity: *Panegyrici latini* 7(6).3.3, celestial features, 14.5, addressed to Constantius: "this is your particular immortality, a son similar in appearance"; also *Panegyrici latini* 6(7).4.3, "formae similitudo"; with Wright (1987), discussing changes in Constantine's appearance. Constantine's nose: *Vita Constantini*, ed Guidi (1907) 319, τὴν ῥῖνα ἐπίγρυπον. One panegyrist claimed that as soon as Constantine rejoined his father, he had been seen "not as a candidate for imperial rule but as the designated [successor]": see *Panegyrici latini* 6(7).4.2.

earlier Diocletian himself had left the capital in disgust. Although he had arrived to celebrate the twentieth anniversary of his accession and to assume a consulship, the people of Rome had driven him away with their outspoken abuse. He had assumed his consulship instead at Ravenna. Constantine furthermore wanted to distinguish himself from the Herculian dynasty of Maximian and Maxentius. So he presented himself as a Flavian. That identification in addition offered Constantine a symbolic link with the earlier imperial dynasty of the first Flavian emperors, Vespasian (officially known as Titus Flavius Vespasianus) and his two sons, Titus and Domitian.[17]

The first Flavian dynasty had lasted only two generations, from Vespasian's acclamation in 69 to Domitian's assassination in 96. In Roman historiography it had started well, since the "Flavian family" was credited with rescuing the empire after a period of civil wars and instability on the imperial throne. By the end, however, its reputation was considerably tarnished, largely because of Domitian's cruel policies and scandalous behavior. Contemporaries savaged him for having terrorized the senatorial elite. Christian historians denounced him as one of the first emperors to persecute Christians. During Constantine's reign both Eusebius and Lactantius denigrated Domitian as a persecuting emperor, a true successor to the vilified Nero. In addition, later in the fourth century his personal behavior was still remembered to have been so dissolute that even Julian, another opponent of Christianity in his own way, nevertheless thought he should have been locked up. Constantine may have appreciated the traditions that praised the first Flavian dynasty for stabilizing the empire after civil wars, but he certainly did not want to revive those other memories about antagonism toward senators (especially at Rome), hostility to Christianity, and bad behavior.[18]

Instead, he preferred to associate himself with this namesake dynasty's reputation for construction at the capital. Soon after his arrival at Rome

[17]  Abuse of Diocletian: Lactantius, *De mortibus persecutorum* 17.1–3.
[18]  *Gens Flavia* as savior: Suetonius, *Vespasianus* 1.1. Domitian the persecutor: Eusebius, *HE* 3.17–20, Lactantius, *De mortibus persecutorum* 3. Locked up: Julian, *Caesares* 311A.

Vespasian had personally helped to clear the rubble from the Temple of Jupiter Optimus Maximus on the Capitoline Hill that had been burned in the street fighting during the civil wars, and he had encouraged the swift reconstruction of the temple. Both sons had followed his example of extensive building at Rome and throughout Italy. In particular, Domitian had such an obsession for building that his "Midas touch" was thought to have turned everything to stone. At Rome he too had initiated an extensive program of construction. Some buildings he restored, and in the process he set an example for Constantine by conspicuously replacing the names of the original builders with his own. His restorations included the Temple of Jupiter Optimus Maximus, which had burned down again soon after its recent reconstruction by Vespasian. Domitian now rebuilt this temple in lavish style, with columns imported from Athens and expensive gilding on the roof. His new projects included a temple in honor of his family that he constructed on the site of the house in which he had been born. Contemporary poets were duly impressed with this temple in honor of his dynasty. Statius complimented Domitian for having honored his "eternal family" with a "Flavian heaven." The satirist Martial praised the temple as "the lofty splendor of the Flavian family." Despite the recent restoration of his own impressive temple on the Capitoline, even Jupiter had been envious.[19]

In fourth-century Rome this Temple of the Flavian Dynasty was still on conspicuous display, and Domitian retained his reputation as one of the great builders in the city's history. In fact, in the middle of the

[19] Vespasian's Temple of Jupiter Optimus Maximus: Tacitus, *Historiae* 3.72, fire, 4.53, reconstruction by Vespasian; Suetonius, *Vespasianus* 8.5, Vespasian's assistance. Domitian's Temple of Jupiter: Plutarch, *Publicola* 15.3–4, gilding and columns, 5, Midas touch. Replacement of names: Suetonius, *Domitianus* 5. Temple of the Flavian Dynasty: Statius, *Silvae* 4.3.19, "Flaviumque caelum," 5.1.240, "aeternae ... genti"; Martial, *Epigrammata* 9.1.8, "manebit altum Flaviae decus gentis," 9.34, Jupiter's envy; also 9.3.12, 20.1–6. Richardson (1992) 181, and Davies (2000a) 24–27, 79, (2000b) 32–33, suggest that this temple was located possibly off the Alta Semita. Darwell-Smith (1996), provides an excellent comprehensive overview of Flavian construction at Rome; other surveys include Scheithauer (2000) 127–53, and Packer (2003).

century one chronographer listed more buildings for Domitian than for any other emperor, more even than for such other notable builders as Augustus, Nero, Trajan, and Hadrian. Some of the most noticeable of the monuments constructed by the first Flavian dynasty near the city's symbolic center were the Forum Transitorium, located to the east of the other imperial forums; the Temple of Peace and its large colonnaded courtyard adjacent to the Forum Transitorium; the Arch of Titus, at the east end of the old Forum at the foot of the Palatine Hill; the Baths of Titus, on the south flank of the Esquiline Hill; and, of course, the huge Flavian amphitheater, the Colosseum, in the valley below the Esquiline Hill. Many of Maxentius' projects of construction or renovation were located near these monuments, including the colossal statue now probably rededicated in honor of his son Romulus, the Temple of Venus and Roma, the temple in honor of Romulus, and the Basilica Nova. Stretched out in a line northwest from the Colosseum toward the Temple of Peace and just north of the Arch of Titus, Maxentius' buildings and monuments had invaded this Flavian neighborhood. As the most striking manifestation of this intrusion, the Basilica Nova was built on a site that had previously been occupied by Domitian's Horrea Piperataria ("Spice Warehouses").[20]

It was most likely no coincidence that the Arch of Constantine was subsequently located in the same area, just west of the Colosseum and almost in line with the Arch of Titus. The dedicatory inscription on Constantine's arch, carefully inscribed on both the front and the back, named him as Flavius Constantinus. The presence of this arch pointedly emphasized that this entire area again commemorated the Flavians, both the first and the second dynasty. By proximity, Maxentius' projects were also "Flavianized," now appropriated for Constantine and his dynasty. Constantine was the victorious liberator, Maxentius the deposed tyrant, and Rome had become a Flavian capital again.[21]

---

[20] Domitian's reputation in the fourth century: Chronographer of 354, *Chronica urbis Romae*, s.v. Domitianus, ed Mommsen (1892) 146; Anderson (1983), concludes that this list of Domitian's buildings is mostly reliable.

[21] For the significance of the location of Constantine's arch, see Peirce (1989) 405: "neutralise the influence of Maxentius"; and Wilson Jones (2000) 69: "a monumental celebrative space that he endeavored to make his own."

## A DIVINE DYNASTY

In 305 Constantine had been literally pushed aside when new emperors had been introduced to replace Diocletian and Maximian in a reconfig-ured Tetrarchy; in 315 the dedication of a triumphal arch celebrated his success at Rome. During the intervening decade Constantine had trans-formed himself from a discarded presumptive heir of imperial power into the ruler of most of the western empire. In the process he had repeatedly reinvented his image as emperor. In particular, each victory over a rival had allowed him to discard a bit more of the ideological legacy of the Tetrarchy. After Maximian's treachery and death Con-stantine had ordered the destruction of his father-in-law's statues and images. Since Maximian had often been represented in tandem with his fellow emperor Diocletian, the removal of one's images meant the removal of the other's too. The aftermath of Maximian's plot hence allowed Constantine to distance himself from the memories of both senior emperors of the original Tetrarchy. After his victory over Maxen-tius a frieze of relief panels on his triumphal arch at Rome commemo-rated his victorious campaign and his arrival at the capital. One panel depicted Constantine standing on the Rostra in the old Forum as he addressed a group of senators and a larger audience of citizens. At the back of the Rostra the statues of Jupiter and the guardian spirits of four Tetrarchic emperors, each perched on a tall column, were visible over the heads of the senators. Diocletian and Maximian had erected this Monument of Five Columns in the Forum to commemorate both the ideals of Tetrarchic emperorship and the devotion of Tetrarchic emper-ors to Jupiter; and in fact in 305 the new Tetrarchic emperors had been announced in the presence of a statue of Jupiter outside Nicomedia. But as presented on this panel on the arch dedicated at Rome, Constantine faced resolutely forward. Homage to the cult of Jupiter, allegiance to the Tetrarchy and its ideals: all that was now clearly behind him.[22]

---

[22] Lactantius, *De mortibus persecutorum* 19.2, statue of Jupiter, 4, pushed aside, 42.1, destruction of images. Discussion and photographs of the panel: L'Orange and von Gerkan (1939) 80–89 + Tafeln 14–15, Giuliano (1955) Plate 40, and Kähler (1964) Tafel 1; for the Monument of Five Columns, see also Chapters 2, 9. This

Constantine could also begin to formulate plans for succession that were independent of Tetrarchic ideas. Another advantage for Constantine of presenting himself as a Flavian was to promote his own imperial dynasty, separate from the Valerian dynasty of Diocletian and his fellow emperors, separate from the Herculian dynasty of Maximian and Maxentius, separate too from the entire Jovian dynasty of the Tetrarchy and its successors. For a second time Jupiter, a patron deity of the Tetrarchic emperors, would be upstaged by a Flavian emperor.

By the time Constantine arrived in Rome he had already begun to claim descent from Claudius Gothicus, emperor from 268 to 270. Claudius' full official name had been Marcus Aurelius Valerius Claudius. If Constantine had wanted to identify himself with Diocletian and the Tetrarchs, he might have presented his "ancestor" Claudius as another "Valerian" emperor from Illyricum, a tetrarchic emperor before there had been a Tetrarchy. But eventually other legends about Claudius took priority. Although these legends were finally recorded in the *Augustan History* toward the end of the fourth century, they had most likely been in circulation longer. One claimed that Claudius was the descendant of a Trojan king, another that Constantius had been his nephew. Senators supposedly had hailed Claudius' elevation as emperor with acclamations in the Temple of Apollo. He had announced his victories over the barbarians in a letter to the senate. He had received oracles proclaiming that his descendants would reign forever. After his death the senate and people of Rome had voted to set up a gold shield in his honor in the senate house, a gold statue in front of the Temple of Jupiter on the Capitoline, and a silver statue on the Rostra. These legends made Claudius into Constantine's perfect model ancestor, as an associate of the gods, a triumphant general whom the senate and people of Rome had already honored with statues, and, most significantly, the progenitor of a "divine dynasty" that predated the Tetrarchy. To top off this makeover,

depiction of Constantine's speech on the Rostra was hence not an indication of his loyalty to the Tetrarchic system, as suggested by L'Orange and von Gerkan (1939) 89. Maxentius had previously made an alliance with Maximinus, and images of the two were set up together; after his victory over Maxentius, Constantine probably also destroyed these "statues and images" of Maximinus at Rome: see Lactantius, *De mortibus persecutorum* 43.3, 44.10.

Claudius was also thought to have expanded the Temple of the Flavian Dynasty, "as if mindful of the future." Even though he may not have had the official name, Claudius too had been a "Flavian" emperor.[23]

The importance of Claudius as a progenitor in Constantine's imperial pedigree quickly became common knowledge. In poems composed shortly before or just after the defeat of Licinius in 324 Porphyrius neatly linked all four generations of Constantine's imperial dynasty, both past and future. According to one poem Claudius had earned the title of Gothicus, "Conqueror of the Goths," because he had been undefeated in his military campaigns, whereas Constantius had been known for his piety, peace, and justice. Constantine in turn would surpass his ancestors with his even more impressive gifts, and he would earn acclamations through his sons' military campaigns. Another poem claimed that Crispus, Constantine's oldest son, had received his imperial rule directly from "brave Claudius." With this sort of direct continuity over several generations Porphyrius could stress the longevity of the dynasty. "Constantine, through the edict and commands of a god the era of your pious rule will be eternal. You are blessed."[24]

In two dedications in Italy, one of them in Rome, Constantine was identified as both "son of the divine Constantius" and "descendant of

---

[23] SHA, *Claudius* 3.2–6, shield, statues, Flavian Temple, 4.2–4, acclamations, 7.1–5, letter, 10.1–5, oracles, 10.7, "Constantium, divini generis virum," 11.9, Trojan king, 13.2, uncle of Constantius, 18.3, hailed as Valerius; also SHA, *Heliogabalus* 35.2, "auctor tui generis Claudius." SHA, *Claudius* 7.8, *Aurelianus* 17.2, did include Flavius as part of Claudius' name. Lippold (1981) 357–69, (1992), argues that these legends claiming Claudius as an ancestor were in circulation already during Constantius' reign; Baldini (1992), discusses interpretations of Claudius by historians of the fourth century; less likely is the suggestion of Schlange-Schöningen (2004) 182, that Constantine wanted to emphasize his legitimacy as a Tetrarchic emperor by presenting Claudius "als Vorgänger Diokletians." Note that Licinius would try to trump Constantine's pedigree by claiming descent from Philip the Arab, a still earlier emperor of the mid-third century: see SHA, *Gordiani tres* 34.5.

[24] Porphyrius, *Carm.* 8.27–35, generations, pious rule, 10.24–31, Crispus and Claudius. Barnes (1982) 83n.153, suggests that Porphyrius' allusions to the victories of the sons referred to Crispus' campaigns on the Rhine in 323; Barnes (1975b) 184, argues that the collection including these poems was presented to Constantine in autumn of 324.

the divine Claudius." Significantly, in these dedications that mentioned both his father and Claudius, Constantine was named simply as Flavius Constantinus. Claudius, Constantius, and now Constantine defined a new Flavian dynasty, and the name Flavius appeared repeatedly as a distinguishing feature of its members. The official name of Crispus, Constantine's oldest son, was Flavius Julius Crispus, sometimes Flavius Claudius Crispus or Flavius Valerius Crispus. Constantine's second son, Constantine II, was Flavius Claudius Constantinus, sometimes Flavius Julius Constantinus. His next two sons with his wife Fausta, Constantius II and Constans, were Flavius Julius Constantius, sometimes Flavius Valerius Constantius, and Flavius Julius Constans, sometimes Flavius Junius Constans. Even Fausta herself, who had once represented a linkage with her father Maximian's Herculian dynasty, became Flavia Maxima Fausta. One of Constantine's half-brothers was Flavius Dalmatius; one of his sons in turn was named Flavius Julius Dalmatius. The sons of Julius Constantius, another of Constantine's half-brothers, were the future emperors Gallus, known officially as Flavius Claudius Constantius, sometimes Flavius Julius Constantius, and Julian, officially known as Flavius Claudius Julianus.[25]

Another nephew of Constantine was the younger Licinius, son of the emperor Licinius. In the past the emperor Licinius had been Constantine's ally and had married his half-sister Constantia. Then they

[25] Dedications: *ILS* 1:157, no. 699, "Fl. Constantino | ... divi | Claudi nepoti, divi | Constanti filio," at Ravenna, dated after 324, and *ILS* 1:158, no. 702, "Fl. Constanti[n]us ... | filius divi C[o]nstanti, nepos | divi Claudi," at Rome, dated between 312 and 324 = Grünewald (1990) 216, no. 233, 219, no. 256. According to Grünewald (1990) 274, these are the only two Latin inscriptions that described Constantine as Claudius' descendant. But after Constantine's death a dedication at Arles identified him as "grandson of divine Claudius": see *L'année épigraphique 1952* (1953) 37, no. 107, and Amici (2000) 201, no. 6. Historians of antiquity identified Constantius variously as Claudius' son, nephew, grandson, or grandnephew: see Syme (1983). For references to the official names of the other members of the Constantinian dynasty, see the appropriate entries in *PLRE* 1. For the imposition of a new name as a sign of authority, note Aurelius Victor, *De Caesaribus* 42.9, on Constantius' appointment of Gallus as a junior emperor: "he changed Gallus' name to his own."

became rivals and went to war. After Constantine defeated Licinius in 316, they negotiated a treaty. According to this agreement, Constantine's two sons at the time, the teenager Crispus and the infant Constantine II, and Licinius' infant son, the younger Licinius, all became Caesars. Despite this superficial harmony, Constantine nevertheless carefully distinguished his dynasty from Licinius and his son. Not coincidentally, precisely in 317 and 318 mints throughout Constantine's territory, at Trier, Arles, Rome, Aquileia, Siscia, and Thessalonica, issued the first coins that commemorated "Divine Claudius." Constantine and Licinius had already adopted contrasting styles for the official portraits of themselves and their sons. In their respective reliefs and busts and on their coins Constantine's face was long, lean, and cleanshaven, while Licinius' face was plump and heavily jowled, with the light stubble beard that had been characteristic of the official portraits of the Tetrarchs. Tetrarchic in style and appearance, Licinius and his son also remained Tetrarchic in their official names. While the official names of Constantine's sons and nephews made them Flavians, the young Caesar Licinius did not become a Flavian. Even though he too was a nephew of Constantine, his official imperial name included only Valerius.[26]

Eventually of course Constantine eliminated Licinius and his son. In Roman society the official condemnation of a former emperor's memory typically included both the destruction of his images and the abolition

---

[26] For Constantine's admission that he had hoped to eliminate Licinius and his relatives during the war of 316, see Peter the Patrician, *Frag.* 15, ed. Müller (1851) 189–90. *Divus Claudius* on coins: Bruun (1966) 180, 252, 310–12, 394–95, 429–30, 502–3. A few coins and inscriptions did include Flavius in the name of the younger Licinius: see Bruun (1966) 67n.9, and Chastagnol (1992) 322. For the contrasting portraits, see Smith (1997) 191, "opposed personal and physiognomical styles became opposed dynastic styles," and Kolb (2001) 205, "einen eigenen dynastischen Typus in Konkurrenz zum augusteischen Constantin-Apollon." Plumpness was a tricky image, open to conflicting interpretations. Licinius presumably hoped to communicate personal joviality and prosperity for the empire: see Smith (1997) 191–202. Opponents might interpret corpulence as a sign of greed and oppression. Note John the Lydian, *De magistratibus* 3.58, 61: in the early sixth century one portly imperial magistrate with a reputation for extortion was mocked as Maxilloplumbacius, "Jowls of Lead," and Πλατύγναθος, "Plump Cheeks."

of his name. Erasing his name from dedications and removing it from official records transformed honor into infamy: "his very tenure [as emperor] is to be considered as if it had not happened." Through his successes in these civil wars Constantine relentlessly ensured the disappearance of the Tetrarchic name of Valerius. Both the era and the name of the Tetrarchs were meant to vanish from memory and from any usefulness as a paradigm. As a result, when Julius Nepotianus, the son of another of Constantine's half-sisters, would set himself up briefly as emperor at Rome in 350, his primary claim to the throne was explicitly that he was "a relative of Flavius through his mother's family." Julius Nepotianus had every reason to shun the family connection that he had inherited through his mother, because his father had quite likely been a victim in the massacre of Constantine's collateral relatives in 337 that Constantine's sons, his cousins, may have sanctioned. But despite that horror, he nevertheless wanted to identify himself with his uncle's dynasty as a Constantinian emperor. As the new warranty of imperial authority the Constantinian name of Flavius would replace the Tetrarchic name of Valerius.[27]

## LEGITIMATE SONS

Constantine advertised his Flavian connections in order to enhance his standing at Rome, erase memories of Maxentius at the capital, and initiate the foundation of a new line of imperial succession. But defining

---

[27] For the execution of Licinius, see Chapter 6. During the war Licinius had appointed his general Valens as a "Valerian" co-emperor with the official imperial name of Aurelius Valerius Valens; afterward Constantine demanded Valens' removal and execution: see *PLRE* 1:931, "Aur. Val. Valens 13." Tenure: *CTh* 15.14.9, issued in 395 after the execution of Eugenius; with Vittinghoff (1936) 18–43, and Flower (2000), on the abolition of names, and Chapter 12, for Eugenius' reign. Nepotianus, son of Eutropia: Aurelius Victor, *De Caesaribus* 42.6, with *PLRE* 1:316, "Eutropia 2," 625, "Virius Nepotianus 7"; also Barnes (1982) 108, for the identification of his father as most likely Virius Nepotianus, consul in 336, and Barnes (1981) 398n.11, for speculation about his father's execution. Julian included his cousin Nepotianus as a member of "the imperial dynasty": see Julian, *Orat.* 2.58D.

a new Flavian dynasty was the easy task; arranging the actual succession was much more difficult.

Constantine faced two practical problems. One was the precedent of the Tetrarchy. The original Tetrarchy had been an ideological dynasty, a religious dynasty devoted to Jupiter and Hercules in which a Jovian emperor would succeed a Jovian emperor, a Herculian would succeed a Herculian, and all would assume the Tetrarchic name of Valerius. Because the welfare of the state was supposed to take priority through the selection of experienced men as new emperors, the Tetrarchy had not been designed to be a strict family dynasty. Constantius was already married to a daughter of Maximian and Galerius to a daughter of Diocletian before they were promoted as Caesars in 293. But in 305, when new emperors were to be selected following the retirement of Diocletian and Maximian, "new men" were preferred over the "sons of emperors." Galerius was able to arrange the selection of Maximinus, his nephew, and Severus, his friend. Although sons were available, none was selected as a successor. Constantine was in his early thirties, the adult son of an original Tetrarch with considerable military experience from serving with Diocletian and Galerius. Maxentius, although about a decade younger than Constantine, was the son of another original Tetrarch and already the son-in-law of Galerius. Constantius also had three other sons, and Galerius had a son who was about nine years old. All of these imperial sons were passed over for appointment.[28]

Even though Galerius was obviously influential in these decisions, the disavowal of hereditary succession apparently reflected Diocletian's preferences. Diocletian had personally announced the new emperors in 305, and in 308 he had come out of retirement to participate in the conference that selected Licinius as the new senior emperor to replace Severus. After that conference Constantine was also recognized as an

---

[28] See Barnes (1982) 37, 125–26, for Constantius' marriage to Theodora before 293, 38, for Galerius' marriage to Valeria, and Lactantius, *De mortibus persecutorum* 18.9, for Maxentius as Galerius' son-in-law. New men: Orosius, *Historiae adversum paganos* 7.28.14, contrasting Constantine and Maxentius, "filiis Augustorum," with Licinius and Maximinus, "hominibus novis"; also Lactantius, *De mortibus persecutorum* 25.2, for the new Caesars as *ignoti*, "unknowns."

official member of the Tetrarchy. But he had already forced his way in, by compelling recognition from Galerius after Constantius' death in 306. Although Maxentius too had by now been proclaimed as an emperor at Rome, he was still not acknowledged as a member of the Tetrarchy. As long as Diocletian was involved in the selection of new emperors, no true sons were willingly invited to join the Tetrarchy. In one respect Diocletian's opposition to hereditary succession was a consequence of his personal situation, because of all the Tetrarchs, both original and replacement, he had been the only one without a son. One later historian thought that Diocletian would be an appropriate emperor to be reassured that "very few of the great men have left a son who was exceptional and competent." Diocletian had been clearly suspicious of hereditary succession, and in this historian's perspective his lack of a son to promote as a successor had been, in fact, good policy. After decades of Tetrarchic rule under Diocletian's influence, the succession of sons was not a foregone expectation.[29]

The second practical problem for Constantine was too many sons. Without fail, as Diocletian's influence faded and the Tetrarchic system began to disintegrate, the other emperors had ignored Diocletian's preferences by promoting or supporting their own sons, and they had tried to establish true hereditary dynasties. Hereditary succession was

[29] Lactantius, *De mortibus persecutorum* 19.4, proclamation in 305, 29.2, Diocletian's attendance at the conference of Carnuntum in 308 that promoted Licinius. For Diocletian's ideas about succession, see Kolb (1987) 142, "Diocletian keine dynastische Nachfolge im traditionellen Sinne wünschte"; (2001) 30, "Diocletian trennte sorgfältig die göttliche Familie der Herrscher von jener der Blutsverwandten." Note that according to the fanciful dialogue in Lactantius, *De mortibus persecutorum* 18.8–11, in 305 Diocletian was ready to promote Maxentius and Constantine until Galerius objected. Barnes (1981) 25–26, (1996) 544–46, (1997) 102–5, argues that the four original Tetrarchs had met in northern Italy in late 303, where they agreed that Diocletian and Maximian would eventually retire and that Constantine and Maxentius would become the new junior emperors; but in 305 Galerius initiated a different scheme of succession. Great men: SHA, *Severus* 20.4, with Honoré (1987) 163, on ideas about dynastic succession in the *Historia Augusta*. For the re-emergence of the idea of the empire as a family patrimony, especially under Constantine, see Tantillo (1998).

simply the natural order. According to Julian, the gods had voted Marcus Aurelius as the best emperor, even though he had allowed his immoral son Commodus to succeed him. "It is customary to entrust the succession to sons. Everyone vows to do so." Like Valentinian decades later, when he was on the verge of selecting his brother, Valens, as co-emperor, the other Tetrarchic emperors had consistently preferred the promotion of relatives to the interests of the state. "If you love your relatives," one adviser told Valentinian, "you have a brother; if you love the state, look to invest someone else." A few years later Valentinian again privileged his family when he decided to promote his adolescent son Gratian as a senior emperor against the recommendation of his advisers who had commended the virtues of various seasoned magistrates.[30]

The obvious exception to this pattern was Theodosius, whom Gratian promoted as emperor soon after Valens' death in battle against the Goths. Valentinian II, Gratian's juvenile half-brother, was already a senior emperor, proclaimed a few years earlier after their father's premature death by a cabal of court officials and military officers. Gratian had not been happy, and even as he conceded the promotion, he had repeatedly belittled his "little brother." One panegyrist would even praise Gratian, with a dollop of sarcasm, for accepting his brother as a colleague, but "in the guise of a son." In 378, however, when Gratian faced a true threat to the frontiers, Theodosius was an attractive choice because of his military experience: "Gratian selected not his closest relative as the best man, but the best man as his closest relative." But within a few years Theodosius too reverted to form by unilaterally elevating his own young son Arcadius as emperor. During the fourth century blood relationships repeatedly trumped seniority, experience, and ideology, and

---

[30] Marcus Aurelius: Julian, *Caesares* 334D, with Hekster (2001), emphasizing the importance of family connections in the selection of emperors during the second century. Ausonius likewise praised Marcus Aurelius as Plato's philosopher-ruler but criticized his choice of successor: see Ausonius, *Caesares*, M. Antoninus 4, "he harmed his fatherland only by having a son." Valentinian: Ammianus Marcellinus, *Res gestae* 26.4.1, criticism of brother in 364, 27.6, concerns about son in 367.

emperors almost always decided that sons, brothers, or cousins would be the best colleagues or successors.[31]

As a result, whenever the cooperation between emperors collapsed and they became rivals, they had to think about eliminating not only each other, but also their opponent's sons (and other relatives). One preacher even considered such murderous squabbling to be a necessary characteristic of imperial rule. "Without doubt the pavement of the imperial [palace] is always covered with the blood of relatives." Most of the civil wars among Tetrarchic emperors and their successors had become family feuds. In a power struggle at Rome Maxentius forced his father, Maximian, to flee. "No one ever liked Maxentius, not even his father." True to form, Galerius, his father-in-law, also detested Maxentius. Constantine was responsible for the deaths of his imperial in-laws, Maximian and Maxentius. After Maxentius' death, however, his mother supposedly admitted that Maximian had in fact not been his true father. Since this surprising announcement abruptly redefined Maximian as an important former emperor without a natural son of his own, Constantine could eventually rehabilitate the reputation of his father-in-law and claim him as his own ancestor. After Licinius defeated Maximinus, he made a point of hunting down Maximinus' young son and daughter, Severus' son, Galerius' son, and, for good measure, Diocletian's widow and daughter. After Constantine defeated Licinius, he executed him and his son, even though the young boy's mother was Constantine's half-sister. Sparing the son of a former rival was a sign of extraordinary imperial clemency. Usually the widows of emperors lived with a constant gnawing apprehension about the safety of their children. "One [emperor's] widow who had a fatherless son trembled and fretted that one of the [current] emperors would remove her son out of fear for the future." Because the survival of sons (and daughters, wives, and mothers) from other imperial families might generate

---

[31] Valentinian II: Augustine, *De civitate Dei* 5.25, "parvulum . . . fratrem"; Ausonius, *Gratiarum actio* 2, "instar filii." Selection of Theodosius: Themistius, *Orat.* 14.182b; also Pacatus, *Panegyrici latini* 2(12).12.1, addressed to Theodosius: "you were not related to the emperor's family."

dangerous expectations about the possibility of alternative emperors and an alternative dynastic succession, new rulers wanted to exterminate rival dynasties entirely.[32]

[32] Pavement: John Chrysostom, *Hom. in epistulam ad Philippenses* 15.5 (*PG* 62.295). *Epitome de Caesaribus* 40.14, Maxentius and his father; Lactantius, *De mortibus persecutorum* 26.4, Galerius and Maxentius, 28, confrontation between Maximian and Maxentius. Note that Constantine was also responsible for the death of Bassianus, the husband of his half-sister Anastasia. Constantine had proposed that his brother-in-law should become the Caesar in Italy, but Licinius refused. After Bassianus then revolted, Constantine had him executed in 316: see *Origo Constantini imperatoris* 5.14–15, with Barnes (1981) 66–67, Callu (2002) 111–18, and Lenski (2006b) 73, on the political calculations, and Chapter 6. Denial of Maximian's paternity: *Panegyrici latini* 12(9).3.4, 4.3–4; *Epitome de Caesaribus* 40.13; *Origo Constantini imperatoris* 4.12; with Grünewald (1990) 122–24, on the rehabilitation of Maximian as a Constantinian ancestor. Licinius' executions: Lactantius, *De mortibus persecutorum* 50–51, with Varner (2001) 85–86, (2004) 221, noting that the memories of Diocletian's wife and daughter were obliterated so thoroughly that modern scholars cannot positively identify a sculpted portrait of either. Execution of the younger Licinius: Eutropius, *Breviarium* 10.6.3; for speculation about the fate of the widow Constantia, see below. Licinius may also have had an illegitimate son who was eventually reduced in rank and sent to work in an imperial textile mill in Carthage: see *CTh* 4.6.2–3 (both edicts dated to 336). For the debate over this boy's paternity, see Barnes (1982) 44, arguing that he was Licinius' bastard son, Chastagnol (1992) 317–23, arguing that he was not, and Corcoran (1996) 291, "no relation of Licinius at all." Clemency: Julian, *Orat.* 1.49A, 2.99A, praising Constantius for sparing the young son of the usurper Silvanus; also Ambrose, *Ep.* 74(40).32, praising Theodosius' piety for sparing the mother and daughters of the usurper Magnus Maximus. Imperial widow: John Chrysostom, *Ad viduam iuniorem* 4. *PLRE* 1:201, "Charito," suggests that this fearful woman may have been the widow of Jovian, *PLRE* 1:111–12, "Artemisia," and Lenski (2002) 113, that she was Artemisia, widow of the usurper Procopius, and Grillet and Ettlinger (1968) 138–39n.1, that she was Justina, widow of Valentinian I.

The behavior of Constantina succinctly illustrates the opportunities and the dangers of an unmarried woman in the imperial family. Constantina was a daughter of Constantine and sister of Constantius and Constans. She was first married to her cousin Hannibalianus, presumably at the initiative of her father; then her husband was killed in the massacre of Constantine's relatives in 337. In 350 she apparently encouraged the general Vetranio to oppose the usurper Magnentius, who had killed Constans. Supposedly she even bestowed upon Vetranio the title

After eliminating his rivals and their sons, Constantine still had to deal with his own sons. Constantine had four sons, with two (or, less likely, three) mothers. The only previous emperor with more sons had been Marcus Aurelius, and most of his sons had died young. He had promoted two as Caesars while they were children, although only one, Commodus, had survived to become emperor as an adult. Constantius had also had four sons, with two mothers. Although all the sons had been present at their father's deathbed, only the oldest, Constantine himself, had become an emperor. Later traditions, both favorable and hostile, sometimes were at a loss to explain Constantine's sole succession. One hostile historian hinted at a military coup. According to this account, the soldiers at Constantius' deathbed decided that none of his "legitimate sons" was capable and instead hailed Constantine. In contrast, favorable accounts stressed the predictability of primogeniture. Only a few years after his succession one panegyrist claimed there had been no doubt that Constantine would be his father's sole heir because the "fates" had bestowed him upon Constantius as his "first son." According to a later account, Constantine alone had inherited his father's entire share of the empire through his seniority, which was a "law of nature."[33]

of Caesar: see Philostorgius, *HE* 3.22, "she seemed to have the power to do this, because during his life their common father [Constantine] had crowned her with a diadem and called her Augusta." At first Constantius recognized Vetranio as an emperor; then he compelled him to retire. Magnentius had already offered to marry Constantina, and in addition he suggested that Constantius marry his daughter: see Peter the Patrician, *Frag.* 16, ed. Müller (1851) 190. Instead, even before Constantius finally defeated Magnentius, he promoted his cousin Gallus as Caesar and had him marry Constantina. From a perspective of political expediency Constantina had been used, twice, to bind her father's nephews more closely into his direct lineage; but from a perspective of personal advancement Constantina had been remarkably successful at promoting her own standing, even in comparison with her brothers and cousins. Perhaps it is no surprise that during her marriage to Gallus, Constantina had a reputation for "excessive arrogance": see Ammianus Marcellinus, *Res gestae* 14.1.2, with Bleckmann (1994), for an excellent discussion of Constantina's political influence.

[33] For the mothers of Constantine's sons, see the contrasting positions of Barnes (1982) 42–43, arguing for only two, Minervina, mother of Crispus, and Fausta,

In fact, the other three sons might well have been seen to have had a stronger dynastic claim on the throne. Rumors had long been circulating that Helena, Constantine's mother, had been only the mistress of Constantius, not his lawful wife. Whatever her status, Constantine had certainly been born before Constantius became an emperor, even before he had served as Maximian's praetorian prefect. In contrast, his half-brothers were quite likely *porphyrogeniti*, "born to the purple" as the offspring of Constantius' service with the Tetrarchic emperors. Their blood pedigree furthermore included an extra imperial ancestor. While Constantine claimed Maximian as his father-in-law, his half-brothers were Maximian's direct grandsons through their mother. But despite these credentials, the half-brothers kept a low profile. Although Julius Constantius, one of these half-brothers, was indeed thought to have been more suitable for imperial rule, he remained loyal to Constantine. Rather than presenting himself as an alternative, he became a wanderer, "like Odysseus." During the early years of Constantine's emperorship both he and his brother Dalmatius effectively banished themselves to out-of-the-way provincial cities. Julius Constantius lived at Corinth and Dalmatius at Toulouse, "quarantined in virtual exile." Only toward the end of his reign in the mid-330s did Constantine feel confident enough to honor both of these half-brothers with consulships and to include some of their children in his plans for succession.[34]

mother of Constantine II, Constantius II, and Constans, and *PLRE* 1:223, "Fl. Claudius Constantinus 3," suggesting that Constantine II was illegitimate. But Julian, *Orat.* 1.9C-D, claimed that Fausta had been the mother of three emperors. For Marcus Aurelius' children, at least fourteen, see Birley (2000) 154, 157, 165, 170, 179; in the later sixth century the emperor Maurice had six sons, but Phocas, his successor, had his entire family executed: see *Chronicon Paschale* s.a. 602, with Dagron (1984) 179–80, for mockery of Maurice's procreative powers. Soldiers, legitimate sons: Zosimus, *Historia nova* 2.9.1. Fates, first son: *Panegyrici latini* 6(7).4.2. Sons at deathbed, law of nature: Eusebius, *Vita Constantini* 1.21.2. Julian later attributed Constantine's succession to Constantius' decision and a vote by the army: see Julian, *Orat.* 1.7D.

[34] For a survey of the conflicting sources concerning Helena's status, see Drijvers (1992) 17–19, concluding that she had been Constantius' concubine. For the argument that Theodora, the mother of Dalmatius, Julius Constantius, and

But Constantine could not have anticipated the same harmony and deference among his own sons. Even if he had tried to promote only one

Hannibalianus, was the daughter and not the stepdaughter of Maximian, see Barnes (1982) 33–34, 37. For the use of *purpuratus* as a synonym for "emperor," see Eutropius, *Breviarium* 9.24, with Kolb (2001) 49–50.

During the negotiations leading up to the war with Licinius in 316 Constantine used Constantius as his envoy: see *Origo Constantini imperatoris* 5.14. Since his half-sister Constantia was already married to Licinius, Constantine perhaps likewise chose his half-brother to approach his rival, and this envoy Constantius may have been Julius Constantius: see Barnes (1981) 66, but also Chapter 7, for Flavius Constantius. As a result, Kent (1981) 4, even suggests that these half-siblings "may have taken on the aspect of partizans of Licinius in these dangerous years." But at the same time Constantine was emphasizing his own dynasty, and once his son Constantine II was born in August 316, Julius Constantius and the other half-siblings apparently fell from favor. Julius Constantius and his brother Dalmatius went into exile; their sister Constantia most likely did likewise after the execution of her husband, Licinius; and their sister Anastasia, after the execution of her husband, Bassianus, eventually retired to Constantinople, where her name was attached to some baths: see Ammianus Marcellinus, *Res gestae* 26.6.14. Since Julian, a son of Julius Constantius, would later characterize Helena as "unscrupulous," perhaps her concern for the succession of her own grandchildren contributed to the displacement of these half-siblings: see Libanius, *Orat.* 14.30.

Favorable evaluation of Julius Constantius: Libanius, *Orat.* 18.8. Julius Constantius as Odysseus and at Corinth: Julian, *Fragmenta breviora* 3, Libanius, *Orat.* 14.30–31; Julius Constantius may also have lived in Etruria, where his son Gallus was born in the mid-320s: see Ammianus Marcellinus, *Res gestae* 14.11.27. Dalmatius quarantined at Toulouse: Ausonius, *Professores* 16.11–12; also 17.9–11, on the education of Dalmatius' sons. Since Ausonius, *Professores* 16.11, mentioned that *Constantini fratres*, "Constantine's brothers," resided at Toulouse, *PLRE* 1:226, "Iulius Constantius 7," suggests that Julius Constantius had also lived there before moving to Corinth. Barnes (1981) 251, suggests that both half-brothers were recalled in 326, Wiemer (1994) 517, that both accompanied Constantine to Rome in 326; according to a story in Libanius, *Orat.* 19.19, Constantine once consulted with his two half-brothers about how to react to insults from the people at Rome. Dalmatius was consul in 333 and Julius Constantius in 335; Dalmatius also served as an imperial envoy and perhaps as a military commander on the eastern frontier during the mid-330s: see *PLRE* 1:240–41, "Fl. Dalmatius 6." Since their brother Hannibalianus was not credited with any offices or children, perhaps he had died young: see *PLRE* 1:407, "Hannibalianus 1."

of his sons, rivalries among them, and among their respective supporters, were almost inevitable. Memories of the first Flavian dynasty would have provided a relevant warning, because centuries earlier Vespasian's two sons were rumored to have hated each other, and Domitian was thought to have connived at Titus' death. In 326 Constantine had sanctioned the execution of Crispus, his oldest son, in mysterious circumstances that apparently revolved somehow around concerns over succession. Constantine was then about fifty or a few years older. In terms of the expectations, and realities, of ancient society he was already an old man, with a life expectancy of only another decade or so. As a preview of his own mortality he could remember that his father had died in his mid- or late fifties. But he could not yet be sure about the future, since his oldest surviving son was still only about ten. During the final decade of his reign Constantine was looking for ways of ensuring both the succession of his sons and harmony among his successors.[35]

In late 324 Constantine gave Helena the title of Augusta: see Barnes (1982) 9. Helena also became a Flavian, since her official imperial name was Flavia Julia Helena. Constantine might have promoted his mother's rank in part to demote the standing of his half-brothers, because while he was one of four sons of Constantius, he was the only son of Helena: see Grünewald (1990) 138–39, and Chapter 11. In contrast, Theodora, the mother of Constantine's half-siblings, never received the title of Augusta during her lifetime: see Kent (1981) 3–7, 126, 234, 442, and Vanderspoel and Mann (2002) 354–55, for coins depicting Theodora Augusta minted after Constantine's death. Nor was she a Flavian. A few coins minted at Rome and Trier did name her as Flavia Maxima Theodora. But these coins were issued apparently in 337 during the confusion soon after Constantine's death, perhaps as an attempt to enhance the Flavian pedigree of her grandson Flavius Julius Dalmatius, who was already a Caesar and expected to succeed as a co-emperor with Constantine's three sons: see Kent (1981) 7, 79, 126, 143–44, 234, 250–51, for the coins, and the discussion in Drijvers (1992) 43–44. The massacre of most of Theodora's descendants, including the Caesar Dalmatius, ended that expectation.

[35] Titus and Domitian: Dio, *Historiae Romanae* 66.26. Death of Crispus: for additional discussion, see Chapter 11; also Barnes (1981) 220–21, on the rumors and accusations; Elliott (1996) 233, "the suggestion that dynastic considerations were critical at this moment is attractive"; Woods (1998), arguing that Crispus had committed adultery with Fausta, his stepmother; and, for comprehensive surveys

## Constans and Flavia Constans

Throughout the empire Constantine was publicizing his dynasty. One time-tested tactic he used was new names for cities. Constantinople, the "city of his cognomen," was only the most conspicuous example of his tendency to sanction new names for cities that recalled his family by including Flavia or some variant of Constan-. Already in 311 a Gallic panegyrist not only reminded Constantine that Autun had once appealed for the assistance of the emperor Claudius Gothicus, but also emphasized with pride that the city had now renamed itself with "your name" as Flavia Aeduorum. The citizens of Arles would later claim that their city had been honored by Constantine and "received the name Constantina from his name." In Italy, Portus was renamed Flavia Constantiniana. In Africa, Cirta was renamed Constantina, and Constantine himself issued instructions for the construction of a new church. One fortress on the Danube frontier was named Constantia. After the Persians destroyed a frontier town in Osrhoene between the Euphrates and Tigris Rivers, Constantine had it rebuilt and renamed as Constantina. Since this town had previously been named after the emperor Galerius, this new name both promoted the new dynasty and obliterated the memory of one of its earlier opponents.[36]

of the possible interpretations, Pohlsander (1984) 99–106, Drijvers (1992) 60–63, and Paschoud (1979–2000) 1:234–37. Julian, *Orat.* 1.45C, hinted to Constantius that Constantine had considered him the most capable of his sons: "your father entrusted to you alone supervision of affairs concerning the empire and your brothers, even though you were not the oldest of the children"; *Orat.* 2.94B, "at the end of his life he [Constantine] ... entrusted him [Constantius] with all affairs regarding the empire." Old age and life expectancy: Saller (1994) 12–25.

[36] Name of Constantinople: *ILS* 1:165, no. 736, lines 5–6, "hoc decus ornatum genitor cognominis urbis | esse volens," referring to the obelisk Constantius erected at Rome. Autun: *Panegyrici latini* 5(8).1.1, 2.5, 14.5. Arles: Pope Leo I, *Ep.* 65.3 (*PL* 54.882A) = *Epistolae Arelatenses* 12, ed. Gundlach (1892) 19. Note also Honorius' edict of 418: *Epistolae Arelatenses* 8, ed. Gundlach (1892) 14, with the discussion of Klingshirn (1994) 53, Burgess (1999a) 278–79, and Chapter 2. The ancient name for Coutances in western Gaul was Constantia (*Notitia dignitatum in partibus Occidentis* 37.9, 20) or Constantina (Gregory of Tours, *Historiae* 8.31). Portus:

His son Constantius not only continued these activities, but also sometimes seemed to be competing with his father's reputation. On the eastern frontier he rebuilt Amida and "hoped that it would be renamed with his name"; he also refounded another frontier city as Constantia. During much of his reign he resided at Antioch, which was so grateful for his benefactions that it renamed itself with "your name" (perhaps as Constantia). Salamis, a city on Cyprus that had been destroyed in an earthquake, was renamed Constantia after receiving assistance from Constantius. Even at Constantinople Constantius initiated so many construction projects that an orator could claim that "the city named after your father" was now "yours rather than your father's." Constantinople, Constantina, Constantia: the names of these cities celebrated a dynasty, rather than only a specific emperor.[37]

Sometimes these new names were associated with a switch from paganism to Christianity. Because Constantine sent out messengers with imperial letters that encouraged cities to abandon their traditional cults, in the Greek East in particular some towns destroyed their pagan shrines in the hope of receiving imperial favors. "Hereafter peoples and cities willingly converted from their former beliefs." The town of Antaradus was a way station on the road along the coast of southern Syria. Constantine apparently detached it from the control of Aradus, perhaps as a response to its conversion to Christianity. Antaradus furthermore

*CIL* 14, Supplementum, 639, no. 4449. Cirta: see Chapter 2. Constantia on the Danube, near Margum: Priscus, *Frag.* 2. Constantina in Osrhoene, previously named Maximianopolis: John Malalas, *Chronographia* 13.12, with Millar (1993) 209.

[37] Amida: Ammianus Marcellinus, *Res gestae* 18.9.1; Antoni(n)opolis: Theophanes, *Chronographia* a.m. 5832, with the discussion of Burgess (1999a) 274–82. Antioch: Julian, *Orat.* 1.40D, with Downey (1961) 356, 582, and Henck (2001) 297. Salamis: John Malalas, *Chronographia* 12.48, attributing the rebuilding to Constantius I; but for the destruction of Salamis by earthquakes in 331/332 and 341/342, see Theophanes, *Chronographia* a.m. 5824, 5834. Your city: Themistius, *Orat.* 3.40c.

When promoting the village of Drepanum in Bithynia as an independent city, Constantine bestowed the new name of Helenopolis after his mother: see Socrates, *HE* 1.17.1, 18.13; also Philostorgius, *HE* 2.12, with Mango (1994). According to Sozomen, *HE* 2.2.5, he also renamed another city in Palestine after his mother.

received the rank of a city, as well as the new imperial name of Constantina or Constantia, "the name of the emperor." In Palestine the inhabitants of the port town of Maiuma all converted to Christianity. Since Constantine responded with a rescript, they must have appealed for the emperor's patronage. And since bishop Eusebius of Caesarea was familiar with this rescript, they had most likely inscribed it on a public monument. Constantine rewarded their piety by detaching Maiuma from the control of Gaza and bestowing upon it the rank of a city. Maiuma also received the new imperial name of Constantia, a "superior name" reminiscent of the emperor's "pious sister." Eusebius quickly realized the dual implications of this enhancement in the city's standing, since Constantia "was thought worthy of greater honor both with God and with the emperor." This city's new name reflected both divine sanction and imperial patronage.[38]

---

[38]   Sozomen, *HE* 2.5.2, letters, 7, peoples and cities. Antaradus: *Itinerarium Burdigalense* 582.10, "mansio Antaradus"; name of the emperor: Sozomen, *HE* 2.5.8, "Constantina among the Phoenicians"; also Theophanes, *Chronographia* a.m. 5838, Constantia; with Jones (1971) 267, 459n.54, and Rey-Coquais (1974) 141, 196. Maiuma: Eusebius, *Vita Constantini* 4.37, βασιλεὼς ἀντιφώνησις, 38, superior name, sister, honor; Socrates, *HE* 1.18.13, "from the name of his sister Constantia"; with Van Dam (1985b) 6–13.

  Papal tradition claimed that Constantia, Constantine's half-sister, was baptized with her niece Constantina in a baptistery attached to the Church of St. Agnes in Rome: see *Liber pontificalis* 34.23. But the new name of Maiuma was perhaps an indication of her presence in Palestine, where she may have retired after the murder of her husband, the emperor Licinius. Constantia's residence in the area might explain her request for an icon of Christ from Eusebius of Caesarea: see Eusebius, *Epistula ad Constantiam Augustam*, ed. *PG* 20.1545–49, and ed. Hennephof (1969) 42–44, with Gero (1981), arguing that the letter was genuine, and Lenski (2004), for the tendency of widowed or estranged imperial women to retire to Palestine.

  Note that one tradition claimed that Constantine had renamed Maiuma after his son Constantius, not his sister Constantia: see Sozomen, *HE* 2.5.8, "the dearest son of his children," 5.3.6, "he named it for his son Constantius." This alternative etymology is worthy of consideration because Sozomen and his family were from the vicinity. Sozomen's grandfather had been among the first Christians at Bethelea, a town near Gaza, and he and his family had been persecuted under Julian: see Sozomen, *HE* 5.15.14–17. On the other hand, contemporaries were probably

In the case of Hispellum, rather than bestowing a new name as a marker of conversion to Christianity, Constantine seems to have used it as another tactic in promoting his dynasty. Hispellum was close to the homeland of the first Flavian dynasty in central Italy. Vespasian had been born in Reate, forty miles to the south, his mother had been from Nursia, and the town of Vespasiae, only about twenty miles to the south-east, was filled with monuments to the family. The rise of Vespasian's family had marked the culmination to the process of promoting notables from Italian cities that had been so marked a feature of the policies of Augustus and his Julio-Claudian successors. One long-term outcome of Augustus' Roman revolution had been the establishment of emperors from an old Italian family. As he now allowed the foundation of a temple and a festival at Hispellum, Constantine could advance his dynastic ambitions by associating his second Flavian dynasty with the Italian homeland of the first Flavian dynasty. In the process, this association with the first dynasty of Italian emperors would effectively "Italianize" his provincial family from the Balkans. One outcome of Constantine's Roman revolution was the establishment of another apparently "Italian" dynasty of Flavian emperors.[39]

Constantine furthermore agreed that Hispellum could rename itself as Flavia Constans, a name that was reminiscent of Flavius Julius Constans, his youngest son. Constans had been born in the early 320s, and was proclaimed a Caesar on December 25, 333. This rescript to the cities of Umbria was likely one of the first to list him as a member of the imperial college with his father and his surviving older brothers, Constantine II and Constantius. In the mid-330s, when he was about sixty, their father was finally making official arrangements for the succession. In September 335 Constantine promoted a nephew, the younger Dalmatius, as a fourth Caesar. By then assigning the four Caesars to particular regions of the empire, Constantine set up his own family tetrarchy of junior emperors. These Caesars were now the team of "four

all too ready to take advantage of the similarity of names in the Constantinian dynasty to claim affiliation with a particular emperor.
[39] Vespasian's family: Suetonius, *Vespasianus* 1.3, 2.1.

colts" hitched to "the one yoke of the imperial chariot." The younger Constantine took up residence at Trier and administered Britain, Gaul, and Spain. Dalmatius was given responsibility for the frontier along the lower Danube in the Balkans, and Constantius took up residence at Antioch, a staging point for campaigns on the eastern frontier. The original Tetrarchy may not have offered a precedent for family succession, but it had defined a model for dealing with multiple successors as concurrent legitimate emperors.[40]

Constans seems to have grown up at Constantinople. There he had received a proper education in classical culture, so that he was "skillful in the practice of that rhetoric that is suitable for Romans." Unlike the original Tetrarchs, Constans was civilized, not a semi-barbarian. Even though he had grown up in an eastern city, his education had nevertheless significantly included study in Latin with a rhetorician from Gaul. Constans was not just being educated; he was being groomed as an emperor for the West, specifically as an Italian emperor. By allowing Hispellum to be named after Constans, Constantine was preparing the way. First he authorized a city in Italy to rename itself after one of his sons; then he sent the son himself.[41]

After the mid-330s Constans came to Italy, where initially he resided probably at Milan. At Rome a dedication praised him for enhancing the public welfare with his virtues, and he may have visited the capital. Dedications elsewhere hailed him as son of Constantine, grandson of

---

[40]   Both *PLRE* 1:220, "Fl. Iul. Constans 3," and Barnes (1982) 45, suggest that Constans was born in 320 or 323. For Constantine's plans for succession in the mid-330s, see Eusebius, *Vita Constantini* 4.51–52, and for the division of the empire among the four Caesars, see *Epitome de Caesaribus* 41.20, *Origo Constantini imperatoris* 6.35, with Barnes (1982) 84–87, 198–200. Four colts, chariot: Eusebius, *De laudibus Constantini* 3.4. Chantraine (1992) 17, proposes that Constantine intended his four successors to form a true Tetrarchy, with Constantine II and Constantius as the senior emperors and Constans and Dalmatius as the junior emperors; Kolb (2001) 63, suggests that he may have intended all three sons to be senior emperors and only Dalmatius to become a junior emperor.

[41]   Rhetoric: Libanius, *Orat.* 59.34. For Constans' (likely) study with Arborius, see Ausonius, *Professores* 16.13–15, with *PLRE* 1:98, "Aemilius Magnus Arborius 4."

Constantius, and a descendant of Claudius. Since the reputation of
Maximian had by now been rehabilitated, Constans could be hailed
as his grandson too. Constans was now the full heir to the legacy of a
pre-Tetrarchic emperor, two original Tetrarchs, and the Flavian dynasty
of Constantine.[42]

Hispellum soon began to use its new name of Flavia Constans. Eventually "the entire urban population of Flavia Constans" honored one
of its local notables as a "most worthy patron." Among this notable's
many services to his community was his tenure as "priest of the Flavian
dynasty." This priesthood was presumably an indication that Hispellum
had indeed constructed its new temple in honor of Constantine and his
family. By now the city was also celebrating its new festival, since this
laudatory inscription praised this priest as a "producer of happiness in
the theater." This notable's career neatly paralleled the change in status,
and the rise in prominence, of Hispellum and the region of Umbria.
Previously this notable had served as an official, most likely a priest, of
the consolidated district of Tuscia and Umbria when the two regions
had shared a festival. Then he had become the priest of the imperial cult
located at Hispellum. Rather than having to make the arduous trip to
Volsinii, this priest could now preside in his hometown. Umbria now
had its own regional festival, and Hispellum had its own temple and
priest in honor of the Flavian dynasty.[43]

---

[42] Dedication at Rome: *ILS* 1:163, no. 726. For the possibility of a visit by Constans
to Rome, see *Passio Artemii* 9 = Philostorgius, *HE* 3.1[a]: Constantine II "advanced
upon the inheritence of his youngest brother [Constans] who was away visiting
Rome." Constantine II was killed near Aquileia in early 340: see Barnes (1975a)
327–28, (1993) 315n.47, suggesting that Constans visited Rome after this battle, and Gasperini (1988), discussing a dedication at Ostia, reprinted in *L'année
épigraphique 1988* (1991) 61, no. 217. Dedications elsewhere: *ILS* 1:162–63, nos. 723,
725, 730.

[43] Patron: *ILS* 2.1:631, no. 6623, in honor of C. Matrinius Aurelius Antoninus,
*coronatus Tusciae et Umbriae*, then *pontifex gentis Flaviae*. The office of a *coronatus*
is difficult to define. During Julian's reign a governor of Numidia ranked officials
in the order they were to receive greetings: see "Edictum de ordine salutationis
sportularumque," in Riccobono (1941) 331–32, no. 64. The *coronati provinciae*
ranked after senators, *comites*, former *comites*, administrators, the chief of staff

## "The Family of the Highest Distinction"

After Constantine's death in 337 some of his arrangements for succession were modified. The Constantinian version of a new family-based tetrarchy never had a chance to be established. Once troops at Constantinople decided that only his three "legitimate sons" would be emperors, they massacred many collateral members of the family, including the Caesar Dalmatius and Constantine's two surviving half-brothers. Almost four months after his death Constantine was finally succeeded by a "trinity" of sons, not a tetrarchy that would have included a nephew.[44]

Nor did Constantine's three sons rule in harmony. Even though they had held imperial titles already for years, upon their succession they were still quite young, Constantine II and Constantius barely

of the governor's bureau, the secretary of the bureau, and palatine officials, but before the other bureaucrats on the governor's staff. After identifying the *coronatus* as "le grand-prêtre du conseil fédéral de Tuscie et d'Ombrie," Gascou (1967) 640, suggests that Matrinius had held this office before the split between the two regions, and that he had become *pontifex gentis Flaviae* afterward; Tabata (1995) 384–85, suggests that Matrinius may have initiated the petition to Constantine. For the importance of the imperial cult in promoting imperial families rather than only particular emperors, see Price (1984) 159–62.

[44] Eusebius, *Vita Constantini* 4.40.2, three sons as trinity, 71.2, legitimate sons. For the dynastic politics behind this massacre, see above and Chapter 11, with Klein (1999a), for an excellent analysis of the competing factions.

Gossip about the bad blood within the Constantinian dynasty lingered for centuries. Julian was thought to have had a long memory. In a later fanciful account Julian explained his rationale for rebelling against his cousin Constantius II: see *Passio Artemii* 41, "Imperial rule is more appropriate for our [ = my] family. For my father, [Julius] Constantius, was born to my grandfather Constans [i.e. Constantius I] by Theodora, daughter of Maximian. But Constantine was born to him [Constantius I] by Helena, who was a common woman no different from prostitutes. This [birth of Constantine] happened not when he [Constantius I] was a Caesar, but while he was in the rank of a private citizen. Constantine then seized imperial rule through the boldness of his ambition, and he unjustly killed my father and both of his brothers." Bidez (1913) XLIV, and Kotter (1988) 187, date the composition of this *Passio* sometime before the tenth century; one of its primary sources was Philostorgius' *HE*.

into their twenties, Constans only a teenager. Personal animosity was one upsetting factor. In 340 Constantine II was killed after invading Constans' territory. Constantius promptly belittled "our enemy" as a "public enemy," and both he and Constans sanctioned the erasure of their brother's name from public dedications. Constantine II now disappeared from official memories. Within a few years the orator Libanius delivered a panegyric in which he pretended that Constantius and Constans had been Constantine's only sons. Religion was another divisive factor. Because they supported different Christian doctrines, Constans and Constantius almost came to blows, and Constans once threatened his brother with war over the restoration of some deposed bishops. After Constans was killed in 350 following Magnentius' coup, Constantius supposedly had to be warned in a dream by Constantine himself to avenge "the descendant of many emperors, my son and your brother."[45]

Perhaps Constantius needed a pointed reminder from his father's ghost about the fragility of hereditary succession, since he was now the last survivor of Constantine's sons and, in his mid-thirties, still had no son of his own. When Constantius conceded the need for a co-emperor, he had no choice but to appoint his cousins, first Gallus in 351 because of his "relationship to the imperial dynasty," then Julian in 355. As he presented Julian to the army, Constantius was supposed to have addressed his cousin as his "most beloved brother." Despite this pledge

---

[45] Enemy: *CTh* 11.12.1, issued in April 340; for Constans' challenge to the priority of Constantine II, see Bruun (1987); for the erasure of the name of Constantine II, see Chastagnol (1976), and Cahn (1987). Only two sons: Libanius, *Orat.* 59.43, 75. For the disappearance of Constantine II from official memories, note also Athanasius, *Vita Antonii* 81.1, claiming that Antony had received a letter from Constantine and his two sons, Constantius II and Constans. At Constantinople a statue with three heads was identified as a composite of Constantine flanked by Constantius II and Constans: see *Parastaseis syntomoi chronikai* 43, with Cameron and Herrin (1984) 231–32, and Bassett (2004) 239–40. Constans' threat: Socrates, *HE* 2.22, with Barnes (1993) 89–90, Portmann (1999), and Kolb (2001) 243–49, on the discord between the brothers. Constantius' dream: Peter the Patrician, *Frag.* 16, ed. Müller (1851) 190.

of fraternal cooperation, a few years later they too were on the verge of a civil war. Personal rivalries had undermined Constantine's hopes first for fraternal harmony among his successors, and then for the long-term survival of his dynasty.[46]

The death of Julian marked the end of the hereditary dynasty of Flavian sons. Julian was a grandson of Constantius I and a nephew of Constantine. In a dream he himself had once foreseen the truncated future of his family: he would be the last sapling to sprout from this root. In the extended Flavian dynasty Julian's generation had included at least eleven sons, including Constantine's four sons (Crispus, Constantine II, Constantius II, and Constans), Dalmatius' two sons (the younger Dalmatius and the younger Hannibalianus), Julius Constantius' three sons (Gallus, his unnamed older brother, and their half-brother Julian), Constantia's son with Licinius (the younger Licinius), and Eutropia's son (Julius Nepotianus). But this large generation of cousins was notably unable to produce more sons.[47]

One reason was lethal rivalries over succession. Constantine himself authorized the execution of Crispus and various in-laws; several of these cousins were murdered in the elimination of dynastic rivals that followed Constantine's death, apparently before they had had any children; Constantine II was killed in a conflict with his brother Constans; Constantius was later responsible for the execution of his cousin Gallus. One retrospective evaluation knew exactly what had gone wrong: "the impressive fertility of this dynasty was destroyed through an obsession with [acquiring] sole rule."[48]

---

[46] Ammianus Marcellinus, *Res gestae* 14.1.1, promotion of Gallus, 15.8.12, most beloved brother.

[47] Julian's dream at Paris: Julian, *Ep.* 4. Julian noted that the massacre of his relatives had included his father (Julius Constantius), his oldest brother (in fact, an unnamed half-brother), an uncle (Dalmatius), and six cousins: see Julian, *Epistula ad Athenienses* 270C–271A, with Barnes (1981) 398nn.10–11, for suggestions about the identity of these cousins. Julian also claimed that Constantius himself blamed his failure to have children on his role in this massacre.

[48] Impressive fertility: Themistius, *Orat.* 6.74c. Julian likewise attributed the demise of "the multitude of sons" to the ambition of each to reign as sole emperor, "just like his father": see Julian, *Orat.* 7.228A-B.

A second reason for the end of the dynasty was its vulnerability to basic handicaps of Roman demography, including a late age of first marriage for men and high mortality rates for young children. Of Constantine's sons, Crispus had had one daughter, and perhaps another child; his daughter was quite possibly the mother of the emperor Valentinian's second wife. Constantine II was married but had no recorded children, and Constans died in his late twenties before marrying. Constantius' first marriage, to a cousin who was the daughter of Julius Constantius, was childless; he subsequently married Eusebia "in order to produce children who would inherit his prestige and his power," but that marriage too was childless. With his third wife, Faustina, he did have a daughter, although she was born after his death. Of Julius Constantius' sons, Gallus was married to Constantina, a daughter of Constantine, and they had a daughter. Julian was the last son of the Constantinian dynasty. For a few years he had been married to Helena, another of Constantine's daughters. They had a child, who died immediately after birth; Helena herself died in 360. Contemporaries could sense that this family had run out of heirs. Less than a year after his death Julian was already seen as merely the "residue of Constantine's succession."[49]

[49] Daughter of Crispus and Helena: see Barnes (1981) 72–73, (1982) 44. If Justina was in fact a granddaughter of Crispus, then the emperor Valentinian II, one of her four children with Valentinian, was a great-great-grandson of Constantine by direct descent. For different explanations of Justina's connection to the Constantinian family, see Lenski (2002) 103 (Justina's father was a cousin of Gallus), and Frakes (2006) 97 (Justina's mother was a sister of Gallus). Wife of Constantine II and first marriage of Constantius: Eusebius, *Vita Constantini* 4.49. As a teenager Constans was engaged to Olympias, daughter of Flavius Ablabius, a powerful prefect under Constantine: see Ammianus Marcellinus, *Res gestae* 20.11.3, with Chausson (2002a) 211–17, suggesting that Olympias' mother was a niece of Constantine. While waiting for their marriage Constans supported Olympias "as his own wife": see Athanasius, *Historia Arianorum* 69.1. After Constantine's death Constantius had Ablabius executed; after Constans' death Olympias was married instead to king Arsaces of Armenia: see *PLRE* 1:3–4, "Fl. Ablabius 4," 642, "Olympias 1." Constantius' marriage to Eusebia: Julian, *Orat.* 3.109B; Constantius was thought to have sought a cure for his wife's infertility: see Philostorgius, *HE* 4.7, with Holum (1982) 21–44, on the importance of childbearing in the

According to Libanius, one of the emperor's champions, Julian subsequently complimented himself for not remarrying and having any
children because he had deliberately wanted to end hereditary succession. "When his supporters urged him to remarry so that he might
produce sons who would inherit the empire, he said that this prospect
was terrifying, because they might be evil but would legally succeed and
destroy the state." Julian was still young enough at his death that he had
probably not thought much about imperial succession. If he had, perhaps he would have concluded that the most important qualifications
for a new emperor were the same qualities that he hoped to privilege
in the appointment of imperial magistrates, familiarity with classical
culture and devotion to paganism. "Philosophy, not dynastic tradition,
was the legitimization of his rule." Reviving the empire through the
promotion of his religious and cultural agenda would most likely have
taken priority over the continuation of his uncle's Flavian dynasty.[50]

The idea of a Flavian imperial dynasty nevertheless dominated the
remainder of the fourth century and into the fifth century and beyond:
"even after the end of his life Constantine's own name was heard." Constantine's dynastic legacy became the touchstone for subsequent emperors and pretenders. Jovian, Valentinian and his sons, Valens, and Theodosius and his sons, as well as usurpers like Magnentius and Eugenius,

representation of imperial women. Daughter of Gallus and Constantina: Julian,
*Epistula ad Athenienses* 272D. Death of Julian's child: Ammianus Marcellinus, *Res
gestae* 16.10.19, suggesting that the miscarriage was due to the plotting of Eusebia,
Constantius' wife, who was unable to bear children herself. John Chrysostom,
*Hom. in epistulam ad Philippenses* 15.5 (*PG* 62.295), once listed recent misfortunes
of emperors: "Another [emperor] watched his wife be destroyed by drugs. Because
she did not conceive, she was a wretched and miserable wife. In her misery and
despair she hoped to produce a gift from God [i.e., a child] through her own
cleverness. By dispensing drugs, she destroyed an emperor's wife and was herself
likewise destroyed." This story might be a garbled memory of Eusebia and Helena.
Residue: Themistius, *Orat.* 5.65b, in an oration honoring Jovian's consulship in
January 364; with Chausson (2002b), for important speculation about collateral
descendants of Constantine's children.
[50] Libanius, *Orat.* 18.157–59, qualifications of magistrates, 181, remarry. Quotation
about philosophy from Elm (2003) 500.

all adopted Flavius as part of their official imperial nomenclature. Even the usurper Procopius, who as a distant maternal relative of Julian might have been hostile to the Constantinian side of the family, nevertheless posed as the true heir to "the family of the highest distinction" by appearing with Constantius' widow and infant daughter. After Gratian, a son of Valentinian, subsequently married that daughter of Constantius, he presented a new consul with a robe embroidered with an image of his deceased father-in-law, whom he could now claim as "my ancestor." In the mid- and later fourth century the orator Themistius carefully ingratiated himself with each new emperor by pronouncing favorable comparisons to Constantine. Jovian was "wholly Constantine," in fact a truer Constantine than even his son Constantius and his nephew Julian had been; Valentinian and Valens would be able to exceed Constantine through the justice of their behavior in Constantinople; Theodosius would become a third founder for Constantinople, surpassing both the legendary Byzas and Constantine himself. Subsequent emperors wanted to associate themselves with Constantine, if possible through their activities or family connections, but at the very least through their names. The official images of these emperors complemented their official names, since they also had their portraits resemble those of Constantine. They were all Flavian offspring.[51]

During the fourth century Flavius had become essentially an imperial title, similar to Augustus. Later Byzantine emperors continued

---

[51] Constantine's name: Eusebius, *Vita Constantini* 4.72. Ammianus Marcellinus, *Res gestae* 26.7.10, widow and daughter, 16, family, 29.6.7, marriage of Gratian and Constantia; with Lenski (2002) 98–104, on claims to the Constantinian dynasty. The sources cited in *PLRE* 1:401, "Fl. Gratianus 2," do not support the suggestion that Gratian and Constantia had a son. Robe: Ausonius, *Gratiarum actio* 11. Themistius, *Orat.* 5.70d, Jovian; 6.83b-c, Valentinian and Valens; 18.223b, Theodosius; with the survey of Constantine's reputation in Magdalino (1994). Galla Placidia, a granddaughter of Valentinian I, niece of Valentinian II, and daughter of Theodosius, emphasized her ties to the dynasty of Constantine: see Brubaker (1997), and Chapter 12, for Theodosius' marriage into the Constantinian dynasty. On the continuity of imperial images, see Smith (1985) 221: "the direct connection with Constantine was kept before the eyes of the empire's subjects by the virtually unbroken continuity of the emperor's portrait image."

to use it in their official names, as one way of associating themselves with "the golden glow of Constantine's legacy." Some of the barbarian kings in post-Roman western Europe, in particular kings of the Visigoths, Ostrogoths, and Lombards, even used it as a royal title. But unlike Augustus, Flavius was furthermore a name that ordinary people might adopt too. In the late third and early fourth century Roman magistrates, commanders, and soldiers had adopted Valerius as an onomastic marker of status and rank that linked them with Diocletian and the Tetrarchs. After the reign of Constantine, however, the use of Flavius largely replaced Valerius as an indication of privilege and a courtesy title of prestige, adopted especially in the eastern empire by imperial magistrates, generals, up-and-coming municipal notables, and even soldiers. The first volume of *The Prosopography of the Later Roman Empire* includes about 270 magistrates and other notables outside Constantine's family with Flavius in their names during the fourth century, the second volume well over 200 men for the fifth and early sixth centuries; thereafter the third volume simply stopped cross-referencing this ubiquitous name.[52]

An imperial-sounding name might even be enough of a credential to make an emperor. In the far north the army in Britain proclaimed Constantine III as an emperor in 407. Since this new emperor had previously been merely an ordinary soldier, one historian thought that his only claim to the throne was "hope in his name." This new emperor had adopted an official name that made him a double of the original Constantine: Flavius Claudius Constantinus. In the face of renewed barbarian invasions on the northern frontier, his supporters presumably hoped that this new Constantine might recreate the military successes of the original Constantine. Since one of the emperor's sons was named Julian and another Constans, his supporters may have furthermore

---

[52] Glow: Brubaker (1999) 171, commenting on the attempts of emperor Basil I to claim Constantine for his new dynasty. For the use of Flavius, see the overview in Mócsy (1964), the detailed elaboration in Keenan (1973–1974), (1983), and the summation in Salway (1994) 137–41. For questions about whether Flavius should be considered part of a name or simply a courtesy title, see Bagnall et al. (1987) 36–40, reprised in Cameron (1988) 33: "the hallmark of the *newly* important."

hoped that this new Constantine also had a new Constantinian dynasty of his own in the making. At a moment of danger, perhaps there might be another Constantinian dynasty of Flavian emperors.[53]

## "YOUR ENTIRE FAMILY"

In the early years of his reign Constantine had worried about his legitimacy. One solution was the invention of a Flavian dynasty that included both his father and the earlier emperor Claudius Gothicus, and that was quite distinct from the Valerian dynasty of Diocletian and the Tetrarchs. In the later years of his reign Constantine fretted about succession. This time one solution was the promotion of the Flavian dynasty, in his sons and a nephew as successors, in the names of cities, in the names of ordinary people. A new Flavian dynasty was the answer to concerns about legitimacy and worries about succession, since it provided Constantine with both a past and a future, both distinguished imperial ancestors and worthy imperial heirs from his own family. Even Julian, who had strong disagreements with his uncle Constantine's behavior and religious policies, still appreciated being a member of the dynasty that had started with Claudius. "All the gods granted imperial rule to Claudius' family. They thought it proper that the descendants of such a patriot should remain in power for as long as possible." Julian may have had misgivings about hereditary succession after he became emperor, but he nevertheless valued the role of dynastic connections in his own accession. Once a Flavian pedigree had been a legacy from Claudius and Constantius; then it had become a destiny for Constantine's descendants.[54]

---

[53] Hope in his name: Orosius, *Historiae adversum paganos* 7.40.4, with *PLRE* 2:316–17, "Fl. Claudius Constantinus 21." Also Sozomen, *HE* 9.11.2: the soldiers of Britain "thought that because he had this name, he would rule the empire with firmness."

[54] Gods: Julian, *Caesares* 313D; also *Orat.* 1.6D, 2.51C, "the affairs of our family began with Claudius"; with Castritius (1969) 43–47, on Julian's appreciation for his dynastic legacy. On the other hand, this supposed descent from Claudius may not have had wide circulation after Constantine's reign. Note that some of Julian's contemporaries were unaware of or unimpressed by the dynastic connection. In an oration addressed to Constantius and Constans probably in 344 Libanius claimed

In their petition Hispellum and the other cities of Umbria were hoping to revive an earlier intimacy with emperors by issuing an indirect invitation for Constantine to visit. In order to advance their request these cities seem to have sensed that Constantine was more concerned about the future of his family than about the imposition of a particular religion. The emperor's reply permitted the construction of a new temple of the Flavian dynasty. This concession seems odd in the context of his support for Christianity, but quite predictable in the context of his single-minded promotion of his dynasty. Dynastic succession trumped religion. Starting out as a usurper seems to have heightened Constantine's awareness of the need for legitimacy for himself and his descendants, and his political needs repeatedly took priority over any religious preferences.[55]

Churchmen likewise had to acknowledge this priority. Almost a century after Constantine's death bishop Augustine of Hippo offered a reinterpretation of Roman history in his *City of God*. Augustine may have been one of the most influential contributors to a distinctively Christian perspective on history, but even he had to concede the importance to emperors of political concerns over religious issues. As the first Christian emperor Constantine posed a tricky problem of evaluation, and when Augustine defined "Christian emperors," he admitted that

that the empire belonged to them "from the third generation" and compared the brothers to men who inherited "their father's and grandfather's possessions": see Libanius, *Orat.* 59.13, with Lieu and Montserrat (1996) 161–62, for the date. In an oration addressed to Constantius in the late 340s or early 350s Themistius likewise characterized him as representative of only "the third generation of imperial rule": see Themistius, *Orat.* 1.2b, with Heather and Moncur (2001) 69–71, on the date. In the 370s Epiphanius, bishop of Salamis on Cyprus, claimed that Constantius I had been the son of the emperor Valerian, a predecessor of Claudius: see Epiphanius, *Panarion* 69.1.3.

55 For similar conclusions about Constantine's priorities concerning the cult at Hispellum, see de Dominicis (1963) 211: "un carattere prevalentemente civile e laico"; and Gascou (1967) 654: "le culte de la famille impériale n'a pas un caractère d'adoration religieuse, mais seulement de fidélité dynastique." For Constantine's constant obsession with dynastic succession, see Grünewald (1990) 157: "dem ältesten Thema der konstantinischen Propaganda ..., der Dynastie."

dynastic succession was still a crucial characteristic of success. According to his interpretation, only Christian emperors who "feared, loved, and worshipped God" could be considered happy and prosperous. Because Constantine had exemplified such devotion, God had rewarded him with "gifts in this world" that included the foundation of a new capital, the administration of the entire Roman world as the sole emperor, great victories in his military campaigns, and a long life. The last of these blessings had been the succession of his sons as emperors.[56]

Augustine listed these gifts even though they came close to undermining his ideas about an ideal Christian monarch. In his perspective, these gifts had been incidental consequences of Constantine's love of God. In Constantine's own perspective, however, these consequences, dynastic succession in particular, had been his primary objectives all along. As a result, this obsession with preserving his renown through the continuation of his family's imperial rule might well be taken instead as an indication of the cravings that Augustine hoped to eliminate from Christian rulership. Dynastic succession was a sign of an emperor's "desire of praise," "passion for glory," and even "love of self." As a bishop Augustine of course had misgivings about such selfish desires and instead highlighted love of God. But the realities of imperial rule demanded that every emperor, even a Christian emperor, would not ignore his own and his family's future reputation.[57]

Even in the middle of his conversion to Christianity, his early visits to Rome, and his participation in ecclesiastical disputes, Constantine had consistently highlighted his family, and in particular his sons. Three small episodes succinctly emphasized his obsession with dynastic succession. First, he himself later insisted that before his campaign against

---

[56] Augustine, *De civitate Dei* 5.24, Christian emperors, 25, gifts for Constantine; with McLynn (1999) 32, on Augustine's attitudes about emperors, and Dagron (2003) 23–24, on dynastic succession as a sign of God's approval.

[57] Augustine, *De civitate Dei* 5.12, desire and passion, 14.28, love of God and love of self. Note that Lactantius had already listed dynastic succession as a reward of Constantine's support for Christianity: see Lactantius, *Institutiones divinae* 1.1.14, with Bowen and Garnsey (2003) 3, 48–51, on Lactantius' last thoughts about Constantine.

Maxentius in 312 he had seen a vision of a cross in the sky. Immediately afterward, he furthermore claimed, he had constructed a military standard in the shape of a cross. This standard was more than a religious symbol, however, because in addition to other decorations it displayed a "golden portrait of the emperor, God's friend, and of his sons." Since in 312 Constantine had had only one son, a later version of this military standard had clearly drifted into his subsequent retellings of the original vision and its consequences. According to Eusebius of Caesarea, this "sign of salvation," the military standard, "enhanced the emperor's entire house and dynasty." Because the political aspects of his conversion were as important to publicize as the religious affiliation, Constantine used both the story about his vision of the cross and the construction of a military standard to sanction the succession of his sons. Second, during his visit to Rome in the summer of 315 Constantine issued an edict in the names of himself and the Caesar. The incongruity here is that although he still had only one son, he had yet to appoint him as a Caesar. He was already clearly planning ahead to the promotion of his son. Third, at some time Constantine composed a prayer for his army. This prayer was similar to, and may have been modeled on, a prayer that the emperor Licinius had once composed for his army. But Constantine's version pointedly differed from his rival's prayer by including a telling additional entreaty for his troops to recite as a guarantee of their loyalty to his entire dynasty: "we pray that our emperor Constantine and his sons, God's friends, be preserved safe and victorious for us for a very long time." This prayer, with its petition about Constantine's imperial family, was the liturgical equivalent of the military standard, with its portrait of Constantine's imperial family. Constantine's concern over dynastic succession permeated his relationship with the army, his political authority, and even the celebration of the liturgy. The military standard, the edict, and the military prayer advertised not just Constantine himself, but also his dynasty of sons.[58]

[58]  Military standard: Eusebius, *Vita Constantini* 1.31.2. Sign of salvation: Eusebius, *De laudibus Constantini* 9.18, with Drake (1976) 72, commenting on the monogram of the Chi-Rho depicted on the military standard: "during Constantine's lifetime

Constantine would bend his religious policies, and perhaps even his own personal piety, to fit circumstances. But dynastic succession was the one commitment that he would not compromise, and his family name became a marker not necessarily of religious conformity, but of political loyalty. His support for a particular Christian orthodoxy, even for Christianity itself, was of secondary importance. Hispellum and the other cities of Umbria had successfully played upon this concern about dynastic succession to receive permission to construct a new pagan temple. Christian churchmen likewise could sense the advantage of appealing to this obsession. Two years after the council of Nicaea had anathematized his theological teachings, the infamous priest Arius asked Constantine for reconciliation. After outlining their revised doctrines he and an associate came to the clinching argument: once they were reinstated, they could join the rest of the church in praying "for your entire family." Their petition was successful.[59]

---

the monogram was associated not with Christ but ... with the Emperor and his house." Edict issued on September 13, 315: *CTh* 10.1.1, "Imp. Constantinus A. et Caes. ad populum"; in 315 there was no Caesar in the imperial college: see Barnes (1982) 7. Constantine's prayer: Eusebius, *Vita Constantini* 4.20.1; Licinius' prayer: Lactantius, *De mortibus persecutorum* 46.6; with Sozomen, *HE* 1.8.10–11, for Constantine's assignment of clerics as chaplains for army units.

[59] Letter from Arius and Euzoius to Constantine, late 327: Urkunde 30.5, ed. Opitz (1934–1935) 64, quoted in Socrates, *HE* 1.26, Sozomen, *HE* 2.27; with Chapter 10, for additional discussion of Arius' reinstatement. For the absence of religious connotations in the Flavian name, see Mócsy (1964) 259: "es keine religiösen Unterschiede gibt."

# READING AHEAD

## CHAPTER FOUR

I N OUR POSTMODERN TIMES IRONY RULES, AND EVERY READING of the past is presumed to have some validity. To argue their inter- pretations historians resort to various techniques, including the selection, highlighting, and rearranging of texts and artifacts. By those criteria the passage of time can qualify as an interpreter of history, since it too has shuffled the stuff of the past into unexpected configura- tions. The passage of time is not just the subject of history; it has also, in its own mysterious way, provided "readings" and interpretations of the past. Nor are these memories to be dismissed as haphazard, and there- fore meaningless for the historical enterprise. In fact, in some respects the passage of time has provided readings that are truly thought provok- ing in their unpredictable playfulness. While many modern historical narratives are burdened by their own theoretical jargon and ponderous seriousness, the passage of time seems to have a mischievous sense of humor.[1]

---

[1]  For this empirical notion of memory, see Klein (2000) 136: "The new 'materializa- tion' of memory thus grounds the elevation of memory to the status of a historical agent, and we enter a new age in which archives remember and statues forget."

The fate of the inscription at Hispellum is one example of the playfulness of time. The people of Hispellum had wanted their own imperial temple and festival. After Constantine's favorable response they constructed their temple, appointed their priests, celebrated their festival, and renamed their city. They also erected a permanent record of the emperor's rescript on a large stone slab over five feet high and almost two feet wide. Like other ancient cities that displayed the responses of the oracles they had consulted or of the emperors they had petitioned, Hispellum prominently exhibited Constantine's rescript as a guarantee of its new autonomy. This inscription was rediscovered in the early eighteenth century. These days it is displayed on a wall in a meeting room in the Palazzo Comunale Vecchio at Spello, and guidebooks feature it in a short history of the town. Even though the festival is long gone, the stone monument with the emperor's rescript survives as a source of municipal pride, a relic of a better time. Appealing to the past still has its rewards, and the record of Constantine's favorable rescript to Hispellum has again become an emblem of Spello's importance.

At Rome too the passage of time has modified Constantine's reputation in various ways. As Rome became an increasingly Christian and papal city, the churches that Constantine had built on the edges of the old city became more central. Just as late antique Italy was turned upside-down, with northern frontier Italy becoming more important to emperors than Rome and peninsular Italy, so late antique Rome was turned inside out, with the churches near and outside the walls and the saints' shrines in the suburbs becoming more significant than the old pagan temples in the monumental center. In the empire, frontier cities became capitals. At Rome, outlying churches and shrines in the "Christian hinterland around the city" defined new centers of piety. One of these newly important suburban shrines was, of course, the Church of St. Peter, which was outside the city's walls, across the Tiber, on a hill that was not one of the original seven. This Vatican Hill furthermore had such a degraded reputation that one prefect of Rome would dismiss it as merely a place of ill repute where beggars congregated. Then Constantine and his sons funded the construction of an enormous new church that commemorated the martyr's shrine on the hill.

Now outlying cemeteries that had been named after St. Peter and St. Paul were transformed into "the most magnificent monuments."[2]

As new churches overshadowed old temples, observers could imagine the urban topography of Rome differently. Jerome would hint at these new religious and topographical priorities when he recalled his earlier residence at the capital. "The golden sheen of the Capitoline Hill is filthy, and all the temples of Rome are covered with soot and cobwebs. The city is being moved from its foundations. The people rush past the ruins of the temples and hurry to the martyrs' tombs." Jerome himself, when a young schoolboy at Rome during the 360s, used to visit the catacombs on Sundays. For him and his friends it had been a thrill to enter the crypts, creep between the rows of corpses, and shiver in the darkness. From his retreat in Campania in the early fifth century, Paulinus of Nola still conceded the primacy of Rome, but no longer because of its military conquests. "Previously Rome was foremost only because of its empire and its victorious arms; but now it has priority in the world because of the tombs of the apostles." Just as the increasing

---

[2] Quotation about Christian hinterland from Curran (2000) 148; see also Hunt (2003), who associates these suburban churches with the celebration of the liturgy, and the picturesque analogy of Hansen (2003) 43, on the location of these churches: "almost as if they were a siege machine, conquering the city by surrounding it." Krautheimer (1983) 29, argues that Constantine founded churches on the edges of Rome "as part of a policy of sparing pagan sentiment"; also Santangeli Valenzani (2000), contrasting Maxentius' construction in the center of Rome and Constantine's churches on the periphery. For the revival of the shrines at the catacombs under bishop Damasus, see the excellent overview in Trout (2003): "the essence of the city, and the sources of its image and identity, now lay outside its walls" (p. 528). Beggars: Ammianus Marcellinus, *Res gestae* 27.3.6, with the Introduction to "Emperor and God," for additional discussion of the Church of St. Peter.

For the increasing importance of churches at Rome, note the transition from Eusebius' ecclesiastical history to Rufinus' narrative. Writing before Constantine's victory at Rome, Eusebius, *HE* 2.25.5, mentioned "the name of Peter and Paul, which still today prevails at the cemeteries there"; almost a century later when Rufinus translated this passage, he omitted any reference to cemeteries and instead highlighted "still today the most magnificent monuments."

importance of Second Rome rearranged the dynamics of the empire, so the rising significance of the Vatican and other suburban Christian shrines reordered the symbolic topography of First Rome.[3]

The reputation of Constantine's secular monuments at Rome did not fare as well. The huge Constantinian Basilica next to the old Forum became a quarry, especially for medieval popes and Renaissance builders. One seventh-century pope neatly articulated the new realignment of priorities when he removed bronze tiles from the basilica to provide a new roof for the Church of St. Peter. Repairing a church outside the city's walls was more important than maintaining an imperial building in the city's heart, even one once associated with the first Christian emperor. As this basilica crumbled over the centuries and was gradually (and literally) deconstructed, its name has reverted to its original patron. These days many guidebooks and exhibition catalogues refer to its imposing remains as the Basilica of Maxentius.[4]

In the fifteenth century the remains of the huge statue of Constantine were found in the ruins of the basilica, including the head, the right hand, the right upper arm, the right knee, the right lower leg, and the feet. These fragments were eventually moved to the Capitoline, and in the seventeenth century relocated to the courtyard of the Palazzo dei Conservatori. This courtyard is now a morgue of miscellaneous body parts that seem to be awaiting reassembly, just as an apocryphal story claimed that long ago Domitian's wife had stitched together the

[3] Capitoline Hill: Jerome, *Ep.* 107.1, with Curran (1994) 49, on "the progress of conversion which left the Capitol less visited than [in] earlier periods." Catacombs: Jerome, *Commentarii in Ezechielem* 12, on Ezekiel 40:5–13, ed. Glorie (1964) 556–57. Tombs of apostles: Paulinus of Nola, *Carm.* 13.29–30, with the excellent survey of poets' images of Rome in Roberts (2001). For the continuation of imperial support for the games and entertainments at Rome, see the perceptive discussion in Lim (1999). As a result, Ammianus Marcellinus, *Res gestae* 28.4.29, classified the Circus Maximus as a "temple" for the spectators at Rome.

[4] Roof tiles: *Liber pontificalis* 72.2, ed. Duchesne (1886) 323, "de templo qui appellatur Romae," with Ward-Perkins (1984) 222, and Coarelli (1993) 171, discussing Duchesne's identification of this Templum Romae with the Constantinian Basilica.

butchered limbs of her husband, the last of the first Flavian emperors. In a wry twist of fate, even though Constantine himself, during one of his visits to Rome, had declined to ascend the Capitoline Hill and participate in a pagan festival, his giant head and limbs have now found a home on the Campidoglio.[5]

## READING A HEAD AND A HAND

Constantine's monumental head and right hand have become prominent relics of his presence at Rome. Moved from their original location, detached from their original context, this head and hand now conjure up at least three different readings of Constantine's role in the capital, as usurper, as ancestor, and as benefactor.

One reading would highlight his standing as an outsider. After his father's death Constantine had proclaimed his elevation as emperor by sending a traditional laurelled image of himself to Galerius, the surviving senior emperor. By accepting the image, however begrudgingly,

---

[5] Domitian's wife: Procopius, *Anecdota* 8.15–20, with Kaldellis (2004) 134, "one of the most macabre passages in ancient literature." Procopius recounted this story because he thought that Justinian resembled this handmade monstrosity! In fact, Domitian's body had been cremated, although some of his statues were beheaded and dismembered: see Suetonius, *Domitianus* 17.5, death; Pliny, *Panegyricus* 52.5, statues. Discussion of Constantine's head and history of fragments: Stuart Jones (1926) 5–6, 11–14, and Fittschen and Zanker (1985) 147–52. Avoidance of festival: Zosimus, *Historia nova* 2.29.5. The bibliography about Constantine's refusal to ascend the Capitoline Hill, in particular regarding the date and the wider meaning, is large; for overviews, see Paschoud (1979–2000) 1:238–40, (1992), and Nixon and Rodgers (1994) 323n.119.

Eight panels from an earlier arch (or arches) dedicated to Marcus Aurelius were reused on the Arch of Constantine. On these panels depicting various imperial activities the emperor's head was recut to resemble Constantine or his father, Constantius: see Chapter 2. Among the panels from the same series that were *not* used on the Arch of Constantine was one depicting Marcus Aurelius performing a sacrifice in front of the Temple of Jupiter on the Capitoline Hill: see Ruysschaert (1962–1963b). For an excellent interpretation of this deliberate suppression of a depiction of the emperor on the Capitoline Hill, see Ruysschaert (1962–1963a): "Païen par ce qu'il exprime, l'arc de Constantin est chrétien par ce qu'il tait" (p. 99).

Galerius welcomed Constantine into the "partnership" of emperors. Other emperors likewise publicized their authority by sending out images, statues, and even gold coins stamped with their portraits. But if portraits, statues, and busts announced the beginning of a new emperor's reign, then his actual bodiless head announced the end. Maxentius had drowned in the Tiber during the battle at the Milvian Bridge. Constantine's troops retrieved his corpse, cut off its head, and carried it into the city in their triumphal procession. Constantine then sent "the tyrant's hideous head" to Africa to demonstrate that he was now in control. The statues of a defeated emperor typically suffered the same fate. "After a tyrant is killed, his images and statues are pulled down. When only the appearance is changed, the [tyrant's] head is removed and the bust of the victor is placed on top [of the statues], so that the body remains but another head is substituted for those that were cut off." A new emperor was a new face and the new head of government; a deposed emperor was defaced and beheaded. Decapitation marked the death both of a failed emperor and of any memories of him. Decapitation was the symbolic equivalent of erasing names and ending a lineage: without its head, the corpse of one usurper was "nameless."[6]

[6] Image of Constantine: Lactantius, *De mortibus persecutorum* 25.1–3; with Zosimus, *Historia nova* 2.9.2, for Maxentius' angry reaction to the display of Constantine's image at Rome, and Bruun (1976), on the transmission and acceptance of images of new emperors. Gold coins: note Ammianus Marcellinus, *Res gestae* 26.7.11, for Procopius' attempt to generate support in Illyricum by distributing gold coins "stamped with the new emperor's portrait"; with López Sánchez (2003), discussing the images on Procopius' coins. Maxentius' head: *Panegyrici latini* 12(9).18, 4(10).31.4, "tyranni ipsius taeterrimum caput," Zosimus, *Historia nova* 2.17.1; sent to Africa: *Panegyrici latini* 4(10).32.6–8; also Praxagoras of Athens, summarized by Photius, *Bibliotheca* 62: "some Romans cut off his head, hung it on a pole, and wandered through the city," with Malosse (2000), arguing that Praxagoras was the source for Libanius, *Orat.* 59. Tyrant's statue: Jerome, *Commentarium in Abacuc prophetam* 2, on Habakkuk 3:14 (*PL* 25.1329A-B), with the commentary in Stewart (1999). Nameless body of Magnus Maximus: Pacatus, *Panegyrici latini* 2(12).45.2; also Rufinus, *HE* 8.13.15, on Maximian's statues: "in public buildings the words of his name were changed." Richlin (1999), is a suggestive meditation on the meaning of decapitation in the Roman world.

Beheading was a common fate for deposed emperors and other rebels during the fourth and early fifth centuries. As Constantius set out to face Julian, he hoped to send his rebellious cousin's head back to Antioch. The usurpers Magnentius and Procopius were beheaded; so were Magnus Maximus, Eugenius, Constantine III and his son Julian, and Jovinus and his brother Sebastianus, and their heads put on display. At Constantinople the head of a renegade Gothic general was on permanent display, carefully preserved in brine. Sometimes the penalty included a hand. The usurper Attalus lost the fingers of his right hand. The usurper Johannes lost his head and a hand. After soldiers killed Rufinus, the prefect of the East who was thought to have designs on the eastern throne, they cut off his head and both hands. They then paraded through Constantinople carrying the prefect's head and his outstretched right hand.[7]

Constantine had certainly tried to ingratiate himself at Rome. But however relieved people were after the overthrow of Maxentius, Constantine was still a military man, another emperor from the Balkans, an invader from the north, an outspoken Christian ruler. At Rome Constantine was an interloper. On one occasion, most likely during his final visit to Rome in 326, "the people mocked him with shouts of ridicule." Perhaps it was these citizens at the capital who pelted an image of the emperor with stones. According to this story, Constantine felt his face and then shrugged off their scorn with a sardonic joke: "I note that there is no dent on my forehead; my head is intact, and my face has no scratches at all." Even as he feigned indifference, however, Constantine may also have misconstrued the discomfort about his presence at the capital. By the time he left Rome for good, "he had made the senate and people hate him."[8]

---

[7] Ammianus Marcellinus, *Res gestae* 22.14.4, Julian and Magnentius, 26.9.9, Procopius. Other usurpers: Olympiodorus, *Frag.* 20. Gainas' head: Philostorgius, *HE* 11.8. Attalus: Olympiodorus, *Frag.* 14. Johannes: Philostorgius, *HE* 12.13. Rufinus: Zosimus, *Historia nova* 5.7.6; head and hand: Claudian, *In Rufinum* 2.433–53, Philostorgius, *HE* 11.3.

[8] Shouts: Libanius, *Orat.* 19.19; also *Orat.* 20.24: "he is noted for enduring the boorish behavior of the Roman people"; with Wiemer (1994) 517–18, locating this

Successors, even emperors from his own family, were not above criticizing him at Rome. Constantine had once decided to honor the capital with the gift of an obelisk from Egypt. When his son Constantius visited Rome in 357, he finally arranged for the obelisk to be erected. But in the dedication inscribed on the base, he subtly distinguished himself by claiming that his father had in fact initially intended the obelisk for Constantinople. Constantine had acquired a reputation for having supplied New Rome at the expense of other cities; in this dedication Constantius could now imply that he had instead returned priority to Old Rome at the expense of New Rome. Finally some of the spoils of the East were coming to Rome again. By tacitly criticizing his father, Constantius had enhanced his own standing at Rome.[9]

In 361 Julian was looking for support in his civil war against Constantius. In a letter to the senate at Rome he bitterly denounced his cousin for his scandalous behavior. This libel had no effect on Constantius' reputation in the capital, since the senators reacted by demanding that

discontent during Constantine's visit in 326. Stones and joke: John Chrysostom, *Homiliae de statuis* 21.11 (*PG* 49.216), preached at Antioch in late April 387. In his sermon John attributed this story about Constantine to an oration he claimed Flavianus, bishop of Antioch, had delivered to the emperor Theodosius at Constantinople a month earlier. Although John noted that "still today everyone praises this joke," that is, presumably at Antioch, he did not locate the episode itself at a particular city. Hatred: Zosimus, *Historia nova* 2.29.5 (but admittedly a hostile source).

9   Erection of Constantius' obelisk: Ammianus Marcellinus, *Res gestae* 17.4.12–15, although claiming that Constantine originally intended it for Rome; its dedication: *ILS* 1:165, no. 736; for discussion, see Fowden (1987), suggesting that Constantine had intended to conciliate the pagans of Rome, Klein (1999b) 60–63, arguing that Constantius was resolving differences with Rome at a time when he was also promoting the standing of Constantinople, Hunt (1998) 21–22, illustrating the uneasy relationship between Constantius and the Roman establishment, and G. Kelly (2003) 603–6, (2004) 154–55, stressing Ammianus' deliberate suppression of any reference to Constantinople. Supply of Constantinople: see Jerome, *Chronicon* s.a. 330, "Constantinople was dedicated by stripping bare almost all other cities."

Julian show some respect for the emperor who had promoted him in the first place. But Julian went on in his letter to censure his uncle Constantine as "an innovator and a disturber of ancient laws and traditional custom." Disrupting antiquity was a powerful accusation at Rome, and Julian knew his audience. This was an indictment with merit. Constantine had come to Rome as an outsider, and he had abandoned it in favor of New Rome. For modern historians the display of Constantine's head and hand is a colossal reminder that he too had been a usurper who never quite fit in at Rome.[10]

At the same time this head can provide an alternative reading of Constantine's standing at Rome, and more generally in imperial history. Prominent Roman aristocrats filled their houses with "images of ancestors," including busts, portraits, and wax masks. These trophies were reminders to themselves of the legacies they had inherited and advertisements to guests of their families' distinction. Often these images were on display in the *atrium*, the inner courtyard where the master of the house would greet visitors. Men with few distinguished ancestors had to finesse their humble lineages. The first Flavian dynasty of emperors had been "obscure and lacking any images of ancestors." Vespasian himself, before starting a military career and holding high offices, had worked as a mule-driver; he was thought to have become emperor through a mere twist of good fortune.[11]

---

[10] Julian's letter: Ammianus Marcellinus, *Res gestae* 21.10.7–8, with Weiss (1978) 136: "L'Apostat veut . . . constituer une sorte de front de défense autour du *mos maiorum*." During his civil war with Constantius, Julian provided grain for Rome from his own resources: see *Panegyrici latini* 3(11).14.1–2. After his final victory he made concessions to senators at Rome: see Ammianus Marcellinus, *Res gestae* 21.12.24–25. He also later explained his abolishment of some of Constantine's edicts as a restoration of "ancient law": see *CTh* 2.5.2, 3.1.3. For Constantine's reputation at Rome, see Kähler (1952) 25: "Dieser Sieger aber ist . . . als Mensch eine die Römer überraschende Erscheinung."

[11] "Maiorum imagines": *CJ* 5.37.22, an edict issued by Constantine in 326 on the legal responsibilities of a guardian. Suetonius, *Vespasianus* 1.1, obscurity of Vespasian's family, 4.3, mule-driver; also 12, for Vespasian's disdain for inventing an ancestry that would have linked him with Hercules. Vespasian's good fortune: Tacitus, *Agricola* 13.5.

The second Flavian dynasty had started out with the same handicap of obscurity. Helena, Constantine's mother, was even rumored to have once worked in a stable or a tavern. But after Constantine's reign subsequent emperors, even those not related to his dynasty, wanted to adopt the Flavian name. Constantine had become their common ancestor. Long ago the Cornelian family had kept an image of Scipio Africanus, the great general who had defeated Hannibal, in the Temple of Jupiter Optimus Maximus on the Capitoline Hill: "for him alone the Capitol is similar to an *atrium*." Much later Constantine's giant head was moved to the Capitoline. Today his head can still be viewed as an oversized ancestral bust now conveniently on display in the *atrium* of the capital, this little courtyard on the Campidoglio. In this reading Constantine was the ancestor of all subsequent emperors.[12]

A final reading returns Constantine to the context of petitions. As they approached with trepidation, petitioners looked most intently at an emperor's face and his hands. Their first hope was that the emperor would extend a hand to receive them and their petitions. One orator noted that when the municipal councilors who had accompanied him from Autun bowed before Constantine, the emperor directed them to stand with a wave from his "invincible right hand." Bishop Eusebius of Caesarea distinguished Constantine from his rivals by noting how he had "extended his right hand of salvation to everyone." Constantine himself once prayed that God would "extend his right hand"; after his death, coins depicted Constantine's reception in heaven "by a right hand extending from above." With an inviting gesture a ruler's hand represented mercy and forbearance.[13]

---

[12] Helena's reputed background as a *stabularia*: Ambrose, *De obitu Theodosii* 42, with the discussion of other texts referring to her insignificant status in Drijvers (1992) 15–19. Scipio's image: Valerius Maximus, *Facta et dicta memorabilia* 8.15.1, with Flower (1996) 48–52, suggesting that this image was an ancestor mask. For the display of ancestral images in houses, see Flower (1996) 185–222; also Hillner (2003) 138–39, for the creation of ancestral galleries by aristocrats at Rome during the fourth century.

[13] *Panegyrici latini* 5(8).1.3, right hand. Eusebius, *HE* 10.9.4, Constantine's right hand, *Vita Constantini* 1.28.1, prayer, 4.73, coins, with the discussion of Cameron

The second hope of petitioners was that the emperor would indicate his assent by nodding or smiling. One orator waited for Constantine's nod before he began to talk about a sensitive topic; another knew that Constantine was sympathetic when he saw the tears in the emperor's eyes; another petitioner recognized that Constantius II had agreed once he smiled. When petitioners approached an emperor, they looked for a gesture from his hand, hopefully of acceptance, and the expression on his face, hopefully of approval. One former supporter of Maxentius hoped to placate the victorious Constantine with the gift of a poem "that has reached your victorious hands, to be read by your gentle eyes." As modern tourists visit the fragments of Constantine's giant statue on the Campidoglio, they still imitate this suppliant with their intent gaze on the emperor's placid face and his folded hand. At Rome the passage of time has now reduced this statue of Constantine to his physical essence as a benefactor: his face and his right hand.[14]

Eusebius of Caesarea knew firsthand the blessings of Constantine's nod of approval, because during one of the bishop's monotonously pro-lix orations the emperor had actually smiled. Eusebius had also enjoyed the emperor's patronage and hospitality. After the ecumenical coun-cil at Nicaea, Constantine celebrated the twentieth anniversary of his accession by hosting a banquet for the bishops. Eusebius was in awe of the imperial bodyguards. His previous experience with soldiers had been consistently terrifying, since they had been the agents for enforc-ing emperors' hostile edicts. In his account of the persecutions under Maximinus he had noted how one martyr in Palestine had been ripped

---

and Hall (1999) 348–50, and Kolb (2001) 253–54, on the appropriation of pagan motifs in this depiction of Constantine's reception in heaven.

[14] *Panegyrici latini* 5(8).9.5, tears; 6(7).14.1, nod. Athanasius, *Apologia ad Constantium* 16, on Constantius' preference about a place to worship in Alexandria: "I know that you prefer the place with your name [Caesarion]. For you are smiling; and by smiling you announce this." Poem: Porphyrius, *Epistula ad Constantinum* 2, with Barnes (1975b) 185, suggesting that Porphyrius had been a supporter of Maxentius and wrote this letter in November or December 312. For Constantine's favorable reply, see Constantine, *Epistula ad Porfyrium*. Nicholson (2001), discusses the heavenward gaze of the statue.

apart by a governor's bodyguards, who had acted "like wild animals." This time, even though the soldiers were standing at the entrance to the palace with drawn swords, Eusebius and the other churchmen walked through their midst "without fear." This was every petitioner's dream, to approach an emperor directly and fearlessly, to offer a petition to the emperor's hand, to await the emperor's smile. Eusebius was so bedazzled at this banquet that in his estimation it had to be a preview of Christ's future rule on earth. Through Constantine's goodwill his own prayer had been answered. This truly was kingdom come.[15]

[15] Eusebius, *Vita Constantini* 3.15, banquet, 4.46, smile; *De martyribus Palaestinae*, recensio brevior 4.10, wild animals; with Elton (2006) 328–29, for the ubiquitous presence of imperial bodyguards.

# A GREEK
# ROMAN EMPIRE

## SECTION TWO

EUSEBIUS OF CAESAREA REFUSED TO CONCEDE ANY CONTINU-
ity between Constantine, the first Christian emperor, and the
Tetrarchs, his pagan predecessors who had initiated persecutions of the Christians. In his biography of the emperor he
instead preferred comparisons with a biblical hero. As a model for the
experiences of the young Constantine he highlighted the early life of
the Old Testament lawgiver Moses, a foundling who had grown up
among foreign "tyrants" before abruptly fleeing their plots. Constantine's conversion to Christianity was supposedly just as sudden, the
consequence of a stunning vision before his battle outside Rome in
312. Eusebius' punctuation of the emperor's early reign with a sharp,
discontinuous moment retains its powerful influence on modern interpretations, and not only of Constantine. This fascination with the novelty of Constantine's support for Christianity affects our evaluation of
the antecedents of his reign too. In terms of structural features, such
as the imperial administration, its offices, and its magistrates, Diocletian and Constantine can be said to have shared a "new empire." In
terms of personal religious beliefs, however, only Constantine was new.
The conventional emphasis on the abruptness of his conversion and

143

the fundamental differences between his religious policies and those of his Tetrarchic predecessors highlights the impression of significant contrast, sudden change, even bold disjunction at the beginning of his reign.[1]

In fact, Constantine was the scrupulous heir of Diocletian and his fellow Tetrarchic emperors, and even though he supported a different religion, he continued core policies of the Tetrarchs. Many of those policies had focused on a stern notion of Romanness. Despite their origins in backward Balkan provinces, Diocletian and his fellow emperors wanted to present themselves as champions of "old laws and the public discipline of the Romans." That strict devotion to Romanness was a foundation for various military and administrative initiatives. The campaigns against the Persian empire seemed to represent, in part, an attempt to extend Romanness into the Middle East. After one notable victory the emperor Galerius vaunted himself as a "second Romulus," the founder of Rome. Diocletian also hoped to centralize aspects of Roman society by developing a larger, more intrusive imperial administration. During the mid-third century pressure on the frontiers had led to repeated usurpations of imperial power, territorial fragmentation, and even the appearance of breakaway regional empires. Diocletian responded to the anarchy of multiple illegitimate emperors by creating a Tetrarchy of multiple legitimate emperors. He likewise hoped to enhance the efficiency of the central administration by expanding its size

---

[1] Constantine as Moses: Eusebius, *De vita Constantini* 1.12, 20. From the extensive discussion of this comparison, see Hollerich (1990) 316–24, Cameron (1997) 157–61, Wilson (1998) 112–21, Rapp (1998), (2005) 129–31, Cameron and Hall (1999) 35–39, and Drake (2000) 376–77. "New empire" is the title of Barnes (1982), which explicitly focuses on emperors, imperial magistrates, and the working of the imperial administration; for continuity from the Tetrarchs, note Cameron (2005) 108, "Constantine himself was a product of the tetrarchic system." For examples of the emphasis on sudden religious change, see Vogt (1963) 39, "the battle of the Milvian Bridge was a turning-point"; Barnes (1981) 43, "the moment of psychological conviction"; MacMullen (1984) 102, "Nothing counts for more than the year 312"; and Odahl (2004) 106, "At this moment, Constantine converted"; Baglivi (1992), analyzes ancient interpretations of the novelty of Constantine. For an argument that Constantine's religious conviction should be interpreted as an extended process of forming an identity, see Van Dam (2003c).

and appointing more magistrates to govern the additional provinces, dioceses, and prefectures. He implemented a new census for registering taxpayers and their property, tightened the collection of taxes, and used those additional revenues to augment the army. He tried to regulate inflation by imposing maximum prices: "the emperors insisted upon cheapness." An enlarged, more centralized administration was now a defining characteristic not just of the realities of Roman rule, but of the idea of Romanness.[2]

Diocletian and the Tetrarchs furthermore explicitly linked their imperial power to the promotion of correct religious practices, and they matched military initiatives and administrative innovations with an insistence on religious traditions and antiquity. They supported the cults of traditional classical deities, for instance by identifying themselves with Jupiter and Hercules and adding the titles of Jovius and Herculius to their official names. Their intimate affiliation with these pagan gods thus ensured the prosperity of the empire. According to one orator, "the golden age is now reborn under the eternal guidance of Jupiter and Hercules." Other cults they outlawed. In the middle of the third century the prophet Mani had initiated a new world religion in Mesopotamia, and his Manichaean teachings then quickly spread from the Persian empire to the eastern provinces of the Roman empire. Diocletian and the Tetrarchs soon issued an edict that labeled the Manichees as opponents of "old religions" and condemned them for infecting the "chaste Roman people" with their malevolence.[3]

---

[2] Lactantius, *De mortibus persecutorum* 9.9, second Romulus, 34.1, old laws, in an edict attributed to Galerius; with Chapter 2, for the cultural prejudices about these emperors. For the impact of the Tetrarchy on the eastern frontier, see Millar (1993) 205: "The physical record of the Roman forces, erecting grandiloquent Latin inscriptions, is more evident than ever before." Cheapness: *Consularia Constantinopolitana* s.a. 302.

[3] Golden age: *Panegyrici latini* 9(4).18.5, with additional discussion of the theology of the Tetrarchy in Chapter 9; also SHA, *Heliogabalus* 35.4, "Diocletian, father of a golden age." Manichees: "Edictum de maleficis et Manichaeis," in *Collatio legum Mosaicarum et Romanarum* 15.3.4. Grant (1980) 95, suggests that Eusebius knew of this edict and hence condemned Manichaeism as a heresy in *HE* 7.31: "Non-Christian readers . . . would become aware that orthodox Christianity was responsibly Roman."

Christianity was another target of religious correctness. Already during an earlier general persecution, one prominent bishop had been executed as an "enemy of the Roman gods." Starting in 303 the Tetrarchic emperors issued a series of edicts that penalized Christians and removed some of their civil rights as Romans. The first edict explicitly stripped them of any official ranks and offices and made them liable to legal penalties; subsequent edicts ordered clerics, and then everyone, to sacrifice to the gods. From the perspective of Christians these were oppressive edicts of persecution that challenged both their religion and their identity as Romans. "Increasingly, Christians were set against a religious world that the central authorities at least could define as *Roman*." From the perspective of the Tetrarchs, however, these edicts were attempts to restore traditional Roman religious practices and to enhance their own standing and the authority of the central imperial administration. In Africa a governor was candid in informing a defiant Christian matron how to avoid execution: "worship the Roman religion observed by our lords, the totally unconquered Caesars." Just as people had to register for the census and receive a receipt for the payment of taxes, so now they also needed verification of having performed sacrifice. By linking political centralization with religious uniformity, the Tetrarchs made correct religion another aspect of Romanness.[4]

---

[4] Enemy: *Acta proconsularia sancti Cypriani* 4.1. Edicts of persecution: Lactantius, *De mortibus persecutorum* 13.1 (first); Eusebius, *HE* 8.2.4 (first), 8.2.5, 6.10 (sacrifice), *De martyribus Palaestinae* 3.1 (everyone), with Digeser (2000) 55: "These measures effectively stripped Christians of their Roman citizenship." Quotation about Christians from Beard, North and Price (1998) 1:241. For the contrasting perspectives on the edicts, see L'Orange (1938) 33: "Was für den Christen *ferocitas* ist, das heißt in der offiziellen staatlichen Propaganda *pietas*." Roman religion: *Passio Crispinae* 2.4. For the connection between census and sacrifice, note in particular Eusebius, *De martyribus Palaestinae*, recensio brevior 4.8: at Caesarea in Palestine soldiers enforced the order to sacrifice by summoning everyone by name from an ἀπογραφή, a census register; with Millar (1993) 193–98, 535–44, on registration for the Tetrarchic tax system. Rives (1999) 152–54, is an excellent discussion of religious orthopraxy as a sign of Romanness; also Rives (1995) 258, "Diocletian clearly believed that there was a distinctly Roman religious identity," and Kolb (1995) 28, for the Tetrarchic emphasis on "eine religiös fundierte Loyalität aller Untertanen zum Herrscherhaus und zum Staat."

Nor did they stop with religious conformity. All of them were native Latin speakers who had served in that most Latin of institutions, the army. The Tetrarchic emperors who reigned in the East, first Diocletian and Galerius, then their successors Maximinus and Licinius, consistently used Latin as the language of power. "The presence of Latin in the East would peak under Diocletian, who included the use of Latin in his political program as the language of administration for the entire empire." Even though these emperors were largely unfamiliar with classical culture, as "Roman" emperors they were supposed to be "Latin." In fact, upon becoming emperor Diocletian was thought to have changed his original "Greek" name of Diocles simply to conform to "Roman custom." The Tetrarchs defined proper Romanness in terms of both religion and culture, both pagan sacrifice and the use of Latin.[5]

Their promotion of Latin hence posed a dilemma for provincials in the Greek East. If the emperors were prepared to compel their subjects to accept their religious preferences, then perhaps they also expected cultural uniformity. Some Greeks had already concluded that knowledge of Latin would improve their prospects for acquiring offices in the imperial administration. Perhaps cities, in their petitions to the court and imperial magistrates, should follow this lead. Constantine too was a native Latin speaker. He could also sense the advantages of linking imperial authority with religion. Even though he eventually decided to promote Christianity rather than pagan cults, his support for a particular religion still followed the Tetrarchic precedent. In fact, he was if anything even more restrictive than the Tetrarchs, since he endorsed

---

[5] Quotation about Diocletian's promotion of Latin translated from Rochette (1997) 9; also 327, "Dioclétien ... s'appliqua à étendre l'usage du latin à toute la *Romania.*" Note also Liebeschuetz (1972) 253, "the government tried to maintain the Latin and Roman character of the empire"; Corcoran (1996) 183: "Most edictal texts of this period are in Latin"; and Corcoran (2002) 229, "the apparent Latin chauvinism of Galerius and other Tetrarchic emperors." Diocletian's new imperial name: *Epitome de Caesaribus* 39.1, "Graium nomen in Romanum morem convertit"; after his abdication he again assumed the name of Diocles: see Lactantius, *De mortibus persecutorum* 19.5, with Cambi (2004) 38–41, on the changes in Diocletian's name. A Greek sophist like Libanius nevertheless preferred to refer to him even during his emperorship as Diocles: see Libanius, *Orat.* 19.45–46.

the idea of an orthodoxy within Christianity. In the Greek East, Constantine's reign hence raised similar concerns about the imposition of religious correctness for both individuals and cities. The additional question was whether it also expected cultural correctness.

During his long reign Constantine fiddled repeatedly in his official representation of himself, first copying Tetrarchic images, then modeling himself after Augustus, and finally portraying himself crowned with a diadem. He likewise vacillated in his attempts to define himself as a Christian emperor, in part because dealing with ecclesiastical disputes compelled him to change his mind and modify his beliefs. Linking imperial authority explicitly with religion and culture was an extended process of experimentation, both for the Tetrarchs and for Constantine, and their subjects had to cope with the emperors' uncertainties. These concerns were particularly acute when individuals and cities submitted petitions to emperors. For their requests to be successful, petitioners wanted to appeal directly to an emperor's preferences. To do so they had to know those preferences.[6]

New emperors were especially problematic, because they had not yet had time to publicize their intentions. In 324 Constantine assumed control of the eastern empire. By then he had already ruled as a Christian emperor in Italy and the western provinces for well over a decade. In Palestine, Eusebius, who had extended his *Ecclesiastical History* to include Constantine's actions in the West, certainly knew that the new emperor had already issued edicts in support of Christianity. But most people in the East would not have known much about him and his policies: "separated by a great distance over land and sea, the inhabitants of the East hear little about Italy." In addition, after imposing his rule over the eastern provinces Constantine still sometimes tolerated pagan cults and allowed pagan practices. In the Greek East Constantine was at first an unknown emperor and subsequently a seemingly fickle emperor whose policies at times wavered. If we modern historians repeatedly disagree about interpreting Constantine's religious intentions, then his contemporaries were no less baffled. And their uncertainties were not

---

[6] Constantine's portraits: Smith (1997) 185–87, with Introduction, for his diadem.

mere academic disputes. For them, a misreading of an emperor might have disadvantageous, even dangerous, consequences.[7]

In the mid-320s Orcistus (now Ortaköy), a small town in central Asia Minor, submitted a petition to Constantine in which it presented its grievances and requested benefactions. The subsequent dialogue between emperor and town included a series of letters and another petition (Chapter 5). In their initial petition the people of Orcistus were vague about their own religious preferences. Because both the Tetrarchic emperors and Constantine were experimenting with the relationship between politics and religion throughout their reigns, cities and individuals were often unsure how to approach them (Chapter 6). In sending its petition to Constantine, Orcistus was hence taking a chance and making a guess about the new eastern emperor. Its petition was based upon two conjectures, one about culture and the other about religion. Orcistus decided to compose the petition in Latin but not to mention Christianity. Since its petition was successful, Orcistus seems to have guessed right. In the long run, however, Orcistus was mistaken about the future of both Christianity and Latin in the eastern Roman empire. Christianity did become the official religion, and the East remained Greek (Chapter 7).

The pillar on which Orcistus inscribed these documents had its own remarkable afterlife (Chapter 8). At the time the city had wanted to display a copy of the documents simply as a warranty of its new imperial patronage. But for those documents to become historical sources, centuries later modern scholars first had to rescue this pillar from a watermill.

---

[7] In the tenth book of his *History* Eusebius cited a series of edicts issued by Constantine alone or with Licinius; for the chronology of Eusebius' revisions of the *History* and his sources, see Chapter 6 and the Introduction to "Emperor and God." Separated: Herodian, *Hist.* 6.7.4.

# CONSTANTINE'S DIALOGUE WITH ORCISTUS

## CHAPTER FIVE

IN SEPTEMBER 324 CONSTANTINE FINALLY DEFEATED LICINIUS and acquired control over the provinces surrounding the eastern Mediterranean. With this victory he had eliminated his last imperial rival and reunited the Roman empire. Constantine had not been in the East for almost twenty years, ever since he had left Nicomedia in mid-305 to join his father in Gaul. Now he was back at Nicomedia to accept Licinius' surrender. He quickly initiated a whirlwind of activity to establish his authority as the emperor in the East and his reputation as a patron of Christianity. Only two months later he consecrated the site of Byzantium in preparation for its transformation into the new capital of Constantinople. During the winter or perhaps in the spring of 325, he traveled across central Asia Minor twice, to and from Antioch. In May and June he participated in the large council of bishops that met at Nicaea. He then remained in or near Constantinople and Nicomedia until the spring of 326, when he traveled to Italy.[1]

---

[1] Constantine was at Nicomedia on February 25, 325: see *CTh* 1.15.1. Bruun (1966) 70, 664–69, dates Constantine's visit to Antioch in late 324 and early 325, Barnes (1978b) 54–56, (1981) 212, (1982) 76, to December 324, before returning

During Constantine's journeys locals along the road in Asia Minor would have had firsthand opportunities to meet him and members of his entourage, or at least learn about his preferences. The accession of a new emperor offered a propitious opportunity for cities and individuals to present petitions and make requests for new honors, new titles, and new amenities. Long ago, various communities and individuals in the Greek East had sent embassies and petitions to Augustus almost immediately after his final victory over his rival Marcus Antonius. King Herod of Judaea met Augustus at Rhodes to apologize for his earlier support for Marcus Antonius and pledge his allegiance; a delegation from Rhosus in Syria met Augustus at Ephesus to present a celebratory crown; a village of fishermen on the tiny island of Gyarus sent an ambassador to Augustus at Corinth to complain about their taxes. Subsequent emperors were typically just as magnanimous. In the mid-first century the city of Perge in Pamphylia had set up a dedication to Vespasian soon after he emerged victorious in the civil war. In the mid-fourth century when the emperor Julian traveled through central Asia Minor, petitioners approached him on the road; and the first court official to hail Valentinian's selection of Gratian as emperor would be promoted on the spot! Not only was a new emperor usually in a gracious mood, but he might in fact have welcomed the opportunity to demonstrate his beneficence and impose his authority by modifying his predecessors' decisions. One small town in the mountainous outback between Phrygia and Galatia now decided to take advantage of Constantine's reappearance in the East by appealing directly for his assistance.[2]

to Nicomedia; Lane Fox (1986) 638–43, argues that Constantine departed from Nicomedia and reached Antioch in April 325; on the date of the council of Antioch see also Burgess (1999a) 189, "no way of being certain." Constantine had apparently hoped to visit Egypt on this trip and mediate the doctrinal conflict between bishop Alexander of Alexandria and his priest Arius: see Chapter 10. Instead he wrote to explain his failure to visit: see Eusebius, *Vita Constantini* 2.72.2, "recently when I stopped at Nicomedia, I eagerly planned [to travel] to the East at once."
[2] King Herod: Josephus, *Bellum Iudaicum* 1.20.1–3, *Antiquitates Iudaicae* 15.187–96, with the discussion of Augustus' travels in the Greek East in Millar (2000): "the communities of the Greek East recognised immediately . . . that their world

## MEMORIES

Although Orcistus claimed that it had once held the rank of a city, it had subsequently slipped into dependence to the neighboring city of Nacolea. Orcistus recalled this memory of its former eminence, as well as its complaints about its current sorry condition, in two petitions to the emperor. Subsequently the town inscribed copies of the first of these petitions and the emperor's favorable responses to both petitions on a pillar that was just over five feet high, about twenty inches wide, and about fifteen inches thick. This dossier of documents included:

1. A decision about the first petition, addressed apparently to the people of Orcistus. This direct response was Constantine's own *adnotatio*, the brief opinion in which he indicated his reaction to the petition. At the end of this opinion he confirmed his decision with an autograph subscription: "I have signed." An emperor might issue an *adnotatio* directly to an individual or a community "to provide exceptions to customary legal and administrative procedures, and ... to convey special privileges." Constantine subsequently mentioned and then cited this *adnotatio* at the end of his letter to Ablabius.[3]
2. A letter from Constantine to Ablabius, a high-ranking imperial magistrate, in which the emperor summarized some of the claims and grievances from the petition and then paraphrased his own *adnotatio*, his decision. Decades earlier Constantine himself had announced that an *adnotatio* was not binding without an accompanying rescript to an imperial magistrate. This letter is largely intact on the pillar, with only a few illegible letters and missing words.[4]

now had a new individual ruler" (p. 20). Rhosus: Sherk (1969) 297–98, no. 58, document III. Gyarus: Strabo, *Geographia* 10.5.3. Dedication by Perge: Eck (2000) 650–55, discussing Sahin (1999) 69, no. 54. Ammianus Marcellinus, *Res gestae* 22.9.8, Julian's trip, 27.6.14, promotion of Eupraxius.

[3] For the identification of this document as an *adnotatio*, see Feissel (1999), especially pp. 261–62, for the emendation of *scribti* to *scrib<s>i*. Quotation from Mathisen (2004) 26. Other discussions include Millar (1977) 266, Chastagnol (1981a) 392–93, and Corcoran (1996) 57–58.

[4] Necessity of rescript: *CTh* 1.2.1, issued in 313, with Mathisen (2004) 27, on issuing "an enabling rescript addressed to an imperial official," and Feissel (1999) 266–67,

3. The first petition. The inscribed version included only the salutation and the first few sentences, before it abruptly stopped in mid-sentence at the bottom of the pillar. The original petition had certainly said more about the amenities of Orcistus and its grievances, since Constantine's letter to Ablabius included a summary.[5]

4. Another letter from Constantine to the municipal council of Orcistus, largely intact, written some years after the first three documents. This letter was obviously a response to another petition from Orcistus, although this second petition was not inscribed on the pillar.[6]

This dialogue between town and emperor extended over several years. Orcistus submitted its first petition (Document 3) between early November 324 and May 326. Soon afterward Constantine noted his decision in an *adnotatio* (Document 1), and then conveyed his decision in a letter to Ablabius (Document 2), who transmitted it to Orcistus. A few years later, probably in the first half of 331, Orcistus sent a second petition to the emperor. This time Constantine replied directly to the citizens of Orcistus in a letter dated on June 30, 331 (Document 4).[7]

(2004) 35–36, for direct rescripts to petitioners supported by indirect rescripts to imperial magistrates.

[5] The stonecutter could have engraved a few more lines of Document 3 on the protruding foot of the right side, as he had done on the foot of the front face of the pillar. In a letter to T. Mommsen, W. M. Ramsay thought that the text of the petition might have been continued on the back side of the pillar, "but after careful examination at several points I could find no trace of letters." Mommsen then suggested that the pillar had originally stood against a wall, and that the text of the petition had been continued on a second stone: see Mommsen (1887) 314, 316. For the circumstances of this correspondence between Mommsen and Ramsey, see Chapter 8.

[6] According to Millar (1977) 544n.40, this second reply was a letter rather than an *adnotatio* because Orcistus had by now acquired the rank of a city. But the emperors nevertheless followed the pattern of the earlier transaction by promising to supplement their direct reply to the city with a supporting rescript to an imperial magistrate, in this case the *rationalis* of the diocese of Asiana, who would then enforce their new decision.

[7] For discussion of the dates, an edition of the Latin text, and a translation of the documents, see Appendix 2.

Document 1 and the first three-quarters of Document 2 were inscribed on the front face of the pillar (Panel 1), the remainder of Document 2 and Document 3 on the right side (Panel 2), and Document 4 on the left side (Panel 3). The most important outcome, Constantine's favorable decision to the first petition, was inscribed twice on the pillar, at the very top of the front panel and near the top of the right panel. In order to highlight this decision the stonecutter ignored both the proper chronological sequence of the first three documents and the order of these documents in the official dossier. In correct chronological sequence, Orcistus first submitted its petition (Document 3), Constantine indicated his decision in his *adnotatio* (Document 1), and he subsequently wrote a letter to Ablabius that summarized the petition and his decision (Document 2). The official dossier containing the emperor's favorable reply would have included first the letter to Ablabius (Document 2), and then "copies . . . attached below" of the emperor's decision (Document 1) and the town's petition (Document 3). Constantine's letter to the council of Orcistus (Document 4) marked a revival of this exchange a few years later and its conclusion. This letter was engraved perhaps on the side of an existing monument that already displayed the first three documents; or its arrival may have been the catalyst for setting up a permanent record of the entire dossier.[8]

Since the stonecutter had so clearly rearranged the order of the first three documents in order to give pride of place to Constantine's decisions, the monument itself was an interpretation of the dialogue

---

[8] For the order of the documents in the official dossier returned to Orcistus by Ablabius, see Feissel (1999) 267. Copies: Document 2, lines 45–46, "subiec[t]a . . . exempla." Other cities had already displayed dossiers of two or three Tetrarchic edicts, rather than only individual documents: see Feissel (1996) 288–89, and Corcoran (2000) 348, 350–52. Chastagnol (1981a) 391–92, suggests that Orcistus decided to display all the documents on the pillar only after receiving Document 4, Constantine's second letter. But Professor Kent Rigsby suggests that Document 4 seems to have been engraved by a different hand; if so, then this later letter may have been added to the left side of an already existing monument. For the addition of a revised version of one chapter to a copy of Diocletian's Prices Edict already inscribed on the facade of a basilica at Aphrodisias, see Crawford (2002).

between emperor and city. This memorial of past imperial decisions was also to be a reminder of future imperial benefits. On the pillar the stonecutter engraved Constantine's initial favorable decision (Document 1) at the top of the front panel on a wide band of protruding molding. Constantine essentially repeated this decision toward the end of his letter to Ablabius (Document 2). But in the layout on the pillar, the stonecutter ensured that the repetition of this same favorable decision in the letter to Ablabius nevertheless appeared at the top of the right panel, starting just below the molding. The stonecutter even engraved four additional lines of this letter on the protruding foot of the front panel in order to ensure that Constantine's decision appeared at the top of the right panel. The top of the left panel displayed the beginning of Constantine's final favorable reply (Document 4) to the second petition from Orcistus, with the date on the molding and the names of Constantine and two of his sons just below. If this pillar was standing on the ground, then the molding at its top would have been easy to read at about eye-level. There was hence no need to read all the panels down to their bottoms. All the important information, including two versions of the initial favorable decision, the names of the emperors who verified it for a second time, and the date of the final favorable reply, was at the very top of the pillar.

The layout of the inscriptions on the pillar was hence a form of interpretive editing that emphasized the truly important bits of the documents, and as a monument the faces of the pillar could be read both down, for all the details, and sideways, for the highlights. Around the top of the pillar, on and just below the protruding molding, the three sides could be read in a horizontal arc that underscored the repeated patronage of Constantine and his sons for Orcistus.[9]

---

[9] Note that because standard editions and translations print the documents as a continuous text, first the front face of the pillar, then the right side, and then the left side, they all overlook the three-dimensional aspects of the pillar and the possibility of reading the faces of the pillar horizontally. The text and translation in Appendix 2 are printed in three columns. For a suggestive discussion of the visual aspects of ancient monuments and the interaction between images and inscriptions, see Woolf (1996).

## HONORS AND SUBORDINATION

In its first petition Orcistus hoped to influence Constantine by using several different arguments and tactics. Those tactics included a recollection of the city's honors and complaints about its current subordination.

Orcistus was a small town in a much-maligned region of central Asia Minor. Phrygia had a longstanding reputation for its deficiency in those hallmarks of Greek civilization, proper cities and classical culture, and along with Galatia it represented "rural Anatolia *par excellence.*" Orcistus was not to be deterred, however, and in its first petition it nevertheless decided to remind the emperor of its distinctions and amenities. Orcistus insisted that it had in fact once held the formal rank and title of a city, a *civitas* (or, in Greek, a *polis*). To prove that it was still worthy of such a rank, the petition noted that the town had citizens, annual magistrates, and decurions (members of the municipal council). It was an important way station on roads that led to four neighboring cities. It had the appropriate municipal buildings, including public baths, a forum, and a theater (if the seats that it claimed its citizens filled were in a theater). It also boasted of its many watermills.[10]

Confirmation for these claims about amenities is, predictably, difficult to find. Watermills were common enough among cities in the East, and Orcistus was situated on an undulating plateau crossed by small rivers that fed into the upper Sangarius River. The importance of Orcistus for ancient travelers is more dubious. The petition claimed that it was a way station on the roads to four cities: Pessinus to its northeast, Midaion to its northwest, Amorium to its south, and another city. Although the inscription broke off before naming this fourth city, it was presumably Nacolea, to the northwest of Orcistus. In fact, none of the extant itineraries mentioned Orcistus as a way station, and the

---

[10] Quotation about rural Anatolia from Mitchell (1993) 1:178, with a photograph of the barren site of Orcistus on p. 6. For a survey of the unfavorable reputation of Phrygia, see Gnoli and Thornton (1997). Chastagnol (1981b) discusses the amenities at Orcistus; see also Yegül (2000), for an excellent overview of the material requirements for cities in Roman Asia Minor.

important roads through central Asia Minor from the west all skirted by Orcistus, to the north through Dorylaeum and Midaion toward Ancyra in Galatia, to the south through Docimium and Amorium toward Ancyra. In its petition Orcistus was no doubt exaggerating its local significance, perhaps in accordance with the expectations about the composition of public eulogies. Perhaps Orcistus was just reminding Constantine that on his recent trips through central Asia Minor he had passed nearby, and that the town had shared in the heavy burden of providing for the emperor and his entourage.[11]

In its petition Orcistus mentioned that statues of former emperors decorated its forum. A block found at a nearby village was apparently the base for a statue of the emperor Commodus. The dedicatory inscription indicated that the statue had originally been set up at Orcistus: "the citizenry and senate of the people of Orcistus [honor] the god Commodus." A tall column from Orcistus inscribed with a dedication for the emperor Marcus Aurelius was most likely the pedestal for a statue of that emperor. This inscription also listed some of the current officials at Orcistus, including "collectors," "managers," and "magistrates."[12]

Another set of inscriptions recorded the deed of a gift to Orcistus from Aurelius Marcus, one of its grateful citizens, and a resolution from the

[11] For watermills in the East, see Wilson (2001), with Horden and Purcell (2000) 256: "such machines [watermills] could add to the cachet of an ancient community in the same way as did the traditional repertoire of buildings for civic munificence." For Nacolea as the fourth city, see Chastagnol (1981a) 403, (1981b) 376. For a survey of roads in central Asia Minor, see Mitchell (1993) 1:127–36. Jacques (1992) compares the claims in this petition with the recommendations of rhetoricians about the content of public orations and concludes that the petition was "un libelle rédigé selon les canons de la rhétorique classique" (p. 436); for the increasing influence of rhetoric on the style of petitions in late antiquity, see Fournet (2004).

[12] Commodus: *MAMA* 1:219, no. 416 = *IGR* 4:204, no. 550, from Baghlija, Θεὸν Κόμμο|δον Ὀρκιστη|νῶν ὁ δῆμος | καὶ ἡ γερουσί|α; in the top of the base is a life-size hollow footprint. Marcus Aurelius: *MAMA* 7:69, no. 304 = *IGR* 4:203, no. 547, from Orcistus, with a dedicatory inscription to Marcus Aurelius Antoninus from the Ὀρκιστηνοί, followed by a list of officials, εἰσηγησάμενοι, ἐπιμεληθέντες, and ἄρχοντες. Price (1984) 85–86, associates these statues with an imperial cult at Orcistus.

people of Orcistus honoring this benefactor. In late May 237 Aurelius Marcus deposited a record of his benefaction in the archives of the *demos*, the community. In appreciation for "Orcistus, my fatherland," Aurelius Marcus donated a sum of money that was to be loaned out for the benefit of his hometown. Part of the interest was to be used for the purchase of grain and the annual distribution of loaves of bread to the other citizens, and part for the funding of an annual festival on the Day of Happiness that was to be celebrated in the town's gymnasium. The first archon (the chief magistrate), two other archons, and a clerk witnessed this gift. A day or two later the community of Orcistus passed a resolution of gratitude in its *ekklesia*, its assembly, with the support of the *gerousia*, the council of elders. This resolution commended Aurelius Marcus for having already held offices and liturgies, praised him for his gift, and proposed the erection of a statue "in the most conspicuous spot." The guarantors of this resolution were the first archon, two other archons, the clerk, and the keeper of the records.[13]

These inscriptions suggest that in the late second and early third centuries Orcistus did have some of the public monuments, political institutions, and municipal magistrates that were characteristic of Greek cities. But at least by 237 it did not have the official rank of a city. In the deed of his gift Aurelius Marcus referred to Orcistus not as *polis*, a formal city, but only as *demos*, a community, and *patris*, his hometown. He also, perhaps, designated it with a word that apparently means "village." At the time Orcistus was "a township not possessing city status."[14]

---

[13] Text and translation of deed and decree, with a careful commentary, in Buckler (1937).

[14] Buckler (1937), filled out the end of the second line of the deed as ἐν Ὀρκιστῷ, Οὐάρ[ιος]; hence, the patron's name would be Varius Aurelius Marcus. Ramsay (1937), read the line instead as ἐν Ὀρκιστῷ οὐᾶι, and interpreted the rare word οὐά as the equivalent of κώμη, "village." Ruge (1939) 1094, is reluctant about both restorations of this line, but concludes that the possession of these institutions and magistrates did imply that Orcistus was already a city. Kolb (1993) 333–38, suggests that not only was Orcistus not a city in the early third century, but that it may have lied in claiming to Constantine that it had once been a city. Quotation about township from Buckler (1937) 10.

Orcistus may once have had the rank of a city, but it was still small and insignificant. At some point it had come under the control of a larger neighboring city. Another tactic that Orcistus used in its petition to Constantine was to complain about Nacolea and its aggrandizement. Nacolea was an impressive city. Its legends had apparently appropriated Hercules as its mythical founder. It had the usual municipal magistrates and institutions. It erected dedications and statues in honor of emperors. Its residents included freedmen and other officials who administered the nearby imperial estates. One of these freedmen was wealthy enough and devoted enough to his "most beloved fatherland" to bequeath funds to ensure the supply of grain and to celebrate a holiday.[15]

The hinterland of Nacolea was very large and included many small villages. These dependent villages were presumably expected to contribute to the city's expenses. In the later second century Nacolea may even have appointed an *exactor rei publicae Nacolensium*, a "collector from the community of the people of Nacolea," to demand the arrears in these contributions. Another means that Nacolea may have used to extend its influence was the cult of Zeus Bronton, Zeus the Thunderer. Many of the tombstones from Nacolea, the neighboring city of Dory-laeum about twenty-five miles to its north, and the surrounding villages included both an epitaph for the deceased and a dedication to Zeus Bronton. Some of the villages set up dedications at the shrine of Zeus Bronton near Marlakkou Kome (modern Avdan), a site in the country-side about midway between Nacolea and Dorylaeum. Nacolea exploited its dominance in this cult to extend its hegemony over neighboring set-tlements. Like other cities at the time, Nacolea was expansionist and domineering toward its neighbors.[16]

---

[15] Legends and institutions: *MAMA* 5:xxvi–xxx. Hercules as founder: Ruge (1935) 1601. Dedications to emperors: *MAMA* 5:92, no. 197, to Commodus; 93, no. 199, to Quietus. Will of P. Aelius Onesimus: *MAMA* 5:95, no. 202 = *ILS* 2.1:734, no. 7196 = Kearsley (2001) 70–71, no. 97.

[16] Extensive territory of Nacolea: *MAMA* 5:xxx–xxxi. *Exactor*: *MAMA* 5:92, no. 197, with the interpretation on pp. xxix–xxx; Mitchell (1993) 1:159, suggests that this *exactor* was another imperial magistrate "concerned with extracting revenue or agricultural products from the local property and transferring it to the treasury."

Somehow Orcistus had become another of these dependencies. One moment for such a change in its standing might be a reorganization of the provinces. Emperors were constantly tinkering with the provincial administration in Asia Minor. A new province that included the regions of Phrygia and Caria was separated from the large province of Asia by the middle of the third century, while under Diocletian Caria became a separate province and Phrygia was split into two provinces, and under Galerius Pisidia became a separate province. Some cities benefited from this sort of reorganization of the provinces, in particular the larger cities that became new metropolitan capitals. Lesser towns might also benefit. Within Phrygia the village of Meirus (about fifty miles west of Orcistus) somehow acquired the official rank of a city (a *polis*), apparently as a result of Diocletian's reorganization. Other towns might fall behind. Orcistus now complained that because Nacolea had "demanded" an alliance, it had lost its privileges "through the plundering of the more powerful."[17]

On the cult of Zeus Bronton at Nacolea and Dorylaeum, see *MAMA* 5:xxxviii–xliii. Dedications from villages: *MAMA* 5:61–63, 74–75, nos. 124–27, 157, and new finds in Drew-Bear and Naour (1990) 1992–2013.

[17] Province of Phrygia and Caria: Roueché (1981), (1989) 2–4, 12–19. Province of Caria: Roueché (1989) 21. Provinces of Phrygia Prima and Phrygia Secunda: *Laterculus Veronensis* 3.3–4, with Barnes (1982) 215, and Mitchell (1993) 2:160–1. Belke and Mersich (1990) 78, suggest that the two Phrygian provinces may have been temporarily reunited under Constantine; note that John Malalas, *Chronographia* 13.11, credited Constantine with the formation of Phrygia Salutaris. For the renaming of Phrygia Secunda as Phrygia Salutaris, see Pietri (1997b) 613. Formation of province of Pisidia dated to late 309 or 310 by Christol and Drew-Bear (1999) 70. Meirus: Anderson (1897) 422–24, for the texts of two dedications, one from the mid-third century describing Meirus as a κατοικία, the other from "after the reorganization of Diocletian" (p. 424) describing Meirus as a πόλις; Jones (1971) 69, dates the second inscription to "the reign of Constantine or one of his immediate successors." As an explanation for the subordination of Orcistus, Chastagnol (1981a) 399–400, suggests a decline in population or a reorganization of the province, Chastagnol (1981b) 373, "peut-être en punition pour motifs politiques ou politico-religieux," and Jones (2006) 161, that Nacolea had previously successfully petitioned for control.

By contrasting its amenities with its grievances Orcistus apparently hoped to activate Constantine's sympathies. The town furthermore seemed to imply that if the emperor responded favorably to its petition, a statue of him would join those of his predecessors in its forum. Other cities had proposed the same exchange of honors for favors. Athens, for instance, paid tribute to Constantine with "a statue with an inscription." By hailing him as *strategos,* "general," this dedication co-opted the emperor as a local municipal magistrate. Constantine was apparently genuinely pleased to be flattered at this most prestigious center of Greek culture: "he was more delighted than if he had been honored with the greatest of awards." In return, he instituted an annual distribution of grain for Athens. During his campaign against Licinius in 324 he assembled his fleet in Athens' harbor of Peireus. Praxagoras, a young historian from Athens, subsequently commemorated Constantine's military successes in an account composed apparently toward the end of the emperor's reign. His laudatory history of Constantine kept good company, since he also wrote histories about the kings of Athens and Alexander the Great. Even though he stressed military history, Praxagoras nevertheless insisted that Constantine had surpassed earlier emperors in virtue, excellence, and good fortune. The people of Athens continued this interaction into the next generation of emperors, when a distinguished sophist who taught at Athens asked one of Constantine's sons to donate some fertile islands to the city.[18]

In a similar fashion this series of requests and replies at Orcistus was another example of the "constant dialogue of petition and response" that had long characterized the relationships between emperors and provincial cities. By hinting at the possibility of honors in exchange for its own autonomy Orcistus was not so much merely soliciting a favor as implicitly negotiating with the emperor, "creating a process of dialogue,

---

[18] Constantine's statue at Athens: Julian, *Orat.* 1.8C-D, with Oliver (1981) 423, suggesting that Constantine in fact held the eponymous archonship at Athens. Peireus: Zosimus, *Historia nova* 2.22.2–3, 23.2. Praxagoras' "two books of history about Constantine the Great": Photius, *Bibliotheca* 62. Proaeresius' request to Constans: Eunapius, *Vitae sophistarum* 492.

and hence an interaction where language was polity, . . . implying some form of parity." Orcistus may have been a tiny, insignificant town, but it was now suggesting that it could award something that even a powerful emperor might find desirable. At a time when small cities were losing their status and importance for the central administration, the citizens of Orcistus could still behave as if they lived in a provincial capital or a noted cultural center like Athens. They were now offering the new emperor an opportunity to demonstrate his generosity and earn their esteem. In return, if Constantine enhanced the standing of Orcistus, the newly-promoted city would elevate his reputation by erecting a statue and a dedicatory inscription. A recently victorious emperor who still needed to consolidate his support in Asia Minor and a small town that was ready to acknowledge a new emperor could benefit each other.[19]

[19]   Quotation about petition and response from Millar (1983) 80; quotation about polity from Ma (1999) 241, in an excellent discussion of the interactions between Hellenistic kings and cities in Asia Minor. For the declining role of ordinary cities, see Liebeschuetz (2001) 38–39: "after the first decades of the fourth century, it was rare for run-of-the-mill cities to put up an inscribed monument to the emperors."

# "THE MOST HOLY RELIGION": PETITIONING THE EMPEROR

## CHAPTER SIX

I N ORDER TO DIFFERENTIATE ITSELF FROM NACOLEA, ONE ARGU-
ment that Orcistus used in this petition was an appeal to religious
affiliation. Constantine himself noted that this plea was the climax
of the petition, and he seems to have been quoting or paraphrasing
when he stated in his letter "that all are said to reside there as supporters
of the most holy religion." This description was obviously rather vague.
In fact, if somehow the inscribed version of this dossier had been mutilated so that the salutations were lost and the letters and petition were
anonymous, it would be quite possible to interpret this description of
the people of Orcistus in terms of a general affiliation to some pagan
cult, certainly something other than Christianity. Perhaps the people of
Orcistus were unsure about how to approach Constantine.

## TOLERATION AND PERSECUTION

Recent history would have made them wary. In the eastern empire
Diocletian, his fellow Tetrarch Galerius, and their successors had been
quite inconsistent in their pronouncements about religions. Not only
had they promoted pagan cults and ordered the persecution of Christians, but they had also flip-flopped repeatedly in their religious policies.

Even when Constantine's immediate predecessors had articulated and tried to enforce clear religious preferences, none of their policies had lasted long without further modifications.

Although he had a reputation for his scrupulous preservation of "the most traditional of religions," for most of his reign Diocletian had apparently been prepared to tolerate Christianity: "persecution was not part of Diocletian's grand design for the Roman Empire." Then Galerius, a junior emperor, pushed him into issuing edicts against Christianity. Diocletian retired in 305, and Galerius became senior emperor in the East. But in April 311 Galerius issued an edict at Nicomedia that ended persecution of Christians. In this edict he insisted that previously he had only wanted to ensure the restoration of "old laws" and "the customs of the ancestors." In the past he had tried to compel Christians to conform; now he asked them to "pray to their own God on behalf of our safety, the safety of the state, and their own safety." He then promised to reinforce his edict of toleration by sending a letter to the "judges," that is, most likely the provincial governors.[1]

Galerius died a few days later, and Maximinus, the junior emperor stationed at Antioch, rushed to take over control of Asia Minor. Even though Maximinus had nominally joined with Galerius in publishing the edict that ended persecution, he was seemingly reluctant to allow religious toleration. In previous years he had been most insistent in his enforcement of imperial edicts of persecution. At Caesarea in Palestine the emperor had even presided in person over the execution of a martyr, and on his own authority he may have issued an additional edict that required everyone to offer sacrifice. Once Maximinus had expanded his authority in 311 to include Asia Minor, however, his prefect Sabinus communicated his new preferences in a letter to provincial governors. In this letter Sabinus ordered that Christians were to be free

---

[1] Religions: Aurelius Victor, *De Caesaribus* 39.45. Quotation about Diocletian from Barnes (1981) 19. Galerius as instigator: Lactantius, *De mortibus persecutorum* 10.6, 31.1, Eusebius, *HE* 8, Appendix 1, 4, with Chapter 9. Galerius' edict of 311: Lactantius, *De mortibus persecutorum* 34, and the Greek version in Eusebius, *HE* 8.17.3–10.

from danger, and he instructed the governors to inform lesser officials that they were now to ignore "that document," that is, presumably an earlier directive ordering persecution. Even though this letter did not include all the concessions of Galerius' edict of toleration, it seems to have corresponded to the letter that Galerius had promised to send as an elaboration of his edict. Maximinus had hence started his reign in Asia Minor by proclaiming, even if begrudgingly, his toleration of Christianity.[2]

By the end of the year he had changed his mind, and he apparently let it be known that he would appreciate a demonstration of support from sympathetic pagans. Petitioners quickly picked up on this revival of the emperor's hostility to Christianity and his patronage for pagan cults. Embassies arrived from various cities, among them one from Nicomedia and another from the people of Antioch in Syria who asked "that he not allow any Christians to reside in their homeland." A petition from the province of Lycia and Pamphylia neatly juxtaposed loyalty to the traditional gods with hostility toward Christians. Addressed to Maximinus and the other emperors, this petition praised the generosity of "the gods, your kindred." It furthermore requested the imposition of restrictions on the Christians that would prevent them from disgracing "the honor that is owed to the gods," and it asked for a "divine and everlasting decree" that would curtail the activities of "the atheists."[3]

[2] Maximinus: Eusebius, *De martyribus Palaestinae* 6, Caesarea, recensio brevior 9.2, imperial edict, with Barnes (1981) 153, dating this edict to autumn of 309. Sabinus' letter: Eusebius, *HE* 9.1.3–6. Eusebius wrote the first, long recension of *De martyribus Palaestinae* between Galerius' edict of toleration and Maximinus' resumption of persecution in late 312: see Barnes (1980) 194, (1981) 149. At the time he thought that persecution was over: see Eusebius, *De martyribus Palaestinae*, recensio prolixior 13.11, referring to "the entire time of the persecution," trans. Lawlor and Oulton (1927–1928) 1:399.

[3] Eusebius, *HE* 9.2, embassy from Antioch, 9.9a.6, embassy from Nicomedia. For the fragmentary text of the petition from Lycia and Pamphylia, see the edition and reconstruction of Sahin (1994) 13–14, no. 12. Earlier reconstructions of this petition include *CIL* 3, Supplementum 3:2056, no. 12132; *OGIS* 2:252–55, no. 569; Grégoire (1922) 95–96, no. 282; *TAM* 2.3:291, no. 785; and *ILCV* 1:1–2, no. 1a-b.

In April 312 Maximinus issued a rescript from Sardis that encouraged cities to expel Christians. According to Eusebius of Caesarea, "the decrees of cities against us [Christians] were set up in the middle of cities, engraved on bronze plates, as well as the rescripts with imperial decisions on these matters." Inscriptions with fragmentary copies of Maximinus' rescript in Latin have been found at Colbasa in Pisidia and at Arycanda in Lycia, and Eusebius provided a Greek translation of part of the copy of the rescript that was on display in Tyre. In the copy of this rescript addressed to the people of Colbasa the emperor agreed that "those who have persisted in this detestable superstition are to be expelled far from your city and your territory, just as you ask." The wide circulation of this rescript suggests that Maximinus considered it to be a general edict, rather than a narrowly targeted response to the concerns of only a few specific delegations.[4]

This persecution under Maximinus certainly extended to Pontus. Some Christians fled. One bishop in Pontus spent seven years hiding in Palestine. Those who stayed were equally fearful. The paternal grandparents of Basil, who would later become the distinguished bishop of Caesarea in Cappadocia, concealed themselves for seven years in the mountains of Pontus during what Basil's brother Gregory of Nyssa would call "the time of the persecutions." Their resistance conferred such great prestige upon their family that when Gregory of Nazianzus later commemorated his friend Basil's life, he would compliment him as the descendant of "living martyrs." This resistance also became a point of reference for subsequent opposition from an uncongenial emperor, since Gregory would pointedly characterize the emperor Valens and the other imperial magistrates who had opposed Basil during the 370s as "Tetrarchs." The grandparents' lengthy seclusion would have extended during the reigns of various Tetrarchs who had controlled Asia Minor.

---

[4] Eusebius, *HE* 9.7.1, decrees, 3–14, translation. For the fragmentary texts of the rescript published at Colbasa and Arycanda, see the editions and reconstructions of Mitchell (1988) 108, 110, reprinted in *L'année épigraphique 1988* (1991) 281–82, nos. 1046–47, with the minor correction of one reading in Konrad (1989). Mitchell (1988), provides an excellent discussion of Maximinus' religious policies; for the impact of those policies at Ancyra, see Mitchell (1982).

But the only emperor whom Gregory mentioned by name was Maximinus. The persecution that he initiated "made all [previous persecutions] seem gentle by comparison, since it gushed with excessive force and was eager to assume the power of impiety."[5]

In addition to encouraging the expulsion of Christians, Maximinus actively promoted pagan cults and sacrifices. He hoped to establish a hierarchical clergy of pagan priests. Each city was to have a chief priest who would perform daily sacrifices to all the gods and, in association with the current priests of various cults, prevent Christians from meeting. For each province there was to be a priest of even higher rank, "a pontiff of sorts," who was to wear a white cloak. This hierarchical supervision of local priests was another manifestation of two distinctive characteristics of Tetrarchic rule: the extension of the reach of the imperial administration and the association of religion with imperial decisions. Maximinus expected local priests, both traditional and new, to carry out his centralizing policies, both administrative and religious.[6]

During the spring of 312 Maximinus traveled through western and southern Asia Minor on his way to Antioch in Syria. In part this procession was a public affirmation of his revitalized devotion to pagan cults, and in particular to cults of Zeus. In Caria he visited Stratonicaea, where his "divine nature" somehow "eradicated banditry." During this journey the emperor apparently visited the shrine of Zeus at Panamara, where the high priest provided a demonstration of how priests were

---

[5] Eusebius, *HE* 7.32.26–28, bishop Meletius of Pontus, 8.12.1, 6, tortures in Cappadocia and Pontus. Gregory of Nyssa, *Vita Macrinae* 2, persecutions. Gregory of Nazianzus, *Orat.* 43.5, "living martyrs," Maximinus' persecution, 6–8, seven years, mountains, 31, Tetrarchs; also the evaluation in *Orat.* 4.96: Diocletian was the first to discredit Christians, Galerius was worse, and Maximinus surpassed both as a persecutor. For the memories of persecution in Basil's family, see Van Dam (2003a) 15–18, 34–39.

[6] Priests: Eusebius, *HE* 9.4.2–3; pontiff: Lactantius, *De mortibus persecutorum* 36.4–5, with Nicholson (1994) 9, "Traditional worship was being adapted to new political fashions and realities." For one prominent pagan priest in Phrygia, see Mitchell (1993) 2:47, 64.

expected to behave under this new regime by subsidizing an especially lavish celebration. Like the other Tetrarchs, Maximinus seems to have cultivated a special relationship, even identification, with the highest deity, Zeus or Jupiter. Devotion to Zeus or Jupiter was a sign of political loyalty, not just to Diocletian but also to the ideals of the Tetrarchy: "a friend of Zeus was his friend; an enemy of Zeus, his enemy." Just before his death Diocletian had supposedly acknowledged Maximinus as his preferred heir. Maximinus had already been selected as a junior emperor in the presence of a statue of Jupiter, and he had already received the imperial title of Jovius that associated him with Jupiter or Zeus. One local tradition claimed that Sardis had been the birthplace of Zeus; in the rescript that Maximinus had issued just recently at Sardis he had praised Zeus as the protector of cities, cults, and families. In his final battle against Licinius he would make a vow to Jupiter to exterminate the Christian name if he were victorious. Now, after his visit to Caria, the dedication listing the accomplishments of the high priest at Panamara pointedly honored Maximinus as "Jovius."[7]

By now Maximinus was the only Jovian emperor left in the eastern provinces. Since cults of Zeus, in various guises, were so common throughout the Greek East, other cities too would most likely have noted the emperor's patronage for cults of Zeus or Jupiter. At Antioch one of Maximinus' supporters erected a statue of Zeus Philios, Zeus the Friend, and produced oracles against the Christians. With its cult of Zeus Bronton perhaps Nacolea too was feeling flush enough to try to tighten its control over dependent towns like Orcistus.[8]

[7] Dedication for M. Sempronius Auruncius Theodotus at Panamara: Sahin (1981) 170–1, no. 310; earlier edition in *SIG*[3] 2:617–19, no. 900. Friend and enemy: Libanius, *Orat.* 18.125, in a description of Julian's religious policies. True heir: *Epitome de Caesaribus* 39.7, "Diocletian repeatedly insisted that he had favored Maxentius and now favored Maximinus." Statue of Jupiter: Lactantius, *De mortibus persecutorum* 19.2. Sardis as birthplace of Zeus: *Anthologia graeca* 9.645, with the excellent commentary of Weiss (1995). Rescript at Sardis: Eusebius, *HE* 9.7.7. Vow: Lactantius, *De mortibus persecutorum* 46.2.

[8] Zeus Philios at Antioch: Eusebius, *HE* 9.3, 9.11.5, with Mitchell (1993) 2:22, "The most widely worshipped god in central Asia Minor was certainly Zeus."

By the end of 312, however, Maximinus was again backpedaling. After his victory over his imperial rival Maxentius at Rome in October, Constantine joined with Licinius, the emperor in the Balkans, to issue another law on behalf of Christians. Maximinus responded with a letter in which he again ordered the provincial governors to tolerate Christians, even if again in a rather indirect manner: "no one has the authority to harass our provincials with insults and blows." Yet the emperor himself was apparently the worst offender against his subjects: "he treated the East as his toy." After Licinius attacked and defeated his forces in the early spring of 313, Maximinus made one last attempt to save himself by issuing yet another edict of toleration. In this edict he allowed freedom of religious belief generally, and more specifically the right for Christians to build churches and reclaim confiscated properties. By now Maximinus had run out of options, and he soon suffered a miserable death. Some of his supporters were executed. His memory was literally erased, as public portraits and statues were smashed and disfigured. Decades later in Cappadocia "his icons are still on display in public places, and they publicize the mutilation of his body." Cities in the eastern empire that had honored Maximinus had to start over. Now they set up public proclamations that declared him to be "the enemy of all" and "the tyrant who hated God." They also had to deal with a new emperor and his preferences.[9]

In the summer of 313 Licinius started his reign in the eastern empire by promulgating his version of the edict of toleration that he and Constantine had agreed upon some months earlier. Licinius was perhaps

---

[9] Eusebius, *HE* 9.9.12, law of Constantine and Licinius, 9a.1–9, Maximinus' letter of late 312 (quotation from 9.9a.9), 10.6–11, Maximinus' edict of May 313, 11.2–6, supporters, portraits, proclamations. Lactantius, *De mortibus persecutorum* 38.7, toy, 50, execution of Maximinus' supporters. For an imperial edict limiting accusations of treason, see Riccobono (1941) 458–61, no. 94, and *CTh* 9.5.1, with Corcoran (1996) 190–91, 288–91, (2000) 349–52, discussing the attribution of this edict to Licinius in the aftermath of the purges of Maximinus' supporters in early 314, although Corcoran (2002), (2004) 66–70, now assigns this edict to the initiative of Galerius in the summer of 305. Icons in Cappadocia: Gregory of Nazianzus, *Orat.* 4.96.

purposefully vague about his underlying religious orientation, since this edict justified its directives by insisting upon respect only for "the divinity" or "the highest divinity." It did nevertheless allow everyone, Christians specifically, to worship as they pleased, and it insisted upon the restoration of property to Christians. Now it seemed safe to be a Christian. In Asia Minor bishops resumed meeting in councils to discuss doctrinal issues and church order, at Caesarea perhaps in 314, at Ancyra most likely in 314, at a city in Bithynia to evaluate the teachings of Arius. Since many of the canons of the council of Ancyra considered penalties for clerics and others who had lapsed and performed sacrifices, these bishops presumably thought that the persecutions were over and it was time to deal with their aftermath. Becoming a bishop was now a more attractive career for municipal notables. Marcus Julius Eugenius had married a senator's daughter and was serving on the staff of the governor of Pisidia. When Maximinus had issued an edict that "Christians were to sacrifice and not to leave the civil service," Eugenius endured "very many ordeals, often repeated" under his governor. Severus, "a glorious prize winner of the Father in heaven," apparently did not survive this persecution. Eugenius did, but abandoned his career in the imperial bureaucracy. Instead, "at the wish of the almighty God" he soon became bishop of Laodicea Catacecaumene in Pisidia, most likely in succession to Severus. During his episcopacy Eugenius celebrated his new local distinction by constructing a magnificent church surrounded by colonnades, courtyards, a fountain, and an entrance gate, all decorated with paintings, mosaics, and sculptures.[10]

Eugenius built this church perhaps during the decade of Licinius' reign in Asia Minor. But since he served as bishop for twenty-five years, he may also have waited until the reign of Constantine. For over the

[10] Licinius' edict: Lactantius, *De mortibus persecutorum* 48.2–12, *summa divinitas*, Eusebius, *HE* 10.5.1–14, τὸ θεῖον. Council of Caesarea: Barnes (1981) 65, and Parvis (2001a). Council of Ancyra: Logan (1992), and Chapter 11, for the role of bishop Marcellus. Council in Bithynia: Sozomen, *HE* 1.15.10 = Urkunde 5, ed. Opitz (1934–1935) 12, with Chapter 10, on the Arian controversy. *MAMA* 1:89–92, no. 170, epitaph of Eugenius, no. 171, epitaph of Severus, with Wischmeyer (1990), emphasizing the larger context of municipal notables, and Tabbernee (1997a) 426–44, linking the two epitaphs in a single narrative.

years, as Licinius' tension with Constantine increased, so did his intolerance of Christians. With the hope of victory over his rival Licinius was thought to have turned to pagan sacrifices and to have consulted the famous oracle of Apollo at Didyma. By the early 320s he had ordered soldiers and imperial magistrates to offer sacrifices during pagan festivals or lose their ranks and offices, and he had imposed restrictions on bishops and their Christian communities. Eventually provincial governors sanctioned the destruction of churches and the execution of some bishops in Pontus, and some people again fled into the mountains.[11]

The original Tetrarchic emperors and their successors in the East, Diocletian, Galerius, Maximinus, and Licinius, had all oscillated between tolerating Christianity and persecuting Christianity. In the mid-fourth century the pagan orator Themistius would comment to the Christian emperor Jovian that in matters of religious piety the "human edicts" of emperors were "momentary constraints," "as often removed by the passage of time as imposed." The religious policies of the Tetrarchic emperors had certainly exemplified that tendency to vacillation. As a result, because the emperors' preferences about pagan cults and Christianity had fluctuated so rapidly, cities in the eastern provinces could never be sure about how, or even whether, to refer to religion in their petitions.[12]

## CONSTANTINE'S DUPLICITY

Constantine had meanwhile not been seen in the eastern provinces for decades. He had served in the army as a tribune, a junior officer, and seems to have spent most of his time at the courts of Diocletian or Galerius as they had traveled throughout the East, campaigned in Mesopotamia, or resided at various cities such as Antioch. In early 303 Diocletian and Galerius had begun issuing a series of edicts that had revived persecution of Christians. Some soldiers, including tribunes, had destroyed the church at Nicomedia; Constantine himself would

---

[11] Pagan sacrifices, oracle of Apollo: Sozomen, *HE* 1.7.2–3; Licinius' intolerance: Eusebius, *HE* 10.8.10–19, *Vita Constantini* 1.51–53, 2.1–2, with Barnes (1981) 70–72.

[12] Constraints: Themistius, *Orat.* 5.67c-d.

later admit that he had been at Diocletian's court in Nicomedia at the time. In the spring of 305, shortly after Diocletian's retirement, Constantine had left to join his father in Gaul. His previous appearances in the eastern empire had not hinted at support for Christianity. If anything, Christians might have remembered Constantine as yet another loyal supporter of a hostile imperial regime.[13]

Years later, when he finally returned to the East after his victory over Licinius in 324, Christians in Asia Minor might well be cautious of their new emperor's intentions. Both Maximinus and Licinius had initially tolerated Christianity when they had assumed control over Asia Minor, and both had ended up, sooner or later, harassing Christians. Even a churchman like Eusebius of Caesarea who admired Constantine was all too aware of the fickleness of imperial patronage with regard to religion. When he published the first edition of his *Ecclesiastical History* in 313 or soon afterward, he claimed that Constantine had summoned the assistance of God and Jesus Christ in his victory over Maxentius at Rome in 312, and he credited both Constantine and Licinius with having forced Maximinus to end his persecution of Christians. A few years later, before autumn 316, he produced a revised edition of *History* that included a new book in which he cited six imperial letters issued in support of Christianity. Constantine was the sole author of five, but he and Licinius together issued the letter that granted religious toleration to both Christians and everyone else in 313. Since by then Licinius had become the emperor for all the eastern provinces, at the time Eusebius would presumably have been more concerned about his patronage for Christianity, and not necessarily about Constantine's support. Licinius' edicts affected him and his see directly, not Constantine's.[14]

---

[13]  Tribunes and church: Lactantius, *De mortibus persecutorum* 12.2. Constantine at Nicomedia: Constantine, *Oratio ad sanctorum coetum* 25.2.

[14]  Eusebius, *HE* 9.9.2, Constantine's summons, 12, Constantine and Licinius; 10.5–7, new letters; Latin version of Constantine's and Licinius' rescript in Lactantius, *De mortibus persecutorum* 48.2–12. For the first edition of Eusebius' *HE*, published in 313–314, see Louth (1990) and Burgess (1997) 483–86, accepted by Drake (2000) 356; for subsequent revisions and editions, Barnes (1981) 150; with additional discussion in the Introduction to "Emperor and God."

But by the time Eusebius revised his history once more, Licinius had turned against Christians, and Constantine had defeated him. Once Eusebius had seen the future, he quietly corrected his earlier account by transforming Licinius from a patron of Christianity into a persecutor. In this case he could simply slip into his historical narrative a few additional derogatory chapters and pejorative comments about Licinius. The possibility of rewriting and revising his earlier interpretations ensured that Eusebius' historical perspective would never be totally wrong. In real life, however, choosing the wrong side had more bloody consequences. As among Maximinus' supporters at the end of his reign, now another bloodletting among Licinius' supporters followed his defeat.[15]

Constantine moved swiftly to reassure people in the eastern empire by trying to recruit some of Licinius' supporters. Since Licinius had been reigning alone in the East for over a decade, by now all of the imperial magistrates in the eastern provinces were his appointees. Rather than replacing them immediately, Constantine decided to use their expertise and networks of patronage. As the most notable example of his policy of reconciliation, he now honored Julius Julianus with a consulship in 325. Julius Julianus had served for almost a decade as praetorian prefect under Licinius. During his long tenure he had been "an upright and wise prefect whom his victorious enemy [Constantine] had respected and whom he had encouraged his own magistrates to consider as a model for administration." Soon Constantine even blended him and his family into his own family, when Julius Julianus' daughter married Julius Constantius, one of Constantine's half-brothers. After his victory Constantine had pointedly reached out to one of Licinius' most prominent supporters. Julius Julianus hence became the namesake of a future emperor in the Constantinian dynasty, his grandson Julian.[16]

---

[15] Executions: Eusebius, *Vita Constantini* 2.18; for the execution of Martinianus, who served as Licinius' *magister officiorum* and briefly as Caesar, see *PLRE* 1:563, "Martinianus 2."

[16] Wise prefect and marriage of Basilina: Libanius, *Orat.* 18.9; with Barnes (1982) 102–3, for Julius Julianus' career, Grünewald (1990) 135–36, for Constantine's accommodation, and Kelly (2006), on Constantine's overtures to provincial notables in the East. The pagan philosopher Sopater, who had visited the court of

At the same time, however, Constantine quickly distinguished himself from his predecessor. He recalled Licinius' opponents from exile and restored confiscated property. He soon issued edicts that invalidated or modified Licinius' edicts. He also sent letters to the provincials in the East. In one he explained his support for Christianity and attributed his military success to the support of the Christian God. With the assistance of the all-powerful God he had been able to eliminate "the evil that had previously subjected all mankind," that is, Licinius and his regime. As Eusebius commented when he quoted this letter, then "people in our regions" received confirmation of what "they had previously learned through hearsay about what was happening in the other half of the Roman empire." From now on Constantine's opinion mattered in the eastern provinces. Eusebius cited the copies of the letters that had been sent specifically to the provincials of Palestine, or perhaps directly to himself. Presumably the court had sent similar copies to other regions and other bishops. Perhaps the publication of these letters and edicts, with their promise of the emperor's new accessibility and generosity, now motivated the people of Orcistus to appeal for Constantine's assistance.[17]

But people could also see that the new emperor's word might nevertheless be suspect. Throughout his reign Constantine seemed to treat marriages less as guarantees of alliances with fellow emperors and more as pretexts for hostility. His hands were thoroughly stained with "the blood of relatives." During his rise as emperor in the western provinces he had allied himself with Maximian and Maxentius by marrying Maximian's daughter. Then he had turned against his in-laws. In 316 he had proposed that his brother-in-law Bassianus should become the Caesar in Italy; but after Bassianus was soon accused of conspiring

Licinius, later became an adviser to Constantine: see Eunapius, *Vitae sophistarum* 462–63, with the discussion of Barnes (1978a).

[17]  Invalidation: *CTh* 15.14.1–2. Modification: see Barnes (1982) 234–37, for an edict issued in autumn of 324 that changed the age of exemption from fiscal burdens. Eusebius, *Vita Constantini* 2.22, confirmation, 30–39, exiles and property, 42, the evil. For Constantine's presentation of himself after his victory over Licinius, see Pietri (1997a) 263–72.

with Licinius, Constantine ordered his execution. His relationship with Licinius, another brother-in-law, followed a similar pattern of initial friendship followed by open hostility. Critics blamed the emperor's customary deceitfulness: "as usual, Constantine disregarded his agreement with Licinius."[18]

For people in the East the final fate of Licinius in particular contradicted any claims about Constantine's trustworthiness. In the past Licinius had sealed an alliance by marrying Constantia, Constantine's half-sister; then he had become Constantine's rival. After his victory in September 324, Constantine had at first displayed his clemency. He granted Constantia's request for mercy on behalf of her husband, shared a meal with Licinius, and then sent him to Thessalonica. But by the end of the year he issued an edict that branded Licinius as a "tyrant" and rescinded all of his rival's legislation. Soon he had his brother-in-law executed. The circumstances of this execution may have been murky, connected perhaps with a riot among soldiers or the possibility of rebellion, but it was certainly apparent that Constantine had broken the sanctity of his promise. His detractors even thought that this particular change of mind was indicative of a fundamental flaw in the emperor's character. "He trampled on his oath; this was customary for him." Even Constantine's close advisers were concerned about trying to control his "impulsiveness" and his tendency to behave like "an undisciplined mob." As a result, if it was apparent that his personal and political guarantees were unreliable, if his decisions seemed consistently fickle and mutable, then the durability of his religious patronage was perhaps equally suspect.[19]

---

[18] Blood of relatives: Julian, *Caesares* 336B, explaining Constantine's interest in the promise of cleansing offered by Jesus. For Constantine's treatment of Maximian and Maxentius, see Chapter 3. Bassianus, husband of Constantine's half-sister Anastasia: *Origo Constantini imperatoris* 5.14–15, with additional discussion in Chapter 3. As usual: Zosimus, *Historia nova* 2.18.1. But note that Praxagoras of Athens claimed that it had been Licinius who had violated his oaths to Constantine about preserving their treaty: see Photius, *Bibliotheca* 62.

[19] Mercy, meal, and execution: *Origo Constantini imperatoris* 5.28–29, with Barnes (1981) 214, for speculation about the circumstances. For the possible role of bishop

## SECTARIANISM

The people of Orcistus could hence view the beginning of Constantine's reign with both high hopes and wary concern. They could anticipate having ready access to the imperial court, since the new emperor had already traveled near their town on his journeys through Asia Minor to and from Antioch, and the ecumenical council planned for mid-325 was scheduled to be held at Ancyra (but then of course moved to Nicaea). They had done their homework in order to learn about Constantine's most recent imperial titles and the current ranks of his sons. They probably knew that Constantine had pointedly distinguished himself from some of Licinius' policies and had announced his preference for Christianity. On the other hand, his recent predecessors had been fickle in their religious policies, and Constantine had already shown that he was untrustworthy with regard to his oath to Licinius. Once he changed his mind, Constantine furthermore wanted to pretend that nothing was different. After his victory over his rival he ordered the removal of images of Licinius and his son: "even their names were forgotten." If he were to be as dismissive about cults, then a petition that included a specific appeal to a particular religious affiliation was risky. As a result, although the people of Orcistus wanted to take advantage of Constantine's goodwill at the beginning of his reign in the eastern empire, their description of themselves as "supporters of the most holy religion" was perhaps intentionally cryptic.[20]

Eusebius of Nicomedia in these negotiations, see Chapter 10. Tyrant: *CTh* 15.14.1, with the emendation of the date to December 16, 324, by Seeck (1919) 99. Broken promise: Eutropius, *Breviarum* 10.6.1, "contra religionem sacramenti"; Jerome, *Chronicon* s.a. 323, "contra ius sacramenti." Customary: Zosimus, *Historia nova* 2.28.2. Note also Themistius, *Orat.* 6.83b, for a contrast between Constantine, who stripped the purple robe from his brother-in-law, and Valentinian, who shared it with his brother. Eunapius, *Vitae sophistarum* 462, impulsiveness, 464, mob.

[20] For the confusion over Constantine's titles after 324, see Grünewald (1990) 136: "Bei den Provinzialen gab es nach dem *victor*-Erlaß anfänglich Unsicherheiten im Umgang mit der neuen Kaisertitulatur." Council originally scheduled for Ancyra: Urkunde 18.15, 20, ed. Opitz (1934–1935) 40–42. Names: Eusebius, *HE* 10.9.5,

Modern scholars consistently state that the people of Orcistus were Christians. Such an interpretation assumes that by now Constantine would deal favorably only with Christians. In fact, the emperor was apparently still quite open-minded, and in another letter sent to the eastern provincials soon after his victory over Licinius he had preached religious toleration. Even though he again stated his preference for Christianity, he did not insist upon universal conversion. "Those who persist in their errors are to receive a similar gift of peace and tranquility as the believers." Constantine did continue to support non-Christians occasionally. He allowed the people of Hispellum in Italy to construct a new temple, and one pagan priest from Athens thanked him for having funded some of his research in Egypt: "I am grateful to the gods and to the most pious emperor Constantine." Soon after the council at Nicaea the emperor issued an edict to all the provincials in which he hoped to secure the goodwill of "the highest divinity." Even though Constantine of course promoted Christianity, he also tolerated pagan cults and used ambiguous language to describe his own beliefs. At the beginning of his reign in the East, Constantine was as vague about his religious preferences as Licinius had been at first; and memories of how Licinius had subsequently backpedaled on his toleration for Christianity were still fresh.[21]

with Corcoran (1993), (1996) 274–92, on the removal of Licinius' name from the collections of laws.

[21] For the common, but unwarranted, assumption that the people of Orcistus were Christians, see Dörries (1954) 214, "vor allem ist es ... das christliche Bekenntnis der Petenten als ausschlaggebendes Argument"; Lane Fox (1986) 587, "its totally Christian population"; Tabbernee (1997a) 99, "no reason to doubt that Orkistos was, at least, predominantly Christian"; Mitchell (1998) 53, "its inhabitants were all Christians"; Galsterer (2000) 356, "the people were fervent Christians"; Bleckmann (2006) 17, "the Christian community of Orcistus"; and Edwards (2006) 139, "the unanimous Christianity of the inhabitants ... of Orcistus." Having suggested that Orcistus may have exaggerated in claiming that it had once had the rank of a city, Kolb (1993) 339, must conclude that Constantine's favorable response was motivated entirely by religion: "Er wollte den Orkistenern den polis-Status verleihen, weil sie Christen waren." Letter to provincials: Eusebius, Vita Constantini 2.56.1, with Drake (1976) 63, stressing that Constantine distinguished his personal

Since the citizens of Orcistus may have been uncertain, or uneasy, about Constantine's religious beliefs, they apparently decided that the best tactic was to respond with similar vagueness about their own religious allegiance. Such an imprecise indication was certainly open to different interpretations. In the rugged highlands of central Asia Minor, including Phrygia, many cities still retained their pagan cults. "The inscriptions ... bear eloquent witness to the vitality of paganism at Dorylaeum and Nacolea." These cities might have thought that it was still permissible, even preferable, to honor Constantine through a pagan cult. In Pisidia the citizens of Termessus set up a statue of Constantine, dedicated to him as "all-seeing Helios." They were not alone in associating Constantine with the Sun-god. Shortly after Licinius' defeat the aristocratic poet Porphyrius hoped to ensure his return from exile by presenting the victorious Constantine with a collection of poems. Rather than highlighting Constantine's Christianity, these poems placed his achievements in the context of allusions to classical literature and pagan deities: "in the glow of his purple robes the conqueror must be venerated as the Sun." Porphyrius was in fact successful with his praise of Constantine as the Sun, since he was allowed to return. Likewise, since Constantine himself continued his devotion to the Sun-god Helios well after his victory over Licinius, the citizens of Termessus may have thought that their dedication flattered the emperor. The long-term endurance of Constantine's current preference for Christianity was not readily apparent so quickly after his takeover of the eastern empire. As a result, even though Orcistus referred to its religious devotion in its first petition requesting autonomy from Nacolea, it is not necessary to

beliefs from his imperial policy. For the temple at Hispellum, see Chapters 1–3. Pagan priest Nicagoras: *OGIS* 2:462, no. 721, with Fowden (1987), arguing that Constantine sent Nicagoras to Egypt in 326 to negotiate the acquisition of an obelisk from a shrine at Thebes, Lane Fox (1986) 640–41, speculating that Constantine had sent Nicagoras as an ornithologist to find the mythical phoenix, and Bassett (2004) 43, suggesting that Nicagoras was scouting for monuments to be moved to Constantinople. "Summa divinitas": *CTh* 9.1.4, issued from Nicomedia in September 325, with Digeser (2000) 125–33, for a survey of Constantine's inclusive religious policies after 324.

conclude that that affiliation was without doubt Christianity. Perhaps its citizens were in fact hinting at a lingering devotion to paganism behind the vague description of their religious affiliation. In that case their petition was not an attempt to identify with Constantine's Christianity, but a test of his declaration of toleration.[22]

Even if the citizens of Orcistus were Christians, the exact nature of their Christianity is open to question. Phrygia in particular had a reputation for both the variety and the intermingling of its many religious cults. "In Phrygia pagan, Christian, and Jew, living together in the same communities, . . . found ways and devices to accommodate one another's beliefs." As in other provinces throughout the Roman empire, in Phrygia too over the centuries Christians had adapted to local circumstances by adopting, modifying, and opposing local beliefs. The vague description of religious devotion in this petition from Orcistus could have embraced, and disguised, different scenarios about their Christianity.[23]

One possibility is that the citizens of Orcistus had only recently converted. After Constantine sent out letters in which he suggested that people should abandon their temples, all the citizens of Maiuma on the coast of Palestine converted to Christianity. They must then have appealed for the emperor's assistance, since he responded with a rescript in which he detached the town from the control of Gaza and bestowed upon it the rank of a city. In central Asia Minor some provincials likewise now suddenly took stock of the future. Gregory

---

[22] Quotation about paganism from *MAMA* 5:xxxiii. Dedication at Termessus: *TAM* 3.1:39, no. 45: Κωνσταντείνω Σεβ(αστῶ) | Ἡλίω | Παντεπόπτη | ὁ δῆμος; with Wallraff (2001), on Constantine and Helios after 324. Constantine as Sol: Porphyrius, *Carm.* 18.25, with Chapter 2, for the date. For a suggestion that Christianity did not exist at Orcistus before Constantine's reign, see *MAMA* 7:xxxviii: "but for Constantine's statement, it would have to be classed . . . as a blank on the early-Christian map of Phrygia." Mitchell (1998), emphasizes Constantine's limited role in the transformation of cities in Asia Minor: "central imperial decisions were not a decisive factor in determining local religious practices" (p. 66).

[23] Quotation from Mitchell (1993) 2:49, in by far the best survey of religious cults in central Asia Minor.

the Elder, the father of the famous theologian Gregory of Nazianzus, was a local notable at Nazianzus in Cappadocia who belonged to a sect of Hypsistarians. These "worshippers of the Most High" had formed a syncretistic religious cult by combining Jewish practices with pagan monotheism. But once Gregory the Elder observed all the bishops who had joined the Christian emperor at the council of Nicaea, he seems to have sensed that Christians, and in particular bishops and clerics, were about to benefit from imperial patronage. Gregory the Elder quickly converted to Christianity, and in 329 became bishop of his hometown. His conversion had certainly helped to improve his local standing. In a similar fashion, and at about the same time, the citizens of Orcistus may have hoped that a new devotion to Christianity would be the clinching argument in favor of autonomy and promotion. Like Maiuma, their town too could be liberated from the domination of a neighboring city. In this scenario their petition represented a celebration of their own fresh conversion.[24]

Another possibility is that they had been Christians of some sort for a long time. Christianity had spread to much of Phrygia already by the second century, although in many different versions that later ecclesiastical historians, once they had seen the new standards of orthodoxy, of course dismissed as "outlandish heresies" that "slithered over Asia and Phrygia like poisonous serpents." Perhaps the most notorious of these older versions of Christianity was the "New Prophecy," later known as Montanism but repeatedly stigmatized as the "Phrygian heresy." The prophet Montanus had begun preaching in northwestern Phrygia in the later second century, and by the third century there were Montanist communities in Dorylaeum and Cotiaeum, neighboring cities to the north and west of Nacolea and Orcistus. It is worth noting in passing that whatever the theological value of Montanist teachings, the acceptance of this new cult might confer some of the same political rewards

---

[24] Maiuma: see Chapter 3. Gregory the Elder: Gregory of Nazianzus, *Orat.* 18.5, with Van Dam (2003a) 41–47, on Gregory the Elder and the Hypsistarians; for the various cults of the Highest God, see Trebilco (1991) 127–44, 163–64, and Mitchell (1993) 2:49–51, (1999).

that Orcistus would later request from Constantine. Lacking amenities or direct access to major roads, small cities might try to enhance their standing by appealing for the patronage of an emperor or an imperial magistrate or by becoming the center of a new religious cult. Pepousa and Tymion, both thoroughly nondescript towns in Phrygia, could claim a huge improvement in their local reputations once Montanus renamed each of them as "Jerusalem." In the delirium of his ecstatic visions Montanus even hoped to assemble people "from everywhere" in these two "tiny cities in Phrygia."[25]

Other distinctive Christian communities in Phrygia before Constantine's reign can be distinguished by unique phrases on their inscriptions, such as the "Christians for Christians" sectarians in western Phrygia and the group in southern Phrygia using the "Eumeneian formula" that left grave robbers to God's judgment. By the reign of Constantine the schismatic Novatian church had become prominent in Phrygia. Although its theology was quite similar to the doctrines eventually approved as orthodox, Novatian Christians differentiated themselves by their rigorous standards of conduct and moral discipline. Phrygia was one notable stronghold for Novatian Christianity, in particular at Cotiaeum. In fact, later in the fourth century some Novatian bishops met in a council at a small Phrygian town located in the headwaters of the Sangarius River near Orcistus. As a result, already in the early fourth century, and indeed in subsequent centuries too, there was certainly no uniform version of Christianity in Phrygia or in neighboring regions in the central highlands. Near Laodicea Catacecaumene, for instance, the priest commemorated on his tombstone as a member of "the holy church of the orthodox" cannot be assigned with confidence to any particular version of Christianity. All Christian sects thought of themselves as "orthodox," "catholic," and "apostolic." In Phrygia likewise diverse

---

[25] Montanism: Eusebius, *HE* 5.14.1, heresies, serpents, 18.2, Jerusalem, tiny cities, 19.2, New Prophecy. For the survival of Montanism in Phrygia before and during Constantine's reign, see Trevett (1996) 198–232, and Tabbernee (1997a) 219–334, 345–47, 359–444; the location of Pepouza and Tymion, Trevett (1996) 15–26, and Tabbernee (2003). Strobel (1980), emphasizes the distinctly Phrygian character of Montanism.

Christian communities, whose respective beliefs and behavior differed considerably, dotted the entire region around Nacolea and Orcistus.[26]

Under the Tetrarchs some Christian communities in Phrygia had suffered. During one outbreak of hostility soldiers had burned a village in Phrygia and slaughtered all its inhabitants. "Everyone in the village was a Christian." Even though such persecution ended under Constantine, his reign now posed a different problem for Christians, since it was not obvious which variety of Christianity he would endorse as orthodox. Orcistus sent its first petition at about the time of the council of Nicaea. At a moment of such doctrinal instability, when it was not clear that the emperor himself had a definite sense of his theological preferences, even a town that had been Christian for some time might have wanted to dissemble about its beliefs. If its version of Christianity was considered heterodox, then its inhabitants could still hope to be treated like Acesius, one of the leaders of the Novatian church. At the council of Nicaea, Acesius insisted that differences over discipline, even when there were no differences over doctrine, might still be grounds for schism. Constantine was nonplussed, but nevertheless respectful. On the other hand, if its version of Christianity was considered orthodox, then the inhabitants of Orcistus could present their oppression under Nacolea as the equivalent of persecution. In that case they could hope to appear before Constantine like the Egyptian bishop who had suffered grievously during the Tetrarchic persecutions. At the council of Nicaea, Constantine honored this bishop and kissed his scars.[27]

[26] Novatianism: survey in Mitchell (1993) 2:96–104. Council at Pazon: Socrates, *HE* 4.28.18, commenting that the bishop of Cotiaeum, who did not attend, was one of the leaders of the Novatian church. Belke and Mersich (1990) 357, suggest that the council may be dated to ca. 368; for a proposed location of Pazon, see the map in Mitchell (1993) 2:94. Priest: *MAMA* 1:154, no. 290, dated to the later fourth century; with Hübner (2005) 197, for other examples from nearby.

[27] Burning of village: Eusebius, *HE* 8.9.1; also Lactantius, *Institutiones divinae* 5.11.10, noting that one man had demonstrated his impiety by "burning an entire community in Phrygia with its meeting house." The suggestion of Chastagnol (1981a) 411, that this burned village was Orcistus, is quite implausible. Acesius: Socrates, *HE* 1.10, Sozomen, *HE* 1.22; also *CTh* 16.5.2, Constantine's grant of concessions

A longstanding commitment to some form of Christianity, a recent conversion, a lingering devotion to pagan cults: for whatever reason, in their petition the citizens of Orcistus were quite vague in their description of their religious preferences. They wanted to use their devotion to "the most holy religion" as an argument for receiving autonomy from the control of Nacolea, but they were also seemingly reluctant to be too precise about its exact characteristics. They could be certain about the current imperial titles of Constantine and his sons, but not about his religious preferences. In their petition the citizens of Orcistus had apparently decided to let Constantine understand their religious affiliation to be whatever he wanted to think. Vagueness had its rewards. As long as they were liberated from the control of Nacolea, their new benefactor could believe whatever he wished about their religious beliefs.

to the Novatians issued in September 326. Bishop Paphnutius: Rufinus, *HE* 10.4, Socrates, *HE* 1.11. Note that the council of Nicaea also did not condemn Montanism by name: see Jerome, *Ep.* 84.4.

At some time Constantine did issue to provincial governors an edict against heretics, and he sent a letter "to heretics" that criticized their practices and explained the penalties of the edict. In the letter he mentioned, among other heretics, the Novatians and "those named from the regions of Phrygia" (i.e. "Cataphrygians"): see Eusebius, *Vita Constantini* 3.63–66. If dated just before or after the council of Nicaea, then the edict preceded Constantine's subsequent toleration; but if dated to the later 320s, then it marked a shift toward intolerance: see the survey of possible dates in Cameron and Hall (1999) 306–7. Whether dated early or late, the edict and the accompanying letter again indicated Constantine's vacillation about religious affairs.

# "THE ROMAN LANGUAGE": LATIN AND THE GREEK EAST

## CHAPTER SEVEN

O RCISTUS USED YET ANOTHER SHREWD TACTIC IN ITS PETI- tion. This tactic was unstated but readily apparent: the petition was in Latin. In its petition Orcistus described itself as located on the frontier between eastern Phrygia and western Galatia. In this borderland several languages were common. The native language of Phrygian remained in use well into the Roman empire. Not only were some dedications inscribed in Phrygian, but in the later fourth century a bishop whose mother was from the region was still able to preach in Phrygian. Latin was the language of Roman imperial administration. Some local inscriptions were in Latin, primar- ily milestones and some of the dedications to emperors. The imperial slaves and freedmen who settled in Nacolea presumably used Latin in their official communications, and one freedman inscribed some of the provisions of his will in Latin. But "in Phrygia Latin never became a popular language." Greek culture trumped imperial administration, even Roman administration. The common spoken language, certainly for local notables and probably for most ordinary people too, was now

Greek, and most municipal and private inscriptions in the region were in Greek.[1]

## LANGUAGE OF CULTURE AND LANGUAGE OF POWER

Since languages were such pointed indicators of essential ideas about power, administration, culture, and religion, their imposition and inter-action were always contested. As in other empires, the use of a new, unfamiliar language was a sign of cultural and political domination, as the conquerors insisted that the conquered conform to their prefer-ences, or as new subjects decided it was to their advantage to follow the lead of their rulers. At the beginning of the fifth century bishop Augus-tine of Hippo would candidly acknowledge that the use of Latin in the imperial administration had reflected political superiority. "The ruling city imposed not only its authority but also its own language on con-quered peoples, as a means of ensuring peace in society." In the eastern provinces earlier emperors had remained committed to the use of Latin, even when it undermined the effectiveness of administration in regions where Latin was not the common spoken language. Later emperors maintained this awkward policy, despite the bothersome consequences. In the later fourth century, for instance, the famous Greek rhetorician Libanius would simply dismiss one governor of Syria, a native of north-ern Italy who knew no Greek, as a "fraud." Augustine himself recognized the contradiction when he conceded that this shortsighted policy was self-defeating, since in fact an inability to communicate had led to wars and bloodshed. Elevating a symbolic display of power over the need for practicality could become a liability, for both imperial administrators and their subjects in the provinces. As a result, in the East the provincials

[1] For the borderland between Phrygia and Galatia, note also Zosimus, *Historia nova* 4.7.3, "Galatia next to Phrygia." Preaching in Phrygian: Socrates, *HE* 5.23.8. *MAMA* 1:xiii, "Roman citizens and officials in the Imperial service generally wrote Greek"; *MAMA* 7:x, neo-Phrygian inscriptions at Orcistus, xxx, overwhelming percentage of inscriptions in Greek, xxxii, quotation about Latin. On the survival of (late or neo-) Phrygian, see Neumann (1980) 174–76, and Mitchell (1993) 1:174; also Petrie (1906), for "Phrygian Greek," and Brixhe (2002), for "Phrygianized Greek."

might well prefer the appointment of locals, any locals, over the imposition of outsiders, in particular non-Greeks. "A man would be happier
with his dog than with a foreigner." A dog that barked in Greek was
more appealing than a Latin-speaking magistrate.[2]

From the later third century several factors reinforced or modified
the taut relationship between Latin and Greek in the eastern empire.
One was the decisions of emperors about the proper language of imperial administration. Through their various reforms Diocletian and the
Tetrarchs tried to enhance their own authority as emperors. In the Greek
East that objective apparently included the use of Latin as the language
of imperial rule. During their extensive residences in the eastern empire
Diocletian, Galerius, and Maximinus would certainly have learned and
used at least some Greek. But since they were native Latin speakers from
the Balkan regions, Latin remained their preferred language. According
to a later apocryphal story, when the ghost of the illustrious Greek sage
Apollonius had appeared to Aurelian at Tyana, he had considerately
addressed the emperor in Latin, "so that a man from Pannonia might
understand."[3]

This preference for Latin during the reigns of Diocletian and his
fellow Tetrarchs appeared in different guises throughout the eastern
provinces. Soldiers and their commanders tended to use Latin. At Luxor

---

[2] Festus, governor of Syria: Libanius, *Orat.* 1.156. Ruling city, dog: Augustine, *De
civitate Dei* 19.7, with Lafferty (2003), an excellent survey of the development
of the Latin liturgy at Rome and Milan. For Latin as a language of power, see
Adams (2003) 545–76: "Greek was regularly chosen, even in the army. But Latin
was in the wings, to be called on *ad hoc* for the forceful symbolising of Roman
power" (p. 557); and Eck (2004), stressing the tension in the early empire between
the arrogance of using Latin and the pragmatic need to be understood. For the
ongoing tension over the identity of Greek provinces in the early empire, see
Woolf (1994) 130: "Romans were never wholly reconciled to Greek culture, and
Greeks never stopped being Greek."

[3] Apollonius' ghost: SHA, *Aurelianus* 24.3. Diocletian nevertheless could respect
Greek culture. When listing emperors who had honored philosophers Themistius
twice included Diocletian, who had promoted "the founder of my family" (*Orat.*
5.63d) and praised "a philosopher at that time in Byzantium" (*Orat.* 11.173b). This
founder and philosopher was most likely Themistius' grandfather: see Vanderspoel
(1995) 33.

in Egypt one officer set up a series of dedications to Tetrarchic emperors
in Latin, perhaps as a reminder of the authority of Diocletian and
subsequent Tetrarchic emperors after a failed revolt. Dedications in
Latin accompanied a reform in the procedures for collecting taxes in
Egypt. Imperial magistrates, and especially provincial governors, erected
dedications to emperors in Latin. At Antioch in Pisidia, for example,
one such dedication hailed Galerius, in Latin, as the "restorer of the
Roman empire." The emperors themselves likewise seemed to have
identified Romanness with the use of Latin. In their official edicts the
Tetrarchs repeatedly proclaimed their devotion to "Roman dignity and
majesty," "the chaste and peaceful Roman people," "Roman law," "the
Roman name," and "the prosperity of the Roman world." Throughout
the eastern empire communities erected copies of these edicts in Latin.
Copies of the famous Prices Edict, for instance, have been found in
almost forty locations in the Greek East. One provincial governor did
try to make this Latin imperial edict more accessible for a city in Phrygia
by adding his own edict in Greek in which he extolled the emperors'
intentions. But only in Achaea was the lengthy list of prices translated
into Greek, perhaps on the initiative of the governor for the benefit of
the Greek-speaking provincials. Even in this case, however, the preamble
to the edict, in which the emperors ranted about the baneful affects of
greed and lust, remained in Latin. Although economic realities alone
quickly doomed this ambitious attempt to fix prices, publishing it in
Latin had certainly not improved its chances for success in the eastern
empire. This edict had more to do with broadcasting power than with
mending the economy, and its publication in Latin was instead a bold
statement about the essence of Romanness. The use of Latin defined
the preferred political (and, in this case, economic) correctness under
the Tetrarchs.[4]

---

[4] For the inscriptions at Luxor, see Chapter 9, with the interpretation of Lacau
(1934) 43: "Il s'agit d'une unification voulue et systématique, car personne ne
comprenait le latin en Egypt." For the new tax system in Egypt, see Barnes (1982)
230–1. Dedication to Galerius: Levick (1967) 105, no. 9 = L'année épigraphique
1967 (1969) 156, no. 494 = Christol and Drew-Bear (1999) 65–66, "restau|ratori
imperii Roma|ni," with additional examples on p. 70: "dans les provinces d'Orient
ce sont les fonctionnaires de l'Empire, et surtout les gouverneurs, qui nous ont

In the later books of his *Ecclesiastical History* Eusebius cited many official edicts and letters, most issued by Tetrarchs, a few by imperial magistrates. In several cases he mentioned explicitly that he was quoting a Greek translation: "these [are the contents] according to the language of the Romans, translated into the Greek language as far as possible." By implication, the other imperial pronouncements too had been issued originally in Latin. Even when the emperors received petitions in Greek, they responded in Latin. When Diocletian received envoys from Antioch, their spokesman presented the petition in Greek, and the emperor replied in Latin. Another telling example is the bilingual dialogue between Maximinus and the cities in the regions he controlled. The emperor had solicited petitions, which various cities and provinces submitted in Greek. Maximinus issued his rescript in Latin. Cities then erected copies of this rescript in Latin. To help the readers of his *History* Eusebius quoted his own Greek translation of the copy on display at Tyre. But at the city itself most of the residents would have been mere spectators of this decree in Latin, and not readers. They could look at the public monument and deduce its symbolic message about the majesty of imperial power, but most of them could not comprehend its actual words. Throughout the Greek East the Tetrarchs preferred to publicize themselves and their policies in a foreign language.[5]

laissé à l'époque tétrarchique des inscriptions latines élogieuses pour les princes de leur temps." *Edictum de pretiis*, praef., "Romana dignitas maiestasque," ed. J. Reynolds, in Roueché (1989) 266, with the excellent discussion in Corcoran (1996) 205–33. "Edictum de maleficis et Manichaeis," in *Collatio legum Mosaicarum et Romanarum* 15.3.4, "Romanam gentem modestam atque tranquillam." "Edictum de nuptiis," in *Collatio legum Mosaicarum et Romanarum* 6.4.1, "Romanis legibus," "Romano nomini," with the comment of Evans Grubbs (1995) 101, on this edict: "the preservation of the Empire itself is at stake." First edict about Caesariani, ed. Feissel (1996) 285, "beatitudo <o>rbis Roman<i>," with Feissel (1995) 51–52, justifying the correction from *urbis Romanae*, and Corcoran (2000) 347–48, for a survey of opinions. Edict of Fulvius Asticus at Aezani: see Crawford and Reynolds (1975), with the corrections of Oliver (1976).

5 Quotation from Eusebius, *HE* 8.17.11, referring to Galerius' edict of toleration in 311; for the Latin original, see Lactantius, *De mortibus persecutorum* 34. Eusebius included the preamble listing the emperors who issued the decree with Galerius;

A second factor affecting the relationship between Greek and Latin was the increased size of the central administration. Even though the central administration may have once been imposed by foreigners, by now it offered opportunities for Greek provincials to hold offices. Diocletian and the Tetrarchs had dramatically enlarged the imperial administration with the creation of more provinces and dioceses and the presence of more imperial courts resident in the eastern provinces. This larger administration needed more provincial magistrates and court officials, as well as many lesser functionaries and secretaries. In anticipation of acquiring these jobs the sons of provincial Greek notables increasingly began to study Latin and Roman law, as well as shorthand for the clerical positions. Diocletian apparently encouraged their expectations. By conferring exemption from municipal duties upon young law students at Beirut, the emperor himself supported the study of Latin and Roman law in the Greek East.[6]

Every spring the sons of local notables at Antioch and other cities in the eastern provinces left to study Roman law at Beirut or Latin at Rome. At first Libanius was prepared to refer potential students to his friend Domnio, who taught law at Beirut: "it is the prevailing opinion

for a detailed comparison of translation with original, see Coleman-Norton (1966) 1:20–22. Other explicit translations in Eusebius' *HE*: 9.1.2, "a Roman letter whose translation follows this form"; 9.7.2, "copy of a translation"; 9.9.13, "copy of a translation"; 9.10.6, "copy of a translation made from the Roman language into the Greek"; 10.2.2, "the pronouncements translated from the language of the Romans into the Greek"; 10.5.1, "translations of the imperial decrees of Constantine and Licinius made from the language of the Romans." Diocletian's dialogue: *CJ* 10.48.2. For discussion of the use of Latin under the Tetrarchy, see Feissel (1995) 34, "la prépondéronce du latin est d'autant plus frappante que notre documentation épigraphique est presque entièrement orientale"; Corcoran (1996) 254–55; and Adams (2003) 636, "The choice of Latin on occasions before Greeks as an act of power was not a Diocletianic invention, but had its roots back in the Republic." For some limits to the use of Latin in the administration of Egypt, see Turner (1961), and Bagnall (1993) 231: "more Latin was used in the fourth century than earlier, ... but still the main text is in Greek."

[6] Exemption: *CJ* 10.50.1, with Butcher (2003) 230–36, on the Latin characteristics of Beirut in late antiquity.

that an advocate who has not sipped from there is ineffective." To a father at Tarsus he recommended that the future rewards of his son's education in law were well worth the high cost of tuition, because his son now had "hopes of wealth, offices, and other power." These hopes were often rewarded with advisory positions in the civil service. "Learned men from Beirut assist provincial governors throughout the entire world, and as experts in the law they protect the provinces." Some went on to hold higher offices. At Aphrodisias, for instance, a dedication from the municipal council honored a governor of the province of Caria in the later fourth century. Even though this governor was apparently a native Greek, the very first line of the dedication praised him for his knowledge of laws and his facility with "the Italian Muse." In this dedication familiarity with Roman law and Latin ranked higher than even the "honey sweetness of his spoken Attic [Greek]." In a discussion of the importance of education John Chrysostom inadvertently conceded the advantage of knowing Latin for young Greeks. Familiarity with Greek culture allowed a man to hold high offices, marry a wealthy wife, and construct a magnificent house. But knowledge of "the language of the Italians" allowed a man to become influential at the imperial courts. Expertise in Latin and Roman law had become a practical means for social advancement, a sign of loyalty and political correctness, but also a marker of a new cultural correctness.[7]

By the later fourth century, however, Libanius was increasingly appalled at this abandonment of Greek culture (and the accompanying decline in the number of his students) in favor of studying a rival language and culture or, in the case of shorthand, a mere technical skill. Libanius wanted Greeks to return to the old ways, as in fact members

---

[7] Libanius, *Orat.* 48.22, every spring; *Ep.* 1203.1, prevailing opinion, 1539.1, hopes, with Liebeschuetz (1972) 242–55, for an excellent overview of Libanius' ideas about the rival studies: "a deliberate and sustained attempt of the Roman government to make the Roman character of the empire prevail against all difficulties" (p. 252). Learned men: *Expositio totius mundi et gentium* 25. Dedication to Oecumenius: Sevcenko (1968), and Roueché (1989) 54–55, with the excellent discussion of the statue in Smith (2002). Language of the Italians: John Chrysostom, *Adversus oppugnatores vitae monasticae* 3.5 (*PG* 47.357).

of his family had done. One of his great-grandfathers had known Latin well enough that some had thought he was a native of Italy. But the generation of Libanius' father, born about the time of Diocletian's accession as emperor, had reverted to knowing only Greek. One of Libanius' uncles knew no Latin and could converse with imperial magistrates only through interpreters. Libanius himself did not read Latin. Despite the increasing intrusiveness of the central administration and the opportunities it offered for provincials from the eastern provinces, teachers like Libanius wanted to preserve the study of Greek and Greek culture. In their perspective, even if the imperial administration was to be Latin, the dominant literary and rhetorical culture in the eastern provinces should remain Greek.[8]

Libanius' cultural preference received support from unexpected allies. A final factor influencing the relationship between Latin and Greek was the growing prominence of Christianity and the opportunities it offered for careers in the clergy. Over the centuries service in the ecclesiastical hierarchy had become increasingly appealing, and men from locally prominent families had begun to serve as clerics and bishops. Constantine's patronage for Christian clerics made church administration even more attractive in eastern cities. Such clerical service required no new language skills beyond a knowledge of Greek. In fact, because early Christianity in the eastern empire had been so strongly influenced by Greek culture, few Greek Church Fathers knew Latin at all. According to Basil of Caesarea, not only was Latin simply inadequate for expressing the subtleties of theology, but even Latin churchmen conceded the "narrow limits of their own language." Gregory of Nazianzus admitted that he did not know Latin: "I am not 'Roman' with regard to language." Even though John Chrysostom may have once considered following his father's career and entering the imperial civil service,

---

[8] Libanius, *Orat.* 1.3, great-grandfather; *Orat.* 49.29, uncle; for letters in Latin, Libanius summoned translators: see Libanius, *Ep.* 1004.4, 1036.2. The most stimulating discussion of the interplay between Greek and Latin in the eastern empire during the fourth century is still Dagron (1969); for overviews, see Jones (1964) 986–91, Zgusta (1980) 131–35, and Rochette (1997) 116–41. For Libanius' attempt to promote a "Greek Roman empire," see Van Dam (forthcoming).

he had not formally studied Latin. He instead became a priest and a bishop.[9]

Service in the ecclesiastical hierarchy as a cleric or bishop was hence more than a religious choice. Like service in the imperial administration it also represented a cultural dilemma for local Greek aristocrats. In the mid-third century a young notable like Gregory Thaumaturgus had faced exactly this choice between Greek and Latin. Gregory was an older contemporary of Libanius' great-grandfather, who had been fluent in Latin. Gregory now left his homeland of Pontus to study Roman law at Beirut. Since he had ambitions of becoming an advocate, perhaps of serving in the imperial administration, he rationalized his decision by insisting that Roman law was "very Greek" because of its wisdom and precision. But to study Roman law, he also had to master Latin, "the language of the Romans." That was a bit more than he could endure. Latin was off-putting: "it seemed vulgar to me." So Gregory instead moved on to study Christian doctrines with Origen, an illustrious Greek theologian at Caesarea in Palestine. When Gregory returned to Pontus, he eventually became bishop at Neocaesarea. Although his career would hence be an early example of the increasing attractiveness of clerical service over imperial service for local Greek aristocrats, the significant conversion in his life was not necessarily his adoption of Christian asceticism or his acceptance of an episcopal see. Instead, it was his decision to abandon Latin in favor of Greek. Studying Roman law would have required him to become a "Latin" Roman. Studying Christian theology allowed him to remain a "Greek" Roman. Gregory

---

[9] Narrow limits: Basil of Caesarea, *Ep.* 214.4. Not a Roman: Gregory of Nazianzus, *Ep.* 173.1. For John Chrysostom's education and early ambitions, see Kelly (1995) 5–16. For the limited familiarity with Latin among churchmen in the East, see Rochette (1997) 150–54: "les évêques et les théologiens de langue grecque ne surent jamais le latin" (p. 153). One exception was bishop Athanasius of Alexandria, who spent several years in exile in Latin-speaking provinces: see Barnes (1993) 13. Another might be Eusebius, who served successively as bishop of Beirut, a center for the study of Roman law, Nicomedia, an imperial capital under Diocletian, and Constantinople, an imperial capital under Constantine. Perhaps knowledge of Latin contributed to Eusebius' influence with emperors: see Chapter 10.

Thaumaturgus' devotion to Christianity marked a cultural decision, rather than a strictly religious conversion.[10]

At the same time that Christianity was becoming more prominent, the central administration was becoming more intrusive, and cities in the eastern provinces were now suspended between imperial courts that used Latin and their bishops who used Greek. Since the Tetrarchs preferred to use Latin, their hostility to Christians in the eastern empire might have seemed to be less a persecution of their religion and more a dismissal of their Greekness. The use of Latin was not only a sign of political and cultural correctness; it was also a marker of religious correctness. In the eastern provinces familiarity with Latin was now associated with the political authority of the emperors, the cultural skills needed for holding offices in the imperial administration, and opposition to Christianity. The Tetrarchs' promotion of a Latin Romanness, in its many dimensions, was an incentive for cities in the Greek East to start using Latin.

The pretensions of Latin-speaking emperors and the seduction of service in the imperial administration would have promoted the spread of Latin among aristocrats and cities in the Greek East, while the rise of Christianity and the complaints of pagan teachers like Libanius would have pushed Greek notables and cities toward remaining Greek. In a letter to Libanius, bishop Gregory of Nyssa shared the great sophist's disdain for those who had "mistakenly abandoned Greek in favor of that barbarous language." Such deserters were no better than mercenaries, since they preferred to sell their service rather than to pursue the study of their own Greek culture and rhetorical eloquence. In the face of this threat from the intrusive spread of Latin, in the eastern provinces Christian churchmen and pagan rhetoricians had formed an odd alliance in support of the use of Greek.[11]

---

[10] Law and Latin: Gregory Thaumaturgus, *Oratio panegyrica in Origenem* 1.7, with Van Dam (1982) 272–73, and Millar (1999) 105–8, on Greeks studying Roman law.

[11] Gregory of Nyssa, *Ep.* 14.6. This alliance of course had its limits. After commiserating with Libanius about the neglect of *logoi*, "culture," Gregory offered an argument about "our Logos," Jesus Christ the "Word."

## CONSTANTINE AND GREEK

Two emperors in particular, Constantine and his nephew Julian, neatly embodied this tension about the respective roles of Latin and Greek in the eastern empire during the fourth century. Constantine had been born at Naissus in Dacia, just on the Latin-speaking side of the line dividing Latin and Greek speakers in the Balkans, and he too had grown up in the army. When he later composed a prayer for his troops, it was in Latin, "the Roman language." But he also spoke and read Greek. His mother, Helena, was said to have been a native of Bithynia. During most of his twenties and early thirties Constantine had served as a military officer under Diocletian and Galerius throughout the Greek East. At the council of Nicaea he participated in the theological debates by speaking Greek. Constantine could also appreciate public orations and panegyrics in Greek. After one of Eusebius' interminable orations the emperor offered his own critique. During another he even smiled. Although a native Latin speaker, Constantine obviously knew, understood, and spoke Greek.[12]

Yet as emperor in the Greek East Constantine nevertheless seems to have conducted most of his official business in Latin. When he presided over a legal procedure held before his imperial consistory of advisors, the litigant spoke in Greek, and he replied in Latin. Soon after his victory over Licinius in 324 he sent out a series of letters. One was a general letter to the provincials. Eusebius quoted the version of this "imperial law" sent specifically to the provincials of Palestine, of which he claimed

---

[12] For the distinction between Latin-speaking and Greek-speaking regions in the Balkans, see the maps in Gerov (1980) 149, and Rochette (1997) 391. Helena's birth in Drepanum, later renamed Helenopolis: Eusebius, *Vita Constantini* 4.61.1, Procopius, *De aedificiis* 5.2.1–2, with the skeptical discussion in Drijvers (1992) 9–12. Constantine's Latin and Greek: Eusebius, *Vita Constantini* 3.13.2, at the council of Nicaea "he spoke Greek, since he was not ignorant of that language"; 4.19, prayer, 33.1, critique, 46, smile. Limited education: *Origo Constantini imperatoris* 2.2, "litteris minus instructus"; in contrast, the historian Praxagoras of Athens claimed that Constantius had sent Constantine to Diocletian's court at Nicomedia to be educated, presumably in Greek culture: see Photius, *Bibliotheca* 62.

to have in his possession an "authentic" copy with the emperor's actual
signature. He also claimed that this and Constantine's other letters had
been composed in "both the Roman language and the Greek language."
This description seems to imply that the imperial chancery had had the
letter translated into Greek before sending out copies (perhaps bilingual
copies) to various regions. Constantine also sent another general letter to
the provincials in the East. Eusebius quoted this letter from an autograph
copy, "translated from the Roman language." This description seems to
imply that one of Eusebius' secretaries had translated this letter from
an original version in Latin. Yet another of Constantine's letters went
to Shapur, ruler of the Persian empire. Eusebius claimed that a copy
of this letter, "written by the emperor in person," was available "to me
in the Roman language." He then suggested that this letter would be
more comprehensible if it were translated "into the Greek language."
Presumably one of his secretaries supplied this translation too.[13]

Eusebius' firsthand familiarity with Constantine's letters suggests
that the emperor and his staff composed them in Latin. The imperial
chancery then translated some into Greek before circulating them; others the provincials themselves, or imperial magistrates in the provinces,
had to translate. At public occasions Constantine also apparently preferred to give his own orations in Latin. At the council of Nicaea he
delivered his opening speech in Latin. When he delivered formal orations about his theology, he spoke in Latin, and interpreters translated
his words into Greek, perhaps on the spot. In his biography of the
emperor Eusebius indicated that he planned to include in an appendix
one of Constantine's speeches, "as an example of his translated orations."
This speech, which Eusebius entitled "To the Assembly of the Saints,"
can be identified with an extant oration attributed to Constantine. Since
Constantine had most likely delivered this oration originally in Latin,

---

[13] Court case: *CTh* 8.15.1, with Corcoran (1996) 259–60. Letter to provincials of
Palestine: Eusebius, *Vita Constantini* 2.23. Letter to provincials in the East: Eusebius, *Vita Constantini* 2.47.2. Letter to Shapur: Eusebius, *Vita Constantini* 4.8. On
the quality of Eusebius' translations, note Lawlor and Oulton (1927–1928) 2:37:
"his knowledge of Latin was not great," and Carriker (2003) 18, "when necessary,
he could translate a Latin text into Greek."

the extant version in Greek was a later translation. He also apparently preferred to read theological treatises in Latin. He once thanked Eusebius for a copy of his treatise on Easter. Since the version he read was in Latin, he in addition thanked Eusebius' secretary, "who translated your work into the Roman language." Even though he may have spent increasingly more of his time in the Greek East, as emperor Constantine was still a typical Roman administrator who used Latin in his official business.[14]

Constantine hence could have read a petition in Greek. But Orcistus seems to have decided that it would demonstrate its Romanness by submitting its petition in Latin. After an earlier civil war another Greek city had done the same in its public declaration of allegiance. Decades earlier when the citizens of Perge in Pamphylia erected a dedication for Vespasian, they had, exceptionally, used Latin: "in the context of a civil war Latin seemed to be the proper language for an expression of political loyalty." Perhaps the people of Orcistus were now influenced by seeing other dedications to the new emperor. At Ancyra the praetorian prefect Flavius Constantius set up a short dedication in honor of "the most clement and perpetual emperor, our Lord, Constantine, Maximus, Victor, always Augustus." The prefect most likely erected this dedication when he accompanied Constantine on his trip across Asia Minor to Antioch in late 324 or early 325. Flavius Constantius was an influential member of Constantine's entourage, perhaps even a relative, and the smallest details of his behavior would have been scrutinized for clues about the new emperor's preferences. In this dedication, just as the

---

[14] Eusebius, *Vita Constantini* 3.13.1, council of Nicaea; 4.32, example, orations in Latin and translation, 35.3, treatise on Easter. The debate about the original language of Constantine's oration, entitled *Oratio ad sanctorum coetum*, focuses on his familiarity with a Greek translation of Virgil's Fourth Eclogue. Bardy (1948) 124–25, Wigtil (1981), Rochette (1997) 315–19, and Edwards (1999) 254–60, (2003) xxvi, argue that Constantine delivered this oration in Latin, Lane Fox (1986) 629–54, in Greek. For the date of this oration, see Chapter 11. In the mid-sixth century John the Lydian, a civil servant at Constantinople, found a copy of Constantine's discourses "written in his own language" (i.e. Latin): see John the Lydian, *De magistratibus* 2.30, with Dubuisson (1992), on John's familiarity with Latin.

prefect's emphasis on the emperor's clemency probably reflected the new regime's ideology of forgiveness, so his use of Latin may have seemed significant. Ancyra was about one hundred miles northeast of Orcistus, and the people of Orcistus may have concluded that if a high-ranking imperial magistrate commemorated Constantine in Latin, they should do the same. Even if the town was still apprehensive about the new emperor's religious preferences or disingenuous about its own religious affiliations, it could share Latin Romanness with the emperor.[15]

---

[15] Quotation about Perge translated from Eck (2000) 652. Dedication at Ancyra: *CIL* 3, Supplementum 1:1234, no. 6751 = Grünewald (1990) 244, no. 417, "[C]leme[n]tissimo adqu|e perpetuo imperatori | d. n. Co[nsta]ntino | maxi[mo] victori sem|[p]er A[ug.] Fl. Constantiu[s] | v. c. praefectus praetorii [*sic*] | pietati eius semper | dicatis[sim]u[s]." Note the similarities between this dedication and the salutation to the first petition from Orcistus: "domini impp. Constantine | [maxi]me victor semper Aug. et . . . " For the novelty of the choice of Latin, see Feissel (1995) 47n.79: "Ce n'est apparemment pas avant l'époque constantinienne que les pétitions elles-mêmes seront rédigées en latin."

Chausson (2002b) 138–40, 145–46, suggests that Flavius Constantius had been Constantine's envoy to Licinius in 316: see Chapter 3. He also argues that Flavius Constantius was another son of Constantius and Helena and hence Constantine's full brother, and that he might have been the father of Crispus' wife, also named Helena. If so, then because Flavius Constantius remained prefect until 327, he may have had to assist in the awkward task of removing Crispus, his son-in-law, and Fausta, Constantine's wife: see Chapter 11. For the close relationship between Constantine and Flavius Constantius, see Grünewald (1990) 135.

Flavius Constantius was a prefect already in December 324: see *CTh* 15.14.1, with the corrected date in Seeck (1919) 99, 174, and Barnes (1982) 131. In August or September 325 he received *CTh* 1.5.1. According to the subscription, this edict was "dat. . . . . Antiochiae." In late summer and early autumn of 325 Constantine was at or near Nicomedia: see Barnes (1982) 76. So rather than being "issued at Antioch," perhaps this edict was "posted at Antioch." In that case, Flavius Constantius had presumably remained at Antioch after accompanying Constantine there: see Barnes (1982) 139, suggesting that as prefect at Antioch he "operated independently of an emperor."

According to John Malalas, *Chronographia* 13.3, when Constantine left Antioch after a war against the Persians, he appointed Plutarch as "governor of Antioch in Syria." *PLRE* 1:707, "Plutarchus 2," suggests that Plutarch was probably the provincial governor; but since Constantine visited Antioch only during the winter

Since in its petition the town was coy about its religion but conspicuous about its new culture, its choice of Latin over Greek was more significant than any conversion from paganism to Christianity. Orcistus had made the opposite choice from the decision of Gregory Thaumaturgus. Orcistus was instead the municipal equivalent of all those Greek aristocrats who were now learning Latin and studying Roman law in order to get ahead. For them, both city and notables, the reign of Constantine seemed to mark more of a cultural revolution than a religious revolution. Orcistus looked at the reign of Constantine and decided that the future lay not necessarily with Christianity, but with the use of Latin.

This petition was successful, because Constantine ordered Ablabius to grant Orcistus the rank of a city. Yet significantly, in his response the emperor did not frame his decision in terms of religion by highlighting his patronage for Christianity. Already in his *adnotatio*, his initial response to the petition from Orcistus, he had stressed his reverence for "ancient honor." In his letter to Ablabius he elaborated by locating his decision in the context of his general regard for cities. "[For us] whose desire is either to found new cities or to civilize ancient cities or to revive lifeless cities, this petition was most welcome." At the time of this petition Constantine certainly had the foundation and revival of cities on his mind. One immediate concern was to surpass Licinius, his predecessor as emperor in the East, who had acquired a reputation for "helping the cities to flourish." Another concern was the foundation of Constantinople, since in late 324 he had marked out the boundaries for the new capital and in the later 320s he was preparing for its formal dedication. Between his defeat of Licinius and the dedication of Constantinople in 330, the emperor was clearly thinking about his legacy in

of 324–325 and never led a Persian campaign, the chronology is uncertain. John Malalas claimed that Plutarch melted down a bronze statue of Poseidon to make a statue of Constantine, which he set up outside his official residence. Beneath the statue he inscribed a dedication: "To the good Constantine." Although John cited the dedication in Greek letters (Βόνω Κωνσταντίνω), the original was obviously in Latin. Downey (1961) 349n.144, doubts when John actually saw this statue and dedication.

terms of cities. Orcistus' request about its municipal rank had reached him at just the right moment.[16]

This petition from Orcistus could also tap into a much longer tradition of imperial patronage for cities, and in this respect Constantine was reacting like his non-Christian predecessors. The town of Tymandus in the borderland between southern Phrygia and western Pisidia had likewise once petitioned an emperor for promotion to "the legal standing and rank of a city." In his response this (anonymous) emperor had highlighted his regard for the welfare of cities. "It is inherent for us that throughout our entire world the honor and number of cities be increased." Since at the end of his letter this emperor appealed to "the favor of the immortal gods," he was certainly a pagan. In late 307 or early 308 the emperors Galerius and Maximinus responded to a petition from Heraclea Sintica in Macedonia by granting the rank of a city. They too advertised a "concern for our republic," and they predicted that the state would flourish when "cities have been enhanced by the goodwill of our foresight and benevolence." All emperors shared a concern for the welfare of cities. This concern even seemed to take priority over religious preferences.[17]

Cities that lost out in these disputes might decide to ignore an emperor's decision and assume that overworked or compliant local imperial administrators would overlook any indiscretions. In its dispute

---

[16] Licinius' reputation: Libanius, *Orat.* 30.6.

[17] Tymandus: *MAMA* 4:86–87, no. 236 = *ILS* 2.1:526, no. 6090 = Riccobono (1941) 454–55, no. 92. Since the titulature and preamble of this letter are lost, so is any indication of the date and the emperor (or emperors) who sent this response. Feissel (1995) 37, argues that the letter should be dated before Constantine's conversion because of the invocation of "immortal gods." The recipient of the rescript was "most dear Lepidus." Riccobono (1941) 454, and Corcoran (1996) 139, suggest that Lepidus was the governor of Pisidia in the late third or early fourth century; this suggestion implies that the emperor may have been Diocletian or one of his immediate pagan successors in the East. But *PLRE* 1:504, "Lepidus 2," suggests that Lepidus may instead have served under Julian. Rescript to Heraclea Sintica: Mitrev (2003), reprinted in *L'année épigraphique 2002* (2005) 454, no. 1293, with the commentary of Lepelley (2004), dating the rescript between December 10, 307 and April 30, 308.

with Orcistus, Nacolea seems to have been a sore loser. Even after Constantine's first decision it had apparently continued to demand a levy for the funding of its cults. Orcistus must have sent a second petition to the emperor, since in 331 Constantine again responded to "your pleas and your petition." This time he reasserted the rights and autonomy of Orcistus as a city and openly challenged "the wrongdoing of the people of Nacolea that has endured beyond the benefits of our indulgence." The enforcer of this decision was to be the *rationalis*, the chief administrator responsible for supervising the imperial properties in the diocese of Asiana. Constantine now instructed this imperial magistrate to ensure the immunity of Orcistus from Nacolea's demands.[18]

## JULIAN AND LATIN

Even then Nacolea may have continued to dream about regaining control over Orcistus. Just as Orcistus had finally benefited from a sympathetic emperor, perhaps all Nacolea had to do was wait for a new emperor with different preferences. The reign of Julian seemed to offer that opportunity to reverse earlier decisions, in particular about religion. Constantine had rewarded the port town of Maiuma for its conversion to Christianity by making it an independent city; after becoming sole emperor Julian rescinded that decision and made Maiuma again a dependency of Gaza. In 362 Julian traveled across central Asia Minor on his way to Antioch. At the beginning of the year he had been praised at Constantinople for his assistance in restoring an "unexpected youthfulness" to cities in the Balkans and the Greek peninsula. He had already publicized his patronage for pagan cults and pagan deities, and he was attempting to promote the influence of local priests and provincial high priests. In his public portraits and his philosophical treatises he furthermore seemed to be reviving aspects of Tetrarchic political theology by associating himself with Jupiter and Hercules.[19]

[18] Chastagnol (1981a) 412, interprets the *pecunia pro cultis* that Orcistus still paid as "un impôt local."
[19] Julian and Maiuma: Sozomen, *HE* 5.3.6–7, with Van Dam (1985b) 10–17, and Chapter 3. Assistance for cities in Macedonia, Illyricum, and the Peloponnesus:

Since Nacolea promoted the cult of Zeus Bronton and claimed Hercules as its founder, it may have sensed an opportunity to promote its claims. One governor in Phrygia pandered to Julian's preference for pagan cults by ordering that a temple at Meirus (about twenty-five miles southwest of Nacolea) should be reopened and its statues cleaned. When some zealous Christians smashed the statues, the indignant governor had them executed. As Julian traveled through central Asia Minor toward Ancyra, his presence made pagan cults an issue. During his journey he made a quick detour to the shrine of Cybele, the Mother of the gods, at Pessinus, which was about fifty miles east of Nacolea and not far from Orcistus. Julian was a devoté of Cybele, and his oration in her honor was an attempt to combine pagan religion and ancient philosophy into a comprehensive scheme. By presenting himself as a philosopher priest, the emperor could offer this religious synthesis "as an encyclical addressed to the higher pagan clergy by their hierarch." He also pointedly linked his munificence and goodwill to the community's devotion to its goddess. As a result, his explicit preferences may have emboldened a neighboring town in Phrygia. Just as the citizens of Orcistus had once petitioned the Christian emperor Constantine at about the time he had been traveling through central Asia Minor, so the citizens of Nacolea may now have tried to take advantage of a pagan emperor's proximity. Nacolea set up a short dedication in honor of Julian: "To our lord Flavius Claudius Julianus, Victor and Celebrator of triumphs, Perpetual Augustus."[20]

Despite its brevity, this dedication had significant implications. First, its wording was almost identical to the dedication on a milestone located outside Laodicea Catacecaumene, about 135 miles southeast of Nacolea: "To Flavius Claudius Julianus, Victor and Celebrator of triumphs,

---

Claudius Mamertinus, *Panegyrici latini* 3(11).9. For Julian and Tetrarchic ideology, see Chapter 9, and Epilogue.

[20] Meirus: Socrates, *HE* 3.15, Sozomen, *HE* 5.11.1–3. Visit to Pessinus: Ammianus Marcellinus, *Res gestae* 22.9.5. Quotation about Julian, *Orat.* 5, from Athanassiadi (1981) 141. Munificence and devotion: Julian, *Ep.* 22.432A. Dedication at Nacolea: *CIL* 3.1:62, no. 350 = Conti (2004) 91, no. 46, "d(omino) n(ostro) | F[l(avio)] C[l(audio)] | Iuliano | victori ac | t[r]iumfatori | perpetuo Aug|usto."

Perpetual Augustus." During the fourth century milestones too became "an apparatus for imperial communication between the centralized state and its subjects." Emperors typically ensured the formulaic repetition of their titles and achievements on milestones in order to broadcast their legitimacy and authority, while local communities could use the dedications on milestones to advertise their loyalty. Other milestones in the vicinity no doubt used similar dedications for the new emperor Julian. The duplication in phrasing hence suggests that the people of Nacolea may have borrowed the wording of their dedication from an official road marker, because they were otherwise unsure how to address the emperor. Second, even if they were uncertain about Julian's titles, they still wanted to make a statement about their devotion to a pagan cult. Other cities claimed to be the guardian of a famous old temple or welcomed Julian with sacrifices; the people of Nacolea engraved their dedication on a large marble altar. This dedication was hence an indication of their loyalty to both the new emperor and his pagan religious preferences. Finally, this dedication was somewhat similar to the opening line of the petition from Orcistus to Constantine over thirty-five years earlier. Perhaps the similarity was deliberate, although not as a respectful reminiscence but rather as a slightly sarcastic pun, with the expectation of an opposite outcome. Perhaps Nacolea was hinting that in return for this honor, Julian might restore control over a former dependency like Orcistus. In the past this sort of appeal had worked against the interests of Nacolea; with a different emperor it might now work to its advantage.[21]

[21] For the similar dedication on a milestone on the road east of Laodicea Catacecaumene, see *MAMA* 7:2, no. 9 = Conti (2004) 89, no. 43: "Fl. Cl. Iuliano | victor(i) ac | triumfatori | [p]erpet(uo) Aug(usto). | Mi(lia) θ." Quotation about milestones from Laurence (2004) 56, in a suggestive discussion of the Roman "road as an arena of communication and propaganda" (p. 57). Arce (1984) 111, 163–64, and Conti (2004) 91, state that the inscription at Nacolea was on a milestone; in fact, it was apparently a dedication on an altar: see Christol and Drew-Bear (1986) 53, "L'inscription est gravée sur un grand autel de marbre gris," 55, "notre dédicace fut érigée par les autorités municipales à l'occasion du séjour de l'empereur dans cette partie de la Phrygie." Miletus as guardian of temple of Apollo at Didyma: *SIG*³ 2:624, no. 906a = Conti (2004) 85, no. 36. Sacrifices for Julian at Batnae: Julian, *Ep.* 58.400c.

Nacolea was not alone in Asia Minor in honoring Julian. Secundus Salutius, the prefect of the East, erected a dedication, and probably a statue, at Ancyra. Although Secundus Salutius was a native of Gaul, Julian himself praised the prefect for his familiarity with Greek rhetoric and philosophy. Yet as a high-ranking imperial magistrate, Secundus Salutius nevertheless set up this dedication in Latin. In the eastern provinces dedications to Julian sponsored by a provincial governor might be in Greek (as at Aphrodisias) or in Latin (as at Ephesus and near Pergamum). But when a city itself took the initiative, its dedication was in Greek. At Magnesia the city honored Julian as the "most divine emperor," at Miletus as "the ruler of land, sea, and the entire race of men." At Iasos in Caria the council and people honored Julian for "ruling through philosophy." In this case a compliment that Gregory of Nazianzus applied to the learned rhetorician Themistius only a few years later was probably more directly appropriate to Julian. Iasos had essentially hailed Julian as "the emperor of culture." Its dedication commemorated him precisely as an emperor who was following the dictates of philosophy. Iasos flattered Julian as a student and patron of Greek culture.[22]

In contrast, the dedication of Nacolea was in Latin. Perhaps this city too was now trying to establish its "Roman" credentials. But in this case the use of Latin rather ruined the effect. Julian was the other emperor of the fourth century who crystallized the tension between Latin and Greek in the eastern empire. But just as he was the opposite of Constantine in religious preferences, so he had different cultural

---

[22] Secundus Salutius' familiarity with Greek culture: Julian, *Orat.* 8.252A-B; his dedication at Ancyra: *ILS* 1:168, no. 754 = Conti (2004) 73, no. 20. Dedication to Julian at Aphrodisias: Roueché (1989) 39, no. 20 = Conti (2004) 82, no. 33, with illustration in Smith (1999) 163, and discussion of the statue in Smith (2001). At Ephesus: Börker and Merkelbach (1979) 114, no. 313A = Conti (2004) 77, no. 26, and Meriç, Merkelbach, Nollé, and Sahin (1981) 1:19, no. 3021 = Conti (2004) 78, no. 27. Near Pergamum: *ILS* 1:167, no. 751 = Conti (2004) 79, no. 28. At Magnesia: *SIG*³ 2:624, no. 906b = Conti (2004) 84, no. 35. At Miletus: *SIG*³ 2:624, no. 906a = Conti (2004) 85, no. 36. At Iasos: *OGIS* 2:174–75, no. 520 = Blümel (1985) 1:33–34, no. 14 = Conti (2004) 83, no. 34, lines 2–3, τὸν ἐκ φιλοσοφίας βα|σιλεύοντα. Description of Themistius: Gregory of Nazianzus, *Ep.* 24.1, βασιλεὺς . . . τῶν λόγων; Gallay (1964–1967) 1:32, dates this letter between 365 and 369.

preferences. Julian prided himself as a thoroughly "Hellenic" emperor, not just devoted to pagan cults but also deeply learned in Greek culture. In fact, his familiarity with Greek culture was a direct legacy from the non-Constantinian side of his family. Julius Constantius, Julian's father and Constantine's half-brother, had been killed during the massacre of Constantine's relatives that followed his death. Of the three sons of Constantine who became emperors, Constantius assumed responsibility for his young cousin. The mentors and tutors he chose for Julian were churchmen, including Eusebius, bishop of Nicomedia and later of Constantinople, and Georgius, later bishop of Alexandria. "The emperor Constantius decided that Julian would not deviate into superstition after studying with a 'Greek' teacher." In contrast, the teacher who had first introduced him to the delights of Homer's poems was Mardonius, the tutor whom his grandfather Julius Julianus had originally hired to teach his daughter, Julian's mother. As a result, Julian always resented Constantius for having forced him to leave "the schools" of his classical education in order to study Christian texts with churchmen. The Julianic side of Julian's family represented Greek culture, and the Constantinian side Christianity. Already as a teenager Julian had used his familiarity with classical Greek culture as a way of distinguishing himself from his own Constantinian pedigree.[23]

As emperor Julian reasserted this distinction regarding both culture and family. His identification with Greek culture now allowed him to bury the "western," Constantinian, side of his family's background: "although my family was Thracian, I am a Greek in my behavior." Julian had read and studied Latin texts already during his early years, since his education had included "much of the Greek language and not a little of the other language." During his military command in Gaul

---

[23] Constantius' decision: Socrates, *HE* 3.1.11. Julian's tutor Mardonius: Julian, *Misopogon* 352A-353A, with Athanassiadi (1981) 14–21, on Julian's devotion to Mardonius. Julian was not alone on his mother's side of the family in discarding aspects of the Constantinian legacy. Note that Julianus, Julian's maternal uncle, also rejected Christianity during Julian's reign: see Philostorgius, *HE* 7.10. Schools: Julian, *Epistula ad Athenienses* 271B, with Van Dam (2002) 98–99, 159–60, 163–64, on Julian's education.

he had certainly displayed "an adequate fluency in speaking Latin." But even though he was familiar with some aspects of Latin culture and had become a Latinized *miles*, Julian nevertheless always chose to present himself as a *Graecus*. Unlike many of his recent predecessors as emperors, who had been primarily military men with little familiarity with classical culture, Julian was both an officer and a gentleman. Since he had options, he preferred to present himself as a learned Greek intellectual rather than as a native of the Latin-speaking Balkans or as a Latinized soldier. Julian was defiantly Greek rather than Latin, a man of culture rather than a military man. In contrast to Constantine, when Julian addressed his imperial consistory of advisors, he spoke in Greek. Julian clearly distinguished himself from Constantine and his imperial dynasty not just through his rejection of Christianity, but even more significantly through his assertion of Greekness.[24]

Once Julian became sole emperor, he could furthermore try to turn his cultural preferences into official policy. Since he too was interested in reviving the cities in the eastern empire, his proposals included the promotion of Greek culture, and his sense of "Hellenism" combined culture and religion. According to Libanius, Julian announced that Greek culture and veneration for pagan cults were "brothers." His journey through central Asia Minor was meant to be a triumphant demonstration of the potential success of his ambitions to revive cities, their councils, and their municipal notables, revitalize pagan cults, and promote the teaching of classical Greek culture. Unlike the Tetrarchs, whose enhancement of the power of the central administration had undermined the role of cities, Julian was trying to promote the vitality of cities by restoring some of their local autonomy and resources. As a result, although he did resemble the Tetrarchs in his promotion of pagan cults, he did not share their priorities about languages and

---

[24] Thracian and Greek: Julian, *Misopogon* 367c. Other language: Libanius, *Orat.* 18.21. Ammianus Marcellinus, *Res gestae* 16.5.7, fluency, 31.16.9, soldier and Greek, with Adams (2003) 609, on "the use of Latin at key moments to symbolise the Romanness of command." Julian and his consistory: *CTh* 11.39.5, dated March 23, 362, at Constantinople.

culture. Whatever was to be the language of imperial administration, Julian expected Greek cities to use Greek.[25]

Julian preferred Greekness as a reaction against his Constantinian pedigree, as a tactic for reviving cities and urban life, and as a general expression of his cultural and religious priorities. Since not all of these intentions would have been readily apparent, provincials often had to guess about his preferences. Decades earlier Constantine had ordered the destruction of pagan temples in the region of Phoenicia, including shrines of Aphrodite at Aphaca and Heliopolis. Since for Heliopolis he issued a "new law," sent a "personal letter," and funded the construction of a new church, presumably he had responded to a petition from local citizens. Under Julian, however, other locals tried a different approach. Now the provincial assembly of the region of Phoenicia honored Julian as "the liberator of the Roman world, the restorer of temples, and the renewer of [municipal] councils and the republic." In part this dedication was a petition in disguise, an attempt to flatter Julian into enhancing the standing of Tyre, the most prominent city in the region. Like the people of Nacolea, who had readily demonstrated that their city's pagan cults still flourished by engraving their dedication to Julian on an altar, the assembly of Phoenicia had neatly highlighted some of the emperor's significant religious and administrative ambitions, such as promoting pagan cults and strengthening municipal institutions. But also like the dedication at Nacolea, this dedication was in Latin. Both the citizens of Nacolea and the people of Phoenicia presumably hoped to demonstrate their "Romanness" to the emperor by using Latin. In both cases, however, the use of Latin may have been a misstep. Since Julian was presenting himself as a "Greek" rather than a "Latin" Roman emperor, a Greek city and a Greek assembly should have set up a dedication in Greek. Julian was killed in battle before he could respond to the dedication from the Phoenician assembly. And since Orcistus retained its autonomy, Nacolea's attempt to reassert its hegemony by pandering to Julian was unsuccessful.[26]

---

[25] Brothers: Libanius, *Orat.* 18.157. For Julian's ideas about Greekness and Romanness, see Bouffartigue (1991), and Van Dam (2002) 163–80.

[26] Shrines at Aphaca (= Aphrodite Aphakitis) and Heliopolis (Baalbek): Eusebius, *Vita Constantini* 3.55, 58, with Sartre (2001) 853–54, on the limits of Latin in

Within a few years the people of Nacolea would have received an unmistakable confirmation of their faulty judgment. A year after Julian's death the emperor Valentinian selected his brother Valens to become co-emperor for the eastern provinces. Valens was a supporter of Christianity and a native Latin speaker from the Balkans who never became familiar with Greek culture and the Greek language, despite his years of residence at Constantinople and Antioch. At the beginning of his reign his support in the eastern provinces was limited. In late 365 Procopius was hailed as a usurping emperor in Constantinople. Procopius was a relative of Julian, most likely on his mother's side of the family. In an attempt to present himself as Julian's legitimate heir he stressed his support for Greek culture by representing himself as another Greek philosopher emperor, a look-alike of Julian, in contrast to Valens, a Latin Christian emperor who was the antithesis of Julian. Since Procopius and Valens were both browsing for support in Phrygia and central Asia Minor in general, Nacolea might have hoped that its earlier attempt to honor Julian would resonate with the usurper. Instead, within a year Valens had defeated and beheaded Procopius. The final confrontation between their two armies took place outside Nacolea. At that moment the inhabitants of the city would not have had to guess about the preferences of a distant emperor. Instead, they could follow the lead of the commanders who

Syria and the Roman Near East. Dedications in Phoenicia, one from Byblus (now in Beirut), the other from the vicinity of Caesarea Philippi (Paneas): for texts and discussion, see Dietz (2000), commenting on the surprising use of Latin: "Zweifellos sollte die Verwendung der Reichssprache den offiziellen charakter der Äußerung des *Foenicum genus* betonen, vermutlich wollte man dadurch das «römische» Element Phöniziens zusätzlich herausstellen" (p. 812); the text from near Caesarea Philippi was confirmed by Eck (2000); both texts are reprinted in Conti (2004) 70–71, nos. 17–18: "Dabei betonte der Landtag, dass er sowohl hinter den politischen wie religiösen Beschlüssen des Kaisers stand" (p. 72). On the political intention of the dedications, see Gordon (2003) 266: "such a vow was undertaken by the élite of Tyre not merely in support of Julian's religious reforms but in the hope of obtaining some political advantage over Antioch from the emperor." Note that not all reactions were so polite. At Heliopolis a deacon who had destroyed pagan statues during Constantine's reign was now killed during Julian's reign: see Theodoret, *HE* 3.7.2–3.

had defected from Procopius and start rethinking their relationship with Valens at once.[27]

## GUARANTEES OF AUTONOMY

Once Constantine's goodwill had liberated the community of Orcistus, the citizens decided to publicize their success by inscribing the documents on a thick pillar. "The setting up of a monument with a text inscribed in Latin in a place that would be noticed by fellow members of the community was just one part of the general adoption of Roman urban culture by provincial subjects." Since Constantine himself had stressed the dramatic differences his reign portended for the eastern provinces, this monument became a visible token of the city's new Roman identity in a new empire. Such moments of distinctive political, cultural, or religious transformation marked eras when communities and individuals commonly redefined themselves in public monuments and buildings: "periods of monumentalization often seem to characterize the formative periods of cultures, civilizations, or states, rather than their apogees." On this monument Orcistus created a sparkling new identity for itself as an independent city that participated in Latin culture and enjoyed the patronage of Constantine and his sons.[28]

Orcistus soon found yet other means of ensuring its standing as an autonomous city. Once it had emphasized its Romanness by appealing for the emperor's patronage in Latin; then it discovered the blessings of big bureaucracy. The region of Phrygia had previously been part of the large province of Asia, and then of the smaller province of Phrygia and Caria. In the reorganization of provinces under Diocletian Phrygia had become two separate provinces, Phrygia Prima (Pacatiana) in the west and Phrygia Secunda (Salutaris) in the east. Phrygia Secunda included the cities of Midaion, Nacolea, and Dorylaeum. Cities a bit farther east, such as Pessinus, Amorium, and Orcistus, had in the past likewise been

---

[27] Battle at Nacolea: Ammianus Marcellinus, *Res gestae* 26.9.7, Zosimus, *Historia nova* 4.8.3; on Procopius' revolt, see Van Dam (2002) 103–6, and Lenski (2002) 68–115.

[28] Quotation about monument and text from Edmondson (2002) 47, commenting on Latin inscriptions in Lusitania; quotation about monumentalization from Woolf (1996) 30–31.

included in the older, larger provinces. But now their administrative assignment was in question.

At the end of the fourth century the large neighboring province of Galatia was also divided into smaller provinces, Galatia Prima in the east and Galatia (Secunda) Salutaris in the west. Pessinus became the metropolitan capital of the new province of Galatia Salutaris, which now also included Amorium and Orcistus. Once a Phrygian town, Orcistus had become a Galatian town. Since the reign of Diocletian provinces had furthermore been grouped into larger administrative units, the dioceses. Asia Minor was partitioned diagonally into two large dioceses. Phrygia Secunda was in the diocese of Asiana, which included the provinces in western and southwestern Asia Minor, and Galatia Salutaris in the diocese of Pontica, which included the provinces in central, northern, and eastern Asia Minor. Orcistus obviously benefited from these administrative realignments. By being moved to a different province, which in turn was assigned to a different diocese, Orcistus was free from any possibility of being subordinated again to Nacolea. A double administrative boundary, provincial and diocesan, now separated the two cities.[29]

Orcistus also acquired its own bishop. In 325, at about the time that Orcistus was preparing or sending its petition, Constantine had summoned the bishops of the eastern empire to meet in a great council. Originally this ecumenical council was scheduled to meet at Ancyra to the northeast of Orcistus; then it was moved to Nicaea, to the northwest of Orcistus. Since many of the bishops from the Levant would have traveled to this council overland on the roads through central Asia Minor, the people of Orcistus could see that churchmen now enjoyed the use of the imperial system of transportation. This assistance with transportation was such a notable perk that its excessive use by churchmen would infuriate one pagan observer. Among the attendees at this council were a few bishops from Phrygia. Most came

[29] For lists of the cities in these provinces, see Jones (1971) 530–33. For the division of Galatia, see Belke and Restle (1984) 55; the creation of Galatia Salutaris, Pietri (1997b) 623–27. Note the clear observation in Ammianus Marcellinus, *Res gestae* 26.9.1, on the reassignment of Pessinus: "Phrygiae quondam, nunc Galatiae oppidum."

from cities in western and southern Phrygia; from northern Phrygia the bishop of Dorylaeum attended. Once Orcistus became a proper city, however, it also became an episcopal see, and bishops from Orcistus started showing up in the lists of churchmen at councils during the fifth and later centuries. Bishops from Nacolea also attended these later councils. But since the ecclesiastical administrative structure tended to follow the imperial structure, these bishops were in different ecclesiastical provinces, each the suffragan of a different metropolitan bishop. Both the imperial administration and the ecclesiastical hierarchy now ensured the standing of Orcistus as a free city.[30]

Modern scholars have provided the final guarantee of the autonomy of Orcistus. In *Tabula Imperii Byzantini*, the lavish survey of cities in the Byzantine empire, the entry for Orcistus is in the volume on Galatia and Lycaonia and the entry for Nacolea in the volume on Phrygia and Pisidia. Now that the hardcovers of modern scholarly books have separated the two cities, Orcistus need no longer worry about subordination to Nacolea. A different civil province, a different civil diocese, its own bishopric in a different ecclesiastical province, discussion by modern historians in different volumes of *TIB*: Orcistus probably never dreamed that its petition to Constantine would be so successful.[31]

[30] Constantine's invitation to use imperial transportation: Eusebius, *Vita Constantini* 3.6.1. Indignation: Ammianus Marcellinus, *Res gestae* 21.16.18. For the Phrygian bishops at the council of Nicaea, see Gelzer, Hilgenfeld, and Cuntz (1898) 36–37, 67. Later bishops of Orcistus: Belke and Restle (1984) 211; of Nacolea: Belke and Mersich (1990) 344–46.

As episcopal sees, these Christian cities could now start competing with each other over the acquisition of relics and the construction of shrines. Nothing is known about any Christian shrines at Orcistus. But at least by the fifth century Germia, a city in Galatia about thirty-five miles east of Orcistus, had built a large church dedicated to the archangel St. Michael. Julian had once detoured to visit the nearby shrine of Cybele at Pessinus; this shrine of St. Michael eventually became so important that in 563 the emperor Justinian visited: see Theophanes, *Chronographia* a.m. 6056, with Mitchell (1993) 2:128–29.

[31] Orcistus has also prevailed in standard reference handbooks of the ancient world such as *Paulys Real-Encyclopädie der classischen Altertumswissenschaft*, in which discussion of its correspondence with Constantine makes its entry almost twice as long as that for Nacolea: see Ruge (1935) and (1939).

## "OUR LANGUAGE"

Despite this success, Orcistus was nevertheless wrong about the future. Even though Constantine increasingly clarified his preference for Christianity, Orcistus would continue to hedge by saying nothing specific about its own religious affiliations. With regard to religion, the emperor could read whatever he wanted in the vague remarks of the petition. In contrast, Orcistus had wagered explicitly on culture, Greek or Latin. At the time its petition in Latin had been successful. The use of Latin in the East furthermore retained imperial support during the fourth century, since subsequent emperors in the eastern provinces, with the notable exception of Julian, were likewise native Latin speakers. Jovian and Valens were from frontier zones in the Balkans, like the Tetrarchs and the family of Constantine, and Theodosius was a native of Spain. Their knowledge of Greek and sympathy with Greek culture were quite limited. Jovian had Julian's library at Antioch burned down "with all its books." Greek panegyrists would have to apologize to Valens for using a language he could not understand. Theodosius did try to enhance his limited education by learning enough Roman history to avoid the overbearing behavior of famous Roman generals like Marius and Sulla. But his knowledge of Greek was still so rudimentary that he used his stumbling recitation of the Greek alphabet as a technique to soften his anger. Even though provincial magistrates used Greek in their daily activities and the imperial courts often used Greek in letters and rescripts to cities and individuals, during the reigns of these western emperors Latin was still the official language of the imperial administration in the eastern empire.[32]

During the fourth century familiarity with Latin remained an important qualification for service in the imperial administration. Many of the men whose skill in both languages had assisted their careers were natives

---

[32] Jovian and Julian's library: Eunapius, *Fragmenta historica* 29.1 = *Suda* I.401. For Valens' ignorance of Greek, see Van Dam (2002) 107–8, 119–21, and Lenski (2002) 94–96. Theodosius' education: *Epitome de Caesaribus* 48.11–12, 15. For the relationship between Latin and Greek in the imperial administration, see Jones (1964) 988: "In effect...Latin was used for very limited purposes only."

of eastern Greek provinces who had learned Latin. Already as a young man Hermogenes had served at an imperial court as a secretary. Afterward he studied Greek rhetoric and philosophy; in addition he learned "Italian," that is, Latin. As a result, he became an adviser to Constantine, "the most just emperor," at Constantinople. Later, probably during the reign of Constantius, he became governor of Achaea, and eventually perhaps prefect of the East. Strategius was known for "his facility in both languages." After he served as an interpreter in the investigation of various religious cults in the East, Constantine and Constantius promoted him to increasingly more powerful offices, including a prefecture during the mid-350s. Although a career military man himself, Constantine nevertheless appreciated this magistrate's learning, and he even changed his military name of Strategius (derived from the Greek word for "general") to Musonianus, a name that reflected his familiarity with learned culture. Musonianus was now a man of the Muses. Flavius Domitius Leontius, who served as prefect of the East and consul during the early 340s, received a laudatory dedication from the municipal council at Beirut, probably his hometown. Since Beirut was noted as a center for the study of Roman law, this dedication was in Latin. Two relatives from a distinguished family at Beirut were both successful at advancing their careers. Anatolius studied Roman law at Beirut before moving to Rome and eventually becoming prefect of Illyricum in the mid-340s. His relative, also named Anatolius, likewise studied Roman law. After declining appointment as prefect of Rome, he became prefect of Illyricum in the later 350s. In a letter to this Anatolius, Libanius recommended Theodorus, a native of Arabia who had studied law at Beirut. A few years later Theodorus served as a provincial governor in western Asia Minor. Julianus was a native of Syria whom Libanius recommended for imperial offices during the 360s, in part because of his distinction in both Greek rhetoric and "the language of the rulers." Greeks who held offices in the West had certainly learned Latin. Martinianus was a native of Cappadocia who served as governor of Sicily and vicar of Africa during the later 350s and prefect of Rome in 378. Publius Ampelius was a native of Antioch who served as governor of Africa in 364 and prefect of Rome in the early 370s. Flavius Hypatius was a native of Thessalonica. His sister married the emperor Constantius II, and his brother served as governor of some eastern provinces. He himself served as prefect of Rome in 379 and prefect of Italy in the early 380s.[33]

Eventually of course Greek replaced Latin as the official language of the imperial administration in the eastern provinces. As a preview of this trend, increasingly during the fourth century the bilingual office holders were more commonly native Latin speakers who learned Greek and held offices in the East. Aradius Rufinus was a native of Rome who served on an embassy from the "eternal city" to Julian at Antioch. Because these ambassadors were supporters of pagan cults, the emperor rewarded most of them with high offices in the West. But because Aradius Rufinus was in addition familiar with "the ancient wise men, both those of your [Latin] language and those of the Greek language,"

[33] Hermogenes: Himerius, *Orat.* 48.18, imperial court, 28, "Greek and Italian," emperor at Constantinople, with *PLRE* 1:424–25, "F. Hermogenes 9." If he can be identified with the Hermogenes who served as prefect of the East in the later 350s, then he was a native of Pontus: see Ammianus Marcellinus, *Res gestae* 19.12.6, with *PLRE* 1:423, "Hermogenes 3." Strategius Musonianus: Ammianus Marcellinus, *Res gestae* 15.13.1–2, with *PLRE* 1:611–12, and Drijvers (1996), suggesting that Strategius knew Aramaic in addition to, or perhaps instead of, Latin. Leontius: *ILS* 1:271–72, no. 1234, with *PLRE* 1:502–3, "Fl. Domitius Leontius 20." Anatolius, prefect during 340s: Eunapius, *Vitae sophistarum* 490; Anatolius, prefect during 350s: Libanius, *Ep.* 391.13–14, prefecture at Rome; with Bradbury (2000), distinguishing these two men, against the conflation in *PLRE* 1:59–60, "Anatolius 3." Theodorus: Libanius, *Ep.* 339.6–7, with *PLRE* 1:897, "Theodorus 11." Julianus: Libanius, *Ep.* 668.1, language of the rulers, 1296.1, a Syrian, 2, "knowledgeable in our culture and also familiar with the culture of the Italians"; with *PLRE* 1:472, "Iulianus 15." For Beirut as a legal center during the fourth century, see Hall (2004) 195–209, 282–83. Martinianus: Van Dam (2002) 58–59, 120–21. According to Gregory of Nazianzus, *Epitaph.* 52 (*PG* 38.36) = *Anthologia Graeca* 8.116, Martinianus had become the "leader of the noble Cappadocians of Rome"; interpreted by Métivier (2005) 344, as an indication of a community of Cappadocians at Rome. Publius Ampelius: Ammianus Marcellinus, *Res gestae* 28.4.3, with *PLRE* 1:56–57, and Van Dam (1996) 27–28. Flavius Hypatius: Julian, *Orat.* 3.106B–107D, from Thessalonica; with *PLRE* 1:308–9, "Fl. Eusebius 40" (his brother), 448–49, "Flavius Hypatius 4."

Julian kept him at his court by appointing him as count of the East in 363. As governor of Achaea he appointed Vettius Agorius Praetextatus, a distinguished senator at Rome who was known for his translations of Greek poetry and philosophical treatises. Nicomachus Flavianus was the scion of a prominent senatorial family at Rome who served as governor of the province of Asia in the early 380s. While traveling through Greece to take up his governorship he received three orations in Greek from Himerius, a famous teacher at Athens. Postumianus was a native most likely of Italy who held various offices before becoming prefect of the East in 383, when Gregory of Nazianzus praised him for his marvelous facility in "both cultures." Flavius Rufinus was a native of southern Gaul who served as *magister officiorum*, chief of staff, at the court of Theodosius. Shortly after his appointment in 388 he needed a translator to read a letter from Libanius; but by the time he visited Antioch as the prefect of the East during the winter of 392–393, he was able to have a conversation with Libanius in "our language."[34]

The use of Greek gradually became more common in the imperial administration of the East. Libanius' fears about the rise of a rival culture turned out to be unfounded, because by the reign of Theodosius almost 80 percent of the top imperial magistrates in the East, prefects, vicars, and governors, had had advanced study in Greek culture. At the end of the fourth century the emperors Arcadius and Honorius conceded that provincial governors could publish their judicial decisions in either Latin

---

[34] Aradius Rufinus: Ammianus Marcellinus, *Res gestae* 23.1.4, embassy; Libanius, *Ep.* 1493.2, wise men, 5, "you are an offshoot of the best Rome." Aradius Rufinus returned to Italy to serve as prefect of Rome in 376; in the early fifth century his daughters still owned estates in southern Italy: see Symmachus, *Ep.* 7.126, with *PLRE* 1:775–76, "Aradius Rufinus 11." Praetextatus: see his epitaph, *ILS* 1:278–279, no. 1259, *a tergo* 8–12, for his skill as an editor in "either language"; with Bloch (1945) 203–9, and *PLRE* 1:722–24, for his translations of Themistius' commentary on treatises by Aristotle. Flavianus: Himerius, *Orat.* 12, 36, 43, with Barnes (1987) 213–14, 224–25. Flavianus' father, Virius Nicomachus Flavianus, translated Philostratus' *Life of Apollonius* into Latin: see Sidonius, *Ep.* 8.3.1. Postumianus: Gregory of Nazianzus, *Ep.* 173.1, with *PLRE* 1:718, "Postumianus 2." Flavius Rufinus: Libanius, *Ep.* 865.3, translator, 1106.5, our language; with *PLRE* 1:778–81, "Flavius Rufinus 18."

or Greek. At Beirut the law school began to teach in Greek, and famous jurists wrote text books and commentaries on Roman law in Greek. By the later 430s Cyrus, prefect of the East, was issuing his official decrees in Greek. During the long reign of Theodosius II the court entourage increasingly used Greek. When the western emperor Valentinian III wished to communicate with the court at Constantinople, he sent as his envoy Consentius, a native of southern Gaul who nevertheless spoke Greek like a native. In the early sixth century the prefect John the Cappadocian decided that even the official business for the parts of Italy still under the rule of the eastern empire would be conducted in Greek.[35]

The expansion of Christianity in the eastern empire should hence be interpreted as an aspect of a larger cultural phenomenon, and not as simply a religious transformation. In the early empire Greek cities had had to accommodate a Latin imperial administration. Orcistus guessed, correctly, that it was still doing so under Constantine's reign. In contrast, although Nacolea appealed to Julian's preferred religious preferences, it guessed incorrectly about culture. Greek was the future in the Greek East. Not only, of course, did Greek remain as the language of municipal administration. Eventually it would also become the preferred language of imperial administration in the Greek East, and Latin would be gradually demoted to the standing of an antiquarian language, necessary for reading older imperial legislation but not the primary language for new legislation. In the Byzantine empire Greek would become the "language of the Romans." Even though Constantine had defined the future of religion in the East by promoting Christianity, Julian had nevertheless previewed the future of both culture and administration with his support of Greekness. Constantine's religious preference and

[35] For the percentage of "élites cultivées et sensibles aux impératifs de la paideia" among imperial magistrates, see Petit (1955) 368–70, 413. Latin or Greek: *CJ* 7.45.12, dated to 397. Rochette (1997) 173–74, suggests that at Beirut instruction switched from Latin to Greek between 381/382 and 410/420; for the teachers, see Hall (2004) 210–13. John the Lydian, *De magistratibus* 2.12, 3.42, Cyrus, 3.68, John the Cappadocian, with C. Kelly (2004) 32–36, for John the Lydian's distaste for Cyrus' reform. Consentius: Sidonius, *Carm.* 23.228–40, with *PLRE* 2:308–9.

Julian's cultural preference each shaped the inheritance of the Byzantine empire that was the successor to the eastern Roman empire, and they should be credited as co-founders of Byzantine society. After the fourth century cities in the eastern provinces had to deal with a Roman administration that was both Christian and Greek.[36]

---

[36] For the reassertion of Greek in the East, see Zgusta (1980): "die stärkere Rolle des Lateinischen in der Zeit von Diokletian und Konstantin war nur vorübergehend" (p. 136), and Millar (1998), on the Roman Near East after Constantine: "neither a 'Roman' ethnicity nor the Latin language . . . played any significant part in determining personal or group identity in the Near East in this period, either in society in general or within the Christian church" (p. 160). For Greek as the "language of the Romans," see Dagron (1994) 220n.6.

# FALLING WATER

## CHAPTER EIGHT

S A PERMANENT MEMORIAL TO THEIR SUCCESS THE CITI-
zens of Orcistus had inscribed their petition and the letters
from Constantine on a large pillar that may have served as
the pedestal for a statue of the emperor. Initially this monument had been erected to announce the autonomy of the city, warn off
neighboring cities, and publicize the generosity of Constantine. It also
commemorated the city's surprising good fortune. At a time when it
was difficult to expect even a reply from imperial magistrates who were
overwhelmed with requests, somehow this small city had received not
one, but two favorable responses directly from the emperor himself.[1]

Then the pillar faded into obscurity for well over a millennium, until
Richard Pococke stumbled upon it during a trip through central Asia
Minor in the late winter and early spring of 1740. In a large plain "of a
very barren white clay" he discovered some ruins and a few inscriptions,
"one of them in Latin . . . of the time of Constantine." Almost a century
later William Hamilton returned to the site and found the pillar again,

---

[1] For the obstacles for petitioners, see C. Kelly (2004) 128: "easy access to government
in the Roman Empire remained a grand ideal rather than an administrative reality."

but this time being used as a cornerstone in a new dam for a watermill. Because it was upside-down and under the falling water, he could read only enough of the inscription to confirm it was the one published by Pococke. In 1859 when the indefatigable Theodor Mommsen was collecting Latin inscriptions from Asia Minor for inclusion in the third volume of the *Corpus Inscriptionum Latinarum*, he sent J. Mordtmann to the site to make another copy. Mordtmann searched four mills, but left without finding the pillar. At the time Mommsen was deeply disappointed, almost embarrassed, as if he had failed his duty as editor. Since he hence had to base his edition on the earlier partial transcriptions of Pococke and Hamilton, in his introduction he hoped that other visitors would keep looking.[2]

William Ramsay and J. R. S. Sterrett soon arrived to search for the pillar. Their visit in 1883 represented a somewhat disconcerting mixture of cultural romanticism about the East and intellectual superiority about their own Western scholarship. Sterrett described their journey as a visit to a fairytale world: "There is ever a charm about the quaint unchanging Orient." Ramsay was pleased to explain how they inveigled the local elders: "it is a universal rule in the east that if you wish to get anything you must show complete indifference about it." These days their condescending attitudes would make them vulnerable to an accusation of Orientalism. After hosting a feast of roast sheep, they convinced the locals to lead them to the correct mill. Additional expansion of the causeway had by now hidden the stone from view.

---

[2]  Discovery: Pococke (1745) 85. Pococke published a partial transcription of the text, primarily the front panel, in Pococke (1752) 10. Mill: Hamilton (1842) 1:447, discovery, 2:432–33, no. 154, partial transcription of text. Disappointment: Mommsen (1887) 309.

On the recycling of monuments already in late antiquity, note a pillar from Hadrianopolis in northern Asia Minor, described in Feissel and Kaygusuz (1985). This pillar, slightly taller, wider, and thicker than the pillar at Orcistus, was initially inscribed with a dedication to Commodus on its front face in the early 180s and used as the base for a statue of the emperor. Eventually this pillar was moved to a nearby village, where in the mid-sixth century a letter to local landowners from the imperial court was engraved on its other three faces.

Ramsay paid the mill's owner to remove the pillar, but found it covered with encrusted scale. In the ancient world the markers on tombs often warned against grave robbing. In Cappadocia, for instance, Gregory of Nazianzus would compose a whole series of such admonitory epitaphs that allowed tombstones to speak for themselves. "Once I was an untouched tomb. . . . Now a wild beast from my own household has demolished me for the sake of gold." Ramsay now worried that if he showed too great an interest the locals would conclude there was gold inside the pillar and destroy it. So he had the pillar restored to its place in the embankment.[3]

Three years later Ramsay returned. This time he distributed some token gifts (including "small revolvers"!) and paid to have the pillar removed again. Although he and Mommsen had hoped to have it shipped to Germany, Ramsay arranged to have the incrustation chipped away on the spot. His transcription formed the basis for a new edition by Mommsen. In 1928 William Calder and his companions checked the pillar once more. They exposed more of the front panel by chipping away a layer of mason's mortar, and in 1956 Calder published a complete text.

This pillar has had many lives. Initially it celebrated the success of the petition from Orcistus and the subsequent enhancement of the city's rank. Then the stone itself became more valuable than the words, and it was cemented into a building. Once the small village of Orcistus had puffed up its reputation by mentioning its watermills; fifteen hundred years later the pillar recording its successful petition had become a prop in the construction of a new mill. Sometimes the passage of time does seem to have its own mischievous sense of humor. The documents finally

[3] Sterrett (1889) 3. Ramsay's account of his two visits was printed in Mommsen (1887) 310–14, and partially reprinted in Sterrett (1889) 11–12; for an appreciation of the pioneering explorations of Ramsay and his collaborators in Asia Minor, see Frend (1996) 91–107, 130–37. Epitaph: Gregory of Nazianzus, *Epigram.* 51 (*PG* 38.110) = *Anthologia Graeca* 8.178, with Morrisson (1981), on the plundering of tombs and the legislation about windfall discoveries during the Byzantine period, and Rebillard (2003) 73–95, on the concern for protecting tombs. For an overview of the modern history of the inscription, see Chastagnol (1981a) 381–84.

regained their historical importance once scholars found and edited the texts. Now the petition and Constantine's responses are central to academic discussions of the emperor's religious and cultural policies in the Greek East. Unfortunately the pillar itself can no longer share in its modern reputation. Sometime after Calder's visit the locals did smash it to pieces in the expectation of finding gold inside. These days the fragments are apparently just heaped in a wooden crate. This coffin is in a museum in Afyon Karahisar, ancient Akroenos, about fifty miles southwest of Orcistus. In the early fourth century a petition had liberated Orcistus from subordination to a neighboring city; now, in an ironic twist of fate, a neighboring city has claimed the fragments of the inscription of that petition. The only consolation is that at least it is not Nacolea.[4]

The various fates of this inscription are a reminder of how far our scholarly interest in the content of the texts diverges from the concerns of the locals, both ancient and modern. Long ago the people of Orcistus had erected the pillar in order to display the words of their petition and the imperial responses. In modern times the local residents seem to have thought that the ancient words were an indication of hidden treasure. Greek citizens then, Turkish citizens now: in both cases most of the locals could not actually read the Latin texts. Far more important than the content of the texts was what the words represented, imperial patronage back then, the hope of great wealth now.

---

[4] When Calder revisited the monument in 1951, it was already broken, and its pieces "were helping to prop the leaking lade of the *aquimolina* beside which Pococke, Hamilton, and Ramsay saw it": see Calder (1954) 285. For the fragments and the museum, see the letter of T. Drew-Bear quoted in Chastagnol (1981a) 383. On Akroenos, see Belke and Mersich (1990) 177–78, and Brixhe and Drew-Bear (1997) 80–83.

# EMPEROR AND GOD

## SECTION THREE

FTER HIS VICTORY IN 312 CONSTANTINE INITIATED CON-
struction of a series of churches and shrines at Rome. The
most impressive was an enormous monumental complex on
the Vatican Hill. The approach to this complex eventually
included an expansive courtyard and a porch leading to a large church
dedicated to St. Peter. Within the church a transept divided the long
central nave and its side aisles from the apse. In front of the apse, at
the center of the transept, was a shrine commemorating the tomb of
St. Peter. This church quickly became a favorite recipient of imperial
patronage. Later traditions claimed that Constantine endowed it with
extensive properties, and that he and his mother, Helena, presented the
shrine with a large cross of gold.[1]

Although primarily a remembrance of St. Peter, this church also commemorated Constantine. On the arch that separated the nave from the
transept an inscription recalled his success and generosity. "Under your

---

[1] *Liber pontificalis* 34.17, cross, 19–20, endowments, with Krautheimer (1937–1980)
5:171–285, for a comprehensive overview of the church, and Curran (2000) 109–14,
for a survey of the sequence of construction: "an example of Constantine's self-
promotion through a monumental Christian medium" (p. 112). Holloway (2004)
120–55, summarizes recent archaeology of the tomb site.

leadership the world has raised itself triumphant to the stars. As a result, Constantine the victor has built this hall for you." With a dedication that attributed the emperor's military victories to God's guidance this arch became the equivalent of a Christian response to the Arch of Constantine that stood in the symbolic heart of the city. On that triumphal arch the senate and people of Rome had interpreted the emperor's victory in a "Republican" context as the liberation of the capital. On this ecclesiastical arch the victorious emperor had instead expressed his gratitude for God's leadership.[2]

In the apse of the church another inscription celebrated the building itself. "This [church] that you see is a seat of justice, a house of faith, and a hall of modesty. All piety possesses it. This celebrated [church] rejoices in the virtues of father and son, and it makes its own *auctor* equal in the praises of the *genitor*." The suggestively imprecise wording of this dedication is open to conflicting interpretations. One intriguing possibility is that the dedication celebrated the virtues of Father and Son, that is, God and Jesus Christ, and that it essentially equated Jesus Christ the "Creator" with God the "Progenitor." In this perspective the dedication was a theological statement, a pointed contribution to the ongoing controversies among churchmen about the exact formulation of the relationship between God the Father and Jesus Christ the Son. Another possibility is that the son of Constantine who controlled Italy after his father's death, either Constans until his death in 350 or Constantius afterward, wanted due recognition for completing the church. In that case the dedication equated the son, the "builder" who finally finished the project, with his father, the "founder" of the church. This reading of the inscription would then transform the church into yet another monument highlighting successive generations of the imperial dynasty,

---

[2] Dedication on arch: *ICUR* 2.1:20, no. 6 = *ICUR* nova series 2:5, no. 4092 = *ILCV* 1:340, no. 1752 = Grünewald (1990) 221, no. 263. The use of the title of *victor* suggests that this dedication was added after Constantine's victory over Licinius in 324: see Appendix 2; for the Republican context of the Arch of Constantine, see Chapter 2. Accompanying the dedicatory inscription was a mosaic that depicted Constantine presenting a model of the church to Jesus Christ and St. Peter: see Frothingham (1883), and Krautheimer (1937–1980) 5:177.

and it would again hint at a latent tension between Constantine and one of his sons at Rome. Since by the end of his reign Constantine's popularity at the capital had faded, a son might want to distinguish himself even in the completion of this church.[3]

This dedication is hence open to a theological interpretation as a claim about the fundamental equality of Father and Son, or a political interpretation as a comment on the uneasy dynamics between father and son. Yet another interpretation would shuffle some of these actors into a different combination by suggesting that the dedication recognized Constantine, the builder of the church, as the equal of his Begetter, God the Father. In that case the dedication was equating emperor and God. Perhaps the ambiguity was deliberate, and ancient readers were meant to understand all these meanings simultaneously. If so, then rather than trying to resolve the interpretive tension by insisting upon just one perspective, modern scholars must understand the role of the ambiguity itself in late Roman society. Father and Son, the emperor and one of his sons, God and emperor: these dueling interpretations suggest that in late Roman society the discourse about the political philosophy of a Christian emperor had merged with arguments over the Trinitarian theology of the Christian God.

In the early fourth century a Christian emperor was certainly a novelty. Three centuries after the crucifixion of its founder Christianity was still a comparatively small cult in the Roman world, and under the Tetrarchic emperors Christians had recently been persecuted. Eusebius of Caesarea, for instance, had been imprisoned during a visit to Egypt and apparently challenged to perform a pagan sacrifice. This outburst of direct imperial hostility was also influential in the formation of Eusebius

---

[3] Dedication in apse: *ICUR* 2.1:21, no. 10 = *ICUR* nova series 2:6, no. 4094 = *ILCV* 1:340, no. 1753. Ruysschaert (1967–1968), interprets the dedication in terms of God the Father and God the Son and suggests that it was added to the apse as an affirmation of Nicene theology after Constantius' death; Krautheimer (1937–1980) 5:177–78, (1987), prefers a reference to Constantine and a son; for an overview, see Pietri (1976) 56–57. Bowersock (2002), argues that Constans initiated construction of the church. For the promotion of the Constantinian dynasty, see Chapter 3; for Constantine's reputation at Rome, Chapter 2.

as a historian, because at the same time he was assembling documents and organizing his thoughts about the history of the early church. He collected accounts of local martyrs in a treatise entitled *Martyrs of Palestine*. He included a condensed version of this treatise as the eighth book and an account of the persecutions under the emperor Maximinus as the ninth (and final) book of the first published edition of his *Ecclesiastical History*. Persecution and martyrdom were obviously important themes in Eusebius' life and in his historical vision. In the eastern provinces that hostility finally ended with the defeat of Maximinus in 313.[4]

Eusebius published this first edition of *History* soon after Maximinus' death. Already then he seemed to have recognized that Constantine was a different sort of emperor, even if he had no personal familiarity with him. Eusebius mentioned in passing Constantine's proclamation as emperor by his father's troops, with the claim that he had previously been destined for imperial rule by God himself. He noted that Constantine had advanced on Rome after praying for the assistance of "God in heaven and his Word, the Savior of all, Jesus Christ." He compared

---

[4] For the rumors about Eusebius' suspect behavior, see Athanasius, *Apologia contra Arianos* 8.3, who claimed that Eusebius had been accused of sacrificing, and Epiphanius, *Panarion* 68.8.3–5, for a story about Potamon, a bishop in Egypt who later wondered how Eusebius had survived imprisonment: "During the persecution, were you not with me in prison? I lost an eye for the sake of the truth. But you do not seem to have been maimed in your body, and you were not martyred. Instead, you are alive and unmarked. How did you leave the prison, if you did not promise those inflicting the torture of persecution on us to perform something wicked, or if you did not do so?" See Grant (1980) 114–25, on Eusebius' interest in persecution and martyrdom, and Tabbernee (1997b), for an excellent account of the development of Eusebius' thinking about persecution in the successive editions of his *History*.

According to Sirinelli (1961), Eusebius explained the chronological coincidence of Jesus' birth and Augustus' establishment of the Roman empire as a manifestation of divine providence only after 313: "L'affirmation, après 313, d'une action divine dans un domaine tout autre, ... celui de la politique, représente un élément nouveau" (pp. 407–8). Sirinelli's extended analysis of Eusebius' historical perspective before the council of Nicaea is distinctively odd because it never mentions Constantine.

Constantine, who had been victorious at the Milvian Bridge over the Tiber River, to Moses, who had destroyed the pharaoh's army at the Red Sea. He described a statue of Constantine at the capital and its dedicatory inscription, in which the emperor asserted that he had liberated Rome through the power of the cross, "the sign of salvation." At the conclusion of this first edition Eusebius praised both Constantine and Licinius, the emperor who had defeated Maximinus, for their "piety toward the Deity."[5]

In this first edition of *History* Eusebius was most relieved that the persecutions were over in the eastern provinces. A few years later he expanded *History* by adding a tenth book that included a long sermon he had recently delivered at the dedication of a church in Tyre and a series of imperial constitutions issued in favor of Christianity. In the sermon he barely mentioned the emperors, praising them merely in passing for honoring the One and Only God and Christ, the Son of God, and for serving as the agents of the Word, the Savior. Most of the imperial edicts catalogued a series of gifts and privileges from Constantine for churches and their clergy in western provinces. Only one constitution was directly relevant for the eastern provinces, the edict of toleration agreed upon jointly by Constantine and Licinius. Even with the benefit of a few more years' hindsight Eusebius was apparently still not thinking about the significance of a Christian emperor in the eastern provinces.[6]

---

[5] For the contents and the dating of the first edition of Eusebius' *History*, see Chapter 6. Eusebius, *HE* 8.13.14, proclamation, 9.9.2, prayer, 5–8, Moses, 11, sign of salvation, 9.11.8, piety. Although Eusebius heard about Constantine's victory in 312 very quickly, his source is not obvious. Christensen (1989) 287–92, argues that Eusebius based his narrative of Constantine's triumphant arrival in *HE* 9.9.9–11 on a "politically inspired account of pagan origin" that he modified with comments about the role of Christianity.

[6] Eusebius, *HE* 10.4.16, emperors, 59–60, Logos, 10.5–7, constitutions. For Eusebius' expansion of *History* before autumn 316, see Barnes (1981) 150. Warmington (1985) 93–94, suggests that Eusebius acquired these imperial documents from a Christian imperial bureaucrat who was traveling in the East, Barnes (1992) 648, from Syracuse, Carriker (2003) 285, perhaps from a bishop involved in the Donatist controversy.

In 324 Constantine defeated Licinius and took control of the East. A year later Eusebius met Constantine for the first time at the council of Nicaea, where he was defending his theological doctrines. Over a decade later in his posthumous *Life* of Constantine he remembered the emperor at the council as a "heavenly angel of God," and he sometimes seemed to compare him to Jesus Christ. These comparisons suggest that by the time he composed this *Life*, and probably already at the council, Eusebius was evaluating the meaning of a Christian emperor in combination with his doctrines of Jesus Christ.[7]

Modern scholarship typically discusses the development of Christian theology separately from political philosophy. In terms of actual behavior, in the early empire some emperors opposed Christianity, in the later empire some emperors meddled in the disputes over orthodoxy and heresy, and their political intrigues certainly reinforced the infighting among bishops. In contrast, analyses of the idea of a Christian emperor and the idea of a Christian God are kept resolutely distinct. In modern scholarship *The Search for the Christian Doctrine of God* parallels but rarely intersects with the simultaneous development of *Early Christian and Byzantine Political Philosophy*.[8]

In terms of both the realities of late Roman society and the effectiveness of modern research, this is an odd separation. Not only did the same emperors and the same churchmen participate in the concurrent arguments over both political philosophy and theology during the fourth and subsequent centuries. In addition, the issues, the vocabulary, and the imagery overlapped considerably. Thinking about God (or gods) and thinking about emperors were two aspects of the same discourse about the intersection of divine and human in Roman society, and hence about the acquisition of authority, the representation of power, and the imposition of proper religious and political beliefs. Religious doctrines,

---

[7] Heavenly angel: Eusebius, *Vita Constantini* 3.10.3, with Chapter 11.

[8] For the titles, see the magisterial surveys of Hanson (1988) and Dvornik (1966). Since political philosophy and theology were both techniques of representation, the scholarship of art historians about the iconography of emperors is also highly relevant: see L'Orange (1984).

both pagan and Christian, provided symbolic idioms for constructing emperors and their power; images of emperors, whether Tetrarchic or Christian, likewise provided symbolic idioms for constructing deities, both pagan gods and Christian God. Each could be used to imagine the other.

The chapters in this section discuss the overlapping of these concurrent dialogues. The invention of a Tetrarchy, four emperors ruling simultaneously, had led to a reconsideration of two longstanding issues, the relative ranking of co-emperors and the affiliation between emperors and pagan deities (Chapter 9). A generation later doctrinal controversies among Christians over the relationship between God the Father and Jesus Christ the Son sometimes used ideas and terminology similar to the language and images employed in defining this college of co-emperors (Chapter 10). Articulating the role of Constantine then revisited the problem of the correlation between emperor and divinity, although now between Christian emperor and Christian God, and in his panegyrics and biography Eusebius fashioned the emperor according to his theology. Eusebius did not endorse simply a generic Christian emperor; he instead promoted a particular sort of Christian emperor that conveniently corresponded to his own doctrines (Chapter 11). Constantine's death did not end his role in this process of rethinking emperors and God, however. Even as churchmen responded to changed circumstances through their new readings of a classic text like Eusebius' *Life of Constantine*, emperors like Theodosius presented themselves as imitators of Constantine. Both *Life of Constantine* and Constantine's life influenced later generations (Chapter 12). By then, of course, the historical Constantine had long since disappeared into the competing agendas of historians, churchmen, and successor emperors. The foundation of Constantinople as New Rome had modified the significance of First Rome. In the same way every imitator of Constantine was a new Constantine, and every new Constantine further altered the meaning of the first Constantine.

# "BEGOTTEN OF THE GODS": THE IMPERIAL TETRARCHY

## CHAPTER NINE

DIOCLETIAN WAS YET ANOTHER IN THE LONG LINE OF USUR-
pers during the third century who became emperors through
military coups. After the mysterious death of the emperor
Numerianus in Bithynia, military commanders selected
Diocletian, a fellow officer, as emperor in the East in late 284. By the next
spring he and his troops were poised for a battle with the emperor Carinus, Numerianus' brother, near the middle Danube. After his victory
Diocletian had to face occasional rival usurpers and barbarian unrest
on the frontiers. He responded by selecting fellow emperors to share his
rule. Already later in 285 he appointed Maximian as a junior emperor,
and in the next year he promoted him as a co-emperor who shared
his title of Augustus. In 293 these two senior emperors appointed two
junior emperors, Constantius and Galerius, each with the title of Caesar.
Diocletian's reign was known for his ruthless suppression of challengers
and his generous promotion of co-emperors into a Tetrarchy, a college
of four emperors. This odd combination of repression and collegiality
was successful, and Diocletian's long reign of more than twenty years
restored stability to imperial rule.

It is doubtful whether Diocletian had a plan for a Tetrarchy from the beginning, either in its institutional details or as a derivative from earlier examples of shared emperorship. His immediate objectives were deeply practical: survival as an emperor, legitimation of his authority, effective administration of a vast state, reform of the system of taxation, and protection of the beleaguered frontiers. The Tetrarchic system of government was hence a pragmatic response in which Diocletian, through thoughtful deliberation or improvised good fortune, seemingly solved some of the systemic problems of the mid-third century. In terms of administration, the persistent tendency toward regional separatism now became the division of current provinces into smaller provinces and the imposition of more governors and additional layers of higher magistrates who assumed oversight for larger administrative regions. In terms of finances, irregular requisitions of commodities now became regular payments of taxes in both commodities and money. In terms of imperial rulership, anarchy now became Tetrarchy, multiple illegitimate emperors became multiple legitimate emperors, and each emperor could campaign on a frontier without worrying that the troops on another frontier might feel abandoned and support their own rival emperor. Diocletian had a knack for rejiggering problems into their own solutions.[1]

But the existence of a Tetrarchy also raised new challenges. One involved the underlying justification of imperial rule. Because Diocletian and his fellow emperors continued the trend toward associating imperial rule with religious and divine support, their reign sharpened the issue of articulating the correspondence between emperors and gods. A second, related concern involved the relationships among the emperors

---

[1] The historian Eutropius, writing in the later 360s, thought that the joint rule of Marcus Aurelius and Lucius Verus had been the first shared emperorship: see Eutropius, *Breviarium* 8.9.2: "then for the first time the Roman state obeyed two men governing the empire with equal authority, whereas up to that time it had always had individual emperors." For a survey of the arguments over Diocletian's intentions, see Kolb (1987) 1–9; for the contrasting opinions, see Kolb (1995) 31, "Diocletian recht früh weitreichende Reformen in Angriff nimmt"; Rees (2004) 89, "a makeshift alliance of affiliated emperors"; and Bowman (2005) 88, "a judicious blend of conservatism and reaction to pressing problems."

themselves. An emphasis on harmony and collegiality somehow kept the emperors together, and it even allowed for the continuation of the Tetrarchic system through retirement and replacement in 305. But even as the emperors stressed their concord and unfaltering cooperation, they also accepted a fundamental hierarchy. Not only were there two senior emperors and two junior emperors, but Diocletian ranked higher than the other senior emperor, Maximian. The awareness of this ranking might have seemed to be a recipe for disaster, since it raised the potential for disagreement, feuding, and even fragmentation. Four emperors could easily have been matched by four distinct empires. Instead, the Roman empire remained unified, "partitioned into four" but still one. In the past the oneness of the emperor had guaranteed the unity of the empire; now the harmony of the emperors would ensure the integrity of the empire. Even though there were multiple emperors, the prevailing ideology of imperial rule insisted that the Roman world remained an "undivided patrimony."[2]

## A THEOLOGY OF EMPERORSHIP

Diocletian and Maximian soon identified themselves with divinities, Jupiter (or Zeus), the lord of the gods, and his assistant Hercules. According to one panegyrist, Jupiter was the "heavenly founder or father of your family." In particular, because Jupiter was the "creator of Diocletian," Diocletian added the name of Jovius; and because Maximian shared the "power of your Hercules," he added the name of Herculius. After their promotions Galerius added the name of Jovius, and Constantius of Herculius. Jupiter in particular was the patron deity of this first Tetrarchy, from beginning to end. In 305, before retiring to his villa at Split, Diocletian removed his purple robes on a hill a few miles outside Nicomedia. A statue of Jupiter perched on a column presided over the ceremony of his abdication.[3]

---

[2] Aurelius Victor, *De Caesaribus* 39.30, "quadripartito imperio"; *Panegyrici latini* 11(3).6.3, "indiviso patrimonio."

[3] *Panegyrici latini* 11(3).3.2, heavenly founder, 3, "Diocletiani auctor," 6, your Hercules. Diocletian's retirement: Lactantius, *De mortibus persecutorum* 19.2. For

Diocletian and his fellow emperors had strong reasons to highlight their selection by and support from these key deities. In previous centuries emperors had commonly justified their authority through association with the prestige of the senate at Rome, the power of the army, or their benevolent concern for their subjects, especially those in Italy and at Rome. Augustus had established himself as the sole ruler and the first emperor after eliminating his rivals and essentially reconquering much of Rome's Mediterranean empire. In order to disguise his military coup he himself had insisted that he had in fact revived the institutions and values of the old Republic, and after the early years he generously honored the senate and the people of Rome. Because senators often presented themselves as the guardians of the Republic's traditions, subsequent emperors likewise paid their respects.

But by the mid-third century this notion of having revived the Republic was wearing thin. Senators were increasingly excluded from military commands, and then from provincial governorships. They had little say in the selection of new emperors: "the power of the army grew, and the empire and the right of selecting an emperor were snatched from the senate." In addition, by now almost all of the emperors were from the provinces, usually military men who spent most of their time on the frontiers and visited Italy only infrequently. Such soldier-emperors could not easily integrate themselves with the traditional mythology of the Roman Republic, its senate at Rome, and its earlier conquests. Their power came from the support of the troops. "Enrich the soldiers," one emperor was supposed to have advised his sons, "and ignore everyone else." Yet that support too came with a price, because the chaotic events of the mid- and later third century had proved conclusively that emperors who failed to maintain the loyalty of their troops soon lost their lives. Emperors were looking for an ideology of imperial power that

Diocletian's early association with Jupiter, see Kolb (1987) 19–21; for the role of Jupiter in Tetrarchic succession, note Kolb (1997) 37: "Im Prinzip . . . ist nicht Diocletian der *auctor imperii* der anderen Herrscher, sondern Jupiter." Themistius, *Orat.* 11.145b, once referred to Diocletian as "the name derived from Dios." Since Δῖος, "god," was Zeus, Themistius was here presumably punning on Dio-cletian, or his earlier Greek name of Dio-kles.

could transcend any dependence on outdated Republican sentiments, senatorial pretensions, and the fickleness of military loyalties.[4]

One alternative was an ideology that located the source of imperial power in its association or even identification with divine power. In the provinces communities had already founded cults in honor of emperors and members of their families. By the later third century, however, emperors themselves were taking the lead in identifying themselves more closely with divine power and sometimes directly with gods. Pagan emperors affiliated themselves with the leading pagan gods. In the later third century the emperor Aurelian was thought to have once deflected an uprising among some soldiers by arguing that they had no say in the making or ending of his rule. "He said that the soldiers were mistaken if they supposed that the destiny of emperors was in their hands. For he said that god [Jupiter] alone had bestowed the purple robe and had measured the length of a reign." In this perspective the sanction of divine authority trumped military power.[5]

---

[4] Power of army: Aurelius Victor, *De Caesaribus* 37.5, with Curran (2000) 26–35, on soldiers and senate, and Kulikowski (2006), on the link between usurpations and barbarian invasions. Septimius Severus' advice: Dio, *Historiae Romanae* 77.15.2. During the civil wars both Licinius and Constantine offered financial concessions to veterans: see the letter of Licinius issued in 311, ed. Riccobono (1941) 456–58, no. 93, and Constantine's pronouncement in *CTh* 7.20.2, dated to 320 by Corcoran (1996) 257–59.

[5] Aurelian's claim: Anonymus post Dionem (= Dio Continuatus), *Frag.* 10.6 = [Peter the Patrician], *Frag.* 178, with Watson (1999) 186–87.

Note that the involvement of the army in proclaiming Christian emperors lingered as a concern among churchmen. When Eusebius first described the accession of Constantine, he highlighted the role of the army alone: see Eusebius, *HE* 8, Appendix 5, "he was proclaimed immediately at the beginning as greatest emperor and Augustus by the soldiers." But in his revised version of this passage published a few years later before autumn 316, he downplayed the army's role in favor of God's selection: see Eusebius, *HE* 8.13.14, "Constantine . . . was proclaimed immediately at the beginning as greatest emperor and Augustus by the soldiers and long before them by God himself, the Emperor over all." For discussion of this revision, see Christensen (1983) 186, 198–99, 203–4, (1989) 121–22; also Chapter 6, for the editions of Eusebius' *HE*. Decades later after Constantine's death Eusebius emphasized only God's role: see Eusebius, *Vita Constantini* 1.24, "On his own

A generation later Diocletian and the other Tetrarchic emperors continued this trend of highlighting their association with gods. But rather than merely claiming that their power derived from gods, they openly identified themselves with Jupiter, "the ruler of heaven," and Hercules, "the pacifier of the earth." "Diocletian was using the new nomenclature to indicate that he and his partners somehow participated directly in the divine nature of Jupiter and Hercules." At a time when earlier representations of imperial power were ineffective or unacceptable, the emperors appropriated an idiom of pagan deities in order to articulate their authority. This religious language provided a medium through which they could fashion their authority and negotiate relationships with senators, local notables, and the army. In reality of course they certainly still needed the support of their army, and dynastic succession remained a powerful endorsement for assuming imperial rule. But in theory their standing as gods allowed them to transcend dependence on the affirmation of the senate at Rome and the acclamation of the troops. Now any opposition to their rule could be represented as not just seditious, but also sacrilegious, impious, even unbelief. A theology of Tetrarchic emperorship could help stabilize the politics of Tetrarchic emperors.[6]

Subsequent emperors intuitively appreciated the effectiveness of identifying with deities, and this Tetrarchic theological idiom remained attractive for non-Christian emperors throughout the fourth century. After Diocletian and Maximian abdicated in 305, Constantius and Galerius, the new senior emperors, promoted Maximinus and Severus as the new junior emperors, who in turn adopted the names of Jovius and Herculius, respectively. When Licinius became an emperor, he added the name of Jovius; for a short time while he was allied with Maximian and Maxentius, Constantine added the name of Herculius. Soon,

God, the ruler of the entire universe, selected Constantine." By then Eusebius had transformed the commander of a military coup into God's chosen ruler.

[6] Jupiter and Hercules: *Panegyrici latini* 10(2).11.6. Quotation about nomenclature from Digeser (2000) 27; also Kolb (1987) 90, "Teilhabe am göttlichen Wesen," 93, "eine göttliche Familie."

however, Constantine discarded this name with pagan overtones, and subsequent Christian emperors of course followed his lead. But even these Christian emperors maintained the Tetrarchic paradigm, because while they may have disavowed any association with pagan gods, they retained a close connection to, even an identification with, the Christian God. A theology of Tetrarchic emperorship could readily mutate into a theology of Christian emperorship.[7]

It is not surprising that during his brief reign Julian would revive these earlier associations with Tetrarchic gods. By converting from Christianity to paganism he was the opposite of his uncle Constantine. As a result, his ideological ancestors in some respects were the Tetrarchic emperors. Julian hence emphasized his connections with divine support in public portraits that depicted "Jupiter as he appeared from heaven to offer him the imperial insignia, a diadem and a purple robe." He also associated himself with Hercules in his roles as mediator with the gods and savior of mankind. Julian effectively presented himself as a neo-Tetrarchic emperor who was reviving aspects of the Tetrarchic political theology that had defined an influential model of authority by linking emperors directly with pagan gods. For both Christians and pagans, sanction from, association with, and even identification with deities now provided a powerful idiom for constructing imperial rule during the fourth century.[8]

## HARMONY

Multiple emperors, even when they all acknowledged each other to be legitimate, nevertheless always had the potential to initiate civil wars. Diocletian in fact was thought to have been so preoccupied with a "fear of conflicts" that he kept secrets from his colleagues. For a

---

[7] For Maximinus and Jupiter, see Chapter 6.

[8] Julian's portraits: Sozomen, *HE* 5.17; also Gregory of Nazianzus, *Orat.* 4.81, "he had gods painted on his icons." On Julian and Hercules, see Athanassiadi (1981) 132–33, in a discussion of philosophy and Greek religion. In accordance with his support for Tetrarchic political theology it is not surprising that Julian would claim that Constantine's former soldiers still "continued to venerate him like a god": see Julian, *Orat.* 1.8A.

Christian emperor like Constantine the existence of multiple pagan gods offered a telling parallel of the inevitable outcome for multiple emperors: "Pride and greediness shattered the harmony and agreement of everything.... Whom would prayers and entreaties [honor] first, and whom last?" But one oddity of the college of emperors founded by Diocletian was its apparent immunity from divisive conflicts. In order to encourage that cooperation, Diocletian and his fellow emperors promoted an image of themselves that tried to minimize differences and highlight harmony as a distinctive, even natural, characteristic of a multiple emperorship.[9]

Before there was a Tetrarchy, Diocletian and Maximian ruled together for eight years. During this period of "Dyarchy," the rule of two emperors, they publicized their harmony in various ways. Previous emperors had specified their chosen successors as "sons"; Diocletian now acknowledged that Maximian was a true co-emperor by designating him as "brother." The legends on their coins commemorated the concord, the prosperity, the peace, and the victory "of two senior emperors," and they stressed that both emperors were under the protection of Jupiter the Defender. At least one Christian intellectual intuitively sensed that the theological terminology that was being deployed in the concurrent dispute over the relationship between God the Father and Jesus Christ his Son might also be used to describe this relationship between emperors. Lactantius, a Christian rhetorician who knew Diocletian, could discern no difference between the two emperors: "Maximian was not dissimilar from Diocletian."[10]

In Gaul, orators commemorated the successes of the two emperors in public panegyrics. Since the two surviving panegyrics from this period were addressed to Maximian, they tended to highlight his achievements and reputation, sometimes seemingly even at the expense of

---

[9] Fear: Aurelius Victor, *De Caesaribus* 39.46. Pride: Constantine, *Oratio ad sanctorum coetum* 3.2–3.

[10] *Panegyrici latini* 6(7).15.6, adoption as brother, with Kolb (1987) 47, "*Augusti fratres* hatten sich vor der tetrarchischen Epoche nur M. Aurelius and L. Verus genannt." Coins: Webb (1933) 221–95. Not dissimilar: Lactantius, *De mortibus persecutorum* 8.1.

Diocletian. As a result, both panegyrics presented Maximian as a coordinate emperor with Diocletian, in particular by stressing that they were "brothers." One panegyrist, in an oration delivered at Trier probably in 289, emphasized Maximian's association with Hercules. Since Diocletian associated himself with Jupiter, the highest of the gods, their respective divine identities would seem to suggest that Maximian had become Diocletian's helper. "You [Maximian] assisted the tottering Roman name at the side of the emperor [Diocletian] with that same opportune assistance as your Hercules once assisted your Jupiter as he struggled in a war against the earthborn [Giants]." In fact, in this orator's perspective Maximian, under his adopted name of Herculius, was the equal of Diocletian, under his adopted name of Jovius. Since some legends had given Hercules a role in the foundation of Rome, Maximian could furthermore be thought of as a founder of the capital. More significantly, this orator claimed that Maximian should be considered a founder and restorer of the empire along with Diocletian, "your brother." Because Maximian had willingly accepted the responsibilities offered by "the best of brothers," "you govern an equal portion of the state." When the two emperors had recently met, their conversation had been "brotherly," and they had "clasped together their invincible right hands." As "brothers in virtue," they ruled together "in concord."[11]

The other panegyrist, in an oration delivered probably at Trier and probably in 291, reinforced these themes. Maximian again was presented as the peer of Diocletian: "the immortal gods cannot divide their benefactions between you; whatever belongs to one, belongs to the other." Their military victories had made them into "brothers," and even though they were not the same age, they shared a "dual consensus." Each of them had the capacity to protect the Roman empire through his divine nature. "This world can be filled with Jupiter, and also with Hercules."[12]

---

[11] *Panegyrici latini* 10(2).1.5, your brother, 4.1, best of brothers, 4.2, Roman name, 9.1, hands, conversation, 9.3, virtue, concord, 9.4, equal portion, with Nixon and Rodgers (1994) 43, dating this panegyric to April 21, 289.

[12] *Panegyrici latini* 11(3).7.3, immortal gods, 7.5, brothers, 7.7, consensus, 14.4, this world, with Nixon and Rodgers (1994) 76–79, for the date of the panegyric.

Soon after the promotion of Maximian as a fellow senior emperor with Diocletian a usurper tried to muscle his way in as a third emperor. Carausius was serving as a naval commander along the Atlantic coast of Gaul when he was hailed as an Augustus, a senior emperor, in Britain. After a military stalemate Diocletian and Maximian seem to have tolerated his rule. Carausius responded by inserting himself into the language and imagery of his fellow emperors. Some of his coins depicted profiles of three emperors, identified as "Carausius and his brothers," and hailed the "peace of three senior emperors." The legends on other coins mentioned the various virtues, such as the prosperity, the providence, the salvation, and the strength, of "three senior emperors." This wishful propaganda of equality with his brother emperors was unsuccessful, however, and eventually Carausius was assassinated by one of his own magistrates. By 296 Constantius' troops had regained Britain. Diocletian and Maximian had declined to admit Carausius into their imperial fraternity. Instead, they would promote their "sons" as junior emperors.[13]

In 293 Constantius and Galerius joined this dynamic duo of emperors to form a Tetrarchy. As Caesars these new emperors were of course subordinate in seniority, and one historian even characterized them as mere "attendants." Despite these obvious distinctions in rank and status, the ideology of harmony and collegiality was extended to accommodate four coordinate emperors. Now the legends on coins advertised the "concord of two senior emperors and two junior emperors." In a panegyric to Constantius delivered in the later 290s, most likely at Trier, the orator stressed the correspondence between heaven and earth. "The kindred majesty of Jupiter and Hercules demanded a similarity between the entire world and celestial affairs in Jovian and Herculian emperors." Because Constantius had added the name of Herculius to his official nomenclature and Galerius the name of Jovius, all four emperors were Jovian and Herculian. This correlation allowed the orator to associate the emperors with various fourfold marvels of nature and the heavenly order: the four natural elements, the four seasons of a year, the four zones of the world, the four horses that pulled the chariot of the sun, the four heavenly bodies of sun, moon, morning star, and evening star.

---

[13] Carausius' coins: Webb (1933) 442–43 ("pax Auggg"), 550–56, with Carson (1987).

As complementary rulers the four emperors were different but the same, essentially manifestations of a single emperorship whose unity ensured a consolidated empire: "that immensity finally fuses in an intact empire." Despite the existence of multiple emperors, the empire was now as "solid" as one of the new coins of pure gold, known as a *solidus*, that would be minted to stabilize the imperial finances.[14]

When Diocletian and Maximian met at Rome in late 303, they dedicated a monument to commemorate their devotion to Jupiter and the anniversaries of the accessions of the emperors in the Tetrarchy. This monument consisted of five columns erected at the back of the Rostra in the old Forum. A statue of Jupiter was atop the middle column, and a statue of the guardian spirit of an emperor atop each of the other four. An inscription on one of the pedestals commemorated the "happy twentieth anniversary of the Augusti." Even though Maximian had in fact become an Augustus over a year after Diocletian's accession, the two shared an anniversary as senior emperors. Another dedicatory inscription commemorated the "happy tenth anniversary of the Caesars." Even though Constantius had apparently been appointed a junior emperor a bit before Galerius, they too shared an anniversary. Yet another dedicatory inscription commemorated the "twentieth anniversary of the emperors." This dedication had been inscribed most likely on the pedestal of the middle column that displayed the statue of Jupiter. In this case all four emperors, whether senior or junior, were included to share a common anniversary of collective emperorship. Even as this monument acknowledged distinctions of rank and seniority among the emperors, it also emphasized, under the aegis of Jupiter, their concord and harmony. The discrepancies of calendar dates posed no obstacles to their fundamental similarity.[15]

---

[14] Attendants: Ammianus Marcellinus, *Res gestae* 14.11.10. "Concordia Augg et Caess": Sutherland (1967) 279, 300, 310. *Panegyrici latini* 8(5).4.1, majesty, 4.2, fourfold phenomena, 20.2, "solido...imperio," with Nixon and Rodgers (1994) 105–6, dating this panegyric to 297, or otherwise 298. For the significance of the *solidus*, see Depeyrot (2006) 237–44.

[15] Dedications: *CIL* 6.1:251, no. 1203 = 6.4.2:3081, no. 31261, "Caesarum | decennalia | feliciter" (still extant); 6.1:251, no. 1204 = 6.4.2:3081, no. 31262, "Augustorum

## HIERARCHY

Within two years of his acclamation as emperor Diocletian had shared his title of Augustus with Maximian, his co-emperor. But he does not seem to have shared all of his power. Even though Maximian most likely had the authority to send official letters and issue rescripts and probably could publish edicts, in fact, Diocletian himself seems to have initiated all the edicts known from their joint reign. And even though these edicts were issued with the names of both emperors in the headings, Diocletian's name was always first. Despite the similarity of their official titles and their partnership in imperial authority, Diocletian nevertheless remained the senior of the two senior emperors. Diocletian's authority was preeminent, "in the manner of the great god," like that of Jupiter: "everything was administered at his nod."[16]

In 293 Diocletian and Maximian selected Constantius and Galerius as additional emperors. Even though they now shared the titles of conquest that all the emperors assumed when one was victorious, these new appointees were clearly junior emperors with the title of Caesar. Constantius was furthermore the son-in-law of Maximian, and Galerius the son-in-law of Diocletian. Ideology matched reality, since among the four emperors Diocletian and Maximian were now each a "father" and Constantius and Galerius were each a "son." Underlying this symmetry, however, was still the tacit acknowledgement that Diocletian was

---

| vicennalia | feliciter" (now lost); 6.1:252, no. 1205 = 6.4.2:3081, no. 31262, "vicennalia | imperatorum" (now lost); with Alföldy (1996) 4335, for recent bibliography, and L'Orange (1938) 20–31, discussing these inscriptions and conjectures about the two additional dedications that were never found: "die Nebeneinanderreihung der vier Imperatoren und ihre symmetrische Unterordnung unter Jupiter" (p. 28). For additional interpretation of the Monument of Five Columns, see Chapters 2–3. A town in Numidia likewise celebrated the twentieth anniversary with a dedication to all four emperors, Augusti and Caesars: see *ILS* 1:147, no. 644.

[16] Aurelius Victor, *De Caesaribus* 39.1, acclamation, 29, "dei magni ... modo," 36, "cuius nutu." For the dispute over Maximian's titles and the dates of his promotions, see the thorough review in Kolb (1987) 22–67.

somehow the progenitor of them all. "The emperors always thought of Valerius [Diocletian] as a father."[17]

Of these four emperors, apparently only Diocletian issued edicts. In some instances another emperor may have proposed a policy, but Diocletian nevertheless initiated the edicts. In his account of the outbreak of persecution in 303 Lactantius claimed that during consultations at Nicomedia, Galerius convinced the "uncommitted old man" to oppose Christianity. Diocletian finally agreed and issued a series of edicts. But he seems not to have consulted with his fellow emperors in the western provinces. Instead, he simply sent letters to Maximian and Constantius with instructions to follow his lead. According to Christian historiographical tradition, Constantius may have been reluctant to do so. His application of these edicts was superficial, just enough "so that he would not appear to dissent from the instructions of his superiors."[18]

Iconography reinforced this ranking of the emperors. On the commemorative arch that Galerius constructed at Thessalonica one panel depicted all four emperors, surrounded by images of various deities. The four emperors were all wearing the same costumes, belted tunics and cloaks, and they were about the same size. But Diocletian and Maximian were seated in the middle, and Diocletian was furthermore distinguished from his colleague by the tall scepter that he held in his left hand. Standing on each side were Galerius and Constantius. Even as this panel celebrated the harmony of the four emperors, it clearly

---

[17] Aurelius Victor, *De Caesaribus* 39.29, "ut parentem"; also *CTh* 13.10.2, "sub domino et parente nostro Diocletiano seniore A(ugusto)," with Corcoran (1996) 151–52, arguing that this edict was issued by Maximinus in 312. For Diocletian as an "uncle" to Constantius, see *Panegyrici latini* 8(5).1.3. For the assumption of victory titles by all members of the Tetrarchy, see Barnes (1982) 27.

[18] Lactantius, *De mortibus persecutorum* 10.6, old man, 15.6, letters, 15.7, dissent; also 10.4, for letters to military officers. Note that over the years Eusebius increasingly minimized Constantius' involvement: see *De martyribus Palaestinae*, recensio brevior 11.12, persecution in Gaul for only the first two years; *HE* 8.13.13, "he did not participate in the war against us"; *Vita Constantini* 1.13.2, "he kept his hands clean from their abominable impiety." For the authority of Tetrarchic emperors other than Diocletian, see Corcoran (1996) 270–74.

elevated Diocletian over Maximian, and both of them over the junior emperors.[19]

At Luxor in southern Egypt a fresco depicted a similar hierarchy of emperors. Long ago the pharaohs had repeatedly enlarged and remodeled the large temple of Amun at this city that the Greeks called Thebes or Diospolis Magna, the Great City of Zeus. In 297 Diocletian campaigned in Egypt against various revolts, and in the next year he sailed up the Nile to make treaties with local tribes. He then reorganized both the provincial administration of Egypt and the defense of its southern frontier. Perhaps as part of this reorganization Roman troops enclosed the ancient shrine of Amun with a wall and turned it into a garrison. This reconstruction included a new monument in honor of the emperors that consisted apparently of statues of the four original Tetrarchs, each perched on a column standing at each of the four corners of the intersection of two streets. The dedications inscribed on the bases of the columns are fragmentary, but each was clearly directed to a particular emperor, and each ended with a vow of eternal devotion to "his divine authority and majesty." A few years later, after the retirement of Diocletian and Maximian and other changes in the college of emperors, a similar monument of four columns and statues at another intersection commemorated the revamped Tetrarchy of the senior emperors Galerius and Licinius and the junior emperors Constantine and Maximinus. The dedications on the bases of the columns commemorated each emperor in particular roles, Galerius as "propagator of eternal peace and guardian of the public security," Licinius as "promoter of piety and destroyer of barbarian peoples," and Constantine as "promoter of youth and guardian of eternal peace." But these inscriptions furthermore respected the emperors' shared authority, since each dedication to an individual emperor ended with an expression of devotion to "*their* divine authority and majesty." This newer monument included

---

[19] For discussion of this panel, see Laubscher (1975) 69–78, with Tafeln 51, 58–60: "Das Bild der Wiederherstellung des Römischen Reiches ist zugleich Ausdruck der den Tetrarchen von Jupiter verliehenen Kosmokratie" (p. 78); with the excellent summary in Kolb (2001) 158–162.

a clearer commemoration of both individuality and collegiality in the Tetrarchy.[20]

These two monuments at prominent intersections within the camp celebrated the rule of the Tetrarchy, both the original version and a subsequent revised version. The temple of Amun was furthermore remodeled to highlight the Tetrarchic system and its individual emperors. Inside the temple one room was adapted into an imperial chamber. From a courtyard an entryway passed through the rows of columns in an inner hall to the entrance of this chamber. Within the chamber across from this entrance a doorway that led to additional rooms within the sanctuary was now blocked and reconstructed as a small apse, flanked on each side with a decorative column. On the side walls of the chamber paintings depicted processions of soldiers and horses that advanced toward the front of the chamber. On the front wall paintings on each side of the apse depicted groups of magistrates, or perhaps military commanders, who were gathered to pay their respects perhaps to a pair of emperors seated on their thrones. Within the apse itself a painting depicted four emperors, standing and facing forward. The two outer emperors were slightly shorter than the two inner emperors. One of the two inner emperors was holding a globe in his left hand and gripping a long staff (or scepter) in his right hand. This emperor was most likely Diocletian, holding the symbol of his universal rule and the scepter he had received from Jupiter himself. The ceiling of the apse depicted an eagle with outstretched wings, clutching a wreath in its talons. Since the eagle was a symbol of Jupiter, the apse represented the four emperors of the Tetrarchy ruling beneath the divine sanction of the highest deity. This imagery stressed the roles of one deity and

---

[20] For Diocletian's actions in Egypt following the revolts of 297, see Barnes (1981) 17–18, (1982) 54–55, 211, 230–31. For the dedications, see Lacau (1934) 22–23 (second monument), and Deckers (1979) 604–6n.16. Lacau and Deckers date the second monument between November 308 (proclamation of Licinius as Augustus) and May 309 (promotion of Constantine from Caesar to Augustus). In fact, the date of the recognition of Constantine as an Augustus in the eastern provinces is uncertain: see Grünewald (1990) 57–58.

four distinct emperors, and it carefully differentiated the emperors by rank.[21]

The sense of hierarchy among the emperors certainly survived after the abdications of Diocletian and Maximian in May 305. According to Lactantius' account, Diocletian had once offered to make Galerius an Augustus too. Galerius responded that the current arrangement should be preserved, with two "greater" emperors in charge of affairs and two "lesser" emperors to assist them. He also argued that to make way for his promotion, Diocletian should retire. After Diocletian and Maximian did retire, Constantius and Galerius moved up to replace them as senior emperors, each with the title of Augustus.[22]

But despite the similarity of their titles, Galerius had to concede, to his scornful dismay, that Constantius nevertheless still had priority between them. All along Galerius seems to have been deeply annoyed that from the beginning he had been "the lesser [Caesar] and the last [among the original four emperors]." During his tenure as a Caesar not only had he resented his standing as the most junior of the four emperors, but he was also publicly humiliated by a senior emperor. Angry that their combined armies had been defeated by the Persians in early 297, Diocletian had tried to deflect the blame by forcing his subordinate, while still wearing his purple robe, to march beside his carriage. This attempt to "scrape away the corrosion of his imperial arrogance" perhaps backfired,

---

[21] The figure of the other inner emperor was erased. This figure had represented most likely Maximian, whose images Constantine later had removed or destroyed: see Lactantius, *De mortibus persecutorum* 42.1, with Chapter 3. Kalavrezou-Maxeiner (1975), argues that the wall paintings depicted a ceremony celebrating Diocletian's arrival, that the four emperors in the apse were the original four Tetrarchs, and that the painted room served as an audience chamber: "at Luxor, Diocletian sat in front of the austere figures of the Tetrarchs" (p. 250). Deckers (1979), adds more details about the paintings on the front wall on each side of the apse and provides the best drawing of how they should be reconstructed. Kolb (2001) 175–86, suggests that the paintings on the walls represented a ceremony of homage for new emperors following a change in the membership of the Tetrarchy and that the painting in the apse depicted Diocletian and Maximian as retired emperors, flanked by the two current senior emperors.

[22] Lactantius, *De mortibus persecutorum* 18.4–7, Diocletian and Galerius.

because Galerius repeatedly challenged the imperial hierarchy. According to the emperor Julian, Galerius "never sang in harmony with the melody of four notes." Instead, he identified himself with Dionysus, one of the more incorrigible and disruptive of the pagan gods. After a subsequent victory over the Persians, achieved without Diocletian's assistance, Galerius supposedly claimed descent from Mars, the god of war, and then complained that he was still only a Caesar. The triumphal arch that he erected at Thessalonica commemorated his personal successes over the Persians. One panel on this arch certainly celebrated collective accomplishments by depicting all four emperors. At the same time, however, the iconography on the arch subverted the Terarchic ideology of collegiate emperorship by glorifying Galerius' leading role in the campaigns against the Persians. Other panels highlighted his impressive individual accomplishments, such as leading a charge of the Roman cavalry, capturing the Persian king's harem, receiving captives, processing into a city in victory, demonstrating his clemency, addressing his troops, negotiating with a Persian delegation, and sacrificing with Diocletian. As the culmination of his personal success one panel depicted him defeating the Persian king in direct hand-to-hand combat. Although this confrontation was completely imaginary, the image elevated Galerius as the champion of the classical world. He was now the new Alexander, the prototypical conqueror of the Persians. The lesser Caesar had seemingly surpassed his more senior colleagues.[23]

---

[23] Lactantius, *De mortibus persecutorum* 9.8–9, Mars, complaint, 18.6, "minor et extremus." Humiliation of Galerius: Eutropius, *Breviarium* 9.24, Ammianus Marcellinus, *Res gestae* 14.11.10, with the reconstruction of the Persian campaigns in Barnes (1976a) 182–86, and the corrected chronology in Zuckerman (1994), endorsed by Barnes (1996) 543–44. Corrosion: Orosius, *Historiae adversum paganos* 7.25.10. Melody: Julian, *Caesares* 315c. Association with Dionysus: Nicholson (1984). For excellent discussion of the panels on the arch, see Pond Rothman (1977), with Pond Rothman (1975) 21, on the panel of the enthroned emperors: "an illustration of the dogma, not the history, of the Tetrarchy." Mayer (2002) 47–65, notes the absence of allusions to the senate and its Republican traditions; Kolb (1987) 159–76, interprets the arch as an indication of the enduring attractiveness of the Tetrarchic system and minimizes Galerius' prominence. But already as a Caesar

Although promoted as an Augustus in 305, Galerius was technically still junior to his colleague Constantius. As a result, he was also a frustrated Augustus with ambitious plans. After their promotion the new senior emperors selected Severus and Maximinus as the new junior emperors. In fact, Galerius seems to have controlled these choices, since Severus was his friend and Maximinus a relative, while Constantius' adult son Constantine was overlooked. Although his intrigues seemed to respect Tetrarchic protocols, Galerius was also apparently already scheming about a future in which he would have priority as the senior Augustus. According to Lactantius' account, although Galerius wanted his friend Licinius to become an emperor, he did not want to appoint him as a Caesar, so that he could avoid having to designate him as his "son." Instead, he hoped soon to replace Constantius with Licinius as a fellow Augustus, so that he could designate him as his "brother." Then he would finally be the senior of the senior emperors, supported both by Licinius as his sidekick Augustus and by Maximinus and his own young son as Caesars holding the "second name." Galerius' scheming was a pointed indication of the underlying reality of rank and hierarchy in the Tetrarchy, both the original configuration and its sequel. Although at first the ranking of emperors was an obstacle to his plan to promote his friend, in the end he hoped to use that hierarchy to his advantage.[24]

After the usurpation of Constantine upset his plans for the realignment of the Tetrarchy following Constantius' death in 306, Galerius again professed his loyalty to the system. He declined to bring in Licinius as a new Augustus from outside the existing college of emperors,

---

Galerius had a statue of himself set up at Antioch, holding a globe: see Ammianus Marcellinus, *Res gestae* 25.10.2, with Srejovic (1994) 146–52, discussing a similar statue of Galerius at his palace in Romuliana (Gamzigrad, about forty miles north of Constantine's birthplace at Naissus). Galerius apparently did associate himself with the mythology of Alexander: see *Epitome de Caesaribus* 40.17.

[24] Lactantius, *De mortibus persecutorum* 20, Galerius' schemes, with Chapter 3, on the selection of new Caesars in 305. In this second Tetrarchy Constantius had priority perhaps because in 293 he had been appointed as a Caesar before Galerius, even though they later shared the same anniversary: for the debate, see Kolb (1987) 72–85, and Nixon and Rodgers (1994) 112n.8.

and instead promoted the current Caesar Severus. Licinius became an Augustus only in 308 after Severus' death. Although Galerius did recognize Constantine as a Caesar, he declined to acknowledge Maxentius after his usurpation at Rome. In this case ideology trumped family. Maxentius may have been his son-in-law, but "he could not appoint three Caesars." A Tetrarchy was supposed to have only four emperors, who were all clearly ordered by rank.[25]

Galerius' obsession with preserving a proper hierarchy of emperors was unlikely of success, however, in part because after 305 there were retired emperors who remained influential. Since emperors were expected to rule for life, both the traditional ideology and the conventional terminology of emperorship were unable to accommodate former emperors. As a result, after their abdications Diocletian and Maximian were classified with an oddly hybrid label as "private-citizen emperors." Although no longer officially ruling, they took the titles of "more-senior senior emperors" and "fathers of the emperors and the junior emperors." In ideological terms Diocletian and Maximian were now, literally, "grandfathered" into the Tetrarchic hierarchy. They also continued to meddle in imperial affairs, Maximian by returning to help his son Maxentius and his son-in-law Constantine, Diocletian by presiding over Galerius' selection of Licinius as a new senior emperor. Since Maximinus and Constantine were miffed at being only junior emperors, eventually they assumed the title of Augustus too. By 310 there were six senior emperors (four active, two nominally retired), as well as Maxentius at Rome, and no junior emperors. Diocletian was content to return to tending his vegetable garden during his retirement; the other emperors immediately started plotting and fighting against each other. The ironical outcome of this extended experiment in collegiate emperorship was a return to the pre-Tetrarchic era of civil wars between emperors.[26]

---

[25] Lactantius, *De mortibus persecutorum* 25.4–5, promotion of Severus, 26.4, three Caesars.

[26] Maximian as "privatus princeps": *Panegyrici latini* 7(6).10.5. Diocletian and Maximian as "seniores Augg., patres impp. et Caess.": *ILS* 1:148, no. 646, the dedication

Keeping up with all these changes in seniority and ideology must have been confusing already in the ancient world. At the garrison in Luxor one monument of four columns and statues commemorated the original four Tetrarchs. But a separate statue of the junior emperor Galerius was also set up, perhaps in honor of his victories on the eastern frontier. A second monument of four columns and statues commemorated the revised Tetrarchy between late 308 and 309. At that moment of unanimity Galerius and Licinius as senior emperors and Constantine and Maximinus as junior emperors shared the honors of imperial rule. But after Licinius defeated Maximinus in 313, the entire dedication to Maximinus was chiseled off the base of his column. After Constantine defeated Licinius in 324, Licinius' name was chiseled out of his dedication. Three statues of Constantine were meanwhile set up, perhaps in anticipation of a visit to Egypt that the emperor had already announced. At this camp the imperial magistrates, officers, and soldiers scrambled to keep the monumental expressions of their loyalty as current as possible. To do so, not only did they want to know the outcomes of civil wars; they also had to learn the relative ranks of the emperors.[27]

on the baths of Diocletian at Rome. Diocletian as "patrem Augustoru[m]": *CIL* 3, Supplementum 2:2046, no. 12049. Multiple emperors: Lactantius, *De mortibus persecutorum* 29.2, "at one time there were six." Medallions on pilasters found at Romuliana depicted three pairs of emperors, most likely the Tetrarchy after 305 plus Diocletian and Maximian: for discussion, see Srejovic (1994) 145–46, "a sixfold image of the same person," and Kolb (2001) 163–67, 186–91. Diocletian's vegetables: *Epitome de Caesaribus* 39.6, with Nakamura (2003), arguing that Diocletian died in December 312. Bleckmann (2004), stresses the frequency of civil wars between emperors after Diocletian: "die fatalen Folgen des Mehrherrschaftssystems bereits zu einer irreversiblen Schädigung der Integrität des Reiches geführt haben" (p. 75).

[27] For these changes at Luxor, including the dedications inscribed on the bases of the statues of Galerius and Constantine, see Lacau (1934); the three dedications for Constantine are reprinted in Grünewald (1990) 257–58, nos. 489–91. Grünewald dates the dedications and statues between ca. 312 and 315, but Lacau associates them with Constantine's proposed visit a decade later. For preparations for the aborted visit to Egypt in early 325, see Barnes (1981) 212.

## ONENESS AND FOURNESS, ONENESS AND THREENESS

A religious idiom was a powerful medium for articulating the ruler-ship of the Tetrarchic emperors. It legitimated their imperial authority through their identification with gods; it separated their possession of power from the fickle support of senate, people, and army; it hoped to eliminate personal disputes among the emperors by clearly defining their respective ranks; and it tried to maintain the unity of the empire by insisting upon a fundamental concord among the emperors. Tetrar-chic political theology insisted that the Oneness of a single emperorship was compatible with the Fourness of emperors. For all its success under the primacy of Diocletian, however, this underlying theology of Tetrar-chic rule was also unstable from the beginning as the emperors tried to reconcile such powerful opposing forces as hierarchy and harmony. Tetrarchic ideology could be readily misconstrued or manipulated, in particular by disgruntled or ambitious emperors. As a result, a religious idiom that was so effective at constructing relationships was equally powerful for deconstructing them.

The rise of Constantine overlapped with the end of the Tetrarchic era, and Constantine himself only gradually disengaged from Tetrarchic political ideology and its related theology. His emergence as a Christian emperor certainly undermined the significance of the Tetrarchic theol-ogy of emperors who had identified with Jupiter and Hercules by adopt-ing the names of Jovius and Herculius: "truly the Lord destroyed these [names] and erased them from the earth." But the underlying issue about the correspondence of emperors and gods remained, although now in the format of the correlation between Christian emperor and Christian God. To talk about one was to talk about the other: in this Christian context the political discourse about emperors remained a simultaneous religious discourse about God. At the same time during this period of transition Greek theologians were arguing about doctrines of the Trinity. In some respects these churchmen had seemingly transposed the debate about the multiple emperors who held a single emperorship into a con-troversy about the multiple manifestations of one God. Sameness and difference, hierarchy and harmony, defining the intervention of divine power in human affairs: Christian theologians and their congregations were now trying to articulate the relationship between God the Father and Jesus Christ the Son, as well as the role of the Holy Spirit in the Trinity. Like the political and religious discourse about emperors and their divinity, this Christian theological discourse was also attempting to accommodate multiple manifestations of divine power. And since both discussions used similar terms and ideas, a debate about doctrines was simultaneously a debate about Christian emperorship.[28]

Tetrarchic emperors were always concerned about legitimacy, both their own and that of their chosen successors. Because they themselves had not inherited the throne as sons of emperors, and because they overlooked their own true sons when choosing successors, they could not rely upon the buttress of straightforward dynastic succession. Instead, the emperors' descent from gods would provide a substitute pedigree. One panegyrist emphasized that Diocletian and Maximian were "begotten of the gods." A dedication at Colossae in western Phrygia likewise commemorated Constantius and another emperor as "begotten of the gods." Having inherited divinity, these emperors could also bequeath divinity. If the association of Diocletian and Maximian with Jupiter and Hercules was confirmation of their right to rule, then through their identification with those gods they could pass on divinity to their successors. A dedication set up near Dyrrhacium on the Adriatic coast hence commemorated Diocletian and Maximian as "begotten of the gods and creators of gods." This perspective lingered into the early years of the rise of Constantine. In Italy a dedication at Saepinum commemorated Constantine in similar terms shortly after his victory at Rome in 312: "to the restorer of public liberty, begotten of the gods, our lord emperor Caesar, Flavius Valerius Constantine, pious, fortunate, unconquered Augustus, by decree of the town councilors."[29]

---

[28] Names: Lactantius, *De mortibus persecutorum* 52.3.

[29] Begotten of the gods: *Panegyrici latini* 11(3).2.4, "vos dis esse genitos... approbatis." Colossae: *MAMA* 6:15, no. 38 = *L'année épigraphique 1940* (1941) 58, no. 182, "diis genitis | orbis terra|rum domino | nostro Fl(avio) | Valerio |

These municipal notables at Saepinum seem to have decided that the use of customary terminology and a by now routine ideology was a safe way to commemorate a new emperor who was still largely unknown in Italy, and they continued to view Constantine through a Tetrarchic perspective. They had apparently not heard that he was a new-fangled Christian ruler. But if pagan notables were still prepared to imagine Constantine as yet another Tetrarchic emperor, Christians were likewise uncertain about how to define him. Because Jesus was their prototype of a Christian ruler on earth, the appearance of a Christian emperor in their midst compelled them to reconsider both notions of imperial rulership and doctrines about divine Rulership. Now they suddenly had to redefine both Jesus Christ and Roman emperor. The consequent

Constantio | p(io) f(elici) invicto | Aug(usto) [et . . . " Dyrrhacium (modern Durrës in Albania): *ILS* 1:141, no. 629, "diis genitis et | deorum creatoribus | dd. nn. Diocletiano et | [Maximiano invict]is Augg." Saepinum: *L'année épigraphique 1984* (1987) 94, no. 367 = Grünewald (1990) 222, no. 272, dated between October 28, 312 and ca. 315, "Restitutori | p(ublicae) libertatis | di(i)s genito d(omino) n(ostro) | imp(eratori) Caes(ari) Flavio | Val(erio) Constantino | pio felici inv(icto) Aug(usto) | d(ecreto) d(ecurionum)." For additional discussion of Tetrarchic notions of succession, see Chapter 3.

This description of emperors as "begotten of the gods" might seem to have put them on a collision course with Christians and their ideas about God the Father and his only-begotten Son. For one possible consequence, see Kolb (2001) 37, suggesting a motive for the initiation of persecutions: "Die Tetrarchie war mithin eine *domus divina* von fleischgewordenen Göttersöhnen und somit natürlicher Rivale des christlichen Gottessohnes; die diocletianische Christenverfolgung war schon aus diesem Grunde unvermeidlich"; also Kolb (1987) 113, "Die tetrarchischen 'Göttersöhne' konnten den Monopolanspruch des christlichen Gottessohnes nicht tolerieren." For an explicit connection between persecution and blasphemy against Jesus Christ, note the appearance of *Memoirs of Pilate and Our Savior*, a spurious account apparently of Jesus' trial before Pilate. Eusebius claimed that this hostile account had been published recently, "yesterday or the day before" (*HE* 1.9.3), during the persecution of Maximinus in 312. Maximinus himself ordered that *Memoirs* was to be circulated widely and taught by grammarians. As a result, "every day children in schools recited [the names of] Jesus and Pilate, as well as the *Memoirs* that had been falsified as an insult": see Eusebius, *HE* 9.5.1, 7.1, with Carriker (2003) 281–82, on *Acts of Pilate*.

confusion over these interrelated issues meant that the making of Christian theology overlapped with the making of a new political philosophy. As a result, Christian theologians who were trying to verbalize their doctrines about the Oneness and Threeness of God might well have been intrigued by a Tetrarchic theology that combined both "begetting" and "creating" in definitions of the divine origin of rulers and the promotion of successors.

# "BEGOTTEN FROM THE FATHER": THE CHRISTIAN TRINITY

## CHAPTER TEN

D URING THE EARLY FOURTH CENTURY THE TEACHINGS OF
Arius and like-minded theologians offered many attractive qualities. These theologians were careful interpreters
of Scripture, and they respectfully used numerous biblical
citations and allusions to support their doctrines about the essential
subordination of Jesus Christ the Son to God the Father. They argued
that God's preexistent Logos and Sophia, "Word" and "Wisdom,"
were not merely divine attributes but had been embodied as a distinct divine entity, the Son. They invoked the authority of earlier
distinguished theologians. They engaged with the concepts of classical philosophers. They were concerned about the practical concerns
of ordinary believers and defined appropriate doctrines of soteriology and ecclesiology. With its appeals to the Bible, tradition, reason, and discipleship, Arian theology would have made a perfectly
respectable orthodox Christianity. In retrospect, modern historians
of doctrine would have seen its enshrinement as orthodoxy as a

logical, even necessary, outcome of the theological trends of early Christianity.[1]

Instead, Arianism ended up reviled as thoroughly heterodox, "the prince of heresies." The council of Nicaea in 325 accepted the fundamental coordination of God and Jesus Christ; it also set the tone of vicious antagonism by supplementing its creed with anathemas that pointedly detonated Arius' teachings. Despite this hostility, Arian and neo-Arian doctrines nevertheless survived and even flourished. During the mid-fourth century Arianizing bishops were more successful at acquiring imperial patronage, including the support of Constantine, Constantius, and Valens, and for a time Arianizing theology (in the guise of Homoian Arian doctrines) seemed on the verge of success. Then the council of Constantinople in 381 reaffirmed Nicene (or neo-Nicene) theology as orthodoxy. Theodosius and subsequent emperors reinforced that declaration with authoritarian legislation against "those evil habits that are detestable to God and mankind." In retrospect, modern accounts now see Nicene doctrines as the only possible outcome of earlier theological trends.[2]

But a retrospective explanation is not identical with, not even similar to, a proper historical interpretation of this controversy over Christian doctrine and its outcome, and a catalogue of intellectual antecedents and ecclesiastical consequences cannot substitute for a true critical analysis. The fundamental difficulty is readily apparent: the Nicene Creed is both a "symbol of normative Christian truth" and "an explicit repudiation of Arius," simultaneously transcendent and transient. Our explanations of the development of doctrinal orthodoxy struggle to reconcile the

---

[1]  For sympathetic readings of Arius, see especially the survey in Williams (1987) 1–25, and Wiles (1996) 9–26; of later "Arianism," the contributions in Barnes and Williams (1993); of Aetius and Eunomius, Vaggione (2000), and Van Dam (2003b) 15–45. For Arian soteriology, see Gregg and Groh (1981) 43–76. For the underlying popularity of Arius' teaching about the precedence of the Father over the Son, see Williams (1993) 162: "as if, in this matter, the theology of the bishops was becoming increasingly out of step with popular sentiment."

[2]  Quotation about prince of heresies from Wiles (1996) vi. Evil habits: *CTh* 16.5.12, issued in 383.

timeless perspective of normative religious truths with the time-bound perspective of historical criticism. Our history of theology sometimes begins to resemble the object of that theology, simultaneously impassible God and "a man who shared our passions," simultaneously eternal and a participant in our ephemeral experiences, simultaneously divine and human. Bishop Eusebius of Caesarea neatly hinted at this tension by beginning his *Ecclesiastical History* with a doctrinal confession of his version of correct theology, and then conceding that doctrines about Jesus Christ were "beyond man." As a result, his *History* offered a prototypical confessional, pietistic narrative. Because Jesus had once intruded in human history, Eusebius concluded that he could evaluate changing human affairs against the standards of an unchanging realm outside those human affairs. In his perspective, "orthodoxy" and "heresy" were simply normative, uncontested categories of description that were suitable terms of social analysis. Eusebius had clearly not yet read Foucault and his postmodern progeny.[3]

In order to reconcile this tension between transcendence and transience, modern narratives typically adopt contrasting approaches to the study of orthodoxy and heresy. Whether acknowledged or not, Eusebius' *History* is the model. In Eusebius' perspective, orthodoxy was singular but heresies were plural. Heresies were ephemeral, and their history could be presented as a sequence of faddish innovations attributed to a series of misguided teachers. Heresies multiplied and changed over time. In contrast, even though orthodoxy was only gradually exposed, elaborated, and clarified over time, it was still unique and unchanging. Orthodoxy was prior and original. During the 370s bishop Epiphanius

---

[3] Quotations about Nicene Creed from Wiles (1996) 2. Eusebius, *HE* 1.1.1, innovation, 1.1.7, beyond man, 1.2.1, passions; with Williams (1987) 243, on the theological implications of "Jesus' involvement in the necessarily tragic limitations of history." For other attempts at formulating and resolving this tension, see Elm et al. (2000) XVII, contrasting "orthodoxy as a durable category" and "specific formulations of orthodoxy"; Vaggione (2000) 374–75, contrasting matter and rhythm, propositions and "the frameworks governing their choice"; and Ayres (2004) 429, contrasting "wider faith commitments" and "objective historiographical criteria."

of Salamis even argued that orthodox doctrines had existed "from the beginning," that is, already at the moment of creation: "Adam knew about God the Father, the Son, and the Holy Spirit, for he was a prophet." Adam had been a Nicene Christian. Such an inert perspective does not allow a proper interpretive history of orthodoxy, both as a conceptual construct and as an emerging consensus about specific doctrines. Like Eusebius' *History*, modern historical criticism falters at coping with the presumed permanence and timelessness of orthodox theology.[4]

The paradoxical result is that heresies can have a true critical history, in which they responded to external events, changed, fluctuated in popularity, and perhaps disappeared. Modern historians have successfully located various heresies in social and cultural history by highlighting the interaction between cities and countryside, the claustrophobic pressures of small communities, the use of accusations of otherness at public hearings to enforce conformity, the influence of gender roles, and the significance of networks of patronage. Many of the most interesting studies of the social dimensions of early Christianity have been books about heresies, such as Gnosticism, Montanism, Donatism, Priscillianism, Origenism, and Monophysitism. Even if the conclusions of these studies can be disputed, it is obvious that heterodoxy often brings out the best in scholars of late antiquity. But regrettably, there are no similar self-consciously social and cultural interpretations of the development of orthodoxy. Orthodoxy is typically presented as simply the proper outcome of a rational process, the anticipated goal of a single true linear narrative. The titles of modern books are a revealing indication of this contrast. Books about heresies stress "construction" and "making"; books about orthodoxy stress "emergence" and "search." While early

---

[4] For Eusebius' commitment to a fixed orthodoxy, see Grant (1980) 87, "His ideas were controlled by the notion of a fixed deposit"; also Barnes (1981) 132, on "his inability to contemplate theological development. For Eusebius there could be no improvement on the truths revealed imperfectly in the Old Testament and fully in the New." Adam: Epiphanius, *Panarion* 2.3–4. For an excellent critique of the notion that "orthodoxy" was prior, pure, and unified, see King (2003) 218–36.

heresies were made over and over, orthodoxy was apparently begotten only once, and then gradually revealed.[5]

The priest Arius publicized his theology in opposition to Alexander, his bishop at Alexandria. Even though other churchmen quickly took sides, many were caught in the middle. At the council of Nicaea Eusebius of Caesarea, for instance, struggled to explain how his own subordinationist doctrines nevertheless could fit in a Nicene framework. But this dispute involved more than merely theology, however, because in the background were the concurrent political developments of the demise of the Tetrarchic emperors and the rise of a Christian emperor. Tetrarchic emperorship had itself raised theological issues over the imagining of emperors as gods; the controversy over Arian and Nicene Christianity was also a political dispute over the representation of a Christian emperor; and at the intersection of all these discourses was Constantine.

## WHY NOT ARIANISM?

Already during the fourth century Arianism was difficult to categorize as a coherent doctrinal movement. Arius himself was ordained a priest at Alexandria at about the time that Licinius was preparing to campaign against Maximinus, his rival emperor in the eastern provinces. After the persecutions under the Tetrarchs the rise of Licinius seemed to promise open acceptance for all Christians in the East, whatever their beliefs, since he now publicized the edict of toleration that had been agreed upon with his fellow emperor Constantine. Several years later Arius openly disagreed with the theology of his new bishop, Alexander of Alexandria, about the relationship between God the Father and the Son. Alexander may have initiated this theological discussion in order to evaluate the credentials of his priests and hence extend his own episcopal authority. In return, Arius' apparent disrespect for his bishop may have

---

[5] Cultural construction: Clark (1992); making: Burrus (1995); search: Hanson (1988); emergence: Pelikan (1971). For a better sense of the making of orthodoxy, see Williams (1987) 25, "Orthodoxy continues to be *made*. . . . this need not involve a wholly relativist view of doctrinal truth"; reflected in the title and preface of Williams (1989) ix, "Orthodoxy is *constructed*, in the processes of both theological and political conflict."

been as important a catalyst of the subsequent hostility as any oddities in his doctrines. The dispute between the two simmered for years and quickly spilled over outside Egypt. A council at Alexandria, perhaps in 321, excommunicated Arius and some supporters; other councils of bishops in Bithynia and Palestine supported him and his teachings. Soon after his defeat of Licinius in 324, Constantine sent a long letter to Arius and Alexander that insisted on their reconciliation. Even though the new emperor in the eastern provinces did not fully understand the circumstances of the dispute, he wanted it to stop. "Return to mutual friendship and goodwill, and restore the proper intimacy to all the people." Having reunified the empire politically, Constantine was not prepared to tolerate the possibility of theological fractures.[6]

Constantine was certainly not alone in his bafflement about the theological issues. Arius' own doctrines are obscure. Few of his writings have survived, and his opponents so maligned him in their treatises that he and his ideas were soon reduced to a caricature. The circumstances of his death in 336 only reinforced the satire. Arius died in Constantinople, apparently while sitting in a public latrine. Bishop Athanasius of Alexandria, one exceptionally harsh critic, considered his death to have been the providential answer to a prayer, and he pointedly compared his squalid fate to the shameful death of Judas, the betrayer of Jesus. Later historians reiterated the circumstances of his death with glee and foreboding, as if his sordid demise had been an indication of divine judgment on his life and doctrines. "It is rumored that for a long time afterward no one used the seat on which he had died." One tradition claimed that at the end of the fourth century the emperor Theodosius set up statues of Arius and other infamous heretics on this site in the

---

[6] Alexander's initiative: Socrates, *HE* 1.5. Constantine's letter: Urkunde 17.14, ed. Opitz (1934–1935) 35, quoted in Eusebius, *Vita Constantini* 2.71.8, with S. G. Hall (1998) 86–97, suggesting that Constantine in fact sent this letter to the bishops at the council of Antioch in 325. For Arius' early career, see Williams (1987) 29–61, and Hanson (1988) 3–5. The "Urkunden" (documents) edited in Opitz (1934–1935), provide the foundation for determining the chronology of events before 325. Hanson (1988) 129–38, discusses and summarizes Opitz' conclusions; for revisions, see Williams (1987) 48–66, and Burgess (1999a) 183–91.

capital and invited people to spatter them with urine and excrement. Already in his lifetime a vilified apocryphal Arius had overshadowed the vilified historical Arius.[7]

In addition, even like-minded churchmen were reluctant to give Arius much credit. Arius had been a very effective preacher, and his supporters in Egypt had included deacons, priests, and even bishops, not to mention hundreds of virgins. After his death, however, churchmen were more circumspect, and during the early years of the controversy "Arius' teachings were not yet assigned to the founder's name." Since Arius had been only a priest, even the bishops who endorsed his ideas refused to be called his followers, and some were resentful that the infamy of his lingering reputation seemingly precluded an honest evaluation of their own doctrines. The bishops who had gathered at a council at Antioch in 341 were quite indignant. "We were not followers of Arius. Since we are bishops, how do we follow a priest?" Opponents likewise struggled to come to terms with the enormous variety of theological opinions. "Arianism" was apparently first used as a collective noun designating a doctrinal system in a sermon by Gregory of Nazianzus shortly before the ecumenical council that met at Constantinople in 381 reaffirmed the orthodoxy of the Nicene creed. In order to be condemned, Arianism had had to be turned into an orderly system, typically by its opponents. During the fourth century the making of orthodox theology and the construction of a coherent non-orthodoxy called Arianism were complementary processes.[8]

7　Arius' death: Athanasius, *Epistula ad episcopos Aegypti et Libyae* 19 (*PG* 25.581B–584C), *Epistula de morte Arii* 3.3 (drawing upon the eyewitness account of the priest Macarius); with Leroy-Molinghen (1968), for discussion of the sources. Arius died in summer of 336: see Barnes (1981) 242. Rumor: Sozomen, *HE* 2.30.6. Statues: *Parastaseis syntomoi chronikai* 39, with Dagron (1984) 141–43. For the obscuring of the historical Arius, note Kannengiesser (1997) 225, "a phantom Arianism," "a dogmatic ghost."
8　Supporters: Epiphanius, *Panarion* 69.3.2. Arius' teachings: Sozomen, *HE* 2.32.1. Council of Antioch: Athanasius, *De synodis* 22.3. For the attitudes of non-Nicene theologians toward Arius, see Hanson (1988) 123–28, and Vaggione (2000) 37–49; Lienhard (1999) 28–46, discusses the difficulties in characterizing the opposing

The controversy over Trinitarian doctrines during the early fourth century focused on several important themes. The most consequential concerned the relationship between God the Father and Jesus Christ the Son. From texts in the Old Testament, reinforced by the Gospel stories about Jesus and the apostle Paul's teachings about Christ, early Christians had long emphasized the notion of a God who consisted of a Father and a Son. The celebration of the liturgy had repeated and reinforced this paternal and filial imagery. But defining the details of the relationship between Father and Son was deeply contested. Not only were these theologians discussing concepts, such as eternity and the nonexistent, for which words seemed inadequate. By wanting to preserve both a sense of connection and a sense of distinction between Father and Son, both coordination and subordination, both monotheism and a divinity that Father and Son somehow shared, they were trying to combine seemingly antithetical perspectives.[9]

Arius and his supporters clearly emphasized the distinction between the two, and hence the inferiority and the subordination of the Son to the Father. Arius himself phrased this distinction and subordination in various ways. In a letter to his supporter Eusebius, bishop of Nicomedia,

viewpoints and parties during the fourth century. The only example of Ἀρειανισμός cited in Lampe (1961) 224, is Gregory of Nazianzus, *Orat.* 21.22, critiquing the outcome of the council of Seleucia in 359: "substituting an Arianism that had no support in the Bible." Bernardi (1968) 155, dates Gregory's sermon to May 379, Mossay and Lafontaine (1980) 99–103, more generally to his pastoral tenure in Constantinople between 379 and 381. For the correlation of the making of orthodoxy and non-orthodoxy, see Cameron and Hall (1999) 258, on the council of Nicaea: "its effect was rather to crystallize something that could be labelled 'Arianism' than to condemn an existing sect."

[9] Ayres (2004) 41, identifies two distinct trends among theologians of the fourth century: "some prefer language that emphasizes the *sameness* of Father and Son, while others emphasize *diversity* between the two." Many early Christian theologians were subtle thinkers; a few were just muddled. To understand both the nuances and the obscurities, non-specialists like me are grateful for the guidance of modern patristics scholarship. Especially invaluable are the comprehensive surveys of the development of theology by Kelly (1960), Pelikan (1971), Ayres (2004), and, in particular, Hanson (1988).

he agreed that "God exists before the Son without a beginning." He elaborated by claiming that "the Son is not unbegotten, not a part of an unbegotten [God] in any way, and not from any substrate. Instead, he exists by a will and a decision before time and before ages. He is God, only-begotten, immutable. Before he was begotten, created, determined, or established, he was not. He was not unbegotten." In a letter to his rival Alexander, bishop of Alexandria, Arius emphasized the uniqueness of God, who was "one, alone unbegotten, alone eternal, alone without beginning." This God begat an only-begotten Son who was the "offspring of the Father" and "a perfect creature of God, but not like one of the [other] creatures."[10]

In these statements Arius insisted that the Son was somehow derivative from the Father, both after in time and inferior in essence. In order to define this subordination Arius had already focused on two common modes of generation, one highlighting birth and begetting, the other creating and making. For theologians the notion of begetting was an obvious corollary with the titles of Father and Son, while the process of creation had been necessary for the existence of people and animals. Arius essentially linked the two processes and concluded that both indicated subordination and dependence. He furthermore insisted upon a priority in sequence for God the Father. The Son may have been "begotten by the Father outside time and created before the ages," but "before his begetting he was not." As begetter and creator God was before the begotten and the creature: "God is prior to the Son." To clinch his arguments Arius claimed, rather presumptuously, that his authority was bishop Alexander himself: "we learned this from you, as you were preaching in the middle of the church."[11]

---

[10] Arius' letter to Eusebius of Nicomedia: Urkunde 1, in Opitz (1934–1935) 1–3, quoted in Epiphanius, *Panarion* 69.6. For the views of Eusebius of Nicomedia, see his letter to bishop Paulinus of Tyre: Urkunde 8, ed. Opitz (1934–1935) 15–17, quoted in Theodoret, *HE* 1.6.1–8. Arius' letter to Alexander: Urkunde 6, ed. Opitz (1934–1935) 12–13, quoted in Epiphanius, *Panarion* 69.7.

[11] Arius' letter to Alexander: Urkunde 6, in Opitz (1934–1935) 13, quoted in Athanasius, *De synodis* 16, and Epiphanius, *Panarion* 69.7–8.

Alexander himself summarized some of the teachings of what he already called "a heresy that was the enemy of Christ." According to a letter in which he explained his opposition to Arius and his supporters, these "apostates" had claimed that "there was a time when God was not a Father." Then God created the Son as a creature "out of the nonexistent." As a result, since the Son "was not similar to the Father according to essence," he was "mutable and alterable in his nature, like all other rational beings." According to Alexander's formulation, these suspect teachings claimed that the Son became an intermediary between God and us, in particular in the process of creation: "the Son was made for us, so that God might create us by him, as by an instrument." Even though the highest of creatures, the Son was still a part of the created world. This emphasis then spilled over to affect Arius' view of soteriology. The salvation of mankind certainly required the participation of God, even the suffering of God, but that participation had to be by God the Son, Jesus Christ, a creation of the divine will whose divinity had been already somehow diminished. The divine essence of God the Father had to be buffered from any exposure to human passions. In terms of cosmology, ontology, and soteriology, Arius and his supporters were clearly determined not to allow the transcendent essence of God the Father to be compromised in any way.[12]

In contrast, their opponents were equally intent on ensuring the exalted status of the Son by emphasizing his coordination and partic-ipation with the Father. In one of his letters Arius summarized some teachings that Alexander had stated in public. "Always God, always Son; at once God, at once Son; the Son coexists with God without gen-eration, always-begotten, ungenerated-created; God does not precede the Son either by a thought or by some instant [of time]; always God, always Son, the Son [is] from God himself." With this insistence on coordination, coexistence, even identity, Alexander rejected the priority of God the Father, any dissimilarity in essence, any mutability of the

---

[12] Alexander's letter to other bishops: Urkunde 4b, in Opitz (1934–1935) 6–10, quoted in Socrates, *HE* 1.6.4–30. Οὐσία and its cognates are typically translated as "essence" or "substance."

Son, and the notion that the Son was created or made. Even though usage of the terms of Father and Son might suggest a priority and a superiority between the two, from the perspective of Alexander being a Father seemed to require the eternal presence of a Son. As he wrote to one of his supporters, "the Son is an exact and identical image of the Father." Even though theologians like Alexander and Arius obviously understood Fatherhood and Sonship in different ways, they both wanted to claim the terminology for their own interpretations. "Just as the orthodox prefer 'Son' because it guarantees the status of the Son, while the Arians object because it compromises the nature of the Father, so the Arians prefer creature because it guarantees the uniqueness of the Father, and the orthodox object because it compromises the status of the Son."[13]

In his initial letter to Alexander and Arius, Constantine was both irritated and bemused, in part because of the apparent mismatch between the pettiness of the issues and the passion of the dispute. "It is surely not proper nor at all lawful for so many of God's people to disagree while you argue with one another about small details and completely insignificant matters." The emperor's frustration was not simply an indication of his preoccupation with military affairs or a sign of theological ignorance. Modern historians too can wonder why eastern theologians were so fanatical about this particular issue of Trinitarian theology at this specific moment.[14]

## REPRESENTING GOD

Defining orthodoxy and heresy was obviously problematic already in the early church. Once Constantine became a sympathetic participant, the

---

[13] Arius' summary: Urkunde 1, in Opitz (1934–1935) 2, quoted in Epiphanius, *Panarion* 69.6. Alexander's counterarguments: Urkunde 4b.11–15, in Opitz (1934–1935) 8–9. Alexander's letter to bishop Alexander: Urkunde 14.47, ed. Opitz (1934–1935) 27, quoted in Theodoret, *HE* 1.4.47. Quotation about Father and Son from Osborne (1993) 165.

[14] Constantine's letter: Urkunde 17.9, ed. Opitz (1934–1935) 34, quoted in Eusebius, *Vita Constantini* 2.71.1, not proper; note Gregg and Groh (1981) 162, "a scriptural illiterate like the Emperor Constantine."

stakes were all the higher, because then churchmen were also contending for the emperor's patronage. Long before he assumed control of the eastern provinces Constantine had become familiar with the ferocity of ecclesiastical disputation, because after his victory at Rome in 312 he had inherited an ongoing dispute among Christians in North Africa. In fact, in his letter to Alexander and Arius he had alluded to the "intolerable madness that gripped all of Africa" and his own desire "to heal that sickness." This reference was an odd way to advertise his skill as a mediator. Not only had the issues been different, but Constantine's involvement had been quite unconvincing.[15]

One significant issue underlying this dispute in Africa was bad behavior during the Tetrarchic persecutions. Opponents of Caecilianus, the bishop of Carthage, claimed that he had been consecrated by a collaborator, a bishop who had surrendered a copy of the Bible during a persecution. A council of bishops that met at Carthage soon declared Caecilianus' consecration invalid and selected a replacement bishop. But in a series of letters sent during the winter of 312–313 Constantine nevertheless supported bishop Caecilianus. In particular, in one letter to the provincial governor he explicitly noted that Caecilianus presided over the "catholic church" in Africa. When Caecilianus' opponents petitioned for a hearing before arbitrators from Gaul, Constantine selected three Gallic bishops to attend a council at Rome. In his letter to the bishop of Rome the emperor noted his respect for the "legitimate catholic church" and hoped for the elimination of this schism. During the autumn of 313 this council exonerated Caecilianus and condemned his rival Donatus. Caecilianus' opponents, by now known as Donatists, appealed again to the emperor, this time in person. In response Constantine summoned bishops from the western provinces to meet at a council at Arles in August 314. This council reaffirmed the decision of the previous council. After yet more appeals Constantine commissioned an investigation by imperial magistrates in Africa, and he summoned

[15] Urkunde 17.2, ed. Opitz (1934–1935) 32, quoted in Eusebius, *Vita Constantini* 2.66, madness, sickness; with Barnes (1981) 54–61, for an excellent synthetic narrative of the early years of the Donatist controversy.

Caecilianus and his antagonists to court. At Milan in October 315 he again supported Caecilianus. Subsequently he announced that he would soon be visiting Africa to demonstrate to both Caecilianus and his opponents the proper form of "veneration for the highest divinity."[16]

Despite Constantine's repeated professions of support for bishop Caecilianus, his interventions had been inconclusive. He never visited Africa, and in subsequent years he vacillated in his attitude toward the Donatists. At first he imposed legal penalties, including the confiscation of churches. In the long run this sort of intolerance boomeranged, because the Donatists could argue that the opposition of an emperor, even a Christian emperor, proved that they were the authentic heirs of the martyrs who had once confronted pagan emperors and their magistrates. For building popular support imperial patronage was useful, but imperial opposition was even better. The Donatists could now claim to be the true "church of the martyrs." After a few years Constantine reversed course and permitted the return of Donatist exiles. In a letter to the bishops of Africa he explained that his clemency reflected the "mercy of omnipotent God." In fact, he was trying to reconcile a persistent squabble in the West as he prepared to confront Licinius in the East. For the moment political and military concerns took priority over ecclesiastical issues.[17]

The Donatist controversy had highlighted consequential issues concerning the value of martyrdom, the importance of ritual purity, and the

---

[16] Letter to governor Anullinus: Eusebius, *HE* 10.7.2, catholic church. Letter to bishop Miltiades of Rome: Eusebius, *HE* 10.5.20, legitimate. Council of Rome: Optatus, *Contra Donatistas* 1.23–25. Personal appeal: Optatus, Appendix 3.30a. Council of Arles: Optatus, Appendix 4. Letter to vicar Celsus: Optatus, Appendix 7.34a, Africa. For the chronology of the documents in the Donatist controversy, see Barnes (1982) 238–47.

[17] Legal penalties: *Sermo de passione Donati et Advocati*, with Maier (1987–1989) 1:198–200; also *CTh* 16.6.2, "lege divali . . . Constantini," with *PLRE* 1:347, "Virius Nicomachus Flavianus 15." Church of the martyrs: *Passio Dativi, Saturnini presbyteri et aliorum* 22. Letter to bishops: Optatus, Appendix 9.35a. On the tradition of Donatist martyrs, see Frend (1952) 315–32, still a classic account of contrasting worldviews.

need for rebaptism. It had also originated from allegations of specific acts of betrayal during the persecutions. The controversy over Arianism highlighted equally consequential issues about the theology of the Trinity. But unlike Donatism, there was no precipitating act of singular defiance or specific outrage. In fact, before the acrimonious dispute between bishop Alexander and his priest Arius in Egypt crystallized the issues, subordinationist doctrines were widespread and common. "There is no theologian in the Eastern or the Western Church before the outbreak of the Arian Controversy, who does not in some sense regard the Son as subordinate to the Father." Before Arius all theologians were "Arian." In the early fourth century it was Alexander's teachings that should have seemed novel and out of step with the current doctrinal consensus.[18]

The controversy over Arianism hence poses two pointed questions for modern historians. Why was the dispute about these particular issues? Why did it happen at this particular time? Grand surveys of the development of doctrine in early Christianity often adopt the devotional viewpoint of Eusebius' *Ecclesiastical History* by evaluating various doctrinal formulations against a fixed, transcendent standard of orthodoxy. These surveys tend to describe a sequence of ideas that seemingly appeared and developed according to a preordained intelligent design. The greatest concern is to avoid any hint of random selection. One such survey warns against "a historicism that relativized the development of Christian doctrine in such a way as to make the distinction between authentic growth and cancerous aberration seem completely arbitrary." This is a fair warning; it is also disingenuous, because it does not define the ancient criteria for distinguishing authenticity and aberration, and it does not provide a warrant for the modern use of such prejudicial

---

[18] Quotation from Hanson (1988) 64. In the early fifth century Philostorgius composed a continuation of Eusebius' *Ecclesiastical History* that did highlight this dispute in Egypt. According to the Byzantine bishop Photius, Philostorgius started his narrative with "the quarrel, as he calls it, by Arius against Alexander; for he [Philostorgius] claims that this quarrel was the source of the heresy": see Philostorgius, *HE* 1, prol. Some modern accounts likewise highlight the importance of this quarrel: see Ayres (2004) 15, "these [theological] controversies began with a dispute between the priest Arius and his bishop Alexander."

language. Even though these modern surveys are prodigiously learned and insightful, there is often little that ties their narratives specifically to the society and culture of the later Roman empire. Despite references to names, dates, and places, these disputes might have been happening anywhere, anytime. Teleology is timeless, and reading these modern accounts can lead to the same bewildered reaction of one ecclesiastical historian from antiquity who thought that the outcome of doctrinal controversies had been a bit haphazard, "as if these were contests not over piety and faith but over a choice and type of colors." As a result, despite their concerns over relativism, pietistic narratives that presuppose a rational linearity in fact make the whole process seem disengaged from actual events. The process of formulating orthodoxy and heresy seems to have been as faddish as an intellectual fashion, as transient as an interpretive flair, as fickle as a critical style.[19]

Confessional narratives of the sequence of doctrines are inadequate for explaining the emergence and resolution of disputes over particular issues at specific times. A better strategy is the adoption of a symbolic reading of the many varieties of early Christianity as cultural systems. Even though early Christianity in general became more sophisticated and more widespread than the local cults that modern anthropologists often study, each version can still be analyzed like other religious cults as "an historically transmitted pattern of meanings embodied in symbols...by means of which men communicate, perpetuate, and develop their knowledge about and attitudes toward life." Theological

---

[19] Quotation about historicism from Pelikan (1971) 9. Contests: Philostorgius, *HE* 9.3. For examples of the difficulty in explaining particular disputes and specific times, see Kelly (1960) 232, "We have little or no first-hand evidence of the reasons animating the fathers of Nicaea in their repudiation of Arianism"; and Hanson (1988) xx, "In the fourth century there came to a head a crisis."

Confessional histories are not unique in these shortcomings. Note that some of the more recent postmodern readings of early Christian theology are just as ahistorical and unaware of social and cultural contexts. Even as they sidestep an appeal to the timelessness of normative religious truths, they rely on similar transcendent ideological truths, which these days are often Foucauldian or feminist interpretations. The use of critical theory has become our new postmodern confessional history. For a comprehensive survey of the various types of critical theory, see Clark (2004).

doctrines were modeled on aspects of human society; but once formulated, those doctrines could become models for human behavior. Doctrines were not simply statements or beliefs about God. Because religion was a symbolic language, an idiom, a medium, a logic of classification, and a form of knowledge, doctrines also helped people find meaning and identity in their daily lives and represent themselves within their communities. Churchmen and ordinary believers did not just think about God; in addition, they thought with God as a symbolic category. Talking about God was a strategy for articulating a self, a community, and a society. Since orthodoxy and heresy, as variously defined by different churchmen, butted up against opposite sides of the same conceptual boundaries, the construction of one always entailed the concurrent construction of the other. Examining all versions of Christianity, both "orthodox" and "heterodox," as legitimate cultural systems allows us to shift the focus from abstract beliefs about a transcendent deity to more immediate concerns over meaning and identity.[20]

Another advantage of this approach to early doctrinal controversies is a heightened sensitivity to the fundamental contingency and unpredictability of the process. Contingency is not to be confused with random selection, which would defy any attempt at historical analysis. But it is also the opposite of teleology, which equally precludes any critical historical analysis. In retrospect the path of doctrine might seem to have been preordained; but as the participants at the time looked forward,

[20] Quotation about cultural system from Geertz (1975) 89; also Price (1984) 247, on the imperial cult in the Greek world: "the imposition of the conventional distinction between religion and politics obscures the basic similarity . . . : both are ways of systematically constructing power." Note that although Ayres (2004) 274–78, does suggest a similar definition of Christian beliefs as "a system of learned patterns of behaviour . . . , ideas, and products that together shape conceptions of the order of existence and interactions with other cultures" (p. 274), his subsequent discussion is limited only to "the structure of pro-Nicene orthodoxy" (p. 276). This self-imposed restriction defeats the purpose of defining religion as a cultural system, which is to make possible meaningful comparisons not only between Christianity and another cultural system such as pagan cults or Greek culture (i.e. "Greekness"), but also within Christianity among different doctrinal formulations. For the reciprocity of orthodoxy and heresy, see King (2003) 24: "This discourse not only determines the self but constructs the other as well."

there was no certainty about the outcome. "There was no predetermined orthodoxy that was simply there, waiting to be more carefully defined." The development of theology was not determined outside (or before) historical events; instead, it interacted with and responded to both religious and nonreligious factors. In the early fourth century two factors in particular influenced thinking about Christian theology. One was the lingering influence of a Tetrarchic theology that identified emperors and gods. The other was the appearance of a Christian emperor who in his own way might likewise be identified with God. Constantine now seemed to be fulfilling roles once anticipated for a triumphant Jesus Christ, while Jesus Christ now seemed to be in competition with a Christian emperor.[21]

Identification with pagan gods had been an effective symbolic language for imagining and constructing a new form of imperial rulership, a Tetrarchy of four emperors, and for articulating both rank and concord among co-emperors. A Christian emperor was just as difficult to imagine as a college of multiple emperors. As a result, the emergence of Constantine as a Christian emperor continued and expanded the

---

[21] Quotation about orthodoxy from King (2003) 25. Even distinguished patristics scholars now concede the inadequacy of a simple linear narrative of doctrines; see, e.g., Wiles (1996) 180, critiquing Hanson (1988), "he is able to present the controversy as one . . . apparently little affected by its immediate historical context"; Vaggione (2000) 98, "the propositions by themselves cannot explain the debate"; and R. Williams (2001) 248, "As patristic studies in general . . . moved away from a simple 'history of ideas' model into the bracing new climate of cultural, political and gender-oriented interpretation, it became harder to isolate issues of 'pure' intellectual influence and development." But it remains difficult to avoid a sense of teleological direction in the development of theology: note Williams (1987) 91, on the possibility that Arius represented "a theological style doomed to spiritual sterility." On contingency in the development of theology, note the appreciation of Bauer (1972) by Le Boulluec (2000) 308: "L'une des conséquences du travail de W. Bauer est d'attirer l'attention sur le caractère contingent du concept d'hérésie et, corrélativement, du concept d'orthodoxie." For a fine critique of the conventional periodization of the history of early Christianity, see Nasrallah (2003) 11–19, 201–4, rejecting a straightforward transition from charismatic beginnings to routinized institutions.

Tetrarchic discourse over emperors and gods. At least initially, among churchmen most of the subsequent reconsideration took place in doctrinal terms. Early theologians had already developed extensive traditions about doctrinal issues, but they had no explicitly Christian notions ready to help articulate the idea of a Christian emperor. Until they developed that sort of separate Christian political philosophy, theological debates would have to substitute as a symbolic medium. Suddenly a local debate over theology between Alexander and Arius, a bishop and his priest in Egypt, had larger implications. Direct disputation about Father and Son could serve as an indirect discourse about a Christian emperor.[22]

## MAN OF GOD

Alexander and Arius were certainly not the only churchmen searching for the proper terminology to describe Jesus Christ the Son as a manifestation of God the Father. The analogies and nuances ranged from

---

[22] Several valuable earlier studies offer inspiration for trying to connect theological controversies with the discourse over Christian emperors during the fourth century. Williams (1951a), (1951b), argues that the controversy over Arianism was simultaneously an attempt to clarify the relationship between the church and Christian magistrates, including the emperor; see also the excellent, though equally schematic, critique of Beskow (1962) 313–30. Leach (1972) argues that Arian theology implied support for local autonomy and Nicene doctrines support of a centralized regime. Leach was one of the foremost social and cultural anthropologists of the twentieth century; for an appreciation of his structuralist analysis of doctrinal cosmologies by an equally distinguished anthropologist, see Tambiah (2002) 319–28. Patristics scholars tend to ignore these earlier studies, or at best disparage them. Williams (1987) 15, dismisses Leach's argument as "inaccurate and impressionistic," but then restates the contrasting implications of the controversy for episcopal authority in terms of a fissiparous "Academic" model that focused on the personality of a teacher and a homogenizing "Catholic" model that highlighted the common practice of worship (pp. 86–87). By calling one of the options "Catholic" this formulation again begs the question of orthodoxy and heresy. Other important pioneers include Pagels (1979) 55–56, suggesting that "varying beliefs about the nature of God inevitably bear different political implications"; and Gager (1982) 361, arguing that doctrines were body-symbols with "the power . . . to shape reality."

ingenious to unintentionally comic: "Second God," "Son-Father," "off-shoot," "belch," a "power of God" similar to a locust or a caterpillar, the rust that appeared on iron. Some churchmen even questioned the suitability of the terms "Father" and "Son" to characterize the relation-ship. If, as their opponents claimed, the Son was eternal and coexisted with the Father, then should they not be . . . Brothers? Such mischievous skepticism was probably inevitable in the mingling of dialectics and rhetorical metaphors that characterized theological controversies. Per-haps it is also possible to speculate about the influence of the debates over paternal hierarchy and fraternal harmony that had characterized the theology of the Tetrarchy. In the early fourth century churchmen argued Christian theology under a Tetrarchic shadow.[23]

In June 325 an heir of that Tetrarchic imperial system presided over sessions of an ecumenical council of bishops. Constantine himself had moved this council to Nicaea "so that I might attend as a spectator and a participant in events." Although the emperor argued that Nicaea had better weather and was more accessible to bishops coming from western provinces, it is significant that the city also seems to have had a close asso-ciation with the Tetrarchic emperors. Nicaea claimed Hercules, a patron deity of the Tetrarchy, as a mythological founder. In the city, or perhaps on a nearby hill, was a triumphal arch commemorating Diocletian's victories over the Alamans. During the council the churchmen met in

---

[23] Second God, attributed to bishop Narcissus of Neronias: see Eusebius, *Contra Marcellum* 1.4.53 = Urkunde 19, ed. Opitz (1934–1935) 41. Eusebius of Caesarea also referred to Christ as "Second God": see Kopecek (1979) 47n.2. Son-Father, as taught by Sabellius: Urkunde 6.3, ed. Opitz (1934–1935) 12, quoted in Athanasius, *De synodis* 16.3, and Epiphanius, *Panarion* 69.7.6, with Feige (1993), on the misuse of this term against Marcellus of Ancyra. Belch and offshoot, attributed by Arius to some opponents: Urkunde 1.3, ed. Opitz (1934–1935) 2, quoted in Epiphanius, *Panarion* 69.6.4; "offshoot" explained in Socrates, *HE* 1.8.32, "like sprouts from roots." Locust and caterpillar, as taught by Asterius, based on Joel 2:25: Athanasius, *De synodis* 18.3, 7, Socrates, *HE* 1.36.2; with Wiles and Gregg (1985) 115–18. Iron and rust: *Historia acephala* 4.6, in a creed attributed to Aetius, with Martin (1985) 55–62, and Vaggione (2000) 283–84. Brothers: Athanasius, *Orat. contra Arianos* 1.14: "The Father and the Son were not begotten from someone's preexisting origin, so that they are considered Brothers."

a large room of an imperial palace that had been constructed perhaps by a Tetrarchic emperor. In previous centuries Nicaea had competed with its neighboring city of Nicomedia over titles, ranks, privileges, and amenities. Tetrarchic emperors like Diocletian and Galerius, as well as their successor Licinius, had favored Nicomedia as an imperial residence; Constantine himself would occasionally visit. In this case, although Constantine distanced himself from his Tetrarchic predecessors by avoiding Nicomedia, he nevertheless convened this council at a city filled with reminders of the Tetrarchic era.[24]

Bishop Alexander of Alexandria was in attendance along with a few hundred other bishops, almost all from sees in the eastern provinces. Although a handful of the bishops still supported Arius and his theology, by the conclusion of the sessions the council had rejected his doctrines. The creed they issued explicitly stated that Jesus Christ, the Son of God, was "begotten from the Father," "only begotten, that is, from the essence of the Father," "true God from true God," "begotten not made," and "of the same essence as the Father." In addition, a series of anathemas condemned statements characteristic of the theology of Arius and his supporters. No longer was it appropriate to say of the Son that "there was [a time] when he was not," "he did not exist before he was begotten," and "he came into being out of the nonexistent." The council of Nicaea emphasized the identity and coordination of God the Father and Jesus Christ the Son.[25]

This combination of creed and anathemas should have served as an obituary for Arius' doctrines. The emperor then added his own endorsement. A letter from the council to the churches in Egypt and Libya stressed that Arius' "impiety and lawlessness" had been condemned

[24] Constantine's letter: Urkunde 20, ed. Opitz (1934–1935) 41–42. For Hercules as a founder of Nicaea, see Mitchell (1993) 1:207. For discussion of the fragmentary reliefs from the arch, see Laubscher (1993): "Seine Aussage läßt sich nur aus der Ideologie des tetrarchischen Systems schlüssig erklären" (p. 378). Imperial palace: Eusebius, *Vita Constantini* 3.10.1; also Sozomen, *HE* 1.19.1, Theodoret, *HE* 1.7.7; with Robert (1977), on the longstanding rivalry between Nicomedia and Nicaea.
[25] Nicene creed and anathemas: Urkunde 24, ed. Opitz (1934–1935) 51–52, quoted in Athanasius, *De decretis Nicaenae synodi* 33.8.

"in the presence of Constantine, an emperor who is most beloved of God." Constantine himself sent a letter to the church of Alexandria in which he acknowledged his relief for the elimination of schisms and the restoration of unity around "one and the same confession." In his estimation, "Arius alone" had been the cause of all evil. As corroboration for the council's decision to excommunicate Arius, Constantine apparently now issued an edict that sent him into exile. In a general letter he furthermore praised another decision of the council about the date of Easter. Having recently eliminated Licinius, his last rival as emperor, Constantine was obsessed with reinforcing the unity of his empire. Perhaps he now sensed that the imposition of an "Easter standard time" would be a solid foundation. In this combination of religious harmony and political unity Constantine was again adapting the model of the Tetrarchic emperors. The Tetrarchs had used religion to ensure political centralization by insisting that everyone perform pagan sacrifices. Constantine now endorsed the decision of the council that all Christians everywhere should celebrate the sacrifice of Jesus Christ on the same day. One orthodoxy, one Easter, one empire: the celebration of a single synchronized Easter would commemorate both the resurrection of Jesus Christ and the reunification of the empire.[26]

Almost immediately, however, these Nicene doctrines were contested, and theological disputation continued. Constantine himself seemed to waver in his doctrinal preferences, and he often preferred Arian or

---

[26] Letter of council: Urkunde 23.2, ed. Opitz (1934–1935) 47, quoted in Athanasius, *De decretis Nicaenae synodi* 36.2, and Socrates, *HE* 1.9.3. Constantine's letter to Alexandria: Urkunde 25.1–2, 5, ed. Opitz (1934–1935) 52–53, quoted in Athanasius, *De decretis Nicaenae synodi* 38, and Socrates, *HE* 1.9.17–25. Constantine's edict: Socrates, *HE* 1.8.33. Constantine's general letter: Urkunde 26, ed. Opitz (1934–1935) 54–57, quoted in Eusebius, *Vita Constantini* 3.17–20, and Socrates, *HE* 1.9.31–46, with Petersen (1992), for Eusebius' ideas on Easter.

Note that some Christians suggested that Easter should be celebrated each year on Constantine's birthday, February 27: see Epiphanius, *Panarion* 70.9.4, with Barnes (1982) 39, for the date. Later emperors considered an unwillingness "to meet together in obedient religious observance on the day of Easter" as a sure sign of deviance: see *CTh* 16.5.9, issued in 382.

Arianizing churchmen who temporized over rigid supporters of Nicene doctrines. His apparent ambivalence after the council was a return to his neutrality in this dispute during the previous year. In a letter written soon after his victory over Licinius he had blamed both bishop Alexander for putting his priests on the spot and Arius for his candid response: "it was not proper either to ask about these matters in the beginning, or to answer when asked." Because Constantine's overriding concern had been unity in the empire, his initial reaction to hearing about the controversy had been simply to try to match a single perspective on God with harmony in the empire.[27]

But at the council of Nicaea he had joined the bishops in opposing Arian doctrines. One contributing factor may have been his hostility toward bishop Eusebius of Nicomedia. After the emperor Licinius had lost control of the Balkans to Constantine, he established his primary residence at Nicomedia in 317. At about the same time Eusebius had moved from his see of Beirut to become bishop of Nicomedia. Eusebius of Nicomedia now acquired influence at Licinius' court, perhaps primarily because of his persuasiveness with the emperor's wife, Constantia. During these later years of Licinius' rule in the eastern provinces Eusebius had apparently tried to turn his political influence into ecclesiastical prominence. At a time when the organization of the church was still in flux, Eusebius seemed to conclude that the bishop of an imperial residence could claim overall leadership in ecclesiastical

---

[27] Constantine's letter to Alexander and Arius: Eusebius, *Vita Constantini* 2.65.1, one perspective and harmony, 69.2, not proper = Urkunde 17, ed. Opitz (1934–1935) 32–35.

Constantine discussed his ideas about philosophy and theology in an oration entitled *Oratio ad sanctorum coetum.* The precise date and location of this oration are contested: see Chapter 11. So are its theological implications: see Barnes (1985) 390, noting that one comment "brings him close to the theology of Eusebius of Caesarea, whom his opponents consistently regarded as an Arian"; Bleckmann (1997) 200, "die arianisierenden Passagen"; and Edwards (2003) xxvii, "All claims to have discerned an Arian tenor in the speech are . . . ill-founded." Davies (1991) suggests that Eusebius himself interpolated the dubious theological remarks when he attached the speech to his *Life of Constantine.*

affairs. According to his bitter opponent Alexander, bishop of Alexandria, "Eusebius thinks that the affairs of the church are dependent on his opinion." Because Eusebius had openly supported Arius, Alexander could malign him as the leader of "this disgraceful heresy that is an enemy of Christ." As a result, once Constantine defeated Licinius in 324, Eusebius' outdated political loyalties may have become a religious liability too. Constantine may now have turned against Arius' doctrines in part as a reprisal for Eusebius' collaboration with Licinius. In the process of demoting a supporter of Licinius, Constantine became an opponent of his theology at the council of Nicaea. In this perspective the emperor's early opposition to the doctrines of Arius and Eusebius of Nicomedia may have reflected not strictly theological evaluation, but primarily political retaliation.[28]

In fact, a few months after the council at Nicaea Constantine sent a letter to the church at Nicomedia, in which he reminded the congregation of the new orthodoxy. He also listed a series of charges against bishop Eusebius. Constantine linked Eusebius with Licinius by claiming that he had been an "accomplice in the tyrant's cruelty" and a "client of the tyrant." During the war of the previous year Eusebius had allegedly sent "eyes" to spy on Constantine, and he had all but recruited armed men to help Licinius. After the council he had given hospitality to deposed churchmen. These were serious accusations, both political

---

[28] Letter of Alexander about Eusebius of Nicomedia: Urkunde 4b, ed. Opitz (1934–1935) 6–11, quoted in Socrates, *HE* 1.6.4–30. Influence at court: Socrates, *HE* 1.6.33, "At that time Eusebius was especially influential, because the emperor then resided at Nicomedia." Eusebius and Constantia: Socrates, *HE* 1.25, Sozomen, *HE* 2.27, Philostorgius, *HE* 1.9, with Chapter 6, for discussion of Constantia and her half-brother Constantine. Later traditions claimed that bishop Eusebius of Nicomedia was also involved in the negotiations over Licinius' surrender in September 324. According to a Byzantine *Life of Constantine*, Licinius requested the assistance of Eusebius of Nicomedia in appealing for Constantine's mercy: see *Vita Constantini* 17, ed. Opitz (1934) 555; also printed in Bidez' edition of Philostorgius, *HE*, p. 180.

Ammianus Marcellinus, *Res gestae* 22.9.4, claimed that Eusebius of Nicomedia was a distant relative of the emperor Julian. Barnes (1981) 321n.79, suggests that the kinship was through Julian's mother, a daughter of Julius Julianus, who served as a prefect under Licinius and a consul under Constantine: see Chapters 6–7.

and doctrinal, and Constantine now sent Eusebius of Nicomedia and others into exile. "I ordered them to be arrested and banished as far away as possible."[29]

But a few years later Constantine allowed Eusebius to return as bishop of Nicomedia. First, however, he invited Arius to visit the court and learn about his kindness. In late 327 Arius and a supporter brought a creed for the emperor's inspection. This statement of their doctrines carefully avoided most of the contentious terminology of the Nicene creed. Constantine then examined their beliefs in person. "Many were present when I talked to them about the meaning of life." With his blessing, a council readmitted Arius. Eusebius of Nicomedia and a colleague then asked to be reinstated too, and Constantine ordered their recall in an imperial edict.[30]

In 328 Athanasius succeeded Alexander as bishop of Alexandria and as an outspoken opponent of Arius and his doctrines. As a powerful advocate of Nicene theology he was also hostile toward Eusebius of Nicomedia, whom he pointedly called the "leader of the Arian heresy." Not surprisingly, Athanasius and Eusebius now competed for Constantine's support. Not only did Eusebius soon insist that Athanasius receive Arius back into communion, but to deflect attention from suspicions about his own past disloyalty he also accused Athanasius of having "plotted against the emperor's affairs." After Constantine wrote with a threat of exile, Athanasius visited Constantinople in 332 for a hearing on charges about his highhanded actions in Egypt. Eusebius and his allies in Egypt promoted these accusations; but this time Constantine

---

[29] Constantine's letter: Urkunde 27.9 10, accomplice, client, eyes, armed men, 16, hospitality, arrest, ed. Opitz (1934–1935) 58–62, quoted in Athanasius, *De decretis Nicaenae synodi* 41.

[30] Constantine's letter to Arius: Urkunde 29, ed. Opitz (1934–1935) 63, quoted in Socrates, *HE* 1.25.7–8. Letter from Arius and Euzoius: Urkunde 30.5, ed. Opitz (1934–1935) 64, quoted in Socrates, *HE* 1.26, Sozomen, *HE* 2.27. Conversation: Urkunde 32.3, ed. Opitz (1934–1935) 66, with Barnes (1978b) 60–61, (1981) 229, arguing that the council met at Nicomedia. Letter of Eusebius of Nicomedia and Theognius of Nicaea: Urkunde 31, ed. Opitz (1934–1935) 65–66, quoted in Socrates, *HE* 1.14.2–6, Sozomen, *HE* 2.16.3–7. Imperial edict: Socrates, *HE* 1.14.1.

supported Athanasius, and in a letter to the church at Alexandria he praised their bishop as a "man of God." Two years later the emperor ordered bishops to meet at Caesarea in Palestine to hear more charges against Athanasius, this time including murder. Eusebius of Nicomedia planned to attend this council. But after Athanasius wrote to Constantine that the man presumed dead had been found alive, the emperor halted the inquiry. In 335 Eusebius again joined with Athanasius' opponents in Egypt to present yet more accusations. This time a council at Tyre deposed Athanasius; it also sent Eusebius of Nicomedia as one of the delegates to present its findings to Constantine. When these bishops arrived at Constantinople, they discovered that Athanasius was at the capital and had already talked with the emperor. Constantine now invited all the bishops who had attended the council at Tyre to appear before his court and demonstrate "the purity of your judgement." The delegates from the council instead claimed that Athanasius had threatened to interfere with the shipment of grain from Egypt to the capital. Eusebius insisted in public that Athanasius was capable of such a threat; Athanasius protested; but Constantine was so angry at even a hint of possible meddling with the grain supply that he sent Athanasius into exile to Trier. By now Eusebius of Nicomedia had clearly overcome the antagonism of his early relationship with Constantine to become a significant influence at the court. In spring of 337 he baptized the emperor on his deathbed. After Constantius succeeded his father as emperor for the eastern provinces, he helped Eusebius become bishop at Constantinople. Under Licinius, Eusebius had become bishop at the imperial residence of Nicomedia; now he was bishop of Constantinople. His episcopal career had taken him from a Tetrarchic capital to the new Constantinian capital.[31]

---

[31] Athanasius, *Apologia contra Arianos* 9.3, grain supply, 9.4, protests, 59.4, leader, Eusebius' letter, 59.6, Constantine's threatening letter to Athanasius, 60.4, hearing and accusations, 62.5, man of God, 65.4, end of inquiry, 86.9, purity, 87.1, delegation, grain supply, 87.2, emperor's anger; with Williams (1987) 75–81, on the "ecclesiastical civil war" between Eusebius of Nicomedia and Athanasius. Accusation of plotting: Socrates, *HE* 1.27.9, Sozomen, *HE* 2.22.8. Even though Athanasius was accused of sending a "bag full of gold" to Philumenus, a high-ranking imperial

In these intrigues among powerful bishops Arius was often just a pawn. In 332 he wrote to Constantine and complained about his continuing exclusion from the Egyptian church. He also included another statement of his beliefs that was much more strident than his earlier attempt at accommodation. Arius now agreed that there was "one God," but assigned a "foreign substance" to the Son. This formulation emphasized not just the subordination of the Son, but also a clear distinction between the Son and the Father. Constantine responded with anger. Not only did he reassert the Nicene doctrine that Father and Son shared "one essence"; he also scorned Arius' request and mocked his haggard appearance: "wash yourself in the Nile." Along with this letter the emperor issued a general edict ordering Arius' books to be burned. From his treatment of the rival emperors he had already deposed Constantine certainly knew how to erase memories: "absolutely no memorial of Arius is to be preserved." But at another meeting Arius was able to convince Constantine of his orthodoxy, and in 335 the emperor recommended to a council at Jerusalem that Arius should be readmitted to communion. In the next year the emperor again questioned Arius in person at Constantinople and asked if he would endorse the doctrines of the council of Nicaea. Arius agreed, signed a statement, and took an oath. Only his untimely death precluded his readmission.[32]

## A PERFECT CREATURE OF GOD

Another churchman who benefited from Constantine's patronage was Eusebius of Caesarea. Eusebius had backed Arius early in the

magistrate, the basis for this allegation is obscure. Barnes (1993) 21, suggests a connection with an attempt by a bodyguard to assassinate Constantine: see Socrates, *HE* 1.13.4–10. Translation of Eusebius: Socrates, *HE* 2.7.

[32] In his reply Constantine quoted from Arius' letter: Urkunde 34.13, one God, 14, foreign substance, one essence, 37, Nile, ed. Opitz (1934–1935) 69–75, quoted in Athanasius, *De decretis Nicaeae synodi* 40; dated to winter of 332–333 by Barnes (1981) 232–33. Edict: Urkunde 33, ed. Opitz (1934–1935) 66–68, quoted in Athanasius, *De decretis Nicaeae synodi* 39, and Socrates, *HE* 1.9.30–31. Council of Jerusalem: Athanasius, *Apologia contra Arianos* 84, *De synodis* 21. Examination at Constantinople: Socrates, *HE* 1.38.

controversy, and in his letter to bishop Alexander, Arius had claimed Eusebius as one of his supporters. By then Eusebius was bishop of Caesarea in Palestine. Already in his fifties, he had previously served as a priest for over twenty years, and he had a deserved reputation as a meticulous biblical scholar. His doctrines about the subordination of the Son to the Father were quite similar to Arius' teachings. In one letter Eusebius had argued that because the Father existed before the Son, the Son did not coexist with the Father. As a result, "one is considered prior and better than the second in rank and prestige." According to Eusebius, the Son was God, but not true God; at best, the true Son was an image of the true God. In another letter Eusebius had chided bishop Alexander of Alexandria for misrepresenting Arius' doctrines. Eusebius agreed with Arius that the Son of God was "a perfect creature of God, but not like one of the other creatures." But as Alexander gathered more supporters, Eusebius was increasingly isolated. In early 325 he attended the council at Antioch that explicitly supported Alexander and condemned Arius. The creed of this council proclaimed that the Lord Jesus Christ was the only-begotten Son, begotten from the Father not as if something made, but as if something truly begotten. All but three bishops supported this creed. After questioning them, the council condemned them as "sympathetic to the teachings of Arius." One of these dissenters was Eusebius.[33]

Eusebius had hence arrived at the council of Nicaea as a condemned heretic. He came prepared to make his case. He brought his own creed, which was most likely the baptismal creed in use at his see of Caesarea.

---

[33] Arius' letter to Eusebius of Nicomedia: Urkunde 1.3, "Eusebius, your brother in Caesarea, [and other churchmen in the East] say that God existed before the Son without a beginning," ed. Opitz (1934–1935) 2, quoted in Epiphanius, *Panarion* 69.6. Eusebius' letter to bishop Euphration of Balanea: Urkunde 3, ed. Opitz (1934–1935) 4–5. Letter to Alexander: Urkunde 7, ed. Opitz (1934–1935) 14–15. Council of Antioch: Urkunde 18, ed. Opitz (1934–1935) 36–41. Some modern scholars try to salvage Eusebius' reputation by distancing him from Arius: note Luibhéid (1981) 122, "He was a loser, not because he followed the same road as Arius"; and Hanson (1988) 59, "a theological stance which could be called modified Arianism."

This creed was quite neutral, stating that the Lord Jesus Christ was the Word of God, "the only-begotten Son, the firstborn of all creation, begotten from the Father before all ages, through whom everything came into existence." Blandness had its attractions, especially in the presence of the emperor. Eusebius claimed that when he presented this creed at the council, there was no opposition. In fact, Constantine himself "was the first to admit that this creed included the most correct statements." Furthermore, according to Eusebius, the emperor "confessed that he thought the same, and he urged everyone there to agree and subscribe to these doctrines." Constantine's only suggestion was to include the adjective *homoousios*, "of the same essence," to describe Jesus Christ in his relationship with God the Father. Whatever Constantine's true role in resolving these doctrinal disputes, Eusebius could now at least claim that this vital term was simply an elaboration of his own doctrines.[34]

Eusebius' creed perhaps provided a starting point for the structure and style of the council's final creed. But the vocabulary and the intentions of that Nicene creed were in fact quite different from Eusebius' doctrines, and he now scrambled to justify his acceptance of it. In an awkward letter to his congregation at Caesarea he carefully explained his understanding of controversial terminology, including, of course, the notion "of the same essence." This term implied, he argued, only that the Son "is from the Father, not that he exists as a part of the Father." He also accepted the notion of the Son as "begotten not made" by arguing that he shared an essence that was greater than that of any creature. Eusebius may have insisted to his congregation that he had been defiant "up to the last hour," but now he could save face. Once all these issues had been satisfactorily explained in Constantine's presence, he had endorsed the Nicene creed. Nominally at least, Eusebius was now a Nicene bishop.[35]

---

[34] Eusebius' letter to Caesarea: Urkunde 22.4, only-begotten Son, 7, the first, *homoousios*, ed. Opitz (1934–1935) 42–47, quoted in Athanasius, *De decretis Nicaenae synodi* 33.1–17, and Socrates, *HE* 1.8.35–54.

[35] Eusebius' letter to Caesarea: Urkunde 22.9, from the Father, 11, essence, 14, emperor's presence, 17, last hour.

Despite that clumsy endorsement, Eusebius of course always retained his fundamental subordinationist doctrines about the relationship of Jesus Christ the Son with God the Father. For a few years after the council of Nicaea he seems to have carefully moderated his theological terminology. Then he was increasingly successful in finding support. Perhaps already at the banquet that Constantine hosted for the bishops Eusebius had "taken the stage at the council of God's ministers" to deliver a panegyric that previewed the upcoming twentieth anniversary of the emperor's reign. As a result, one of his supporters was now Constantine, and he was able to triumph over his opponents. Even though bishop Eustathius of Antioch accused him of having "debased" the Nicene creed through his tortured interpretation, Eusebius ended up presiding at a council at Antioch that deposed Eustathius. After Eusebius subsequently turned down the opportunity to become bishop of Antioch himself, Constantine praised his respect for the traditions of church order in a flattering letter. The emperor also asked him to have his scribes compose fifty copies of the Bible; in addition, Eusebius sent the emperor a copy of his treatise on Easter. Even as he benefited from the emperor's patronage, Eusebius had become an important source for Constantine's ideas about Christian theology.[36]

## THE GOD OF WAR

After his victory over Licinius in 324 and until his death in 337 Constantine had been a vigorous participant in the ongoing controversies over doctrinal orthodoxy in the eastern provinces. Not only had he used his imperial authority to promote some churchmen and oppose others; he had also contributed his own theological interpretations. But

---

[36] Eusebius, *Vita Constantini* 1.1.1, stage, 3.15, banquet, 61, Constantine's letter, 4.35, Easter, 36, Bibles; with Skeat (1999), arguing that the Codex Sinaiticus and the Codex Vaticanus were among the copies of the Bible now composed at Caesarea. Conflict with Eustathius: Socrates, *HE* 1.23.8, debase, 24, council; Athanasius, *Apologia contra Arianos* 45.2, presidency of Eusebius; with Barnes (1978b) 59–60, dating this council at Antioch to 327, and Burgess (1999a) 191–96, (2000), to late 328. For Eusebius' moderation of his theology after the council of Nicaea, see Hollerich (1999) 24–26, 61–66.

as a patron and as a theologian he had been remarkably inconsistent. In particular, in his long venomous letter to Arius he had vigorously defended Nicene theology and critiqued Arius' doctrines; but during the last years of his reign he had also reconciled with Arius, his mentor Eusebius of Nicomedia, and a like-minded supporter, Eusebius of Caesarea. The consistency in Constantine's policies had been not doctrines, but the dream of political and religious unity. When Arius had mentioned that he had the support of "all the people of Libya," Constantine had been outraged. By hinting at the potential of schism, Arius seemed to have morphed into "Ares," the god of war on the verge of initiating yet more civil discord. But when Arius was more discreet and conciliatory, Constantine was prepared to recommend his restoration. It had taken Constantine almost two decades to eliminate his imperial rivals. After those wars he expected Christianity to be a unifying force. As a result, in his letter to the bishops at the council of Tyre he had encouraged them to restore "the proper harmony to the provinces" and to offer "the gift of peace to those who are now in contention."[37]

Like his Tetrarchic predecessors, Constantine encouraged a close correlation between religion and imperial rule. Each could reinforce the other, and his dominating performance at the council of Nicaea made him the prototype of an assertive Christian emperor for subsequent generations. In contrast, the bumbling performance of Eusebius of Caesarea at the council should have left him labeled as a turncoat for subsequent generations. Instead, because Constantine eventually patronized bishops like Eusebius of Nicomedia and Eusebius of Caesarea who supported Arius, Arian doctrines remained influential. Eusebius of Caesarea became an honored acquaintance of the emperor, and he continued to promote his theology about the fundamental subordination of Jesus

---

[37] Constantine's letter to Arius: Urkunde 34.6, Arius as Ares, 20, Libya, ed. Opitz (1934–1935) 69–75, quoted in Athanasius, *De decretis Nicaenae synodi* 40. Constantine's letter to council of Tyre: Eusebius, *Vita Constantini* 4.42.1, harmony, 5, peace. For the claim that Constantine was reluctant to use coercion to impose a Christian orthodoxy, see Drake (2000), previewed in Drake (1996), reprised in Drake (2006).

Christ the Son. He also started thinking about the symbolic significance of a Christian emperor. Just as Constantine concluded that theological doctrines had implications about his political standing as an emperor, so Eusebius could sense that ideas about the emperor might support his non-Nicene doctrines. Perhaps a theology of a Christian emperor could strengthen his particular theology of Jesus Christ.

# "ONLY-BEGOTTEN SON": HISTORY BECOMES THEOLOGY

## CHAPTER ELEVEN

USEBIUS COMPLETED HIS *LIFE OF CONSTANTINE* AFTER THE emperor's funeral in 337 and near the end of his own long life. By then of course he had a longstanding reputation as a historian, the author of *Chronicle* and *Ecclesiastical History*. But the primary composition of those historical works had been decades in the past, and even the most recent revisions were by now quite dated. The final entry in his revised *Chronicle* had mentioned the celebration of the twentieth anniversary of Constantine's reign in 325–326, and the final revisions to *History* had perhaps included the deletion of references to Crispus, Constantine's oldest son, after his execution in 326. For the narrative of Constantine's early years in *Life*, Eusebius of course used his *History* as a source and often simply repeated his earlier account with a few alterations. But by the time he compiled his *Life of Constantine*, writing history was not his most pressing concern.[1]

---

[1] For the final revisions to *Chronicle* and *Ecclesiastical History*, see Barnes (1981) 113, 150, and Burgess (1999a) 56–57, 66–74; also Grant (1980) 164–67, suggesting that Eusebius rewrote passages in *HE* 1–7 after the Council of Nicaea, and Barnes (1984), arguing that he did not change his mind on important issues in *HE* 1–7.

Instead, Eusebius spent his final years defending himself and his non-Nicene doctrines. By then one primary opponent was Marcellus, the bishop of Ancyra who was a devoted champion of Nicene theology. Eusebius composed both a merciless critique of Marcellus' doctrines and an extended treatise, entitled *Ecclesiastical Theology*, that presented his own theology. At about the same time that he was writing these theological treatises, he was composing *Life*. This context suggests that Eusebius was writing *Life* with theology, not history, predominantly on his mind. As a result, rather than instinctively thinking of *Life* as a continuation of, even a conclusion to, his *Ecclesiastical History*, it is appropriate to consider it as a supplemental treatise that reinforced the doctrinal arguments in his *Ecclesiastical Theology*.

Modern scholars have often read *Life* as a political apology that provided a rationale for a Christian emperor who ruled in the image of God. There is no doubt that in *Life*, as in his other writings, Eusebius blended religion and politics. But during his final years doctrinal controversies certainly took priority, and it is possible to read *Life* instead as

For Eusebius' use of his earlier writings as sources for *Vita Constantini*, see Hall (1993).

Eusebius mentioned Crispus by name in *HE* 10.9.4, 6. The Syriac translation of *HE*, composed perhaps ca. 400, omitted these references to Crispus: for the date, see Schwartz (1909) XLII. Schwartz (1909) L, followed by Barnes (1980) 197–98, and other modern scholars, concludes that Eusebius himself had already removed these references. Another possibility is that the Syriac translator was responsible, and in part for theological rather than political reasons. In *HE* 10.9.6 Eusebius had described Crispus as "similar to his father in all respects." In 359 the emperor Constantius promulgated a statement of Trinitarian orthodoxy, now often known as the Dated Creed, that carefully avoided any use of the contentious term "essence" by claiming that the Son was "similar to the Father in all respects": see Athanasius, *De synodis* 8.7. This creedal formulation was later discarded. As a result, a Syriac translator who was aware of the future development of orthodoxy may have wanted to correct the political philosophy too. When Eusebius recycled these passages from *HE* in *Vita Constantini* 2.3.2, 19.2, he certainly ignored Crispus. But he may have left the references in *HE*. Note that later Greek historians continued to include Crispus' name in their citations of these passages: see Evagrius, *HE* 3.41, quoting Eusebius, *HE* 10.9.6.

a theological apology that provided a rationale for Eusebius' doctrines about the subordination of Jesus Christ to God. In this perspective the Constantine of *Life* was less the subject of a biography and more a constructed character in an ongoing theological discourse. Even as Eusebius defended his version of Constantine's legacy, he was defending himself and his doctrines. Eusebius did not just think *about* Constantine; he also thought *with* him as another symbolic category to help articulate his own theology. In various panegyrics he had already started manipulating his image of a Christian emperor to correspond to his doctrines; in this biography the emperor was now another representation of the author's own theology. An apology for Constantine's reign could become an apology for Eusebius' theology. In *Life* the author could imagine the emperor as a medium to promote his own doctrines.[2]

Nor was Eusebius alone in constructing a biography. After the council of Nicaea Constantine had become increasingly interested in the life of Jesus Christ in Palestine, and he soon funded the building of churches

---

[2] For *Life* as a political apology for Constantine, see Cameron (1997) 152: "The work as we have it has a clear and single thread running through every part, namely the desire to defend Constantine, present all his actions and motives in the best possible light from Eusebius' point of view, and to claim and commend the continuation of his policies." For an effective critique of this characterization of Eusebius as mere political propagandist, see Hollerich (1990), (1999) 192–93.

Subsequent readers in late antiquity and the Byzantine period often praised Eusebius as a learned historian but criticized him as a heterodox theologian. In accordance with this distinction they tended to classify his *Life of Constantine* as a doctrinal treatise rather than a historical treatise: see Winkelmann (1964) 111, "Die Vita Constantini gehörte nicht zu den historisch-objektiven Schriften Eusebs, sie wirkte außerdem nicht dogmatisch einwandfrei, galt als unerwünscht." As one example, note that in the ninth century Photius, bishop of Constantinople, was especially critical of Eusebius' misleading account of the theological controversies in *Life*: see Photius, *Bibliotheca* 127, "with regard to the Arian heresy, he does not say clearly if he shared that doctrine." Photius thought that this theological dissemblance had hence tainted Eusebius' historical interpretation of Constantine. "Eusebius states that a 'dispute' broke out between Arius and Alexander. By describing this heresy in this way, he dissimulates. For the emperor, God's friend, was much troubled with this 'dispute.' . . . The narrative is neither accurate nor clear."

that commemorated the highlights of Jesus' life on earth, including his birth, death, resurrection, and ascension. Constantine's patronage helped transform sites in Palestine into a Christian Holy Land. In the process he promoted himself and his dynasty. Constantine appropriated Jesus' life to serve his political goals; Eusebius appropriated Constantine's life to serve his theological objectives.

## PANEGYRIC AS THEOLOGY

After the council of Nicaea Eusebius had slowly worked himself into Constantine's good graces, despite his theology. But other bishops continued to oppose Eusebius, precisely because of his theology. One rival was Marcellus, the bishop of Ancyra who had been a prominent theologian for decades. Marcellus had most likely presided at the council that met at Ancyra probably in 314, soon after the emperor Licinius took control of Asia Minor. Leadership at this council would have enhanced his wider contacts, since the bishops who attended represented sees from throughout central and eastern Asia Minor, and even from Syria. Marcellus then seems to have become a supporter of bishop Alexander of Alexandria, in opposition to Arius and his doctrines. His own theology emphasized a rather extreme form of monotheism: "the divinity of the Father and the Son is indivisible." In his interpretation the Logos, the "Word," was eternal with God and unbegotten, although after his incarnation he was called Son, Jesus Christ, Savior, or King. At first "silent," the Word became "articulate" as the incarnated Son. "If the addition of the flesh is examined with regard to the Savior, the Divinity seems to be expanded only by activity. Hence it is most likely a truly undivided oneness." After finally abandoning this body, the Word would return to God. Marcellus clearly wanted to circumvent having to make any distinctions within "the one God." As a result, by trying "to avoid . . . any doctrine that would subordinate the Son to the Father," he "failed to distinguish the Son from the Father."[3]

---

[3] For the confusion about Marcellus' leadership at the council of Ancyra, see Hanson (1988) 217, and Parvis (2001b). The primary sources for Marcellus' doctrines are the fragmentary quotations from his treatise as cited in Eusebius' treatises, and

During these earlier years of jockeying for position, Eusebius of Caesarea made clear his opposition to Marcellus by traveling to preach in support of Arius' doctrines. He was certainly welcomed at Laodicea in Syria, where bishop Theodotus was a friend and a like-minded supporter of Arius. But in Marcellus' backyard in central Asia Minor the reception was different. In the church at Ancyra, Eusebius delivered a sermon in which he criticized the people of Galatia for rejecting his doctrine that there were "two essences, two entities, two powers, and two Gods." Marcellus was apparently in attendance and may well have taken offense at these inflammatory comments. Over a decade later, when he remembered and attributed these remarks to Eusebius, he was still "irritated."[4]

In early 325 a council at Antioch supported Alexander of Alexandria and opposed Arius. Even though Marcellus did not attend this council, his rather extreme theological viewpoint seems to have influenced the outcome. Marcellus may well have suggested that the council should focus on the issue of divine essence. At this council some bishops were questioned about exactly this issue. One said he believed in three distinct essences; Eusebius admitted again that he believed in two. Eusebius had been boxed into a difficult position, and because he was unable to accept the creed from this council, he left under a cloud of suspicion. Nor could he have been optimistic about the future of his doctrines, since his next opportunity to clear himself would

the letter he wrote to bishop Julius of Rome (Fragment 129), quoted in Epiphanius, *Panarion* 72.2–3. Marcellus, Fragment 71, Savior, quoted in Eusebius, *De ecclesiastica theologia* 2.4.1; Fragment 128, one God, quoted in Eusebius, *Epistula ad Flacillum*; Fragment 129, indivisible, quoted in Epiphanius, *Panarion* 72.3.2. For comprehensive summaries of Marcellus' theology, see Luibhéid (1981) 64–97, Hanson (1988) 217–35, Lienhard (1999) 47–68, and Ayres (2004) 62–69; quotation about Son and Father from Hanson (1988) 235.

4 Eusebius' sermons: Eusebius, *Contra Marcellum* 1.4.42, 45–46 (= Marcellus, Fragment 83), with Logan (1992) 436–38, arguing that Eusebius of Nicomedia had organized this tour of Arius' supporters during 322–323. Eusebius dedicated to Theodotus both his *Praeparatio evangelica* and his *Demonstratio evangelica*, which he composed between 313 and 324: see Barnes (1981) 178, and Carriker (2003) 72–73.

be at Marcellus' own see. Marcellus may have already suggested that Ancyra should be the host for a "great council of churchmen," which would now provide disgraced bishops like Eusebius "a place for repentance and acknowledgement of the truth." Even though the emperor soon moved the council to Nicaea, Marcellus was nevertheless again an important participant. While Eusebius strained to harmonize his doctrines with the Nicene creed, Marcellus pointedly rejected the doctrines of Arius and his supporters: "I refuted them at the council of Nicaea."[5]

During the 320s Marcellus and Eusebius had hence already clashed, directly and repeatedly, over doctrines, over the emperor's support, over personal pride. Their animosity lingered throughout the later years of Constantine's reign. In 335 Marcellus declined to accept the decisions of two councils that the emperor himself had summoned. The council of Tyre had ordered the removal of bishop Athanasius of Alexandria, a firm supporter of Nicene theology, and the council of Jerusalem had agreed to readmit Arius to communion. Marcellus was upset at what he considered to be a retreat from Nicene theology, and in response he composed an enormous treatise that promoted his doctrines and condemned various opponents. Among these misguided theologians he mentioned Eusebius of Caesarea by name as having taught that God consisted of two distinct essences. In his estimation, Eusebius' theology was similar to those earlier doctrines of Gnostic Christians that had postulated the existence of multiple Gods. Marcellus then sent this treatise to the emperor, with the hope that Constantine would reprimand his opponents. The emperor referred the matter to a council of bishops that met in his presence at Constantinople in July 336. At this council Marcellus' treatise was unsuccessful, since these bishops again

[5] Great council: Urkunde 18.15, ed. Opitz (1934–1935) 40; two or three essences: Urkunde 19.1, ed. Opitz (1934–1935) 41 = Marcellus, Fragment 81, quoted in Eusebius, *Contra Marcellum* 1.4.39; with Logan (1992) 434–36, highlighting Marcellus' influence in formulating the doctrinal issues at the council of Antioch. Refutation: Marcellus, Fragment 129, quoted in Epiphanius, *Panarion* 72.2.1; also Athanasius, *Apologia contra Arianos* 23.3, 32.2, for Marcellus' presence at the council of Nicaea.

decided to reinstate Arius. In addition, this time they also deposed Marcellus himself.[6]

Eusebius reacted to Marcellus' criticisms in different media. One rejoinder was the composition of two detailed treatises that attacked his opponent and promoted his own theology. Since Eusebius had attended the council of Constantinople, he had participated in the decision against Marcellus. As a result, one of his treatises, *Against Marcellus*, was an attempt to "defend the decisions of the holy council." In this long critique Eusebius quoted extensively from Marcellus' treatise in order to condemn his opponent by citing verbatim his own, supposedly outrageous, claims. "Rather than [proposing] a comprehensive alternative, I assembled a clear refutation of his words from the words themselves." These citations focused, predictably, on the status of God the Son. "This holy council of God rejected his [Marcellus'] treatise, and properly so, because he did not confess either the beginning or the pious consummation of the Son of God." This collection of Marcellus' sayings apparently did not have enough of an impact, however, and Eusebius soon decided to supplement it with a more positive discussion in a matching treatise, *Ecclesiastical Theology*, that was a reassertion of his own doctrines. In a dedicatory letter to bishop Flacillus of Antioch he explained his new intention of disputing Marcellus' "frivolous and verbose treatise" with his own "brief writings." "We who venerate the all-holy and thrice-blessed Trinity have collected our entire argument in the same number [of books, i.e., the three books of this treatise], avoiding verbosity and presenting the true theology in short summaries." As usual, however, Eusebius underestimated his predilection for verbosity, since each of these treatises was in fact quite substantial and garrulous.[7]

---

[6] Eusebius, *Contra Marcellum* 1.3, Marcellus' enormous treatise. Criticism of Eusebius: Marcellus, Fragment 81, two essences, quoted in Eusebius, *Contra Marcellum* 1.4.39 (= Urkunde 19); Fragment 85, similarity to the Gnostic teacher Valentinus, quoted in Eusebius, *Contra Marcellum* 1.4.41. Deposition at council of Constantinople: Socrates, *HE* 1.36, Sozomen, *HE* 2.33.

[7] Eusebius, *Contra Marcellum* 2.4.29–31, decisions, council; *Epistula ad Flacillum*, clear refutation. Because Eusebius, *Contra Marcellum* 2.4.29, described Constantine as "thrice-blessed," Barnes (1978b) 64–65, argues that Eusebius wrote this

Eusebius also adopted another tactic to complement this refutation of his opponent's doctrines. In his own treatise Marcellus had combined an apologetic exposition of his theology with flattery of Constantine. Like a panegyrist, he hoped to earn the emperor's support through his compliments. "Because of the tributes about the emperor, he perhaps somehow hoped to acquire the emperor's goodwill for himself and to have the bishops whom he had slandered subjected to a penalty." Even though Marcellus' appeal was unsuccessful, it had most likely alerted Eusebius to the importance of winning the emperor's patronage through flattery. After the council in 336 he stayed in Constantinople to celebrate the thirtieth anniversary of the emperor's accession on July 25, and during the festivities he delivered a panegyric in honor of Constantine.[8]

Eusebius' panegyric of "imperial hymns" of course flattered the emperor. But even as he was "weaving garlands of words," he was also, once more, promoting his own doctrines. Eusebius started his pane-gyric with a segue from the "Great Emperor," God the Father who was shrouded in his heavenly palace, to "our emperor." Ruling with the Great Emperor was his only-begotten Logos, the "Word." This Logos may have been "the only-begotten Son," "governor of the entire cos-mos," "older than all time," and even a "fellow Emperor with his Father," but Eusebius also emphasized that he was nevertheless subordinate to God. The Logos was "distinguished with second place in his Father's kingdom." Corresponding to the Logos was the emperor, "the friend of

---

treatise after Constantine's death in May 337. Because Eusebius, *De ecclesiastica theologia* 2.22.4, mentioned that Marcellus "had grown old in the episcopacy of Christ's church," Barnes (1981) 263–65, argues that Eusebius started writing this treatise too only after Constantine's death when his sons pardoned all deposed bishops. In contrast, Hanson (1988) 217–18, suggests, more plausibly, that Euse-bius started composing *Contra Marcellum* immediately after Marcellus' deposi-tion in the summer of 336. Constantine had once invited Eusebius to send him more of his recent treatises: see Eusebius, *Vita Constantini* 4.35.3. Since Marcellus had already sent his treatise to Constantine, perhaps Eusebius likewise had the emperor in mind as a potential reader. Drake (2000) 355, implies that Eusebius had completed both treatises before Constantine's death.

[8] Eusebius, *Contra Marcellum* 2.4.30, emperor's goodwill.

God" who promoted true piety on earth. While the Logos commanded the armies of heaven, Constantine commanded the armies that defeated both the barbarians and the demons of pagan cults.[9]

This parallelism with the Logos of the Great Emperor certainly complimented the emperor during the celebration of his jubilee. But these comparisons were furthermore a reflection of Eusebius' particular subordinationist theology about God and his Logos, and also a reinforcement of those doctrines. In this panegyric Eusebius never mentioned Jesus Christ by name. As a result, he seems to have left the impression that Constantine had been God's sole representative on earth, an analogue to God's Logos in heaven. Eusebius was furthermore quite explicit about the similarity between the two by using the same simile. In his perspective, the Logos who commanded the heavenly hosts and Constantine who advanced against his defeated enemies were each acting "like a prefect of the Great Emperor." At the conclusion of his panegyric Eusebius mentioned just three rulers, God the Great Emperor, the one only-begotten Savior, and the one emperor on earth. In this triad Constantine was not subordinate to both God and the Logos; instead, "the hierarchy . . . is not so much God-Logos-Emperor as God working through two coordinate powers in Heaven and on earth." Constantine apparently had the same direct access to God that the Logos enjoyed. According to Eusebius, "God himself, the Great Emperor, was extending his right hand to him from above." Even as he flattered the emperor by correlating him with the Logos, Eusebius clearly stressed that both the Logos and the emperor were subordinate to God the Father. The coordination of the emperor and the Logos implied the subordination of both to God the Father. Flattery of the emperor was at the same time theology about God the Father and the Logos.[10]

[9] Eusebius, *De laudibus Constantini* Prologus 2, hymns; 1.1, Great Emperor, 1.3, our emperor, 1.6, governor, older, second place, 2.1, fellow emperor, 3.6, only-begotten Son; *Vita Constantini* 1.1.1, garlands. For the argument that Eusebius delivered this oration in Constantinople during the summer of 336, see Drake (1976) 30–45.

[10] Eusebius, *De laudibus Constantini* 3.5, Logos as prefect, 7.13, emperor as prefect, 10.6–7, three rulers, right hand. Quotation about hierarchy from Drake (1976) 57, who argues that Eusebius did not mention Jesus Christ in this oration because

Less than a year earlier Eusebius had delivered another oration before Constantine at Constantinople. Although the primary subject of that oration had been the new Church of the Holy Sepulcher at Jerusalem, Eusebius also complimented the emperor as the patron of its construction. Constantine had stood and listened carefully to the oration, and at the end he had "asserted the truth of its theological doctrines." Now, in this more recent panegyric about the thirtieth anniversary of Constantine's reign Eusebius again included statements about his own doctrines, this time intertwined with flattery of the emperor. Constantine certainly welcomed the adoration. "While he listened, the friend of God resembled a happy man. After listening, he said as much while he dined and talked with the bishops who were in attendance." Eusebius was no doubt hoping that Constantine, in appreciation for the panegyric, would likewise again endorse the theology.[11]

Marcellus' treatise that combined doctrinal apology and imperial flattery had been a powerful catalyst for several of Eusebius' final writings, and perhaps also a model to imitate. Eusebius had tried to bury Marcellus' doctrines beneath the barrage of his two theological treatises, and he had countered with his own accolades of Constantine in a panegyric celebrating the emperor's thirtieth anniversary. In this oration Eusebius had carefully emphasized that the emperor was an analogue of the Logos, and that both were subordinate to God the Father. Because the Constantine honored in this panegyric made sense only in the context of Eusebius' subordinationist doctrines, this panegyric had become a theological treatise in disguise.

In addition, other opponents had written to various churches with instructions to search for and destroy copies of Marcellus' treatise. But

---

Constantine himself had yet to endorse Christ as a principle of imperial policy; for a slightly different formulation, see Drake (2000) 529n.98: "in practice Constantine appears as much coordinate with as subordinate to the Logos." Also Barnes (1981) 254, "The greater part of the *Panegyric* consists of variations and elaborations on a single theme: the similarity of Constantine to Christ," and Kolb (2001) 69, on Constantine as "die dritte Person in einer göttlichen Trinität."

[11] Eusebius, *Vita Constantini* 4.33.1, truth, 46, happy man. For additional discussion of Eusebius' oration about the Church of the Holy Sepulcher, see below.

despite this strong opposition Marcellus nevertheless remained a challenging rival, and after Constantine's death in May 337 he was allowed to return to his former see of Ancyra. Because Basil had already been appointed as the new bishop in Ancyra, Marcellus' return now led to retribution and outbreaks of violence. His opponents accused him of burning houses, parading priests and virgins naked in the forum, and profaning the liturgical elements. The exaggerated hysteria of these charges was perhaps a sign of Marcellus' success. As a result, Marcellus again had the standing to broadcast his theology, and he and his teachings were a revived threat to Eusebius and his doctrines. Having already tried to dispute Marcellus through two theological treatises and an imperial panegyric, Eusebius now considered promoting his theology through a new literary genre, a *Life* of a Christian ruler.[12]

## His Mother's Son

As a young military officer Constantine had visited the ruined sites of Memphis and Babylon. Long ago Memphis had been a capital and a religious center in the Old Kingdom of the Egyptian pharaohs, and Babylon had been the capital of the ancient Babylonian and Chaldaean empire. After their decline each city had come to represent the faded splendor of ancient civilizations, Memphis of the powerful kingdoms in Egypt along the Nile, Babylon of the great kingdoms in Mesopotamia along the Euphrates and Tigris. Constantine had explored each city most likely during campaigns with emperors, Galerius when he invaded the Persian empire during 297–298, and Diocletian when he visited Egypt during the winter of 301–302. Decades later Eusebius would still remember that on this last trip he had glimpsed Constantine as the imperial entourage passed through Palestine.[13]

---

[12] Search and destroy: Sozomen, *HE* 2.33.1. Violence at Ancyra: *Decretum sinodi orientalium apud Serdiciam* [*sic*] *episcoporum a parte Arrianorum* 9, cited in Hilary of Potiers, *Excerpta ex opere historico deperdito*, ed. CSEL 65, p. 55; Barnes (1993) 71, dates this council of Serdica to late summer of 343.

[13] Constantine, *Oratio ad sanctorum coetum* 16.2, Memphis and Babylon: "I do not say this based on hearsay; instead, I myself was present as an eyewitness investigating the lamentable misfortune of these cities." Entourage in Palestine:

In late antiquity the pyramids of Egypt and the walls of Babylon had become evocative symbols of extravagance, of "wealth, possessions, luxury, and a mind burning with ambition." But when Constantine subsequently recalled his visits in a public oration, he adopted a Christian perspective and thought only about the religious implications. For cities so devoted to ancestral gods, destruction and abandonment were the predictable, and proper, fates. He furthermore linked these cities with paradigmatic events from the Old Testament, Moses' victory over the armies of the pharaoh and Daniel's confrontations with king Nebuchadnezzar. One possibility is that Constantine's interest in the biblical implications of these sites went back to his original visits. If so, then it might be appropriate to suggest that he had been sympathetic to Christianity already before his rise as an emperor. Another possibility is that he began to sense the usefulness of biblical prototypes only during his reign. By the time he delivered this oration, he had already defeated some, perhaps even all, of his imperial rivals. In those circumstances he might well have started to imagine himself, a victorious Christian emperor, as a new Moses or a new Daniel.[14]

However early Constantine became interested in Christianity, it is notable that initially he was concerned primarily with heroes and events from the Old Testament. As Diocletian's court trekked through Palestine, Constantine would have passed through or near various cities and

Eusebius, *Vita Constantini* 1.19.1, with Barnes (1982) 41–42, for a reconstruction of Constantine's early career.

[14] Wealth: Julian, *Orat.* 2.83C. Constantine, *Oratio ad sanctorum coetum* 16.2, Moses, 17.2–3, Daniel. The date of this oration is uncertain: for a selection of possibilities, see Edwards (2003) xxiii–xxix, arguing for Easter 315, Barnes (1976b), for Good Friday in April 317, Barnes (1981) 323n.115, for 321, Drake (2006) 126, for a few months after the victory over Licinius, Lane Fox (1986) 631–35, for Good Friday in April 325, Barnes (2001), for Easter celebrations in April 325, and Bleckmann (1997), for spring of 328. Barnes (1985) 380, cites the visit to Babylon to suggest that "the young Constantine was already interested in biblical history"; Elliott (1996) 29–38, likewise argues that Constantine was a Christian before becoming emperor. Constantine was later credited with decorating one of the forums at Constantinople with "a [statue of] Daniel with the lions, fashioned from bronze and gleaming with gold leaf": Eusebius, *Vita Constantini* 3.49.

regions associated with the life of Jesus Christ. But the landscape itself would have provided few reminders, since there were still hardly any memorials or relics of Jesus' life. The most notable that Eusebius mentioned were ancient bronze statues of Jesus and a woman he had healed, located in the interior highlands at Caesarea Philippi (Paneas). "They said that this statue presented an image of Jesus; it has survived even to our own age." On display at Jerusalem was the throne of Jacobus (James), the first bishop of the city who was said to have been Jesus' brother. Overall, these were insignificant tributes to Jesus' life. When Constantine visited, Palestine was not a noticeably Christian holy land.[15]

Instead, most of the biblical memorials he might have seen commemorated people and events from the Old Testament. Along the coastal road between Caesarea and Beirut he could have visited Mt. Carmel, where the prophet Elijah had challenged the priests of Baal, and the site where Elijah had been fed by the widow. A bit inland was the plain where David had killed Goliath and the mountain where Abraham was said to have sacrificed. Further inland were the sites of Joseph's tomb, Jacob's well, and Jacob's dream. In the vicinity of Jerusalem were memorials of great kings, such as David and Solomon, and tombs of great prophets, such as Isaiah. In the early fourth century Palestine was still an Old Testament landscape.[16]

Under Roman rule, however, the Jews had already had to modify their sense of their promised land. Most conspicuously, at Jerusalem all that was left of Solomon's great temple were charred ruins. The future emperor Titus had destroyed the temple in 70 after suppressing a Jewish revolt; after another revolt in the mid-130s the emperor Hadrian had constructed a new city. Although he planned to replace the temple with a shrine to Jupiter and did have two statues of himself erected on the

---

[15] Eusebius, *HE* 7.18, statue, 19, throne.

[16] *Itinerarium Burdigalense* 583.12–13, Elijah and widow, 585.1, Mt. Carmel, 586.6, David and Goliath, 587.3, Abraham,, 587.5–588.1, Joseph's tomb, 588.3–4, Jacob's well, 588.9–10, Jacob's dream, 589.7–9, Solomon's pools, 590.5, Solomon's palace, 592.6, David's palace, 595.2–4, tomb of Isaiah; with Bowman (1999), on the role of the *Itinerarium* in explaining the typological and historical relationships between Old Testament and New Testament.

site, Hadrian situated the new city to the west of the devastated Temple
Mount. This new city was called Aelia Capitolina, named after both
the emperor's Aelian dynasty and the patron deities worshipped on the
Capitoline Hill in Rome. "Jewish Jerusalem, it seemed, was extinct."
By the early fourth century the Roman name of Aelia Capitolina was so
commonplace that a Roman magistrate no longer remembered the city's
earlier name. During the persecution in Palestine in 310 one Christian
defiantly announced that his hometown was Jerusalem, "a fatherland
only for the pious," located "in the East, toward the rising sun." The
provincial governor was baffled by the unfamiliar name and "thought
that the Christians had founded a city somewhere that was very dangerous and hostile to the Romans." This governor had interpreted the
Christian's vision of a heavenly Jerusalem as a reference to a secret rebel
base. The promised land, a terrorist camp: notably missing from this
dialogue was any recognition of a Jerusalem associated with the life of
Jesus.[17]

The idea of a Christian Jerusalem finally appeared at the council of
Nicaea in 325, when the bishops discussed the relative rank of the bishop
of Jerusalem. Even though they still referred to the city as Aelia, they
decided that its bishop should have a higher status, while nevertheless
respecting the rank of the metropolitan bishop of Caesarea. The organization of ecclesiastical provinces tended to follow the organization of
the Roman civil provinces, and since Caesarea was the capital of the
province of Palaestina, its bishop was the metropolitan. But because
this promotion of the standing of Jerusalem and its bishop now disregarded its lowly standing as an ordinary provincial city, it presumably
reflected a new, alternative understanding of the city's importance as a
Christian center. At the council of Nicaea the bishops were apparently

[17] Foundation of Aelia Capitolina: Goodman (2000) 671–75. Temple of Jupiter:
Dio, *Historiae Romanae* 69.12.1; two statues: *Itinerarium Burdigalense* 591.4; quotation from Wilken (1992a) 43. Fatherland: Eusebius, *De martyribus Palaestinae*
11.1l (recensio prolixior), 9–12; for the governor Firmilianus, see *PLRE* 1:338, "Firmilianus 2." In *Demonstratio evangelica* 8.3 (*PG* 22.636B), Eusebius claimed that
Romans were farming the Temple Mount, and that he had seen it being plowed
by oxen.

beginning to imagine a Palestine in which Christian history took priority over Roman administration. Then Constantine added his support. Since the emperor had attended sessions of the council, his interest was a natural consequence of hearing debates about the doctrines of Jesus Christ the Son and his Father. Perhaps the emperor was now curious about the historical Jesus behind the theological Jesus.[18]

After the council Constantine soon acted on his interest in the sites of Jesus' life. He issued an edict ordering the demolition of buildings on Golgatha in Jerusalem and encouraged the excavation that uncovered a cave identified as Jesus' tomb. He directed the imperial magistrates in the eastern provinces to contribute to the construction of a magnificent church on the site. In a letter he instructed Macarius, the bishop of Jerusalem, to request whatever was necessary, craftsmen, laborers, columns, marble panels, and gold plating, to build "a church more spectacular than any other anywhere." The final result was an extended complex of buildings and memorials. At the west end was the tomb itself, surrounded by colonnades. In one corner of the large courtyard fronting the tomb a rocky outcrop marked the spot of the crucifixion. Across this courtyard was the huge Church of the Holy Sepulcher. At the east end of this church was another courtyard that opened into a busy street. According to Eusebius, the church, the courtyards, the colonnades, and the glorification of the crucifixion and the tomb had all contributed to the making of "New Jerusalem."[19]

Constantine's interest in Jesus' life had quick results. "At his order" churches were constructed not only in Jerusalem at the site of Jesus' crucifixion and tomb, but also in Bethlehem at the site of his birth and on the Mount of Olives at the site of his ascension to heaven. Soon shrines and monuments also memorialized other holy sites in Jesus'

---

[18]  Rank: Council of Nicaea, Canon 7.

[19]  Eusebius, *Vita Constantini* 3.26.7, edict, 27–28, excavation and cave, 29.2, magistrates, 30–32, letter to Macarius, 33.1–2, new Jerusalem, 34–40, description of complex, with Wilkinson (1981) 39–46, 164–71, discussing the buildings; Hunt (1982) 7–8, and Holum (1996) 141–43, emphasizing the leading role of Macarius; and Wilken (1992a) 88–100, (1992b), for excellent analysis of Eusebius' reinterpretation of biblical prophecies to accommodate these Christian shrines.

life. When a pilgrim from Bordeaux traveled to Palestine in 333, he of course visited those three great churches, which were most likely still under construction. In addition, during his trip he visited, or at least noted, the spot of Jesus' baptism by John the Baptist, the tomb of Lazarus, the pinnacle where Jesus had been tempted, the palm tree whose branches had covered the road during Jesus' triumphal entry, the hill where Moses and Elijah had appeared to Jesus, the rock where Judas had betrayed Jesus, the house of Pontius Pilate, and the column on which Jesus had been whipped. In September 335 an ecclesiastical council celebrated the dedication of the Church of the Holy Sepulcher at Jerusalem. In a series of sermons various bishops explicated biblical passages, discussed theology, and praised the church. Those preachers included Eusebius, the metropolitan bishop of Caesarea, who delivered several sermons.[20]

Constantine's patronage was a "pious and devout confession," and his true piety need not be doubted. But his devotion nevertheless intersected with supplementary political motives for his promotion of the cult of Jesus Christ in Palestine. One was his need to distance himself, again, from the precedents, imagery, and actions of his Tetrarchic predecessors. In his letter to bishop Macarius he had stressed his veneration

[20] "Iussu Constantini": *Itinerarium Burdigalense* 594.2, tomb, 595.6, Mount of Olives, 598.7, Bethlehem. Other sites: *Itinerarium Burdigalense* 589.11–590.2, pinnacle, 592.4–5, column, 593.2–3, Pilate's house, 594.7, Judas, 595.1–2, palm tree, 595.6–596.1, hill, 596.1–3, Lazarus, 598.1–2, baptism; with the excellent discussion of the conceptual innovation of the *Itinerarium* in Elsner (2000b): "the remarkable elevation of an obscure provincial village in the middle of nowhere into the ideological centre of the Christian Empire" (p. 194). Eusebius, *Vita Constantini* 4.45, sermons at Jerusalem. Later in 335 Eusebius delivered a sermon about the Savior's tomb to Constantine in the palace at Constantinople: see Eusebius, *Vita Constantini* 4.33. For the context of Eusebius' surviving oration about this church, *De laudibus Constantini* 11–18, see Drake (1976) 30–45. Holum (1990) 75, suggests that "Constantine was attempting to work out a new conception of the empire, with Jerusalem in some sense at its physical center"; Wharton (1995) 85–100, offers a perceptive discussion of Constantine's appropriation of Hadrian's city as an example of "colonized territory" (p. 97); Jacobs (2004) 139–99, locates the Christian development of Jerusalem in the theories of postcolonial studies.

of martyrs. Long ago the crucifixion of Jesus had provided the paradigm for martyrdom as an act of defiance toward Roman rulers. In early Christianity the tradition of martyrdom had a distinguished reputation, and at Rome Constantine had been ready to honor some of the earliest martyrs, St. Peter and St. Paul. He also had firsthand experience of the making of more martyrs. The legislation of the Tetrarchic emperors against Christians had been enforced primarily in eastern provinces, and their persecutions, as well as the more recent hostility under Licinius, had produced new martyrs. Christians remembered Tetrarchic rule for the persecutions. As a result, Constantine's decision to venerate martyrs was another explicit disavowal of one distinctive Tetrarchic policy. He respected "the memorials of dead bodies and their tombs," even in the face of complaints; he dedicated Constantinople, "his city," to "the God of the martyrs"; and at Jerusalem he venerated the original exemplary martyr, Jesus Christ. His great Church of the Holy Sepulcher in Jerusalem was hence also known as Martyrium, "the place of martyrdom." By honoring the victims, Constantine could repudiate the authors of persecutions.[21]

Constantine furthermore dissociated himself from memories of Tetrarchic rule with his patronage for the construction of Christian churches in Jerusalem. In the process of clearing the ground for the Church of the Holy Sepulcher the builders had removed a pagan shrine from the site of the buried tomb of Jesus Christ. This shrine may have been a "murky sanctuary" dedicated to Aphrodite, or a statue of Jupiter. Since Jupiter had been a patron deity of the Tetrarchic emperors, the replacement of his shrine by a new church that commemorated Jesus' death and resurrection would have been another clear indication of Constantine's different preferences. At Rome, Diocletian and Maximian had once met in the Temple of Jupiter on the Capitoline Hill; but Constantine later declined to participate in a pagan festival on the

---

[21] Eusebius, *De laudibus Constantini* 11.3, memorials, 18.2, confession; *Vita Constantini* 3.48.1, Constantinople. Martyrium: Egeria, *Itinerarium* 30.1: "[the church] is called Martyrium because it is on Golgatha, that is, behind the cross where the Lord suffered."

hill. Now, at Aelia Capitolina he would repeat his disavowal of Jupiter by demolishing this imitation Capitoline shrine. Not only would there be no more persecutions of Christians, but his patron deity was now the Christian God. In the eastern provinces too Constantine was now trying to bring the Tetrarchic era to an end.[22]

The shadow of Tetrarchic rule was one of Constantine's political considerations; another was his concern for the promotion of his dynasty and the problem of succession. In July 326 he ordered the execution of Crispus, his oldest son, for undisclosed reasons. Crispus may in fact have been a casualty of a scheme engineered by Fausta, Constantine's current wife, who was perhaps intent on promoting the prospects of her sons over Crispus, her stepson. Once the intrigue was exposed, Fausta was soon forced to commit suicide. Within a year of the council of Nicaea Constantine had lost his oldest son and the mother of his three remaining sons. At that council he had desperately tried to reinforce the political unity of his empire by enforcing religious harmony within Christianity. Now he had to deal with discord in his own family.[23]

Constantine responded by using the development of Christian shrines in Palestine as a medium for clarifying and publicizing his ideas about succession. First, there was Eutropia, mother of Fausta. Both women had helped his early rise to power. His marriage to Fausta in 307 had bolstered his alliance with the emperors Maximian and Maxentius, her father and brother. After Constantine defeated Maxentius in 312, Eutropia conveniently acknowledged that her son's father had in fact been an anonymous Syrian; this opportune confession allowed Constantine to rehabilitate Maximian, his father-in-law, as his own distinguished ancestor. After defeating Licinius, however, Constantine

---

[22] Aphrodite's sanctuary: Eusebius, *Vita Constantini* 3.26.3. Jupiter's statue: Jerome, *Ep.* 58.4: "During the approximately 180 years from the time of Hadrian until the reign of Constantine a statue of Jupiter was worshipped on the spot of the resurrection, and a marble statue of Venus was erected by the pagans and worshipped on the rock of the cross."

[23] For the legends about the deaths of Crispus and Fausta, see Barnes (1981) 220–21; Frakes (2006) 95, connects Crispus' execution with the elimination of Licinius' supporters.

no longer needed this particular imperial pedigree. With regard to the past, Fausta's death was yet another confirmation of his separation from old Tetrarchic emperors and their ideology. With regard to the future, moreover, Fausta was also expendable, because descent from her mother was just as exclusive. Eutropia hence retained some political importance as a grandmother of Constantine's three surviving sons. He allowed her to retire to Palestine, and he continued to honor her as his "most holy mother-in-law." In Palestine Eutropia apparently visited biblical sites. After she wrote to Constantine about the pagan sacrifices that defiled the site of Mamre, south of Jerusalem, the emperor sent letters to local bishops, including Macarius of Jerusalem and Eusebius of Caesarea, and recommended the construction of a new church.[24]

Eutropia had become an important contributor to Constantine's patronage in Palestine. But it is significant that her role was limited to the site of a famous event in the Old Testament that eventually was interpreted as a foretelling of New Testament theology. According to the account in the book of Genesis, at Mamre three strangers had appeared to Abraham and prophesied his seminal role in the settlement of Israel. Since Christian theologians would interpret these three visitors as an early theophany, so did the emperor. "At that place the Savior himself with two angels for the first time bestowed an appearance of himself to Abraham," Constantine noted. "At that place God first appeared to men." Eutropia's role as a patron in Palestine hence matched her earlier political role. In the past she had helped establish her son-in-law's

---

[24] For discussion of the earlier dynastic intrigues, see Chapter 3. Constantine's letter: Eusebius, *Vita Constantini* 3.52, most holy mother-in-law; also Sozomen, *HE* 2.4. Cameron and Hall (1999) 300, suggest that Constantine's flattery of Eutropia "becomes more comfortable if the visit [to Palestine] took place before the death of her daughter Fausta in 326." It is more likely that Eutropia retired to Palestine after Fausta's death. In his letter to the bishops Constantine instructed Acacius, "our most distinguished *comes*," to help with construction of the church; Acacius was still serving as *comes* during the later 320s: see Eusebius, *Vita Constantini* 3.62.1, with *PLRE* 1:6, "Acacius 4," dating his tenure as *comes* to ca. 326/330. For the "marvelous beauty" of Constantine's church at Mamre, see *Itinerarium Burdigalense* 599.5–6.

credentials as an heir to the Tetrarchic imperial system that he had subsequently repudiated. Now she was promoting a site important to Jewish history that Christians would venerate as a preview of the new era of Jesus Christ. Even as Constantine honored his mother-in-law for her contribution to his early career, she would not have an important personal role in shaping his plans for the future. In religion as in politics, she consistently represented an old dispensation that had been superseded.[25]

Second, there was his mother, Helena. After Crispus' execution the oldest of Constantine's three surviving sons, Constantine II, was not yet ten years old. If Constantine were to die, the obvious adult successors would be Flavius Dalmatius and Julius Constantius. These two half-brothers had an impressive pedigree. Like Constantine himself, they were sons of Constantius; like Constantine's sons, they were grandsons of the emperor Maximian. In order to prepare his plans for succession, Constantine hence had to decide which ancestors to highlight and which to diminish. He had already devalued the significance of Maximian in favor of Eutropia, who was the grandmother of his three sons but not of his half-brothers. He might now also have preferred to minimize the importance of his father, Constantius, whom he shared with his half-brothers. Instead, Constantine could underscore the importance of his mother. Descent from Helena again excluded the half-siblings and their sons; her only direct descendants were Constantine, his three surviving sons, and his two daughters, one of whom was in fact named Helena. In his ideological representation of himself Constantine had in the past been his father's son. Now he became primarily his mother's son.[26]

Constantine was already a teenager when his father, Constantius, had married Maximian's daughter Theodora in the later 280s. His mother, Helena, had subsequently disappeared from view for decades. She only

---

[25] Eusebius, *Vita Constantini* 3.53.3, at that spot. In *Demonstratio evangelica* 5.9 (*PG* 22.384A-B), Eusebius noted that at Mamre a painting depicted Abraham's three visitors; because the middle guest was larger, Eusebius concluded he had been the Lord and Savior. In *HE* 1.2.7–8, Eusebius suggested that the Lord God who had appeared at Mamre could only have been "his Logos."

[26] For Constantine's relationship with his half-brothers, see Chapter 3.

reappeared once her son became an emperor, living perhaps at his court at Trier, perhaps at Rome after 312. In late 324, after defeating his final rival, Constantine promoted her rank by giving her the title of Augusta, and her image started appearing on his coinage. Perhaps more significantly, at least one community now acknowledged the legitimacy of her earlier relationship with Constantius. A dedication at Salerno described her not just as the mother of Constantine and grandmother of the Caesars, but also as the "most chaste wife of Constantius." Recognition of Helena's marriage was additional reinforcement for the legitimacy of Constantine and his dynasty. In the summer of 326 she met Constantine after the execution of Crispus and apparently convinced him of Fausta's complicity. In Italy the news traveled quickly, and the people of Sorrento were quick to acknowledge Helena's new prominence in the imperial family. On a dedication in honor of Constantine's family they carefully chiseled out the words "Fausta" and "wife" and replaced them with "Helena" and "mother." Soon afterward Helena left to visit the eastern provinces, with her son's full support. On her journey she distributed gifts to individuals, cities, and soldiers, she cared for the poor and imprisoned, and she was generous to churches and shrines. Her most significant contributions supported the new Church of the Nativity at Bethlehem and the new Church of the Ascension at the Mount of Olives. After the council at Nicaea, after the turmoil within the dynasty following Crispus' execution, Helena became the most visible representative of Constantine's rule in the eastern provinces.[27]

---

[27] Barnes (1982) 37, 125–26, argues that Constantius was married to Theodora before April 289; for a survey of the issues, see Nixon and Rodgers (1994) 70n.38. Title of Augusta: see Chapter 3. Dedication at Salerno: *ILS* 1:160, no. 708. Helena and Fausta: *Epitome de Caesaribus* 41.12, Zosimus, *Historia nova* 2.29.2, with Chapter 2, on the possibility of Helena's residence at Rome. Dedication at Sorrento: *ILS* 1:160, no. 710, with Drijvers (1992) 49. Eusebius, *Vita Constantini* 3.43, Bethlehem and Mount of Olives, 44, gifts, 45, churches, 47.2, Augusta, coins, with Bruun (1966) 26, and Barnes (1982) 9, for the coinage; Drijvers (1992) 39–54, for coins and inscriptions; and Hunt (1997a) 418, on the "public and official character" of Helena's journey. Later traditions gave Helena much more credit for this construction in the Holy Land, including the discovery of the True Cross: see Drijvers (1992) 79–145, and Pietri (2001).

The ongoing disputes among Christian theologians about God the Father and his Son neatly merged with this new focus on Constantine's mother. At Bethlehem one esteemed mother, Helena, honored another blessed mother, the Virgin Mary, when "the most pious empress adorned the pregnancy of the 'God-Bearer' with marvelous memorials." At the Mount of Olives a "true account" claimed that Jesus had instructed his disciples there before his ascension. Helena now patronized these two sites associated in particular with birth and ascension, the very beginning and the very end of Jesus' life on earth. For Constantine and his dynasty she represented the same transition points, the birth of her "son, such a great emperor," and the handover to his successors, "her grandsons." Featuring Helena hence emphasized the long continuity of Constantine's dynasty and its merger with a new sibling. The outcome was the construction of an intriguingly symbolic makeshift "family" consisting of a Father, a mother and her Son, and another mother and her son and grandsons. This imagined family was similar to various blended imperial families, such as those of Constantius or Constantine himself, which consisted of an emperor, successive wives, and a series of sons. In this case, through his mother Constantine now seemed to be claiming affiliation with another ruling family that had divine connections.[28]

A decade later when Eusebius was recounting the activities of Helena in Palestine, he seemed still to encourage this elusiveness about the family connections of Constantine and his mother. According to his depiction of the end of her life, Helena had bequeathed her possessions "to her only-begotten son, the emperor who alone ruled the world, and to his sons, the Caesars who were her grandsons." In the context of ongoing doctrinal disputes a reference to "only-begotten Son" would have conjured up Jesus Christ; but in this case, this "only-begotten son" was Constantine. In addition, in attendance at her deathbed was "such a

---

[28] Eusebius, *Vita Constantini* 3.42.1, son and grandsons, 43.2, empress, 43.3, true account. Note that Jesus too, according to later traditions, was thought to have grown up in a blended family. His half-brothers "according to the flesh" included Jacobus and Judas (Jude), sons of Joseph: see Eusebius, *HE* 2.1.2, 2.23.1, 3.19–20, 7.19. Jacobus was thought to have been elected the first bishop of Jerusalem. His successor was Simon, a "cousin of the Savior," whose father, Clopas, was a brother of Joseph: see Eusebius, *HE* 3.11, 32.6.

great son, who comforted her and held her hands." If Helena had indeed died in Constantine's presence, then this son too was the emperor. But Eusebius' description was simultaneously so imprecise and so marinated in the technical terminology of theological disputation that he also left the impression that the Son himself had been present. As Helena made the transition from "life on earth" to "life in heaven," her soul "was transformed into the incorruptible essence of an angel." As she was "taken up to her Savior," Helena seemed to have experienced her own ascension and recovered her divine essence. Perhaps all along she had been a divine Mother.[29]

In the mid-320s Constantine had the opportunity to rewrite his life, both its past and its future. The defeat of Licinius, his final rival, allowed him to reevaluate his ancestors; the execution of his son Crispus compelled him to reconsider the role of his surviving sons as successors. One new public text was the Holy Land in Palestine, where at Jerusalem and other sites he inscribed an account of his reign. By honoring central moments in the life of Jesus, he could also highlight significant aspects of his own life. The important transitional figure was his mother. Through her patronage for various churches Helena seemed to provide a link between her son, Constantine, and the Son, Jesus Christ, that positioned her descendants as members of a divine ruling dynasty. The shrines at and near Jerusalem hence commemorated both the biography of Jesus and the autobiography of Constantine.

## SON OF A VIRGIN BIRTH

Another medium for autobiography was Constantinople, which Constantine was simultaneously developing. Just as Constantine had needed repeatedly to reinvent his imperial ancestry, this new imperial capital likewise required an instant history that properly located the city in Greek and Roman antiquity. To be accepted as a new capital,

[29] Eusebius, *Vita Constantini* 3.46.1, ἐπὶ μονογενεῖ υἱῷ βασιλεῖ, 2, great son; for μονογενής applied to the Son of God, see *Vita Constantini* 1.32.2. Note that Cameron and Hall (1999) obscure this parallelism with different translations of μονογενής: "the Onlybegotten Son" (p. 82) when applied to Jesus, but "her only son" (p. 139) when applied to the emperor. The place and date of Helena's death are uncertain: see Drijvers (1992) 73, and Chapter 2.

Constantinople had to appear to be old. Constantine hence imported ancient statues and monuments from Rome and provinces throughout the eastern Mediterranean. Many of these confiscated antiquities were put on display in the hippodrome, among them the Serpent Column from Delphi that had commemorated a famous victory of the Greeks over the Persians and a bronze statue from Nicopolis that had memorialized Augustus' final victory. These famous monuments confirmed Constantine's standing as an authentic protector of the Greeks and the true heir of the Roman emperors. He furthermore acknowledged his own imperial pedigree, including his Tetrarchic background. A statue of Diocletian was located somewhere in the hippodrome, and in the senate house Constantine placed a bronze statue of himself and his wife Fausta. He also, of course, commemorated his mother. In particular, he renamed an existing plaza that was at the center of the city adjacent to the hippodrome, the imperial palace, and the church of Hagia Sophia. This large open plaza was now known as the Augusteum, in honor of Helena Augusta. Next to the Augusteum, Constantine erected a statue of his mother.[30]

In the representation of his life at both Jerusalem and Constantinople, Constantine clearly emphasized the important role of his mother. A notable contrast was a corresponding vagueness about his father. After 324, when he no longer had to worry about imperial rivals who represented alternative dynasties, fewer dedications commemorated him as "son of the divine Constantius." Nor was there a public memorial to his father in Constantinople. Constantine too now seemed to be the son of a virgin birth.[31]

---

[30] For the Serpent Column and the statue of driver and donkey, see Bassett (2004) 62, 213, 224–27, in an excellent account of both the individual monuments and the meaning of Constantine's entire collection. Statues of Fausta and Diocletian: *Parastaseis syntomoi chronikai* 43, 76, with Cameron and Herrin (1984) 232, 270. Augusteum: *Notitia urbis Constantinopolitanae* 5.7, 16.52, with Cameron and Herrin (1984) 262–63. Statue of mother "on a slim porphyry column": John Malalas, *Chronographia* 13.8.

[31] Son of Constantius: for a calculation of the inscriptions, see Grünewald (1990) 122n.59, 146.

Instead, during his later years the emperor developed new ideas about his special standing and intimacy with God the Father and Jesus Christ, and he sometimes even appropriated divine roles. In 330 he indicated his despair about the schismatic Donatist bishops in Africa whose stubbornness, in his estimation, had blinded them to the need of thinking about their future salvation. In his letter the emperor seemed to attribute to himself a soteriological power that could have benefited these bishops if only they had listened. Instead, despite his invitations and warnings, his greatest frustration was his inability to rescue them. "If they had decided to submit to my orders, they would be saved from all evil." A few years later Constantine sent a long letter to the disgraced priest Arius that included an unsettling mixture of mockery and conciliation. At the end of the letter the emperor offered Arius assistance in cleansing his conscience. "Come to me, come, I say, to a man of God. Believe that through my questions I will examine the mysteries of your heart. And if some madness seems to be lurking there, I will summon God's grace and restore you." This invitation to visit sounded like a summons to confess sins. In these doctrinal controversies the emperor now presented himself as a savior.[32]

Constantine furthermore developed a strong interest, especially toward the end of his reign, in associating himself directly with Jesus Christ. He donated ornaments and embroideries to the new churches at Bethlehem and on the Mount of Olives, and he certainly enhanced the Church of the Holy Sepulcher at Jerusalem. From birth to death to ascension, Constantine had essentially incorporated Jesus' entire life on earth into his own family's traditions. Nor would death keep them apart. After the ceremony of dedication for the Church of the Holy Sepulcher in 335, one of the bishops went so far as to proclaim that Constantine, having been deemed worthy of imperial rule in this life,

[32] Donatist bishops: Optatus, Appendix 10.37a, dated to February 330. Constantine's letter to Arius: Urkunde 34.42, ed. Opitz (1934–1935) 74, quoted in Athanasius, *De decretis Nicaenae synodi* 40.42. For Constantine's initiative in defining a Christian emperor, see Pietri (1997a) 280: "C'est l'empereur qui a consciemment donné le départ à toute cette imagerie du roi chrétien."

would in the future reign with the Son of God. Together they would reign as Dyarchs, like Diocletian and Maximian decades earlier, indistinguishable brothers.[33]

Reminders of this intimate association between emperor and Jesus Christ filled the new capital. Although named after the emperor, Constantinople was also known as "Christoupolis," "Christ's city." In a new forum the emperor erected a giant statue of himself on top of a tall porphyry column. The residents of the city later believed that he had also placed a relic of the True Cross in his statue, and some even offered prayers to it "as if to a god." Over the entrance to the palace Constantine hung a portrait depicting himself and his sons with a cross over their heads and a serpent beneath their feet. This portrait commemorated the emperor's military success over Licinius, an imperial rival whom he had himself once characterized as a "serpent." It also presented the emperor as another savior who had defeated evil with the assistance of the cross. As a result, Eusebius pointedly interpreted this portrait in terms of a prophecy from the Old Testament that was conventionally applied to the soteriological role of Jesus Christ.[34]

---

[33] Eusebius, *Vita Constantini* 3.41–43, churches at Bethlehem and the Mount of Olives, 3.25–40, 4.43–46, Church of the Holy Sepulcher, 48, bishop, with Walker (1990) 184–98, on the theology of these three sites in Palestine, 235–81, on the meaning of the tomb and the Church of the Holy Sepulcher.

[34] Constantinople as Christ's city: Sozomen, *HE* 2.3.8. Statue and relic: Socrates, *HE* 1.17, with Fowden (1991). Prayers: Philostorgius, *HE* 2.17. Eusebius, *Vita Constantini* 3.3, portrait (citing Isaiah 27:1), with 2.46.2, Constantine's description of Licinius in a letter to Eusebius; also Eusebius, *Commentarii in Isaiam* 27.1 (*PG* 24.280A-B), for Eusebius' commentary on this verse: "As he instructs, God wishes not to destroy those who have repented, but to cleanse and sanctify them." For Eusebius' interpretation of Isaiah, see Leeb (1992) 51, on the portrait: "Im Konstantinopler Bild setzte sich aber Konstantin an die Stelle Christi und vollbringt dessen Werk"; Wilken (1992a) 79, on the commentary: "Eusebius uses the triumphant imagery of Isaiah about the messianic age to describe the reign of the new Christian emperor"; and Hollerich (1999) 200, on the verse: "This was the expression of Christ's ultimate triumph."

One monument at Constantinople might have been intended to depict Constantine's new "family." According to a later tradition, near a new church dedicated

Eventually Constantine constructed a shrine, either a mausoleum or a church, to serve as his funerary memorial in the new capital. This shrine contained a niche for his sarcophagus surrounded by twelve cenotaphs that represented, and were possibly inscribed with the names of, the twelve apostles. Since the emperor himself had presented to the Church of the Holy Sepulcher at Jerusalem the twelve columns that encircled the apse and commemorated the twelve apostles, he was certainly aware of the significance of placing his own tomb in the middle of these twelve symbolic tombs. During his final illness Constantine acknowledged that he had always hoped to imitate the Savior by being baptized in the Jordan River. Now, even after his death, the placement of his sarcophagus would continue to remind people of his standing as the equivalent of Jesus Christ.[35]

One of Constantine's contributions to the ongoing doctrinal disputes was to publicize this correspondence between Jesus Christ the Son and himself. By promoting the holy sites of Jesus' ministry in Palestine, by commemorating Jesus at his new capital, and by hoping to relive moments from Jesus' career, Constantine had inscribed himself in Jesus' life as both patron and likeness. His sincere piety was no doubt one compelling motive; equally powerful objectives were the enhancement of his own imperial authority and the promotion of his plans for succession. In the process, however, he had thoroughly mingled political philosophy and Christian theology. Since the reign of Augustus historians and intellectuals had used *basileus*, "king," as the proper equivalent in Greek for "emperor"; Christian preachers had long been applying this same title to both God and Jesus; now Constantine seems to have appropriated some divine functions. The end result was a Jesus Christ who was emperor-like and an emperor who was Christ-like.

to the Theotokos, the Virgin Mary in her role as the God-Bearer, Constantine erected statues of himself, his mother, Jesus, and the Virgin: see *Parastaseis syntomoi chronikai* 53, with Cameron and Herrin (1984) 240.

[35] Eusebius, *Vita Constantini* 3.38, twelve columns in the Church of the Holy Sepulcher, 4.58–60, shrine, 62.2, Jordan River; with Dagron (1974) 407, on the "prétentions véritables de Constantin qui, dans sa ville, se veut l'égal du Christ"; and Krautheimer (1983) 3, on the "political topography" of Constantinople.

## BIOGRAPHY AS THEOLOGY

Eusebius may have had mixed feelings about Constantine's patronage for these holy places in Palestine. He certainly appreciated the emperor's promotion of doctrines about Jesus Christ and his support for the construction of new churches. On the other hand, he could sense that the increasing reputation of the Church of the Holy Sepulcher might inspire the bishop of Jerusalem to challenge the metropolitan authority of himself, the bishop of Caesarea. Eusebius would also face objections to his doctrines from the likes of Marcellus of Ancyra, despite his eventual attempt to defame his opponent's theology. In fact, it was possible for some to read Eusebius' treatises against Marcellus as yet more evidence that he was himself truly an "Arianizer" after all.[36]

After the council at Nicaea Eusebius had benefited from Constantine's support. In return, he had hoped to shape the emperor's actions and thinking through letters, occasional panegyrics, and doctrinal treatises. After the emperor's death he furthermore composed a biography of Constantine. He seems to have been collecting the material for this *Life* for a long time. He reread his own writings, and at various points in *Life*, in particular in the first two books, he recycled passages from earlier works such as *Ecclesiastical History*. He inserted in *Life* many of Constantine's letters that he had received or acquired over the years. He also included stories that he had heard directly from the emperor. This *Life* was hence a sometimes jumbled combination of biography, panegyric, dossier of imperial documents, and anthology of oral traditions. Eusebius had apparently invented a new literary genre.[37]

---

[36] Eusebius as Arianizer: Socrates, *HE* 2.21.1. Marcellus lived into the 370s: see Barnes (1993) 93.

[37] On *Life* as "an experiment in hagiography," see Barnes (1989b) 110, arguing that Eusebius combined a draft of a panegyric composed after Constantine's death with an earlier historical narrative that already included a collection of historical documents: "the *Life of Constantine* originated as a continuation of or sequel to the final edition of the *Ecclesiastical History*" (p. 114); elaborated in Barnes (1994b). Drake (1988), (2000) 374–75, argues that Eusebius did research in Constantinople after the summer of 336, perhaps during Easter 337.

Finding a model for the life of a Christian emperor was likewise not easy, and Eusebius considered several different possibilities. For the first part of the reign in particular he compared Constantine to Moses, the great Old Testament leader. When he recounted the emperor's victory over Maxentius, for instance, Eusebius immediately thought of Moses' triumph over the pharaoh. At the beginning of the biography he also considered, but decided against, using comparisons with king Cyrus, the founder of the Persian empire, or with Alexander the Great. The only Roman emperor he mentioned as worthy of imitation was Constantius, Constantine's father. He furthermore toyed with the possibility of presenting the emperor as the secular equivalent of bishops. As he looked for an appropriate model for a Christian emperor, Eusebius thought of an Old Testament champion, great conquerors, a Roman emperor, and even bishops like himself.[38]

Another possible paradigm for a great Christian ruler was Jesus Christ. Jesus was a natural analogue, for two reasons. One was the traditions of Greek political philosophy. Greek philosophers had already articulated a political philosophy, even a political theology, of monarchs that later authors had eventually applied to Roman emperors. Their ideas had identified the ruler as the lawmaker, or even with the law itself by making him the "animate law." They had suggested not only that a ruler represented or imitated a god, or gods, on earth, but that he might also become divine himself. And they had argued that because a ruler attained perfect internal harmony, he could become virtually a savior through his capacity for passing on this harmony to his kingdom and its subjects. The ideas of Greek political philosophy hence seemed to be applicable both to a Christian emperor and to Jesus Christ. As a result, a second reason Eusebius might have found this analogy attractive was, not so surprisingly, as an apology for his own theology. The

[38] Eusebius, *Vita Constantini* 1.7, Cyrus and Alexander, 12, Constantius, 38, Moses and pharaoh, 44.2, "like a common bishop established by God," 4.24, "I am a bishop established by God for those outside." For the experimental nature of *Life of Constantine*, see Cameron and Hall (1999) 27–34; the comparison with Moses, the Introduction to "A Greek Roman Empire"; the comparison with bishops, Rapp (1998), (2005) 129–31.

more Jesus Christ and Constantine resembled each other, the more Jesus was distinctly different from and subordinate to God the Father.[39]

In *Life* Eusebius sometimes described Constantine with terminology used in the ongoing doctrinal controversies. He consistently described the emperor as a "friend of God," and he claimed that God alone had selected Constantine as ruler. When the emperor had addressed the provincials in an edict, Eusebius compared him to "a very loud herald of God." When the emperor had entered the council of bishops at Nicaea, Eusebius, who had been in attendance, compared him to "a heavenly angel of God." In the confession of faith at the beginning of *Ecclesiastical History* Eusebius had described Jesus Christ the Son as "the angel of great guidance." In a panegyric celebrating the emperor's thirtieth jubilee in 336 he again described the Logos as an "angel of great guidance." In Eusebius' interpretive perspective, and in his theology, both Jesus Christ and the emperor were "angels," messengers of God on earth. The culmination of his depiction of Constantine as God's special representative was his ecstatic description of the banquet that the emperor hosted for the bishops after the council. Eusebius was among the guests: "one might think that an image of Christ's kingdom was becoming apparent." As in Eusebius' panegyrics, so also in *Life*, Jesus Christ and Constantine were similar, and both were subordinate to God the Father.[40]

Eusebius' *Life* was hence another theological treatise in disguise, another attempt to defend his own doctrines this time by turning Constantine into the embodiment of his theology. Eusebius had transformed

---

[39] See Dvornik (1966) 243–77, on Greek political philosophy, 614–22, on its application by Eusebius to Jesus Christ and Constantine, and Drake (2000) 384–92, on Eusebius' attempt to redefine good rulership in terms of evaluation by bishops.

[40] Eusebius, *Vita Constantini* 1.24, selection, 2.61, herald, 3.10.3, heavenly angel, 15.2, Christ's kingdom, with additional discussion of the banquet in Chapter 4; *HE* 1.2.3, angel; *De laudibus Constantini* 3.6, angel of great guidance, with Van Dam (2003c), for Eusebius' motives in highlighting this similarity. For the frequent descriptions of Constantine as ὁ τῷ θεῷ φίλος and θεοφιλής, see Winkelmann (1991) 195, 226, with Drake (1976) 158n.1, on the grammar; for Eusebius' use of "angel," see Hanson (1988) 48–49.

the subject of *Life* into a medium for representing his doctrines. After the council of Nicaea Constantine had supported Eusebius; after the emperor's death Eusebius converted him into a personification of his own theology. In *Life* he imagined a Constantine who could be understood only within the context of an Arian subordinationist theology that allowed him to be seen as an analogue of Jesus Christ.

This analogy with Jesus Christ offers modern historians an intriguing additional option for finding an antecedent for the new literary genre of *Life*. If Constantine was like Jesus Christ, then Eusebius' *Life* had become something like a Gospel of a Christian emperor. This *Life* was a true witness to the emperor, both a confession of faith and an exhortation to readers. As a result, just as the New Testament Gospels had concluded with the appearances of Jesus after his death and resurrection, this *Life* likewise included an account of the emperor's afterlife. Constantine's sons were not declared senior emperors until more than three months after their father's death. Eusebius neatly glossed over this extended interregnum by insisting that Constantine himself had continued as emperor: "alone of mortals the blessed one ruled even after his death." In fact, Eusebius even hinted at the possibility of a resurrection: "he governed the entire empire as if after restoration to life." Just as the Savior had appeared to his disciples after his resurrection, so Constantine ensured his continuing rule through the succession of his sons. He himself, however, like Jesus, had then ascended to heaven. Upon hearing the news of his death, people at Rome set up a color portrait that depicted Constantine "enjoying an ethereal repose above the arches of heaven." This portrait was erected presumably in anticipation of celebrating the emperor's funeral and burial. But to their dismay, a portrait was all the citizens of Rome would have, because Constantine's body was not to be buried in the mausoleum with his mother. Like Jerusalem, Rome could now commemorate only an empty tomb.[41]

---

[41] Eusebius, *Vita Constantini* 4.67.3, alone, 69.2, portrait, 71.2, after restoration, 72, "like his Savior," with Cameron and Hall (1999) 348, "the dead Emperor's apotheosis comes near to becoming a Christian resurrection."

## THE BAPTIST

As he lay dying, Constantine recalled that once he had hoped to imitate Jesus by being baptized in the Jordan River. In 337 he had become ill soon after celebrating Easter in Constantinople. Looking for relief, he visited the baths outside Helenopolis, a nearby city renamed after his mother, where he probably also prayed in a shrine dedicated to martyrs. After journeying on to the outskirts of Nicomedia he summoned bishops and announced his wish for baptism. "Once I intended to accept the seal of salvation at the waters of the Jordan River where the Savior is remembered to have received baptism as an example for us." Instead, he would now accept baptism from these bishops. Constantine died soon afterward on May 22, the day of Pentecost.[42]

The soldiers in the imperial entourage immediately hailed Constantine as "master, lord, and emperor," and some mourned the loss of their "good shepherd." Constantine's body lay in state in the imperial palace at Constantinople until his son Constantius arrived to lead the funeral cortege. Eusebius' description of the funeral was so vibrant that he left the impression that he himself had attended. If he had, perhaps he would have thought about a missed opportunity.[43]

Constantine's patronage for the development of Palestine as a Christian Holy Land had considerably upgraded the status of Jerusalem. It had also elevated the prestige of the bishop of Jerusalem, who might begin to present himself as a peer of the metropolitan bishop of Caesarea, Eusebius himself. And if Constantine had indeed been healthy enough to travel to Palestine, he certainly would have toured the important shrines in and near Jerusalem with the local bishop. But that visit would also have given Eusebius one more chance to shine. If Constantine had now been able to follow Jesus' lead by being baptized in the Jordan

---

[42] Eusebius, *Vita Constantini* 4.60.5–64.2, death and baptism, 62.2, Jordan River; with Burgess (1999a) 219–32, (1999b), clarifying the details of Constantine's final journey. Constantine would presumably have detoured to Palestine before or after his planned invasion of the Persian empire: see Fowden (2006).

[43] Eusebius, *Vita Constantini* 4.65.1–2, acclamations, 66–71, funeral, with Cameron and Hall (1999) 346, "writes as if he was there himself."

River, then Eusebius, as the metropolitan bishop, would probably have presided over the ceremony. In that case Eusebius would have played the role of John the Baptist, the harbinger of Constantine's reign as a Christian ruler and, perhaps, the herald of the emperor's theology.

Bishops like Eusebius, who saw Constantine as the fulfillment of Christian history and the embodiment of proper Christian theology, had clearly appreciated the rise of a Christian emperor. But then as now, historians and theologians were more adept at reconfiguring the past than at predicting the future. Even though subsequent emperors continued to patronize the Holy Land, they also subtly undermined its prestige. Not only did they fail to visit as pilgrims; they also gradually removed more and more relics. In the Church of the Holy Apostles at Constantinople, which was part of the precinct that included Constantine's mausoleum, the emperor Constantius dedicated relics of the apostle Andrew, the evangelist Luke, and the missionary Timothy. In the later fourth century the emperor Theodosius imported the head of John the Baptist. Then the new capital contained shrines that commemorated both Jesus' precursor and his successors. Eventually Constantinople acquired so many biblical relics that it seemed to have replaced the Holy Land itself. New Rome had also become "New Jerusalem."[44]

Eusebius had thought that the Christian Jerusalem that replaced Roman Aelia was New Jerusalem. He would probably not have imagined that eventually another New Jerusalem on the Bosphorus might become a counterweight, even a rival, to Jerusalem in Palestine. Nor would his conviction that the establishment of a Christian emperorship was a sign of divine providence have allowed him to sympathize with the tense confrontations that would develop between some bishops and emperors. In those cases too John the Baptist could again serve as a spiritual model, because he had once defied a disreputable overlord.

---

[44] Burgess (2003), suggests that already in 336 Constantine had imported the relics of Andrew and Luke for what became his mausoleum, and that Constantius moved them to the new Church of the Holy Apostles in 357 to join the relics of Timothy; Hunt (1997b), stresses Theodosius' lack of involvement with the Holy Land. For the relics of John the Baptist, see Chapter 12. Constantinople as New Jerusalem: *Vita Danielis stylitae* 10.

In their willingness to oppose even a Christian emperor these later churchmen were ready, like John the Baptist, to become martyrs. As an honored relic, the head of John the Baptist was hence a reminder of his very distinctive dual roles as both a precursor of a new era and an opponent to a wicked regime. Churchmen could interpret the paradigm of his life in contrasting ways, as adulation for an admirable emperor or as opposition to a despotic emperor. Eusebius could imagine himself as the Baptist who had previewed the teachings of God's chosen monarch; subsequent bishops might instead imagine themselves as the Baptist who had challenged an overbearing ruler.[45]

---

[45] For the comparison applied to bishop Basil of Caesarea, see Gregory of Nyssa, *In Basilium fratrem* 14, "John [the Baptist] spoke candidly to [king] Herod, and Basil to [emperor] Valens," with Van Dam (2002) 118–35, for the context.

# THE SEARCH FOR THE CHRISTIAN DOCTRINE OF THE EMPEROR

## CHAPTER TWELVE

AFTER HIS EXECUTION JOHN THE BAPTIST HAD BEEN BURIED, according to legend, in Sebaste (formerly Samaria), on the west bank of the Jordan River. During the reign of Julian opponents of Christianity desecrated his tomb and scattered his bones. According to the historian Rufinus, monks from Jerusalem were able to collect John's venerable relics and bring them back to their monastery. They then sent the relics for safekeeping to Athanasius, the bishop of Alexandria. According to the historian Sozomen, monks from Jerusalem who had migrated to Cilicia eventually found John's head. The emperor Valens ordered it to be brought to Constantinople, but it was moved only as far as a village near Chalcedon. Toward the end of his reign the emperor Theodosius visited this village and took the head to Constantinople. By then John the Baptist was being hailed as a revered founder of monasticism and the ascetic lifestyle. Now a disheveled prophet who had once lived on locusts and wild honey in the wilderness was honored in a new church at the eastern capital.[1]

---

[1] Burial at Sebaste: Jerome, *Ep.* 46.13, 108.13. Desecration: Rufinus, *HE* 11.28, with Thélamon (1981) 290–94, on Rufinus' notion of pagan sacrilege; also Philostorgius,

Eusebius had concluded the final edition of his *Ecclesiastical History* with Constantine's victory over his last imperial rival. Once it became apparent in subsequent years that Christianity would continue to enjoy imperial support, much of his history of the early church had to be reconsidered. That reevaluation included the significance of Constantine. Eusebius himself, in his *Life* of the emperor and his panegyrics, acknowledged the need for reassessment by essentially equating Constantine with Jesus Christ. His hope was to use biography and panegyric as reinforcement for his theology.

Because of this correlation between history and theology, Christians who disapproved of Eusebius' doctrines were predisposed to modify his interpretation of Constantine too. After Constantine's death Eusebius had transformed the emperor into an embodiment of his own theology; now Eusebius' theological critics had to construct their own historical versions of Constantine. Contesting theology necessitated rewriting history. Not surprisingly, the same groups, sometimes the same men who were most responsible for adapting the legendary history of John the Baptist, also took the lead in rewriting the history of the life and times of Constantine in order to promote their own interests.

Bishop Athanasius of Alexandria certainly opposed Eusebius' doctrines. But to publicize his own theology he nevertheless followed Eusebius' rhetorical strategy by inscribing his doctrines into the life of an acclaimed warrior, this time not an emperor, but Antony, a famous Egyptian monk. At the same time he proposed an entirely different historical framework for the Tetrarchic and Constantinian periods by substituting an Age of Antony. Athanasius replaced Constantine with Antony as an alternative symbolic medium for articulating both theology and history. Ecclesiastical historians such as Rufinus, Socrates, and Sozomen likewise reconsidered the significance of Constantine even as they worked directly with Eusebius' historical writings, by translating his *History*, continuing his *History* through the fourth century, or using his *Life* as a source. But unlike Athanasius, who had rewritten the period

HE 7.4. Sozomen, *HE* 1.12.9, John as founder of "the best philosophy," 7.21.1–5, Valens and Theodosius. New church at Hebdomon: *Chronicon Paschale* s.a. 391.

in terms of the importance of Egyptian asceticism, these historians continued to focus on the role of emperors, and they reinterpreted the Age of Constantine as a prelude to subsequent imperial reigns. Eusebius had seemed to imagine Constantine as the fulfillment of history; these later historians knew that his reign had instead marked the beginning of a sequence of Christian emperors. One important successor in the later fourth century was Theodosius, who both presented himself as an imitator of Constantine and thoroughly modified the idea of a Christian emperor through his actions. His reign soon became a new template for evaluating Christian emperors, including earlier emperors like Constantine. The reigns of Theodosius and of every subsequent emperor who imagined himself as a new Constantine remodeled the memories of the first Christian emperor.

Over time many details of Constantine's reign were forgotten. In a sermon at Antioch in 387 the priest John Chrysostom attributed a particular joke to Constantine but knew little else. "He founded many great cities and he conquered many barbarians. We remember none of them." But theological disputes kept history alive. Because Eusebius had so thoroughly conflated history and theology, in the process of rejecting or modifying his doctrines bishops, ecclesiastical historians, and successor emperors all discovered the need to rewrite the life of Constantine. Long after the emperor's death images of Constantine remained central to disputes over both theology and the political philosophy of a Christian emperor.[2]

## "He Is a Man"

Antony grew up in a small Egyptian village on the west bank of the Nile. If it is correct that he lived to be a centenarian, then he had been born in the early 250s. This chronology made him a contemporary of the emperors in the original Tetrarchy, a few years younger than Diocletian, about the same age as Maximian and Constantius, and a few years

---

[2] Remember: John Chrysostom, *Hom. de statuis* 21.11 (*PG* 49.216), with Chapter 4, for Constantine's joke, and Van Dam (forthcoming), for the context of John's sermons.

older than Galerius. Antony's parents were prosperous landowners who raised their son as a Christian. They died in the early 270s, and Antony assumed responsibility for his younger sister. A few months later he changed the direction of his life completely by entrusting his sister to a community of virgins, dispersing his family's possessions, and adopting a life of strict ascetic discipline. At about the same time Constantius was celebrating the birth of his first son, Constantine. While one family could look forward to dynastic continuation, the continuity of the other was already ended. Antony's family would have no next generation.[3]

At first Antony lived near his hometown under the supervision of a spiritual master; eventually he resided in a graveyard farther away, where he repeatedly fought against temptations. In the mid-280s he moved again to a more distant site in the desert. At about the time that Diocletian and Maximian were establishing their joint imperial rule, Antony "hurried to the mountain." On the Outer Mountain east of the Nile he took up residence in a deserted fort. For twenty years, the entire joint reign of Diocletian and Maximian, almost no one saw him. Finally, at about the time those emperors retired in 305, Antony emerged to be greeted by visitors who viewed him as completely unaffected by his physical trials and who were hoping to receive healings through his intercession. More men now followed his lead to become monks living in the desert or the mountains. Even though Antony did not establish a dynasty of sons, he did have ascetic offspring. As he visited the monasteries and settlements of his spiritual progeny, Antony "guided all the monks like a father."[4]

---

[3] According to Athanasius, *Vita Antonii* 89.3, Antony claimed to be almost 105 years old when he died; according to Jerome, *Chronicon* s.a. 356, he died in 356. Sozomen, *HE* 1.13.2, noted that he had been born in Koma, across the river and a few miles south of Aphrodito. Athanasius, *Vita Antonii* 1, parents, 2.1, their death when Antony was "about eighteen or twenty years old," 3.1, sister. For the ages of emperors, see Barnes (1982) 30–32, 35, 37, 39–41.

[4] Athanasius, *Vita Antonii* 3.2, "not far from his hometown," 8.1, "the tombs located far from his hometown," 10.4, "he was then about thirty-five years old," 11.2, mountain, 12.3, deserted fort, 14.1, "almost twenty years," 14, emergence, 15.3, father.

A few years later Antony decided to transform his life again, this time by exchanging his asceticism for martyrdom. During the persecutions initiated by the emperor Maximinus, most likely in 312, he traveled to Alexandria with a "yearning to become a martyr." Although he tried to earn execution by confronting an imperial magistrate, in the end he was content to help the Christians who had been imprisoned or condemned to the mines before returning to his solitary residence. Soon afterward he moved again to escape the crowds of visitors, this time to the Inner Mountain farther east toward the Red Sea. Decades later Antony descended from his fortress of solitude once more. In the summer of 338 he revisited Alexandria, where he denounced Arian doctrines and performed miracles of healing before "returning to the mountain, as if to his own home." Eventually he also revisited his original retreat in response to pleas from magistrates and ordinary people for assistance. But Antony had critics and opponents too, including pagan philosophers, some imperial magistrates, and even some churchmen. Once he warned a belligerent military commander about God's wrath; this officer was soon mortally injured in a riding accident, probably in 345. Antony died in 356, less than a year after the emperor Constantius had promoted his cousin Julian as a junior emperor. This bashful monk had almost outlived the entire Constantinian dynasty of emperors.[5]

---

[5] Athanasius, *Vita Antonii* 46.1, Maximinus' persecution, Alexandria, 46.2, yearning, prisons, 69.2, Alexandria, 71.2, own home, 86, death of Valacius. For the persecutions under Maximinus, see Chapter 6; the date of Antony's second visit to Alexandria, Barnes (1993) 45, and Brakke (1995) 204–6; the date of Valacius' death, Barnes (1993) 96.

Note that Athanasius mentioned Antony only once in his other writings. In *Historia Arianorum* 14, he criticized Gregorius, who had replaced him as bishop of Alexandria from 339 to 345. Athanasius censured Gregorius as "a friend of imperial magistrates rather than of bishops and monks." Not only did Gregorius ignore Antony's letters, but he also convinced the general Valacius to spit on one of them. Valacius was soon killed by his horse. This account of Antony's role in Valacius' death differed from the version in *Vita Antonii*, in which Athanasius never mentioned Gregorius. Athanasius wrote *Historia Arianorum* in late 357, a year or so after Antony's death: for the date, see Barnes (1993) 126.

One of the bishops who welcomed Antony to Alexandria in 338 was Athanasius. As a young deacon he had attended the council of Nicaea to assist bishop Alexander. In 328 he had succeeded his mentor, and as bishop of Alexandria he became a prominent champion of Nicene theology and an opponent of the doctrines of Arius and his like-minded allies. Those allies included Eusebius of Caesarea, who in 335 participated in a council at Tyre that voted to depose Athanasius. In response Athanasius resorted to direct personal criticism of Eusebius' "capricious behavior." In his opinion, Eusebius had maliciously misrepresented his own theology in order to appear to conform at the council of Nicaea. Athanasius also looked for backing among the monks in Egypt. One motive for Antony's visit to Alexandria was to show his support for Athanasius, who had just returned from defending himself before the emperor Constantius. Athanasius was most grateful, and as the celebrated monk departed, "we escorted him." Perhaps on this occasion Athanasius presented Antony with a new cloak.[6]

After Antony's death Athanasius wrote a *Life* of the monk. In early 356 imperial magistrates had forced him into exile once again, and the emperor Constantius was supporting creeds that undermined Nicene theology. Athanasius defended himself and his Nicene doctrines in many treatises, including this *Life*. Even as this *Life* combined a biography of Antony's career with a defense of his behavior, it also advocated the author's own objectives. By the time Antony died, Athanasius was asserting the authority of bishops like himself to intervene in monastic affairs. During his exile Athanasius in fact lived in monasteries throughout Egypt. He also hoped to integrate the desert monks more fully into ecclesiastical affairs by appointing some of them as bishops. As a complement to this integration of monks, Athanasius articulated a more comprehensive spirituality that promoted the relevance of the values of desert ascetics for ordinary Christians. All of these goals in turn further reinforced his arguments in favor of his doctrines and his involvement

---

[6] Athanasius, *De synodis* 13.2–3, Eusebius' behavior; *Vita Antonii* 71.1, escort, 91.8, new cloak; with Chapter 10, for additional discussion of Athanasius' career during Constantine's reign.

in larger theological controversies. Just as Eusebius had appropriated the life of Constantine in order to articulate and promote his theology, so Athanasius now appropriated the life of Antony for the same reason. The Antony that Athanasius imagined in *Life* could likewise become a medium for expressing theology.[7]

In his *Life* Athanasius rewrote the history of the later third and early fourth century from a distinctively different viewpoint. He first offered a geographical outlook that contrasted with Eusebius' view from Palestine and Constantine's from Constantinople. "By birth Antony was an Egyptian." In *Life* Athanasius highlighted an Egyptian perspective on events in which the monks of Egypt, and in particular Antony, had inherited the prestige of the martyrs. Second, he imposed a different chronological pattern. Eusebius had located ecclesiastical events in a framework of emperors and their activities; Athanasius now almost entirely ignored emperors, their political maneuvering, and their military campaigns. He never mentioned Diocletian and the Tetrarchy, the rise of Constantine as a Christian emperor, his removal of imperial rivals, his foundation of Constantinople, or his patronage for Jerusalem. Instead, by attributing great longevity to Antony, Athanasius was able to discuss the same period in terms of decisive moments in the monk's life. Those turning points often conveniently corresponded to important transitions in imperial history. Antony's adoption of his ascetic lifestyle, for instance, coincided with the birth of Constantine, and the decades during which he lived in a deserted fort coincided with Diocletian's entire reign. Most important, the highlights of Antony's ascetic career could replace the framework of Constantine's reign. At about the time that Constantine was hailed as emperor, Antony was thought to have been "inspired by God" when he emerged from seclusion. At about the time that Constantine was victorious at Rome, Antony visited

---

[7] For confirmation of Athanasius as the author of the Greek *Vita Antonii* and of its priority to subsequent Syriac and Coptic versions, see Bartelink (1994) 27–42, Brakke (1994), and Rubenson (1995) 126–32. For Athanasius' goals of integrating both asceticism and ascetics, see the excellent discussion in Brakke (1995). Barnes (1993) 121–35, surveys Athanasius' apologetic treatises from the later 350s.

324 THE ROMAN REVOLUTION OF CONSTANTINE

Alexandria with the hope of becoming a martyr. Soon after Constantine's death he revisited Alexandria to denounce Arianism and other heresies. Athanasius' account hence retained the basic chronological narrative for the period, even as Antony's miraculously long life provided an alternative framework of significant transitional moments. Eusebius' emphasis on Constantine's reign had linked the emperor's patronage for Christianity with military success; Athanasius' focus on Antony's career connected God's blessing with ascetic discipline. Athanasius essentially replaced the entire Tetrarchic and Constantinian eras with an Age of Antony.[8]

Once Athanasius had reconstructed the historical narrative of the period on this monastic and Egyptian scaffolding, he could present Antony as a powerful spokesman for Nicene theology. Eusebius had been impressed with Constantine's orations; Athanasius now attributed to Antony various comments and sermons, in particular warnings against Arian doctrines. "He despised the Arian heresy, and he recommended that no one approach them or accept their perverse faith." When Antony visited Alexandria in 338, he publicly disparaged Arian doctrines. According to this *Life*, even though Antony had only a limited education and spoke only "the Egyptian language," he had somehow mastered the sophisticated terminology of the doctrinal controversy. He now taught that the Son of God was not a creature, that he had not been made out of the nonexistent, and that he was the eternal Word

---

[8] Athanasius, *Vita Antonii* 1.1, by birth, 14.2, inspired. The historicity of aspects of Antony's life is disputable, in particular during the first half of Antony's life before Athanasius became a cleric at Alexandria during the early 320s. Especially problematic is Antony's great age at death. Athanasius certainly had the freedom to manipulate the chronology, since Antony himself probably did not know his age: see Rubenson (1995) 43. Athanasius also had an obvious motive for extending Antony's age, since it allowed him to replace the Tetrarchic period, Constantine's reign, and the reigns of almost the entire Constantinian dynasty with a chronological framework based exclusively on Antony's adult ascetic life. But the probability of becoming a centenarian in ancient society was very low: see Frier (2000) 796–97, and Parkin (1992) 105–11, (2003) 50, "only a very select few ancient Greeks and Romans could have genuinely boasted of passing the century mark."

and Wisdom from the Father's essence. "All the people were happy to hear such a man condemn this heresy that belittled Christ." In a final conversation in anticipation of his death Antony again recommended that his companions avoid contact with Arians.[9]

Antony's doctrines corresponded not only with the theology adopted at the council of Nicaea, but also with Athanasius' own doctrines. In this *Life* Antony was presented as a mouthpiece of Athanasius' theology. But Athanasius' rhetorical techniques surpassed merely inserting denunciations of Arian doctrines and endorsements of his own Nicene theology into Antony's mouth. He also transformed Antony into an embodiment of those Nicene doctrines. Just as Eusebius had presented an emperor who made sense only in terms of Arian theology, so Athanasius now imagined a monk who could be understood only within the context of Nicene theology. Arian doctrines claimed that Jesus Christ, even though he was part of the created world, a creature like other men, had nevertheless been elevated to a perfected Sonship that was "a reward for performance." This theology that emphasized progress in obedience and divine favor offered in turn the possibility that a similar sonship by adoption was available to all true believers, and in particular to such distinctive strivers for disciplined perfection as monks and ascetics. Athanasius, of course, rejected both this Arian theology and its implications for interpreting Antony's life, and in *Life* he fashioned an Antony whose achievements were instead wholly dependent on God's grace. Antony himself was thought to have acknowledged his need for divine support by declining to accept credit for healing a young girl. "This success is not mine. . . . Instead, the healing is due to the Savior." In this perspective, although Antony's life was a model of discipline and striving, his reputation for goodness was wholly a gift from God: "Antony's holiness is not achieved, it is received." Antony supposedly said so; and Athanasius pointedly interpreted his entire career likewise. "It was evident to everyone that he was not performing [these cures],

---

[9] Athanasius, *Vita Antonii* 16.1, language (i.e. Coptic), 68.2, despised, 69.3, teachings, 70.1, all the people, 73, mockery of Antony as uneducated, 89.4, final recommendation.

but that it was the Lord who was generous to mankind and healing the suffering through Antony."[10]

Even though Eusebius had not been a familiar intimate of Constantine, he had nevertheless appropriated the emperor's life in order to publicize his own doctrines. Athanasius had likewise not been a close companion of Antony, and he overlooked some of the monk's accomplishments. In his own letters Antony in fact revealed himself to have been literate and educated, a leader of monastic communities who was versed in some of the doctrines of the earlier theologian Origen and neo-Platonic ideas about the importance of self-knowledge as the path toward salvation. But like Eusebius, Athanasius now converted the life of his subject into a symbolic medium for asserting theology: "the major feature is not the rejection of anything authentic, but the transformation of it for a new purpose." Like Eusebius' *Life of Constantine*, this *Life of Antony* was an implicit theological treatise about the relationship between God the Father and Jesus Christ his Son. In order to promote his Arian doctrines Eusebius had constructed an emperor who was an analogue of Jesus Christ and subordinated both to God the Father. In order to promote his Nicene doctrines Athanasius had coordinated Father and Son and depicted a monk who was clearly dependent upon Jesus Christ.[11]

Athanasius was not content, however, merely to present a "Nicene" image of a monk like Antony as a contrast to an "Arian" image of an emperor like Constantine. Although he rarely mentioned emperors, his

---

[10] Athanasius, *Vita Antonii* 58.4, success, 84.1, evident. Quotations from Gregg and Groh (1981) 57, reward, 147, holiness, in an outstanding discussion of the interplay between dogma and biography in *Life*. "Antony's *acta* have been fashioned and narrated in such a way as to preclude the Arian understanding of Christ" (p. 153). Note also the excellent analyses in Brakke (1995) 216–44, on the insertion of Athanasius' own doctrines in *Life*, 248–49, on the pivotal role of the image of Antony in the development of Christian thought "from a theology emphasizing human freedom and virtue to one emphasizing divine power and grace."

[11] Quotation from Rubenson (1995) 144, in an outstanding comparison of *Life* and Antony's letters; but Rousseau (2000), downplays any differences in the portraits of Antony as a master of pedagogical technique depicted in his letters and *Life*.

*Life* nevertheless offered an alternative perspective on Christian emperors. In particular, Athanasius seems to have used his *Life* as a direct response to claims about the potential divinity of a Christian emperor by suggesting that Constantine too, like Antony, had in fact not been an analogue of Jesus. According to one story, Antony once made a clear distinction between himself and Jesus Christ. When a military officer requested a miraculous cure for his daughter, Antony demurred: "I am a man, just like you." He recommended that the officer instead pray to Christ. In another story Antony applied the same distinction to the emperor when he received a letter from Constantine and two of his sons. As he discussed this letter with his fellow monks, Antony was unimpressed. "Why are you surprised if the emperor writes to us? He is a man. Instead, marvel that God has written the law for mankind and has spoken it to us through his Son." When Antony did agree to send a reply, he encouraged the emperors to venerate Christ and to remember that "Christ is the only true and eternal Emperor." This story was a miniature "Life of Constantine," in which an Antony who had criticized Arian theology was now also presented as critical of an Arianizing political philosophy. According to Antony's alternative perspective, only God the Father and his Son were coordinate, while emperors, like monks and in fact like other people too, were subordinate to Jesus Christ. In *Life* Antony's support for Nicene theology had generated a Nicene political philosophy about Christian emperors.[12]

Athanasius was most likely not familiar with Eusebius' *Life of Constantine*. But in his *Life of Antony* he had seemingly responded to Eusebius' image of a Christian ruler. In some respects his Antony became an inverted reflection of Eusebius' Constantine, with the monk's every activity carefully subverting fundamental aspects of the emperor's reign. For Antony the acquisition of spiritual virtue was more important than military successes. In Eusebius' *Life* Constantine had fought against rival emperors; in Athanasius' *Life* Antony fought against demons. Constantine had turned the cross into a military standard for his troops. Antony provided a theological interpretation of the cross and crucifixion

---

[12] Athanasius, *Vita Antonii* 48, military officer, 81, emperor's letter and reply.

in terms of Jesus' incarnation and the possibility that people might "share in the holy and spiritual nature." Most notably, Antony too, like Constantine, had become the founder of a new city. Constantine's Constantinople had been simply a larger version of the conventional classical city that was so central to traditional notions of the realization of the good life, and he had bolstered the standing of his new political capital by importing monuments and trophies that commemorated great events in Greek and Roman history. But in Athanasius' perspective, as an imperial capital Constantinople was just another negligible aspect of that imperial historical narrative that he had replaced in his *Life of Antony*. His new narrative had no place for Constantinople. Instead, in *Life* Antony had looked entirely outside the world of classical cities into the wastelands of Egypt: "the desert became a city of monks." By attracting more supporters to become monks, Antony deserved credit for turning the desert into "a city of asceticism." Over the decades this representation of the role of the desert in promoting ascetic values became increasingly more dominant in Roman society, and one influential model for a true Christian city was now the desert. In fact, as monks moved to urban areas, they soon seemed to transform cities into desert. With the expanding influence of ascetic values, with the arrival of monks and the foundation of monasteries, even Constantinople, Constantine's new imperial city, might eventually come to resemble Antony's new city of monks, the desert.[13]

Athanasius' *Life of Antony* was highly inspirational and extensively read. It was soon translated into two Latin versions, one quite literal but another by Evagrius, a priest at Antioch, that was more of a paraphrase. These Latin translations circulated widely in the western provinces. At Trier a court official who read "a book in which the life of Antony was

---

[13] Athanasius, *Vita Antonii* 8.2, city of asceticism, 14.7, the desert, 74.4, share, with Rubenson (1995) 119, "an urbanization of the desert." Cameron (2000) discusses both *Lives* as political works and suggests that Athanasius was responding to Eusebius: "Could the Greek *Life of Antony* possibly itself be an answer to the *Life of Constantine*?" (p. 85). For monasticism at the eastern capital, see the excellent survey of Dagron (1970): for monks, "Constantinople fascine et inquiète" (p. 260).

written" abruptly decided to abandon his imperial career: "behold, I am becoming a friend of God right now." The Greek *Life* was read just as widely in the eastern provinces, and for churchmen throughout the empire *Life of Antony* became a standard literary model for the composition of hagiographical *Lives* of bishops and monks. In addition, the highly stylized pattern of Antony's life defined a model lifestyle that presupposed the acceptance of a theology of coordination and identity between God and his Son, an acknowledgment of dependence upon Jesus Christ, and an expectation of obedience to bishops and clerics. This paradigmatic life in turn was influential beyond the world of churchmen and monks. Not only did it inspire monks and ascetics by deflecting the impact of Arian theology and extending episcopal supervision. It also gradually became an exemplar for the life of a Christian emperor.[14]

## READING *LIFE OF CONSTANTINE*

Athanasius died in May 373, and scuffles soon broke out in Alexandria over the episcopal succession. One witness to these controversies was Rufinus, who had come to Alexandria to study with Didymus, a famous theologian who had once met Antony. During his stay in Egypt Rufinus visited the monks in the desert, including some of the master's disciples who still lived on "Antony's mountain." Later he moved to Palestine, where he lived in a monastery on the Mount of Olives and became a priest. In 397 he returned to his homeland of Italy, where he eventually resided in Aquileia.[15]

Since Rufinus already had a reputation as a translator of Greek ecclesiastical texts into Latin, the bishop of Aquileia soon suggested that he translate Eusebius' *History*. The result was not a strict translation, a faithful rendition of Eusebius' narrative. Instead, Rufinus composed "a kind of paraphrase which gives the general sense." In particular, he

---

[14] Bartelink (1994) 68–70, literary influence, 95–98, Latin translations. Trier: Augustine, *Confessiones* 8.6.15. For the impact among monks, see Williams (1987) 89: "Arianism failed to capture the ascetic movements of the fourth century."

[15] Rufinus, *HE* 11.4, visit to monks, 7, Didymus, 8, mountain.

omitted much of the tenth book of Eusebius' *History*, including a long sermon and a series of imperial edicts, and combined "whatever history remained" with the ninth book. To this condensed version of Eusebius' ten books he then added two books of his own as a sequel that covered the period "from the era of Constantine after the [ending of] persecution to the death of the Augustus Theodosius." Just as Jesus had once fed the multitude with five loaves and two fish, so Rufinus claimed he would nourish his readers with a version of Eusebius' "twice-five loaves" and his own "two small fish."[16]

In his *History* Eusebius had first mentioned Constantine in the eighth book upon his acclamation as emperor and then of course discussed additional events of his reign in the ninth and tenth books. Because Eusebius' Greek narrative is still extant, it is most advantageous that Rufinus did not merely translate it verbatim. Instead, the differences

---

[16]    For bishop Chromatius' request in later 401, see Murphy (1945) 158, and Hammond (1977) 392. Quotation about paraphrase from Oulton (1929) 150. For Rufinus' description of his own *HE*, see his *Prologus*, ed. Mommsen, pp. 951–52. Because he had condensed Eusebius' ninth and tenth books into one (ninth) book, Rufinus called his own two additional books the tenth and the eleventh. To avoid confusion, references to Rufinus' translation of Eusebius' tenth book will use references to Eusebius, *HE* 10.

One possible source was another continuation of Eusebius' *History* by Gelasius of Caesarea, in Greek. Gelasius' continuation is now lost; but since he had died apparently a few years before Rufinus wrote his continuation, he had worked independently of Rufinus. The nature of the relationship between these two continuations is much contested. The spectrum of hypotheses is wide: that Rufinus' entire continuation was simply a translation of Gelasius' *History* without attribution, that Rufinus translated Gelasius' *History* to its end (perhaps at the death of Arius, or during the reign of Julian, or in the mid-370s) and then himself added the rest, that Rufinus wrote independently of Gelasius, that Rufinus himself composed a Greek version of his original additions that was then combined with Gelasius' *History* to provide a narrative of the entire fourth century, or that someone else translated all of Rufinus' continuation into Greek; for a survey of the scholarship, see Drijvers (1992) 95–98, and Amidon (1997) xiii–xvii. Thélamon (1981) 20, is rightly skeptical of this stubborn commitment to recreating a lost history: "un leurre qui conduit à l'abandon d'un objet réel pour la quête stérile d'un objet perdu."

between the two versions, the additions and omissions, reflected Rufinus' own reading of the significance of Constantine's reign from a perspective about sixty-five years after the emperor's death. Rufinus had seen the future, and the idiosyncrasies of his narrative reflected his own contemporary ideal of a Christian emperor.

Two characteristics of Rufinus' account of Constantine's early reign were especially significant. One was his characterization of Constantine as a "religious emperor." When Eusebius had published the first edition of his *History*, he had been concerned primarily about the ending of persecution with the death of Maximinus. In his first reference to Constantine he had described the new emperor simply as Constantius' "legitimate son." Decades later, when successor emperors were all claiming to be Constantine's heirs, legitimacy was no longer an issue. Instead, Rufinus introduced Constantine as the "more religious son" of a "religious father." In his perspective, Constantine had been a devoutly Christian emperor from the beginning. At the end of the final edition of his *History*, after Constantine had defeated Licinius, Eusebius had stressed the emperor's piety toward the churches. Rufinus again described Constantine as a "religious emperor."[17]

A second important characteristic of Rufinus' reading of Constantine was his emphasis on the emperor's respect for bishops. As Constantine set out for his final campaign against Licinius, Eusebius had described the emperor as "the friend of God." This designation suggested an exclusive intimacy with God, as if Constantine were his special representative. Not surprisingly, Eusebius furthermore claimed that Constantine extended his right hand to offer salvation through his military campaign. Constantine was God's "agent," "a great light-giver and savior for everyone." Rufinus included none of these exalted descriptions in his translation. Instead, in his version of the buildup to war he stressed Constantine's reverence for bishops and clerics. As a "religious emperor" Constantine "did not think it was appropriate for the clerics of God if

---

[17] Rufinus, *HE* 8.13.14, more religious emperor; Rufinus, *apud* Eusebius, *HE* 10.9.6, "religiosi imperatoris"; with Thélamon (1981) 185, 311–12, for Rufinus' use of *religio* as "Christianity."

he presented himself as an equal or if he did not greatly privilege them." At the end of the war Constantine "bestowed many privileges upon the churches and high honors upon the clerics."[18]

Throughout his *History* Eusebius had consistently promoted a theology that subordinated Jesus Christ the Son to God the Father. Jerome, a sometime friend of Rufinus, recognized the difficulty later readers would have in admiring the history but rejecting the theology. In his estimation, even though Eusebius had composed a magnificent account of ecclesiastical history, he was nevertheless "the most outspoken advocate of Arius' impiety." This was a truly "bittersweet" *History* that combined a delectable historical narrative with a sour theology. Eusebius' doctrines had been especially evident in the introduction to his *History* and in the long sermon that he included in the tenth book. Rufinus knew that that sort of Arianizing theology had eventually been condemned, and in his translation of the introduction he repeatedly modified Eusebius' unacceptable comments to sound more orthodox. He also simply excluded Eusebius' sermon. This concern to diminish or omit Eusebius' heterodox doctrines furthermore affected Rufinus' representation of the first Christian emperor. Just as he rejected Eusebius' theology, he likewise rejected his political philosophy. Eusebius' Constantine had been a savior, similar to Jesus Christ. Rufinus' Constantine was a loyal servant of the church and its bishops.[19]

Rufinus could have continued his translation of Eusebius' *History* with a translation of Eusebius' *Life of Constantine*. Quite probably he was familiar with this *Life*. In fact, in his translation of one episode in Eusebius' *History* Rufinus seems to have been influenced by the more elaborate version in *Life*. When Eusebius had narrated Constantine's victory over Maxentius in *History*, his account had first mentioned Constantine's initial prayer to God and Jesus Christ, "the Savior of all," and then described military affairs, such as the battles in northern Italy, Maxentius' advance outside the walls of Rome, the collapse of the

---

[18] Eusebius, *HE* 10.8.19, savior, agent, 9.2, friend, 4, salvation. Rufinus, *apud* Eusebius, *HE* 10.8.1–2, appropriate, 9.8, privileges.

[19] For Rufinus' modifications of Eusebius' theology, see Oulton (1929) 153–56. Advocate: Jerome, *Ep.* 84.2.

bridge, and Maxentius' drowning. Decades later in *Life*, Eusebius had provided an expanded narrative in which Constantine's famous vision of a cross in the sky and his construction of a military standard in the shape of a cross preceded his victory over Maxentius. In his translation of this episode in *History* Rufinus now inserted an account of this vision and the military standard that seemed to borrow from the expanded narrative in *Life*. In particular, he quoted in Greek the slogan that Eusebius claimed had appeared with the cross in the sky: "conquer in this." Of course, true to form Rufinus also added details not found in either Eusebius' *History* or his *Life*, such as the angels who were reciting the slogan and the gold cross that the emperor thereafter carried in his right hand.[20]

Rufinus nevertheless preferred to overlook this *Life*, perhaps because like the sermon in the tenth book of *History*, it was too contaminated with Eusebius' ideas about the subordination of Jesus Christ to God the Father and the similarities between Jesus and Constantine. Instead, he continued his translation of Eusebius' *History* with an account that he based on "the writings of ancestors" and his own memory. Even though he never mentioned his predecessor in his additional books, Rufinus' observations in his additional books were a further repudiation of Eusebius' theology. He criticized both Arius, whose theology Eusebius had supported, and Eusebius of Nicomedia, another partisan of Arius. He praised the outcome of the council of Nicaea and cited its creed and its denunciations of Arian doctrines. He admired bishop Alexander, who had resisted "the threats of Eusebius [of Nicomedia] and Arius' intimidation." He especially admired Athanasius, Alexander's successor as bishop of Alexandria and an outspoken critic of Eusebius of Caesarea. Until Athanasius' death in 373, Rufinus could use the bishop's loyalty

---

[20] Victory over Maxentius: Eusebius, *HE* 9.9.1–8, *Vita Constantini* 1.28–38. Rufinus, *HE* 9.9.1–4, vision, slogan, military standard, cross, with Christensen (1989) 293, "Rufinus must have known the *Vita Constantini*, or at any rate a similar source," 295n.301, "Rufinus relied on a tradition here, which despite all the similarities, is independent of Eusebius's account in *Vita Constantini*." Rufinus' narrative may also have included local legends he had heard during his years in Rome. Note that unlike Eusebius in both his *Ecclesiastical History* and his *Life of Constantine*, Rufinus mentioned the Milvian Bridge by name.

to Nicene doctrines as a framework for his narrative of theological controversies and a benchmark for evaluating the behavior of emperors. Good emperors like Jovian understood the importance of "petitioning Athanasius with a complimentary and most respectful letter." By enhancing Athanasius' reputation Rufinus ensured that his extension of Eusebius' *History* represented a Nicene historical perspective. Eusebius would have been stunned to discover that the Age of Constantine had been only a preview of the Age of Athanasius.[21]

Rufinus also greatly admired the emperor Theodosius. In his opinion, Theodosius had fought against usurpers in order to defend "the catholic faith" against Arianism or against paganism. He had furthermore shown his deference to the ecclesiastical hierarchy by performing penance "after being reproved by the bishops of Italy." According to Rufinus, an emperor now demonstrated his piety through his respect for bishops and other churchmen. Only Constantine and Theodosius had lived up to that expectation. At the beginning of his continuation Rufinus had again praised Constantine as a "religious emperor" for having summoned bishops to the council at Nicaea. Subsequently he praised Theodosius as Constantine's true heir: "by Constantine's order the cult of idols had begun to be neglected and destroyed; it collapsed during Theodosius' reign." He concluded his narrative with Theodosius' death in 395, when "he migrated to a better situation to receive the rewards of his virtues with the most pious of emperors." Eusebius had started his historical narrative by discussing "Jesus Christ, our Savior and Lord," at the side of God, and he had ended the final edition of his *History* with a description of the celebrations in honor of God, the Emperor of all, and the victorious Constantine. In contrast, Rufinus did not correlate Jesus and Constantine as comparable companions of God. The analogous bookends of his own narrative were instead Constantine and Theodosius, the two ideal Christian emperors of the fourth century.[22]

---

[21] Rufinus, *HE* 10.1, Arius, 5, Eusebius of Nicomedia, 6, creed, 14, threats, 11.1, letter, with Barnes (1993) 159, on the authenticity of Jovian's letter.

[22] Rufinus, *HE* 10.1, 3, Constantine as *religiosus imperator*, 11.17, catholic faith, 18, bishops, 19, cult, 34, migrated, with Thélamon (1970), on Rufinus' image of an

## Doorkeepers for the Fishermen

About forty years later Socrates wrote another ecclesiastical history of the fourth century that he extended to the later 430s. Socrates was born, grew up, and worked in Constantinople. Two predecessors inspired him to become a historian. One was Eusebius. In the opening chapter Socrates mentioned both Eusebius' *History* and his *Life of Constantine*, and he started his narrative with a reprise of Constantine's famous vision before his battle against Maxentius, which he seems to have drawn from Eusebius' account in *Life*: "it is useful for our project to recall how the emperor Constantine came to Christianity." The other stimulating model was Rufinus, whose continuation of Eusebius' *History* became a primary source for Socrates' own account. To these two exemplars Socrates offered a respectful tribute: the first word of his first book was "Eusebius," and the first word of his second book was "Rufinus."[23]

The writings of Eusebius and Rufinus were certainly important sources for Socrates. He referred to specific books of Eusebius' *History* and *Life*, and he conceded that initially he had been far too dependent on Rufinus' narrative of the fourth century. But as he weighed their information, Socrates also had to evaluate their analyses, because Eusebius and Rufinus had not shared the same interpretive stance, in particular about Constantine. Socrates then added to this mixture of competing perspectives by using other sources too. One was the writings

ideal emperor: "Rufin est donc bien loin ... de la théologie politique d'Eusèbe" (p. 313). Eusebius, *HE* 1.1.2, Jesus Christ, 10.9.7–8, celebrations. For Rufinus' correlation of the era of Constantine with the era of Theodosius, see Thélamon (1981) 467: "L'*Histoire ecclésiastique* est comprise entre ces deux moments privilégiés."

[23] Socrates, *HE* 1.1.1–2, Eusebius' writings, 4, useful; with Urbainczyk (1997) 13–39, and Wallraff (1997) 209–21, for the few biographical details known about Socrates himself, and Leppin (1996) 274–79, dating the composition of his *HE* to the mid-440s. Since Socrates described Rufinus' account as "the ecclesiastical history in the language of the Romans," he had presumably read it in Latin: see Socrates, *HE* 2.1.1, with Urbainczyk (1997) 51–52; Wallraff (1997) 186–90, argues that Socrates considered Rufinus' account to be original and the account in Greek by Gelasius of Caesarea to be a translation.

of Athanasius, in which the bishop had described his hardships due to the intrigues of his opponents. Once Socrates discovered Athanasius' treatises, he completely revised his first book, which had concluded with Constantine's death, to give more weight to the outlook of "someone who had suffered." As a second supplementary source for Constantine's reign he found "various letters of that time," including "letters of the emperor." When he revised his first book, Socrates quoted many of these letters in their entirety so that his readers would know "what the emperors wrote in their own words" and "what the bishops decided at various councils."[24]

These additional literary sources distanced Socrates' account even farther from Eusebius' vision. Athanasius had been an opponent of Eusebius, and by highlighting his travails Socrates reinforced his preference for Nicene doctrines over the theology of Arius and his supporters, among them Eusebius. The letters that Socrates cited indicated Constantine's own vacillation over Athanasius and Arius, and Eusebius himself had quoted some of these letters in his *Life*. But Socrates also quoted the long letter in which Eusebius had tried to justify to his congregation at Caesarea why he had finally accepted the doctrinal creed of the council at Nicaea. Athanasius, predictably, had already quoted this letter in his collection of documents about the council, perhaps just to revel in Eusebius' squirming explanation. But Eusebius himself, in all his writings, had never quoted or mentioned this embarrassing letter. In *Life* his account of the aftermath of the council had simply omitted any reference to his own change of mind. Even though Socrates clearly appreciated Eusebius' writings as sources, by citing this letter and highlighting his rival Athanasius he quietly undermined the

---

[24] Citations from Eusebius' writings: Socrates, *HE* 1.7.2, 8.4, 8.20, 8.31, 16.4, 22.2. New sources: Socrates, *HE* 2.1.1, Rufinus' mistakes about chronology, 2, Athanasius' suffering, 4, letters, revision of first book, 6, bishops and emperors; with the excellent discussion of Socrates' revisions in Wallraff (1997) 163–72: "Die Tendenz änderte sich ... nicht grundlegend, weil auch Rufins Darstellung schon von der athanasianischen Perspektive geprägt war" (p. 172). Socrates, *HE* 1.23.6, 38.4, also mentioned these new letters.

authority of his illustrious predecessor's interpretation of Constantine's reign.[25]

In fact, as he prepared to launch his account of Constantine, Socrates was already skeptical about the perspective and tone of Eusebius' *Life*. In his estimation, this *Life* had been far too laudatory. "Eusebius wrote a biography of Constantine in which he offered a partial recollection of the events concerning Arius. He was concerned more about his eulogies of the emperor and the grandiloquence of the words in his panegyric, as if in an encomium, than about an accurate narrative of events." Socrates' account of Constantine was hence much more subdued, and his retelling of two important moments was distinctly different from Eusebius' perspective.[26]

One was his narrative of the council at Nicaea. Much of Socrates' account was based directly on Eusebius' account in *Life*. He quoted two passages from Eusebius' *Life* verbatim, first concerning Constantine's convening of the council, then concerning the emperor's role in finding unanimity. "We have not cited these [words of Eusebius] inappropriately, but have quoted them as witnesses for what was said by him [Constantine]." But more significant was what Socrates omitted. Between the two quoted passages Eusebius had described Constantine as he arrived in the assembly of bishops "like a heavenly angel of God." Eusebius had then cited the emperor's speech in which he exhorted the bishops to find unanimity. After the second quoted passage Eusebius had described Constantine's banquet for the bishops as similar to "an image of Christ's kingdom." These descriptions had contributed to Eusebius' construction of Constantine as an analogue of Jesus Christ. In Socrates' version, however, all that was left was the emperor's respectful reluctance to sit until the bishops had assented. A council that in Eusebius' account had spotlighted the emperor's role in presiding over the bishops

[25] Eusebius' letter: Urkunde 22, ed. Opitz (1934–1935) 42–47, quoted in Athanasius, *De decretis Nicaenae synodi* 33, and Socrates, *HE* 1.8.35–54. Eusebius, *Vita Constantini* 3.13.2, claimed that Constantine's leadership produced harmony among the participants at the council; Socrates, *HE* 2.21.3, hence quoted this passage as proof that Eusebius was *not* an "Arianizer"!
[26] Socrates, *HE* 1.1.2, biography.

had now become a council of bishops attended by the emperor. Because Socrates had reversed the dynamic between emperor and bishops, he even interpreted one of Constantine's letters that defended Nicene theology and criticized Arius as confirmation of the emperor's support for bishops: "he called the opinion of all who had assembled there [at the council] the opinion of God."[27]

In his account of Constantine's funeral and burial at Constantinople, Socrates again emphasized the emperor's reverence for bishops. This respect would have surprised both Constantine and Eusebius. Eusebius had used his description of Constantine's funeral to suggest that Constantine had continued to rule even after his death. Constantine had underscored his similarity to Jesus Christ by constructing a funerary shrine in which his tomb was surrounded by twelve empty tombs that commemorated the apostles. In contrast, Socrates called attention to the other incumbents in this mausoleum. Already by the mid-fourth century the imperial mausoleum had been overshadowed by the adjacent Church of the Holy Apostles. Whether Constantine had constructed the mausoleum and his son Constantius had initiated construction of the church, or whether Constantine had had himself buried in the church and his tomb had later been moved to the mausoleum, the prominence of the church soon shifted the emphasis from the tombs of emperors to commemoration of the apostles. Constantius' installation of the relics of Andrew, Luke, and Timothy in the church had strengthened that new orientation. A few years after Constantius' death one priest had already acknowledged this shift in perspective by describing the imperial mausoleum as "the celebrated shrine of the apostles who have welcomed and protected this revered [imperial] family." According to John Chrysostom, who became bishop of Constantinople in the late fourth century,

---

[27]   Council of Nicaea: Socrates, *HE* 1.8.5–11, 21–23 = Eusebius, *Vita Constantini* 3.7–9, 13–14, with Wallraff (1997) 41–55, on Socrates' use of sources for the council. Eusebius, *Vita Constantini* 3.10.3, angel, 12, speech, 15.2, kingdom, with Chapters 4, 11. Socrates, *HE* 1.9.27, opinion, commenting on Urkunde 25, ed. Opitz (1934–1935) 52–54, a letter to the people of Alexandria but not cited by Eusebius in *Vita Constantini*. For Socrates' reluctance to describe Constantine as a "friend of God," see Leppin (1996) 46, 197–202.

even the emperors conceded that they had been demoted. Now they were overjoyed to think they would be buried merely in the vestibule of the church. "Thereafter the emperors were the doorkeepers for the fishermen [the apostles]." In addition, eventually the emperors had to share this space, because by the time Socrates wrote his historical narrative the bishops of Constantinople were also being buried in this mausoleum. As a result, when Socrates described Constantine's burial, he even suggested that Constantine had constructed this shrine "so that emperors and bishops might not be far from the relics of the apostles." According to this interpretation, all along Constantine had intended to honor bishops as well as emperors.[28]

At almost the same time Sozomen was writing another ecclesiastical history that covered almost the same period as Socrates' narrative. Sozomen's ancestors had been prominent in a small town near Gaza and had converted to Christianity in the mid-fourth century. Sozomen himself, like the educated sons of so many provincial families, eventually made his way to Constantinople, where he apparently became an advocate in the law courts during the reign of Theodosius II. He also resolved to become a historian. Because celebrated Greek historians had already written about regions, cities, and mythology, Sozomen chose to write an ecclesiastical history. His initial plan was to survey all events "from the beginning." Then he discovered the accounts of earlier church historians, among them, in particular, Eusebius, "a very

---

[28] Shrine: Gregory of Nazianzus, *Orat.* 5.17, with Chapter 11. Fishermen: John Chrysostom, *Contra Iudaeos et gentiles quod Christus sit Deus* 9 (*PG* 48.825); also *Hom. in epistulam 11 ad Corinthios* 26.5 (*PG* 61.582): "What the doorkeepers are for emperors in their palaces, the emperors are for the fishermen in the tomb." Mango (1990), Effenberger (2000), Henck (2001) 289–91, and Dagron (2003) 138–41, distinguish Constantine's mausoleum from the later Church of the Holy Apostles; Leeb (1992) 93–103, and Odahl (2004) 269–71, argue that Constantine built the church and that his tomb was later moved to an adjacent mausoleum; Burgess (2003) 30, suggests that Constantine's tomb was eventually separated from the relics of the apostles because of "an important public or private sense of inappropriateness." Relics: Socrates, *HE* 1.40.2. In 438 Proclus, bishop of Constantinople, convinced the emperor Theodosius II to let him bury the body of John Chrysostom in the Church of the Holy Apostles: see Socrates, *HE* 7.45.2–4.

learned scholar of holy scriptures and of Greek poets and historians."
For this early period of church history Sozomen instead composed an
epitome in two books that covered events "from Christ's ascension into
the heavens to the destruction of Licinius." Rather than rewriting or
competing with Eusebius' *History*, Sozomen was content to abridge it.
His own original narrative of ecclesiastical history would be another
continuation of Eusebius' *History*.[29]

In his dedication to Theodosius II, Sozomen stated that he intended
to begin his narrative precisely in 324. This starting date coincided with
the end of the final edition of Eusebius' *History*, which had concluded
with Constantine's victory over Licinius in September 324. Sozomen
included his own version of Licinius' defeat. But he also included some
flashbacks to earlier events. One was the story of Constantine's visions
before his battle against Maxentius in 312. Since Sozomen explicitly
cited Eusebius as his source for Constantine's comments, he was familiar with Eusebius' *Life of Constantine*. He also modified that source
by highlighting the role of churchmen. In Eusebius' version Constantine had summoned Christian clerics to explain his visions. Sozomen
now supplemented Eusebius' account by letting these clerics add general comments about resurrection, salvation, and repentance. A second
flashback, to even earlier events, was a reference to Constantius, Constantine's father, who had confirmed and praised the Christian devotion
of court officials.[30]

Even though Sozomen planned to write a continuation of Eusebius'
*History* from 324, familiarity with Eusebius' *Life* had led him to a series
of false starts, going back first to Constantine's visions, then even farther

[29] Sozomen, *HE* 1.1.11–12, early plans, 2.3.10, mentioning an acquaintance "who is
working with us and arguing law cases in the same courts," 5.15.14–17, ancestors
in Palestine; with Grillet (1983), on Sozomen's life, and Leppin (1996) 279–81,
suggesting that Sozomen wrote his *HE* in the later 440s.
[30] Sozomen, *HE, Praefatio ad Theodosium imperatorem* 19, from third consulship of
Caesars Crispus and Constantine II to seventeenth consulship of Theodosius II,
i.e. from 324 to 439; *HE* 1.2.1, "when the Caesars Crispus and Constantine were
consuls," 1.3.2, cites Eusebius, 5–6, clerics, 1.6.1–3, Constantius, 1.7, Licinius'
defeat.

THE SEARCH FOR THE CHRISTIAN DOCTRINE 341

back to Constantius' support for Christianity. Thereafter Eusebius' *Life* was an important source for Sozomen's account of Constantine's reign. But Sozomen extensively supplemented his narrative with lengthy accounts of the spread of Christianity in the Persian empire and among the barbarians and of the importance of monks and ascetics, including Antony. His doctrinal preferences resembled those of his contemporary Socrates, including rejection of Arius' doctrines and acceptance of Nicene theology. He also agreed with Socrates' interpretation of Constantine's burial by stressing the presence of the bishops buried with the emperors in the mausoleum attached to the Church of the Holy Apostles. "Thereafter Christian emperors who died at Constantinople were buried [there]. So were bishops. The dignity of the priesthood, I think, is equal to that of the emperor, and in holy shrines it even takes precedence."[31]

A century after the emperor's death ecclesiastical historians were dubious about both Eusebius' theology and Constantine's depiction of his own tomb. This reappraisal then affected their estimation of the emperor himself. Eusebius had equated Jesus Christ and Constantine in order to promote his own theology. Constantine seems to have used the Church of the Holy Sepulcher in Jerusalem as the model for his mausoleum at Constantinople, in which he could likewise represent himself as the equivalent of Jesus Christ. But once other emperors and bishops were also buried with him, the mausoleum instead resembled the precincts around Jerusalem that were littered with tombs of both Old Testament kings and prophets. At Jerusalem the tomb of Jesus was always the primary attraction: "Constantine's Church [of the Holy Sepulcher] is in the middle of the city." But at Constantinople, once the relics of the apostles interred in the Church of the Holy Apostles had become the central focus, the tombs of Constantine and other emperors were off to the side. As a result, in the early fifth century historians

---

[31] Sozomen, *HE* 1.1.18, Persians, barbarians, monks, 1.13, Antony, 2.34.6, Christian emperors. For Sozomen's relationship with Socrates, see Hansen (1995) xlvi: "An der 'Tendenz' des Socrates brauchte er nicht viel zu ändern"; also Sabbah (1983), for an excellent comparison of Socrates' and Sozomen's treatments of Constantine.

who rejected Eusebius' theology also modified their views on Constantine. "Nicaean writers might be much cooler in their assessment of Constantine than the Arian Eusebius had been."[32]

These later historians furthermore adjusted their perspectives on Constantine in the light of subsequent emperors. In particular, in the later fourth century Theodosius would establish new paradigms for Christian emperorship. Rufinus hence explicitly linked Constantine and Theodosius, and Socrates and Sozomen read Constantine in the image of successor emperors like Theodosius. One emperor had merged into the other. But if Theodosius was now the touchstone for interpreting Constantine, the oddity is that Theodosius had fashioned his own emperorship after Constantine's example. Constantine remained a model for later emperors, even as in historical narratives he became a model of those same emperors. For these historians of the early and mid-fifth century, as Theodosius made himself into a "new Constantine," Constantine was increasingly seen as a "prior Theodosius."[33]

## READING THE LIFE OF CONSTANTINE

In ancient society a legacy was a powerful form of legitimacy. Constantine was thought to have resolved the uncertainty of his sole succession and the displacement of his half-brothers by emerging from Constantius' death chamber wearing "his father's purple robe." According to the biography composed by Athanasius, at the end of his life Antony had left a precious bequest for the beleaguered bishop: "give bishop

---

[32] Middle of the city: *Breviarius de Hierosolyma*, forma a, 1; this short survey was composed apparently in the early sixth century. For the representation of the Church of the Holy Sepulcher at the topographical center of Jerusalem on the Madaba Map, see Tsafrir (1999) 143: "In order to depict such a central position for the entrance to the church . . . , the artist had to distort the geographical reality." Quotation about Nicaean writers from Fowden (1994) 152.

[33] For later legends about Constantine, see Winkelmann (1973), (1978), Kazhdan (1987), and Lieu (1998), (2006) 317, "Constantine was reshaped to fit an imperial ideal suited to the demands of contemporary politics and culture." For a similar reinterpretation of the council of Nicaea in light of the council of Constantinople in 381, see Lim (1995) 182–216.

Athanasius one of the sheepskins and the cloak I used as a blanket. He gave the cloak to me new, and I wore it out." At his inauguration as emperor Theodosius was thought to have worn the cloak of Constantine. Clothed in the mantle of a significant predecessor, each emperor and each bishop wanted to present himself as the heir of a great tradition, whether imperial or ascetic.[34]

In late summer of 378 a force of Goths had defeated Valens and his army near Hadrianople in Thrace. Earlier in the year Valens had returned to Constantinople after an extended residence at Antioch; now his death left both the eastern frontier facing the Persian empire and the Balkan frontier regions exposed. Gratian, the senior emperor in the western provinces, soon appointed Theodosius as a general for troops along the Danube. There he revived his reputation for military success, and he was acclaimed as emperor in January 379. Because of the threat from the Goths in the Balkans, at first Theodosius resided primarily in Thessalonica.[35]

At the beginning of his reign Arian, neo-Arian, and so-called Homoian Arian theologies were still common and influential. Some of the successors to Constantine, such as his son Constantius in particular, had preferred to support Arianizing doctrines, and with their imperial patronage Arianizing bishops were often able to dominate their Nicene rivals. These emperors seem to have sensed that their imperial authority might benefit from the political implications of even modified versions of Arius' sort of subordinationist theology. If Jesus Christ the Son was still somehow subordinate to God the Father, "similar in essence" or merely "similar" but not fully "identical in essence," then it was still possible to imagine that an emperor might be coordinate to the Son. Constantius, for instance, referred to himself as "My Eternity" when he dictated his official documents. In return, Arianizing bishops might be

---

[34] Constantius' robe: Eusebius, *Vita Constantini* 1.22.1. Antony's cloak: Athanasius, *Vita Antonii* 91.8. Constantine's cloak: George the Monk, *Chronicon* 9.8, ed. de Boor (1978) 2:563.

[35] For the suggestion that Theodosius' acclamation as emperor was unsanctioned, see McLynn (2005) 88–100.

more deferential to an emperor whom they linked so closely with God. In fact, Nicene opponents complained that Arianizing bishops seemed to pay more respect to the emperor than to Jesus Christ. Athanasius once mocked the preface to the "Dated Creed," a confession that had claimed that the Son was merely "similar in all respects" to the Father. Athanasius was upset that the authors of this creed had been so deferential to Constantius: "those who called him 'eternal emperor' refused [to call] the Son 'everlasting.'" "They address Constantius, rather than Christ, as 'Lord.'"[36]

The eastern emperor Valens had likewise supported Arianizing doctrines, in particular during the final years of his reign. Although his primary concern was the establishment of concord within Christianity, the bishops whose doctrines he favored were eager to taunt their opponents by citing the emperor's authority: "you are opposing imperial edicts and the desire of the emperor Valens." This intimidation tainted Valens' reputation, and already during his reign Nicene clerics had classified him as a persecutor, similar to the Tetrarchic emperors. Then divine providence seemed to reinforce that judgment. Once Valens was killed in battle against the Goths in 378, Nicene churchmen and historians were quick to argue that his heterodox theology had contributed to the disaster.[37]

In contrast, Theodosius expressed his firm support for Nicene (or neo-Nicene) theology from the beginning. In an edict issued about a year after his accession he promoted the "evangelical doctrine" of "a

---

[36] "Aeternitas mea": Ammianus Marcellinus, *Res gestae* 15.1.3, with Pietri (1989) 146–50, on Constantius' pretensions, and Humphries (1997), (1998), for the demonization of Constantius by Nicene churchmen. Athanasius' taunts: Athanasius, *De synodis* 3.2, eternal emperor, 4.3, Lord, quoted in Socrates, *HE* 2.37.35, 48, paraphrased in Sozomen, *HE* 4.17.10; with Hanson (1988) 362–71, discussing this creed drawn up in 359. For the deference of Arian bishops toward Constantius, see Setton (1941) 78–88, Williams (1951a) 19–26, (1951b) 6–15, and Dvornik (1966) 724–62.

[37] Imperial edicts: Epiphanius, *Panarion* 69.34.1, with Lenski (2002) 241–63, surveying Valens' support for Homoian Arianism, and Brennecke (1988) 240: "In vieler Hinsicht ist die Kirchenpolitik des Valens der des Konstantin fast näher als der des Konstantius." For the characterization of Valens and his magistrates as "Tetrarchs," see Chapter 6. For reactions to Valens' defeat, see Lenski (1997).

single divinity of the Father, Son, and Holy Spirit." Early in 381 he issued another edict that condemned the "poison of the Arian sacrilege" and endorsed the "Nicene faith" of an "undivided essence of the unadulterated Trinity." Later in that year he summoned bishops to meet in a council at Constantinople that reaffirmed Nicene doctrines. Unlike Constantine at the council of Nicaea, Theodosius did not attend the sessions of this council. But his subsequent behavior might seem to suggest that he intended to follow Constantine's lead by championing a particular orthodoxy and likening himself to a bishop. Immediately after the council he issued an edict that backed those bishops who confessed the "Nicene faith" by stating that "the Father, the Son, and the Holy Spirit are of one majesty and power, of the same glory, and of one splendor." While attending services in churches he differentiated himself from other lay members by sitting with the clerics, and he occasionally confronted bishops over religious issues. Eventually Theodosius transformed this legacy into a form of imperial legitimation. After the death of his first wife he married Galla, a sister of the emperor Valentinian II and a half-sister of the emperor Gratian. Establishing a link with the dynasty of his fellow emperors was one important concern; but Galla was also attractive as a bride because she was quite likely a great-great-granddaughter of Constantine. Through this marriage Theodosius blended Constantine into his own family and made him an ancestor of his own imperial dynasty. As a result, when Theodosius was imagined to be rejoined with his family members in heaven after his death, the reunion included Constantine.[38]

Despite this awareness of Constantine's legacy, Theodosius seems not to have shared his predecessor's pretensions of so explicitly identifying himself with Jesus Christ. Arian Christianity had opened the possibility that an emperor might be an analogue of Jesus Christ, and with his preference for retaining the identification of emperor and deity

---

[38] *CTh* 16.1.2, single divinity; 16.1.3, one majesty, issued July 30, 381; 16.5.6, poison. Seating: Sozomen, *HE* 7.25.9, with Van Dam (2002) 136–53, on Theodosius' behavior at Constantinople. For the pedigree of Galla and Valentinian II, see Chapter 3; also Chausson (2002b) 149–50, for the suggestion that Theodosius was a distant descendant of Constantius I. Reunion: Ambrose, *De obitu Theodosii* 40.

Constantine had been a Christian version of a Tetrarchic emperor. In contrast, Theodosius accepted a model of imperial rulership derived from Nicene theology, and he opposed both the Tetrarchic paradigm and the Arian model. With his acknowledgment of the dependence of emperors on bishops and monks, Theodosius instead became a Christian version of an Old Testament king.

Theodosius had several models of emperorship to evaluate. One represented a political philosophy that corresponded to orthodox Nicene theology. In 383 Theodosius offered some heterodox churchmen one last opportunity to win his support. One participant in this "council of all heresies" was Eunomius, a noted Cappadocian theologian. Because Eunomius championed a neo-Arian theology that argued that the Son was not just subordinate to God the Father but totally dissimilar, he probably knew he had little chance of convincing the emperor. So he adopted a more oblique tactic. In addition to presenting his doctrines, Eunomius delicately appealed to the emperor's vanity. In his exposition of his faith Eunomius claimed that the Son of God had only shared "the paternal empire," and that he had received glory from the Father but without partaking in the Father's own glory. Earlier in that year Theodosius had proclaimed his son Arcadius as an Augustus, a senior emperor. Arcadius was still a young child, about five or six years old. Eunomius now seemed to be implying, through an unspoken analogy with his own Trinitarian theology, that even though Theodosius and his son had the same nominal standing as senior emperors, in fact Theodosius could think that he still far outranked his young son with whom he had shared some of his glory. Eunomius was essentially inviting the emperor to consider adopting a subordinationist theology that would have provided a useful parallel for highlighting his own primacy over his co-emperor, his young son, and to make a decision based on political expediency rather than on religious correctness. In presenting his doctrines Eunomius was appealing to current politics and not merely theology.[39]

[39] For the council in 383 and Eunomius' theology, see Van Dam (2003b) 15–45. Son of God: Eunomius, *Expositio fidei* 3, with Peterson (1935) 94, for the political

But Theodosius was not so easily flattered. Another churchman pointedly demonstrated the practical implications of the theological doctrine that God the Son was inferior to God the Father. This churchman greeted Theodosius with respectful deference, but addressed his son as "child" and caressed him with his hand. The emperor was outraged. Rather than elevating himself over his son, he wanted to promote Arcadius' imperial credentials in order to begin establishing a Theodosian dynasty of emperors in the East as a balance to Gratian and Valentinian II, the emperors in the western provinces who were the last survivors of the dynasty of their father, Valentinian I, and their uncle, Valens. To offset their dynasty Theodosius needed his son to be a co-emperor who was of identical standing. Because of these political ambitions, he had no sympathy for a doctrine of subordination, and he now rejected both Eunomius' theology and its political implications. Even as Theodosius endorsed the Nicene doctrine that the Father and the Son were coordinate, he was tacitly acknowledging that he and his son were coequal senior emperors. The subordination of the son to the father was now both heretical theology and heterodox political philosophy.[40]

A second model of imperial rulership was derived from the Old Testament. In 388 Theodosius invaded northern Italy and defeated the usurper Magnus Maximus. Soon after taking up residence in Italy he heard about the destruction of a synagogue at Callinicum, a garrison town on the eastern frontier. When Theodosius ordered the local bishop to rebuild the synagogue and the hooligans to be punished, Ambrose, the popular bishop of Milan, protested and tried to convince the emperor to withdraw these penalties. In a sermon Ambrose recalled a story from the Old Testament about king David, who had repented after the prophet Nathan pointed out his sins. This story was meant

---

implications of Eunomius' theology, and Kopecek (1979) 523–24, for the linkage of Eunomius' doctrines with Theodosius' promotion of Arcadius.

[40] Theodosius' son: Sozomen, *HE* 7.6; Theodoret, *HE* 5.16, identified this churchman as bishop Amphilochius of Iconium. Heather (1991) 172–73, interprets the promotion of Arcadius as Theodosius' tactic for distancing himself from the western emperor Gratian. In 386 Theodosius and Arcadius celebrated a triumph together at Constantinople: see *Consularia Constantinopolitana* s.a. 386.

to be a warning for Theodosius: "I am altering the words [to speak] not only about you but also to you." The emperor obviously listened closely to the bishop's remarks: "You have preached about me." As a display of benevolence he now promised Ambrose, in the middle of this service, that he would abandon his investigation of the incident. In 390 Ambrose held Theodosius responsible for the massacre of civilians at Thessalonica, which had been ordered as reprisal for the murder of a military commander. In a letter to the emperor Ambrose again reminded Theodosius of the penance of king David. Like David, the emperor too should confess his mistake: "I have sinned against the Lord." Then he would enjoy the same outcome: "through that display of humility he became more pleasing to God." By citing these "examples of kings" from the Old Testament, Ambrose had defined a model of Christian emperorship that was based on humility, piety, and gentleness. In this paradigm the emperor was certainly not an analogue of Jesus Christ. As Ambrose pointedly reminded Theodosius, "you are a man, and temptation has come to you." Instead, the emperor was a sinner like king David who would benefit from the reproof of a new Nathan, a bishop such as Ambrose.[41]

A final model of emperorship represented the lingering influence of the Tetrarchic emperors. After returning Valentinian II to power, Theodosius left Italy. Valentinian resided at first in northern Gaul, but in spring of 392 he was found dead in Vienne. Since the circumstances of his death were unclear, the Frankish general Arbogast was blamed as a conspirator. By the end of summer he was supporting Eugenius as emperor at Lyon. Eugenius was a former teacher of Latin rhetoric who had previously served in the palace bureaucracy. In the next year the new emperor moved to Italy, where he was recognized at Rome. Even wary senators nevertheless concluded they could deal with a usurper who

---

[41] Callinicum: Ambrose, *Ep. extra collectionem* 1(41).25, David and Nathan, 26, words, 27, about me, 28, promise; also *Ep.* 74(40).22, "Do you not remember what Christ ordered of the holy David through the prophet Nathan?" Thessalonica: Ambrose, *Ep. extra collectionem* 11(51).7, sinned, 9, humility, 11, examples, man; McLynn (1994) 315–330, interprets Theodosius' ritual humiliation as "a public relations triumph for the emperor" (p. 323).

was prepared to reaffirm the entitlement of Rome to benefit from the provinces. To Symmachus, who was now collecting exotic gladiators to fight in public games in honor of his son's new office, Eugenius presented twenty-nine Saxon warriors, presumably captured during his recent campaigns on the Rhine frontier. Eugenius also reappointed the illustrious senator Virius Nicomachus Flavianus as prefect of Italy and designated him as consul. Flavianus took advantage of the uncertain times to affirm his devotion to traditional pagan cults. At Rome he now ostentatiously celebrated a series of pagan festivals, while his son, who was serving as prefect of Rome, restored a temple of Venus. At Ostia another magistrate rebuilt a temple of Hercules. Flavianus' influence had colored Eugenius' usurpation in a defiantly pagan hue.[42]

Before returning to Constantinople, Theodosius already had issued edicts that outlawed participation in pagan cults. Now he promoted Honorius, his younger son, as a senior emperor and prepared to march west again. In the summer of 394 Theodosius' army met Eugenius' army at the Frigidus River near Aquileia. By now Eugenius was presenting himself effectively as a neo-Tetrarchic emperor, entering battle with the support of Jupiter and Hercules. In the foothills of the Alps overlooking the battlefield he set up statues of Jupiter, each brandishing a thunderbolt fashioned from gold. During the battle his army was led by an image of Hercules. But Theodosius' army, led by a military standard in the shape of a cross, was victorious. Eugenius was defeated, captured, and killed; his supporters Arbogast and Flavianus committed suicide. Now a triumphant Theodosius could mock the false confidence his opponents had placed in their image of Hercules.[43]

---

[42] For Eugenius' early career, see *PLRE* 1:293, "Fl. Eugenius 6," and Kaster (1988) 403–4. Saxon gladiators: Symmachus, *Ep.* 2.46, "hanc munificentiam principis," with Chapter 2, for the campaigns. Virius Nicomachus Flavianus: *Carmen contra paganos* 103–9, pagan festivals, 113–14, temple of Venus, with Matthews (1970), (1975) 238–47, and O'Donnell (1978), for the identification of Flavianus as the subject of this poem. For the dedication of the temple of Hercules at Ostia, see Bloch (1945) 201, (1963) 200, reprinted in *L'année épigraphique 1948* (1949) 50, no. 127.

[43] Edicts: *CTh* 16.10.10–12. Statues of Jupiter: Augustine, *De civitate Dei* 5.26. Theodoret, *HE* 5.24.4, image of Hercules, cross, 17, mockery. Note that bishop

The reign of Theodosius hence marked important changes in the longstanding discourse about emperorship and religion. A whole series of different ideologies was now discarded. First, the customary notion that the rule of emperors still represented a revival of the old Roman Republic was thoroughly destabilized. When the future bishop Paulinus of Nola evaluated Theodosius soon after the emperor's death in 395, he redefined in Christian terms the conventional Republican titles that emperors had long ago purloined. As a senior statesman Augustus had been known as *princeps*, first citizen, and to ensure his association with the army he had used the title of *imperator*, commander. But according to Paulinus' eulogy, Theodosius had owed his standing as *princeps* not to his imperial rule but to his faith; and he should now be hailed not as *imperator*, but simply as *Christi servus*, a "servant of Christ" noted for his humility. Augustus' Roman revolution had reached its end. Augustus had appropriated traditional terminology to characterize his standing as a Republican emperor; Paulinus now subverted the same terminology to define Theodosius' standing as a Christian emperor.[44]

Second, more recent notions of emperorship were also now obsolete. With the defeat of Eugenius the Age of the Tetrarchs was definitively over, and emperors would no longer be identified with pagan deities like Jupiter and Hercules. With the reassertion of Nicene theology at the council of Constantinople Eusebius' Age of Constantine was also over, and emperors would no longer support Arian-style doctrines or identify themselves with Jesus Christ. After the council of Constantinople, emperors, historians, and churchmen all rejected Eusebius' construction of a Christian emperor whose standing as an analogue of Jesus Christ could reinforce Arian theology. Augustus the Republican emperor, Diocletian the Tetrarchic emperor, Constantine the Arian

Ambrose explained his absence to Eugenius by citing an ancient story about the reluctance of Jews to contribute to a sacrifice for Hercules: see Ambrose, *Ep. extra collectionem* 10(57).9.

[44] Eulogy: Paulinus of Nola, *Ep.* 28.6, with Chapter 3, for Maxentius' use of *princeps*, and Van Dam (1985a) 155–56, for the concurrent process of the Christian redefinition of traditional aristocratic values.

emperor as imagined by Eusebius: all these models for a Christian emperor were now outdated.[45]

## VISIONS

The contrast between Constantine and Theodosius was most apparent in their visions. Before his battle at the Milvian Bridge over the Tiber River, Constantine had claimed that he had had a vision of a cross in the sky and subsequently another vision in which Christ himself had urged him to use the symbol as protection against his enemies. Before his battle at the Frigidus River, Theodosius also claimed to have had a vision in which he had seen two men, clothed in white and riding white horses. These men identified themselves as the evangelist John and the apostle Philip and offered to help. In their respective dreams, while Constantine had talked with Jesus Christ himself, Theodosius now spoke only with Jesus' disciples. Theodosius was furthermore thought to have prepared for this battle by praying with clerics at the shrines of martyrs and apostles. He also requested the advice of John of Lycopolis, a monk in Egypt who had been blessed with the "gift of prophecy." As an analogue of Jesus Christ, Constantine had been considered a "friend of God"; but Theodosius was now only a "friend of Christ" who consulted with God's other representatives on earth, bishops and monks.[46]

[45] For the end of Tetrarchic ideology, see Kolb (2004) 36: "Ambrosius von Mailand entsakralisiert den Herrscher. . . . Damit endete das göttliche Wesen des tetrarchischen Kaisertums." These older models of emperorship did not disappear entirely, however. The attractions of the "Arian" model in particular lingered for centuries. In sixth-century Italy the Arian Ostrogothic kings were separated from ordinary parishioners during the celebration of mass by drinking from a separate chalice: see Gregory of Tours, *Historiae* 3.31. For the persistent notion in the Middle Ages of a king as human by nature but "a Christ by grace," see Kantorowicz (1957) 42–61.

[46] Constantine's visions: Eusebius, *Vita Constantini* 1.28.2–29. Theodoret, *HE* 5.24.1–2, John of Lycopolis, 2, ὁ φιλόχριστος . . . βασιλεύς, 5–6, Theodosius' vision, with Paschoud (1979–2000) 2.2:474–500, for a thorough discussion of the different accounts of the battle at the Frigidus River, and Bloch (1945) 240: "The battle . . . symbolizes the end of an age with unusual clarity." Praying with clerics: Rufinus, *HE* 11.33. Gift: Palladius, *Historia Lausiaca* 35.2.

In his historical writings Eusebius had compared Constantine to
Moses, who had liberated his people from the oppression of tyrants.
Constantine had likewise promoted an exalted standing for himself as
a Christian emperor, by lightheartedly identifying himself as a bishop,
by presiding at the council of Nicaea, by seeming to appropriate some
of the functions of Jesus Christ. In contrast, Ambrose had compared
Theodosius to king David, who had acknowledged his sins and sought
forgiveness. By the end of his reign Theodosius himself seems to have
accepted this new image of an emperor who was respectful of bishops and monks. One tradition even claimed that after his victory over
Eugenius this "Christian emperor" had acknowledged his respect for
Ambrose by kneeling at the bishop's feet. Both Constantine and Eusebius would have been astonished at this deference. With regard to behavior, expectations, and image, Constantine would have hardly recognized
Theodosius as a Christian emperor.[47]

Thereafter this new paradigm defined Christian emperorship. At
the council of Chalcedon in 451 the emperor Marcian decided to take
"Constantine of divine memory as a guide." By leading one session
Marcian was imitating Constantine's role of presiding at the council
of Nicaea; and in fact, after the emperor's oration to the council the
assembled bishops did hail him as "new Constantine." At the end of
the session after the approval of a statement of faith the bishops again
hailed him as "new Constantine." But this time they also elaborated with
two additional acclamations. One was "new David." This acclamation
honored the emperor as an associate of Jesus Christ's royal lineage, and
it also reminded him of the respect he was to show for the bishops
themselves. The second additional acclamation was "new Paul." This
acclamation implied that the emperor was to take the lead in spreading
and enforcing the new definition of orthodox Christianity. Marcian,
the most recent "new Constantine," was now an analogue, not of Jesus
Christ, but of the greatest king of the Old Testament, the ancestor of
the Messiah, and the most important apostle of the New Testament, the

---

47   Christian emperor: Paulinus of Milan, *Vita Ambrosii* 31.

messenger of the Christian faith. Eusebius had constructed an image of Constantine that both derived from and supported his theology. Now bishops constructed an image of a New Constantine that was modeled on biblical exemplars.[48]

---

[48] Council of Chalcedon, *Actio* 6.4, guide, 5, New Constantine, 11, New Constantine, New David, New Paul, ed. Schwartz (1933–1935) 2:140, 155.

# ONE EMPEROR

## EPILOGUE

ITHIN CLASSICAL GREEK CULTURE PERHAPS NO POEMS
were more venerated than the *Iliad* and the *Odyssey*.
Because of their prestige, these Homeric epics soon
became revered texts for religious mythologies and political ideologies. In the Roman empire the citation of a single verse from
the *Iliad* still offered an opportunity both to comment on political
affairs and to shape them. The *Iliad* had once described a challenge to
king Agamemnon's leadership over the Greek coalition that was resolved
with the assertion that he had received his scepter directly from Zeus. In
the early first century the emperor Gaius alluded to this dispute when
he announced that "there should be one ruler and one *basileus*." In its
immediate context, a quarrel among bickering client kings, this citation seemed quite relevant, since the emperor was clearly establishing his
priority as the dominant *basileus*, "king." Yet in a larger context Gaius'
citation of this Homeric verse was also quite disconcerting, because the
legitimating ideology of the newly established emperors had emphasized their restoration of the old Roman Republic, whose own political
ideology had always opposed the revival of a kingship. Gaius' use of this

quotation was hence openly supportive of his imperial authority and implicitly subversive to the prevailing Republican political ideology.[1]

Eventually *basileus* became the standard Greek term for "emperor" in the eastern provinces, and people could cite this verse without concern for its overtones about kingship. Yet this Homeric verse retained its potentially challenging implications. In the early fourth century a Christian in Palestine quoted this same verse in a confrontation with imperial magistrates who had ordered him to sacrifice to pagan gods and make an offering to the emperors. By citing this verse the Christian intended to demonstrate his exclusive allegiance to his God, the "Emperor" of all; but the magistrates understood his citation as a seditious comment about the Tetrarchy, the college of four emperors who then shared joint rulership. In this situation too this quotation carried a dual significance. The magistrates executed the Christian for political insubordination in seeming to endorse only one emperor at a time when there happened to be four, while the Christian thought he was earning his martyrdom through single-minded loyalty to his Emperor in heaven. In both of these cases, Gaius' demented arrogance and the Christian's passion for martyrdom, the participants were appealing to conflicting interpretations of a revered verse. Soon Christians would replace this controversy over a Homeric verse with new disputes over biblical verses that were equally open to multiple interpretations.[2]

During the reign of Constantine the arena of this interaction between religion and political philosophy was largely transferred from pagan cults and classical mythology to Christian doctrines and liturgical festivals. At first a discourse over Trinitarian theology provided a medium for defining the essence of a Christian emperor in Roman society; eventually discussion of Christian doctrines helped people to articulate all aspects

---

[1] Gaius: Suetonius, *Gaius Caligula* 22.1, citing Homer, *Iliad* 2.204–5, εἷς βασιλεύς, with Peterson (1935), a path-breaking commentary on the political implications of monotheism that takes its inspiration from this Homeric verse.

[2] Persecution: Eusebius, *De martyribus Palaestinae* 1.1, with Carriker (2003) 131–33, for Eusebius' familiarity with Homer.

of Roman society, both ecclesiastical and imperial. In 357 while visiting Rome, the emperor Constantius responded to a petition to resolve a dispute over the city's episcopacy. Constantius' solution was to allow two bishops, until people ridiculed his proposal in their acclamations: "One God, one Christ, one bishop." In the later fourth century the Gallic teacher Ausonius celebrated Easter with a poem about the members of the Trinity, who included a Beloved Father, "your Son" who was "completely similar and equal," and the Spirit. Ausonius hence emphasized a "threefold faith" but only "one maker." He then flattered the emperor Valentinian with a comparison to this Trinity. Valentinian too was the "progenitor" who had made twin emperors by promoting first his brother, Valens, and then his son, Gratian. Valentinian had shared his "one empire" but without dividing it; the emperors flourished with "a threefold piety." In the later seventh century soldiers from central Asia Minor were so upset at the plan of Constantine IV to deprive his two brothers of participation in imperial rule that they threatened a mutiny: "We believe in a Trinity; let us crown three emperors." In all these cases important issues of Trinitarian disputes, ideas about Oneness and Threeness, had spilled over to become slogans that shaped opinions about bishops and emperors.[3]

In this discourse over Christian theology and political philosophy Constantine had had a unique standing. He was not just a symbolic medium like Jesus Christ, whom churchmen like Eusebius of Caesarea represented in doctrines and images that reinforced their own beliefs. Constantine was also a direct participant who had his own ideas about orthodox theology, as well as about his reign as emperor. Already during his lifetime churchmen were constructing various images of Constantine; but at the same time Constantine was constructing himself, by joking that he too was a bishop, by respectfully listening to bishops' sermons, by presenting himself as an analogue of Jesus Christ.

---

[3] Constantius: Theodoret, *HE* 2.17.6. Valentinian: Ausonius, *Versus paschales* 16–31. Constantine IV: Theophanes, *Chronographia* a.m. 6161, with the commentary in Mango and Scott (1997) 492; Constantine IV eventually deposed and mutilated his brothers.

Constantine was looking for an identity; he too was trying to imagine a Christian emperor.

But Christianity, or even religion in general, was not the only strategy available, to Constantine and to others, for imagining the emperor. As the chapters in the first two sections of this book have demonstrated, Constantine had to decide whether he should be a Roman emperor who ignored Rome in favor of New Rome, or a Latin emperor in the Greek East. Some of his subjects had already made up their minds. The people of Hispellum appealed to Constantine with the hope that he would return to central Italy and Rome; the people of Orcistus wanted to show themselves as Latin Romans in their petition to the emperor. Constantine furthermore had to decide which of his ancestors to highlight, and who would be his successors. For constructing Constantine, both then and now, we modern historians need to respect all these different options and decisions.

In the end Constantine seems to have concluded that perhaps Christianity was incompatible with emperorship. After his baptism he appeared like a typical initiate dressed in white, clothed in "bright imperial robes that gleamed like light." In contrast, he now declined to touch his purple robes. Like Diocletian, Constantine seems to have abdicated. Now he was no longer a Christian emperor; instead, he had resolved the tension between Christianity and emperorship by giving up his imperial rule. Now he was just a baptized Christian.[4]

## JULIAN THE THEOLOGIAN

Julian was one of the few Roman emperors who had carefully studied Christian theology. Before he had been allowed to study classical Greek culture with famous teachers, he had been raised as a Christian. During his teenage years he had been exiled to Cappadocia, where he had read the Christian books in the library of a local churchman. Those books

---

[4] Robes: Eusebius, *Vita Constantini* 4.62.5, with Speck (1995) 144, on the implications of Constantine's baptism: "Daß man ihn kurz vor seinem Tode . . .getauft hat, war bereits der erste Schritt zu seiner Reduzierung auf ein christliches Normalmaß."

had apparently included some of Eusebius' apologetic treatises. After Julian revealed his support for pagan cults, however, he of course tried to exorcize that Christian upbringing. Now he dismissed Eusebius as a "scoundrel" for an exaggerated assertion. Now he repeatedly belittled Christians as "Galilaeans," as if they were members of only a small regional sect. Most importantly, now he hoped to destroy those "many volumes of the doctrines of the impious Galilaeans" that he had once read.[5]

The reign of Julian provides a concise summation of the themes discussed in this book. Julian was the first emperor to have been born in Constantinople. As a young man he studied in cities around the old Greek world of the Aegean; as a junior emperor he commanded troops on the Rhine frontier; as a senior emperor he marched through the Balkans to Constantinople, and then through Asia Minor to Antioch in anticipation of a campaign against the Persian empire. Rome was peripheral in Julian's empire, and he never visited the old capital. Instead, Julian wanted to present himself as a Greek emperor who promoted classical culture and pagan cults. Even though he had clearly benefited from his membership in the Constantinian dynasty, Julian begrudged his uncle Constantine and his cousin Constantius. His preference for Greekness was one way to distinguish himself from both the Latin background of Constantine and his sons and their Christianity. Julian's reign hence complements Constantine's reign as another demonstration of the rise of Constantinople at the expense of Rome, the increasing importance of the northern and eastern frontiers, the tension between Latin and Greek culture in the eastern provinces, and the uncertainties of imperial support for Christianity or pagan cults.

Julian was furthermore a keen observer of emperors and imperial rule. Not only had he obviously thought about Constantine and his sons;

---

[5] Eusebius the scoundrel: Julian, *Contra Galilaeos* 222A, objecting to the claim of Eusebius, *Praeparatio evangelica* 11.5 (*PG* 21.852D), that Moses and David had written "what the Greeks call heroic verse." Many volumes: Julian, *Ep.* 23; also *Ep.* 38, with Van Dam (2002) 173–74, for Julian's use of Georgius' library in Cappadocia.

he had also analyzed the Tetrarchic system. Because he had started out as a junior emperor appointed by his cousin Constantius, then been proclaimed as an Augustus by his troops, and finally emerged in 361 as the only emperor, Julian had personal experience of subordination, insubordination, and preeminence. When he wrote a treatise about his predecessors, he could hence appreciate the intuitive blend of hierarchy and harmony in the original Tetrarchy. Diocletian's three colleagues had "clasped hands, but did not walk beside him; instead, they surrounded him like a chorus." At the same time, however, "when they wished to precede him like bodyguards, he objected, because he did not consider himself worthy of having more [authority]." But Julian also knew that the Tetrarchic system of multiple emperors, a "perfectly harmonious chorus of four," had been flawed from the beginning by its inherent ideological and practical contradictions. As a junior emperor he had himself rebelled; as the sole emperor he did not designate a co-emperor even when he was about to set out on a dangerous invasion of the Persian empire. Julian was a neo-Tetrarchic emperor who resolved the tension between hierarchy and harmony by not appointing any imperial colleagues.[6]

Thinking about emperors was an additional incentive to think about religions, both his preferred pagan cults and the Christianity he had rejected. The political ideology of the Tetrarchic system had had theological underpinnings, and the ongoing controversies over Christian doctrines had likewise combined theology with political philosophy. Because Julian too tended to define himself and Roman society in religious terms, he understood that a discourse about theology was also a discourse about emperorship. Eventually he adopted a new tactic in his disparagement of Christianity. Rather than simply denying his Christian education, he would use his familiarity with biblical texts and ecclesiastical controversies to compose an intellectual refutation of "Galilaean" beliefs. As he explained to a bishop, he hoped to demonstrate that "that

---

[6] Julian, *Caesares* 315A-C, with Introduction, for additional discussion of the circumstances for the composition of this treatise. Note that Julian was the last emperor with the title of Caesar: see Kolb (2001) 105.

new Galilaean God had been stripped of his divinity by his disgraceful death and burial." In the process, however, Julian also reconceptualized the pagan theology of the Tetrarchy.[7]

Julian wrote his book about Christianity during the winter at Antioch when he wrote his satirical treatise about Roman emperors. On the eve of his campaign against the Persian empire, the two topics on his mind were emperorship and Christianity. In his book he criticized Christianity for its rejection of the teachings of both "Hellenes" and "Hebrews." He considered Christianity to be a "heresy" twice over, once for discarding the claims of Greek philosophers and the pagan cults that together defined Greekness, and again for distorting the beliefs of Judaism in the Old Testament. He hence aimed his attacks directly at contemporary Christian doctrines about the divinity of Jesus Christ. In his estimation, Christians had ignored the Jewish commandment prohibiting worship of other gods. "If God wishes that no [other] god be worshipped, why do you worship his bastard Son?" In subsequent arguments Julian disputed claims about a "second God, whether similar or dissimilar," assertions about the "only-begotten Son of God," and explanations about the standing of the Virgin Mary as "Theotokos," the God-Bearer. The New Testament only confirmed his skepticism. "Neither Paul nor Matthew nor Luke nor Mark dared to call Jesus 'God.'" Despite his distaste for Christianity, Julian was quite well-informed about ongoing debates over theology.[8]

---

[7] New Galilaean God: Julian, *Ep.* 55.

[8] Julian, *Contra Galilaeos* 43A, "heresy of the Galilaeans," 155C, commandment, 159E, bastard Son, 253C, second God, 262D, only-begotten Son of God, Theotokos, 327A, Paul, with the discussion of Smith (1995) 190–218. For the moment of composition, see Libanius, *Orat.* 18.178: "while winter extended the nights, he engaged those books that presented the man from Palestine as a god or a son of god."

Julian's devotion to classical philosophy has overshadowed his familiarity with Christian theology. Although Bouffartigue (2004) 129, characterizes the emperor as "un théologien curieux," he carefully argues that Julian relied entirely on his earlier study of philosophy when writing *Contra Galilaeos*. As a result, modern handbooks of the development of Christian doctrines consistently overlook Julian's writings. His skill as an anti-Christian theologian nevertheless deserves

This familiarity with Christian doctrines also affected Julian's elaboration of pagan beliefs, and in one of his odder arguments he recast Zeus in the image of the Christian God. Just as some Christian churchmen argued that Jesus Christ was begotten from God, so Julian claimed that Zeus had begotten Asclepius, a god of healing, "from himself." Like Jesus, Asclepius had then appeared "in the guise of a man," and "over the entire earth he had stretched out his right hand of salvation." In the process of disputing Christian doctrines Julian articulated pagan theology by using Christian terminology and concepts.[9]

Although he had grown to adulthood in a Tetrarchic environment, Constantine had become a post-Tetrarchic Christian emperor with strong opinions about both the godliness of his emperorship and the importance of an orthodox Christian theology. As a neo-Tetrarchic pagan emperor Julian was equally fluent in the discourse about emperors and gods. Since he had been raised as a Christian, he also had an inkling of how political philosophy and Christian theology had intersected over the previous decades. The crucial prelude to the controversy over Arian and Nicene doctrines had not been the confrontation between bishop Alexander and his priest Arius. Instead, it had been the use of pagan theology as a medium to explain the rule of the multiple emperors in the Tetrarchy. Constantine's gradual conversion to Christianity had then shifted this discourse from pagan theology to Christian theology, from Jupiter and his offspring to God, his Son, and his emperor. Julian was now continuing the debate by reversing the interaction. In the past Christian theologians had been influenced

more study. One source for his familiarity with Christian doctrines was probably Aetius, a theologian and sometime bishop who focused on the rational metaphysics of the relationship between God the Father and his Son: see Julian, *Contra Galilaeos* 347B, "one of the most knowledgeable bishops said this to me," with Van Dam (2003b) 15–30, for Aetius' career and interaction with Julian. In addition, the churchmen of late antiquity certainly took him seriously; for the threat posed by Julian's knowledge of the Bible, see Wilken (1999).

[9] Julian, *Contra Galilaeos* 200A, Zeus and Asclepius. Note that Julian's ideas about the roles of pagan priests were likewise modeled on the example of Christian altruism: see Van Dam (2002) 171–73.

by the ideas of a Tetrarchic theology, and they had articulated their own ideas about Christian emperorship through the medium of their disputes over Christian theology. Now the interplay between Christian theology and pagan doctrines had rotated, and Julian was restating neo-Tetrarchic theology under the influence of Christian doctrines. Even as he hoped to refute Christian doctrines, he appropriated Christian terminology to articulate relationships among pagan gods. One outcome of Constantine's Roman revolution was the lingering influence of a Christian perspective on the religious outlook of even a post-Christian emperor.

# HISPELLUM: DATE, TEXT, AND TRANSLATION

## APPENDIX ONE

THE BEST TEXTS OF CONSTANTINE'S RESCRIPT TO HISPELLUM are in *ILS* 1:158–59, no. 705, and Gascou (1967) 610–12, both derived from the edition of E. Bormann in *CIL* 11.2.1:768, no. 5265. Gascou's text is printed and translated here. Also included here is a summary of Gascou's important comments about the numerous oddities in grammar and spelling. For photographs, see Andreotti (1964), facing p. 288, and Lenski (2006a), Figure 4, with the comprehensive survey of earlier scholarship in Amann (2002).

Constantine himself had insisted that edicts and constitutions that did not include an exact date were invalid: see *CTh* 1.1.1, issued in 322. Even though his original rescript to Hispellum had undoubtedly included a date, the inscribed copy erected in the town did not. The dating of the rescript hence depends upon interpretation of the college of emperors in its heading. The heading described Constantine as Augustus, mentioned his three sons, Constantine, Constantius, and Constans, but gave them no titles. Constans joined his two older brothers as a Caesar after his investiture on December 25, 333: for the date, see *Consularia Constantinopolitana* s.a. 333. The younger Dalmatius, Constantine's nephew, joined his three cousins as a Caesar after his investiture on

September 18, 335: for the date, see *Consularia Constantinopolitana* s.a. 335. Grünewald (1990) 150–53, hence dates the rescript between these two dates.

Suggestions for other dates, earlier or later, require too much special pleading. Tabata (1995) 371–86, proposes an earlier date. Because the inscribed version of the rescript did not include titles for the three sons, Tabata suggests that this copy was inscribed before Constans became a Caesar in late 333. The engraver included Constans' name in anticipation of his investiture and eventually planned to fill in the blank space at the end of the preamble (line 6) with the identical titles for all the sons. Tabata furthermore suggests that the cities of Umbria had presented their petition to Constantine already in 326, when the emperor visited Rome to celebrate the twentieth anniversary of his accession.

Gascou (1967) 617–23, proposes a later date. He points out that other inscriptions from after September 335 still mentioned only the three brothers as Caesars, and that on one inscription that included Dalmatius as a fourth Caesar his name was later erased: see *L'année épigraphique 1934* (1935) 42, no. 158 = Grünewald (1990) 220, no. 260; for the date of this inscription, see Barnes (1983) 229, suggesting after December 10, 336, (1982) 23, suggesting ca. February 337. Dalmatius was murdered in the massacre of family members following Constantine's death on May 22, 337. According to Eusebius, *Vita Constantini* 4.67.3, during the long interregnum between Constantine's death and the proclamation of his three sons as Augusti (senior emperors) on September 9, "the blessed [Constantine], alone of mortals, reigned even after his death, and the customs were maintained as if he were still alive." Imperial edicts in Constantine's name were certainly issued during this interregnum: see *CTh* 13.4.2, dated in August. Gascou hence offers two possibilities for the date of the rescript. One is the last months of Constantine's reign. In that case, although Dalmatius' name may have been included in the heading to the rescript, it was suppressed when the inscription was erected after his murder. The other, even more implausible, possibility is the interregnum. In that case Dalmatius' name had not been included in the heading to the rescript because he was dead, the deceased Constantine still "reigned," and the failure to describe the three sons as either Augusti or Caesars was an indication of uncertainty over their interim rank. For a survey of the issues, see Andreotti (1964) 250–57.

Gascou (1967) 612–15, attributed the oddities in grammar and spelling to idiosyncrasies in pronunciation, mistakes by the copyist of the rescript, or mistakes by the engraver:

line 8: *societate* in place of *societatem*

lines 8–9: *curae* to be understood as *curarum*

line 10: *maximus* in place of *maximum*

line 12: *hac* in place of *ac* (cf. line 37)

lines 12–13: *distinguitur* in place of *distinguit*

line 15: *probeantur* in place of *provehantur*

line 16: *inistituto* in place of *instituto* (cf. line 55)

line 17: in his edition in *ILS* Dessau prints *singulos*

line 19: *civitate* in place of *civitatem*

line 20: *schenicos* in place of *scaenicos*

lines 21–22: *difficultates itinerum saltuosa* should be *difficultates itinerum saltuosas*, or *difficultates itinerum saltusque*, or *difficultates itinerum saltuosaq(ue)*; Dessau suggests that *difficultates* should be deleted.

line 29: *amplitudinem* in place of *amplitudine*

line 30: *exsurgere* in place of *exsurgeret*

line 30: *his* in place of *is*

line 32: *scenicorum* in place of *scaenicorum*

line 33: *exhibere* in place of *exhiberet*

line 34: *Tuscia* in place of *Tusciam*

lines 36–37: *frequentare* in place of *frequentaret*

line 37: *praecationi* in place of *precationi*

line 37: *hac* in place of *ac* (cf. line 12)

line 44: *pereici* in place of *perfici*. Although Dessau prints *perfici*, Gascou insists that "Le second E de PEREICI ne peut être lu comme un F."

lines 46–47: *contagiose* in place of *contagiosae*

line 49: *exhibendorum* in place of *exhibendarum*

line 53: *creati* in place of *creatis*

# TEXT AND TRANSLATION:

E(xemplum) S(acri) R(escripti).
Imp(erator) Caes(ar) Fl(avius) Constantinus
Max(imus) Germ(anicus) Sarm(aticus) Got(icus) victor
triump(hator) Aug(ustus) et Fl(avius) Constantinus
et Fl(avius) Iul(ius) Constantius et Fl(avius)
Constans:
omnia quidem, quae humani generis societate tuentur, pervigilium curae cogitatione complectimur; sed pro-
visionum nostrarum opus maximus
est, ut universae urbes, quas in luminibus provinciarum hac regionum omnium species et forma distinguitur, non modo dignitate pristinam teneant,
sed etiam ad meliorem statum beneficentiae nostrae munere probeantur. Cum igitur ita vos Tusciae adsereretis esse coniunctos, ut inistituto
consuetudinis priscae per singulas annorum vices a vobis [a]dque praedictis sacerdotes creentur,
qui aput Vulsinios Tusciae civitate ludos
schenicos et gladiatorum munus exhibeant,
sed propter ardua montium et difficultates itinerum saltuosa inpendio posceretis, ut indulto
remedio sacerdoti vestro ob editiones cele-
brandas Vulsinios pergere necesse non esset,
scilicet ut civitati, cui nunc Hispellum nomen
est quamque Flaminiae viae confinem adque con-
tinuam esse memoratis, de nostro cognomine
nomen daremus, in qua templum Flaviae gentis
opere magnifico nimirum pro amplitudinem
nuncupationis exsurgere, ibidemque his
sacerdos, quem anniversaria vice Umbria de-
disset, spectaculum tam scenicorum ludorum
quam gladiatorii muneris exhibere, manente
per Tuscia ea consuetudine, ut indidem cre-
atus sacerdos aput Vulsinios ut solebat
editionum antedictarum spectacula frequentare, praecationi hac desiderio vestro
facilis accessit noster adsensus. Nam civitati Hispello aeternum vocabulum nomenq(ue)
venerandum de nostra nuncupatione conces-
simus, scilicet ut in posterum praedicta urbs
Flavia Constans vocetur; in cuius gremio
aedem quoque Flaviae, hoc est nostrae gentis, ut desideratis, magnifico opere pereici

Copy of the sacred rescript.
Imperator Caesar Flavius Constantine
Maximus, conqueror of the Germans, Sarmatians, and Goths, Victor,
Celebrator of triumphs, Augustus, with Flavius Constantine
5 and Flavius Julius Constantius and Flavius
Constans:
In our survey of vigilant concerns
we embrace everything that upholds the
society of mankind. But
10 it is the greatest concern of our foresight
that all cities that appearance and shape classify
among the ornaments of provinces and of all regions
not only should retain their original prestige,
but should be advanced to a better standing through
15 the generosity of our beneficence. You claim that you are
joined to Tuscia in such a way that according to the tradition
of ancient custom each year priests are selected
by both you and the aforementioned in turn.
These priests present theatrical shows
20 and gladiator games at Volsinii, a city in Tuscia.
But because of the hardships of the mountains and the difficulties of
the roads through the forests you urgently request that a remedy
be granted and that it not be necessary for your priest to travel
to Volsinii for the celebration of the games.
25 In addition, [you request] that we give a name derived from our
cognomen to the city that now has the name [of] Hispellum
and that you declare to be adjacent and next to the
Via Flaminia. In this city a temple dedicated to the Flavian dynasty
should be built, whose craftsmanship is truly distinguished
30 for the grandeur of its name. In the same place this priest
whom Umbria has provided for the annual duty
should present the festival of the theatrical shows
and the gladiator games. In Tuscia the custom
should survive, so that the priest
35 selected from that place might celebrate the festivals
of the aforementioned games as is customary at Volsinii.
Since [you ask this], our approval has readily supported
your prayer and your desire. For we allow
to the city of Hispellum an eternal name, a
40 venerable name [derived] from our name,
so that in the future the aforementioned city
is to be called Flavia Constans. In the center of this city
we furthermore wish that a shrine of the Flavian [dynasty], that is, of
our dynasty, be constructed of distinguished craftsmanship,

volumus, ea observatione perscripta, ne aedis nostro nomini dedicata cuiusquam contagiose superstitionis fraudibus polluatur;
consequenter etiam editionum in praedicta civitate exhibendorum vobis
licentiam dedimus; scilicet ut, sicuti
dictum est, per vices temporis sollem-
nitas editionum Vulsinios quoque non de-
serat, ubi creati e Tuscia sacerdotibus memo-
rata celebritas exhibenda est. Ita quippe nec
veteribus institutis plurimum videbitur
derogatum, et vos, qui ob praedictas causas
nobis supplices extitistis, ea quae inpendio postulastis, impretrata esse gaude-
bitis.

45 as you wish. This restriction is noted, that a shrine
dedicated to our name not be polluted
with the deceits of any contagious superstition.
We likewise grant you permission for the games
to be presented in the aforementioned city,
50 although, as was said,
the celebration of the games will also
not depart from Volsinii at the time of the year
when priests have been selected from Tuscia and
the aforementioned festival should be celebrated. In this way
55 there will of course not appear to have been much
modification from the old institutions. But you who have been
petitioners to us on behalf of the aforementioned concerns
will rejoice that those requests you urgently submitted
have been obtained.

# ORCISTUS: DATES, TEXT, AND TRANSLATION

## APPENDIX TWO

T HE BEST COMPLETE EDITION OF THE PETITION FROM ORCIS-
tus and Constantine's responses is by W. M. Calder in *MAMA*
7:69–72, no. 305, with rather murky photographs in Plate 20.
The English translation in Johnson, Coleman-Norton and
Bourne (1961) 240–1, no. 304, is based on Calder's text. Chastagnol
(1981a) 384–91, essentially reprints Calder's text and provides a French
translation; Feissel (1999) 256–57, likewise reprints Calder's text, but
also provides an improved edition of Document 1. The text printed and
translated here combines Feissel's edition of Document 1 with Calder's
edition of the other documents.

Earlier editions include Th. Mommsen, in *CIL* 3.1 (1873) 63–66,
no. 352, and again (with O. Hirschfeld and A. Domaszewski) in *CIL* 3,
Supplementum 1 (1902) 1266–68, no. 7000; Mommsen (1887) 316–18;
H. Dessau, in *ILS* 2.1:526–27, no. 6091 (only Constantine's two letters);
Abbott and Johnson (1926) 491–93, no. 154; and Riccobono (1941) 462–
64, no. 95.

The dating of these documents covers the spectrum from exact to
a bit speculative. The date for the first petition (Document 3) at the
beginning of the process can be narrowed to sometime within a period
of about eighteen months. The salutation of the petition addressed
Constantine as "Maximus ['the Greatest'], Victor, always Augustus."

According to Eusebius, after his victory over Licinius in September 324 Constantine took this commemorative title of *Victor* "as the most appropriate name for himself because of the victory that God had given him over all his opponents and enemies." The salutation of the petition also addressed three of Constantine's sons, Crispus, Constantine II, and Constantius II, as Caesars (junior emperors). Apparently immediately after the victory over Licinius cities in the East realized that they were expected to celebrate the entire Constantinian dynasty, both "the pious emperor and his God-beloved sons." Constantius, the youngest of the three sons, was proclaimed Caesar on November 8, 324, while Crispus was executed in May 326. So Orcistus sent its first petition to the court after early November 324 and before May 326.[1]

But the chronology for Constantine's decision about this first petition (Document 1) and his letter to Ablabius (Document 2) is contested. The cause of this chronological uncertainty is uncertainty over the office Ablabius was holding when he received Constantine's letter and applied the emperor's decision.

One solution is to identify him as a prefect, and then try to pin down the date when he began his tenure in this office. Ablabius was certainly a prefect by November 330, and he served as prefect through the remainder of Constantine's reign until shortly after the emperor's death in 337. The Theodosian Code included several laws that were addressed to Ablabius during his tenure as prefect during the 330s. In addition, the Code included three other laws that were addressed to him, two explicitly as a prefect. The subscriptions to these three laws mentioned dates in May 315, June 326, and September 326. If these dates were correct, then Ablabius served as prefect for an exceptionally long tenure either of over twenty years or, if the first law is redated, of over a decade. As prefect he could then have transmitted Constantine's decision to Orcistus soon after the city had submitted its petition in 325 or 326. In

---

[1] *Victor* (Νικητής): Eusebius, *Vita Constantini* 2.19.2, with Barnes (1982) 24. Celebration: Eusebius, *HE* 10.9.7; recycled in *Vita Constantini* 2.19.3, with the sons described as Caesars. Constantius and Crispus: Barnes (1982) 84–85. For a possible source for these titles for Constantine, see Chapter 7. Orcistus could have learned the names of the three Caesars from milestones: e.g. *MAMA* 4:5, no. 13.1 = Grünewald (1990) 253, no. 468, from near Docimium in Phrygia.

# Text:

## Panel 3: Left side of pillar

## Panel 1: Front of pillar

Doc. 1    [S]ac(rae) li[tte]r(ae)(?). Hae(c) quae in precem
              con[tu]lis[tis et nominis]
       et dignitatis reparationem iure qua[erunt obtine-]
       re. Proinde vicari intercessione qua[e fuerant mu-]
       [t]ilata ad integrum prisgi honoris r[educi san-]
5     cimus ut et vos oppidumque dilig[entia tui-]
       tum expetito legum adque appellationis s[plendore]
       *vacat*   perfruamini. Infra: scrib<s>i (?).   *vacat?*

Doc. 4    [S]cr(iptum) prid.
       Kal. Iulias
       [C]onstantinopoli.

Imp. Caes. Consta[n]tinus
5  maximus Guth. victor ac trium-
    fator Aug. et Fl. Clau. Constantinus
    Alaman. et Fl. Iul. Const(ant)ius nnbb.
    Caess. s[al]utem dicunt
    ordini civit. Orcistanorum.
10 Actum est indulgentiae nos-
    trae munere ius vobis civita-
    tis tributum non honore modo
    verum libertatis etiam privi-
    legium custodire. Itaque Na-
15 colensium iniuriam ultra in-
    dulgentiae nostrae beneficia
    perdurantem praesenti re-
    scribtione removemus idque
    oratis vestris petitionique
20 deferimus ut pecuniam quam
    pro cultis ante solebatis in-
    ferre minime deinceps dependa-
    tis. Hoc igitur ad virum perfe-
    [c]tissimum rationalem Asia-
25 nae dioeceseos lenitas nostra
    perscribsit, qui secutus for-
    [mam] indulgentiae concessae
    vobis pecuniam deinceps pr[o]
    supra dicta specie expeti a vo-
30 bis postularique prohibeb[it.]
    Bene valere vos cupim[us.]
    Basso et Ablabio cons.

Doc. 2    Have Ablabi carissime nobis.
    Incole Orcisti iam nu(n)c oppidi et
10 civitatis iucundam munificien-
    tiae nostrae materiem praebue-
    runt, Ablabi carissime et iucundiss[i-]
    me. Quibus enim studium est urbes vel n[o-]
    vas condere vel longaevas erudire vel in-
15 termortuas reparare, id quod petebatur acc[e-]
    ptissimum fuit. Adseruerunt enim vicum suum
    spatiis prioris aetatis oppidi splendore flouru-
    isse ut et annuis magistratum fascibus orn[a-]
    retur essetque curialibus celebre et popul[o]
20 civium plenum. Ita enim ei situ ad[q]ue ingenio
    locus opportunus esse perhib[e]tur ut ex qu-
    attuor partibu[s e]o totidem in sese confluan[t]
    viae, quibus omnibus publicis mansio tamen [u-]
    tilis adque accomo[da] esse dicat[u]r, aquaru[m]
25 ibi abundantem aflu[en]tiam, labacra quoqu[e]
    publica priva[taqu]e, forum istatuis veterum
    principum ornatum, populum comm[a]nentium
    adeo celebrem [ut se]dilia [qu]ae ibidem sunt [fa-]
    cile conpleantur, pr[aeter]ea ex decursibus
30 praeterfluentium [a]quarum aquim(o)lin[a-]
    rum numerum copiosum. Quibus cum omni-
    bus memoratus locus abundare dicatur, c[on-]
    [t]ligisse adseruerunt ut eos Nacolenses si[bi]
    [a]dnecti ante id temporis postularent. Quo[d]
35 [es]t indignum temporibus nostr(i)s, ut tam o[p-]
    [p]ortunus locus civitatis nomen amittat,
    et inutile commanentibus ut depraeda-
    [t]ione potiorum omnia sua commoda utilit[a-]
    [tes]que deperdant. Quibus omnibus quasi
40 quidam cumulus accedit quod omnes
    [i]bidem sectatores sanctissimae religi-
    onis habitare dicantur. Qui cum praeca-
    rentur ut sibi ius antiquum nomenque
    civitatis concederet nostra clementia,
45 sicuti adnotationis nostrae subiec[t]a
    cum precibus exempla testantur, huius mo-
    di sententiam dedimus. Nam haec quae in pre-
    cem contulerunt et nominis et dignitatis

## Panel 2: Right side of pillar

reparation[em iure quae-]
runt obtinere. P[roinde gra-]
vitatis tuae inte[rcessione]
quae fuerant mu[tilata]
5 [a]d integrum prisgi [honoris]
[re]duci sancimus ut et [ipsi]
[o]ppidumque diligent[ia sua]
[t]uitum expetito legum [ad-]
[q]ue appellationis splen-
10 [d]ore perfruantur. Par es[t]
[i]gitur sinceritatem tuam i[d]
[q]uod promptissime pro tem[po-]
[ri]s nostri dignitate conces-
[si]mus erga supplicantes fes-
15 [ti]nanter implere. Vale Abla[bi]
[ca]rissime ac iucundissime n[obis].
       *leaf*      *leaf*

Doc. 3    Exemplum precum.
    [A]d auxilium pietatis vestrae
    [conf]ugimus, domini impp. Constantine
20 [maxi]me victor semper Aug. et Crispe et
    [Con]stantine et Constanti nobb. Caess.
    [Patri]a nostra Orcistos vetusti[s-]
    [sim]um oppidum fuit et ex antiquis[si-]
    [m]is temporibus ab origine etiam
25 [civ]itatis dignitatem obtinuit
    [e]t in medio confinio Gal[a]tiae P(h)ri[g-]
    iae situm est, nam quattuor viar[um]
    [t]ransitus exhibet id est civita[tis]
    [P]essinuntesium, quae civita[s dis-]
30 [ta]t a patria nostra tricensim[o fe-]
    [re l]apide necnon etiam civitat[is Mi-]
    [d]aitanorum, quae et ipsa est a [patria]
    [n]ostra in tricesimo miliario e[t civi-]
    [t]atis Amorianorum quae posita

       *vacat*

# TRANSLATION:

## PANEL 3, Left side of pillar

## PANEL 1, Front of pillar

Doc. 1 Sacred letter (?). These concerns that you mentioned in your request rightly demand (that you) obtain the restoration of both your name and your rank. Therefore, we decree that through the intercession of the vicar whatever has been diminished be restored to the wholeness of the ancient honor, 5 so that both you and your town, protected by diligence, might enjoy that splendor you requested of the laws and of your name. Below: I have signed (?).

## PANEL 2, Right side of pillar

Doc. 4 Recorded on the day before July 1, at Constantinople.

Emperor Caesar Constantine 5 Maximus, conqueror of the Goths, Victor and Celebrator of triumphs, Augustus, along with Flavius Claudius Constantine, conqueror of the Alamanni, and Flavius Julius Constantius, [both] most noble Caesars, sends greetings to the council of the city of the people of Orcistus.

10 Through the gift of our indulgence it has been granted to you to protect not only the right of a city attributed as an honor but also the privilege of liberty. Therefore, 15 through the present rescript we remove the wrongdoing of the people of Nacolea that has endured beyond the benefits of our indulgence, and we grant this to your pleas and your petition, 20 that you no longer pay the levy that you were previously accustomed to pay for the cults. Our gentleness has written this to the *rationalis* 25 of the diocese of Asiana, a most distinguished man, who will follow the formula of the indulgence that has been granted to you and will then prevent the levy to be sought 30 or demanded from you for the aforementioned pretext. We wish you to be well. [Issued] during the consulships of Bassus and Ablabius.

Doc. 2 8 Greetings, Ablabius, you who are most dear to us.

The inhabitants of Orcistus, which is already now a town and 10 a city, have offered a pleasing opportunity to our munificence, most dear and most delightful Ablabius. [For us] whose desire is either to found new cities or to civilize ancient cities or 15 to revive lifeless cities, this petition was most welcome.

They have claimed that during the period of an earlier age their village had flourished with the splendor of a town, so that it was ornamented each year with the symbols of magistrates and that it was celebrated for its decurions and 20 filled with a population of citizens. Its location was stated to be advantageous because of its natural site and human ingenuity, so that as many roads converged together there from four directions. On these [roads] it is said to be a suitable and convenient way station for all public [magistrates]. 25 [It is said that there is] a splendid abundance of water there, as well as public and private baths, a forum decorated with statues of former emperors, a population of inabitants so numerous that the seats that are there are easily filled, and in addition 30 a large number of water mills on account of the torrents of passing streams.

Although the aforementioned place is said to abound with all these [amenities], they have claimed that it happened that before this time the people of Nacolea demanded that they be joined with them. This 35 is unworthy of our times, that such an advantageous place should lose the title of city. This is also injurious for the inhabitants, that they should lose all their privileges and amenities through the plundering of the more powerful. Added to all these [misfortunes] 40 is this culminating [characteristic], as it were, that all are said to reside there as supporters of the most holy religion.

Since they requested that our clemency grant them their ancient legal standing and the title of city, 45 we provided an opinion of this sort, as indicated by the copies of our decision attached below with their requests.

For those concerns that they mentioned in their request

rightly demand (that they) obtain the restoration of both their name and their rank. Therefore, we decree that through the intercession of your dignity whatever has been diminished 5 be restored to the wholeness of the ancient honor, so that both they and their town, protected by their own diligence, might enjoy that splendor they requested of the laws and of their name. 10 It is proper therefore that your sincerity rapidly fulfill for these petitioners what we have most promptly decided on behalf of the dignity of our reign. 15 Farewell, Ablabius, you who are most dear and most delightful to us.

*leaf    leaf*

Doc. 3 17 Copy of the requests.

We have fled to the aid of your piety, Lords and Emperors, Constantine 20 Maximus Victor, always Augustus, and Crispus, Constantine, and Constantius, [all three] most noble Caesars.

Our homeland of Orcistus was a very old town, and from very ancient times, in fact, from its foundation 25 it held the rank of a city. It is located in the middle of the borderland of Galatia [and] Phrygia. It offers passage on four roads: that is, from the city of the people of Pessinus, which is a city 30 about thirty milestones distant from our homeland; also from the city of the people of Midaion, which is also thirty milestones distant from our homeland; also from the city of the people of Amorium, which is located . . .

371

this case, Constantine had responded to the petition quickly. Another solution, however, is to shorten the tenure of Ablabius' prefecture by redating all three laws to 329. But if he is still to be considered as a prefect when he became involved as a mediator, then Constantine's letter to him would have to be dated at the very beginning of his prefecture, "probably 329–330." In this case, Constantine would have delayed his response to the petition for a few years.[2]

A more likely solution is that Ablabius was involved in this transaction between emperor and city before he became prefect. In his *adnotatio*, his initial decision (Document 1), Constantine had stated that Orcistus would receive a favorable response to its request "through the intercession of the vicar." When Constantine repeated this decision in his letter to Ablabius (Document 2), he addressed the phrase directly to Ablabius: "through the intercession of your dignity." Constantine was clearly writing to Ablabius in his capacity as vicar, most likely of the diocese of Asiana that included most of the region of Phrygia. Since the emperor also prided himself for having responded "most promptly," he was most likely writing to Ablabius soon after receiving the petition, probably in 325 or 326. Ablabius was hence a vicar, and through his brokerage Orcistus learned of the emperor's first favorable response very quickly.[3]

The date for Constantine's letter (Document 4) that replied to the second petition from Orcistus at the end of the process is precise. A reference to the day and the consuls firmly dated the issuing of this letter to June 30, 331. Presumably Orcistus had sent its second petition shortly before.

---

[2]  Ablabius as prefect in November 330: *CTh*16.8.2. Three disputed laws: *CTh*11.27.1, "ad Ablavium," dated to May 13, 315; 16.2.6, "ad Ablavium ppo," dated to June 1, 326; 13.5.5, "ad Ablavium ppo," dated to September 18, 326. Ablabius' long career as prefect already in 326: Mommsen (1887) 319. Redating of three laws: Seeck (1919) 54, 64, 179–80. Discussion of Ablabius' short career in Chastagnol (1981a) 393–98, with quotation about dates translated from p. 398; also Chastagnol (1981b) 373, "en 329 ou 330"; accepted by Barnes (1996) 550. For Ablabius' dismissal from office by Constantius after Constantine's death, see Eunapius, *Vitae sophistarum* 464.

[3]  Excellent discussion of Ablabius as vicar in Feissel (1999) 264–66, concluding that Constantine replied in 325 or 326. Earlier discussions of Ablabius' vicariate in 324/326: *PLRE* 1:3–4, "Fl. Ablabius 4," and Barnes (1982) 104, 132, 142. For limitations on the authority of the vicar of Asiana in his own diocese, see Feissel (1998) 92–95.

# EDITIONS AND TRANSLATIONS

✻ ✻ ✻

In this book all translations from Greek and Latin texts are by the author. In this list of editions and translations, full references for books and articles already cited in the notes are in the Bibliography.

*Acta proconsularia sancti Cypriani:* ed. and tr. H. Musurillo, *The Acts of the Christian Martyrs.* Oxford Early Christian Texts (Oxford, 1972), pp. 168–75.

Ambrose —

*De obitu Theodosii* and *De obitu Valentiniani:* ed. O. Faller, *Sancti Ambrosii opera: Pars septima.* CSEL 73 (1955), pp. 329–67, 371–401 – tr. J. H. W. G. Liebeschuetz and C. Hill, *Ambrose of Milan: Political Letters and Speeches.* TTH 43 (2005), pp. 177–203, 364–99.

*Epistulae* and *Epistulae extra collectionem:* ed. O. Faller and M. Zelzer, *Sancti Ambrosii opera, Pars decima: Epistulae et acta,* 3 vols. CSEL 82.1–3 (1968–1990) – tr. M. M. Beyenka, *Saint Ambrose, Letters.* FC 26 (1954) – *Ep.* 10, *Ep. extra collectionem:* tr. J. H. W. G. Liebeschuetz and C. Hill, *Ambrose of Milan: Political Letters and Speeches.* TTH 43 (2005).

Ammianus Marcellinus, *Res gestae:* ed. and tr. J. C. Rolfe, *Ammianus Marcellinus,* 3 vols. LCL (1935–1940).

Anonymus post Dionem ( = Dio Continuatus), *Fragmenta:* ed. and tr. [Latin] Müller (1851), pp. 192–99.

*Anthologia graeca:* ed. and tr. W. R. Paton, *The Greek Anthology,* 5 vols. LCL (1916–1918).

Athanasius —

*Apologia ad Constantium:* ed. and tr. [French] J. M. Szymusiak, *Athanase d'Alexandrie, Deux apologies: A l'empereur Constance, Pour sa fuite.* SChr. 56bis (1987), pp. 86–175.

*Apologia contra Arianos:* ed. H.-G. Opitz, *Athanasius Werke 2.1: Die Apologien* (Berlin and Leipzig, 1935–1941), pp. 87–168.

*De decretis Nicaenae synodi:* ed. H.-G. Opitz, *Athanasius Werke 2.1: Die Apologien* (Berlin and Leipzig, 1935–1941), pp. 1–45.

*De synodis Arimini in Italia et Seleuciae in Isauria:* ed. H.-G. Opitz, *Athanasius Werke 2.1: Die Apologien* (Berlin and Leipzig, 1935–1941), pp. 231–78.

*Epistula ad episcopos Aegypti et Libyae:* ed. *PG* 25.537–93.

*Epistula de morte Arii:* ed. H.-G. Opitz, *Athanasius Werke 2.1: Die Apologien* (Berlin and Leipzig, 1935–1941), pp. 178–80.

*Historia Arianorum:* ed. H.-G. Opitz, *Athanasius Werke 2.1: Die Apologien* (Berlin and Leipzig, 1935–1941), pp. 183–230.

*Orationes contra Arianos* 1–3: ed. W. Bright, *The Orations of St. Athanasius against the Arians according to the Benedictine Text* (Second edition: Oxford, 1884), pp. 1–221.

*Vita Antonii*: ed. and tr. [French] Bartelink (1994) – tr. T. Vivian and A. N. Athanassakis, *The Life of Antony by Athanasius of Alexandria*. Cistercian Studies Series 202 (Kalamazoo, 2003).

Athanasius' writings tr. A. Robertson, *Select Writings and Letters of Athanasius, Bishop of Alexandria*. NPNF, Second series 4 (1892; reprinted 1991).

Augustine —

*Confessiones*: ed. J. Gibb and W. Montgomery, *The Confessions of Augustine* (Cambridge, 1908) – tr. R. S. Pine-Coffin, *Saint Augustine, Confessions* (Harmondsworth, 1961) – ed. J. J. O'Donnell, *Augustine, Confessions*, Vol. 1 (Oxford, 1992).

*De civitate Dei*: ed. B. Dombart and A. Kalb, *Sancti Aurelii Augustini De civitate Dei*. CChr., Series latina 47–48 (1955) – tr. H. Bettenson, *Augustine: Concerning the City of God against the Pagans* (Harmondsworth, 1967).

Augustus, *Res gestae*: ed. and tr. P. A. Brunt and J. M. Moore, *Res gestae divi Augusti: The Achievements of the Divine Augustus* (Oxford, 1967).

Aurelius Victor, *De Caesaribus*: ed. F. Pichlmayr and R. Gruendel, *Sexti Aurelii Victoris Liber de Caesaribus*. Teubner (1970), pp. 77–129 – tr. H. W. Bird, *Liber de Caesaribus of Sextus Aurelius Victor*. TTH 17 (1994).

Ausonius: ed. and tr. H. G. Evelyn White, *Ausonius*, 2 vols. LCL (1919–1921) – ed. R. P. H. Green, *The Works of Ausonius* (Oxford, 1991).

Basil of Caesarea, *Epistulae*: ed. and tr. R. J. Deferrari, *Saint Basil: The Letters*, 4 vols. LCL (1926–1934) – ed. and tr. [French] Y. Courtonne, *Saint Basile: Lettres*, 3 vols. Budé (1957–1966).

*Breviarius de Hierosolyma*: ed. R. Weber, in *Itineraria et alia geographica*, Vol. 1. CChr., Series latina 175 (1965), pp. 109–12.

Callinicus, *Vita Hypatii*: ed. and tr. [French] G. J. M. Bartelink, *Callinicos, Vie d'Hypatios: Introduction, texte critique, traduction et notes*. SChr. 177 (1971).

*Carmen contra paganos*: ed. D. R. Shackleton Bailey, *Anthologia Latina I: Carmina in codicibus scripta. Fasc. 1: Libri Salmasiani aliorumque carmina*. Teubner (1982), pp. 17–23.

*Chronicon Paschale*: ed. L. Dindorf, *Chronicon Paschale ad exemplar Vaticanum*, Vol. 1. Corpus Scriptorum Historiae Byzantinae (Bonn, 1832) – tr. M. Whitby and M. Whitby, *Chronicon Paschale 284–628 AD*. TTH 7 (1989).

Chronographer of 354, *Chronica urbis Romae*: ed. Mommsen (1892), pp. 143–48.

*CJ* = *Codex Justinianus*: ed. P. Krueger, *Codex Iustinianus*. Corpus Iuris Civilis 2 (11th ed., 1954; reprinted Hildesheim, 1989).

Claudian, *De bello Gothico, De consulatu Stilichonis, De quarto consulatu Honorii, De sexto consulatu Honorii, In Rufinum*: ed. and tr. M. Platnauer, *Claudian*, 2 vols. LCL (1922).

Claudius Mamertinus, *Panegyrici latini*: see *Panegyrici latini*

*Collatio legum Mosaicarum et Romanarum*: ed. J. Baviera, *Fontes iuris Romani antejus-tiniani, Pars altera: Auctores* (Florence, 1940), pp. 544–89.

Constantine —
  *Epistula ad Porfyrium*: ed. Polara (1973), Vol. 1:4–6.
  *Oratio ad sanctorum coetum*: ed. I. A. Heikel, *Eusebius Werke 1: Über das Leben Constantins. Constantins Rede an die heilige Versammlung. Tricennatsrede an Constantin.* GCS 7 (1902), pp. 154–92 – tr. Edwards (2003) 1–62.

*Consularia Constantinopolitana*: ed. R. W. Burgess, *The* Chronicle *of Hydatius and the* Consularia Constantinopolitana: *Two Contemporary Accounts of the Final Years of the Roman Empire* (Oxford, 1993), pp. 215–45.

*Consultatio veteris cuiusdam iurisconsulti*: ed. J. Baviera, *Fontes iuris Romani antejus-tiniani, Pars altera: Auctores* (Florence, 1940), pp. 594–613.

*CTh* = *Codex Theodosianus*: ed. T. Mommsen, *Codex Theodosianus 1.2: Theodosiani libri XVI cum Constitutionibus Sirmondi[a]nis* (Berlin, 1905) – tr. C. Pharr et al., *The Theodosian Code and Novels and the Sirmondian Constitutions* (1952; reprinted Westport, 1969), pp. 3–486.

Dio, *Historiae Romanae*: ed. and tr. E. Cary, *Dio's Roman History*, 9 vols. LCL (1914–1927).

Egeria, *Itinerarium*: ed. A. Franceschini and R. Weber, in *Itineraria et alia geographica*, Vol. 1. CChr., Series latina 175 (1965), pp. 37–90 – ed. and tr. [French] P. Maraval, *Egérie: Journal de voyage (Itinéraire)*. SChr. 296 (1982) – tr. Wilkinson (1981), pp. 91–147.

Epiphanius, *Panarion*: ed. K. Holl, *Epiphanius (Ancoratus und Panarion)*, 3 vols. GCS 25, 31, 37 (1915–1933) – tr. F. Williams, *The Panarion of Epiphanius of Salamis*, 2 vols. Nag Hammadi and Manichaean Studies 35–36 (Leiden, 1987–1994) – selection tr. P. R. Amidon, *The* Panarion *of St. Epiphanius, Bishop of Salamis: Selected Passages* (New York and Oxford, 1990).

*Epistolae Arelatenses*: ed. W. Gundlach, in *Epistolae Merowingici et Karolini aevi*, Vol. 1. MGH, Epistolae 3 (1892), pp. 5–83.

*Epitome de Caesaribus*: ed. F. Pichlmayr and R. Gruendel, *Sexti Aurelii Victoris Liber de Caesaribus*. Teubner (1970), pp. 133–76.

Eunapius –
  *Fragmenta historica*: ed. and tr. R. C. Blockley, *The Fragmentary Classicising Historians of the Later Roman Empire: Eunapius, Olympiodorus, Priscus and Malchus, II: Text, Translation and Historiographical Notes.* ARCA Classical and Medieval Texts, Papers and Monographs 10 (Liverpool, 1983), pp. 6–127.
  *Vitae sophistarum*: ed. and tr. W. C. Wright, *Philostratus and Eunapius: The Lives of the Sophists.* LCL (1921), pp. 342–565.

Eunomius, *Expositio fidei*: ed. and tr. R. P. Vaggione, *Eunomius: The Extant Works* (Oxford, 1987), pp. 150–59.

Eusebius of Caesarea –

    *Contra Marcellum*: ed. E. Klostermann, *Eusebius Werke 4: Gegen Marcell, Über die kirchliche Theologie, Die Fragmente Marcells.* GCS 14 (1906; Second edition 1972); Third edition rev. G. C. Hansen, GCS (1991), pp. 1–58.

    *De ecclesiastica theologia* and *Epistula ad Flacillum*: ed. E. Klostermann, *Eusebius Werke 4: Gegen Marcell, Über die kirchliche Theologie, Die Fragmente Marcells.* GCS 14 (1906; Second edition 1972); Third edition rev. G. C. Hansen, GCS (1991), pp. 60–182.

    *De laudibus Constantini*: ed. I. A. Heikel, *Eusebius Werke 1: Über das Leben Constantins. Constantins Rede an die heilige Versammlung. Tricennatsrede an Constantin.* GCS 7 (1902), pp. 195–259 – tr. Drake (1976), pp. 83–127.

    *De martyribus Palaestinae*, "Recensio brevior": ed. E. Schwartz, in E. Schwartz and T. Mommsen, ed., *Eusebius Werke 2: Die Kirchengeschichte*, Vol. 2. GCS 9, Neue Folge 6.2 (1908; reprinted 1999), pp. 907–50 – "Recensio prolixior" and "Recensio brevior": tr. Lawlor and Oulton (1927–1928) 1:327–400.

    *HE = Historia ecclesiastica*: ed. E. Schwartz, in E. Schwartz and T. Mommsen, ed., *Eusebius Werke 2: Die Kirchengeschichte*, Vols. 1–2. GCS 9, Neue Folge 6.1–2 (1903–1908; reprinted 1999) – tr. K. Lake, J. E. L. Oulton, and H. J. Lawlor, *Eusebius: The Ecclesiastical History*, 2 vols. LCL (1926–1932).

    *Vita Constantini*: ed. Winkelmann (1991) – tr. Cameron and Hall (1999).

Eutropius, *Breviarium*: ed. H. Droysen, *Eutropi Breviarium ab urbe condita cum versionibus graecis et Pauli Landolfique additamentis.* MGH, Auctores antiquissimi 2 (1879) – tr. H. W. Bird, *Eutropius: Breviarium.* TTH 14 (1993).

*Expositio totius mundi et gentium*: ed. and tr. [French] Rougé (1966).

Filastrius, *Diversarum hereseon liber*: ed. F. Heylen, in *Eusebius Vercellensis, Filastrius Brixiensis et al.* CChr., Series latina 9 (1957), pp. 217–324.

Fredegar, *Chronica*: ed. B. Krusch, *Fredegarii et aliorum chronica. Vitae sanctorum.* MGH, Scriptores rerum Merovingicarum 2 (1888), pp. 18–168.

Gregory of Nazianzus —

    *Epistulae*: ed. P. Gallay, *Gregor von Nazianz: Briefe.* GCS 53 (1969) – ed. and tr. [French] Gallay (1964–1967) – tr. [German] M. Wittig, *Gregor von Nazianz: Briefe.* Bibliothek der griechischen Literatur, Abteilung Patristik, Bd. 13 (Stuttgart, 1981) – selection tr. C. G. Browne and J. E. Swallow, in *S. Cyril of Jerusalem. S. Gregory Nazianzen.* NPNF, Second series 7 (1894; reprinted 1978), pp. 437–82.

    *Orationes 4–5*: ed. and tr. [French] J. Bernardi, *Grégoire de Nazianze: Discours 4–5, Contre Julien.* SChr. 309 (1983) – tr. C. W. King, *Julian the Emperor: Containing Gregory Nazianzen's Two Invectives and Libanius' Monody with Julian's Extant Theosophical Works* (London, 1888), pp. 1–121 – *Orat.* 18: ed. *PG* 35.985–1044 – *Orat.* 21: ed. and tr. [French] Mossay and Lafontaine (1980) – *Orat.* 43: ed. and tr. [French] J. Bernardi, *Grégoire de Nazianze: Discours 42–43*. SChr. 384 (1992) – *Orat.* 18, 21, 43: tr. C. G. Browne and J. E. Swallow, in *S. Cyril of Jerusalem. S. Gregory Nazianzen.* NPNF, Second series 7 (1894; reprinted 1978), pp. 255–80, 395–422.

Gregory of Nyssa —

*Epistulae:* ed. G. Pasquali, *Gregorii Nysseni Epistulae*. Gregorii Nysseni opera 8.2 (Leiden, Second edition 1959) – ed. and tr. [French] P. Maraval, *Grégoire de Nysse: Lettres*. SChr. 363 (1990) – selection tr. W. Moore, H. C. Ogle, and H. A. Wilson, in *Select Writings and Letters of Gregory, Bishop of Nyssa*. NPNF, Second series 5 (1893; reprinted 1976), pp. 33–34, 382–83, 527–48.

*In Basilium fratrem:* ed. and tr. J. A. Stein, *Encomium of Saint Gregory Bishop of Nyssa on His Brother Saint Basil Archbishop of Cappadocian Caesarea*. Catholic University of America Patristic Studies 17 (Washington, D.C., 1928) – ed. O. Lendle, in *Gregorii Nysseni sermones, pars II*. Gregorii Nysseni opera 10.1 (Leiden, 1990), pp. 107–34.

*Vita Macrinae:* ed. V. W. Callahan, in *Gregorii Nysseni opera ascetica*. Gregorii Nysseni opera 8.1 (Leiden, 1952), pp. 370–414 – tr. V. W. Callahan, *Saint Gregory of Nyssa: Ascetical Works*. FC 58 (1967), pp. 163–91 – ed. and tr. [French] P. Maraval, *Grégoire de Nysse: Vie de sainte Macrine*. SChr. 178 (1971).

Gregory Thaumaturgus, *Oratio panegyrica in Origenem:* ed. and tr. [French] H. Crouzel, *Grégoire le Thaumaturge: Remerciement à Origène, suivi de la lettre d'Origène à Grégoire*. SChr. 148 (1969), pp. 94–183 – tr. M. Slusser, *St. Gregory Thaumaturgus: Life and Works*. FC 98 (1998), pp. 91–126.

Gregory of Tours —

*De passione et virtutibus sancti Iuliani martyris:* ed. B. Krusch, in W. Arndt and B. Krusch, ed., *Gregorii Turonensis opera*. MGH, Scriptores rerum Merovingicarum 1 (1885), pp. 562–84 – tr. Van Dam (1993), pp. 163–95.

*Historiae:* ed. B. Krusch and W. Levison, *Gregorii episcopi Turonensis libri historiarum X*. MGH, Scriptores rerum Merovingicarum 1.1, Second Edition (1937–1951) – tr. O. M. Dalton, *The History of the Franks by Gregory of Tours* (Oxford, 1927), Vol. 2.

*Vita patrum:* ed. B. Krusch, in W. Arndt and B. Krusch, ed., *Gregorii Turonensis opera*. MGH, Scriptores rerum Merovingicarum 1 (1885), pp. 661–744 – tr. E. James, *Gregory of Tours: Life of the Fathers*. TTH 1 (Second edition, 1991).

Herodian, *Historia:* ed. and tr. C. R. Whittaker, *Herodian*, 2 vols. LCL (1969–1970).

Hilary of Potiers, *Excerpta ex opere historico deperdito:* ed. A. Feder, *S. Hilarii episcopi Pictaviensis opera, Pars quarta*. CSEL 65 (1916), pp. 41–193 – tr. L. R. Wickham, *Hilary of Poitiers: Conflicts of Conscience and Law in the Fourth-Century Church*. TTH 25 (1997), pp. 15–103.

Himerius, *Orationes:* ed. A. Colonna, *Himerii declamationes et orationes cum deperditarum fragmentis* (Rome, 1951).

*Historia acephala*: ed. & tr. [French] Martin (1985), pp. 138–69.

Hydatius, *Chronica*: ed. and tr. R. W. Burgess, *The* Chronicle *of Hydatius and the Consularia Constantinopolitana: Two Contemporary Accounts of the Final Years of the Roman Empire* (Oxford, 1993), pp. 70–123.

Isidore of Seville, *Etymologiae*: ed. W. M. Lindsay, *Isidori Hispalensis episcopi Etymologiarum sive Originum libri XX*, 2 vols. Oxford Classical Texts (Oxford, 1911).

*Itinerarium Burdigalense*: ed. P. Geyer and O. Cuntz, in *Itineraria et alia geographica*, Vol. 1. CChr., Series latina 175 (1965), pp. 1–26.

Jerome —

    *Apologia contra Rufinum*: ed. P. Lardet, *S. Hieronymi presbyteri opera, Pars III: Opera polemica*. CChr., Series latina 79 (1982), pp. 1–116 – tr. W. H. Fremantle, in *Theodoret, Jerome, Gennadius, Rufinus: Historical Writings, Etc.* NPNF, Second series 3 (1892; reprinted 1989), pp. 482–541.

    *Chronicon*: ed. R. Helm, *Eusebius Werke 7: Die Chronik des Hieronymus. Hieronymi Chronicon*, Second Edition. GCS 47 (1956) – *Chron.* s.a. 327 to end: tr. M. D. Donalson, *A Translation of Jerome's* Chronicon *with Historical Commentary* (Lewiston, 1996), pp. 39–57.

    *Epistulae*: ed. I. Hilberg, *Sancti Eusebii Hieronymi epistulae*, 3 vols. CSEL 54–56 (1910–1918) – ed. and tr. [French] J. Labourt, *Jérôme: Correspondance*, 8 vols. Budé (1949–1963) – selection tr. W. H. Fremantle, *St. Jerome: Letters and Select Works*. NPNF, Second series 6 (1892; reprinted 1954), pp. 1–295.

John Chrysostom, *Ad viduam iuniorem*: ed. and tr. [French] Grillet and Ettlinger (1968), pp. 112–59.

John the Lydian, *De magistratibus reipublicae Romanae*: ed. and tr. A. C. Bandy, *Ioannes Lydus: On Powers, or The Magistracies of the Roman State. Introduction, Critical Text, Translation, Commentary, and Indices* (Philadelphia, 1983), pp. 2–257.

John Malalas, *Chronographia*: ed. J. Thurn, *Ioannis Malalae Chronographia*. Corpus Fontium Historiae Byzantinae 35, Series Berolinensis (Berlin, 2000) – tr. E. Jeffreys, M. Jeffreys, and R. Scott, *The Chronicle of John Malalas: A Translation*. Byzantina Australiensia 4 (Melbourne, 1986).

Josephus —

    *Antiquitates Iudaicae*: ed. and tr. H. St. J. Thackeray, R. Marcus, A. Wikgren, and L. H. Feldman, *Josephus*, Vols. 4–10. LCL (1930–1965).

    *Bellum Iudaicum*: ed. and tr. H. St. J. Thackeray, *Josephus*, Vols. 2–3. LCL (1927–1928).

Julian, *Caesares, Contra Galilaeos, Epistula ad Athenienses, Epistulae, Fragmenta breviora, Misopogon, Orationes*: ed. and tr. W. C. Wright, *The Works of the Emperor Julian*, 3 vols. LCL (1913–1923).

Lactantius —

    *De mortibus persecutorum*: ed. and tr. J. L. Creed, *Lactantius: De Mortibus Persecutorum*. Oxford Early Christian Texts (Oxford, 1984).

*Institutiones divinae*: ed. S. Brandt, *L. Caeli Firmiani Lactanti opera omnia, Pars I*. CSEL 19 (1890), pp. 1–672 – Books 1–2, 4–5: ed. and tr. [French] P. Monat, *Lactance, Institutions Divines*. SChr. 204–205, 326, 337, 377 (1973–1992) – tr. Bowen and Garnsey (2003).

*Laterculus Veronensis*: ed. O. Seeck, *Notitia Dignitatum accedunt Notitia urbis Constantinopolitanae et Laterculi provinciarum* (Berlin, 1876), pp. 247–53.

Libanius —
  *Epistulae*: ed. R. Foerster, *Libanii opera*, Vols. 10–11. Teubner (1921–1922) – selection ed. and tr. A. F. Norman, *Libanius: Autobiography and Selected Letters*, 2 vols. LCL (1992) – selection tr. S. Bradbury, *Selected Letters of Libanius from the Age of Constantius and Julian*. TTH 41 (2004).
  *Orationes*: ed. R. Foerster, *Libanii opera*, Vols. 1–4. Teubner (1903–1908) – *Orat.* 1: ed. and tr. A. F. Norman, *Libanius: Autobiography and Selected Letters*, Vol. 1. LCL (1992), pp. 52–337 – selection ed. and tr. A. F. Norman, *Libanius: Selected Works*, 2 vols. LCL (1969–1977) – selection tr. A. F. Norman, *Antioch as a Centre of Hellenic Culture as Observed by Libanius*. TTH 34 (2000).

*Liber pontificalis*: ed. Duchesne (1886) – tr. R. Davis, *The Book of Pontiffs (*Liber Pontificalis*): The Ancient Biographies of the First Ninety Roman Bishops to AD 715*. TTH 6 (Revised edition, 2000).

Marcellinus Comes, *Chronicon*: ed. T. Mommsen, *Chronica minora saec. IV. V. VI. VII*, Vol. 2. MGH, Auctores antiquissimi 11 (1894), pp. 60–104 – tr. B. Croke, *The Chronicle of Marcellinus: A Translation and Commentary (with a Reproduction of Mommsen's Edition of the Text)*. Byzantina Australiensia 7 (Sydney, 1995).

Martial, *Epigrammata*: ed. and tr. D. R. Shackleton Bailey, *Martial: Epigrams*, 3 vols. LCL (1993).

*Notitia Dignitatum*: ed. O. Seeck, *Notitia Dignitatum accedunt Notitia urbis Constantinopolitanae et Laterculi provinciarum* (Berlin, 1876), pp. 1–225.

*Notitia urbis Constantinopolitanae*: ed. O. Seeck, *Notitia Dignitatum accedunt Notitia urbis Constantinopolitanae et Laterculi provinciarum* (Berlin, 1876), pp. 229–43.

Olympiodorus, *Fragmenta*: ed. and tr. R. C. Blockley, *The Fragmentary Classicising Historians of the Later Roman Empire: Eunapius, Olympiodorus, Priscus and Malchus, II: Text, Translation and Historiographical Notes*. ARCA Classical and Medieval Texts, Papers and Monographs 10 (Liverpool, 1983), pp. 152–209.

Optatus —
  Appendix: ed. C. Ziwsa, *S. Optati Milevitani libri VII*. CSEL 26 (1893), pp. 185–216 – tr. M. Edwards, *Optatus: Against the Donatists*. TTH 27 (1997), pp. 150–201.
  *Contra Donatistas*: ed. and tr. [French] M. Labrousse, *Optat de Milève, Traité contre les Donatistes*. SChr. 412–413 (1995–1996) – tr. M. Edwards, *Optatus: Against the Donatists*. TTH 27 (1997), pp. 1–149.

*Origo Constantini imperatoris* ( = *Anonymus Valesianus*, Pars prior): ed. and tr. J. C. Rolfe, *Ammianus Marcellinus*, Vol. 3. LCL (1939), pp. 508–31 – tr. J. Stevenson, in Lieu and Montserrat (1996), pp. 43–48.

Orosius, *Historiae adversum paganos*: ed. and tr. [French] M.-P. Arnaud-Lindet, *Orose, Histoire (Contre les païens)*, 3 vols. Budé (1990–1991) – tr. R. J. Deferrari, *Paulus Orosius: The Seven Books of History against the Pagans*. FC 50 (1964).

Pacatus, *Panegyrici latini*: see *Panegyrici latini*

Palladius, *Historia Lausiaca*: ed. C. Butler, *The Lausiac History of Palladius, II: The Greek Text Edited with Introduction and Notes*. Texts and Studies 6.2 (Cambridge, 1904) – tr. R. T. Meyer, *Palladius: The Lausiac History*. ACW 34 (1964).

*Panegyrici latini*: ed. and tr. [French] E. Galletier, *Panégyriques latins*, 3 vols. Budé (1949–1955) – ed. R. A. B. Mynors, *XII Panegyrici latini*. Oxford Classical Texts (Oxford, 1964) – tr. Nixon and Rodgers (1994), pp. 41–516.

*Parastaseis syntomoi chronikai*: ed. T. Preger, *Scriptores originum Constantinopolitanarum*, Vol. 1. Teubner (1901), pp. 19–73 – tr. Cameron and Herrin (1984), pp. 56–165.

*Passio Artemii*: ed. Kotter (1988), pp. 202–45 – selection tr. M. Vermes, in Lieu and Montserrat (1996), pp. 224–56.

*Passio Crispinae*: ed. and tr. H. Musurillo, *The Acts of the Christian Martyrs*. Oxford Early Christian Texts (Oxford, 1972), pp. 302–9.

*Passio Dativi, Saturnini presbyteri et aliorum*: ed. and tr. [French] Maier (1987–1989) 1:59–92.

Paul the Deacon, *Historia Romana*: ed. H. Droysen, *Eutropi Breviarium ab urbe condita cum versionibus graecis et Pauli Landolfique additamentis*. MGH, Auctores antiquissimi 2 (1879), pp. 183–224.

Paulinus of Milan, *Vita Ambrosii*: ed. and tr. M. S. Kaniecka, *Vita sancti Ambrosii Mediolanensis episcopi, a Paulino eius notario ad beatum Augustinum conscripta: A Revised Text, and Commentary, with an Introduction and Translation*. Catholic University of America Patristic Studies 16 (1928).

Paulinus of Nola —

    *Carmina*: ed. G. de Hartel, *Sancti Pontii Meropii Paulini Nolani carmina*. CSEL 30 (1894) – tr. P. G. Walsh, *The Poems of St. Paulinus of Nola*. ACW 40 (1975).

    *Epistulae*: ed. G. de Hartel, *Sancti Pontii Meropii Paulini Nolani epistulae*. CSEL 29 (1894) – tr. P. G. Walsh, *Letters of St. Paulinus of Nola*, 2 vols. ACW 35–36 (1966–1967).

Peter the Patrician, *Fragmenta*: ed. and tr. [Latin] Müller (1851), pp. 184–91.

Philostorgius, *HE* = *Historia ecclesiastica*: ed. Bidez (1913); Second edition rev. F. Winkelmann (1972), Third edition (1981) – tr. E. Walford, *The Ecclesiastical History of Sozomen, Comprising a History of the Church, from A.D. 324 to A.D. 440: Translated from the Greek. With a Memoir of the Author. Also the Ecclesiastical*

*History of Philostorgius, as Epitomised by Photius, Patriarch of Constantinople.*
Bohn's Ecclesiastical Library (London, 1855), pp. 429–521.

Photius, *Bibliotheca*: ed. and tr. [French] R. Henry, *Photius: Bibliothèque*, 8 vols., and Index, ed. J. Schamp. Budé (1959–1991).

Pliny the Elder, *Historia naturalis*: ed. and tr. H. Rackham, W. H. S. Jones, and D. E. Eichholz, *Pliny: Natural History*, 10 vols. LCL (1938–1963).

Pliny the Younger, *Epistulae* and *Panegyricus*: ed. and tr. B. Radice, *Pliny: Letters and Panegyricus*, 2 vols. LCL (1969).

Plutarch, *Publicola*: ed. and tr. B. Perrin, *Plutarch's Lives*, Vol. 1. LCL (1914), pp. 502–65.

Polemius Silvius, *Laterculus*: ed. Mommsen (1892), pp. 518–23, 535–51.

Porphyrius, *Carmina*: ed. Polara (1973), Vol. 1.

Priscus, *Fragmenta*: ed. and tr. R. C. Blockley, *The Fragmentary Classicising Historians of the Later Roman Empire: Eunapius, Olympiodorus, Priscus and Malchus, II: Text, Translation and Historiographical Notes.* ARCA Classical and Medieval Texts, Papers and Monographs 10 (Liverpool, 1983), pp. 222–377.

Procopius, *Anecdota, Bella, De aedificiis*: ed. and tr. H. B. Dewing, *Procopius*, 7 vols. LCL (1914–1940).

Prudentius, *Peristephanon*: ed. and tr. H. J. Thomson, *Prudentius*, Vol. 2. LCL (1953), pp. 98–345.

Rufinus, *HE = Historia ecclesiastica*: ed. T. Mommsen, *Die lateinische Übersetzung des Rufinus*, in E. Schwartz and T. Mommsen, ed., *Eusebius Werke 2.1–2: Die Kirchengeschichte.* GCS 9, Neue Folge 6.1–2 (1903–1908; reprinted 1999) – *HE* 10–11: tr. Amidon (1997).

Rutilius Namatianus, *De reditu suo*: ed. and tr. J. W. Duff and A. M. Duff, *Minor Latin Poets.* LCL (1934), pp. 764–829.

Salvian, *De gubernatione Dei*: ed. and tr. [French] G. Lagarrigue, *Salvien de Marseille, Oeuvres, Tome II: Du gouvernement de Dieu.* SChr. 220 (1975) – tr. J. F. O'Sullivan, *The Writings of Salvian, The Presbyter.* FC 3 (1947), pp. 25–232.

*Sermo de passione Donati et Advocati*: ed. and tr. [French] Maier (1987–1989) 1:201–11 – tr. M. A. Tilley, *Donatist Martyr Stories: The Church in Conflict in Roman North Africa.* TTH 24 (1996), pp. 52–60.

SHA = Scriptores Historiae Augustae, *Aurelianus, Carus et Carinus et Numerianus, Claudius, Gallieni duo, Gordiani tres, Heliogabalus, Severus*: ed. and tr. D. Magie, *The Scriptores Historiae Augustae*, 3 vols. LCL (1921–1932).

Sidonius, *Carmina* and *Epistulae*: ed. and tr. W. B. Anderson, *Sidonius: Poems and Letters*, 2 vols. LCL (1936–1965).

Socrates, *HE = Historia ecclesiastica*: ed. G. C. Hansen, with M. Sirinian, *Sokrates: Kirchengeschichte.* GCS, Neue Folge 1 (1995) – tr. A. C. Zenos, in *Socrates*,

*Sozomenus: Church Histories.* NPNF, Second series 2 (1890; reprinted 1973), pp. 1–178.

Sozomen, *HE = Historia ecclesiastica*: ed. J. Bidez, *Sozomenus: Kirchengeschichte.* GCS 50 (1960); rev. G. C. Hansen. GCS, Neue Folge 4 (Second edition 1995) – tr. C. D. Hartranft, in *Socrates, Sozomenus: Church Histories.* NPNF, Second series 2 (1890; reprinted 1973), pp. 236–427.

Statius, *Silvae*: ed. and tr. D. R. Shackleton Bailey, *Statius: Silvae.* LCL (2003).

Strabo, *Geographia*: ed. and tr. H. L. Jones, *The Geography of Strabo*, 8 vols. LCL (1917–1932).

*Suda*: ed. A. Adler, *Suidae Lexicon*, 5 vols. (1928–1938).

Suetonius, *Augustus, Domitianus, Gaius Caligula, Vespasianus*: ed. and tr. J. C. Rolfe, *Suetonius*, 2 vols. LCL (1914).

Symmachus —

   *Epistulae*: ed. O. Seeck, *Aurelii Symmachi quae supersunt.* MGH, Auctores antiquissimi 6.1 (1883), pp. 1–278 – Books 1–8: ed. & tr. [French] J. P. Callu, *Symmaque: Lettres*, 3 vols. Budé (1972–1995).

   *Orationes*: ed. O. Seeck, *Aurelii Symmachi quae supersunt.* MGH, Auctores antiquissimi 6.1 (1883), pp. 318–39.

   *Relationes*: ed. O. Seeck, *Aurelii Symmachi quae supersunt.* MGH, Auctores antiquissimi 6.1 (1883), pp. 279–317 – ed. and tr. R. H. Barrow, *Prefect and Emperor: The Relationes of Symmachus A.D. 384* (Oxford, 1973).

Tacitus —

   *Agricola*: ed. H. Furneaux and J. G. C. Anderson, *Cornelii Taciti opera minora.* Oxford Classical Texts (Oxford, 1939) – tr. H. Mattingly and S. A. Handford, *Tacitus: The Agricola and the Germania* (Harmondsworth, revised edition 1970).

   *Annales*: ed. C. D. Fisher, *Cornelii Taciti Annalium ab excessu divi Augusti libri.* Oxford Classical Texts (Oxford, 1906) – tr. M. Grant, *Tacitus: The Annals of Imperial Rome* (Harmondsworth, revised edition 1977).

   *Historiae*: ed. C. D. Fisher, *Cornelii Taciti Historiarum libri.* Oxford Classical Texts (Oxford, 1911) – tr. K. Wellesley, *Tacitus: The Histories* (Harmondsworth, 1964).

Themistius, *Orationes*: ed. G. Downey and A. F. Norman, *Themistii orationes quae supersunt*, 2 vols. Teubner (1965–1971) – *Orat.* 1, 3, 5, 6, 14, 15, 16, 17, 34: tr. Heather and Moncur (2001).

Theodoret, *HE = Historia ecclesiastica*: ed. L. Parmentier, *Theodoret: Kirchengeschichte.* GCS 19 (1911); Second edition rev. F. Scheidweiler. GCS 44 (1954); Third edition rev. G. C. Hansen. GCS, Neue Folge 5 (1998) – tr. B. Jackson, in *Theodoret, Jerome, Gennadius, Rufinus: Historical Writings, Etc.* NPNF, Second series 3 (1892; reprinted 1989), pp. 33–159.

Theophanes, *Chronographia*: ed. C. de Boor, *Theophanis Chronographia*, Vol. 1 (Leipzig, 1883) – tr. Mango and Scott (1997).

Urkunde(n): ed. Opitz (1934–1935).

Valerius Maximus, *Facta et dicta memorabilia*: ed. and tr. D. R. Shackleton Bailey, *Valerius Maximus: Memorable Doings and Sayings*, 2 vols. LCL (2000).

*Vita Danielis stylitae*: ed. H. Delehaye, *Les saints stylites*. Subsidia Hagiographica 14 (Brussels, 1923), pp. 1–94 – tr. E. Dawes and N. H. Baynes, *Three Byzantine Saints: Contemporary Biographies Translated from the Greek* (London, 1948), pp. 7–71.

Zosimus, *Historia nova*: ed. L. Mendelssohn, *Zosimi comitis et exadvocati fisci historia nova*. Teubner (1887) – ed. and tr. [French] Paschoud (1979–2000) – tr. R. T. Ridley, *Zosimus: New History. A Translation with Commentary*. Byzantina Australiensia 2 (Canberra, 1982).

# BIBLIOGRAPHY

### ❋ ❋ ❋

Abbott, F. F., and A. C. Johnson (1926). *Municipal Administration in the Roman Empire*. Princeton.

Adams, J. N. (2003). *Bilingualism and the Latin Language*. Cambridge.

Alchermes, J. (1994). "*Spolia* in Roman Cities of the Late Empire: Legislative Rationales and Architectural Reuse." *Dumbarton Oaks Papers* 48:167–78.

——. (1995). "Petrine Politics: Pope Symmachus and the Rotunda of St. Andrew at Old St. Peter's." *Catholic Historical Review* 81:1–40.

Alexander, P. J. (1967). *The Oracle of Baalbek: The Tiburtine Sibyl in Greek Dress*. Dumbarton Oaks Studies 10. Washington, D.C.

Alföldi, A. (1948). *The Conversion of Constantine and Pagan Rome*, tr. H. Mattingly. Oxford.

Alföldy, G., ed. (1996). *Inscriptiones Vrbis Romae Latinae. CIL* 6.8.2. Berlin.

Amann, P. (2002). "Das konstantinische 'Reskript von Hispellum' (CIL XI 5265) und seine Aussagekraft für die etrusko-umbrischen Beziehungen." *Tyche* 17:1–27.

Amici, A. (2000). "*Divus Constantinus*: Le testimonianze epigrafiche." *Rivista storica dell'antichità* 30:187–216.

Amidon, P. R., tr. (1997). *The Church History of Rufinus of Aquileia*. New York.

Anderson, J. C., Jr. (1983). "A Topographical Tradition in Fourth Century Chronicles: Domitian's Building Program." *Historia* 32:93–105.

Anderson, J. G. C. (1897). "A Summer in Phrygia: I." *Journal of Hellenic Studies* 17:396–424.

Andreotti, R. (1964). "Contributo alla discussione del rescritto costantiniano di Hispellum." In *Problemi di storia e archeologia dell'Umbria: Atti del I Convegno di studi umbri, Gubbio, 26–31 maggio 1963*, pp. 249–90. Perugia.

Arce, J. (1984). *Estudios sobre el emperador Fl. Cl. Juliano (Fuentes literarias. Epigrafiía. Numismática)*. Anejos de «Archivo Español de Arqueologia» 8. Madrid.

Arnheim, M. T. W. (1972). *The Senatorial Aristocracy in the Later Roman Empire*. Oxford.

Ashby, T., and R. A. L. Fell (1921). "The Via Flaminia." *Journal of Roman Studies* 11:125–90.

Athanassiadi, P. (1981). *Julian and Hellenism: An Intellectual Biography*. Oxford.

Ausbüttel, F. M. (1988). *Die Verwaltung der Städte und Provinzen im spätantiken Italien*. Europäische Hochschulschriften 343. Frankfurt.

Ayres, L. (2004). *Nicaea and Its Legacy: An Approach to Fourth-Century Trinitarian Theology*. Oxford.

Baglivi, N. (1992). "Da Diocleziano a Costantino: Un punto di riferimento 'storiografico' in alcune interpretazioni tardoantiche." In *Costantino il Grande dall'antichità all'umanesimo: Colloquio sul Cristianesimo nel mondo antico. Macerata 18–20 dicembre 1990*, ed. G. Bonamente and F. Fusco, Vol. 1:59–72. Macerata.

Bagnall, R. S. (1993). *Egypt in Late Antiquity*. Princeton.

Bagnall, R. S., Al. Cameron, S. R. Schwartz, and K. A. Worp (1987). *Consuls of the Later Roman Empire*. Philological Monographs of the American Philological Association 36. Atlanta.

Baldini, A. (1992). "Claudio Gotico e Costantino in Aurelio Vittore ed *Epitome de Caesaribus.*" In *Costantino il Grande dall'antichità all'umanesimo: Colloquio sul Cristianesimo nel mondo antico. Macerata 18–20 dicembre 1990*, ed. G. Bonamente and F. Fusco, Vol. 1:73–89. Macerata.

Barceló, P. (1992). "Una nuova interpretazione dell'Arco di Costantino." In *Costantino il Grande dall'antichità all'umanesimo: Colloquio sul Cristianesimo nel mondo antico. Macerata 18–20 dicembre 1990*, ed. G. Bonamente and F. Fusco, Vol. 1:105–14. Macerata.

Bardy, G. (1948). *La question des langues dans l'église ancienne*. Etudes de théologie historique. Paris.

Barnes, M. R., and D. R. Williams, ed. (1993). *Arianism after Arius: Essays on the Development of the Fourth Century Trinitarian Conflicts*. Edinburgh.

Barnes, T. D. (1975a). "Constans and Gratian in Rome." *Harvard Studies in Classical Philology* 79:325–33.

———. (1975b). "Publilius Optatianus Porfyrius." *American Journal of Philology* 96:173–186. Reprinted in T. D. Barnes, *Early Christianity and the Roman Empire* (London, 1984), Chapter 10.

———. (1975c). "Two Senators under Constantine." *Journal of Roman Studies* 64:40–49. Reprinted in T. D. Barnes, *Early Christianity and the Roman Empire* (London, 1984), Chapter 9.

———. (1976a). "Imperial Campaigns, A.D. 285–311." *Phoenix* 30:174–93. Reprinted in T. D. Barnes, *Early Christianity and the Roman Empire* (London, 1984), Chapter 12.

———. (1976b). "The Emperor Constantine's Good Friday Sermon." *Journal of Theological Studies* n.s. 27:414–23.

———. (1978a). "A Correspondent of Iamblichus." *Greek, Roman and Byzantine Studies* 19:99–106. Reprinted in T. D. Barnes, *Early Christianity and the Roman Empire* (London, 1984), Chapter 17.

———. (1978b). "Emperor and Bishops, A.D. 324–344: Some Problems." *American Journal of Ancient History* 3:53–75. Reprinted in T. D. Barnes, *Early Christianity and the Roman Empire* (London, 1984), Chapter 18.

———. (1980). "The Editions of Eusebius' *Ecclesiastical History*." *Greek, Roman and Byzantine Studies* 21:191–201. Reprinted in T. D. Barnes, *Early Christianity and the Roman Empire* (London, 1984), Chapter 20.

_____. (1981). *Constantine and Eusebius*. Cambridge, MA.

_____. (1982). *The New Empire of Diocletian and Constantine*. Cambridge, MA.

_____. (1983). "Two Victory Titles of Constantius." *Zeitschrift für Papyrologie und Epigraphik* 52:229–35. Reprinted in T. D. Barnes, *From Eusebius to Augustine: Selected Papers 1982–1993* (Aldershot, 1994), Chapter 14.

_____. (1984). "Some Inconsistencies in Eusebius." *Journal of Theological Studies* n.s. 35:470–75. Reprinted in T. D. Barnes, *From Eusebius to Augustine: Selected Papers 1982–1993* (Aldershot, 1994), Chapter 2.

_____. (1985). "The Conversion of Constantine." *Echos du monde classique / Classical Views* 29, n.s. 4:371–91. Reprinted in T. D. Barnes, *From Eusebius to Augustine: Selected Papers 1982–1993* (Aldershot, 1994), Chapter 3.

_____. (1987). "Himerius and the Fourth Century." *Classical Philology* 82:206–25. Reprinted in T. D. Barnes, *From Eusebius to Augustine: Selected Papers 1982–1993* (Aldershot, 1994), Chapter 16.

_____. (1989a). "Christians and Pagans in the Reign of Constantius." In *L'église et l'empire au IV^e siècle*, ed. A. Dihle, pp. 301–37. Fondation Hardt pour l'étude de l'antiquité classique, Entretiens 34. Geneva. Partially reprinted in T. D. Barnes, *From Eusebius to Augustine: Selected Papers 1982–1993* (Aldershot, 1994), Chapter 8.

_____. (1989b). "Panegyric, History and Hagiography in Eusebius' *Life of Constantine*." In *The Making of Orthodoxy: Essays in Honour of Henry Chadwick*, ed. R. Williams, pp. 94–123. Cambridge. Reprinted in T. D. Barnes, *From Eusebius to Augustine: Selected Papers 1982–1993* (Aldershot, 1994), Chapter 11.

_____. (1992). "The Constantinian Settlement." In *Eusebius, Christianity, and Judaism*, ed. H. W. Attridge and G. Hata, pp. 635–57. Detroit. Reprinted in T. D. Barnes, *From Eusebius to Augustine: Selected Papers 1982–1993* (Aldershot, 1994), Chapter 9.

_____. (1993). *Athanasius and Constantius: Theology and Politics in the Constantinian Empire*. Cambridge, MA.

_____. (1994a). "The Religious Affiliation of Consuls and Prefects, 317–361." In T. D. Barnes, *From Eusebius to Augustine: Selected Papers 1982–1993*, Chapter 7. Aldershot.

_____. (1994b). "The Two Drafts of Eusebius' *Life of Constantine*." In T. D. Barnes, *From Eusebius to Augustine: Selected Papers 1982–1993*, Chapter 12. Aldershot.

_____. (1996). "Emperors, Panegyrics, Prefects, Provinces and Palaces." *Journal of Roman Archaeology* 9:532–52.

_____. (1997). "Christentum und dynastische Politik (300–325)." In *Usurpationen in der Spätantike: Akten des Kolloquiums "Staatsstreich und Staatlichkeit," 6.-10. März 1996, Solothurn/Bern*, ed. F. Paschoud and J. Szidat, pp. 99–109. Historia Einzelschriften 111. Stuttgart.

_____. (1998). *Ammianus Marcellinus and the Representation of Historical Reality.* Ithaca.

_____. (1999). "Ambrose and Gratian." *Antiquité tardive* 7:165–74.

_____. (2001). "Constantine's *Speech to the Assembly of the Saints*: Place and Date of Delivery." *Journal of Theological Studies* n.s. 52:26–36.

Bartelink, G. J. M., ed. and tr. (1994). *Athanase d'Alexandrie, Vie d'Antoine.* SChr. 400. Paris.

Bassett, S. (2004). *The Urban Image of Late Antique Constantinople.* Cambridge.

Bastien, P. (1992–1994). *Le buste monétaire des empereurs romains,* 3 vols. Numismatique romaine, Essais, recherches et documents 19. Wetteren.

Bauer, W. (1972). *Orthodoxy and Heresy in Earliest Christianity,* tr. R. A. Kraft et al. London.

Baynes, N. H. (1931). *Constantine the Great and the Christian Church.* The British Academy, The Raleigh Lecture on History 1929. London.

Beard, M., J. North, and S. Price (1998). *Religions of Rome,* 2 vols. Cambridge.

Belke, K., and N. Mersich (1990). *Phrygien und Pisidien.* = *Tabula Imperii Byzantini,* ed. H. Hunger, Bd. 7. Österreichische Akademie der Wissenschaften, philosophisch-historische Klasse, Denkschriften 211. Vienna.

Belke, K., and M. Restle (1984). *Galatien und Lykaonien.* = *Tabula Imperii Byzantini,* ed. H. Hunger, Bd. 4. Österreichische Akademie der Wissenschaften, philosophisch-historische Klasse, Denkschriften 172. Vienna.

Bell, A. J. E. (1997). "Cicero and the Spectacle of Power." *Journal of Roman Studies* 87:1–22.

Bernardi, J. (1968). *La prédication des Pères Cappadociens: La prédicateur et son auditoire.* Paris.

Beskow, P. (1962). *Rex gloriae: The Kingship of Christ in the Early Church.* Stockholm.

Bidez, J., ed. (1913). *Philostorgius Kirchengeschichte: Mit dem Leben des Lucian von Antiochien und den Fragmenten eines arianischen Historiographen.* GCS 21. Leipzig.

_____. (1930). *La vie de l'empereur Julien.* Paris.

Birley, A. R. (2000). "Hadrian to the Antonines." In *The Cambridge Ancient History, Second Edition, Volume XI: The High Empire, A.D. 70–192,* ed. A. K. Bowman, P. Garnsey, and D. Rathbone, pp. 132–94. Cambridge.

Bleckmann, B. (1994). "Constantina, Vetranio und Gallus Caesar." *Chiron* 24:29–68.

_____. (1997). "Ein Kaiser als Prediger: Zur Datierung der konstantinischen 'Rede an die Versammlung der Heiligen.'" *Hermes* 125:183–202.

_____. (2004). "Bemerkungen zum Scheitern des Mehrherrschaftssystems: Reichsteilung und Territorialanspruche." In *Diokletian und die Tetrarchie: Aspekte einer Zeitenwende,* ed. A. Demandt, A. Goltz, and H. Schlange-Schöningen, pp. 74–94. Millennium-Studien zu Kultur und Geschichte des ersten Jahrtausends n. Chr. 1. Berlin and New York.

————. (2006). "Sources for the History of Constantine." In *The Cambridge Companion to the Age of Constantine*, ed. N. Lenski, pp. 14–31. Cambridge.

Bloch, H. (1945). "A New Document of the Last Pagan Revival in the West, 393–394 A.D." *Harvard Theological Review* 38:199–244.

————. (1963). "The Pagan Revival in the West at the End of the Fourth Century." In *The Conflict between Paganism and Christianity in the Fourth Century*, ed. A. Momigliano, pp. 193–218. Oxford-Warburg Studies. Oxford.

Blümel, W., ed. (1985). *Die Inschriften von Iasos*, 2 vols. Inschriften griechischer Städte aus Kleinasien 28.1–2. Bonn.

Börker, C., and R. Merkelbach, with H. Engelmann and D. Knibbe, ed. (1979). *Die Inschriften von Ephesos, Teil II*. Inschriften griechischer Städte aus Kleinasien 12. Bonn.

de Boor, C., ed. (1978). *Georgii Monachi Chronicon*, 2 vols. Corrected edition ed. P. Wirth. Teubner. Stuttgart.

Bouffartigue, J. (1991). "Julien ou l'hellénisme décomposé." In *ΕΛΛΗΝΙΣΜΟΣ: Quelques jalons pour une histoire de l'identité grecque. Actes du colloque de Strasbourg 25–27 octobre 1989*, ed. S. Said, pp. 251–66. Université des sciences humaines de Strasbourg, Travaux du Centre de recherche sur le Proche-Orient et la Grèce antiques 11. Leiden.

————. (2004). "Philosophie et antichristianisme chez l'empereur Julien." In *Hellénisme et christianisme*, ed. M. Narcy and E. Rebillard, pp. 111–31. Lille.

Bowen, A., and P. Garnsey, tr. (2003). *Lactantius, Divine Institutes*. TTH 40. Liverpool.

Bowersock, G. W. (1978). *Julian the Apostate*. London.

————. (1982). "The Imperial Cult: Perceptions and Persistence." In *Jewish and Christian Self-Definition, 3: Self-Definition in the Greco-Roman World*, ed. B. F. Meyer and E. P. Sanders, pp. 171–82, 238–41. Philadelphia.

————. (2002). "Peter and Constantine." In *"Humana sapit": Etudes d'antiquité tardive offertes à Lellia Cracco Ruggini*, ed. J.-M. Carrié and R. L. Testa, pp. 209–17. Bibliothèque de l'Antiquité tardive 3. Turnhout.

Bowman, A. K. (2005). "Diocletian and the First Tetrarchy, A.D. 284–305." In *The Cambridge Ancient History, Second Edition, Volume XII: The Crisis of Empire, A.D. 193–337*, ed. A. K. Bowman, P. Garnsey, and Av. Cameron, pp. 67–89. Cambridge.

Bowman, G. (1999). "'Mapping History's Redemption': Eschatology and Topography in the *Itinerarium Burdigalense*." In *Jerusalem: Its Sanctity and Centrality to Judaism, Christianity, and Islam*, ed. L. I. Levine, pp. 163–87. New York.

Bradbury, S. (1994). "Constantine and the Problem of Anti-Pagan Legislation in the Fourth Century." *Classical Philology* 89:120–39.

————. (1995). "Julian's Pagan Revival and the Decline of Blood Sacrifice." *Phoenix* 49:331–56.

_____. (2000). "A Sophistic Prefect: Anatolius of Berytus in the *Letters* of Libanius."
*Classical Philology* 95:172–86.

Bradley, G. (2000). *Ancient Umbria: State, Culture, and Identity in Central Italy from the Iron Age to the Augustan Era.* Oxford.

Brakke, D. (1994). "The Greek and Syriac Versions of the *Life of Antony.*" *Le Museon* 107:29–53.

_____. (1995). *Athanasius and the Politics of Asceticism.* Oxford.

Brandt, H. (1998). *Geschichte der römischen Kaiserzeit von Diokletian und Konstantin bis zum Ende der konstantinischen Dynastie (284–363).* Berlin.

Brenk, B. (1987). "Spolia from Constantine to Charlemagne: Aesthetics versus Ideology." *Dumbarton Oaks Papers* 41:103–9.

Brennecke, H. C. (1988). *Studien zur Geschichte der Homöer: Der Osten bis zum Ende der homöischen Reichskirche.* Beiträge zur historischen Theologie 73. Tubingen.

Brixhe, C. (2002). "Interactions between Greek and Phrygian under the Roman Empire." In *Bilingualism in Ancient Society: Language Contact and the Written Text,* ed. J. N. Adams, M. Janse, and S. Swain, pp. 246–66. Oxford.

Brixhe, C., and T. Drew-Bear (1997). "Huit inscriptions néo-phrygiennes." In *Frigi e Frigio: Atti del I° Simposio Internazionale Roma, 16–17 ottobre 1995,* ed. R. Gusmani, M. Salvini, and P. Vannicelli, pp. 71–114. Rome.

Brubaker, L. (1997). "Memories of Helena: Patterns in Imperial Female Matronage in the Fourth and Fifth Centuries." In *Women, Men and Eunuchs: Gender in Byzantium,* ed. L. James, pp. 52–75. London.

_____. (1999). *Vision and Meaning in Ninth-Century Byzantium: Image as Exegesis in the Homilies of Gregory of Nazianzus.* Cambridge.

Bruun, C. (1995). "The Thick Neck of the Emperor Constantine: Slimy Snails and 'Quellenforschung.'" *Historia* 44:459–80.

Bruun, P. M. (1954). "The Consecration Coins of Constantine the Great." In *Commentationes in honorem Edwin Linkomies sexagenarii A.D. MCMLV editae,* ed. H. Zilliacus and K.-E. Henriksson. = *Arctos* n.s. 1:19–31.

_____. (1966). *The Roman Imperial Coinage, VII: Constantine and Licinius A.D. 313–337.* London.

_____. (1976). "Notes on the Transmission of Imperial Images in Late Antiquity." In *Studia Romana in honorem Petri Krarup septuagenarii,* ed. K. Ascani, T. Fischer-Hansen, F. Johansen, S. S. Jensen, and J. E. Skydsgaard, pp. 122–31. Odense.

_____. (1987). "Constans Maximus Augustus." In *Mélanges de numismatique offerts à Pierre Bastien à l'occasion de son 75ᵉ anniversaire,* ed. H. Huvelin, M. Christol, and G. Gautier, pp. 187–99. Wetteren.

Buckler, W. H. (1937). "A Charitable Foundation of A.D. 237." *Journal of Hellenic Studies* 57:1–10.

Buckler, W. H., and W. M. Calder, ed. (1939). *Monumenta Asiae Minoris Antiqua, Vol. VI: Monuments and Documents from Phrygia and Caria.* Manchester.

Buckler, W. H., W. M. Calder, and W. K. C. Guthrie, ed. (1933). *Monumenta Asiae Minoris Antiqua, Vol. IV: Monuments and Documents from Eastern Asia and Western Galatia.* Manchester.

Burgess, R. W. (1997). "The Dates and Editions of Eusebius' *Chronici canones* and *Historia ecclesiastica.*" *Journal of Theological Studies* n.s. 48:471–504.

———, with W. Witakowski. (1999a). *Studies in Eusebian and Post-Eusebian Chronography.* Historia Einzelschriften 135. Stuttgart.

———. (1999b). "ΑΧΥΡⲰΝ or ΠΡΟΑΣΤΕΙΟΝ? The Location and Circumstances of Constantine's Death." *Journal of Theological Studies* n.s. 50:153–61.

———. (2000). "The Date of the Deposition of Eustathius of Antioch." *Journal of Theological Studies* n.s. 51:150–60.

———. (2003). "The *Passio S. Artemii*, Philostorgius, and the Dates of the Invention and Translations of the Relics of Sts Andrew and Luke." *Analecta Bollandiana* 121:5–36.

Burrus, V. (1995). *The Making of a Heretic: Gender, Authority, and the Priscillianist Controversy.* Berkeley.

Butcher, K. (2003). *Roman Syria and the Near East.* London.

Cahn, H. A. (1987). "*Abolitio nominis* de Constantin II." In *Mélanges de numismatique offerts à Pierre Bastien à l'occasion de son 75ᵉ anniversaire*, ed. H. Huvelin, M. Christol, and G. Gautier, pp. 201–2. Wetteren.

Calder, W. M., ed. (1928). *Monumenta Asiae Minoris Antiqua, Vol. I.* London.

———. (1954). "William Hepburn Buckler, 1867–1952." *Proceedings of the British Academy* 40:274–86.

———, ed. (1956). *Monumenta Asiae Minoris Antiqua, Vol. VII: Monuments from Eastern Phrygia.* Manchester.

Callu, J.-P. (1995). "A nouveau le savon de Constantin." *Historia* 44:500–2.

———. (2002). "Naissance de la dynastie constantinienne: Le tournant de 314–316." In *"Humana sapit": Etudes d'antiquité tardive offertes à Lellia Cracco Ruggini*, ed. J.-M. Carrié and R. L. Testa, pp. 111–20. Bibliothèque de l'Antiquité tardive 3. Turnhout.

Calza, R. (1959–1960). "Un problema di iconografia imperiale sull'Arco di Costantino." *Atti della Pontificia Accademia Romana di Archeologia* (série III), Rendiconti 32:133–61.

Cambi, N. (2004). "Tetrarchic Practice in Name Giving." In *Diokletian und die Tetrarchie: Aspekte einer Zeitenwende*, ed. A. Demandt, A. Goltz, and H. Schlange-Schöningen, pp. 38–46. Millennium-Studien zu Kultur und Geschichte des ersten Jahrtausends n. Chr. 1. Berlin and New York.

Cameron, Alan (1988). "Flavius: A Nicety of Protocol." *Latomus* 47:26–33.

————. (2004). "Poetry and Literary Culture in Late Antiquity." In *Approaching Late Antiquity: The Transformation from Early to Late Empire*, ed. S. Swain and M. Edwards, pp. 327–54. Oxford.

Cameron, Averil (1997). "Eusebius' *Vita Constantini* and the Construction of Constantine." In *Portraits: Biographical Representation in the Greek and Latin Literature of the Roman Empire*, ed. M. J. Edwards and S. Swain, pp. 145–74. Oxford.

————. (2000). "Form and Meaning: The *Vita Constantini* and the *Vita Antonii*." In *Greek Biography and Panegyric in Late Antiquity*, ed. T. Hägg and P. Rousseau, with C. Høgel, pp. 72–88. The Transformation of the Classical Heritage 31. Berkeley.

————. (2005). "The Reign of Constantine, A.D. 306–337." In *The Cambridge Ancient History, Second Edition, Volume XII: The Crisis of Empire, A.D. 193–337*, ed. A. K. Bowman, P. Garnsey, and Av. Cameron, pp. 90–109. Cambridge.

Cameron, Averil, and S. G. Hall, tr. (1999). *Eusebius, Life of Constantine: Introduction, Translation, and Commentary*. Oxford.

Cameron, Averil, and J. Herrin, with Alan Cameron, R. Cormack, and C. Roueché (1984). *Constantinople in the Early Eighth Century: The* Parastaseis Syntomoi Chronikai. Columbia Studies in the Classical Tradition 10. Leiden.

Campbell, B., tr. (2000). *The Writings of the Roman Land Surveyors: Introduction, Text, Translation and Commentary*. Journal of Roman Studies, Monographs 9. London.

Carriker, A. (2003). *The Library of Eusebius of Caesarea*. Supplements to Vigiliae Christianae 67. Leiden and Boston.

Carson, R. A. G. (1987). "*Carausius et fratres sui* . . . again." In *Mélanges de numismatique offerts à Pierre Bastien à l'occasion de son 75ᵉ anniversaire*, ed. H. Huvelin, M. Christol, and G. Gautier, pp. 145–48. Wetteren.

Castritius, H. (1969). *Studien zu Maximinus Daia*. Frankfurter althistorische Studien 2. Kallmünz.

Chantraine, H. (1992). "Die Nachfolgeordnung Constantins des Großen." *Akademie der Wissenschaften und der Literatur, Abhandlungen der geistes- und socialwissenschaftlichen Klasse*, Jahrgang 1992, Nr. 7:1–25.

Charron, A., and M. Heijmans (2001). "L'obélisque du cirque d'Arles." *Journal of Roman Archaeology* 14:373–80.

Chastagnol, A. (1962). *Les fastes de la préfecture de Rome au Bas-Empire*. Etudes prosopographiques 2. Paris.

————. (1963). "L'administration du Diocèse Italien au Bas Empire." *Historia* 12:348–79.

————. (1973). "Le repli sur Arles des services administratifs gaulois en l'an 407 de notre ère." *Revue historique* 249:23–40.

——. (1976). "Les inscriptions constantiniennes du cirque de Mérida." *Mélanges de l'Ecole française de Rome*, Antiquité 88:259–76. Reprinted in A. Chastagnol, *Aspects de l'antiquité tardive*. Saggi di storia antica 6 (Rome, 1994), pp. 43–59.

——. (1981a). "L'inscription constantinienne d'Orcistus." *Mélanges de l'Ecole française de Rome*, Antiquité 93:381–416. Reprinted in A. Chastagnol, *Aspects de l'antiquité tardive*. Saggi di storia antica 6 (Rome, 1994), pp. 105–42.

——. (1981b). "Les *realia* d'une cité d'après l'inscription constantinienne d'Orkistos." *Ktema* 6:373–79.

——. (1987). "Aspects concrets et cadre topographique des fêtes décennales des empereurs à Rome." In *L'Urbs: Espace urbain et histoire (I$^{er}$ siècle av. J.-C. – III$^e$ siècle ap. J.-C.). Actes du colloque international organisé par le Centre national de la recherche scientifique et l'Ecole française de Rome (Rome, 8–12 mai 1985)*, pp. 491–507. Collection de l'Ecole française de Rome 98. Rome and Paris.

——. (1992). "Quelques mises au point autour de l'empereur Licinius." In *Costantino il Grande dall'antichità all'umanesimo: Colloquio sul Cristianesimo nel mondo antico. Macerata 18–20 dicembre 1990*, ed. G. Bonamente and F. Fusco, Vol. 1:311–23. Macerata.

Chausson, F. (2002a). "La famille du préfet Ablabius." *Pallas* 60:205–29.

——. (2002b). "Une soeur de Constantin: Anastasia." In *"Humana sapit": Etudes d'antiquité tardive offertes à Lellia Cracco Ruggini*, ed. J.-M. Carrié and R. L. Testa, pp. 131–55. Bibliothèque de l'Antiquité tardive 3. Turnhout.

Chioffi, L. (1995). "Equus: Constantius." In *Lexicon Topographicum Urbis Romae*, Vol. 2, ed. E. M. Steinby, p. 227. Rome.

Christensen, T. (1983). "The So-Called *Appendix* to Eusebius' *Historia Ecclesiastica* VIII." *Classica et Mediaevalia* 34:177–209.

——. (1989). *Rufinus of Aquileia and the* Historia Ecclesiastica*, Lib. VIII-IX, of Eusebius*. Det Kongelige Danske Videnskabernes Selskab, Historisk-filosofiske Meddelelser 58. Copenhagen.

Christol, M., and T. Drew-Bear (1986). "Documents latins de Phrygie." *Tyche* 1:41–87.

——. (1999). "Antioche de Pisidie capitale provinciale et l'oeuvre de M. Valerius Diogenes." *Antiquité tardive* 7:39–71.

Clark, E. A. (1992). *The Origenist Controversy: The Cultural Construction of an Early Christian Debate*. Princeton.

——. (2004). *History, Theory, Text: Historians and the Linguistic Turn*. Cambridge, MA.

Coarelli, F. (1986). "L'urbs e il suburbio." In *Società romana e imperio tardoantico, 2. Roma: Politica, economia, paesaggio urbano*, ed. A. Giardina, pp. 1–58, 395–412. Rome.

——. (1993). "Basilica Constantiniana, B. Nova." In *Lexicon Topographicum Urbis Romae*, Vol. 1, ed. E. M. Steinby, pp. 170–73. Rome.

————. (2001). "Il rescritto di Spello e il santuario 'etnico' degli Umbri." In *Umbria cristiana: Dalla diffusione del culto al culto dei santi (secc. IV–X). Atti del XV Congresso internazionale di studi sull'alto medioevo, Spoleto, 23–28 ottobre 2000*, pp. 39–51. Atti dei Congressi 15. Spoleto.

Coleman-Norton, P. R., tr. (1966). *Roman State and Christian Church: A Collection of Legal Documents to A.D. 535*, 3 vols. London.

Conti, S. (2004). *Die Inschriften Kaiser Julians*. Altertumswissenschaftliches Kolloquium, Interdisziplinäre Studien zur Antike und zu ihrem Nachleben 10. Stuttgart.

Corcoran, S. (1993). "Hidden from History: The Legislation of Licinius." In *The Theodosian Code: Studies in the Imperial Law of Late Antiquity*, ed. J. Harries and I. Wood, pp. 97–119. London.

————. (1996). *The Empire of the Tetrarchs: Imperial Pronouncements and Government AD 284–324*. Oxford.

————. (2000). "Additional Notes." In S. Corcoran, *The Empire of the Tetrarchs: Imperial Pronouncements and Government AD 284–324*, Revised Edition, pp. 343–53. Oxford.

————. (2002). "A Tetrarchic Inscription from Corcyra and the Edictum de Accusationibus." *Zeitschrift für Papyrologie und Epigraphik* 141:221–30.

————. (2004). "The Publication of Law in the Era of the Tetrarchs – Diocletian, Galerius, Gregorius, Hermogenian." In *Diokletian und die Tetrarchie: Aspekte einer Zeitenwende*, ed. A. Demandt, A. Goltz, and H. Schlange-Schöningen, pp. 56–73. Millennium-Studien zu Kultur und Geschichte des ersten Jahrtausends n. Chr. 1. Berlin and New York.

Cox, C. W. M., and A. Cameron, ed. (1937). *Monumenta Asiae Minoris Antiqua, Vol. V: Monuments from Dorylaeum and Nacolea*. Manchester.

Crawford, M. H. (2002). "Discovery, Autopsy and Progress: Diocletian's Jigsaw Puzzles." In *Classics in Progress: Essays on Ancient Greece and Rome*, ed. T. P. Wiseman, pp. 145–63. Oxford.

Crawford, M. H., and J. Reynolds (1975). "The Publication of the Prices Edict: A New Inscription from Aezani." *Journal of Roman Studies* 65:160–63.

Cullhed, M. (1994). *Conservator urbis suae: Studies in the Politics and Propaganda of the Emperor Maxentius*. Skrifter Utgivna av Svenska Institutet i Rom, 8°, 20. Stockholm.

Curran, J. (1994). "Moving Statues in Late Antique Rome: Problems of Perspective." *Art History* 17:46–58.

————. (2000). *Pagan City and Christian Capital: Rome in the Fourth Century*. Oxford.

Dagron, G. (1969). "Aux origines de la civilisation byzantine: Langue de culture et langue d'Etat." *Revue historique* 241:23–56.

————. (1970). "Les moines et la ville: Le monachisme à Constantinople jusqu'au concile de Chalcédoine (451)." *Travaux et mémoires* 4:229–76.

———. (1974). *Naissance d'une capitale: Constantinople et ses institutions de 330 à 451.* Bibliothèque byzantine, Etudes 7. Paris.

———. (1984). *Constantinople imaginaire: Etudes sur le recueil des "Patria".* Bibliothèque byzantine, Etudes 8. Paris.

———. (1994). "Formes et fonctions du pluralisme linguistique à Byzance (VIII^e^-XII^e^ siècle)." *Travaux et mémoires* 12:219–40.

———. (2003). *Emperor and Priest: The Imperial Office in Byzantium,* tr. J. Birrell. Cambridge.

Darwell-Smith, R. H. (1996). *Emperors and Architecture: A Study of Flavian Rome.* Collection Latomus 231. Brussels.

Davies, P. J. E. (2000a). *Death and the Emperor: Roman Imperial Funerary Monuments from Augustus to Marcus Aurelius.* Cambridge.

———. (2000b). "'What Worse Than Nero, What Better Than His Baths?': '*Damnatio Memoriae*' and Roman Architecture." In *From Caligula to Constantine: Tyranny and Transformation in Roman Portraiture,* ed. E. R. Varner, pp. 27–44. Atlanta.

Davies, P. S. (1991). "Constantine's Editor." *Journal of Theological Studies* n.s. 42:610–18.

Deckers, J. G. (1979). "Die Wandmalerei im Kaiserkultraum von Luxor." *Jahrbuch des deutschen archäologischen Instituts* 94:600–52.

De Decker, D. (1968). "La politique religieuse de Maxence." *Byzantion* 38:472–562.

Deichmann, F. W., and A. Tschira (1957). "Das Mausoleum der Kaiserin Helena und die Basilika der Heiligen Marcellinus und Petrus an der Via Labicana vor Rom." *Jahrbuch des deutschen archäologischen Instituts* 72:44–110.

Depeyrot, G. (2006). "Economy and Society." In *The Cambridge Companion to the Age of Constantine,* ed. N. Lenski, pp. 226–52. Cambridge.

Dietz, K. (2000). "Kaiser Julian in Phönizien." *Chiron* 30:807–55.

Digeser, E. D. (2000). *The Making of a Christian Empire: Lactantius and Rome.* Ithaca.

Dörries, H. (1954). *Das Selbstzeugnis Kaiser Konstantins.* Abhandlungen der Akademie der Wissenschaften in Göttingen, Philologisch-historische Klasse, Dritte Folge 34. Göttingen.

Dolbeau, F., ed. (1996). *Augustin d'Hippone, Vingt-six sermons au peuple d'Afrique.* Collection des Etudes augustiniennes, Série antiquité 147. Paris.

de Dominicis, M. (1963). "Un intervento legislativo di Costantino in materia religiosa (Nota a C.I.L., XI, 5265)." *Revue internationale des droits de l'antiquité,* 3^e^ série, 10:199–211.

Downey, G. (1961). *A History of Antioch in Syria from Seleucus to the Arab Conquest.* Princeton.

Drake, H. A. (1976). *In Praise of Constantine: A Historical Study and New Translation of Eusebius' Tricennial Orations.* Berkeley.

———. (1988). "What Eusebius Knew: The Genesis of the *Vita Constantini*." *Classical Philology* 83:20–38.

———. (1996). "Lambs into Lions: Explaining Early Christian Intolerance." *Past and Present* 153:3–36.

———. (2000). *Constantine and the Bishops: The Politics of Intolerance*. Baltimore.

———. (2006). "The Impact of Constantine on Christianity." In *The Cambridge Companion to the Age of Constantine*, ed. N. Lenski, pp. 111–36. Cambridge.

Drew-Bear, T., and C. Naour (1990). "Divinités de Phrygie." In *Aufstieg und Niedergang der römischen Welt, Teil II: Principat, Band 18: Religion, 3. Teilband*, ed. W. Haase, pp. 1907–2044. Berlin.

Drijvers, J. W. (1992). *Helena Augusta: The Mother of Constantine the Great and the Legend of Her Finding of the True Cross*. Brill's Studies in Intellectual History 27. Leiden.

———. (1996). "Ammianus Marcellinus 15.13.1–2: Some Observations on the Career and Bilingualism of Strategius Musonianus." *Classical Quarterly* 46:532–37.

Drinkwater, J. F. (1983). *Roman Gaul: The Three Provinces, 58 BC–AD 260*. Ithaca.

Droge, A. J. (1992). "The Apologetic Dimensions of the *Ecclesiastical History*." In *Eusebius, Christianity, and Judaism*, ed. H. W. Attridge and G. Hata, pp. 492–509. Detroit.

Dubuisson, M. (1992). "Jean le Lydien et le latin: Les limites d'une competence." In *Serta Leodiensia Secunda: Mélanges publiés par les classiques de Liège à l'occasion du 175ᵉ anniversaire de l'Université*, pp. 123–31. Liège.

Duchesne, L., ed. (1886). *Le Liber Pontificalis: Texte, introduction et commentaire*, Vol. 1. Bibliothèque des Ecoles françaises d'Athènes et de Rome, 2ᵉ série. Paris.

Duncan-Jones, R. P. (1982). *The Economy of the Roman Empire: Quantitative Studies*. Second edition, Cambridge.

Dvornik, F. (1966). *Early Christian and Byzantine Political Philosophy: Origins and Background*. Dumbarton Oaks Studies 9. Washington, D.C.

Ebersolt, J. (1929–1930). "Sarcophages impériaux de Rome et de Constantinople." *Byzantinische Zeitschrift* 30:582–87.

Eck, W. (1994). "Kaiserliches Handeln in italischen Städten." In *L'Italie d'Auguste à Dioclétien*, pp. 329–51. Collection de l'Ecole française de Rome 198. Rome and Paris.

———. (2000). "Latein als Sprache politischer Kommunikation in Städten der östlichen Provinzen." *Chiron* 30:641–60.

———. (2003). "The Prosopographia Imperii Romani and Prosopographical Method." In *Fifty Years of Prosopography: The Later Roman Empire, Byzantium and Beyond*, ed. Av. Cameron, pp. 11–22. Proceedings of the British Academy 118. Oxford.

———. (2004). "Lateinisch, Griechisch, Germanisch…? Wie sprach Rom mit seinen Untertanen?" In *Roman Rule and Civic Life: Local and Regional Perspectives*.

*Proceedings of the Fourth Workshop of the International Network, Impact of Empire (Roman Empire, c. 200 B.C.-A.D. 476), Leiden, June 25–28, 2003,* ed. L. de Ligt, E. A. Hemelrijk, and H. W. Singor, pp. 3–19. Amsterdam.

Edmondson, J. (2002). "Writing Latin in the Province of Lusitania." In *Becoming Roman, Writing Latin? Literacy and Epigraphy in the Roman West,* ed. A. E. Cooley, pp. 41–60. Journal of Roman Archaeology, Supplementary Series 48. Portsmouth.

Edwards, M. (1999). "The Constantinian Circle and the *Oration to the Saints.*" In *Apologetics in the Roman Empire: Pagans, Jews, and Christians,* ed. M. Edwards, M. Goodman, and S. Price, with C. Rowland, pp. 251–75. Oxford.

_____, tr. (2003). *Constantine and Christendom: The Oration to the Saints, the Greek and Latin Accounts of the Discovery of the Cross, the Edict of Constantine to Pope Silvester.* TTH 39. Liverpool.

_____. (2006). "The Beginnings of Christianization." In *The Cambridge Companion to the Age of Constantine,* ed. N. Lenski, pp. 137–58. Cambridge.

Effenberger, A. (2000). "Konstantinsmausoleum, Apostelkirche – und keine Ende?" In *Lithostroton: Studien zur byzantinischen Kunst und Geschichte. Festschrift für Marcell Restle,* ed. B. Borkopp and T. Steppan, pp. 67–78. Stuttgart.

Elliott, T. G. (1996). *The Christianity of Constantine the Great.* Scranton.

Elm, S. (2003). "Hellenism and Historiography: Gregory of Nazianzus and Julian in Dialogue." *Journal of Medieval and Early Modern Studies* 33:493–515. Reprinted in *The Cultural Turn in Late Ancient Studies: Gender, Asceticism, and Historiography,* ed. D. B. Martin and P. C. Miller (Durham, 2005), pp. 258–77.

Elm, S., P.-A. Fabre, E. Rebillard, A. Romano, and C. Sotinel (2000). "Introduction." In *Orthodoxie, christianisme, histoire: Orthodoxy, Christianity, History,* ed. S. Elm, E. Rebillard and A. Romano, pp. VIII–XXV. Collection de l'Ecole française de Rome 270. Paris and Rome.

Elsner, J. (2000a). "From the Culture of *Spolia* to the Cult of Relics: The Arch of Constantine and the Genesis of Late Antique Forms." *Papers of the British School at Rome* 68:149–84.

_____. (2000b). "The *Itinerarium Burdigalense:* Politics and Salvation in the Geography of Constantine's Empire." *Journal of Roman Studies* 90:181–95.

_____. (2005). "Sacrifice and Narrative on the Arch of the Argentarii at Rome." *Journal of Roman Archaeology* 18:83–98.

Elton, H. (2006). "Warfare and the Military." In *The Cambridge Companion to the Age of Constantine,* ed. N. Lenski, pp. 325–46. Cambridge.

Engemann, J. (1984). "Die religiöse Herrscherfunktion im Fünfsäulenmonument Diocletians in Rom und in den Herrschermosaiken Justinians in Ravenna." *Frühmittelalterliche Studien* 18:336–56.

Ensoli, S. (2000). "I colossi de bronzo a Roma in età tardoantica: Dal Colosso di Nerone al Colosso di Costantino. A proposito dei tre frammenti bronzei dei Musei

Capitolini." In *Aurea Roma: Dalla città pagana alla città cristiana*, ed. S. Ensoli and E. La Rocca, pp. 66–90. Rome.

Evans Grubbs, J. (1995). *Law and Family in Late Antiquity: The Emperor Constantine's Marriage Legislation*. Oxford.

Evers, C. (1991). "Remarques sur l'iconographie de Constantin: A propos du remploi de portraits des «bons empereurs»." *Mélanges de l'Ecole française de Rome*, Antiquité 103:785–806.

Feige, G. (1993). "Der Begriff υἱοπάτωρ in der antimarkellischen Polemik des 4. Jahrhunderts." In *Studia Patristica Vol. XXVI: Papers Presented at the Eleventh International Conference on Patristic Studies Held in Oxford 1991. Liturgica, Second Century, Alexandria before Nicaea, Athanasius and the Arian Controversy*, ed. E. A. Livingstone, pp. 365–68. Leuven.

Feissel, D. (1995). "Les constitutions des Tétrarques connues par l'épigraphie: Inventaire et notes critiques." *Antiquité tardive* 3:33–53.

———. (1996). "Deux constitutions tétrarchiques inscrites à Ephèse." *Antiquité tardive* 4:273–89.

———. (1998). "Vicaires et proconsuls d'Asie du IVᵉ au VIᵉ siècle: Remarques sur l'administration du diocèse asianique au Bas-Empire." *Antiquité tardive* 6:91–104.

———. (1999). "L'*adnotatio* de Constantin sur le droit de cité d'Orcistus en Phrygie." *Antiquité tardive* 7:255–67.

———. (2004). "Pétitions aux empereurs et formes du rescrit dans les sources documentaires du IVᵉ au VIᵉ siècle." In *La pétition à Byzance*, ed. D. Feissel and J. Gascou, pp. 33–52. Centre de recherche d'histoire et civilisation de Byzance, Monographies 14. Paris.

Feissel, D., and I. Kaygusuz (1985). "Un mandement impérial du VIᵉ siècle dans une inscription d'Hadrianoupolis d'Honoriade." *Travaux et mémoires* 9:397–419.

Fittschen, K., and P. Zanker (1985). *Katalog der römischen Porträts in den Capitolinischen Museen und den anderen kommunalen Sammlungen der Stadt Rom, I: Kaiser- und Prinzenbildnisse*. Beiträge zur Erschließung hellenistischer und kaiserzeitlicher Skulptur und Architektur 3. Mainz.

Flower, H. I. (1996). *Ancestor Masks and Aristocratic Power in Roman Culture*. Oxford.

———. (2000). "*Damnatio memoriae* and Epigraphy." In *From Caligula to Constantine: Tyranny and Transformation in Roman Portraiture*, ed. E. R. Varner, pp. 58–69. Atlanta.

Foss, C. (1995). "Nicomedia and Constantinople." In *Constantinople and Its Hinterland: Papers from the Twenty-Seventh Spring Symposium of Byzantine Studies, Oxford, April 1993*, ed. C. Mango and G. Dagron, with G. Greatrex, pp. 181–90. Society for the Promotion of Byzantine Studies, Publications 3. Aldershot.

Fournet, J.-L. (2004). "Entre document et littérature: La pétition dans l'antiquité tardive." In *La pétition à Byzance*, ed. D. Feissel and J. Gascou, pp. 61–74. Centre de recherche d'histoire et civilisation de Byzance, Monographies 14. Paris.

Fowden, G. (1987). "Nicagoras of Athens and the Lateran Obelisk." *Journal of Hellenic Studies* 107:51–57.

———. (1991). "Constantine's Porphyry Column: The Earliest Literary Allusion." *Journal of Roman Studies* 81:119–31.

———. (1994). "The Last Days of Constantine: Oppositional Versions and Their Influence." *Journal of Roman Studies* 84:146–70.

Fowden, E. K. (2006). "Constantine and the Peoples of the Eastern Frontier." In *The Cambridge Companion to the Age of Constantine*, ed. N. Lenski, pp. 377–98. Cambridge.

Frakes, R. M. (2006). "The Dynasty of Constantine Down to 363." In *The Cambridge Companion to the Age of Constantine*, ed. N. Lenski, pp. 91–107. Cambridge.

Frend, W. H. C. (1952). *The Donatist Church.* Oxford.

———. (1996). *The Archaeology of Early Christianity: A History.* London.

Frier, B. W. (2000). "Demography." In *The Cambridge Ancient History, Second Edition, Volume XI: The High Empire, A.D. 70–192*, ed. A. K. Bowman, P. Garnsey, and D. Rathbone, pp. 787–816. Cambridge.

Frothingham, A. L., Jr. (1883). "Une mosaïque constantinienne inconnue à Saint-Pierre de Rome." *Revue archéologique*, série 3, 1:68–72.

Gager, J. G. (1982). "Body-Symbols and Social Reality: Resurrection, Incarnation and Asceticism in Early Christianity." *Religion* 12:345–63.

Gallay, P., ed. and tr. (1964–1967). *Saint Grégoire de Nazianze: Lettres*, 2 vols. Budé. Paris.

Galsterer, H. (1990). "A Man, a Book, and a Method: Sir Ronald Syme's Roman Revolution after Fifty Years." In *Between Republic and Empire: Interpretations of Augustus and His Principate*, ed. K. A. Raaflaub and M. Toher, pp. 1–20. Berkeley.

———. (2000). "Local and Provincial Institutions and Government." In *The Cambridge Ancient History, Second Edition, Volume XI: The High Empire, A.D. 70–192*, ed. A. K. Bowman, P. Garnsey, and D. Rathbone, pp. 344–60. Cambridge.

Gascou, J. (1967). "Le rescrit d'Hispellum." *Mélanges d'archéologie et d'histoire* 79:609–59.

Gasperini, L. (1988). "Dedica ostiensa di Aurelio Avianio Simmaco all'imperatore Costante." *Miscellanea greca e romana 13 = Studi pubblicati dall'Istituto Italiano per la storia antica* 42:242–50.

Geertz, C. (1975). "Religion as a Cultural System." In C. Geertz, *The Interpretation of Cultures: Selected Essays*, pp. 87–125. London.

Gelzer, H., H. Hilgenfeld, and O. Cuntz, ed. (1898). *Patrum Nicaenorum nomina latine graece coptice syriace arabice armeniace.* Leipzig. Reprinted with a Nachwort by C. Markschies (Stuttgart and Leipzig, 1995).

Gero, S. (1981). "The True Image of Christ: Eusebius' Letter to Constantia Reconsidered." *Journal of Theological Studies* n.s. 32:460–70.

Gerov, B. (1980). "Die lateinisch-griechische Sprachgrenze auf der Balkanhalbinsel." In *Die Sprachen im römischen Reich der Kaiserzeit: Kolloquium vom 8. bis 10. April 1974,* ed. G. Neumann and J. Untermann, pp. 147–65. Beihefte der Bonner Jahrbücher 40. Cologne and Bonn.

Gillett, A. (2001). "Rome, Ravenna and the Last Western Emperors." *Papers of the British School at Rome* 69:131–67.

Giuliano, A. (1955). *Arco di Costantino.* Milan.

———. (1991). "Augustus-Constantinus." *Bollettino d'arte* 68–69:3–10.

Gleason, M. W. (1986). "Festive Satire: Julian's *Misopogon* and the New Year at Antioch." *Journal of Roman Studies* 76:106–19.

Glorie, F., ed. (1964). *S. Hieronymi presbyteri opera 1: Opera exegetica 4: Commentariorum in Hiezechielem libri XIV.* CChr., Series latina 75. Turnholt.

Gnoli, T., and J. Thornton (1997). "Σῶζε τὴν κατοικίαν: Società e religione nella Frigia romana. Note introduttive." In *Frigi e Frigio: Atti del 1° Simposio Internazionale Roma, 16–17 ottobre 1995,* ed. R. Gusmani, M. Salvini, and P. Vannicelli, pp. 153–200. Rome.

Goodman, M. (2000). "Judaea." In *The Cambridge Ancient History, Second Edition, Volume XI: The High Empire, A.D. 70–192,* ed. A. K. Bowman, P. Garnsey, and D. Rathbone, pp. 664–78. Cambridge.

Gordon, R., with J. Reynolds (2003). "Roman Inscriptions 1995–2000." *Journal of Roman Studies* 93:212–94.

Grant, R. M. (1980). *Eusebius as Church Historian.* Oxford.

———. (1992). "Eusebius and Imperial Propaganda." In *Eusebius, Christianity, and Judaism,* ed. H. W. Attridge and G. Hata, pp. 658–83. Detroit.

Gregg, R. C., and D. E. Groh (1981). *Early Arianism: A View of Salvation.* Philadelphia.

Grégoire, H., ed. (1922). *Recueil des inscriptions grecques chrétiennes d'Asie Mineure.* Paris.

Grierson, P. (1962). "The Tombs and Obits of the Byzantine Emperors (337–1042)." *Dumbarton Oaks Papers* 16:1–60.

Grillet, B. (1983). "Introduction: Chapitre I, La vie et l'oeuvre." In B. Grillet, G. Sabbah, and A.-J. Festugière, *Sozomène, Histoire ecclésiastique, Livres I–II: Texte grec de l'édition J. Bidez,* pp. 9–31. SChr. 306. Paris.

Grillet, B., and G. H. Ettlinger, ed. and tr. (1968). *Jean Chrysostome, A une jeune veuve. Sur le mariage unique.* SChr. 138. Paris.

Grünewald, T. (1990). *Constantinus Maximus Augustus: Herrschaftspropaganda in der zeitgenössischen Überlieferung.* Historia Einzelschriften 64. Stuttgart.

Guidi, M. (1907). "Un ΒΙΟΣ di Constantino." *Rendiconti della Reale Accademia dei Lincei, Classe di scienze morali, storiche e filologiche*, Serie quinta, 16:304–40, 637–62.

Gundlach, W., ed. (1892). *Epistolae Merowingici et Karolini aevi*. Monumenta Germaniae Historica, Epistolae 3. Berlin.

Guyon, J. (1987). *Le cimetière aux deux lauriers: Recherches sur les catacombes romaines*. Bibliothèque des Ecoles françaises d'Athènes et de Rome 264. Roma sotterranea cristiana 7. Paris and Rome.

von Haehling, R. (1978). *Die Religionszugehörigkeit der hohen Amtsträger des römischen Reiches seit Constantins I. Alleinherrschaft bis zum Ende der theodosianischen Dynastie (324–450 bsw. 455 n.Chr.)*. Antiquitas, Reihe 3, 23. Bonn.

Hall, L. J. (1998). "Cicero's *instinctu divino* and Constantine's *instinctu divinitatis*: The Evidence of the Arch of Constantine for the Senatorial View of the 'Vision' of Constantine." *Journal of Early Christian Studies* 6:647–71.

———. (2004). *Roman Berytus: Beirut in Late Antiquity*. London and New York.

Hall, S. G. (1993). "Eusebian and Other Sources in Vita Constantini I." In *Logos: Festschrift für Luise Abramowski zum 8. Juli 1993*, ed. H. C. Brennecke, E. L. Grasmück, and C. Markschies, pp. 239–63. Beihefte zur Zeitschrift für die neutestamentliche Wissenschaft und die Kunde der älteren Kirche 67. Berlin and New York.

———. (1998). "Some Constantinian Documents in the *Vita Constantini*." In *Constantine: History, Hagiography and Legend*, ed. S. N. C. Lieu and D. Montserrat, pp. 86–103. London.

Halsall, G. (1996). "Towns, Societies and Ideas: The Not-So-Strange Case of Late Roman and Early Merovingian Metz." In *Towns in Transition: Urban Evolution in Late Antiquity and the Early Middle Ages*, ed. N. Christie and S. T. Loseby, pp. 235–61. Aldershot.

Hamilton, W. J. (1842). *Researches in Asia Minor, Pontus, and Armenia; With Some Account of Their Antiquities and Geology*, 2 vols. London.

Hammond, C. P. (1977). "The Last Ten Years of Rufinus' Life and the Date of His Move South from Aquileia." *Journal of Theological Studies* n.s. 28:372–429. Reprinted in C. P. Hammond Bammel, *Origeniana et Rufiniana*. Vetus Latina: Aus der Geschichte der lateinischen Bibel 29 (Freiburg, 1996), Chapter IV.

Hansen, G. C. (1995). "Einleitung." In *Sozomenus Kirchengeschichte*, ed. J. Bidez and G. C. Hansen, pp. IX–LXVII. GCS, Neue Folge 2. Second edition. Berlin.

Hansen, M. F. (2003). *The Eloquence of Appropriation: Prolegomena to an Understanding of Spolia in Early Christian Rome*. Analecta Romana Instituti Danici, Supplementum 33. Rome.

Hanson, R. P. C. (1988). *The Search for the Christian Doctrine of God: The Arian Controversy 318–381*. Edinburgh.

Harrison, E. B. (1967). "The Constantinian Portrait." *Dumbarton Oaks Papers* 21:79–96.

Heather, P. J. (1991). *Goths and Romans 332–489*. Oxford.

———. (1998). "Senators and Senates." In *The Cambridge Ancient History, Volume XIII: The Late Empire A.D. 337–425*, ed. Av. Cameron and P. Garnsey, pp. 184–210. Cambridge.

Heather, P. and D. Moncur, tr. (2001). *Politics, Philosophy, and Empire in the Fourth Century: Select Orations of Themistius*. TTH 36. Liverpool.

Heberdey, R., ed. (1941). *Tituli Asiae Minoris III: Tituli Pisidiae linguis graeca et latina conscripti*, Fasc. 1. Vienna.

Hedrick, C. W., Jr. (2000). *History and Silence: Purge and Rehabilitation of Memory in Late Antiquity*. Austin.

Heijmans, M. (1998). "Le 'Palais de la Trouille' à Arles: Palais impérial ou palais du préfet? Le centre monumental durant l'antiquité tardive à la lumière des recherches récentes." *Antiquité tardive* 6:209–31.

———. (1999). "La topographie de la ville d'Arles durant l'antiquité tardive." *Journal of Roman Archaeology* 12:142–67.

Hekster, O. (2001). "All in the Family: The Appointment of Emperors Designate in the Second Century A.D." In *Administration, Prosopography and Appointment Policies in the Roman Empire: Proceedings of the First Workshop of the International Network Impact of Empire (Roman Empire, 27 B.C.–A.D. 406). Leiden, June 28–July 1, 2000*, ed. L. de Blois, pp. 35–49. Amsterdam.

Henck, N. (2001). "Constantius ὁ φιλοκτίστης." *Dumbarton Oaks Papers* 55:279–304.

Hennephof, H., ed. (1969). *Textus byzantini ad iconomachiam pertinentes in usum academicum*. Byzantina Neerlandica, Series A, Textus: Fasc. 1. Leiden.

Hillner, J. (2003). "*Domus*, Family, and Inheritance: The Senatorial Family House in Late Antique Rome." *Journal of Roman Studies* 93:129–45.

Hollerich, M. J. (1990). "Religion and Politics in the Writings of Eusebius: Reassessing the First 'Court Theologian.'" *Church History* 59:309–25.

———. (1999). *Eusebius of Caesarea's Commentary on Isaiah: Christian Exegesis in the Age of Constantine*. Oxford.

Holloway, R. R. (2004). *Constantine and Rome*. New Haven.

Holum, K. G. (1982). *Theodosian Empresses: Women and Imperial Dominion in Late Antiquity*. Berkeley.

———. (1990). "Hadrian and St. Helena: Imperial Travel and the Origins of Christian Holy Land Pilgrimage." In *The Blessings of Pilgrimage*, ed. R. Ousterhout, pp. 66–81. Illinois Byzantine Studies 1. Urbana and Chicago.

———. (1996). "In the Blinking of an Eye: The Christianizing of Classical Cities in the Levant." In *Religion and Politics in the Ancient Near East*, ed. A. Berlin, pp. 131–50. Studies and Texts in Jewish History and Culture 1. Bethesda.

Honoré, T. (1987). "Scriptor Historiae Augustae." *Journal of Roman Studies* 77:156–76.

Horden, P., and N. Purcell (2000). *The Corrupting Sea: A Study of Mediterranean History.* Oxford.

Hübner, S. (2005). *Der Klerus in der Gesellschaft des spätantiken Kleinasiens.* Altertumswissenschaftliches Kolloquium 15. Munich.

Humfress, C. (2006). "Civil Law and Social Life." In *The Cambridge Companion to the Age of Constantine*, ed. N. Lenski, pp. 205–25. Cambridge.

Humphries, M. (1997). "In nomine patris: Constantine the Great and Constantius II in Christological Polemic." *Historia* 46:448–64.

———. (1998). "Savage Humour: Christian Anti-Panegyric in Hilary of Poitiers' *Against Constantius.*" In *The Propaganda of Power: The Role of Panegyric in Late Antiquity*, ed. M. Whitby, pp. 201–23. Mnemosyne, Supplementum 183. Leiden.

———. (1999). *Communities of the Blessed: Social Environment and Religious Change in Northern Italy, AD 200–400.* Oxford.

———. (2003). "Roman Senators and Absent Emperors in Late Antiquity." In *Rome AD 300–800: Power and Symbol – Image and Reality*, ed. J. R. Brandt, S. Sande, O. Steen, and L. Hodne. = *Acta ad archaeologiam et artium historiam pertinentia* 17 (n.s. 3):27–46.

Hunt, E. D. (1982). *Holy Land Pilgrimage in the Later Roman Empire AD 312–460.* Oxford.

———. (1997a). "Constantine and Jerusalem." *Journal of Ecclesiastical History* 48:405–24.

———. (1997b). "Theodosius I and the Holy Land." In *Studia Patristica Vol. XXIX: Papers Presented at the Twelfth International Conference on Patristic Studies Held in Oxford 1995. Historica, theologica et philosophica, critica et philologica*, ed. E. A. Livingstone, pp. 52–57. Leuven.

———. (1998). "The Successors of Constantine." In *The Cambridge Ancient History, Volume XIII: The Late Empire A.D. 337–425*, ed. Av. Cameron and P. Garnsey, pp. 1–43. Cambridge.

———. (2003). "Imperial Building at Rome: The Role of Constantine." In *"Bread and Circuses": Euergetism and Municipal Patronage in Roman Italy*, ed. K. Lomas and T. Cornell, pp. 105–24. London.

Innes, M. (2000). *State and Society in the Early Middle Ages: The Middle Rhine Valley, 400–1000.* Cambridge.

Jacobs, A. S. (2004). *Remains of the Jews: The Holy Land and Christian Empire in Late Antiquity.* Stanford.

Jacques, F. (1992). "Les moulins d'Orcistus: Rhétorique et géographie au IVᵉ s." In *Institutions, société et vie politique dans l'empire romain au IVᵉ siècle ap. J.-C.: Actes de la table ronde autour de l'oeuvre d'André Chastagnol (Paris, 20–21 janvier 1989)*, ed. M. Christol, S. Demougin, Y. Duval, C. Lepelley, and L. Pietri, pp. 431–46. Collection de l'Ecole française de Rome 159. Rome.

Johnson, A. C., P. R. Coleman-Norton, and F. C. Bourne, tr. (1961). *Ancient Roman Statutes: A Translation with Introduction, Commentary, Glossary, and Index*. The Corpus of Roman Law 2. Austin.

Johnson, M. J. (1991). "On the Burial Places of the Valentinian Dynasty." *Historia* 40:501–6.

———. (1992). "Where Were Constantius I and Helena Buried?" *Latomus* 51:145–50.

Jones, A. H. M. (1962). *Constantine and the Conversion of Europe*. Revised edition. New York.

———. (1964). *The Later Roman Empire*. Oxford and Norman.

———. (1971). *The Cities of the Eastern Roman Provinces*. Second edition. Oxford.

Jones, C. (2006). "A Letter of Hadrian to Naryka (Eastern Locris)." *Journal of Roman Archaeology* 19:151–62.

Kähler, H. (1952). "Konstantin 313." *Jahrbuch des deutschen archäologischen Instituts* 67:1–30.

———. (1964). *Das Fünfsäulendenkmal für die Tetrarchen auf dem Forum Romanum*. Monumenta artis Romanae 3. Cologne.

Kalavrezou-Maxeiner, I. (1975). "The Imperial Chamber at Luxor." *Dumbarton Oaks Papers* 29:225–51.

Kaldellis, A. (2004). *Procopius of Caesarea: Tyranny, History, and Philosophy at the End of Antiquity*. Philadelphia.

Kalinka, E., ed. (1930–1944). *Tituli Asiae Minoris II: Tituli Lyciae linguis graeca et latina conscripti*, Fasc. 2–3. Vienna.

Kannengiesser, C. (1997). "The Bible in the Arian Crisis." In *The Bible in Greek Christian Antiquity*, ed. P. M. Blowers, pp. 217–28. The Bible through the Ages 1. South Bend.

———. (2001). "L'*Histoire des Ariens* d'Athanase d'Alexandrie: Une historiographie de combat au IV^e siècle." In *L'historiographie de l'église des premiers siècles*, ed. B. Pouderon and Y.-M. Duval, pp. 127–38. Théologie historique 114. Paris.

Kantorowicz, E. H. (1957). *The King's Two Bodies: A Study in Mediaeval Political Theology*. Princeton.

Kaster, R. A. (1988). *Guardians of Language: The Grammarian and Society in Late Antiquity*. The Transformation of the Classical Heritage 11. Berkeley.

Kaufmann-Heinimann, A. (1999). "Eighteen New Pieces from the Late Roman Silver Treasure of Kaiseraugst: First Notice." *Journal of Roman Archaeology* 12:333–41.

Kazhdan, A. (1987). "'Constantin imaginaire': Byzantine Legends of the Ninth Century about Constantine the Great." *Byzantion* 57:196–250.

Kearsley, R. A., with T. V. Evans, ed. (2001). *Greeks and Romans in Imperial Asia: Mixed Language Inscriptions and Linguistic Evidence for Cultural Interaction until the End of AD III.* Inschriften griechischer Städte aus Kleinasien 59. Bonn.

Keenan, J. G. (1973–1974). "The Names Flavius and Aurelius as Status Designations in Later Roman Egypt." *Zeitschrift für Papyrologie und Epigraphik* 11:33–63, and 13:283–304.

————. (1983). "An Afterthought on the Names Flavius and Aurelius." *Zeitschrift für Papyrologie und Epigraphik* 53:245–50.

Kelly, C. (2004). *Ruling the Later Roman Empire.* Revealing Antiquity 15. Cambridge, MA.

————. (2006). "Bureaucracy and Government." In *The Cambridge Companion to the Age of Constantine,* ed. N. Lenski, pp. 183–204. Cambridge.

Kelly, G. (2003). "The New Rome and the Old: Ammianus Marcellinus' Silences on Constantinople." *Classical Quarterly* 53:588–607.

————. (2004). "Ammianus and the Great Tsunami." *Journal of Roman Studies* 94:141–67.

Kelly, J. N. D. (1960). *Early Christian Doctrines.* Second edition. London.

————. (1995). *Golden Mouth: The Story of John Chrysostom – Ascetic, Preacher, Bishop.* London.

Kent, J. P. C. (1981). *The Roman Imperial Coinage, VIII: The Family of Constantine I A.D. 337–364.* London.

King, K. L. (2003). *What Is Gnosticism?* Cambridge, MA.

Klein, K. L. (2000). "On the Emergence of *Memory* in Historical Discourse." *Representations* 69:127–50.

Klein, R. (1999a). "Die Kämpfe um die Nachfolge nach dem Tode Constantins des Grossen." In R. Klein, *Roma versa per aevum: Ausgewählte Schriften zur heidnischen und christlichen Spätantike,* ed. R. von Haehling and K. Scherberich, pp. 1–49. Spudasmata 74. Hildesheim. Reprinted from *Byzantinische Forschungen* 6 (1979), pp. 101–50.

————. (1999b). "Der Rombesuch des Kaisers Constantius II. im Jahre 357." In R. Klein, *Roma versa per aevum: Ausgewählte Schriften zur heidnischen und christlichen Spätantike,* ed. R. von Haehling and K. Scherberich, pp. 50–71. Spudasmata 74. Hildesheim. Reprinted from *Athenaeum* 57 (1979), pp. 98–115.

————. (1999c). "Das Kirchenbauverständnis Constantins des Grossen in Rom und in den östlichen Provinzen." In R. Klein, *Roma versa per aevum: Ausgewählte Schriften zur heidnischen und christlichen Spätantike,* ed. R. von Haehling and K. Scherberich, pp. 205–33. Spudasmata 74. Hildesheim. Reprinted from *Das antike Rom und der Osten: Festschrift für Klaus Parlasca zum 65. Geburtstag,* ed. C. Börker and M. Donderer, pp. 77–101. Erlanger Forschungen, Reihe A, Geisteswissenschaften 56 (Erlangen, 1990).

Kleiner, F. S. (2001). "Who Really Built the Arch of Constantine?" *Journal of Roman Archaeology* 14:661–63.

Klingshirn, W. E. (1994). *Caesarius of Arles: The Making of a Christian Community in Late Antique Gaul.* Cambridge.

Koeppel, G. M. (1986). "Die historischen Reliefs der römischen Kaiserzeit IV: Stadtrömische Denkmäler unbekannter Bauzugehörigkeit aus hadrianischer bis konstantinischer Zeit." *Bonner Jahrbücher* 186:1–90.

Koethe, H. (1931). "Zum Mausoleum der weströmischen Dynastie bei Alt-Sankt-Peter." *Mitteilungen des deutschen archäologischen Instituts, Römische Abteilung* 46:9–26.

Kolb, F. (1987). *Diocletian und die erste Tetrarchie: Improvisation oder Experiment in der Organisation monarchischer Herrschaft?* Untersuchungen zur antiken Literatur und Geschichte 27. Berlin.

————. (1993). "Bemerkungen zur urbanen Ausstattung von Städten im Westen und im Osten des römischen Reiches anhand von Tacitus, Agricola 21 und der konstantinischen Inschrift von Orkistos." *Klio* 75:321–41.

————. (1995). "Chronologie und Ideologie der Tetrarchie." *Antiquité tardive* 3:21–31.

————. (1997). "Die Gestalt des spätantiken Kaisertums unter besonderer Berücksichtigung der Tetrarchie." In *Usurpationen in der Spätantike: Akten des Kolloquiums "Staatsstreich und Staatlichkeit," 6.-10. März 1996, Solothurn/Bern*, ed. F. Paschoud and J. Szidat, pp. 35–45. Historia Einzelschriften 111. Stuttgart.

————. (2001). *Herrscherideologie in der Spätantike*. Berlin.

————. (2004). "Praesens Deus: Kaiser und Gott unter der Tetrarchie." In *Diokletian und die Tetrarchie: Aspekte einer Zeitenwende*, ed. A. Demandt, A. Goltz, and H. Schlange-Schöningen, pp. 27–37. Millennium-Studien zu Kultur und Geschichte des ersten Jahrtausends n. Chr. 1. Berlin and New York.

Konrad, C. F. (1989). "Das Datum der neuen Maximinus-Inschrift von Colbasa." *Epigraphica Anatolica* 13:89–90.

Kopecek, T. A. (1979). *A History of Neo-Arianism*. Patristic Monograph Series 8. Cambridge, MA.

Kotter, B., ed. (1988). *Die Schriften des Johannes von Damaskos 5: Opera homiletica et hagiographica*. Patristische Texte und Studien 29. Berlin.

Krautheimer, R., with W. Frankl, S. Corbett, and A. K. Frazer (1937–1980). *Corpus basilicarum christianarum Romae: The Early Christian Basilicas of Rome (IV–IX Cent.)*, 5 vols. Vatican City.

————. (1983). *Three Christian Capitals: Topography and Politics*. Berkeley.

————. (1987). "A Note on the Inscription in the Apse of Old St. Peter's." *Dumbarton Oaks Papers* 41:317–20.

————. (1992). "The Ecclesiastical Building Policy of Constantine." In *Costantino il Grande dall'antichità all'umanesimo: Colloquio sul Cristianesimo nel mondo antico*.

*Macerata 18–20 dicembre 1990*, ed. G. Bonamente and F. Fusco, Vol. 2:509–52. Macerata.

Kuhoff, W. (1991). "Ein Mythos in der römischen Geschichte: Der Sieg Konstantins des Großen über Maxentius vor den Toren Roms am 28. Oktober 312 n. Chr." *Chiron* 21:127–74.

Kulikowski, M. (2001). "The Visigothic Settlement in Aquitania: The Imperial Perspective." In *Society and Culture in Late Antique Gaul: Revisiting the Sources*, ed. R. W. Mathisen and D. Shanzer, pp. 26–38. Aldershot.

————. (2004). *Late Roman Spain and Its Cities*. Baltimore.

————. (2006). "Constantine and the Northern Barbarians." In *The Cambridge Companion to the Age of Constantine*, ed. N. Lenski, pp. 347–76. Cambridge.

Lacau, P. (1934). "Inscriptions latines du Temple de Louxor." *Annales du service des antiquités de l'Egypte* 34:17–46.

Lafferty, M. K. (2003). "Translating Faith from Greek to Latin: *Romanitas* and *Christianitas* in Late Fourth-Century Rome and Milan." *Journal of Early Christian Studies* 11:21–62.

Lampe, G. W. H., ed. (1961). *A Patristic Greek Lexicon*. Oxford.

Lane Fox, R. (1986). *Pagans and Christians*. New York.

Laubscher, H. P. (1975). *Der Reliefschmuck des Galeriusbogens in Thessaloniki*. Archäologische Forschungen 1. Berlin.

————. (1993). "Ein tetrarchisches Siegesdenkmal in Iznik (Nikaia)." *Jahrbuch des deutschen archäologischen Instituts* 108:375–97.

Laurence, R. (1999). *The Roads of Roman Italy: Mobility and Cultural Change*. London.

————. (2004). "Milestones, Communications, and Political Stability." In *Travel, Communication and Geography in Late Antiquity*, ed. L. Ellis and F. L. Kidner, pp. 41–58. Aldershot.

Lawlor, H. J., and J. E. L. Oulton, tr. (1927–1928). *Eusebius Bishop of Caesarea: The Ecclesiastical History and The Martyrs of Palestine*, 2 vols. London.

Leach, E. (1972). "Melchisedech and the Emperor: Icons of Subversion and Orthodoxy." *Proceedings of the Royal Anthropological Institute*, pp. 5–14. Reprinted in E. Leach and D. A. Aycock, *Structuralist Interpretations of Biblical Myth* (Cambridge, 1983), pp. 67–88.

Leadbetter, B. (1998). "The Illegitimacy of Constantine and the Birth of the Tetrarchy." In *Constantine: History, Historiography and Legend*, ed. S. N. C. Lieu and D. Montserrat, pp. 74–85. London.

Le Boulluec, A. (2000). "Orthodoxie et hérésie aux premiers siècles dans l'historiographie récente." In *Orthodoxie, christianisme, histoire: Orthodoxy, Christianity, History*, ed. S. Elm, E. Rebillard and A. Romano, pp. 303–19. Collection de l'Ecole française de Rome 270. Paris and Rome.

Lee, A. D. (2006). "Traditional Religions." In *The Cambridge Companion to the Age of Constantine*, ed. N. Lenski, pp. 159–79. Cambridge.

Leeb, R. (1992). *Konstantin und Christus: Die Verchristlichung der imperialen Repräsentation unter Konstantin dem Großen als Spiegel seiner Kirchenpolitik und seines Selbstverständnisses als christlicher Kaiser.* Arbeiten zur Kirchengeschichte 58. Berlin.

Lenski, N. (1997). *"Initium mali Romano imperio*: Contemporary Reactions to the Battle of Adrianople." *Transactions of the American Philological Association* 127:129–68.

———. (2002). *Failure of Empire: Valens and the Roman State in the Fourth Century A.D.* The Transformation of the Classical Heritage 34. Berkeley.

———. (2004). "Empresses in the Holy Land: The Creation of a Christian Utopia in Late Antique Palestine." In *Travel, Communication and Geography in Late Antiquity,* ed. L. Ellis and F. L. Kidner, pp. 113–24. Aldershot.

———. (2006a). "Introduction." In *The Cambridge Companion to the Age of Constantine,* ed. N. Lenski, pp. 1–13. Cambridge.

———. (2006b). "The Reign of Constantine." In *The Cambridge Companion to the Age of Constantine,* ed. N. Lenski, pp. 59–90. Cambridge.

Lepelley, C. (2004). "Une inscription d'Heraclea Sintica (Macédoine) récemment découverte, révélant un rescrit de l'empereur Galère restituant ses droits à la cité." *Zeitschrift für Papyrologie und Epigraphik* 146:221–31.

Leppin, H. (1996). *Von Constantin dem Großen zu Theodosius II.: Das christliche Kaisertum bei den Kirchenhistorikern Socrates, Sozomenus und Theodoret.* Hypomnemata 110. Gottingen.

Leroy-Molinghen, A. (1968). "La mort d'Arius." *Byzantion* 38:105–11.

Levick, B. (1967). "Unpublished Inscriptions from Pisidian Antioch." *Anatolian Studies* 17:101–21.

Liebeschuetz, J. H. W. G. (1972). *Antioch: City and Imperial Administration in the Later Roman Empire.* Oxford.

———. (2001). *Decline and Fall of the Roman City.* Oxford.

Lienhard, J. T. (1999). *Contra Marcellum: Marcellus of Ancyra and Fourth-Century Theology.* Washington, D.C.

Lieu, S. N. C. (1998). "From History to Legend and Legend to History: The Medieval and Byzantine Transformation of Constantine's *Vita.*" In *Constantine: History, Hagiography and Legend,* ed. S. N. C. Lieu and D. Montserrat, pp. 136–76. London.

———. (2006). "Constantine in Legendary Literature." In *The Cambridge Companion to the Age of Constantine,* ed. N. Lenski, pp. 298–321. Cambridge.

Lieu, S. N. C., and D. Montserrat (1996). *From Constantine to Julian: Pagan and Byzantine Views. A Source History.* London and New York.

Lim, R. (1995). *Public Disputation, Power, and Social Order in Late Antiquity.* The Transformation of the Classical Heritage 23. Berkeley.

———. (1999). "People as Power: Games, Munificence, and Contested Topography." In *The Transformations of Urbs Roma in Late Antiquity*, ed. W. V. Harris, pp. 265–81. Journal of Roman Archaeology, Supplementary Series 33. Portsmouth.

Lippold, A. (1981). "Constantius Caesar, Sieger über die Germanen – Nachfahre des Claudius Gothicus? Der Panegyricus von 297 und die Vita Claudii der HA." *Chiron* 11:347–69.

———. (1992). "Kaiser Claudius II. (Gothicus), Vorfahr Konstantins d. Gr., und der römische Senat." *Klio* 74:380–94.

Liverani, P. (2004). "L'area lateranense in età tardoantica e le origini del Patriarchio." *Mélanges de l'Ecole française de Rome*, Antiquité 116:17–49.

Lo Cascio, E. (2005). "The Emperor and His Administration." In *The Cambridge Ancient History, Second Edition, Volume XII: The Crisis of Empire, A.D. 193–337*, ed. A. K. Bowman, P. Garnsey, and Av. Cameron, pp. 131–83. Cambridge.

Logan, A. H. B. (1992). "Marcellus of Ancyra and the Councils of AD 325: Antioch, Ancyra, and Nicaea." *Journal of Theological Studies* n.s. 43:428–46.

López Sánchez, F. (2003). "Procope et le bouclier macédonien (365–366 après J.-C.)." *Cahiers numismatiques* 156:57–76.

L'Orange, H. P. (1938). "Ein tetrarchisches Ehrendenkmal auf dem Forum Romanum." *Mitteilungen des deutschen archäologischen Instituts*, Römische Abteilung 53:1–34.

———, with R. Unger (1984). *Das spätantike Herrscherbild von Diokletian bis zu den Konstantin-Söhnen 284–361 n. Chr.* Das römischen Herrscherbild 3, Vol. 4. Berlin.

L'Orange, H. P., and A. von Gerkan (1939). *Der spätantike Bildschmuck des Konstantinsbogens.* Studien zur spätantiken Kunstgeschichte 10. Berlin.

Loseby, S. T. (1996). "Arles in Late Antiquity: *Gallula Roma Arelas* and *Urbs Genesii.*" In *Towns in Transition: Urban Evolution in Late Antiquity and the Early Middle Ages*, ed. N. Christie and S. T. Loseby, pp. 45–70. Aldershot.

Louth, A. (1990). "The Date of Eusebius' *Historia ecclesiastica.*" *Journal of Theological Studies* 41:111–23.

Luibhéid, C. (1981). *Eusebius of Caesarea and the Arian Crisis.* Galway.

Ma, J. (1999). *Antiochos III and the Cities of Western Asia Minor.* Oxford.

MacMullen, R. (1984). *Christianizing the Roman Empire (A.D. 100–400).* New Haven.

Magdalino, P. (1994). "Introduction." In *New Constantines: The Rhythm of Imperial Renewal in Byzantium, 4th-13th Centuries. Papers from the Twenty-Sixth Spring Symposium of Byzantine Studies, St Andrews, March 1992*, ed. P. Magdalino, pp. 1–9. Society for the Promotion of Byzantine Studies, Publications 2. Aldershot.

Maier, J.-L. (1987–1989). *Le dossier du Donatisme*, 2 vols. Texte und Untersuchungen 134–135. Berlin.

Malosse, P.-L. (2000). "Libanios, ses «temoins oculaires», Eusèbe et Praxagoras: Le travail préparatoire du sophiste et la question des sources dans l'*Eloge de Constance et de Constant.*" *Revue des études grecques* 113:172–87.

Mango, C. (1990). "Constantine's Mausoleum and the Translation of Relics." *Byzantinische Zeitschrift* 83:51–61. Reprinted in C. Mango, *Studies on Constantinople* (Aldershot, 1993), Chapter 5.

———. (1994). "The Empress Helena, Helenopolis, Pylae." *Travaux et mémoires* 12:143–59.

Mango, C., and R. Scott, with G. Greatrex, tr. (1997). *The Chronicle of Theophanes Confessor: Byzantine and Near Eastern History AD 284–813.* Oxford.

Marcone, A. (1992). "Costantino e l'aristocrazia pagana di Roma." In *Costantino il Grande dall'antichità all'umanesimo: Colloquio sul Cristianesimo nel mondo antico. Macerata 18–20 dicembre 1990*, ed. G. Bonamente and F. Fusco, Vol. 2:645–58. Macerata.

Markus, R. A. (1970). *Saeculum: History and Society in the Theology of St Augustine.* Cambridge.

———. (1990). *The End of Ancient Christianity.* Cambridge.

Marlowe, E. (2006). "Framing the Sun: The Arch of Constantine and the Roman Cityscape." *Art Bulletin* 88:223–42.

Martin, A., ed. and tr. (1985). *Histoire «acéphale» et Index syriaque des lettres festales d'Athanase d'Alexandrie.* SChr. 317. Paris.

Martindale, J. R. (2003). "*The Prosopography of the Later Roman Empire*, Volume I: A Memoir of the Era of A. H. M. Jones." In *Fifty Years of Prosopography: The Later Roman Empire, Byzantium and Beyond*, ed. Av. Cameron, pp. 3–10. Proceedings of the British Academy 118. Oxford.

Mathisen, R. W. (2003). "*The Prosopography of the Later Roman Empire*: Yesterday, Today and Tomorrow." In *Fifty Years of Prosopography: The Later Roman Empire, Byzantium and Beyond*, ed. Av. Cameron, pp. 23–40. Proceedings of the British Academy 118. Oxford.

———. (2004). "*Adnotatio* and *petitio*: The Emperor's Favor and Special Exemptions in the Early Byzantine Empire." In *La pétition à Byzance*, ed. D. Feissel and J. Gascou, pp. 23–32. Centre de recherche d'histoire et civilisation de Byzance, Monographies 14. Paris.

Matthews, J. F. (1970). "The Historical Setting of the 'Carmen contra paganos' (Cod. Par. Lat. 8084)." *Historia* 19:464–79.

———. (1975). *Western Aristocracies and Imperial Court, A.D. 364–425.* Oxford.

Mayer, E. (2002). *Rom ist dort, wo der Kaiser ist: Untersuchungen zu den Staatsdenkmälern des dezentralisierten Reiches von Diocletian bis zu Theodosius II.* Römisch-Germanisches Zentralmuseum, Forschungsinstitut für Vor- und Frühgeschichte, Monographien 53. Mainz.

Mazzini, I. (1992). "Il sapone di Costantino." In *Costantino il Grande dall'antichità all'umanesimo: Colloquio sul Cristianesimo nel mondo antico. Macerata 18–20 dicembre 1990*, ed. G. Bonamente and F. Fusco, Vol. 2:693–99. Macerata.

McCormick, M. (1995). "Byzantium and the West, 700–900." In *The New Cambridge Medieval History, Volume II: c. 700–c. 900*, ed. R. McKitterick, pp. 349–80. Cambridge.

McLynn, N. B. (1994). *Ambrose of Milan: Church and Court in a Christian Capital.* The Transformation of the Classical Heritage 22. Berkeley.

———— (1999). "Augustine's Roman Empire." In *History, Apocalypse, and the Secular Imagination: New Essays on Augustine's* City of God, ed. M. Vessey, K. Pollmann, and A. D. Fitzgerald. = *Augustinian Studies* 30.2:29–44.

————. (2005). "'*Genere Hispanus*': Theodosius, Spain and Nicene Orthodoxy." In *Hispania in Late Antiquity: Current Perspectives*, ed. K. Bowes and M. Kulikowski, pp. 77–120. The Medieval and Early Modern Iberian World 24. Leiden.

Melucco Vaccaro, A., and A. M. Ferroni (1993–1994). "Chi castrui l'arco di Costantino? Un interrogativo ancora attuale." *Atti della Pontificia Accademia Romana di Archeologia* (série III), Rendiconti 66:1–60.

Meriç, R., R. Merkelbach, J. Nollé, and S. Sahin, ed. (1981). *Die Inschriften von Ephesos, Teil VII,1–2*, 2 vols. Inschriften griechischer Städte aus Kleinasien 17.1–2. Bonn.

Messineo, G., and C. Calci (1989). *Malborghetto.* Lavori e Studi di Archeologia 15. Rome.

Métivier, S. (2005). *La Cappadoce (IV<sup>e</sup>-VI<sup>e</sup> siècle): Une histoire provinciale de l'Empire romain d'Orient.* Byzantina Sorbonensia 22. Paris.

Millar, F. (1977). *The Emperor in the Roman World (31 B.C. – A.D. 337).* London.

————. (1983). "Empire and City, Augustus to Julian: Obligations, Excuses and Status." *Journal of Roman Studies* 73:76–96.

————. (1993). *The Roman Near East 31 BC-AD 337.* Cambridge, MA.

———— (1998). "Ethnic Identity in the Roman Near East, 325–450: Language, Religion, and Culture." In *Identities in the Eastern Mediterranean in Antiquity*, ed. G. Clarke. = *Mediterranean Archaeology* 11:159–76.

————. (1999). "The Greek East and Roman Law: The Dossier of M. Cn. Licinius Rufinus." *Journal of Roman Studies* 89:90–108.

————. (2000). "The First Revolution: Imperator Caesar, 36–28 B.C." In *La révolution romaine après Ronald Syme*, ed. A. Giovannini, pp. 1–30. Fondation Hardt pour l'étude de l'antiquité classique, Entretiens 46. Geneva.

Minoprio, A. (1932). "A Restoration of the Basilica of Constantine, Rome." *Papers of the British School at Rome* 12:1–25.

Mitchell, S. (1982). "The Life of Saint Theodotus of Ancyra." *Anatolian Studies* 32:93–113.

_____. (1988). "Maximinus and the Christians in A.D. 312: A New Latin Inscription." *Journal of Roman Studies* 78:105–24.

_____. (1993). *Anatolia: Land, Men, and Gods in Asia Minor*, 2 vols. Oxford.

_____. (1998). "The Cities of Asia Minor in the Age of Constantine." In *Constantine: History, Hagiography and Legend*, ed. S. N. C. Lieu and D. Montserrat, pp. 52–73. London.

_____. (1999). "The Cult of Theos Hypsistos between Pagans, Jews, and Christians." In *Pagan Monotheism in Late Antiquity*, ed. P. Athanassiadi and M. Frede, pp. 81–148. Oxford.

Mitrev, G. (2003). "Civitas Heracleotarum: Heracleia Sintica or the Ancient City at the Village of Rupite (Bulgaria)." *Zeitschrift für Papyrologie und Epigraphik* 145:263–71.

Mócsy, A. (1964). "Der Name Flavius als Rangbezeichnung in der Spätantike." In *Akte des IV. internationalen Kongresses für griechische und lateinische Epigraphik (Wien, 17. bis 22. September 1962)*, pp. 257–63. Vienna.

Mommsen, T. (1887). "Stadtrechtbriefe von Orkistos und Tymandos." *Hermes* 22:309–22.

_____, ed. (1892). *Chronica minora saec. IV. V. VI. VII*, Vol. 1. MGH, Auctores antiquissimi 9. Berlin.

Monaco, E. (2000). "Il Tempio di Venere e Roma: Appunti sulla fase del IV secolo." In *Aurea Roma: Dalla città pagana alla città cristiana*, ed. S. Ensoli and E. La Rocca, pp. 58–60. Rome.

Morrisson, C. (1981). "La découverte des trésors à l'époque byzantine: Théorie et pratique de l'εὕρεσις θησαυροῦ." *Travaux et mémoires* 8:321–43.

Mossay, J., and G. Lafontaine, ed. and tr. (1980). *Grégoire de Nazianze: Discours 20–23*. SChr. 270. Paris.

Müller, C., ed. (1851). *Fragmenta historicorum graecorum*, Vol. 4. Paris.

Murphy, F. X. (1945). *Rufinus of Aquileia (345–411): His Life and Works*. Washington, D.C.

Nakamura, B. J. (2003). "When Did Diocletian Die? New Evidence for an Old Problem." *Classical Philology* 98:283–89.

Nasrallah, L. S. (2003). *"An Ecstasy of Folly": Prophecy and Authority in Early Christianity*. Harvard Theological Studies 52. Cambridge, MA.

Neumann, G. (1980). "Kleinasien." In *Die Sprachen im römischen Reich der Kaiserzeit: Kolloquium vom 8. bis 10. April 1974*, ed. G. Neumann and J. Untermann, pp. 167–85. Beihefte der Bonner Jahrbücher 40. Cologne and Bonn.

Nicholson, O. (1984). "The Wild Man of the Tetrarchy: A Divine Companion for the Emperor Galerius." *Byzantion* 54:253–75.

_____. (1994). "The 'Pagan Churches' of Maximinus Daia and Julian the Apostate." *Journal of Ecclesiastical History* 45:1–10.

————. (1999). "*Civitas quae adhuc sustentat omnia*: Lactantius and the City of Rome." In *The Limits of Ancient Christianity: Essays on Late Antique Thought and Culture in Honor of R. A. Markus*, ed. W. E. Klingshirn and M. Vessey, pp. 7–25. Ann Arbor.

————. (2001). "*Caelum potius intuemini*: Lactantius and a Statue of Constantine." In *Studia Patristica Vol. XXXIV: Papers Presented at the Thirteenth International Conference on Patristic Studies Held in Oxford 1999. Historica, biblica, theologica et philosophica*, ed. M. F. Wiles and E. J. Yarnold, with P. M. Parvis, pp.177–96. Leuven.

Nicolet, C. (1991). *Space, Geography, and Politics in the Early Roman Empire*. Jerome Lectures 19. Ann Arbor.

————. (1994). "L'Italie comme cadre juridique sous le Haut-Empire." In *L'Italie d'Auguste à Dioclétien*, pp. 377–98. Collection de l'Ecole française de Rome 198. Rome and Paris.

Nixon, C. E. V. (1981). "The Panegyric of 307 and Maximian's Visits to Rome." *Phoenix* 35:70–76.

Nixon, C. E. V., and B. S. Rodgers, tr. (1994). *In Praise of Later Roman Emperors: The Panegyrici Latini. Introduction, Translation, and Historical Commentary with the Latin Text of R. A. B. Mynors*. The Transformation of the Classical Heritage 21. Berkeley.

Nordh, A., ed. (1949). *Libellus de regionibus urbis Romae*. Skrifter Utgivna av Svenska Institutet i Rom 3. Lund.

Odahl, C. M. (2004). *Constantine and the Christian Empire*. London.

O'Donnell, J. J. (1978). "The Career of Virius Nicomachus Flavianus." *Phoenix* 32:129–43.

Oliver, J. H. (1976). "The Governor's Edict at Aezani after the Edict of Prices." *American Journal of Philology* 97:174–75.

————. (1981). "Roman Emperors and Athens." *Historia* 30:412–23.

Opitz, H.-G. (1934). "Die Vita Constantini des Codex Angelicus 22." *Byzantion* 9:535–93.

————, ed. (1934–1935). *Athanasius Werke 3.1: Urkunden zur Geschichte des arianischen Streites 318–328*. Berlin and Leipzig.

Osborne, C. (1993). "Literal or Metaphorical? Some Issues of Language in the Arian Controversy." In *Christian Faith and Greek Philosophy in Late Antiquity: Essays in Tribute to George Christopher Stead*, ed. L. R. Wickham and C. P. Bammel, with E. C. D. Hunter, pp. 148–70. Supplements to Vigiliae Christianae 19. Leiden.

Oulton, J. E. L. (1929). "Rufinus's Translation of the Church History of Eusebius." *Journal of Theological Studies* 30:150–74.

Packer, J. E. (2003). "*Plurissima et amplissima opera*: Parsing Flavian Rome." In *Flavian Rome: Culture, Image, Text*, ed. A. J. Boyle and W. J. Dominik, pp. 167–98. Leiden.

Pagels, E. (1979). *The Gnostic Gospels.* New York.

Palanque, J. R. (1973). "Du nouveau sur la date du transfert de la préfecture des Gaules de Trèves à Arles." *Provence historique* 23:29–38.

Panella, C. (1999). "Tecniche costruttive e modalità di inserimento dell'apparato decorativo." In *Arco di Costantino tra archeologia e archeometria,* ed. P. Pensabene and C. Panella, pp. 43–73. Studia Archaeologica 100. Rome.

Papi, E. (2000). *L'Etruria dei Romani: Opere pubbliche e donazioni private in età imperiale.* Rome.

———. (2004). "A New Golden Age? The Northern *Praefectura Urbi* from the Severans to Diocletian." In *Approaching Late Antiquity: The Transformation from Early to Late Empire,* ed. S. Swain and M. Edwards, pp. 53–81. Oxford.

Parkin, T. G. (1992). *Demography and Roman Society.* Baltimore.

———. (2003). *Old Age in the Roman World: A Cultural and Social History.* Baltimore.

Parvis, S. (2001a). "The Canons of Ancyra and Caesarea (314): Lebon's Thesis Revisited." *Journal of Theological Studies* n.s. 52:625–36.

———. (2001b). "Marcellus or Vitalis: Who Presided at Ancyra 314?" In *Studia Patristica Vol. XXXIV: Papers Presented at the Thirteenth International Conference on Patristic Studies Held in Oxford 1999. Historica, biblica, theologica et philosophica,* ed. M. F. Wiles and E. J. Yarnold, with P. M. Parvis, pp. 197–203. Leuven.

Paschoud, F., ed. and tr. (1979–2000). *Zosime, Histoire nouvelle,* 3 vols. Paris.

———. (1992). "Ancora sul rifiuto di Costantino di salire al Campidoglio." In *Costantino il Grande dall'antichità all'umanesimo: Colloquio sul Cristianesimo nel mondo antico. Macerata 18–20 dicembre 1990,* ed. G. Bonamente and F. Fusco, Vol. 2:737–48. Macerata.

Patterson, J. R. (2003). "The Emperor and the Cities of Italy." In *"Bread and Circuses": Euergetism and Municipal Patronage in Roman Italy,* ed. K. Lomas and T. Cornell, pp. 89–104. London.

Peirce, P. (1989). "The Arch of Constantine: Propaganda and Ideology in Late Roman Art." *Art History* 12:387–418.

Pelikan, J. (1971). *The Christian Tradition: A History of the Development of Doctrine, 1: The Emergence of the Catholic Tradition (100–600).* Chicago.

Pensabene, P. (1999). "Progetto unitario e reimpiego nell'Arco di Costantino." In *Arco di Costantino tra archeologia e archeometria,* ed. P. Pensabene and C. Panella, pp. 13–42. Studia Archaeologica 100. Rome.

Petersen, W. L. (1992). "Eusebius and the Paschal Controversy." In *Eusebius, Christianity, and Judaism,* ed. H. W. Attridge and G. Hata, pp. 311–25. Detroit.

Peterson, E. (1935). *Der Monotheismus als politisches Problem: Ein Beitrag zur Geschichte der politischen Theologie im Imperium Romanum.* Leipzig.

Petit, P. (1955). *Libanius et la vie municipale à Antioche au IV<sup>e</sup> siècle après J.-C.* Institut français d'archéologie de Beyrouth, Bibliothèque archéologique et historique 62. Paris.

Petrie, A. (1906). "Epitaphs in Phrygian Greek." In *Studies in the History and Art of the Eastern Provinces of the Roman Empire*, ed. W. M. Ramsay, pp. 117–34. London.

Pietri, C. (1976). *Roma Christiana: Recherches sur l'église de Rome, son organisation, sa politique, son idéologie de Miltiade à Sixte III (311–440)*. Rome.

———. (1989). "La politique de Constance II: Un premier 'Césaropapisme' ou l'*Imitatio Constantini?*" In *L'église et l'empire au IV<sup>e</sup> siècle*, ed. A. Dihle, pp. 113–72. Fondation Hardt pour l'étude de l'antiquité classique, Entretiens 34. Geneva. Reprinted in C. Pietri, *Christiana respublica: Eléments d'une enquête sur le christianisme antique* (Paris and Rome, 1997), 1:281–340. Collection de l'Ecole française de Rome 234.

———. (1997a). "Constantin en 324: Propagande et théologie imperiales d'après les documents de la *Vita Constantini*." In C. Pietri, *Christiana respublica: Eléments d'une enquête sur le christianisme antique*, 1:253–80. Collection de l'Ecole française de Rome 234. Paris and Rome.

———. (1997b). "Les provinces 'Salutaires': Géographie administrative et politique de la conversion sous l'empire chrétien (IVe s.)." In C. Pietri, *Christiana respublica: Eléments d'une enquête sur le christianisme antique*, 1:609–28. Collection de l'Ecole française de Rome 234. Paris and Rome.

Pietri, L. (2001). "Constantin et/ou Hélène, promoteurs des travaux entrepris sur le Golgotha: Les comptes rendus des historiens ecclésiastiques grecs du V<sup>e</sup> siècle." In *L'historiographie de l'église des premiers siècles*, ed. B. Pouderon and Y.-M. Duval, pp. 371–80. Théologie historique 114. Paris.

Piganiol, A. (1932). *L'empereur Constantin*. Paris.

Pisani Sartorio, G. (2000). "Il Palazzo di Massenzio sulla Via Appia." In *Aurea Roma: Dalla città pagana alla città cristiana*, ed. S. Ensoli and E. La Rocca, pp. 116–19. Rome.

Pococke, R. (1745). *A Description of the East, and Some Other Countries. Volume II, Part 2: Observations on the Islands of the Archipelago, Asia Minor, Thrace, Greece, and Some Other Parts of Europe*. London.

———, ed (1752). *Inscriptionum antiquarum graec. et latin. liber. Accedit, numismatum Ptolemaeorum, imperatorum, Augustarum, et Caesarum, in Aegypto cusorum, e scriniis Britannicis, catalogus*. London.

Pohl, W. (2002). "Gregory of Tours and Contemporary Perceptions of Lombard Italy." In *The World of Gregory of Tours*, ed. K. Mitchell and I. Wood, pp. 131–43. Cultures, Beliefs and Traditions, Medieval and Early Modern Peoples 8. Leiden.

Pohlsander, H. A. (1984). "Crispus: Brilliant Career and Tragic End." *Historia* 33:79–106.

Polara, J., ed. (1973). *Publilii Optatiani Porfyrii carmina*, 2 vols. Corpus scriptorum latinorum Paravianum. Turin.

Pond Rothman, M. S. (1975). "The Panel of the Emperors Enthroned on the Arch of Galerius." *Byzantine Studies* 2:19–40.

———. (1977). "The Thematic Organization of the Panel Reliefs on the Arch of Galerius." *American Journal of Archaeology* 81:427–54.

Portmann, W. (1999). "Die politische Krise zwischen den Kaisern Constantius II. und Constans." *Historia* 48:301–29.

Price, S. R. F. (1984). *Rituals and Power: The Roman Imperial Cult in Asia Minor.* Cambridge.

———. (1987). "From Noble Funerals to Divine Cult: The Consecration of Roman Emperors." In *Rituals of Royalty: Power and Ceremonial in Traditional Societies*, ed. D. Cannadine and S. Price, pp. 56–105. Cambridge.

Purcell, N. (1999). "The Populace of Rome in Late Antiquity: Problems of Classification and Historical Description." In *The Transformations of Urbs Roma in Late Antiquity*, ed. W. V. Harris, pp. 135–61. Journal of Roman Archaeology, Supplementary Series 33. Portsmouth.

———. (2000). "Rome and Italy." In *The Cambridge Ancient History, Second Edition, Volume XI: The High Empire, A.D. 70–192*, ed. A. K. Bowman, P. Garnsey, and D. Rathbone, pp. 405–43. Cambridge.

Ramsay, W. M. (1937). "Note on JHS 1937, p. 1." *Journal of Hellenic Studies* 57: 247.

Rapp, C. (1998). "Comparison, Paradigm and the Case of Moses in Panegyric and Hagiography." In *The Propaganda of Power: The Role of Panegyric in Late Antiquity*, ed. M. Whitby, pp. 277–98. *Mnemosyne*, Suppl. 183. Leiden.

———. (2005). *Holy Bishops in Late Antiquity: The Nature of Christian Leadership in an Age of Transition.* The Transformation of the Classical Heritage 37. Berkeley.

Rebillard, E. (2003). *Religion et sépulture: L'église, les vivants et les morts dans l'antiquité tardive.* Civilisations et sociétés 115. Paris.

Rees, R. (2002). *Layers of Loyalty in Latin Panegyric AD 289–307.* Oxford.

———. (2004). *Diocletian and the Tetrarchy.* Edinburgh.

Rey-Coquais, J.-P. (1974). *Arados et sa pérée aux époques grecque, romaine et byzantine: Recueil des témoignages littéraires anciens, suivi de recherches sur les sites, l'histoire, la civilisation.* Institut français d'archéologie de Beyrouth, Bibliothèque archéologique et historique 97. Paris.

Riccobono, S., ed. (1941). *Fontes Iuris Romani Antejustiniani, Pars prima: Leges.* Florence.

Richardson, L., Jr. (1992). *A New Topographical Dictionary of Ancient Rome.* Baltimore.

Richlin, A. (1999). "Cicero's Head." In *Constructions of the Classical Body*, ed. J. I. Porter, pp. 190–211. Ann Arbor.

Rives, J. B. (1995). *Religion and Authority in Roman Carthage from Augustus to Constantine.* Oxford.

———. (1999). "The Decree of Decius and the Religion of Empire." *Journal of Roman Studies* 89:135–54.

Robert, L. (1977). "La titulature de Nicée et de Nicomédie: La glorie et la haine." *Harvard Studies in Classical Philology* 81:1–39.

Roberts, M. (2001). "Rome Personified, Rome Epitomized: Representations of Rome in the Poetry of the Early Fifth Century." *American Journal of Philology* 122:533–65.

Rochette, B. (1997). *Le Latin dans le monde grec: Recherches sur la diffusion de la langue et des lettres latines dans les provinces hellénophones de l'empire romain.* Collection Latomus 233. Brussels.

Rohman, J. (1998). "Die spätantiken Kaiserporträts am Konstantinsbogen in Rom." *Mitteilungen des deutschen archäologischen Instituts,* Römische Abteilung 105:259–82.

Roueché, C. (1981). "Rome, Asia and Aphrodisias in the Third Century." *Journal of Roman Studies* 71:103–20.

———. (1989). *Aphrodisias in Late Antiquity: The Late Roman and Byzantine Inscriptions Including Texts from the Excavations at Aphrodisias Conducted by Kenan T. Erim.* Journal of Roman Studies, Monographs 5. London.

Rougé, J., ed. and tr. (1966). *Expositio totius mundi et gentium: Introduction, texte critique, traduction, notes et commentaire.* SChr. 124. Paris.

Rousseau, P. (2000). "Antony as Teacher in the Greek *Life.*" In *Greek Biography and Panegyric in Late Antiquity,* ed. T. Hägg and P. Rousseau, with C. Høgel, pp. 89–109. The Transformation of the Classical Heritage 31. Berkeley.

Rubenson, S. (1995). *The Letters of St. Antony: Monasticism and the Making of a Saint.* Studies in Antiquity and Christianity. Minneapolis.

Ruge, W. (1935). "Nakoleia." In *Paulys Real-Encyclopädie der classischen Altertumswissenschaft.* Neue Bearbeitung begonnen von G. Wissowa, ed. W. Kroll, vol. 16.2: col. 1600–4. Stuttgart.

———. (1939). "Orkistos." In *Paulys Real-Encyclopädie der classischen Altertumswissenschaft.* Neue Bearbeitung begonnen von G. Wissowa, ed. W. Kroll, vol. 18.1: col. 1090–97. Stuttgart.

Ruysschaert, J. (1962–1963a). "Essai d'interprétation synthétique de l'Arc de Constantin." *Atti della Pontificia Accademia Romana di Archeologia* (série III), Rendiconti 35:79–100.

———. (1962–1963b). "Les onze panneaux de l'Arc de Marc-Aurèle érigé à Rome en 176." *Atti della Pontificia Accademia Romana di Archeologia* (série III), Rendiconti 35:101–21.

————. (1967–1968). "L'inscription absidale primitive de S.-Pierre: Texte et contextes." *Atti della Pontificia Accademia Romana di Archeologia* (série III), Rendiconti 40:171–90.

Sabbah, G. (1983). "Introduction: Chapitre III, Sozomène et Socrate." In B. Grillet, G. Sabbah, and A.-J. Festugière, *Sozomène, Histoire ecclésiastique, Livres I–II: Texte grec de l'édition J. Bidez*, pp. 59–87. SChr. 306. Paris.

Sahin, M. Ç., ed. (1981). *Die Inschriften von Stratonikeia, Teil I: Panamara*. Inschriften griechischer Städte aus Kleinasien 21. Bonn.

————, ed. (1994). *Die Inschriften von Arykanda*. Inschriften griechischer Städte aus Kleinasien 48. Bonn.

————, ed. (1999). *Die Inschriften von Perge, Teil I (Vorrömische Zeit, frühe und hohe Kaiserzeit)*. Inschriften griechischer Städte aus Kleinasien 54. Bonn.

Saller, R. P. (1994). *Patriarchy, Property and Death in the Roman Family*. Cambridge Studies in Population, Economy and Society in Past Time 25. Cambridge.

Salway, B. (1994). "What's in a Name? A Survey of Roman Onomastic Practice from c. 700 B.C. to A.D. 700." *Journal of Roman Studies* 84:124–45.

Salzman, M. R. (1990). *On Roman Time: The Codex-Calendar of 354 and the Rhythms of Urban Life in Late Antiquity*. The Transformation of the Classical Heritage 17. Berkeley.

————. (2002). *The Making of a Christian Aristocracy: Social and Religious Change in the Western Roman Empire*. Cambridge, MA.

————. (2003). "Topography and Religion in 4th-c. Rome." *Journal of Roman Archaeology* 16:689–92.

————. (2004). "Travel and Communication in *The Letters of Symmachus*." In *Travel, Communication and Geography in Late Antiquity*, ed. L. Ellis and F. L. Kidner, pp. 81–94. Aldershot.

Santangeli Valenzani, R. (2000). "La politica urbanistica tra i Tetrarchi e Costantino." In *Aurea Roma: Dalla città pagana alla città cristiana*, ed. S. Ensoli and E. La Rocca, pp. 41–44. Rome.

Sartre, M. (2001). *D'Alexandre à Zénobie: Histoire du Levant antique, IV^e siècle avant J.-C. – III^e siècle après J.-C.* Paris.

Scheithauer, A. (2000). *Kaiserliche Bautätigkeit in Rom: Das Echo in der antiken Literatur*. Heidelberger althistorische Beiträge und epigraphische Studien 32. Stuttgart.

Schlange-Schöningen, H. (2004). "*Felix Augustus* oder αὐτοκράτωρ δείλαιος: Zur Rezeption Diokletians in der konstantinischen Dynastie." In *Diokletian und die Tetrarchie: Aspekte einer Zeitenwende*, ed. A. Demandt, A. Goltz, and H. Schlange-Schöningen, pp. 172–92. Millennium-Studien zu Kultur und Geschichte des ersten Jahrtausends n. Chr. 1. Berlin and New York.

Schwartz, E. (1909). "Einleitung zum griechischen Text." In E. Schwartz and T. Mommsen, ed., *Eusebius Werke 2.3: Die Kirchengeschichte*, pp. XV–CCXLVIII. GCS 9, Neue Folge 6.3. Reprinted Berlin, 1999.

———, ed. (1933–1935). *Acta conciliorum oecumenicorum, Tomus alter, Volumen primum*, 3 vols. Berlin and Leipzig.

Seeck, O. (1919). *Regesten der Kaiser und Päpste für die Jahre 311 bis 476 n. Chr.: Vorarbeit zu einer Prosopographie der christlichen Kaiserzeit*. Stuttgart.

Setton, K. M. (1941). *Christian Attitude towards the Emperor in the Fourth Century*. New York.

Sevcenko, I. (1968). "A Late Antique Epigram and the So-Called Elder Magistrate from Aphrodisias." In *Synthronon: Art et archéologie de la fin de l'antiquité et du Moyen Age. Recueil d'études par Andre Grabar et un groupe de ses disciples*, pp. 29–41. Bibliothèque des Cahiers archéologiques 11. Paris.

Sherk, R. K. (1969). *Roman Documents from the Greek East*. Baltimore.

Sirinelli, J. (1961). *Les vues historiques d'Eusèbe de Césarée durant la période prénicéenne*. Université de Dakar, Faculté des lettres et sciences humaines, Publications de la section de langues et littératures 10. Dakar.

Skeat, T. C. (1999). "The Codex Sinaiticus, the Codex Vaticanus and Constantine." *Journal of Theological Studies* n.s. 50:583–625.

Smith, R. B. E. (1995). *Julian's Gods: Religion and Philosophy in the Thought and Action of Julian the Apostate*. London.

———. (2003). "'Restored Utility, Eternal City': Patronal Imagery at Rome in the Fourth Century AD." In "*Bread and Circuses*": *Euergetism and Municipal Patronage in Roman Italy*, ed. K. Lomas and T. Cornell, pp. 142–66. London.

Smith, R. R. R. (1985). "Roman Portraits: Honours, Empresses, and Late Emperors." *Journal of Roman Studies* 75:209–21.

———. (1997). "The Public Image of Licinius I: Portrait Sculpture and Imperial Ideology in the Early Fourth Century." *Journal of Roman Studies* 87:170–202.

———. (1999). "Late Antique Portraits in a Public Context: Honorific Statuary at Aphrodisias in Caria, A.D. 300–600." *Journal of Roman Studies* 89:155–89.

———. (2001). "A Portrait Monument for Julian and Theodosius at Aphrodisias." In *Griechenland in der Kaiserzeit: Neue Funde und Forschungen zu Skulptur, Architektur und Topographie. Kolloquium zum sechzigsten Geburtstag von Prof. Dietrich Willers, Bern, 12.-13. Juni 1998*, ed. C. Reusser, pp. 125–36. Hefte des archäologischen Seminars der Universität Bern 4. Zurich.

———. (2002). "The Statue Monument of Oecumenius: A New Portrait of a Late Antique Governor from Aphrodisias." *Journal of Roman Studies* 92:134–56.

Speck, P. (1995). "Urbs, quam Deo donavimus: Konstantins des Großen Konzept für Konstantinopel." *Boreas* 18:43–173.

Speidel, M. P. (1986). "Maxentius and His *Equites Singulares* in the Battle at the Milvian Bridge." *Classical Antiquity* 5:253–62.

Srejovic, D. (1994). "The Representations of Tetrarchs in *Romuliana.*" *Antiquité tardive* 2:143–52.

Sterrett, J. R. S. (1889). "Leaflets from the Notebook of an Archaeological Traveler in Asia Minor." *Bulletin of the University of Texas.* Austin.

Stewart, P. (1999). "The Destruction of Statues in Late Antiquity." In *Constructing Identities in Late Antiquity,* ed. R. Miles, pp. 159–89. London.

Strobel, A. (1980). *Das heilige Land der Montanisten: Eine religionsgeographische Untersuchung.* Religionsgeschichtliche Versuche und Vorarbeiten 37. Berlin.

Stuart Jones, H. (1926). *A Catalogue of the Ancient Sculptures Preserved in the Municipal Collections of Rome: The Sculptures of the Palazzo dei Conservatori.* Oxford.

Sundwall, J. (1915). *Weströmische Studien.* Berlin.

Sutherland, C. H. V. (1967). *The Roman Imperial Coinage, VI: From Diocletian's Reform (A.D. 294) to the Death of Maximinus (A.D. 313).* London.

Syme, R. (1939). *The Roman Revolution.* Oxford.

———. (1971). *Danubian Papers.* Bucharest.

———. (1983). "The Ancestry of Constantine." In R. Syme, *Historia Augusta Papers,* pp. 63–79. Oxford.

———. (1986). *The Augustan Aristocracy.* Oxford.

Tabata, K. (1995). "The Date and Setting of the Constantinian Inscription of Hispellum (CIL XI, 5265 = ILS 705)." *Studi classici e orientali* 45:369–410.

Tabbernee, W. (1997a). *Montanist Inscriptions and Testimonia: Epigraphic Sources Illustrating the History of Montanism.* Patristic Monograph Series 16. Macon.

———. (1997b). "Eusebius' 'Theology of Persecution': As Seen in the Various Editions of His Church History." *Journal of Early Christian Studies* 5:319–34.

———. (2003). "Portals of the Montanist New Jerusalem: The Discovery of Pepouza and Tymion." *Journal of Early Christian Studies* 11:87–93.

Tambiah, S. J. (2002). *Edmund Leach: An Anthropological Life.* Cambridge.

Tantillo, I. (1998). "'Come un bene ereditario': Constantino e la retorica dell'impero-patrimonio." *Antiquité tardive* 6:251–64.

Thélamon, F. (1970). "L'empereur idéal d'après l'*Histoire ecclésiastique* de Rufin d'Aquilée." *Studia Patristica* 10 = *Texte und Untersuchungen* 107:310–14.

———. (1981). *Païens et chrétiens au IV^e siècle: L'apport de l' "Histoire ecclésiastique" de Rufin d'Aquilée.* Paris.

Thomsen, R. (1947). *The Italic Regions from Augustus to the Lombard Invasion.* Classica et Mediaevalia, Dissertationes 4. Copenhagen.

Toebelmann, F. (1915). *Der Bogen von Malborghetto.* Abhandlungen der Heidelberger Akademie der Wissenschaften, Stiftung Heinrich Lanz, Philosophisch-historische Klasse 2. Heidelberg.

Trebilco, P. R. (1991). *Jewish Communities in Asia Minor*. Cambridge.

Trevett, C. (1996). *Montanism: Gender, Authority and the New Prophecy*. Cambridge.

Trout, D. E. (2001). "*Lex* and *Iussio*: The *Feriale Campanum* and Christianity in the Theodosian Age." In *Law, Society, and Authority in Late Antiquity*, ed. R. W. Mathisen, pp. 162–78. Oxford.

———. (2003). "Damasus and the Invention of Early Christian Rome." *Journal of Medieval and Early Modern Studies* 33:517–36. Reprinted in *The Cultural Turn in Late Ancient Studies: Gender, Asceticism, and Historiography*, ed. D. B. Martin and P. C. Miller (Durham, 2005), pp. 298–315.

Tsafrir, Y. (1999). "Byzantine Jerusalem: The Configuration of a Christian City." In *Jerusalem: Its Sanctity and Centrality to Judaism, Christianity, and Islam*, ed. L. I. Irvine, pp. 133–50. New York.

Turner, E. G. (1961). "Latin versus Greek as a Universal Language: The Attitude of Diocletian." In *Language and Society: Essays Presented to Arthur M. Jensen on His Seventieth Birthday*, pp. 165–68. Copenhagen.

Urbainczyk, T. (1997). *Socrates of Constantinople: Historian of Church and State*. Ann Arbor.

Urban, R. (1999). *Gallia rebellis: Erhebungen in Gallien im Spiegel antiker Zeugnisse*. Historia Einzelschriften 129. Stuttgart.

Vaggione, R. P. (2000). *Eunomius of Cyzicus and the Nicene Revolution*. Oxford Early Christian Studies. Oxford.

Van Dam, R. (1982). "Hagiography and History: The Life of Gregory Thaumaturgus." *Classical Antiquity* 1:272–308.

———. (1985a). *Leadership and Community in Late Antique Gaul*. The Transformation of the Classical Heritage 8. Berkeley.

———. (1985b). "From Paganism to Christianity at Late Antique Gaza." *Viator* 16:1–20.

———. (1992). "The Pirenne Thesis and Fifth-Century Gaul." In *Fifth-Century Gaul: A Crisis of Identity?*, ed. J. Drinkwater and H. Elton, pp. 321–33. Cambridge.

———. (1993). *Saints and Their Miracles in Late Antique Gaul*. Princeton.

———. (1996). "Governors of Cappadocia during the Fourth Century." In *Late Antiquity and Byzantium*, ed. R. W. Mathisen. = *Medieval Prosopography* 17:7–93.

———. (2002). *Kingdom of Snow: Roman Rule and Greek Culture in Cappadocia*. Philadelphia.

———. (2003a). *Families and Friends in Late Roman Cappadocia*. Philadelphia.

———. (2003b). *Becoming Christian: The Conversion of Roman Cappadocia*. Philadelphia.

———. (2003c). "The Many Conversions of the Emperor Constantine." In *Conversion in Late Antiquity and the Early Middle Ages: Seeing and Believing*, ed. K. Mills and A. Grafton, pp. 127–51. Rochester.

———. (2005). "Merovingian Gaul and the Frankish Conquests." In *The New Cambridge Medieval History, Volume I: c. 500 – c. 700*, ed. P. Fouracre, pp. 193–231. Cambridge.

———. (forthcoming). "Imagining an Eastern Roman Empire: A Riot at Antioch in 387." In *The Sculptural Environment of the Roman Near East: Reflections on Culture, Ideology, and Power*, ed. Y. Z. Eliav, E. Friedland, and S. Herbert.

Vanderspoel, J. (1995). *Themistius and the Imperial Court: Oratory, Civic Duty, and Paideia from Constantius to Theodosius.* Ann Arbor.

Vanderspoel, J., and M. L. Mann (2002). "The Empress Fausta as Romano-Celtic Dea Nutrix." *Numismatic Chronicle* 162:350–55.

Varner, E. R. (2001). "Portraits, Plots, and Politics: *Damnatio memoriae* and the Images of Imperial Women." *Memoirs of the American Academy in Rome* 46:41–93.

———. (2004). *Mutilation and Transformation: Damnatio memoriae and Roman Imperial Portraiture.* Monumenta Graeca et Romana 10. Leiden.

Verduchi, P. (1995). "Equus: Constantinus." In *Lexicon Topographicum Urbis Romae*, Vol. 2, ed. E. M. Steinby, pp. 226–27. Rome.

Vittinghoff, F. (1936). *Der Staatsfeind in der römischen Kaiserzeit: Untersuchungen zur "Damnatio memoriae."* Neue deutsche Forschungen 84, Abteilung Alte Geschichte 2. Berlin.

Vogt, J. (1963). "Pagans and Christians in the Family of Constantine the Great." In *The Conflict between Paganism and Christianity in the Fourth Century*, ed. A. Momigliano, pp. 38–55. Oxford-Warburg Studies. Oxford.

Vollmer, F., and H. Rubenbauer (1926). "Ein verschollenes Grabgedicht aus Trier." *Trierer Zeitschrift* 1:26–30.

Walker, P. W. L. (1990). *Holy City, Holy Places? Christian Attitudes to Jerusalem and the Holy Land in the Fourth Century.* Oxford.

Wallace-Hadrill, A. (1990). "Roman Arches and Greek Honours: The Language of Power at Rome." *Proceedings of the Cambridge Philological Society* 216, n.s. 36:143–81.

Wallraff, M. (1997). *Der Kirchenhistoriker Sokrates: Untersuchungen zu Geschichtsdarstellung, Methode und Person.* Forschungen zur Kirchen- und Dogmengeschichte 68. Gottingen.

———. (2001). "Constantine's Devotion to the Sun after 324." In *Studia Patristica Vol. XXXIV: Papers Presented at the Thirteenth International Conference on Patristic Studies Held in Oxford 1999. Historica, biblica, theologica et philosophica*, ed. M. F. Wiles and E. J. Yarnold, with P. M. Parvis, pp. 256–69. Leuven.

Ward-Perkins, B. (1984). *From Classical Antiquity to the Middle Ages: Urban Public Building in Northern and Central Italy AD 300–850.* Oxford.

Warmington, B. H. (1985). "The Sources of Some Constantinian Documents in Eusebius' *Ecclesiastical History* and *Life of Constantine*." In *Studia Patristica XVIII,*

*Volume One: Historica-theologica-Gnostica-biblica. Papers of the Ninth International Conference on Patristic Studies, Oxford 1983,* ed. E. A. Livingstone, pp. 93–98. Kalamazoo.

———. (1993). "Eusebius of Caesarea's Versions of Constantine's Laws in the Codes." In *Studia Patristica Vol. XXIV: Papers Presented at the Eleventh International Conference on Patristic Studies Held in Oxford 1991. Historica, theologica et philosophica, Gnostica,* ed. E. A. Livingstone, pp. 201–7. Leuven.

———. (1999). "Some Constantinian References in Ammianus." In *The Late Roman World and Its Historian: Interpreting Ammianus Marcellinus,* ed. J. W. Drijvers and D. Hunt, pp. 166–77. London.

Watson, A. (1999). *Aurelian and the Third Century.* London.

Webb, P. H. (1933). *The Roman Imperial Coinage, V, Part II.* London.

Weiss, J.-P. (1978). "Julien, Rome et les Romains." In *L'empereur Julien de l'histoire à la légende (331–1715),* ed. R. Braun and J. Richer, pp. 125–40. Paris.

Weiss, P. (1995). "Götter, Städte und Gelehrte: Lydiaka und 'Patria' um Sardes und den Tmolos." In *Forschungen in Lydien,* ed. E. Schwertheim, pp. 85–109. Asia Minor Studien 17. Bonn.

———. (2003). "The Vision of Constantine," tr. A. R. Birley. *Journal of Roman Archaeology* 16:237–59. Revised version of "Die Vision Constantins." In *Colloquium aus Anlaß des 80. Geburtstages von Alfred Heuß,* ed. J. Bleicken, pp. 143–69. Frankfurter althistorische Studien 13. Kallmünz.

Wharton, A. J. (1995). *Refiguring the Post Classical City: Dura Europos, Jerash, Jerusalem and Ravenna.* Cambridge.

Whittaker, C. R. (1994a). *Frontiers of the Roman Empire: A Social and Economic Study.* Baltimore.

———. (1994b). "The Politics of Power: The Cities of Italy." In *L'Italie d'Auguste à Dioclétien,* pp. 127–43. Collection de l'Ecole française de Rome 198. Rome and Paris.

Wiemer, H.-U. (1994). "Libanius on Constantine." *Classical Quarterly* 44:511–24.

Wightman, E. M. (1970). *Roman Trier and the Treveri.* New York.

Wigtil, D. N. (1981). "Toward a Date for the Greek Fourth Eclogue." *Classical Journal* 76:336–41.

Wiles, M. (1996). *Archetypal Heresy: Arianism through the Centuries.* Oxford.

Wiles, M. F., and R. C. Gregg (1985). "Asterius: A New Chapter in the History of Arianism." In *Arianism: Historical and Theological Reassessments. Papers from the Ninth International Conference on Patristic Studies, September 5–10, 1983, Oxford, England,* ed. R. C. Gregg, pp. 111–51. Patristic Monograph Series 11. Cambridge, MA.

Wilken, R. L. (1992a). *The Land Called Holy: Palestine in Christian History and Thought.* New Haven.

_____. (1992b). "Eusebius and the Christian Holy Land." In *Eusebius, Christianity, and Judaism*, ed. H. W. Attridge and G. Hata, pp. 736–60. Detroit.

_____. (1999). "Cyril of Alexandria's *Contra Iulianum*." In *The Limits of Ancient Christianity: Essays on Late Antique Thought and Culture in Honor of R. A. Markus*, ed. W. E. Klingshirn and M. Vessey, pp. 42–55. Ann Arbor.

Wilkinson, J. (1981). *Egeria's Travels to the Holy Land*, Revised Edition. Jerusalem and Warminster.

Williams, G. H. (1951a). "Christology and Church-State Relations in the Fourth Century." *Church History* 20.3:3–33.

_____. (1951b). "Christology and Church-State Relations in the Fourth Century." *Church History* 20.4:3–26.

Williams, J. H. C. (2001). *Beyond the Rubicon: Romans and Gauls in Republican Italy*. Oxford.

Williams, R. (1987). *Arius: Heresy and Tradition*. London.

_____, ed. (1989). *The Making of Orthodoxy: Essays in Honour of Henry Chadwick*. Cambridge.

_____. (1993). "Baptism and the Arian Controversy." In *Arianism after Arius: Essays on the Development of the Fourth Century Trinitarian Conflicts*, ed. M. R. Barnes and D. H. Williams, pp. 149–80. Edinburgh.

_____. (2001). "Appendix 1: Arius since 1987." In R. Williams, *Arius: Heresy and Tradition*, Revised Edition, pp. 247–67. London.

Wilson, Andrew (2001). "Water-Mills at Amida: Ammianus Marcellinus 18.8.11." *Classical Quarterly* 51:231–36.

Wilson, Anna (1998). "Biographical Models: The Constantinian Period and Beyond." In *Constantine: History, Hagiography and Legend*, ed. S. N. C. Lieu and D. Montserrat, pp. 107–35. London.

Wilson Jones, M. (2000). "Genesis and Mimesis: The Design of the Arch of Constantine in Rome." *Journal of the Society of Architectural Historians* 59:50–77.

Winkelmann, F. (1964). "Die Beurteilung des Eusebius von Cäsarea und seiner Vita Constantini im griechischen Osten: Ein Beitrag zur Untersuchung der griechischen hagiographischen Vitae Constantini." In *Byzantinische Beiträge*, ed. J. Irmscher, pp. 91–119. Berlin. Reprinted in F. Winkelmann, *Studien zu Konstantin dem Grossen und zur byzantinischen Kirchengeschichte: Ausgewählte Aufsätze*, ed. W. Brandes and J. F. Haldon (Birmingham, 1993), Chapter 15.

_____. (1973). "Ein Ordnungsversuch der griechischen hagiographischen Konstantinviten und ihrer Überlieferung." In *Studia Byzantina 2*, ed. J. Irmscher and P. Nagel, pp. 267–84. Berliner byzantinistische Arbeiten 44. Berlin. Reprinted in F. Winkelmann, *Studien zu Konstantin dem Grossen und zur byzantinischen Kirchengeschichte: Ausgewählte Aufsätze*, ed. W. Brandes and J. F. Haldon (Birmingham, 1993), Chapter 12.

————. (1978). "Das hagiographische Bild Konstantins I. in mittelbyzantinischer Zeit." In *Beiträge zur byzantinischen Geschichte im 9.-11. Jahrhundert: Akten des Colloquiums Byzanz auf dem Höhepunkt seiner Macht, Liblice, 20.-23. September 1977*, ed. V. Vavrínek, pp. 179–203. Prague. Reprinted in F. Winkelmann, *Studien zu Konstantin dem Grossen und zur byzantinischen Kirchengeschichte: Ausgewählte Aufsätze*, ed. W. Brandes and J. F. Haldon (Birmingham, 1993), Chapter 14.

————, ed. (1991). *Eusebius Werke 1.1: Über das Leben des Kaisers Konstantin*, Second Edition. GCS. Berlin.

Wischmeyer, W. (1990). "M. Iulius Eugenius: Eine Fallstudie zum Thema «Christen und Gesellschaft im 3. und 4. Jahrhundert»." *Zeitschrift für die neutestamentliche Wissenschaft und die Kunde der älteren Kirche* 81:225–46.

Woods, D. (1998). "On the Death of the Empress Fausta." *Greece and Rome* 45: 70–86.

Woolf, G. (1990). "Food, Poverty and Patronage: The Significance of the Epigraphy of the Roman Alimentary Schemes in Early Imperial Italy." *Papers of the British School at Rome* 58:197–228.

————. (1994). "Becoming Roman, Staying Greek: Culture, Identity and the Civilizing Process in the Roman East." *Proceedings of the Cambridge Philological Society* 40:116–43.

————. (1996). "Monumental Writing and the Expansion of Roman Society in the Early Empire." *Journal of Roman Studies* 86:22–39.

Wrede, H. (1981). "Der Genius populi Romani und das Fünfsäulendenkmal der Tetrarchen auf dem Forum Romanum." *Bonner Jahrbücher* 181:111–42.

Wright, D. H. (1987). "The True Face of Constantine the Great." *Dumbarton Oaks Papers* 41:493–507.

Yegül, F. K. (2000). "Memory, Metaphor, and Meaning in the Cities of Asia Minor." In *Romanization and the City: Creation, Transformations, and Failures. Proceedings of a Conference Held at the American Academy in Rome To Celebrate the 50th Anniversary of the Excavations at Cosa, 14–16 May, 1998*, ed. E. Fentress, pp. 133–53. Journal of Roman Archaeology, Supplementary Series 38. Portsmouth.

Zachos, K. L. (2003). "The *Tropaeum* of the Sea-Battle of Actium at Nikopolis: Interim Report." *Journal of Roman Archaeology* 16:64–92.

Zanker, P. (1988). *The Power of Images in the Age of Augustus*, tr. A. Shapiro. Jerome Lectures 16. Ann Arbor.

Zecchini, G. (1992). "Dall'*Imperium Daciscum* alla *Gothia*: Il ruolo di Costantino nell'evoluzione di un tema politico e storiografico." In *Costantino il Grande dall'antichità all'umanesimo: Colloquio sul Cristianesimo nel mondo antico. Macerata 18–20 dicembre 1990*, ed. G. Bonamente and F. Fusco, Vol. 2:915–33. Macerata.

Zgusta, L. (1980). "Die Ostgrenze von Armenien über Mesopotamien, Syrien bis Arabien." In *Die Sprachen im römischen Reich der Kaiserzeit: Kolloquium vom 8. bis 10. April 1974*, ed. G. Neumann and J. Untermann, pp. 121–45. Beihefte der Bonner Jahrbücher 40. Cologne and Bonn.

Zuckerman, C. (1994). "Les campagnes des Tétrarques, 296–298: Notes de chronologie." *Antiquité tardive* 2:65–70.

# INDEX

Clopas, 304n
Colbasa, 166
Colonia Augusta Raurica, 73n, 74n
Colossae, 249
Colosseum, 51, 82, 96
Commodus (emperor), 89n, 105, 108, 157,
    159n, 218
Consentius (envoy), 215
Constans (emperor and son of Constantine),
    15, 31, 37n, 50, 56n, 60, 100, 107n, 125n,
    161n; in Italy, 73–74, 115–21, 222–23,
    363–64
Constans (son of Constantine III), 124–25
Constantia (half-sister of Constantine and
    wife of Licinius), 100, 110n, 114, 120,
    175, 273
Constantia, as name for city, 113n. See also
    Antaradus; Antioch; Antoni(n)opolis;
    Coutances; Maiuma; Salamis
Constantina (daughter of Constantine),
    59–60, 107n, 114n, 121
Constantina, as name for city: see Antaradus;
    Arles; Cirta; Coutances;
    Maximianopolis
Constantine (emperor), 71, 241, 247;
    boyhood of, 12n, 15; in Gaul, 37–38, 62,
    83–85; as hairdresser, 2, 17–18; and
    diadem, 16–18; and Augustus, 5–6,
    27–28, 48–49, 88, 148; and Marcus
    Aurelius, 2, 30, 88; and Claudius
    Gothicus, 84–85, 98–100; identity of,
    13–15, 148, 223–27; names and titles of,
    92–96; at Rome, 30–31, 39–40, 45–57,
    80–81, 85–88, 110n, 128, 134–38, 313,
    364; and Constantinople, 57–59, 81,
    299, 305–9, 328; oration of, 195–96,
    273n, 294; death of, 2, 56n, 59, 357;
    tomb of, 59, 309, 315, 338–42. See also
    Hispellum; Orcistus; Theodosius
— laws: on celibacy, 4; on guardianship,
    138n; on heresy, 183n; on marriage,
    10–11; on religious toleration, 172, 177;
    on sacrifices, 30–33
— military victories: as usurper, 36–37;
    visions, 6n, 127–28, 143, 333, 335, 340,

351–53; victory over Maxentius, 15, 30,
    37, 45–47, 55n, 61, 85–88, 93, 97, 135–36,
    169, 172, 224–25, 263, 300, 311, 323,
    332–33; victory over Licinius, 15–16, 31,
    38, 51, 99–102, 110n, 148, 150, 161,
    172–76, 194, 197n, 222n, 232n, 247, 257,
    264, 272–75, 280, 300, 305, 308, 331, 369
— monuments: colossal statue at Rome,
    86–89, 133–41; statue at
    Constantinople, 308; statue at Volsinii,
    27–28. See also Arch of Constantine;
    Church of the Holy Apostles
— religion: and Apollo, 85; and Hercules,
    84, 233; and Sol, 38, 47n, 85, 90n, 178;
    and Tetrarchic theology, 248–51; and
    Christian theological controversies, 257,
    262–65; at council of Nicaea, 20,
    140–41, 194, 270–74, 281, 297, 345; and
    Holy Land, 293–305. See also Palestine
— wives and children: see Constans;
    Constantina; Constantine II;
    Constantius II; Crispus; Fausta; Helena
    (daughter); Minervina
— relatives: see Anastasia; Bassianus;
    Claudius Gothicus; Constantia;
    Constantius I; Constantius, Flavius;
    Constantius, Julius; Dalmatius;
    Dalmatius, Flavius; Eutropia
    (half-sister); Eutropia (mother-in-law);
    Gallus; Hannibalianus; Hannibalianus
    the Younger; Helena (mother); Julian
    (emperor); Licinius; Maxentius;
    Maximian; Nepotianus, Julius;
    Theodora. See also Flavian dynasty
Constantine II (emperor and son of
    Constantine), 15, 50, 60, 62, 100–1,
    110n, 115–21, 302, 340n, 363–64, 369
Constantine III (emperor), 66, 124–25, 136
Constantine IV (emperor), 356
Constantinople, 15, 38–39, 70, 77, 110n,
    196n, 215, 257, 323, 328, 335, 349;
    emperors at, 18n, 33, 57, 112, 116, 123,
    198, 200, 207, 212, 275–77, 292, 298n,
    299, 305–9, 314, 338–43, 358; as New
    Rome or Second Rome, 12, 40, 58, 67,

Breinigsville, PA USA
23 June 2010
240486BV00002B/2/P